D0169316

INTRODUCTION TO

DATA COMMUNICATIONS
AND
NETWORKING

Behrouz Forouzan

with

Catherine Coombs and Sophia Chung Fegan

Boston, Massachusetts   Burr Ridge, Illinois   Dubuque, Iowa
Madison, Wisconsin   New York, New York   San Francisco, California   St. Louis, Missouri

WCB/McGraw-Hill

A Division of The McGraw·Hill Companies

INTRODUCTION TO DATA COMMUNICATIONS AND NETWORKING

This book is printed on acid-free paper.

3 4 5 7 8 9 0 DOC/DOC 9 0 9

ISBN 0-256-23044-7

Editorial director: *Tom Casson*
Executive editor: *Elizabeth A. Jones*
Marketing manager: *John Wannemacher*
Senior project manager: *Beth Cigler*
Production supervisor: *Heather D. Burbridge*
Designer: *Kiera Cunningham*
Typeface: *10/12 Times Roman*
Printer: *R. R. Donnelley & Sons Company*

Library of Congress Cataloging-in-Publication Data
Forouzan, Behrouz A.
    Introduction to data communications and networking / Behrouz
Forouzan.
        p.   cm.
    Includes index.
    ISBN 0-256-23044-7
    1. Data transmission systems.   2. Computer networks.   I. Title
TK5105.F67   1998   96-54907
004.6--dc21

http://www.mhhe.com

To Faezeh with love.

PREFACE

Networks and digital communications may be the fastest growing technologies in our culture today. One of the ramifications of that growth is a dramatic increase in the number of professions where an understanding of these technologies is essential for success —and a proportionate increase in the number and types of students taking courses to learn about them. Today students wanting to understand the concepts and mechanisms underlying telecommunications and networking come from a variety of academic and professional backgrounds. To be useful, a textbook on data communication and networking must be accessible to students without technical backgrounds while still providing substance comprehensive enough to challenge more experienced readers. This text is written with this new mix of students in mind.

Features of the Book

Several features of this book are designed to make it particularly easy for students to understand data communication.

Structure

We have used the seven-layer OSI model as the framework for the text not only because a thorough understanding of the model is essential to understanding most current networking theory but also because it is based on a structure of interdependencies: Each layer builds upon the layer beneath it and supports the layer above it. In the same way, each concept introduced in our text builds upon the concepts examined in the previous sections.

The first eight chapters emphasize the physical layer, which is essential for understanding the rest of the layers. These chapters are particularly needed for students with no background in networking or telecommunication.

Chapters 9 through 13 describe all issues related to the data link layer. Chapters 14 to 20 discuss topics associated with the network layer. Chapter 21 describes the transport layer. Chapter 22 focuses on upper layers, which are normally combined in most protocols.

Chapter 23 describes one of the most important protocols, TCP/IP.

Visual Approach

The book presents highly technical subject matter without complex formulas, using a balance of text and figures. The approximately 700 figures accompanying the text provide a visual and intuitive opportunity for understanding the material. Figures are particularly important in explaining networking concepts, which are based on connections and transmission, both often more easily grasped visually than verbally.

Highlighted Points

Important concepts have been repeated in colored boxes for quick reference and immediate attention.

Examples and Applications

Whenever appropriate, we have included examples that illustrate the concept introduced in the text. Also, real-life applications have been added throughout each chapter to motivate students.

Summary

Each chapter ends with a summary of the material covered by that chapter. The summary is a bulleted overview of all the key points in the chapter.

Practice Set

Each chapter includes a practice set designed to reinforce salient concepts and encourage students to apply them. It consists of two parts: multiple choice questions and exercises. Multiple choice questions are designed to test students' grasp of basic concepts and terminology. Exercises require deeper understanding of the material.

Appendixes

The appendixes are intended to provide quick reference material or a review of materials needed to understand the concepts discussed in the book.

Glossary and Acronyms

The book contains an extensive glossary and a list of acronyms.

How to Use the Book

This book is written for both an academic and a professional audience. The book can be used as a self-study guide for interested professionals. As a textbook, it can be used for a one-semester or one-quarter course. The chapters are organized to provide a great deal of flexibility. The following are some suggestions:

- Chapters 1 through 12 and Chapters 14, 16, 20, 21, and 22 are fundamental to understanding the concepts of data communication and networking.
- Chapters 13, 14, 15, 20, and 23 can also be covered in a quarter or a semester.
- Chapters 17, 18, and 19, which discuss the emerging technologies, can be covered if time permits.

Acknowledgments

It is obvious that the development of a book of this scope needs the support of many people. We must first thank the hundreds of students at De Anza College who have used the text and made useful comments. We must also thank the De Anza staff; their encouragement and support materialized the project and contributed to its success. In particular, we thank Sandy Acebo, Richard Gilberg, Martha Kanter, Anne Oney, John Perry, George Rice, Mark Sherby, Orva Stewart, and John Wanlass.

The most important contribution to the development of a book such as this comes from peer reviews. We cannot express our gratitude in words to the many reviewers who spent numerous hours reading the manuscript and providing us with helpful comments and ideas. We would especially like to acknowledge the contributions of the following reviewers:

Russell J. Clark, *University of Dayton*
Charles K. Davis, *University of Houston*
John W. Gray, *University of Massachusetts at Dartmouth*
James M. Frazier, *University of North Carolina at Charlotte*
Thomas F. Hain, *University of South Alabama*
Paul N. Higbee, *University of North Florida*
Seung Bae Im, *California State University at Chico*
Rose M. Laird, *Northern Virginia Community College*
Jorg Liebeherr, *University of Virginia*
Wallace C. Liu, *California State University at Fresno*
T. Radhakrishnan, *Concordia University*
Peter Maggiacomo, *Sinclair Community College*
Larry D. Owens, *California State University at Fresno*
Michael Peterson, *Iowa Western Community College*
Satya Prakash Saraswat, *Bentley College*
Heidi Schmidt, *San Francisco State University*
Gordon Springer, *University of Missouri at Columbia*

Special thanks go to the staff of McGraw-Hill. Betsy Jones, our senior editor, proved how a proficient editor can make the impossible, possible. Bradley Kosirog, the assistant editor, gave us help whenever we needed it. Beth Cigler, our project manager, guided us through the production process with enormous enthusiasm. We also thank Heather Burbridge in production, Kiera Cunningham in design, and Janet Renard, the copy editor.

Trademark Notices

Throughout the text we have used several trademarks. Rather than insert a trademark symbol with each mention of the trademarked name, we acknowledge the trademarks here and state that they are used with no intention of infringing upon them. Other product names, trademarks, and registered trademarks are the property of their respective owners.

■ Apple, AppleTalk, EtherTalk, LocalTalk, TokenTalk, and Macintosh are registered trademarks of Apple Computer, Inc.

■ Bell and StarLan are registered trademarks of AT&T.

■ DEC, DECnet, VAX, and DNA are trademarks of Digital Equipment Corp.

TABLE OF CONTENTS

CHAPTER 1

INTRODUCTION

When cartoonists and disk jockeys are giving out their e-mail addresses to fans, it is a sign of the increasing interconnectivity that defines the way we communicate with the people and institutions of interest to us. The Internet and the World Wide Web are pointing to the real possibility of collaboration on a global scale. Through a computer and modem, a musician in Minneapolis can gain direct access to the facilities of the Institute pour le Recherche et Coordination Acoustique Musique in Paris. A cancer researcher at Stanford University can compare research findings with colleagues at the National Institutes of Health in Washington. An accounting manager in Dallas can get cost-of-manufacturing data from a subsidiary in Singapore in time to present slides at an important meeting.

Networks are changing the way we do business and the way we live. Business decisions have to be made even more quickly, and the decision makers require immediate access to accurate information. But before we ask how quickly we can get hooked up, we need to know how networks operate, what types of technology are available, and which design best fills which set of needs. When a company adds a new division, the technology has to be flexible enough to reflect changing configurations. Is a particular design robust enough to handle the growth? Understanding what it does and when to use each type of technology is essential to providing the right system in today's dynamically changing information environment.

The development of the personal computer brought about tremendous changes for business, industry, science, and education. Information processing technology, once the domain of highly trained technicians, became friendly enough for nontechnical workers to use. Soon salespeople, accountants, professors, researchers, secretaries, and managers began designing their own spreadsheets, presentations, and databases. Corporations and universities began buying microcomputers to facilitate the management of information. As these microcomputers were installed, the traditional terminals that had provided passive connections to mainframes were removed. Terminal emulation through a PC now provided a new smart link to a central server.

Even with all this new processing power, people had no efficient way to share data. Except for those with computers connected directly to a mainframe, anyone wanting to get or send information had to do it manually. In the 1970s, a Toronto company that handled data processing for a local bank would generate material, write it to tape, and then hire an armored car to transport it three blocks to the bank's computer—every week. (A courier carrying a tape on an airplane was considered the ultimate bandwidth for data communication.) In the newer PC and workstation world, data could be either copied onto a floppy disk and physically reloaded onto another PC—even one as close as the next desk—or printed out; mailed, faxed, or couriered to its destination; then rekeyed into a remote computer. This not only was time-consuming but also created other inconveniences. Retyping data could compound human errors, and the problems associated with floppy disk transfer were sometimes worse. In addition to the size limitations, which often required multiple, carefully sequenced disks to carry one transmission, floppies turned out to be a terrific way for a virus to hop from computer to computer.

And standards of productivity were changing. Why wait a week for that report from Germany to arrive by mail when, if computers could talk to each other, it could appear almost instantaneously? The time had come for connecting personal computers into a computer network.

A similar revolution is occurring in telecommunications networks. Technological advances are making it possible for communications links to carry more and faster signals. As a result, services are evolving to allow use of the expanded capacity, including extensions to established telephone services such as conference calling, call waiting, voice mail, and caller ID; new digital services include video conferences and information retrieval.

Developing the right hardware has been one of the challenges facing network designers but by no means the only one. Designing connections between personal computers, workstations, and other digital devices requires an understanding of the needs of the users. How does information flow? Who is sharing data and what kind is being shared? How much physical distance does the information have to travel? Is data sharing limited to several PCs within one office, or do the data also need to be shared with local field offices, or with an unpredictable number of subscribers all over the world? In fact, to manage their business effectively, many institutions today must have more than one type of network.

1.1 DATA COMMUNICATION

When we communicate, we are sharing information. This sharing can be local or remote. Between individuals, local communication usually occurs face to face, while remote communication takes place over distance. The term *telecommunications*, which includes telephony, telegraphy, and television, means communication at a distance (*tele* is Greek for far).

The word *data* refers to facts, concepts, and instructions presented in whatever form is agreed upon by the parties creating and using the data. In the context of computer information systems, data are represented by binary information units (or bits) produced and consumed in the form of 0s and 1s.

> In computer information system, data are represented by binary information units (or bits) produced and consumed in the form of 0s and 1s.

Data communication is the exchange of data (in the form of 0s and 1s) between two devices via some form of transmission medium (such as a wire cable). Data communication is considered local if the communicating devices are in the same building or a similarly restricted geographical area, and is considered remote if the devices are farther apart.

For data communication to occur, the communicating devices must be part of a communication system made up of a combination of hardware and software. The effectiveness of a data communication system depends on three fundamental characteristics:

1. **Delivery.** The system must deliver data to the correct destination. Data must be received by the intended device or user and only by that device or user.

2. **Accuracy.** The system must deliver data accurately. Data that have been altered in transmission and left uncorrected are unusable.

3. **Timeliness.** The system must deliver data in a timely manner. Data delivered late are useless. In the case of video, audio, and voice data, timely delivery means delivering data as they are produced, in the same order that they are produced, and without significant delay. This kind of delivery is called real-time transmission.

Components

A data communication system is made up of five components (see Figure 1.1).

Figure 1.1   *Data communication system components*

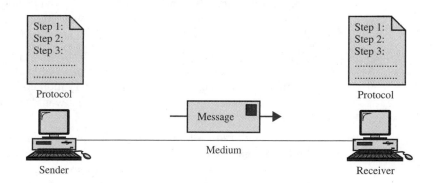

1. **Message.** The message is the information (data) to be communicated. It can consist of text, numbers, pictures, sound, or video—or any combination of these.

2. **Sender.** The sender is the device that sends the data message. It can be a computer, workstation, telephone handset, video camera, and so on.

3. **Receiver.** The receiver is the device that receives the message. It can be a computer, workstation, telephone handset, television, and so on.

4. **Medium.** The transmission medium is the physical path by which a message travels from sender to receiver. It can consist of twisted pair wire, coaxial cable, fiber-optic cable, laser, or radio waves (terrestrial or satellite microwave).

5. **Protocol.** A protocol is a set of rules that govern data communication. It represents an agreement between the communicating devices. Without a protocol, two devices may be connected but not communicating, just as a person speaking French cannot be understood by a person who speaks only Japanese.

1.2   NETWORKS

A network is a set of devices (often referred to as nodes) connected by media links. A node can be a computer, printer, or any other device capable of sending and/or receiving data generated by other nodes on the network. The links connecting the devices are often called communication channels.

Distributed Processing

Networks use distributed processing, in which a task is divided among multiple computers. Instead of a single large machine being responsible for all aspects of a process, each separate computer (usually a personal computer or workstation) handles a subset.
Advantages of distributed processing include the following:

- **Security/encapsulation.** A system designer can limit the kinds of interactions that a given user can have with the entire system. For example, a bank can allow users access to their own accounts through an automated teller machine (ATM) without allowing them access to the bank's entire database.

- **Distributed databases.** No one system needs to provide storage capacity for the entire database. For example, the World Wide Web gives users access to information that may be actually stored and manipulated anywhere on the Internet.

- **Faster problem solving.** Multiple computers working on parts of a problem concurrently can often solve the problem faster than a single machine working alone. For example, networks of PCs have broken encryption codes that were presumed to be unbreakable because of the amount of time it would take a single computer to crack them.

- **Security through redundancy**. Multiple computers running the same program at the same time can provide security through redundancy. For example, in the space shuttle, three computers run the same program so that if one has a hardware error, the other two can override it.

- **Collaborative processing.** Both multiple computers and multiple users may interact on a task. For example, in multiuser network games the actions of each player are visible to and affect all the others.

Network Criteria

To be considered effective and efficient, a network must meet a number of criteria. The most important of these are performance, reliability, and security (see Figure 1.2).

Figure 1.2   *Network criteria*

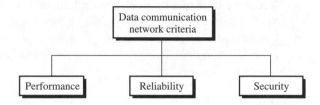

Performance

Performance can be measured in many ways, including transit time and response time. Transit time is the amount of time required for a message to travel from one device to another. Response time is the elapsed time between an inquiry and a response.

The performance of a network depends on a number of factors, including the number of users, the type of transmission medium, the capabilities of the connected hardware, and the efficiency of the software.

- **Number of users.** Having a large number of concurrent users can slow response time in a network not designed to coordinate heavy traffic loads. The design of a given network is based on an assessment of the average number of users that will be communicating at any one time. In peak load periods, however, the actual number of users can exceed the average and thereby decrease performance. How a network responds to loading is a measure of its performance.

- **Type of transmission medium.** The medium defines the speed at which data can travel through a connection (the data rate). Today's networks are moving to faster and faster transmission media, such as fiber optic cabling. A medium that can carry data at 100 megabits per second is ten times more powerful than a medium that can carry data at only 10 megabits per second. However, the speed of light imposes an upper bound on the data rate.

- **Hardware.** The types of hardware included in a network affect both the speed and capacity of transmission. A higher speed computer with greater storage capacity provides better performance.

- **Software.** The software used to process data at the sender, receiver, and intermediate nodes also affects network performance. Moving a message from node to node through a network requires processing to transform the raw data into transmittable signals, to route these signals to the proper destination, to ensure error-free delivery, and to recast the signals into a form the receiver can use. The software that provides these services affects both the speed and the reliability of a network link. Well-designed software can speed the process and make transmission more effective and efficient.

Reliability

In addition to accuracy of delivery, network reliability is measured by frequency of failure, the time it takes a link to recover from a failure, and the network's robustness in a catastrophe.

- **Frequency of failure.** All networks fail occasionally. A network that fails often, however, is of little value to a user.
- **Recovery time of a network after a failure.** How long does it take to restore service? A network that recovers quickly is more useful than one that does not.
- **Catastrophe.** Networks must be protected from catastrophic events such as fire, earthquake, or theft. One protection against unforeseen damage is a reliable system to back up network software.

Security

Network security issues include protecting data from unauthorized access and viruses.

- **Unauthorized access.** For a network to be useful, sensitive data must be protected from unauthorized access. Protection can be accomplished at a number of levels. At the lowest level are user identification codes and passwords. At a higher level are encryption techniques. In these mechanisms, data are systematically altered in such a way that if they are intercepted by an unauthorized user, they will be unintelligible.
- **Viruses.** Because a network is accessible from many points, it can be susceptible to computer viruses. A virus is an illicitly introduced code that damages the system. A good network is protected from viruses by hardware and software designed specifically for that purpose.

Applications

In the short time they have been around, data communication networks have become an indispensable part of business, industry, and entertainment. Some of the network applications in different fields are the following:

- **Marketing and sales.** Computer networks are used extensively in both marketing and sales organizations. Marketing professionals use them to collect, exchange, and analyze data relating to customer needs and product development cycles. Sales applications include teleshopping, which uses order-entry computers or telephones connected to an order-processing network, and on-line reservation services for hotels, airlines, and so on.
- **Financial services.** Today's financial services are totally dependent on computer networks. Applications include credit history searches; foreign exchange and investment services, and electronic funds transfer (EFT), which allows a user to transfer money without going into a bank (an automated teller machine is a kind of electronic funds transfer; automatic paycheck deposit is another).
- **Manufacturing.** Computer networks are used today in many aspects of manufacturing, including the manufacturing process itself. Two applications that use networks to provide essential services are computer-assisted design (CAD) and computer-assisted manufacturing (CAM), both of which allow multiple users to work on a project simultaneously.
- **Electronic messaging.** Probably the most widely used network application is electronic mail (e-mail).

- **Directory services:** Directory services allow lists of files to be stored in a central location to speed worldwide search operations.

- **Information services.** Network information services include bulletin boards and data banks. A World Wide Web site offering the technical specifications for a new product is an information service.

- **Electronic data interchange (EDI).** EDI allows business information (including documents such as purchase orders, and invoices) to be transferred without using paper.

- **Teleconferencing.** Teleconferencing allows conferences to occur without the participants being in the same place. Applications include simple text conferencing (where participants communicate through their keyboards and computer monitors), voice conferencing (where participants at a number of locations communicate simultaneously over the phone), and video conferencing (where participants can see as well as talk to one another).

- **Cellular telephone.** In the past, two parties wishing to use the services of the telephone company had to be linked by a fixed physical connection. Today's cellular networks make it possible to maintain wireless phone connections even while traveling over large distances.

- **Cable television.** Future services provided by cable television networks may include video on request, as well as the same information, financial, and communications services currently provided by the telephone companies and computer networks.

1.3   PROTOCOLS AND STANDARDS

Protocols

In computer networks, communication occurs between entities in different systems. An entity is anything capable of sending or receiving information. Examples include application programs, file transfer packages, browsers, database management systems, and electronic mail software. A system is a physical object that contains one or more entities. Examples include computers and terminals.

But two entities cannot just send bit streams to each other and expect to be understood. For communication to occur, the entities must agree on a protocol. As defined on p. 4, a protocol is a set of rules that govern data communication. A protocol defines what is communicated, how it is communicated, and when it is communicated. The key elements of a protocol are syntax, semantics, and timing.

Syntax

Syntax refers to the structure or format of the data, meaning the order in which they are presented. For example, a simple protocol might expect the first eight bits of data to be the address of the sender, the second eight bits to be the address of the receiver, and the rest of the stream to be the message itself.

Semantics

Semantics refers to the meaning of each section of bits. How is a particular pattern to be interpreted, and what action is to be taken based on that interpretation? For example, does an address identify the route to be taken or the final destination of the message?

Timing

Timing refers to two characteristics: when data should be sent and how fast it can be sent. For example, if a sender produces data at 100 Mbps but the receiver can process data at only 1 Mbps, the transmission will overload the receiver and data will be largely lost.

> In data communication, a protocol is a set of rules (conventions) that governs all aspects of information communication.

Standards

With so many factors to synchronize, a great deal of coordination across the nodes of a network is necessary if communication is to occur at all, let alone accurately or efficiently. A single manufacturer can build all of its products to work well together, but what if some of the best components for your needs are not made by the same company? What good is a television that can pick up only one set of signals if local stations are broadcasting another? Where there are no standards, difficulties arise. Automobiles are an example of nonstandardized products. A steering wheel from one make or model of car will not fit into another model without modification. A standard provides a model for development that makes it possible for a product to work regardless of the individual manufacturer.

Standards are essential in creating and maintaining an open and competitive market for equipment manufacturers and in guaranteeing national and international interoperability of data and telecommunications technology and processes. They provide guidelines to manufacturers, vendors, government agencies, and other service providers to ensure the kind of interconnectivity necessary in today's marketplace and in international communications.

Badly thought-out standards can slow development by forcing adherence to early, possibly inflexible, designs. But today pragmatism and consumer pressure have forced the industry to recognize the need for general models, and there is growing agreement as to what those models are. The intelligence and foresight of designers seem to be such that the standards now being adopted will encourage rather than hinder technical advancement.

Data communication standards fall into two categories: *de facto* (meaning "by fact" or "by convention") and *de jure* (meaning "by law" or "by regulation"). See Figure 1.3.

De jure standards are those that have been legislated by an officially recognized body. Standards that have not been approved by an organized body but have been adopted as standards through widespread use are de facto standards. De facto standards are often established originally by manufacturers seeking to define the functionality of a new product or technology.

Figure 1.3   *Categories of standards*

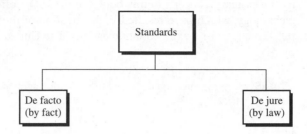

De facto standards can be further subdivided into two classes: *proprietary* and *non-proprietary*. Proprietary standards are those originally invented by a commercial organization as a basis for the operation of its products. They are called proprietary because they are wholly owned by the company that invented them. These standards are also called *closed* standards because they close off communications between systems produced by different vendors. Nonproprietary standards are those originally developed by groups or committees that have passed them into the public domain; they are also called *open* standards because they open communication between different systems.

1.4   STANDARDS ORGANIZATIONS

Standards are developed by cooperation among standards creation committees, forums, and government regulatory agencies.

Standards Creation Committees

While many organizations are dedicated to the establishment of standards, data and telecommunications in North America rely primarily on those published by the following:

- The International Standards Organization (ISO)
- The International Telecommunications Union (ITU-T, formerly the CCITT)
- The American National Standards Institute (ANSI)
- The Institute of Electrical and Electronics Engineers (IEEE)
- The Electronic Industries Association (EIA)
- Bellcore

ISO

The International Standards Organization (ISO; also referred to as the International Organization for Standardization) is a multinational body whose membership is drawn mainly from the standards creation committees of various governments throughout the world. Created in 1947, the ISO is an entirely voluntary organization dedicated to worldwide agreement on international standards. With a membership that currently includes representative bodies from 82 industrialized nations, it aims to facilitate the international exchange of goods and services by providing models for compatibility, improved quality, increased productivity, and decreased prices. The ISO is active in developing cooperation in the realms of scientific, technological, and economic activity. Of primary concern to this book are the ISO's efforts in the field of information technology, which have resulted in the creation of the Open Systems Interconnection (OSI) model for network communications. The United States is represented in the ISO by ANSI.

> The ISO is an organization dedicated to worldwide agreement on international standards in a variety of fields.

ITU-T

By the early 1970s a number of countries were defining national standards for telecommunications, but there was still little international compatibility. The United Nations responded by forming, as part of its International Telecommunications Union (ITU), a committee, the Consultative Committee for International Telegraphy and Telephony (CCITT). This committee was devoted to the research and establishment of standards for telecommunications in general and phone and data systems in particular. On March 1, 1993, the name of this committee was changed to the International Telecommunications Union–Telecommunication Standards Sector (ITU-T).

The ITU-T is divided into study groups, each devoted to a different aspect of the industry. National committees (such as ANSI in the United States and the CEPT in Europe) submit proposals to these study groups. If the study group agrees, the proposal is ratified and becomes part of the ITU-T standard, issued every four years.

The best-known ITU-T standards are the V series (V.32, V.33, V.42), which define data transmission over phone lines; the X series (X.25, X.400, X.500), which define transmission over public digital networks; e-mail and directory services; and the Integrated Services Digital Network (ISDN), which includes parts of the other series and defines the emerging international digital network. Current projects include an extension of ISDN called Broadband ISDN, popularly known as the Information Superhighway.

> ITU-T is an international standards organization related to the United Nations that develops standards for telecommunications. Two popular standards developed by ITU-T are the V series and the X series.

ANSI

Despite its name, the American National Standards Institute (ANSI) is a completely private nonprofit corporation not affiliated with the U.S. federal government. However, all ANSI activities are undertaken with the welfare of the United States and its citizens occupying primary importance. ANSI's expressed aims include serving as the national coordinating institution for voluntary standardization in the United States, furthering the adoption of standards as a way of advancing the U.S. economy, and ensuring the participation and protection of the public interests. ANSI members include professional societies, industry associations, governmental and regulatory bodies, and consumer groups. Current areas of discussion include internetwork planning and engineering; ISDN services, signaling, and architecture; and optical hierarchy (SONET).

ANSI submits proposals to the ITU-T and is the designated voting member from the United States to the ISO. Similar services are provided in the European Community by the Committee of European Post, Telegraph, and Telephone (CEPT) and the European Telecommunications Standards Institute (ETSI).

> ANSI, a nonprofit organization, is the U.S. voting representative to both the ISO and the ITU-T.

IEEE

The Institute of Electrical and Electronics Engineers (IEEE) is the largest professional engineering society in the world. International in scope, it aims to advance theory, creativity, and product quality in the fields of electrical engineering, electronics, and radio as well as in all related branches of engineering. As one of its goals, the IEEE oversees the development and adoption of international standards for computing and communication. The IEEE has a special committee for local area networks (LANs), out of which has come Project 802 (e.g., the 802.3, 802.4, and 802.5 standards).

> The IEEE is the largest national professional group involved in developing standards for computing, communication, electrical engineering, and electronics. It sponsored an important standard for local area networks called Project 802.

EIA

Aligned with ANSI, the Electronic Industries Association (EIA) is a nonprofit organization devoted to the promotion of electronics manufacturing concerns. Its activities include public awareness education and lobbying efforts in addition to standards development. In the field of information technology, the EIA has made significant contributions by defining physical connection interfaces and electronic signaling specifications for data communication. In particular, EIA-232-D, EIA-449, and EIA-530 define serial transmission between two digital devices (e.g., computer to modem).

> EIA is an association of electronics manufacturers in the United States. It is responsible for developing the EIA-232-D and EIA-530 standards.

Bellcore

Bellcore, which stands for Bell Communication Research, is an outgrowth of the Bell Labs. Bellcore provides research and development resources for the advancement of telecommunications technology. It is an important source of draft standards to ANSI.

Forums

Telecommunications technology development is moving faster than the ability of standards committees to ratify standards. Standards committees are procedural bodies and by nature slow moving. To accommodate the need for working models and agreements and to facilitate the standardization process, many special interest groups have developed forums made up of representatives from interested corporations. The forums work with universities and users to test, evaluate, and standardize new technologies. By concentrating their efforts on a particular technology, the forums are able to speed acceptance and use of those technologies in the telecommunications community. The forums present their conclusions to the standards bodies.

Some important forums for the telecommunications industry include the following:

Frame Relay Forum

The Frame Relay Forum was formed by DEC, Northern Telecom, Cisco, and Strata-Com to promote the acceptance and implementation of Frame Relay. Today, it has around 40 members representing North America, Europe, and the Pacific Rim. Issues under review include flow control, encapsulation, translation, and multicasting. Results are submitted to the ISO.

ATM Forum and ATM Consortium

The ATM Forum and the ATM Consortium exist to promote the acceptance and use of Asynchronous Transmission Mode (ATM) technology. The ATM Forum is made up of Customer Premises Equipment (e.g., PBX systems) vendors and Central Office (e.g., telephone exchange) providers. It is concerned with the standardization of services to ensure interoperability. The ATM Consortium is made up of vendors of hardware and software that support ATM.

Internet Society and Internet Engineering Task Force

The Internet Society and the Internet Engineering Task Force (IETF) are concerned with speeding the growth and evolution of Internet communications. The Internet Society concentrates on user issues, including enhancements to the TCP/IP protocol suite. The IETF is the standards body for the Internet itself. It reviews Internet software and hardware. Important contributions include the development of Simple Network Management Protocol (SNMP) and the review of performance standards for bridges, routers, and router protocols.

Regulatory Agencies

All communications technology is subject to regulation by government agencies such as the Federal Communications Commission (FCC) in the United States. The purpose of these agencies is to protect the public interest by regulating radio, television, and wire/cable communications.

FCC

The FCC has authority over interstate and international commerce as it relates to communications. Every piece of communications technology must have FCC approval before it may be marketed (check the bottom of your telephone for an FCC approval code). Specific FCC responsibilities include the following:

- To review rate and service-charge applications made by telegraph and telephone providers.
- To review the technical specifications of communications hardware.

- To establish reasonable common carrier rates of return.
- To divide and allocate radio frequencies.
- To assign carrier frequencies for radio and television broadcasts.

1.5 SUMMARY

- Data communication is the transfer of data from one device to another via some form of transmission medium.
- A data communication system must transmit data to the correct destination in an accurate and timely manner.
- The five basic components of a data communication system are the message, the sender, the receiver, the medium, and the protocol.
- Networks allow shared access to information devices.
- Networks use distributed processing, in which a task is divided among multiple computers.
- Networks are judged by their performance, reliability, and security.
- A protocol is a set of rules that govern data communication; the key elements of a protocol are syntax, semantics, and timing.
- Standards are necessary to ensure that products from different manufacturers can work together as expected.
- The ISO, ITU-T, ANSI, IEEE, EIA, and Bellcore are some of the organizations involved in standards creation.
- Forums consist of representatives from corporations that test, evaluate and standardize new technologies.
- Some important forums are the Frame Relay Forum, the ATM Forum, the Internet Society, and the Internet Engineering Task Force.
- The FCC is a regulatory agency that regulates radio, television, and wire/cable communications.

1.6 PRACTICE SET

Multiple Choice

1. _____ are rules that govern a communication exchange.
   a. Media
   b. Criteria
   c. Protocols
   d. All of the above
2. The _____ is the physical path over which a message travels.
   a. protocol

    b. medium

    c. signal

    d. All of the above

3. Frequency of failure and network recovery time after a failure are measures of the _____ of a network.

    a. performance

    b. reliability

    c. security

    d. feasibility

4. The performance of a data communications network depends on _____.

    a. the number of users

    b. the transmission media

    c. the hardware and software

    d. all of the above

5. Viruses are a network _____ issue.

    a. performance

    b. reliability

    c. security

    d. all of the above

6. Protection of data from a natural disaster such as a tornado is a network _____ issue.

    a. performance

    b. reliability

    c. security

    d. management

7. Which agency is the United States voting member to the ISO?

    a. USO

    b. IEEE

    c. NATO

    d. ANSI

8. Which agency created standards for telephone communications (V series) and standards for network interfaces and public networks (X series)?

    a. ATT

    b. ITU-T

    c. ANSI

    d. ISO

9. Which organization has authority over interstate and international commerce in the communications field?

    a. ITU-T

    b. IEEE

c. FCC

d. Internet Society

10. _____ are special-interest groups that quickly test, evaluate, and standardize new technologies.

   a. Forums

   b. Regulatory agencies

   c. Standards organizations

   d. All of the above

11. Which agency developed standards for electrical connections and the physical transfer of data between devices?

   a. EIA

   b. ITU-T

   c. ANSI

   d. ISO

12. Which organization consists of computer scientists and engineers and is known for its development of LAN standards?

   a. EIA

   b. ITU-T

   c. ANSI

   d. IEEE

Exercises

1. What is the relationship between telecommunications and data communications? Is one a subset of the other? Give reasons for your answers.

2. Give two examples of a product that uses nonstandardized parts. Give two examples of a product that uses standardized parts.

3. Give five instances of how networks were a part of your life today.

4. How can networks be used to make a building secure?

CHAPTER 2

BASIC CONCEPTS

Before examining the specifics of how data are transmitted from one device to another, it is important to understand the relationship between the communicating devices. Five general concepts provide the basis for this relationship:

- Line configuration.
- Topology.
- Transmission mode.
- Categories of networks.
- Internetworks.

2.1 LINE CONFIGURATION

Line configuration refers to the way two or more communication devices attach to a *link*. A link is the physical communication pathway that transfers data from one device to another. For the purposes of visualization, it is simplest to imagine any link as a line drawn between two points. For communication to occur, two devices must be connected in some way to the same link at the same time. There are two possible line configurations: point-to-point and multipoint (see Figure 2.1).

Line configuration defines the attachment of communication devices to a link.

Figure 2.1 *Two categories of line configuration*

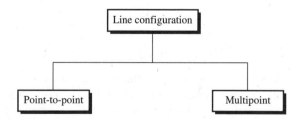

Point-to-Point

A point-to-point line configuration provides a dedicated link between two devices. The entire capacity of the channel is reserved for transmission between those two devices. Most point-to-point line configurations use an actual length of wire or cable to connect the two ends, but other options, such as microwave or satellite links, are also possible (see Figure 2.2). When you change television channels by infrared remote control, you are establishing a point-to-point line configuration between the remote control and the television's control system.

Figure 2.2   *Point-to-point line configuration*

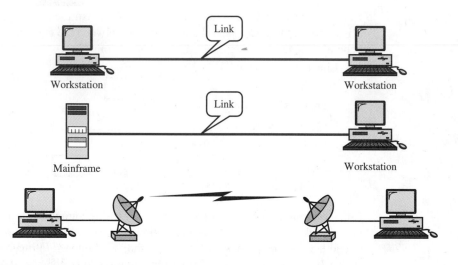

Multipoint

A multipoint (also called multidrop) line configuration is one in which more than two specific devices share a single link (see Figure 2.3).

In a multipoint environment, the capacity of the channel is shared, either spatially or temporally. If several devices can use the link simultaneously, it is a *spatially shared* line configuration. If users must take turns, it is a *time shared* line configuration.

2.2   TOPOLOGY

The term *topology* refers to the way a network is laid out, either physically or logically. Two or more devices connect to a link; two or more links form a topology. The topology of a network is the geometric representation of the relationship of all the links and linking devices (usually called nodes) to each other. There are five basic topologies possible: mesh, star, tree, bus, and ring (see Figure 2.4).

Figure 2.3 *Multipoint line configuration*

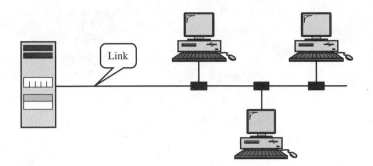

Figure 2.4 *Categories of topology*

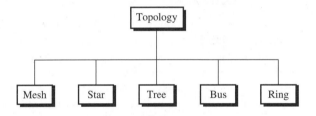

Topology defines the physical or logical arrangement of links in a network.

These five labels describe how the devices in a network are interconnected rather than their physical arrangement. For example, having a star topology does not mean that all of the computers in the network must be placed physically around a hub in a star shape. A consideration when choosing a topology is the relative status of the devices to be linked. Two relationships are possible: *peer-to-peer*, where the devices share the link equally, and *primary–secondary*, where one device controls traffic and the others must transmit through it. Ring and mesh topologies are more convenient for peer-to-peer transmission, while star and tree are more convenient for primary–secondary. A bus topology is equally convenient for either.

Mesh

In a mesh topology, every device has a dedicated point-to-point link to every other device. The term *dedicated* means that the link carries traffic only between the two devices it connects. A fully connected mesh network therefore has $n(n-1)/2$ physical channels to link n devices. To accommodate that many links, every device on the network must have $n-1$ input/output (I/O) ports (see Figure 2.5).

A mesh offers several advantages over other network topologies. First, the use of dedicated links guarantees that each connection can carry its data load, thus eliminating the traffic problems that can occur when links must be shared by multiple devices.

Figure 2.5   *Fully connected mesh topology (for five devices)*

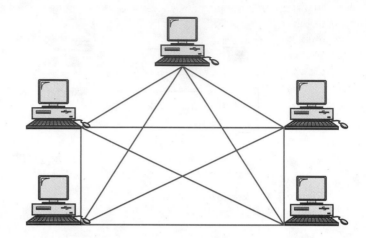

Second, a mesh topology is robust. If one link becomes unusable, it does not incapacitate the entire system.

Another advantage is privacy or security. When every message sent travels along a dedicated line, only the intended recipient sees it. Physical boundaries prevent other users from gaining access to messages.

Finally, point-to-point links make fault identification and fault isolation easy. Traffic can be routed to avoid links with suspected problems. This facility enables the network manager to discover the precise location of the fault and aids in finding its cause and solution.

The main disadvantages of a mesh are related to the amount of cabling and the number of I/O ports required. First, because every device must be connected to every other device, installation and reconfiguration are difficult. Second, the sheer bulk of the wiring can be greater than the available space (in walls, ceilings, or floors) can accommodate. And, finally, the hardware required to connect each link (I/O ports and cable) can be prohibitively expensive. For these reasons a mesh topology is usually implemented in a limited fashion—for example, as a backbone connecting the main computers of a hybrid network that can include several other topologies.

Example 2.1

The Lucky Ducky Corporation has a fully connected mesh network consisting of eight devices. Calculate the total number of cable links needed and the number of ports for each device.

Solution

The formula for the number of links for a fully connected mesh is $n\,(n-1)/2$, where n is the number of devices.

$$\text{Number of links} = n\,(n-1)/2 = 8\,(8-1)\,/\,2 = 28$$

$$\text{Number of ports per device} = n - 1 = 8 - 1 = 7$$

Star

In a star topology, each device has a dedicated point-to-point link only to a central controller, usually called a hub. The devices are not linked to each other. Unlike a mesh topology, a star topology does not allow direct traffic between devices. The controller acts as an exchange: If one device wants to send data to another, it sends to the controller, which then relays the data to the other connected devices (see Figure 2.6).

Figure 2.6   *Star topology*

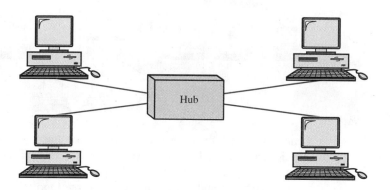

A star topology is less expensive than a mesh topology. In a star, each device needs only one link and one I/O port to connect it to any number of others. This factor also makes it easy to install and reconfigure. Far less cabling needs to be housed, and additions, moves, and deletions involve only one connection: between that device and the hub.

Other advantages include robustness. If one link fails, only that link is affected. All other links remain active. This factor also lends itself to easy fault identification and fault isolation. As long as the hub is working, it can be used to monitor link problems and bypass defective links.

However, although a star requires far less cable than a mesh, each node must be linked to a central hub. For this reason more cabling is required in a star than in some other topologies (such as tree, ring, or bus).

Tree

A tree topology is a variation of a star. As in a star, nodes in a tree are linked to a central hub that controls the traffic to the network. However, not every device plugs directly into the central hub. The majority of devices connect to a secondary hub that in turn is connected to the central hub (see Figure 2.7).

The central hub in the tree is an active hub. An active hub contains a repeater, which is a hardware device that regenerates the received bit patterns before sending them out (repeaters are discussed at length in Chapter 15). Repeating strengthens transmissions and increases the distance a signal can travel between sender and receiver.

Figure 2.7   *Tree topology*

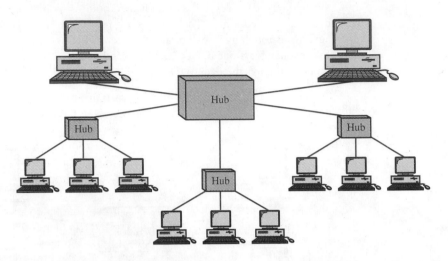

The secondary hubs may be active or passive hubs. A passive hub provides a simple physical connection between the attached devices. Internally, each passive hub contains a set of resistors to balance the circuit linking the connected devices.

The advantages and disadvantages of a tree topology are generally the same as those of a star. The addition of secondary hubs, however, brings two further advantages. First, it allows more devices to be attached to a single central hub and can therefore increase the distance a signal can travel between devices. Second, it allows the network to isolate and prioritize communications from different computers. For example, the computers attached to one secondary hub can be given priority over computers attached to another secondary hub. In this way the network designers and operator can guarantee that time-sensitive data will not have to wait for access to the network.

Bus

The preceding examples all describe point-to-point configurations A bus topology, on the other hand, is multipoint. One long cable acts as a backbone to link all the devices in the network (see Figure 2.8).

Figure 2.8   *Bus topology*

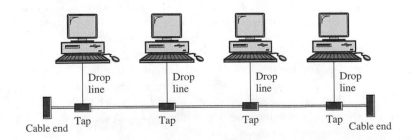

Nodes are connected to the bus cable by drop lines and taps. A drop line is a connection running between the device and the main cable. A tap is a connector that either splices into the main cable or punctures the sheathing of a cable to create a contact with the metallic core. As a signal travels along the backbone, some of its energy is transformed into heat. Therefore, it becomes weaker and weaker the farther it has to travel. For this reason there is a limit on the number of taps a bus can support and on the distance between those taps.

Advantages of a bus topology include ease of installation. Backbone cable can be laid along the most efficient path, then connected to the nodes by drop lines of various lengths. In this way, a bus uses less cabling than mesh, star, or tree topologies. In a star, for example, four network devices in the same room require four lengths of cable reaching all the way to the hub. In a bus, this redundancy is eliminated. Only the backbone cable stretches through the entire facility. Each drop line has to reach only as far as the nearest point on the backbone.

Disadvantages include difficult reconfiguration and fault isolation. A bus is usually designed to be optimally efficient at installation. It can therefore be difficult to add new devices. As mentioned above, signal reflection at the taps can cause degradation in quality. This degradation can be controlled by limiting the number and spacing of devices connected to a given length of cable. Adding new devices may therefore require modification or replacement of the backbone.

In addition, a fault or break in the bus cable stops all transmission, even between devices on the same side of the problem. The damaged area reflects signals back in the direction of origin, creating noise in both directions.

Ring

In a ring topology, each device has a dedicated point-to-point line configuration only with the two devices on either side of it. A signal is passed along the ring in one direction, from device to device, until it reaches its destination. Each device in the ring incorporates a repeater. When a device receives a signal intended for another device, its repeater regenerates the bits and passes them along (see Figure 2.9).

Figure 2.9 *Ring topology*

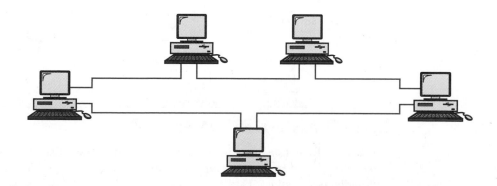

A ring is relatively easy to install and reconfigure. Each device is linked only to its immediate neighbors (either spatially or logically). To add or delete a device requires moving only two connections. The only constraints are media and traffic considerations (maximum ring length and number of devices). In addition, fault isolation is simplified. Generally in a ring, a signal is circulating at all times. If one device does not receive a signal within a specified period, it can issue an alarm. The alarm alerts the network operator to the problem and its location.

However, unidirectional traffic can be a disadvantage. In a simple ring, a break in the ring (such as a disabled station) can disable the entire network. This weakness can be solved by using a dual ring or a switch capable of closing off the break.

Example 2.2

If the devices in Example 2.1 are configured as a ring instead of a mesh, how many cable links are required?

Solution

To connect n devices in a ring topology, we need n cable links. An eight-device ring needs eight cable links.

Hybrid Topologies

Often a network combines several topologies as subnetworks linked together in a larger topology. For instance, one department of a business may have decided to use a bus topology while another department has a ring. The two can be connected to each other via a central controller in a star topology (see Figure 2.10).

Figure 2.10 *Hybrid topology*

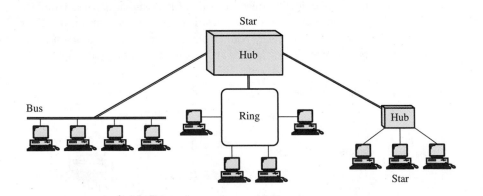

2.3   TRANSMISSION MODE

The term *transmission mode* is used to define the direction of signal flow between two linked devices. There are three types of transmission modes: *simplex*, *half-duplex*, and *full-duplex* (see Figure 2.11).

Figure 2.11   *Transmission modes*

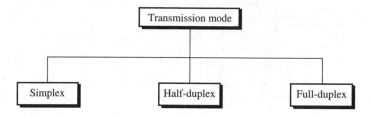

Simplex

In simplex mode, the communication is unidirectional, as on a one-way street. Only one of the two stations on a link can transmit; the other can only receive (see Figure 2.12).

Figure 2.12   *Simplex*

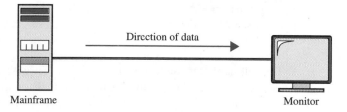

Mainframe   Monitor

The term *transmission mode* refers to the direction of information flow between two devices.

Keyboards and traditional monitors are both examples of simplex devices. The keyboard can only introduce input; the monitor can only accept output.

Half-Duplex

In half-duplex mode, each station can both transmit and receive, but not at the same time. When one device is sending, the other can only receive, and vice versa (see Figure 2.13).

The half-duplex mode is like a one-lane road with two-directional traffic. While cars are traveling one direction, cars going the other way must wait. In a half-duplex transmission, the entire capacity of a channel is taken over by whichever of the two devices is transmitting at the time. Walkie-talkies and CB radios are both half-duplex systems.

Full-Duplex

In full-duplex mode (also called duplex), both stations can transmit and receive simultaneously (see Figure 2.14).

Figure 2.13   *Half-duplex*

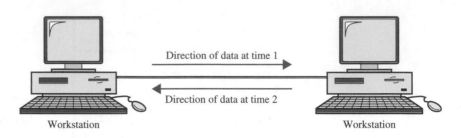

Figure 2.14   *Full-duplex*

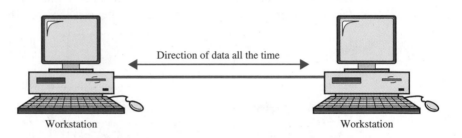

The full-duplex mode is like a two-way street with traffic flowing in both directions at the same time. In full-duplex mode, signals going in either direction share the capacity of the link. This sharing can occur in two ways: either the link must contain two physically separate transmission paths, one for sending and the other for receiving, or the capacity of the channel is divided between signals traveling in opposite directions.

2.4   CATEGORIES OF NETWORKS

Today when we speak of networks, we are generally referring to three primary categories: local area networks (LANs), metropolitan area networks (MANs), and wide area networks (WANs). Which category a network falls into is determined by its size, its ownership, the distance it covers, and its physical architecture (see Figure 2.15).

Local Area Network (LAN)

A local area network is usually privately owned and links the devices in a single office, building, or campus (see Figure 2.16). Depending on the needs of an organization and the type of technology used, a LAN can be as simple as two PCs and a printer in someone's home office, or it can extend throughout a company and include voice, sound, and video peripherals. Currently, LAN size is limited to a few kilometers.

LANs are designed to allow resources to be shared between personal computers or workstations. The resources to be shared can include hardware (e.g., a printer), soft-

Figure 2.15   *Categories of networks*

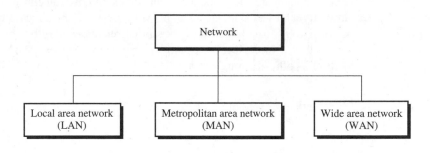

Figure 2.16   *LAN*

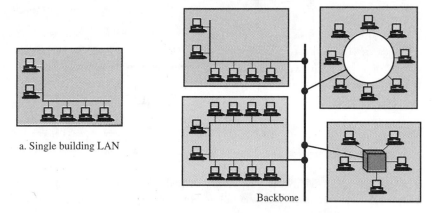

a. Single building LAN

Backbone

b. Multiple building LAN

ware (e.g., an application program), or data. A common example of a LAN, found in many business environments, links a work group of task-related computers, for example, engineering workstations or accounting PCs. One of the computers may be given a large-capacity disk drive and become a server to the other clients. Software can be stored on this central server and used as needed by the whole group. In this example, the size of the LAN may be determined by licensing restrictions on the number of users per copy of software, or by restrictions on the number of users licensed to access the operating system.

In addition to size, LANs are distinguished from other types of networks by their transmission media and topology. In general, a given LAN will use only one type of transmission medium. The most common LAN topologies are bus, ring, and star.

Traditionally, LANs have data rates in the 4 to 16 Mbps range. Today, however, speeds are increasing and can reach 100 Mbps with gigabit systems in development. LANs are discussed at length in Chapter 12.

Metropolitan Area Network (MAN)

A metropolitan area network is designed to extend over an entire city. It may be a single network such as a cable television network, or it may be a means of connecting a number of LANs into a larger network so that resources may be shared LAN-to-LAN as well as device-to-device. For example, a company can use a MAN to connect the LANs in all of its offices throughout a city (see Figure 2.17).

Figure 2.17   *MAN*

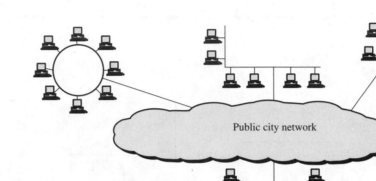

A MAN may be wholly owned and operated by a private company, or it may be a service provided by a public company, such as a local telephone company. Many telephone companies provide a popular MAN service called Switched Multi-megabit Data Services (SMDS), which is discussed in Chapter 13.

Wide Area Network (WAN)

A wide area network provides long-distance transmission of data, voice, image, and video information over large geographical areas that may comprise a country, a continent, or even the whole world (see Figure 2.18).

In contrast to LANs (which depend on their own hardware for transmission), WANs may utilize public, leased, or private communication devices, usually in combinations, and can therefore span an unlimited number of miles.

A WAN that is wholly owned and used by a single company is often referred to as an enterprise network.

Figure 2.18   *WAN*

2.5   INTERNETWORKS

When two or more networks are connected, they become an *internetwork,* or *internet* (see Figure 2.19; in the figure, the boxes labeled R represent routers). Individual networks are joined into internetworks by the use of internetworking devices. These devices which include routers and gateways, are discussed in Chapter 20. The term *internet* (lowercase *i*) should not be confused with *the Internet* (uppercase *I*). The first is a generic term used to mean an interconnection of networks. The second is the name of a specific worldwide network.

Figure 2.19   *Internetwork (internet)*

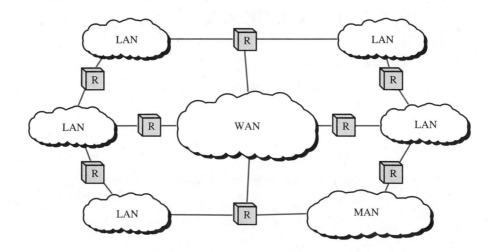

2.6 SUMMARY

- A line configuration defines the relationship of communication devices to a communications pathway.
- In a point-to-point line configuration, two and only two devices are connected by a dedicated link.
- In a multipoint line configuration three or more devices share a link.
- Topology refers to the physical or logical arrangement of a network. Devices may be arranged in a mesh, star, tree, bus, ring, or hybrid topology.
- Communication between two devices can occur in one of three transmission modes: simplex, half-duplex, or full-duplex.
- Simplex transmission means that data flows in one direction only.
- Half-duplex transmission allows data to flow in both directions, but not at the same time.
- Full-duplex transmission allows data to flow in both directions at the same time.
- A network can be categorized as a local area network (LAN), a metropolitan area network (MAN), or a wide area network (WAN).
- A LAN is a data communication system within a building, plant, or campus, or between nearby buildings.
- A MAN is a data communication system covering an area the size of a town or city.
- A WAN is a data communication system spanning states, countries, or the whole world.
- An internet is a network of networks.

2.7 PRACTICE SET

Multiple Choice

1. Which topology requires a central controller or hub?
   a. mesh
   b. star
   c. bus
   d. ring
2. Which topology requires a multipoint connection?
   a. mesh
   b. star
   c. bus
   d. ring

3. Communication between a computer and a keyboard involves _____ transmission.
   a. simplex
   b. half-duplex
   c. full-duplex
   d. automatic
4. In a network with 25 computers, which topology would require the most extensive cabling?
   a. mesh
   b. star
   c. bus
   d. ring
5. A tree topology is a variation of a _____ topology.
   a. mesh
   b. star
   c. bus
   d. ring
6. A television broadcast is an example of _____ transmission.
   a. simplex
   b. half-duplex
   c. full-duplex
   d. automatic
7. In a _____ topology, if there are *n* devices in a network, each device has *n*−1 ports for cables.
   a. mesh
   b. star
   c. bus
   d. ring
8. A _____ connection provides a dedicated link between two devices.
   a. point-to-point
   b. multipoint
   c. primary
   d. secondary
9. In a _____ connection, more than two devices can share a single link.
   a. point-to-point
   b. multipoint
   c. primary
   d. secondary

10. In _____ transmission, the channel capacity is used by both communicating devices at all times.

   a. simplex

   b. half-duplex

   c. full-duplex

   d. half-simplex

11. MacKenzie Publishing, with headquarters in London and branch offices throughout Asia, Europe, and South America, is probably connected by _____.

   a. a LAN

   b. a MAN

   c. a WAN

   d. none of the above

12. BAF Plumbing has a network consisting of two workstations and one printer. This is most probably a _____.

   a. a LAN

   b. a MAN

   c. a WAN

   d. none of the above

Exercises

1. What are the advantages of a multipoint connection over a point-to-point connection?

2. Assume six devices arranged in a mesh topology. How many cables are needed? How many ports are needed for each device?

3. For each of the following four networks, discuss the consequences if a connection fails:

   a. Five devices arranged in a mesh topology.

   b. Five devices arranged in a star topology (not counting the hub).

   c. Five devices arranged in a bus topology.

   d. Five devices arranged in a ring topology.

4. Match the following to a topology type (each can apply to more than one topology):

   a. New devices can be added easily.

   b. Control is through a central device.

   c. Failure of a device does not cause system failure.

   d. Transmission time is spent relaying data through nondestination nodes.

5. Suppose you add two new devices to an existing five-device network. If you have a fully connected mesh topology, how many new cable lines are needed? If, however, the devices are arranged in a single ring, how many new cable lines are needed?

6. Which transmission mode (simplex, half-duplex, or full-duplex) can be compared to the following? Justify your answer.

   a. A heated argument between Lucy and Desi.

   b. A computer to monitor connection.

   c. A polite conversation between Aunt Gertrude and Aunt Rowena.

   d. A television broadcast.

   e. A reversible commuter lane.

   f. A turnstile.

   g. Citizen's band (CB) radio.

7. What are some of the factors that determine whether a communication system is a LAN, MAN, or WAN?

CHAPTER 3

THE OSI MODEL

Established in 1947, the International Standards Organization (ISO) is a multinational body dedicated to worldwide agreement on international standards. An ISO standard that covers all aspects of network communications is the Open Systems Interconnection (OSI) model. An open system is a set of protocols that allows any two different systems to communicate regardless of their underlying architecture. Vendor-specific protocols close off communication between unrelated systems. The purpose of the OSI model is to open communication between different systems without requiring changes to the logic of the underlying hardware and software. The OSI model is not a protocol; it is a model for understanding and designing a network architecture that is flexible, robust, and interoperable.

ISO is the organization. OSI is the model.

3.1 THE MODEL

The Open Systems Interconnection model is a layered framework for the design of network systems that allows for communication across all types of computer systems. It consists of seven separate but related layers, each of which defines a segment of the process of moving information across a network (see Figure 3.1). Understanding the fundamentals of the OSI model provides a solid basis for exploration of data communications.

Layered Architecture

The OSI model is built of seven ordered layers: physical (layer 1), data link (layer 2), network (layer 3), transport (layer 4), session (layer 5), presentation (layer 6), and application (layer 7). Figure 3.2 shows the layers involved when a message is sent from device A to device B. As the message travels from A to B, it may pass through many intermediate nodes. These intermediate nodes usually involve only the first three layers of the OSI model. In developing the model, the designers distilled the process of transmitting data down to its most fundamental elements. They identified which networking

Figure 3.1   *The OSI model*

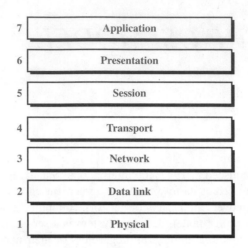

Figure 3.2   *OSI layers*

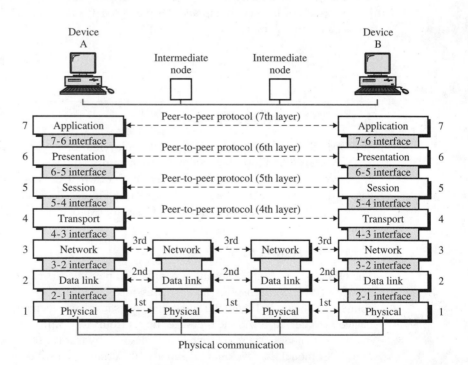

functions had related uses and collected those functions into discrete groups that became the layers. Each layer defines a family of functions distinct from those of the other layers. By defining and localizing functionality in this fashion, the designers created an architecture that is both comprehensive and flexible. Most important, the OSI model allows complete transparency between otherwise incompatible systems.

A mnemonic for remembering the layers of the OSI model is: **Please Do Not Touch Steve's Pet Alligator**, (**P**hysical, **D**ata Link, **N**etwork, **T**ransport, **S**ession, **P**resentation, **A**pplication).

Peer-to-Peer Processes

Within a single machine, each layer calls upon the services of the layer just below it. Layer 3, for example, uses the services provided by layer 2 and provides services for layer 4. Between machines, layer x on one machine communicates with layer x on another machine. This communication is governed by an agreed-upon series of rules and conventions called protocols. The processes on each machine that communicate at a given layer are called peer-to-peer processes. Communication between machines is therefore a peer-to-peer process using the protocols appropriate to a given layer.

At the physical layer, communication is direct: Machine A sends a stream of bits to machine B. At the higher layers, however, communication must move down through the layers on machine A, over to machine B, and then back up through the layers. Each layer in the sending machine adds its own information to the message it receives from the layer just above it and passes the whole package to the layer just below it. This information is added in the form of headers or trailers (control data appended to the beginning or end of a data parcel). Headers are added to the message at layers 6, 5, 4, 3, and 2. A trailer is added at layer 2.

Headers are added to the data at layers 6, 5, 4, 3, and 2. Trailers are usually added only at layer 2.

At layer 1 the entire package is converted to a form that can be transferred to the receiving machine. At the receiving machine, the message is unwrapped layer by layer, with each process receiving and removing the data meant for it. For example, layer 2 removes the data meant for it, then passes the rest to layer 3. Layer 3 removes the data meant for it and passes the rest to layer 4, and so on.

Interfaces between Layers

The passing of the data and network information down through the layers of the sending machine and back up through the layers of the receiving machine is made possible by an *interface* between each pair of adjacent layers. Each interface defines what information and services a layer must provide for the layer above it. Well-defined interfaces and layer functions provide modularity to a network. As long as a layer still provides the expected services to the layer above it, the specific implementation of its functions can be modified or replaced without requiring changes to the surrounding layers.

Organization of the Layers

The seven layers can be thought of as belonging to three subgroups. Layers 1, 2, and 3—physical, data link, and network—are the network support layers; they deal with the physical aspects of moving data from one device to another (such as electrical specifications, physical connections, physical addressing, and transport timing and reliability). Layers 5, 6, and 7—session, presentation, and application—can be thought of as the user support layers; they allow interoperability among unrelated software systems. Layer 4, the transport layer, links the two subgroups and ensures that what the lower layers have transmitted is in a form that the upper layers can use. The upper OSI layers are almost always implemented in software; lower layers are a combination of hardware and software, except for the physical layer, which is mostly hardware.

In Figure 3.3, which gives an overall view of the OSI layers, L7 data means the data unit at layer 7, L6 data means the data unit at layer 6, and so on.The process starts out at layer 7 (the application layer), then moves from layer to layer in descending sequential order. At each layer (except layers 7 and 1), a header is added to the data unit. At layer 2, a trailer is added as well. When the formatted data unit passes through the physical layer (layer 1), it is changed into an electromagnetic signal and transported along a physical link.

Figure 3.3   *An exchange using the OSI model*

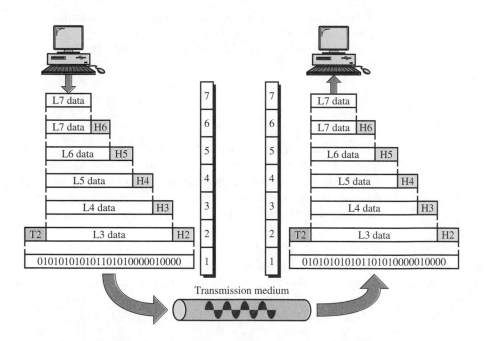

Upon reaching its destination, the signal passes into layer 1 and is transformed back into digital form. The data units then move back up through the OSI layers. As each block of data reaches the next higher layer, the headers and trailers attached to it at the corresponding sending layer are removed, and actions appropriate to that layer are taken. By the time it reaches layer 7, the message is again in a form appropriate to the application and is made available to the recipient.

3.2   FUNCTIONS OF THE LAYERS

Physical Layer

The physical layer coordinates the functions required to transmit a bit stream over a physical medium. It deals with the mechanical and electrical specifications of the primary connections, such as cables, connectors, and signaling options that physically link two nodes on a network.

This first layer receives a data unit from the second layer and puts it into a format capable of being carried by a communications link. It oversees the changing of a bit stream into electromagnetic signals, and their transmission onto and across a medium (see Figure 3.4).

Figure 3.4   *Physical layer*

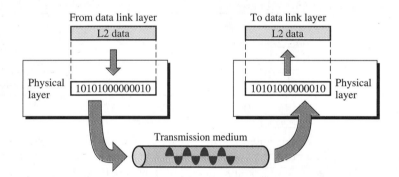

This seemingly simple task requires a number of considerations:

- **Line configuration.** How can two or more devices be linked physically? Are transmission lines to be shared or limited to use between two devices? Is the line available or not?

- **Data transmission mode.** It does transmission flow one way or both ways between two connected devices? Or does it alternate?

- **Topology.** How are network devices arranged? Do they pass data directly to each other or through an intermediary? And by what paths?

- **Signals.** What type of signals are useful for transmitting information?

- **Encoding.** How are bits (0s and 1s) to be represented by available signaling systems? How are data represented by signals?

- **Interface.** What information must be shared between two closely linked devices to enable and facilitate communication? What is the most efficient way to communicate that information?

- **Medium.** What is the physical environment for the transmission of data?

Data Link Layer

The data link layer is responsible for delivering data units (groups of bits) from one station to the next without errors. It accepts a data unit from the third layer and adds meaningful bits to the beginning (header) and end (trailer) that contain addresses and other control information. A data unit with this additional information is called a frame (see Figure 3.5).

Figure 3.5   *Data link layer*

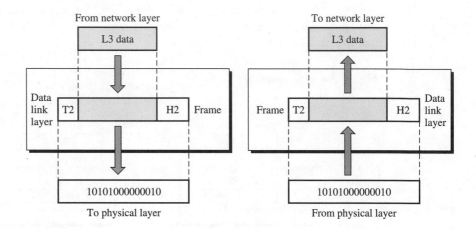

To get to its ultimate destination, a transmission may have to be passed along by a number of intermediate stations, much as a letter from California to Cornell University in Ithaca, New York, may first go to New York City, from there to Syracuse, and from there to Ithaca before finally arriving at Cornell. Data link frame headers and trailers contain the information necessary to move a data unit from one of these stations to the next (information such as the physical address of the station passing along the data unit and that of the next station to which the frame must go on the way to its final destination).

In addition, the data link layer is responsible for flow control and error detection. Protocols in this layer regulate the right of a device to transmit; how to keep transmissions from overwhelming the receiver; and how to ensure that errors introduced during transmission are corrected. To this end, headers and trailers also carry information about synchronization (where one bit stops and another starts), sequencing (what part of the overall transmission is represented by a particular frame), and whether or not the last frame arrived intact.

Headers and trailers at this level are added by the sending node, then checked and interpreted by the receiving node. Once a receiving node accepts a frame, it strips off the header and trailer and passes the remaining data unit on to the network layer.

Specific responsibilities of the data link layer include the following:

- **Node-to-node delivery.** The data link layer is responsible for node-to-node delivery.
- **Addressing.** Headers and trailers added at this layer include the physical addresses of the most recent node and the next intended node.

■ **Access control.** When two or more devices are connected to the same link, the data link layer protocols are necessary to determine which device has control over the link at any given time.

■ **Flow control.** To avoid overwhelming the receiver, the data link layer regulates the amount of data that can be transmitted at one time. It adds identifying numbers to enable the receiving node to control the ordering of the frames.

■ **Error handling.** Data link layer protocols provide for data recovery, usually by having the entire frame retransmitted.

■ **Synchronization.** Headers contain bits to alert the receiving station that a frame is arriving. In addition, these bits provide a pattern to allow the receiver to synchronize its timing to that of the transmission (to know the duration of each bit). Trailers contain bits for error control and also bits that indicate the frame has ended, and that anything to follow is either a new frame or an idle channel.

When the standards were developed for local area networks, the data link layer was subdivided into two sublayers: logical link control (LLC) and media access control (MAC). This subdivision allows for inconsistencies between the protocols of different vendors (see Chapter 12).

Example 3.1

In Figure 3.6 a node with physical address 10 sends a frame to a node with physical address 87. The two nodes are connected by a link. At the data link level this frame contains physical (link) addresses in the header. These are the only addresses needed. The rest of the header contains other information needed at this level. The trailer usually contains extra bits needed for error detection.

Figure 3.6   *Data link layer (Example 3.1)*

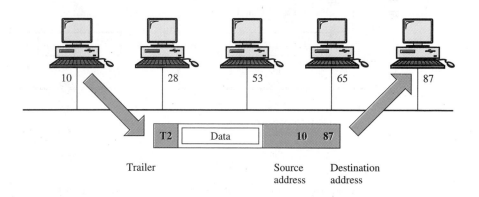

Network Layer

The network layer is responsible for the source-to-destination delivery of a packet across multiple network links. Whereas the data link layer oversees station-to-station (node-to-node) delivery, the network layer ensures that each packet gets from its point of origin to its final destination successfully and efficiently.

To make such end-to-end delivery possible, the network layer provides two related services: *switching* and *routing*. Switching refers to temporary connections between physical links, resulting in longer links for network transmission. A telephone conversation is an example of a switched connection: two lines are temporarily joined into a single dedicated link for the duration of the conversation. In this case each packet is sent by the same route to the destination.

Routing means selecting the best path for sending a packet from one point to another when more than one path is available. In this case, each packet may take a different route to the destination, where the packets are collected and reassembled into their original order. Routing considerations include speed, cost, and the ability to change pathways in midtransmission.

Routing and switching require the addition of a header that includes, among other information, the source and destination addresses of the packet. These addresses are different from the physical (node) addresses included in the data link header. Data link addresses are of the current and next node only (the physical addresses). They change as a frame moves from one node to the next. Network layer addresses are those of the original source and the final destination. They do not change during transmission and are often called the logical addresses. The addition of the network layer header is shown in Figure 3.7.

Figure 3.7   *Network layer*

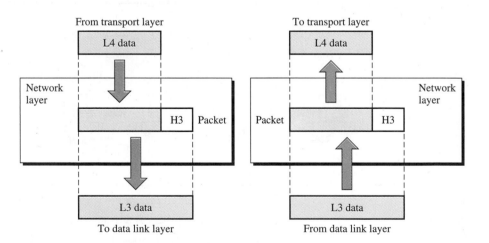

Specific responsibilities of the network layer include the following:

- **Source-to-destination delivery.** Moving a packet (best effort) from its point of origin to its intended destination across multiple network links.
- **Logical addressing.** Inclusion of the source and destination addresses in the header.
- **Routing.** Deciding which of multiple paths a packet should take.
- **Address transformation.** Interpreting logical addresses to find their physical equivalents.

■ **Multiplexing.** Using a single physical line to carry data between many devices at the same time.

Example 3.2

Now imagine that in Figure 3.8 we want to send data from a node with network address A and physical address 10, located on one local area network, to a node with a network address P and physical address 95, located on another local area network. Because the two devices are located on different networks, we cannot use link addresses only; the link addresses have only local jurisdiction. What we need here are universal addresses that can pass through the boundaries of local area networks. The network (logical) addresses have this characteristic. The packet at the network layer contains the logical addresses, which remain the same from the original source to the final destination (A and P, respectively, in the figure). They will not change when we go from network to network. However, the physical addresses will change when the packet moves from one network to another. The box with the R is a router (internetwork device), which we will discuss in Chapter 20.

Figure 3.8 *Network layer (Example 3.2)*

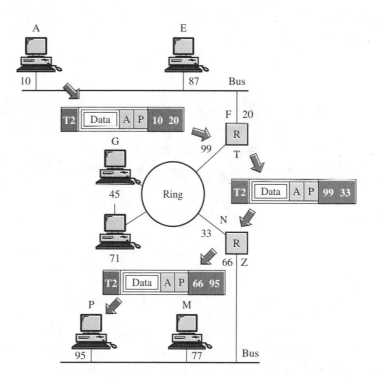

Transport Layer

The transport layer is responsible for source-to-destination (end-to-end) delivery of the entire message. Whereas the network layer oversees end-to-end delivery of individual packets, it does not recognize any relationship between those packets. It treats each one independently, as though each piece belonged to a separate message, whether or not it does. The transport layer, on the other hand, ensures that the whole message arrives intact and in order, overseeing both error control and flow control at the source-to-destination level.

Computers often run several programs at the same time. For this reason, source-to-destination delivery means delivery not only from one computer to the next but also from a specific application on one computer to a specific application on the other. The transport layer header must therefore include a type of address called a service-point address (also called a port address or socket address). The network layer gets each packet to the correct computer; the transport layer gets the entire message to the correct application on that computer.

The transport layer header also contains sequence, or segmentation, numbers. As the transport layer receives the message to be sent from the session layer (layer 5), it divides it into transmittable segments, indicating in the header the sequence of the segments so that they can be reassembled upon receipt at the destination. Figure 3.9 shows the relationship of the transport layer to the network and session layers.

Figure 3.9   *Transport layer*

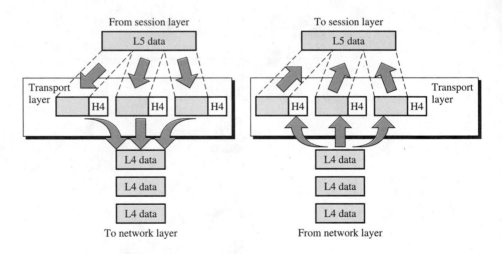

For added security, the transport layer may create a *connection* between the two end ports. A connection is a single logical path between the source and destination that is associated with all packets in a message. Creating a connection involves three steps: connection establishment, data transfer, and connection release. By confining transmission of all packets to a single pathway, the transport layer has more control over sequencing, flow, and error detection and correction.

Specific responsibilities of the transport layer include the following:

- **End-to-end message delivery.** Overseeing the transmission and arrival of all packets of a message at the destination point.

- **Service-point (port) addressing.** Guaranteeing delivery of a message to the appropriate application on a computer running multiple applications.
- **Segmentation and reassembly.** Dividing a message into transmittable segments, and marking each segment with a sequence number. These numbers enable the transport layer to reassemble the message correctly at the destination and to identify and replace packets lost in transmission.
- **Connection control**. Deciding whether or not to send all packets by a single path.

Example 3.3

Figure 3.10 shows an example of a transport layer. Data coming from the upper layers have service-point (port) addresses j and k (j is the address of the sending application, and k is the address of the receiving application). Since the data size is larger than the network layer can handle, the data are split into two packets, each packet retaining the service-point addresses (j and k). Then in the network layer, network addresses (A and P) are added to each packet. The packets may travel on different paths and arrive at the destination either in order or out of order. The two packets are delivered to the destination transport layer, which is responsible for removing the network layer headers and combining the two pieces of data for delivery to the upper layers.

Figure 3.10   *Transport layer (Example 3.3)*

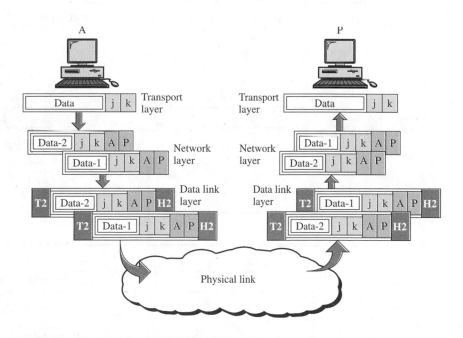

Session Layer

The session layer is the network *dialog controller*. It establishes, maintains, and synchronizes the interaction between communicating devices. It also ensures that each session closes appropriately rather than shutting down abruptly and leaving the user hanging. For example, imagine that a user wants to transfer a file of 200 pages. What happens if the transfer is interrupted after only 52 pages? When the problem is removed and the connection can be made again, should the session be canceled and started all over from page 1? Or should the large session be divided into sub-sessions (of, for example, 10 pages each) so that a problem after page 52 results in only the last two pages (51 and 52) being resent when the session is restored? These issues are concerns of the session layer.

The session layer validates and establishes connections between users. The data unit at this layer may carry the credentials of the host seeking the connection, including password and log-in verification. This is essential whenever a system allows remote access to files. The session layer also controls the exchange of data: whether the exchange occurs in both directions simultaneously or only one direction at a time. If one way at a time, how should turns be taken?

Reliability at the session layer is created by dividing the session into subsessions using checkpoints inserted into the stream. Checkpoints allow a session to backtrack a certain distance without completely starting over when problems occur (as in the file transfer example above). Depending on the requirements of the specific transmission, checkpoints can be either extremely important or ignored altogether.

The header for this layer includes control information such as the type of the data unit being sent and synchronization point information. The relationship of the session layer to the transport and presentation layers is shown in Figure 3.11.

Figure 3.11 *Session layer*

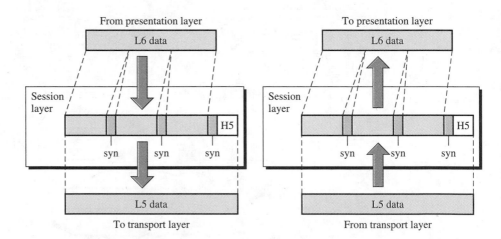

Specific responsibilities of the session layer include the following:

- **Session management.** Dividing a session into subsessions by the introduction of checkpoints and separating long messages into shorter units, called dialog units appropriate for transmission.

- **Synchronization.** Deciding in what order to pass the dialog units to the transport layer, and where in the transmission to require confirmation from the receiver.

- **Dialog control.** Deciding who sends, and when.
- **Graceful close.** Ensuring that the exchange has been completed appropriately before the session closes.

Example 3.4

A computer needs to update a huge file (e.g., a database). The session layer subdivides the tasks into different dialog units.

Presentation Layer

The presentation layer ensures interoperability among communicating devices. Functions at this layer make it possible for two computers to communicate even if their internal representations of data differ (e.g., when one device uses one type of code and the other uses another). It provides the necessary translation of different control codes, character sets, graphics characters, and so on to allow both devices to understand the same transmission the same way.

The presentation layer is also responsible for the encryption and decryption of data for security purposes and for the compression and expansion of data when necessary for transmission efficiency.

Headers added at this layer include information on the type and parameters of the transmission, and the length of the transmission. Figure 3.12 shows the relationship between the presentation layer and the application and session layers.

Figure 3.12 *Presentation layer*

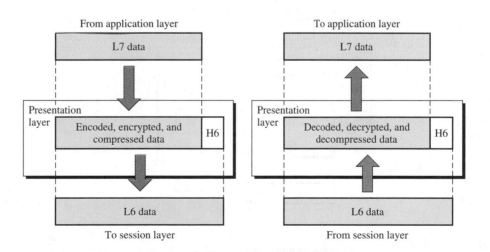

Specific responsibilities of the presentation layer include the following:

- **Translation.** Changing the format of a message from that used by the sender into one mutually acceptable for transmission. Then, at the destination, changing that format into the one understood by the receiver.

- **Encryption.** Encryption and decryption of data for security purposes.
- **Compression.** Compressing and decompressing data to make transmission more efficient.
- **Security.** Validating passwords and log-in codes.

Example 3.5

The sending station uses an encryption algorithm (see Chapter 22) to protect the data from eavesdropping. The encrypted data are decrypted at the destination presentation layer before being delivered to the application layer.

Application Layer

The application layer enables the user, whether human or software, to access the network. It provides user interfaces and support for services such as electronic mail, remote file access and transfer, shared database management, and other types of distributed information services.

The relationship of the application layer to the user and the presentation layer is shown in Figure 3.13. Of the many application services available, the figure shows only three, X.400 (message handling services), X.500 (directory services), and FTAM (file transfer and access management). The user at this moment uses X.400 to send an e-mail message. Note that no headers or trailers are added at this layer.

Figure 3.13   *Application layer*

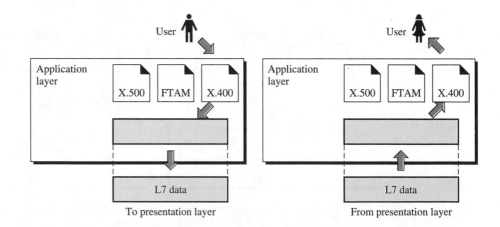

Specific services provided by the application layer include the following:

- **Network virtual terminal.** A software version of a physical terminal. A virtual terminal allows you to log on to a remote host. To do so, the application creates a software emulation of a terminal at the remote host. Your computer talks to the software terminal, which in turn talks to the host, and vice versa. The remote host believes it is communicating with one of its own terminals and allows you to log on.

- **File access, transfer, and management.** Allows a user at a remote computer to access files in another host (to make changes or read data); to retrieve files from a remote computer for use in the local computer; and to manage or control files in a remote computer at that computer.
- **Mail services.** Provides the basis for electronic mail forwarding and storage.
- **Directory services.** Provides distributed database sources and access for global information about various objects and services.

Example 3.6

A user in Beijing, China, wants to send a large proprietary data file to a station in Los Gatos, California. An application service such as FTAM (file transfer and access management) can do the job.

Summary of Layer Functions

The functions of the seven layers are summarized in Figure 3.14.

Figure 3.14   *Summary of layer functions*

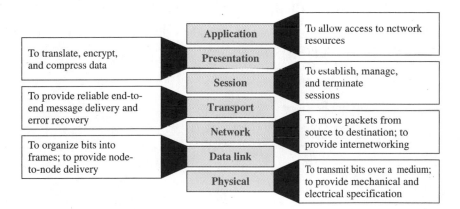

3.3   SUMMARY

- The International Standards Organization (ISO) has created a seven-layer model called Open Systems Interconnection (OSI) to facilitate the development of interactive systems.
- The physical layer coordinates the hardware and software functions required to transmit a bit stream over a physical medium. It deals with the mechanical and electrical specifications of the primary connections.
- The data link layer is responsible for delivering frames from one station to the next without errors. It provides error handling and flow control between one station and the next.

■ The network layer is responsible for the source-to-destination delivery of a data packet. It handles switching and routing.

■ The transport layer is responsible for source-to-destination (end-to-end) delivery of the entire message from one application to another.

■ The session layer is the network dialog controller. It establishes, maintains, and synchronizes the interaction between communicating devices.

■ The presentation layer ensures interoperability among communicating devices. It provides the necessary translation of different control codes, character sets, graphics characters, and so on, to allow two devices to understand the same transmission the same way.

■ The application layer enables the user, whether human or software, to access the network. It provides user interfaces and support for services such as electronic mail, remote file access and transfer, shared database management, and other types of distributed information services.

3.4   PRACTICE SET

Multiple Choice

1. The _____ model shows how the network functions of a computer ought to be organized.
   a. ITU-T
   b. OSI
   c. ISO
   d. ANSI

2. The OSI model consists of _____ layers.
   a. three
   b. five
   c. seven
   d. eight

3. The _____ layer decides the location of synchronization points.
   a. transport
   b. session
   c. presentation
   d. application

4. The end-to-end delivery of the entire message is the responsibility of the _____ layer.
   a. network
   b. transport
   c. session
   d. presentation

5. The _____ layer is the layer closest to the transmission medium.

   a. physical

   b. data link

   c. network

   d. transport

6. In the _____ layer, the data unit is called a frame.

   a. physical

   b. data link

   c. network

   d. transport

7. When different programs are running at the same time on a computer, they can be identified by their _____ addresses.

   a. node

   b. station

   c. service point (port)

   d. source

8. Decryption and encryption of data are the responsibility of the _____ layer.

   a. physical

   b. data link

   c. presentation

   d. session

9. Dialog control is a function of the _____ layer.

   a. transport

   b. session

   c. presentation

   d. application

10. Mail services and directory services are available to network users through the _____ layer.

   a. data link

   b. session

   c. transport

   d. application

11. Node-to-node delivery of the data unit is the responsibility of the _____ layer.

   a. physical

   b. data link

   c. transport

   d. network

12. As the data packet moves from the lower to the upper layers, headers are _____.

   a. added

   b. subtracted

    c. rearranged

    d. modified

13. As the data packet moves from the upper to the lower layers, headers are _____.

    a. added

    b. removed

    c. rearranged

    d. modified

14. The _____ layer lies between the network layer and the session layer.

    a. physical

    b. data link

    c. transport

    d. presentation

15. Layer 2 lies between the physical layer and the _____ layer.

    a. network

    b. data link

    c. transport

    d. presentation

16. When data are transmitted from device A to device B, the header from A's layer 5 is read by B's _____ layer.

    a. physical

    b. transport

    c. session

    d. presentation

17. In the _____ layer, translations from one character code to another occur.

    a. transport

    b. session

    c. presentation

    d. application

18. The _____ layer changes bits into electromagnetic signals.

    a. physical

    b. data link

    c. transport

    d. presentation

19. The _____ layer can use the trailer of the frame for error detection.

    a. physical

    b. data link

    c. transport

    d. presentation

Exercises

1. How are OSI and ISO related to each other?
2. Match the following to one or more layers of the seven OSI layers:
   a. Route determination.
   b. Flow control.
   c. Access to the network for the end user.
   d. Formatting data from one code to another.
   e. Switching.
3. Match the following to one or more of the seven OSI layers:
   a. Provides reliable end-to-end transmission of entire message.
   b. Defines frames.
   c. Provides user services such as electronic mail and file transfer.
   d. Transmits signals across physical medium.
4. Match the following to one or more of the seven OSI layers:
   a. Direct communication with user's application program.
   b. Error correction and retransmission.
   c. Mechanical, electrical, and functional interface.
   d. Responsibility for node-to-node delivery of a frame.
   e. Reassembly of data packets into a message.
5. Match the following to one or more of the seven OSI layers:
   a. Provides format and code conversion services.
   b. Establishes, manages, and terminates sessions.
   c. Oversees end-to-end transmission of data packets.
   d. Provides verification of log-in and log-out.
   e. Provides independence from differences in data representation.
6. Compare and contrast the delivery of data units in the data link layer, the network layer, and the transport layer.

CHAPTER 4

SIGNALS

A major concern of the physical layer is moving information in the form of electromagnetic signals across a transmission medium. Whether you are collecting numerical statistics from another computer, sending animated pictures from a design workstation, or causing a bell to ring in a distant control center, you are working with the transmission of *information* across network connections. Information can be voice, image, numeric data, characters, or code—any message that is readable by and has meaning to the destination user, whether human or machine.

> Information can be in the form of data, voice, picture, and so on.

Generally, the information usable to a person or application is not in a form that can be transmitted over a network. For example, you cannot roll up a photograph, insert it into a wire, and transmit it across town. You can transmit, however, an encoded description of the photograph. Instead of sending the actual photograph, you can use an encoder to create a stream of 1s and 0s that tells the receiving device how to reconstruct the image of the photograph. (Encoding is the subject of Chapter 5.)

But even 1s and 0s cannot be sent as such across network links. They must be further converted into a form that transmission media can accept. Transmission media work by conducting energy along a physical path. So, a data stream of 1s and 0s must be turned into energy in the form of electromagnetic signals (see Figure 4.1).

> To be transmitted, information must be transformed into electromagnetic signals.

4.1   ANALOG AND DIGITAL

Both data and the signals that represent them can take either *analog* or *digital* form. Analog refers to something that is continuous—a set of specific points of data and all possible points between. Digital refers to something that is discrete. Time is an analog quantity. It is a continuous stream that can be divided up into quarters, hundredths, thousandths, and so on ad infinitum. The measurement of time, however, can be either

Figure 4.1   *Transformation of information to signals*

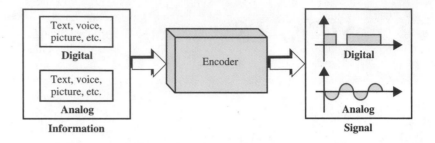

analog or digital. The hands of a traditional, or analog, clock do not jump from minute to minute or hour to hour; they move smoothly through all possible intermediate subdivisions of a 12-hour period. The hour hand is not on the 3 when the time is 3:20; it is one-third of the way from the 3 to the 4. A digital clock, on the other hand, indicates only discrete units of time, usually whole hours and minutes. When a digital clock reads 3:20, the hours indicator (the number to the left of the colon) reads 3 for the entire hour and then changes abruptly to 4 (see Figure 4.2).

Information can be analog or digital. Analog information is continuous. Digital information is discrete.

Digital and analog information can be distinguished by how we think about and refer to them. Analog quantities are generally described using various units of measure, while digital quantities are counted. For example, you may stand five feet, six and a half inches tall, weigh 130 pounds, and own two dogs and one parakeet. Feet, inches, and pounds are units of measure; your height and weight are analog quantities. Two and one are units of counting; the number of pets you own is a digital quantity.

We use measuring units for analog quantities; for example, the length of a room can be 12 feet. We count digital quantities; for example, the number of students in a class can be 56.

Figure 4.2   *Analog and digital clocks*

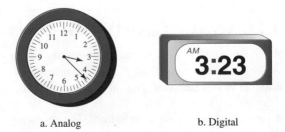

a. Analog   b. Digital

Like the information they represent, signals can be either analog or digital. An analog signal is a continuous wave form that changes smoothly over time. As the wave moves from value A to value B, it passes through and includes an infinite number of values along its path. A digital signal, on the other hand, is discrete. It can have only a limited number of defined values, often as simple as 1 and 0. The transition of a digital signal from value to value is instantaneous, like a light being switched on and off.

We usually illustrate signals by plotting them on a pair of perpendicular axes. The vertical axis represents the value or strength of a signal. The horizontal axis represents the passage of time. Figure 4.3 illustrates an analog and a digital signal. The curve representing the analog signal is smooth and continuous, passing through an infinite number of points. The vertical lines of the digital signal, however, demonstrate the sudden jump the signal makes from value to value; and its flat highs and lows indicate that those values are fixed. Another way to express the difference is that the analog signal changes continuously with respect to time, while the digital signal changes instantaneously.

> Signals can be analog or digital. Analog signals can have any value in a range; digital signals can have only a limited number of values.

Figure 4.3 *Comparison of analog and digital signals*

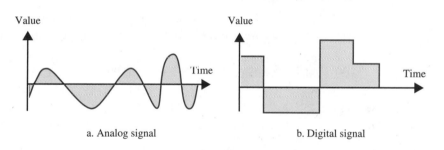

a. Analog signal   b. Digital signal

4.2 APERIODIC AND PERIODIC SIGNALS

Both analog and digital signals can be of two forms: *periodic* and *aperiodic* (nonperiodic).

Periodic Signals

A signal is periodic if it completes a pattern within a measurable time frame, called a period, and repeats that pattern over identical subsequent periods. The completion of one full pattern is called a cycle. A period is defined as the amount of time (expressed in seconds) required to complete one full cycle. The duration of a period, represented by T, may be different for each signal, but is constant for any given periodic signal. Figure 4.4 illustrates hypothetical periodic signals.

> A periodic signal consists of a continuously repeated pattern. The period of a signal (T) is expressed in seconds.

Figure 4.4   *Examples of periodic signals*

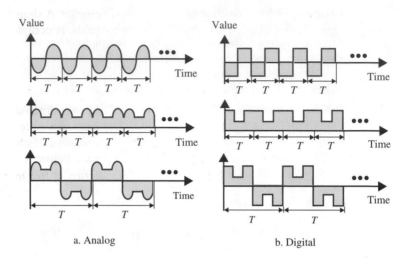

a. Analog   b. Digital

Aperiodic Signals

An aperiodic, or nonperiodic, signal changes constantly without exhibiting a pattern or cycle that repeats over time. Figure 4.5 shows examples of aperiodic signals.

An aperiodic, or nonperiodic, signal has no repetitive pattern.

Figure 4.5   *Examples of aperiodic signals*

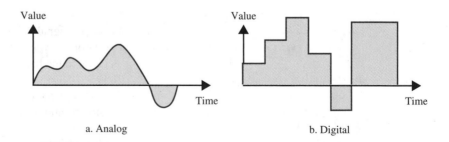

a. Analog   b. Digital

It has been proved, however, by a technique called a Fourier transform (see Appendix E), that any aperiodic signal can be decomposed into an infinite number of periodic signals. Understanding the characteristics of periodic signals, therefore, provides insight into aperiodic signals as well.

An aperiodic signal can be decomposed into an infinite number of periodic signals. A sine wave is the simplest periodic signal.

4.3   ANALOG SIGNALS

Analog signals can be classified as simple or complex. A simple analog signal, or a sine wave, cannot be decomposed into simpler signals. A complex analog signal is composed of multiple sine waves.

Simple Analog Signals

The sine wave is the most fundamental form of a periodic analog signal. Visualized as a simple oscillating curve, its change over the course of a cycle is smooth and consistent, a continuous, rolling flow. Figure 4.6 shows a sine wave. Each cycle consists of a single arc above the time axis followed by a single arc below it. Sine waves can be fully described by three characteristics: *amplitude*, *period* or *frequency*, and *phase*.

Figure 4.6   *A sine wave*

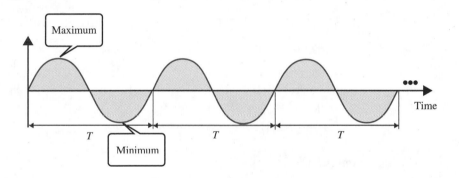

Amplitude

On a graph, the amplitude of a signal is the value of the signal at any point on the wave. It is equal to the vertical distance from a given point on the wave form to the horizontal axis. The maximum amplitude of a sine wave is equal to the highest value it reaches on the vertical axis.

Amplitude is measured in either *volts*, *amperes,* or *watts,* depending on the type of signal. Volts refers to voltage; amperes refers to current; and watts refers to power.

> Amplitude refers to the height of the signal. The unit for amplitude depends on the type of the signal. For electrical signals the unit is normally volts, amperes, or watts.

Period and Frequency

Period refers to the amount of time, in seconds, a signal needs to complete one cycle. *Frequency* refers to the number of periods a signal makes over the course of one second. The frequency of a signal is its number of cycles per second. Mathematically, the relationship between frequency and period is that they are the inverse of each other; if one is given, the other can be derived.

$$\text{Frequency} = 1/\text{Period} \qquad \text{Period} = 1/\text{Frequency}$$

Period is the amount of time it takes a signal to complete one cycle; frequency is the number of cycles per second. Frequency and period are inverses of each other: $f = 1/T$ and $T = 1/f$.

Unit of Frequency   Frequency is expressed in Hertz (Hz), after the German physicist Heinrich Rudolf Hertz. The communications industry uses five units to measure frequency: Hertz (Hz), Kilohertz (KHz=10^3 Hz), Megahertz (MHz=10^6 Hz), Gigahertz (GHz=10^9 Hz), and Terahertz (THz=10^{12} Hz). See Table 4.1.

Unit of Period   Period is expressed in seconds. The communications industry uses five units to measure period: second (s), millisecond (ms=10^{-3} s), microsecond (μs=10^{-6} s), nanosecond (ns=10^{-9} s), and picosecond (ps=10^{-12} s). See Table 4.1.

Table 4.1   *Units of frequency and period*

Frequency		Period	
Unit	*Equivalent*	*Unit*	*Equivalent*
Hertz (Hz)	1 Hz	Second (s)	1 s
Kilohertz (KHz)	10^3 Hz	Millisecond (ms)	10^{-3}s
Megahertz (MHz)	10^6 Hz	Microsecond (μs)	10^{-6} s
Gigahertz (GHz)	10^9 Hz	Nanosecond (ns)	10^{-9} s
Terahertz (THz)	10^{12} Hz	Picosecond (ps)	10^{-12} s

Example 4.1

A sine wave has a frequency of 8 KHz. What is its period?

Solution

Let T be the period and f be the frequency. Then,

$$T = 1/f = 1/8{,}000 = 0.000125 = 125 \ \mu s$$

Example 4.2

A sine wave completes one cycle in 25 μs. What is its frequency?

Solution

Let T be the period and f be the frequency. Then,

$$f = 1/T = 1/(25 \times 10^{-6}) = 40{,}000 = 40 \ \text{KHz}$$

Phase

The term *phase* describes the position of the waveform relative to time zero. If we think of the wave as something that can be shifted backward or forward along the time axis, phase describes the amount of that shift. It indicates the status of the first cycle.

Phase describes the position of the waveform relative to time zero.

Phase is measured in degrees or radians (360 degrees is 2π radians). A phase shift of 360 degrees corresponds to a shift of a complete period; a phase shift of 180 degrees corresponds to a shift of half a period; and a phase shift of 90 degrees corresponds to a shift of a quarter of a period (see Figure 4.7).

Figure 4.7   *Relationship between different phases*

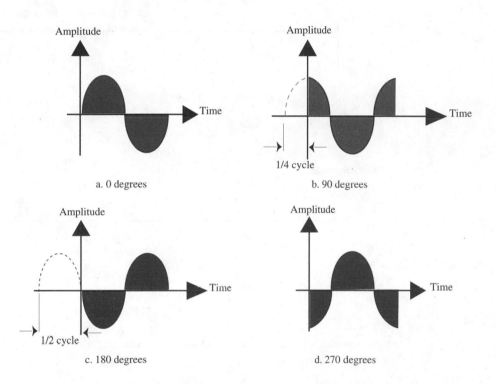

a. 0 degrees

b. 90 degrees

c. 180 degrees

d. 270 degrees

A visual comparison of amplitude, frequency, and phase provides a reference useful for understanding their functions. Changes in all three attributes can be introduced into a signal and controlled electronically. Such control provides the basis for all telecommunications and will be discussed in Chapter 5 (see Figure 4.8, Figure 4.9, and Figure 4.10).

More about Frequency

We know already that frequency is the relationship of a signal to time, and that the frequency of a wave form is the number of cycles it completes per second. But another way to look at frequency is as a measurement of the rate of change. Electromagnetic signals are oscillating wave forms; that is, they fluctuate continuously and predictably above and below a mean energy level. The rate at which a sine wave moves from its lowest to its highest level is its frequency. A 40 Hz signal has half the frequency of an 80 Hz signal; it completes one cycle in twice the time of the 80 Hz signal, so each cycle also takes twice as long to change from its lowest to its highest voltage levels.

Figure 4.8   *Amplitude change*

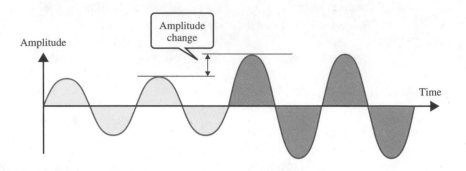

Figure 4.9   *Frequency change*

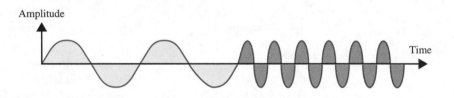

Figure 4.10   *Phase change*

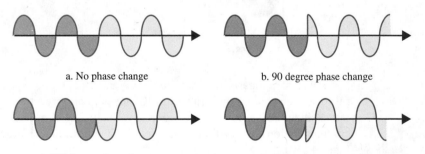

a. No phase change   b. 90 degree phase change

c. 180 degree phase change   d. 270 degree phase change

Frequency, therefore, though described in cycles per second (Hz), is a general measurement of the rate of change of a signal with respect to time.

Frequency is rate of change with respect to time. Change in a short span of time means high frequency. Change in a long span of time means low frequency.

If the value of a signal changes over a very short span of time, its frequency is high. If it changes over a long span of time, its frequency is low.

Two Extremes   What if a signal does not change at all? What if it maintains a constant voltage level the entire time it is active? In such a case, its frequency is zero. Conceptually, this idea is a simple one. If a signal does not change at all, it never completes a cycle, so its frequency is 0 Hz.

But what if a signal changes instantaneously? What if it jumps from one level to another in no time? Then its frequency is infinite. In other words, when a signal changes instantaneously, its period is zero; since frequency is the inverse of period, then in this case, the frequency is 1/0, or infinity.

> If a signal does not change at all, its frequency is zero. If a signal changes instantaneously, its frequency is infinity.

Time versus Frequency Domain   A sine wave is comprehensively defined by its amplitude, frequency, and phase. We have been showing a sine wave using what is called a time-domain plot. The time-domain plot shows changes in signal amplitude with respect to time (it is an amplitude versus time plot). Phase and frequency are not explicitly measured on a time-domain plot.

To show the relationship between the three characteristics (amplitude, frequency, and phase), we can use what is called a frequency-domain plot. There are two types of frequency-domain plots: maximum amplitude versus frequency and phase versus frequency. The first type of frequency-domain plot (maximum amplitude versus frequency) is more common in data communications than the second (phase versus frequency). Figure 4.11 compares the time domain (instantaneous amplitude with respect to time) and the frequency domain (maximum amplitude with respect to frequency).

Figure 4.11   *Time and frequency domains*

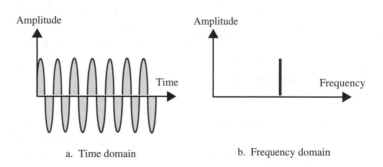

a. Time domain

b. Frequency domain

Figure 4.12 gives examples of both the time-domain and frequency-domain plots of three signals with varying frequencies and amplitudes. Compare the models within each pair to see which sort of information each is best suited to convey.

> A low-frequency signal in the frequency domain corresponds to a signal with a long period in the time domain and vice versa. A signal that changes rapidly in the time domain corresponds to high frequencies in the frequency domain.

Figure 4.12 *Time and frequency domains for different signals*

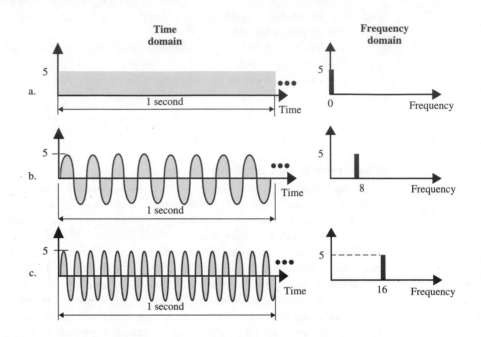

Complex Signals

So far, we have focused attention on simple periodic signals (sine waves). But what about periodic signals that are not sine waves? Many useful wave forms do not change in a single smooth curve between a minimum and maximum amplitude; they jump, slide, wobble, spike, and dip. But as long as any irregularities are consistent, cycle after cycle, a signal is still periodic and logically must be describable in the same terms used for sine waves. In fact, it can be shown that any periodic signal, no matter how complex, can be decomposed into a collection of sine waves, each having a measurable amplitude, frequency, and phase.

To decompose a composite signal into its components, Fourier analysis (discussed in Appendix E) is needed. However, the concept of decomposition can be seen with a simple example. Figure 4.13 shows a periodic signal decomposed into two sine waves. The first sine wave (middle plot) has a frequency of 6 while the second sine wave has a frequency of 0. Adding these two point by point results in the top graph. Notice that the original signal looks like a sine wave that has had its time axis shifted downward. The average amplitude of this signal is nonzero. This factor indicates the presence of a zero-frequency component, a direct current (DC) component. This DC component is responsible for the 10-unit upward shift of the sine wave.

In contrast to the time-domain graph, which illustrates a composite signal as a single entity, a frequency-domain graph shows the composite signal as a series of component frequencies. Instead of showing the impact of each component on the others, it shows the signal as a set of independent frequencies.

Figure 4.13   *A signal with a DC component*

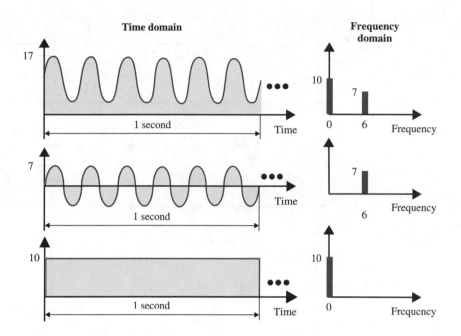

Although the time-domain graph is more useful for understanding the impact of the two signals on each other, the vertical bars of the frequency-domain graph give a more concise view of the relative frequencies and amplitudes of the composite sine waves.

Figure 4.14 shows a composite signal decomposed into four components. This signal is close to a digital signal. For an exact digital signal, we need an infinite number of odd harmonic signals (f, $3f$, $5f$, $7f$, $9f$, …), each with a different amplitude. The frequency-domain graphs are also shown.

Frequency Spectrum and Bandwidth

Two terms need mentioning here: *spectrum* and *bandwidth*. The frequency spectrum of a signal is the collection of all the component frequencies it contains and is shown using a frequency domain graph. The bandwidth of a signal is the width of the frequency spectrum (see Figure 4.15). In other words, bandwidth refers to the range of component frequencies, and frequency spectrum refers to the elements within that range. To calculate the bandwidth, subtract the lowest frequency from the highest frequency of the range.

The frequency spectrum of a signal is the combination of all sine wave signals that make that signal.

Figure 4.14   *Complex waveform*

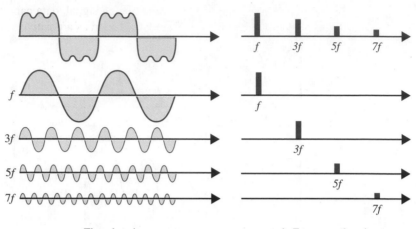

| a. Time domain | b. Frequency domain |

Figure 4.15   *Bandwidth*

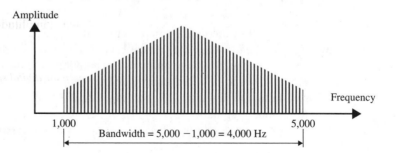

Example 4.3

If a periodic signal is decomposed into five sine waves with frequencies of 100, 300, 500, 700, and 900 Hz, what is the bandwidth?

Solution

Let f_h be the highest frequency, f_l be the lowest frequency, and B be the bandwidth. Then,

$$B = f_h - f_l = 900 - 100 = 800 \text{ Hz}$$

Example 4.4

A signal has a bandwidth of 20 KHz. The highest frequency is 60 KHz. What is the lowest frequency?

Solution

Let f_h be the highest frequency, f_l be the lowest frequency, and B be the bandwidth. Then,

$$B = f_h - f_l \Rightarrow 20 = 60 - f_l \Rightarrow f_l = 60 - 20 = 40 \text{ KHz}$$

4.4   DIGITAL SIGNALS

In addition to being represented by an analog signal, data can also be represented by a digital signal. For example, a 1 can be encoded as a positive voltage, and a 0 as a zero voltage (see Figure 4.16).

Figure 4.16   *A digital signal*

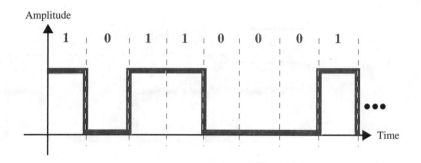

Amplitude, Period, and Phase

The three characteristics of periodic analog signals (amplitude, period, and phase) can be redefined for a periodic digital signal (see Figure 4.17).

Figure 4.17   *Amplitude, period, and phase for a periodic digital signal*

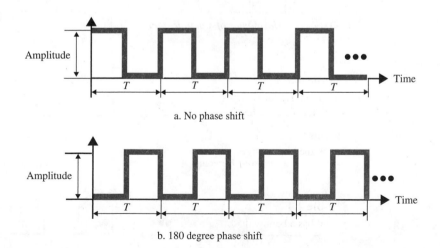

Bit Interval and Bit Rate

Most digital signals are aperiodic and thus period or frequency is not appropriate. Two new terms, *bit interval* (instead of period) and *bit rate* (instead of frequency) are used to describe digital signals. The bit interval is the time required to send one single bit. The bit rate is the number of bit intervals per second. This means that the bit rate is the number of bits sent in one second, usually expressed in bps (bits per second). See Figure 4.18.

Figure 4.18   *Bit rate and bit interval*

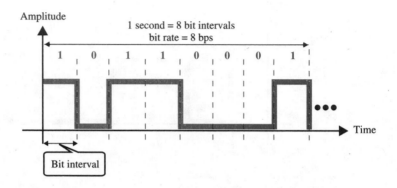

Decomposition of a Digital Signal

A digital signal can be decomposed into an infinite number of simple sine waves called harmonics, each with a different amplitude, frequency, and phase (see Figure 4.19). This means that when we send a digital signal along a transmission medium, we are sending

Figure 4.19   *Harmonics of a digital signal*

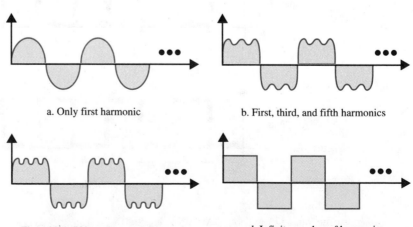

a. Only first harmonic

b. First, third, and fifth harmonics

c. First, third, fifth, and seventh harmonics

d. Infinite number of harmonics

an infinite number of simple signals. To receive an exact replica of the digital signal, all of the frequency components must be faithfully transferred through the transmission medium. If some of the components are not passed through the medium, distortion of the signal at the receiver is the result. Since no practical medium (such as a cable) is capable of transferring the entire range of frequencies, we always have distortion.

Although the frequency spectrum of a digital signal contains an infinite number of frequencies with different amplitudes, if we send only those components whose amplitudes are significant (above an acceptable threshold), we can still recreate the digital signal with reasonable accuracy at the receiver (minimum distortion). We call this part of the infinite spectrum the significant spectrum, and its bandwidth the significant bandwidth (see Figure 4.20).

Figure 4.20   *Exact and significant spectrums*

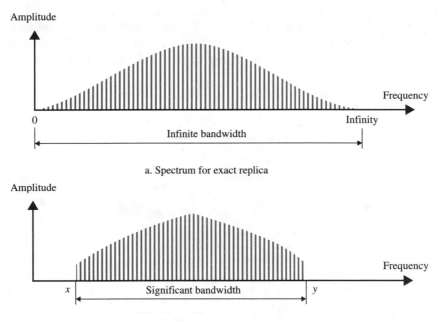

a. Spectrum for exact replica

b. Significant spectrum

The bit rate has a relationship to the significant bandwidth such that when the bit rate increases, the significant bandwidth widens. For example, if the bit rate is 1000 bps, the significant bandwidth can be around 200 Hz (depending on the level of noise in the system). If the bit rate is 2000 bps, the significant bandwidth can be 400 Hz (see Figure 4.21).

Medium Bandwidth and Significant Bandwidth

A transmission medium has a limited bandwidth, which means that it can transfer only some range of frequencies. In other words, a transmission medium with a particular bandwidth is capable of transmitting only digital signals whose significant bandwidth

Figure 4.21 *Bit rates and significant spectrums*

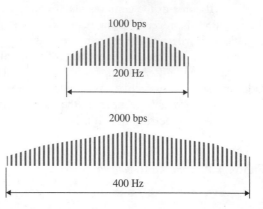

is less than the bandwidth of the medium. If a signal is sent on a transmission medium whose bandwidth is less than the required significant bandwidth, the signal may be so distorted that it is not recognizable at the receiver (see Figure 4.22).

Figure 4.22 *Corruption of a digital signal due to insufficient medium bandwidth*

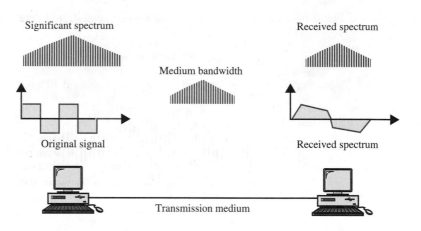

Medium Bandwidth and Data Rate: Channel Capacity

We saw that the significant bandwidth of a signal increases with bit rate. This means when the bit rate is increased, we have a wider significant bandwidth, and consequently we need a medium with wider bandwidth to transfer that signal. Therefore, the medium bandwidth puts a limit on the bit rate. The maximum bit rate a transmission medium can transfer is called channel capacity of the medium. The capacity of a channel depends on the type of encoding technique and the signal-to-noise ratio of the system

Figure 4.23   *Medium bandwidth and data rate*

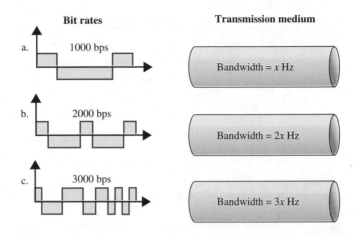

(see Figure 4.23). For example, a normal telephone line with a bandwidth of 3000 Hz is capable of transferring up to 20,000 bps, but other factors can decrease this rate.

Use of Analog Signals to Transmit Digital Data

The following examples show how we can send digital data using analog signals and what bandwidth is needed to do this.

Example 4.5

What bandwidth is required for data being sent at a rate of 10 bps using analog signals? Assume that each signal element is one bit.

Solution

In the worst-case scenario, the data consist of alternating 0s and 1s. This is the situation that will require the largest bandwidth. Each 1 and 0 bit combination can be considered one cycle. Therefore, there are five cycles per second, as shown in Figure 4.24. If we send two bits per each period of analog signal, then the required bandwidth is 5 Hz. However, if each period uses x Hz of bandwidth, then the required bandwidth is 5 times x.

Example 4.6

Compare the bandwidths required for analog data being sent at 1000 and 10,000 bps.

Solution

Similar to Example 4.5, we need a bandwidth of 500 (or multiple of 500) Hz for the first signal and a bandwidth of 5000 (or multiple of 5000) Hz for the second signal. As the data rate increases, the bandwidth also increases.

Example 4.7

We want to transmit 10 pictures per second. Each picture is made of 5-by-5 pixels (picture elements). What is the required bandwidth using digital encoding? See Figure 4.25.

Figure 4.24   *Example 4.5*

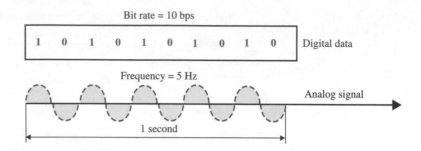

Bit rate = 10 bps

| 1 | 0 | 1 | 0 | 1 | 0 | 1 | 0 | 1 | 0 | Digital data

Frequency = 5 Hz

Analog signal

1 second

Figure 4.25   *Example 4.7*

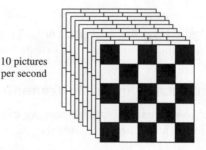

10 pictures
per second

Solution

Each picture is made of 25 pixels. In the worst case, we assume that the pixels are alternating black and white. We also assume that we send one bit per pixel (1 for black, 0 for white). Therefore, we can send 25 bits per picture and 250 bits per second. Using the discussion in Example 4.5, this corresponds to a bandwidth of 125 (or multiple of 125) Hz.

Example 4.8

A television screen is composed of a grid of 525 lines by 700 columns (total of 367,500 pixels). A pixel can be black or white (1 or 0). Thirty complete screens (frames) are scanned in one second. What is the theoretical bandwidth required? The worst case scenario is again alternating black and white (1s and 0s). See Figure 4.26.

Solution

The number of bits that must be sent per second is $30 \times 367,500 = 11,025,000$. If one bit is sent for each pixel, then the number of bits per second is 11,025,000. Using the same argument as in Example 4.5, we get:

$$\text{Bandwidth} = 11,025,000 / 2 = 5,512,500 \Rightarrow 6 \text{ MHz (approximately)}$$

Commercial TVs use 6 MHz for each channel.

Figure 4.26   *Example 4.8*

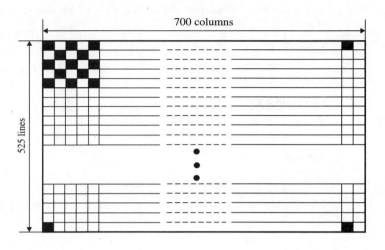

4.5   MATHEMATICAL APPROACH (OPTIONAL)

A sine wave can be mathematically defined as:

$$x(t) = A \sin (2\pi f\, t + \phi)$$

   where
   $x(t)$ is the signal at time t
   A is the maximum amplitude of the signal.
   f represents the number of cycles per second.
   ϕ defines the phase of the signal.
   If the phase shift is −90 degrees (−π/2 radian), the same signal can be expressed as a cosine wave instead of a sine wave:

$$x(t) = A \cos (2\pi f\, t)$$

Example 4.9

The electricity that comes into a house is a good example of a simple sine wave. The maximum amplitude is approximately 155 volts and the frequency is 60 Hz. Write the mathematical equation.

Solution

$$2\, \pi f = 2 \times 3.14 \times 60 = 377 \text{ radians/second}$$

$$x(t) = A \sin (2\pi ft + \phi) = 155 \sin (377\, t + \phi)$$

The phase shift is usually zero.

Example 4.10

The electricity produced by a 6-volt battery is direct current (DC) with frequency zero. It can be described by the following equation, where ϕ is $-\pi/2$ because the voltage starts at +6 volts instead of zero.

Solution

$$x(t) = A \sin (2\pi ft - \pi/2) = A \cos (2\pi ft) = A \cos (0) = A = 6$$

Example 4.11

Your voice is a summation of sine waves, each sine wave having its own frequency, phase, and amplitude. The bandwidth is normally between 300 Hz and 3,300 Hz. Give a general equation.

Solution

$$x(t) = A_1\sin(2\pi f_1 t + \phi_1) + A_2\sin(2\pi f_2 t + \phi_2) + \ldots + A_n\sin(2\pi f_n t + \phi_n)$$

with 300 Hz $< f_n <$ 3,300 Hz f_1, called the fundamental frequency, and $f_2, f_3 \ldots f_n$ called the harmonics.

4.6   SUMMARY

■ Information must be transformed into electromagnetic signals prior to transmission across a network.

■ Information and signals can be either analog (continuous values) or digital (discrete values).

■ A signal is periodic if it consists of a continuously repeating pattern.

■ A periodic signal can be decomposed into a set of sine waves.

■ Each sine wave can be characterized by its

   a. Amplitude—the instantaneous height of the wave.

   b. Frequency—the number of complete cycles per second.

   c. Phase—the shift of the wave along the time axis.

■ Frequency and period are the inverse of each other.

■ A time-domain graph plots amplitude as a function of time.

■ A frequency-domain graph plots each sine wave's peak amplitude against its frequency.

■ The bandwidth of a signal is the range of frequencies the signal occupies. Bandwidth is determined by finding the difference between the highest and lowest frequency components.

■ The spectrum of a signal consists of the sine waves that make up the signal.

■ *Bit rate* (number of bits per second) and *bit interval* (duration of one bit) are terms used to describe digital signals.

■ A digital signal can be decomposed into an infinite number of sine waves (harmonics).

■ The significant spectrum of a digital signal is the portion of the signal's spectrum that can adequately reproduce the original signal.

■ The bit rate of the signal that a transmission medium can transfer (medium capacity) is directly proportional to the bandwidth of that medium.

4.7   PRACTICE SET

Multiple Choice

1. Before information can be transmitted it must be transformed into _____.
   a. periodic signals
   b. electromagnetic signals
   c. aperiodic signals
   d. low-frequency sine waves

2. Which of the following can transform information into signals?
   a. decoder
   b. encoder
   c. modem
   d. all of the above

3. A periodic signal completes one cycle in 0.001 seconds. What is the frequency?
   a. 1 Hz
   b. 100 Hz
   c. 1 KHz
   d. 1 MHz

4. Which of the following can be determined from a frequency-domain graph of a signal?
   a. frequency
   b. phase
   c. power
   d. all of the above

5. Which of the following can be determined from a frequency-domain graph of a signal?
   a. bandwidth
   b. phase
   c. power
   d. all of the above

6. In a frequency-domain plot, the vertical axis measures the _____.
   a. peak amplitude
   b. frequency

   c. phase

   d. slope

7. In a frequency-domain plot, the horizontal axis measures the _____.

   a. peak amplitude

   b. frequency

   c. phase

   d. slope

8. In a time-domain plot, the vertical axis is a measure of _____.

   a. amplitude

   b. frequency

   c. phase

   d. time

9. In a time-domain plot, the horizontal axis is a measure of _____.

   a. signal amplitude

   b. frequency

   c. phase

   d. time

10. If the bandwidth of a signal is 5 KHz and the lowest frequency is 52 KHz, what is the highest frequency?

   a. 5 KHz

   b. 10 KHz

   c. 47 KHz

   d. 57 KHz

11. What is the bandwidth of a signal that ranges from 40 KHz to 4 MHz?

   a. 36 MHz

   b. 360 KHz

   c. 3.96 MHz

   d. 396 KHz

12. When one of the components of a signal has a frequency of zero, the average amplitude of the signal _____.

   a. is greater than zero

   b. is less than zero

   c. is zero

   d. a or b

13. A periodic signal can always be decomposed into _____.

   a. exactly an odd number of sine waves

   b. a set of sine waves

   c. a set of sine waves, one of which must have a phase of zero degrees

   d. none of the above

14. As frequency increases, the period _____.
    a. decreases
    b. increases
    c. remains the same
    d. doubles
15. Given two sine waves A and B, if the frequency of A is twice that of B, then the period of B is _____ that of A.
    a. one-half
    b. twice
    c. the same as
    d. indeterminate from

Exercises

1. Describe the three characteristics of a sine wave.
2. What is the spectrum of a signal?
3. Draw two periods of a sine wave with a phase shift of 90 degrees. On the same diagram draw a sine wave with the same amplitude and frequency but with a 90-degree phase shift from the first. Draw the frequency spectrum.
4. What is the difference between information and signals?
5. Give two examples of analog information. Give two examples of digital information.
6. Contrast an analog signal with a digital signal.
7. Classify the following as analog or digital information:
    a. SAT score.
    b. Amount of milk milked from a cow.
    c. Number of golden eggs laid by Jack's goose.
    d. Length of your foot.
8. What is the bandwidth of a signal that can be decomposed into four sine waves with frequencies at 0 Hz, 20 Hz, 50 Hz, and 200 Hz? All amplitudes are the same. Draw the frequency spectrum.
9. A periodic complex signal with a bandwidth of 2000 Hz has the following characteristics: It is composed of two sine waves. The first one has a frequency of 100 Hz with a maximum amplitude of 20 volts; the second one has a maximum amplitude of 5 volts. Draw the frequency spectrum.
10. Draw the time domain of a sine wave (for only 1 second) with amplitude 15 volts, frequency 5, and phase 270 degrees.
11. Draw two sine waves on the same time-domain axes. The characteristics of each signal are given below:
    Signal A: amplitude 40, frequency 9, phase 0.
    Signal B: amplitude 10, frequency 9, phase 90.

12. Given the frequencies listed below, calculate the corresponding periods. Express the periods in the appropriate units.

    a. 24 Hz

    b. 8 MHz

    c. 140 KHz

    d. 12 THz

13. Given the following periods, calculate the corresponding frequencies. Express the frequencies in the appropriate units.

    a. 5 s

    b. 12 μs

    c. 220 ns

    d. 81 ps

14. Show how a sine wave can change its phase by drawing two periods of an arbitrary sine wave with phase shift of 0 degrees followed by the two periods of the *same signal* with a phase shift of 90 degrees.

15. Imagine we have a sine wave called A. Show the negative of A. In other words, show the signal −A. Can we relate the negation of a signal to the phase shift? How many degrees?

CHAPTER 5

ENCODING

As we discussed in Chapter 4, information must be encoded into signals before it can be transported across communication media.

> We must encode data into signals to send them from one place to another.

How information is encoded depends on its original format and on the format used by the communication hardware. If you want to send a love letter by smoke signal, you need to know which smoke patterns match which words in your message before you actually build your fire. Words are digital information and puffs of smoke are a digital representation of information, so defining the smoke patterns would be a form of digital-to-digital encoding. Communication technology has fundamentally the same requirements with a few additional options.

A simple signal by itself does not carry information any more than a straight line conveys words. The signal must be manipulated so that it contains identifiable changes that are recognizable to the sender and receiver as representing the information intended. First the information must be translated into agreed-upon patterns of 0s and 1s. In the case of textual data, these patterns can belong to either of two conventions: ASCII or EBCDIC (described in Appendix A).

As we saw in Chapter 4, information can be of two types, digital or analog, and signals can be of two types, also digital or analog. Therefore, four types of encoding are possible: digital-to-digital, analog-to-digital, digital-to-analog, and analog-to-analog (see Figure 5.1).

5.1 DIGITAL-TO-DIGITAL ENCODING

Digital-to-digital encoding is the representation of digital information by a digital signal. For example, when you transmit data from your computer to your printer, both the original data and the transmitted data are digital. In this type of encoding, the binary 1s and 0s generated by a computer are translated into a sequence of voltage pulses that can

Figure 5.1   *Different encoding schemes*

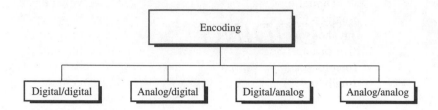

be propagated over a wire. Figure 5.2 shows the relationship between the digital information, the digital-to-digital encoding hardware, and the resultant digital signal.

Figure 5.2   *Digital-to-digital encoding*

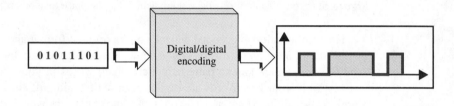

Of the many mechanisms for digital-to-digital encoding, we will discuss only those most useful for data communication. These fall into three broad categories: *unipolar*, *polar*, and *bipolar* (see Figure 5.3).

Figure 5.3   *Types of digital-to-digital encoding*

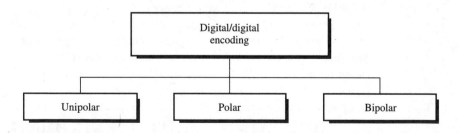

Unipolar encoding is simple, with only one technique in use. Polar encoding has three subcategories, NRZ, RZ and biphase, two of which have multiple variations of their own. The third option, bipolar encoding, has three variations: AMI, B8ZS, and HDB3.

Unipolar

Unipolar encoding is very simple and very primitive. Although it is almost obsolete today, its simplicity provides an easy introduction to the concepts developed with the more complex encoding systems and allows us to examine the kinds of problems that any digital transmission system must overcome.

Digital transmission systems work by sending voltage pulses along a media link, usually a wire or cable. In most types of encoding, one voltage level stands for binary 0 and another level stands for binary 1. The polarity of a pulse refers to whether it is positive or negative. Unipolar encoding is so named because it uses only one polarity. Therefore, only one of the two binary states is encoded, usually the 1. The other state, usually the 0, is represented by zero voltage, or an idle line.

Unipolar encoding uses only one level of value.

Figure 5.4 shows the idea of unipolar encoding. In this example, the 1s are encoded as a positive value and the 0s are idle. In addition to being straightforward, unipolar encoding is inexpensive to implement.

Figure 5.4 *Unipolar encoding*

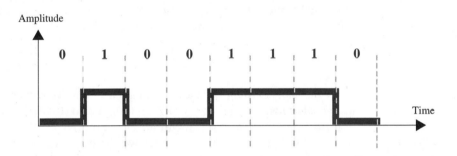

However, unipolar encoding has at least two problems that make it unusable: DC component and synchronization.

DC Component

The average amplitude of a unipolar encoded signal is nonzero. This creates what is called a direct current (DC) component (a component with zero frequency). When a signal contains a DC component, it cannot travel through media that cannot handle DC components, such as microwaves or transformers.

Synchronization

When a signal is unvarying, the receiver cannot determine the beginning and ending of each bit. Therefore, a synchronization problem in unipolar encoding can occur whenever the data stream includes a long uninterrupted series of 1s or 0s. Digital encoding schemes use changes in voltage level to indicate changes in bit type. A signal change also indicates that one bit has ended and a new bit has begun. In unipolar encoding, however, a series of one kind of bit, say seven 1s, occurs with no voltage changes, just an unbroken positive voltage that lasts seven times as long as a single 1 bit. Whenever there is no signal change to indicate the start of the next bit in a sequence, the receiver has to rely on a timer. Given an expected bit rate of 1000 bps, if the receiver detects a positive voltage lasting 0.005 seconds, it reads one 1 per 0.001 seconds, or five 1s.

Unfortunately, propagation delays can distort the timing of the signal so that, for example, five 1s can be stretched to 0.006 seconds causing an extra 1 bit to be read by the receiver. That one extra bit in the data stream causes everything after it to be decoded erroneously. In addition, the receiver's clock can go out of synchronization, causing the receiver to read the bit stream erroneously. A solution developed to control the synchronization of unipolar transmission is to use a separate, parallel line that carries a clock pulse and allows the receiving device to resynchronize its timer to that of the signal. But doubling the number of lines used for transmission increases the cost and so proves uneconomical.

Polar

Polar encoding uses two voltage levels: one positive and one negative. By using both levels, in most polar encoding methods the average voltage level on the line is reduced and the DC component problem of unipolar encoding is alleviated. In Manchester and Differential Manchester encoding (see p. 85) each bit consists of both positive and negative voltages, so the DC component is totally eliminated.

Polar encoding uses two levels (positive and negative) of amplitude.

Of the many existing variations of polar encoding, we will examine only the three most popular: non-return to zero (NRZ), return to zero (RZ), and biphase. NRZ encoding includes two methods: non-return to zero, level (NRZ-L), and non-return to zero-invert (NRZ-I). Biphase also refers to two methods. The first, Manchester, is the method used by Ethernet LANs. The second, Differential Manchester, is the method used by token ring LANs (see Figure 5.5).

Figure 5.5   *Types of polar encoding*

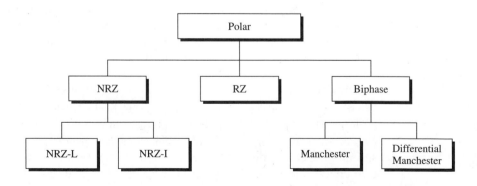

Non-Return to Zero (NRZ)

In NRZ encoding, the level of the signal is always either positive or negative. Unlike in unipolar encoding, where a 0 bit is represented by an idle line, in NRZ systems if the line is idle it means no transmission is occurring at all. The two most popular methods of NRZ transmission are discussed below.

NRZ-L   In NRZ-L encoding, the level of the signal depends on the type of bit it represents. A positive voltage means the bit is a 1, and a negative voltage means the bit is a 0; thus, the level of the signal is dependent upon the state of the bit.

In NRZ-L the level of the signal is dependent upon the state of the bit.

NRZ-I   In NRZ-I, an inversion of the voltage level represents a 1 bit. It is the transition between a positive and negative voltage, not the voltages themselves, that represents a 1 bit. A 0 bit is represented by no change. An advantage of NRZ-I over NRZ-L is that because the signal changes every time a 1 bit is encountered, it provides some synchronization. A series of seven 1s will cause seven inversions. Each of those inversions allows the receiver to resynchronize its timer to the actual arrival of the transmission. Statistically, strings of 1s occur more frequently in transmissions than do strings of 0s. Synchronizing strings of 1s therefore goes a long way toward keeping the entire message synchronized. A string of 0s can still cause problems, but because 0s are not as likely, they are less of a threat to decoding.

In NRZ-I the signal is inverted if a 1 is encountered.

Figure 5.6 shows the NRZ-L and NRZ-I representations of the same series of bits. In the NRZ-L sequence, positive and negative voltages have specific meanings: positive for 1 and negative for 0. In the NRZ-I sequence, the voltages per se are meaningless. Instead, the receiver looks for changes from one level to another as its basis for recognition of 1s.

Return to Zero (RZ)

As you can see, anytime the original data contain strings of consecutive 1s or 0s, the receiver can lose its place. As we mentioned in our discussion of unipolar encoding, one way to assure synchronization is to send a separate timing signal on a separate channel. However, this solution is both expensive and prone to errors of its own. A better solution is to somehow include synchronization in the encoded signal, something like the solution provided by NRZ-I, but one capable of handling strings of 0s as well as 1s.

To assure synchronization, there must be a signal change for each bit. The receiver can use these changes to build up, update, and synchronize its clock. As we saw above, NRZ-I accomplishes this for sequences of 1s. But to change with every bit, we need more than just two values. One solution is return to zero (RZ) encoding, which uses three values: positive, negative, and zero. In RZ, the signal changes not between bits but during each bit. Like NRZ-L, a positive voltage means 1 and a negative voltage means 0. But, unlike NRZ-L, halfway through each bit interval, the signal returns to

Figure 5.6   *NRZ-L and NRZ-I encoding*

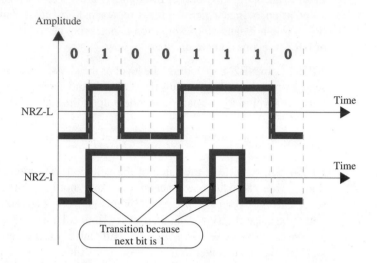

zero. A 1 bit is actually represented by positive-to-zero, and a 0 bit by negative-to-zero, rather than by positive and negative alone. Figure 5.7 illustrates the concept.

Figure 5.7   *RZ encoding*

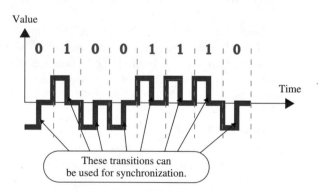

The main disadvantage of RZ encoding is that it requires two signal changes to encode one bit and therefore occupies more bandwidth. But of the three alternatives we have examined so far, it is the most effective.

A good encoded digital signal must contain a provision for synchronization.

Biphase

Probably the best existing solution to the problem of synchronization is biphase encoding. In this method, the signal changes at the middle of the bit interval but does not return to zero. Instead, it continues to the opposite pole. As in RZ, these midinterval transitions allow for synchronization.

As mentioned earlier, there are two types of biphase encoding in use on networks today: Manchester and Differential Manchester.

> Biphase encoding is implemented in two different ways: Manchester and Differential Manchester.

Manchester   Manchester encoding uses the inversion at the middle of each bit interval for both synchronization and bit representation. A negative-to-positive transition represents binary 1 and a positive-to-negative transition represents binary 0. By using a single transition for a dual purpose, Manchester encoding achieves the same level of synchronization as RZ but with only two levels of amplitude.

> In Manchester encoding the transition at the middle of the bit is used for both synchronization and bit representation.

Differential Manchester   In Differential Manchester, the inversion at the middle of the bit interval is used for synchronization, but the presence or absence of an additional transition at the beginning of the interval is used to identify the bit. A transition means binary 0 and no transition means binary 1. Differential Manchester requires two signal changes to represent binary 0 but only one to represent binary 1.

> In Differential Manchester the transition at the middle of the bit is used only for synchronization. The bit representation is shown by the inversion or noninversion at the beginning of the bit.

Figure 5.8 shows the Manchester and Differential Manchester signals for the same bit pattern.

Bipolar

Bipolar encoding, like RZ, uses three voltage levels: positive, negative, and zero. Unlike RZ, however, the zero level in bipolar encoding is used to represent binary 0. Positive and negative voltages represent alternating 1s. If the first 1 bit is represented by the positive amplitude, the second will be represented by the negative amplitude, the third by the positive amplitude, and so on. This alternation occurs even when the 1 bits are not consecutive.

Three types of bipolar encoding are in popular use by the data communications industry: AMI, B8ZS, and HDB3 (see Figure 5.9).

Bipolar Alternate Mark Inversion (AMI)

Bipolar AMI is the simplest type of bipolar encoding. In the name alternate mark inversion, the word mark comes from telegraphy and means 1. So AMI means alternate 1 inversion. A neutral, zero voltage represents binary 0. Binary 1s are represented by alternating positive and negative voltages. Figure 5.10 gives an example.

Figure 5.8   *Manchester and Differential Manchester encoding*

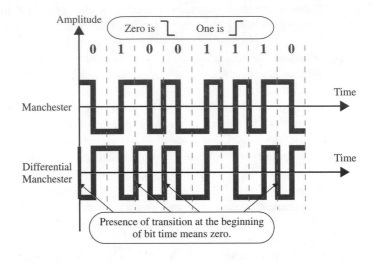

Manchester

Differential Manchester

In bipolar encoding we use three levels: positive, zero, and negative.

Figure 5.9   *Types of bipolar encoding*

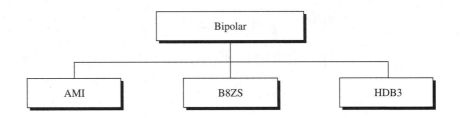

Figure 5.10   *Bipolar AMI encoding*

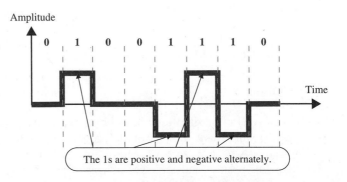

By inverting on each occurrence of a 1, bipolar AMI accomplishes two things: first, the DC component is zero, and second, a long sequence of 1s stays synchronized. There is no mechanism to ensure the synchronization of a long string of 0s.

Two variations of bipolar AMI have been developed to solve the problem of synchronizing sequential 0s. The first, used in North America, is called bipolar 8-zero substitution (B8ZS). The second, used in Europe and Japan, is called high-density bipolar 3 (HDB3). Both are adaptations of bipolar AMI that modify the original pattern only in the case of multiple consecutive 0s.

Bipolar 8-Zero Substitution (B8ZS)

B8ZS is the convention adopted in North America to provide synchronization of long strings of 0s. In most situations, B8ZS functions identically to bipolar AMI. Bipolar AMI changes poles with every 1 it encounters. These changes provide the synchronization needed by the receiver. But the signal does not change during a string of 0s, so synchronization is often lost.

Figure 5.11   *B8ZS encoding*

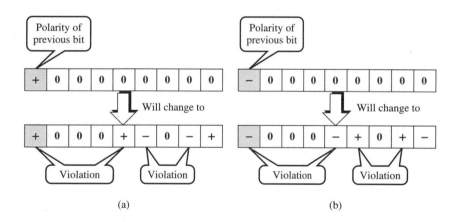

(a)   (b)

The difference between B8ZS and bipolar AMI occurs whenever eight or more consecutive 0s are encountered in the data stream. The solution provided by B8ZS is to force artificial signal changes, called violations, within the 0 string. Anytime eight 0s occur in succession, B8ZS introduces changes in the pattern based on the polarity of the previous 1 (the 1 occurring just before the 0s). See Figure 5.11.

If the previous 1 bit was positive, the eight 0s will be encoded as zero, zero, zero, positive, negative, zero, negative, positive. Remember that the receiver is looking for alternating polarities to identify 1s. When it finds two consecutive positive charges surrounding three 0s, it recognizes the pattern as a deliberately introduced violation and not an error. It then looks for the second pair of the expected violations. When it finds them, the receiver translates all eight bits to 0s and reverts back to normal bipolar AMI mode.

If the polarity of the previous 1 is negative, the pattern of violations is the same but with inverted polarities. Both positive and negative patterns are shown in Figure 5.11.

In B8ZS if eight 0s come one after another, we change the pattern in one of two ways based on the polarity of the previous 1.

High-Density Bipolar 3 (HDB3)

The problem of synchronizing strings of consecutive 0s is solved differently in Europe and Japan than in the United States. This convention, called HDB3, introduces changes into the bipolar AMI pattern every time four consecutive 0s are encountered instead of waiting for the eight expected by B8ZS in North America. Although the name is HDB3, the pattern changes whenever there are four 0s in succession (see Figure 5.12).

In HDB3 if four 0s come one after another, we change the pattern in one of four ways based on the polarity of the previous 1 and the number of 1s since the last substitution.

As in B8ZS, the pattern of violations in HDB3 is based on the polarity of the previous 1 bit. But unlike B8ZS, HDB3 also looks at the number of 1s that have occurred in the bit stream since the last substitution. Whenever the number of 1s since the last substitution is odd, HDB3 puts a violation in the place of the fourth consecutive 0. If the polarity of the previous bit was positive, the violation is positive. If the polarity of the previous bit was negative, the violation is negative.

Whenever the number of 1s since the last substitution is even, HDB3 puts violations in the places of both the first and the fourth consecutive 0s. If the polarity of the previous bit was positive, both violations are negative. If the polarity of the previous bit was negative, both violations are positive. All four patterns are shown in Figure 5.12.

Figure 5.12 *HDB3 encoding*

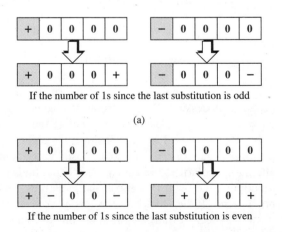

If the number of 1s since the last substitution is odd

(a)

If the number of 1s since the last substitution is even

(b)

As you can see, the point is to violate the standard pattern in ways that a machine can recognize as deliberate, and to use those violations to synchronize the system.

Example 5.1

Compare the bandwidth needed for unipolar encoding and RZ encoding. Assume the worst-case scenario for both.

Solution

The worst-case scenario (the situation requiring the most bandwidth) is alternating 1s and 0s for unipolar. For RZ the worst case is all 1s. As Figure 5.13 shows, RZ needs twice the bandwidth of unipolar encoding.

Figure 5.13   *Solution to Example 5.1*

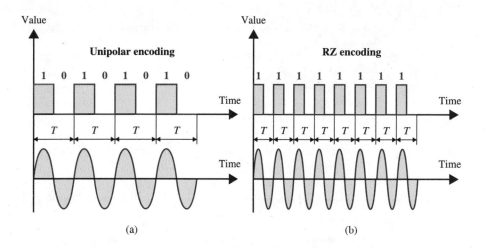

Example 5.2

Compare the bandwidth needed for Manchester and Differential Manchester encoding. Assume the worst-case scenario for both.

Solution

The worst-case scenario for Manchester is consecutive 1s or consecutive 0s. There are two transitions for each bit (one cycle per bit). For Differential Manchester the worst case is consecutive 0s with two transitions per each bit (one cycle per bit). The bandwidths, which are proportional to the bit rate, are the same for each.

Example 5.3

Using B8ZS, encode the bit stream 10000000000100. Assume that the polarity of the first 1 is positive.

Solution

See Figure 5.14.

Figure 5.14   *Solution to Example 5.3*

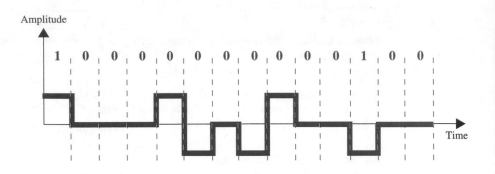

Example 5.4

Using HDB3, encode the bit stream 10000000000100. Assume that the number of 1s so far is odd and the first 1 is positive.

Solution
See Figure 5.15.

Figure 5.15   *Solution to Example 5.4*

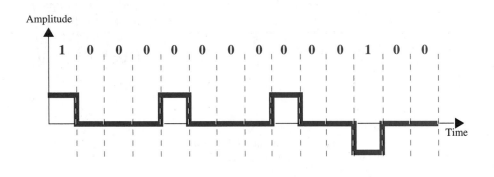

5.2   ANALOG-TO-DIGITAL ENCODING

Analog-to-digital encoding is the representation of analog information by a digital signal. To record a singer's voice onto a compact disc, for example, you use digital means to replicate analog information. To do so you need to reduce the potentially infinite number of values in an analog message so that they can be represented as a digital stream with a minimum loss of information. Several methods for analog-to-digital encoding will be discussed later in this chapter. Figure 5.16 shows the analog-to-digital encoder, called codec (coder-decoder).

In analog-to-digital encoding, we are representing the information contained in a continuous wave form as a series of digital pulses (1s or 0s).

Figure 5.16   *Analog-to-digital encoding*

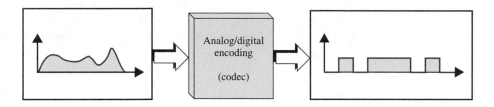

So far, the encoding systems we have been examining have focused on the format of the transporting signal. Analog-to-digital encoding can make use of any of the digital signals discussed in Section 5.1. The structure of the transporting signal is not the problem. Instead, the problem is how to translate information from an infinite number of values to a discrete number of values without sacrificing sense or quality.

Pulse Amplitude Modulation (PAM)

The first step in analog-to-digital encoding is called pulse amplitude modulation (PAM). This technique takes analog information, samples it, and generates a series of pulses based on the results of the sampling. The term *sampling* means measuring the amplitude of the signal at equal intervals.

The method of sampling used in PAM is more useful to other areas of engineering than it is to data communication. However, PAM is the foundation of an important analog-to-digital encoding method called pulse code modulation (PCM).

In PAM, the original signal is sampled at equal intervals as shown in Figure 5.17. PAM uses a technique called sample and hold. At a given moment the signal level is

Figure 5.17   *PAM*

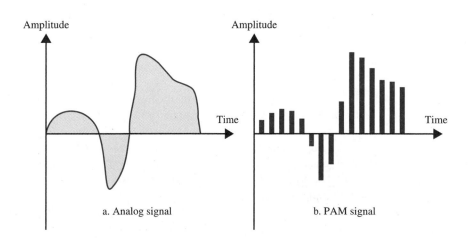

read, then held briefly. The sampled value occurs only instantaneously in the actual wave form, but is generalized over a still short but measurable period in the PAM result.

The reason PAM is not useful to data communications is that, although it translates the original wave form to a series of pulses, these pulses are still of any amplitude (still an analog signal, not digital). To make them digital, we must modify them by using pulse code modulation (PCM).

> Pulse amplitude modulation (PAM) has some applications, but it is not used by itself in data communication. However, it is the first step in another very popular encoding method called pulse code modulation (PCM).

Pulse Code Modulation (PCM)

PCM modifies the pulses created by PAM to create a completely digital signal. To do so, PCM first quantizes the PAM pulses. Quantization is a method of assigning integral values in a specific range to sampled instances. The result of quantization is presented in Figure 5.18.

Figure 5.18   *Quantized PAM signal*

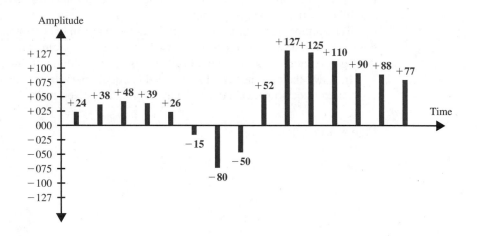

Figure 5.19 shows a simple method of assigning sign and magnitude values to quantized samples. Each value is translated into its seven-bit binary equivalent. The eighth bit indicates the sign.

The binary digits are then transformed into a digital signal using one of the digital-to-digital encoding techniques. Figure 5.20 shows the result of the pulse code modulation of the original signal encoded finally into a unipolar signal. Only the first three sampled values are shown.

PCM is actually made up of four separate processes: PAM, quantization, binary encoding, and digital-to-digital encoding. Figure 5.21 shows the entire process in graphic form. PCM is the sampling method used to digitize voice in T-line transmission in the North American telecommunication system (see Chapter 8).

Figure 5.19 *Quantizing using sign and magnitude*

+024	00011000	−015	10001111	+125	01111101
+038	00100110	−080	11010000	+110	01101110
+048	00110000	−050	10110010	+090	01011010
+039	00100111	+052	00110110	+088	01011000
+026	00011010	+127	01111111	+077	01001101

Sign bit
+ is 0 − is 1

Figure 5.20 *PCM*

+ 024   +038   +048

0 0 0 1 1 0 0 0   0 0 1 0 0 1 1 0   0 0 1 1 0 0 0 0   • • •

Direction of transfer

Figure 5.21 *From analog signal to PCM digital code*

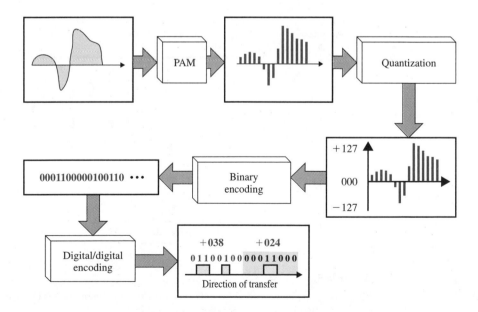

Sampling Rate

As you can tell from the preceding figures, the accuracy of any digital reproduction of an analog signal depends on the number of samples taken. Using PAM and PCM, we can reproduce the wave form exactly by taking infinite samples, or we can reproduce the barest generalization of its direction of change by taking three samples. Obviously, we prefer to find a number somewhere between these two extremes. So the question is, How many samples are sufficient?

Actually, it requires remarkably little information for the receiving device to reconstruct an analog signal. According to the Nyquist theorem, to ensure the accurate reproduction of an original analog signal using PAM, the sampling rate must be at least twice the highest frequency of the original signal. So if we want to sample telephone voice information with maximum frequency 3300 Hz, we need a sampling rate of 6600 samples per second. In actual practice, 8000 samples are taken to compensate for imperfection in later processing.

> According to the Nyquist theorem, the sampling rate must be at least two times the highest frequency.

A sampling rate of twice a frequency of x Hz means that the signal must be sampled every $1/2x$ seconds. Using the voice-over-phone-lines example above, that means one sample every 1/8000 second. Figure 5.22 illustrates the concept.

Figure 5.22   *Nyquist theorem*

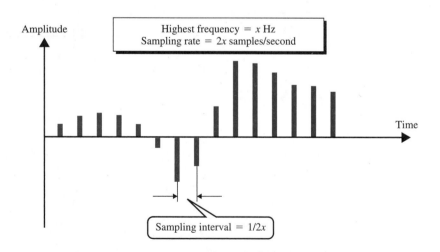

Example 5.5

What sampling rate is needed for a signal with a bandwidth of 10,000 Hz (1000 to 11,000 Hz)? If the quantization is eight bits per sample, what is the bit rate?

Solution

The sampling rate must be twice the highest frequency in the signal:

Sampling rate = 2 (11,000) = 22,000 samples/S

Each sample is quantized to eight bits:

Data rate = (22,000 samples/S) (8 bits/Sample) = 176 Kbps

5.3   DIGITAL-TO-ANALOG ENCODING

Digital-to-analog encoding is the representation of digital information by an analog signal. When you transmit data from one computer to another across a public access phone line, for example, the data start out as digital, but because telephone wires carry analog signals, the data must be converted. The digital data must be encoded on an analog signal that has been manipulated to look like two distinct values that correspond to binary 1 and binary 0. Figure 5.23 shows the relationship between the digital information, the digital-to-analog encoding hardware, and the resultant analog signal.

Figure 5.23   *Digital-to-analog encoding*

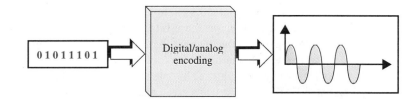

Of the many mechanisms for digital-to-analog encoding, we will discuss only those most useful for data communications.

As discussed in Chapter 4, a sine wave is defined by three characteristics: amplitude, frequency, and phase. When we vary any one of these characteristics, we create a second version of that wave. If we then say that the original wave represents binary 1, the variation can represent binary 0, or vice versa. So, by changing one aspect of a simple electrical signal back and forth, we can use it to represent digital data. Any of the three characteristics listed above can be altered in this way, giving us at least three mechanisms for encoding digital data into an analog signal: amplitude shift keying (ASK), frequency shift keying (FSK), and phase shift keying (PSK). In addition, there is a fourth (and better) mechanism that combines changes in both amplitude and phase called quadrature amplitude modulation (QAM). QAM is the most efficient of these options and is the mechanism used in all modern modems (see Figure 5.24).

Aspects of Digital-to-Analog Encoding

Before we discuss specific methods of digital-to-analog encoding, two basic issues must be defined: bit/baud rate and carrier signal.

Figure 5.24   *Types of digital-to-analog encoding*

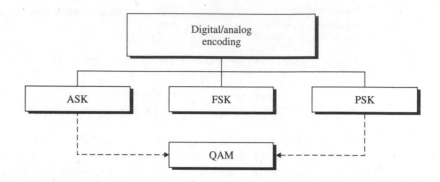

Bit Rate and Baud Rate

Two terms used frequently in data communication are *bit rate* and *baud rate*. Bit rate is the number of bits transmitted during one second. Baud rate refers to the number of signal units per second that are required to represent those bits. In discussions of computer efficiency the bit rate is the more important—we want to know how long it takes to process each piece of information. In data transmission, however, we are more concerned with how efficiently we can move that data from place to place, whether in pieces or blocks. The fewer signal units required, the more efficient the system and the less bandwidth required to transmit more bits; so we are more concerned with baud rate. The baud rate determines the bandwidth required to send the signal.

Bit rate equals the baud rate times the number of bits represented by each signal unit. The baud rate equals the bit rate divided by the number of bits represented by each signal shift. Bit rate is always greater than or equal to the baud rate.

> Bit rate is the number of bits per second. Baud rate is the number of signal units per second. Baud rate is less than or equal to the bit rate.

Carrier Signal

In analog transmission the sending device produces a high-frequency signal that acts as a basis for the information signal. This base signal is called the carrier signal or carrier frequency. The receiving device is tuned to the frequency of the carrier signal that it expects from the sender. Digital information is then encoded onto the carrier signal by modifying one or more of its characteristics (amplitude, frequency, phase). This kind of modification is called modulation (or shift keying) and the information signal is called a modulating signal.

Amplitude Shift Keying (ASK)

In amplitude shift keying (ASK), the strength of the signal is varied to represent binary 1 or 0. Both frequency and phase remain constant while the amplitude changes. Which voltage represents 1 and which represents 0 is left to the system designers. A bit duration is the period of time that defines one bit. The peak amplitude of the signal during each bit duration is constant and its value depends on the bit (0 or 1). The speed of transmission using ASK is limited by the physical characteristics of the transmission medium. Figure 5.25 gives a conceptual view of ASK.

Figure 5.25   *ASK encoding*

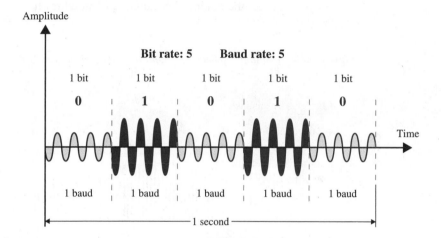

Unfortunately, ASK transmission is highly susceptible to noise interference. The term *noise* refers to unintentional voltages introduced onto a line by various phenomena such as heat or electromagnetic induction created by other sources. These unintentional voltages combine with the signal to change the amplitude. Some types of noise, for example thermal noise, are constant enough not to interfere with the intelligibility of the signal. Impulse noise, however, is a sudden surge of energy that can wipe out an entire section of a transmission by inserting high-amplitude spikes where low amplitude was intended. In that case, a section of the signal that was intended to be received as one or more 0s will read as 1s. You can see how surges in voltage would be especially problematic for ASK, which relies solely on amplitude for recognition. Noise usually affects the amplitude; therefore, ASK is the encoding method most affected by noise.

A popular ASK technique is called on-off-keying (OOK). In OOK one of the bit values is represented by no voltage. The advantage is a reduction in the amount of energy required to transmit information.

Bandwidth for ASK

As you will recall from Chapter 4, the bandwidth of a signal is the total range of frequencies occupied by that signal. When we decompose an ASK-encoded signal, we get a spectrum of simple frequencies. The signal at the center of this spectrum is the carrier f_c. At either side are signals with frequencies $f_c - N_{baud}/2, f_c + N_{baud}/2, f_c - 3N_{baud}/2, f_c + 3N_{baud}/2$, and so on. For practical purposes, however, only the carrier frequency and the two closest side frequencies are needed (see Figure 5.26).

Bandwidth requirements for ASK encoding are calculated using the formula

$$BW = (1 + d) \times N_{baud}$$

where
BW is the bandwidth
N_{baud} is the baud rate
d is a factor related to the condition of the line (with a minimum value of 0)

As you can see, the minimum bandwidth required for transmission is equal to the baud rate.

Figure 5.26   *Relationship between baud rate and bandwidth in ASK*

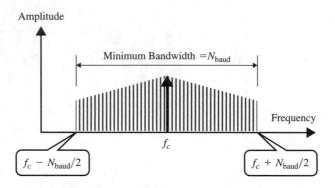

Example 5.6

Find the bandwidth for an ASK signal transmitting at 2000 bps. Transmission is in half-duplex mode.

Solution

In ASK the baud rate and bit rate are the same. The baud rate is therefore 2000. An ASK signal requires a bandwidth equal to its baud rate. Therefore, the bandwidth is 2000 Hz.

Example 5.7

Given a bandwidth of 5000 Hz for an ASK signal, what are the baud rate and bit rate?

Solution

In ASK the baud rate is the same as the bandwidth, which means the baud rate is 5000. But because the baud rate and the bit rate are also the same for ASK, the bit rate is 5000 bps.

Example 5.8

Given a bandwidth of 10,000 Hz (1000 to 11,000 Hz), draw the full-duplex ASK diagram of the system. Find the carriers and the bandwidths in each direction. Assume there is no gap between the bands in two directions.

Solution

For full-duplex ASK the bandwidth for each direction is

$$BW = 10,000/2 = 5000 \text{ Hz}$$

The carrier frequencies can be chosen at the middle of each band (see Figure 5.27).

$$f_{c \text{ (backward)}} = 1000 + 5000/2 = 3500 \text{ Hz}$$

$$f_{c \text{ (forward)}} = 11000 - 5000/2 = 8500 \text{ Hz}$$

Figure 5.27 *Solution to Example 5.8*

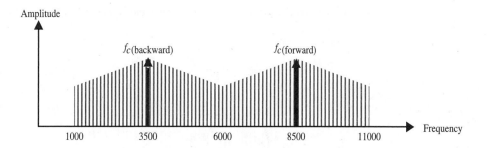

Frequency Shift Keying (FSK)

In frequency shift keying (FSK), the frequency of the signal is varied to represent binary 1 or 0. The frequency of the signal during each bit duration is constant and its value depends on the bit (0 or 1): both peak amplitude and phase remain constant. Figure 5.28 gives the conceptual view of FSK.

FSK avoids most of the noise problems of ASK. Because the receiving device is looking for specific frequency changes over a given number of periods, it can ignore voltage spikes. The limiting factors of FSK are the physical capabilities of the carrier.

Figure 5.28 *FSK encoding*

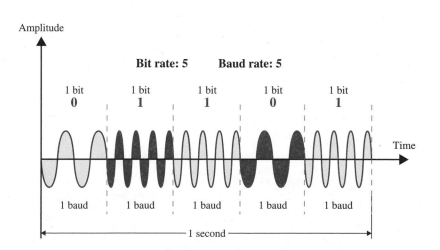

Bandwidth for FSK

Although FSK shifts between two carrier frequencies, it is easier to analyze as two coexisting frequencies. We can say that the FSK spectrum is the combination of two ASK spectra centered around f_{c0} and f_{c1}. BW $= (f_{c1} - f_{c0}) + N_{baud}$. The bandwidth required for FSK transmission is equal to the baud rate of the signal plus the frequency shift (difference between the two carrier frequencies). See Figure 5.29.

Figure 5.29 *Relationship between baud rate and bandwidth in FSK*

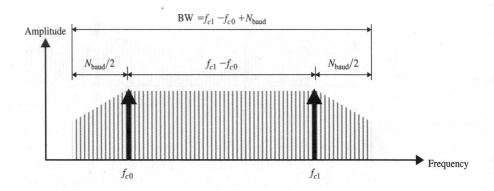

Example 5.9

Find the bandwidth for an FSK signal transmitting at 2000 bps. Transmission is in half-duplex mode and the carriers must be separated by 3000 Hz.

Solution

For FSK, if f_{c1} and f_{c0} are the carrier frequencies, then

$$BW = \text{Baud rate} + (f_{c1} - f_{c0})$$

However, the baud rate here is the same as the bit rate. Therefore,

$$BW \text{ V}= \text{Bit rate} + (f_{c1} - f_{c0}) = 2000 + 3000 = 5000 \text{ Hz}$$

Example 5.10

Find the maximum bit rates for an FSK signal if the bandwidth of the medium is 12,000 Hz and the distance between the two carriers must be at least 2000 Hz. Transmission is in full duplex mode.

Solution

Because the transmission is full duplex, only 6000 Hz is allocated for each direction. For FSK, if f_{c1} and f_{c0} are the carrier frequencies,

$$BW = \text{Baud rate} + (f_{c1} - f_{c0})$$

$$\text{Baud rate} = BW - (f_{c1} - f_{c0}) = 6000 - 2000 = 4000$$

But because the baud rate is the same as the bit rate, the bit rate is 4000 bps.

Phase Shift Keying (PSK)

In phase shift keying (PSK), the phase is varied to represent binary 1 or 0. Both peak amplitude and frequency remain constant as the phase changes. For example, if we start with a phase of 0 degrees to represent binary 0, then we can change the phase to 180 degrees to send binary 1. The phase of the signal during each bit duration is constant and its value depends on the bit (0 or 1). Figure 5.30 gives a conceptual view of PSK.

Figure 5.30 *PSK*

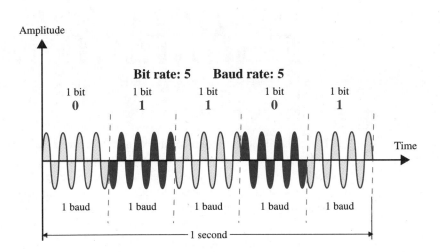

Figure 5.31 *PSK constellation*

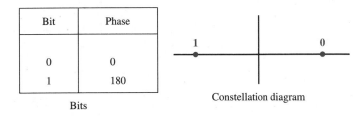

The above method is often called 2-PSK, or binary PSK, because two different phases (0 and 180 degrees) are used in the encoding. Figure 5.31 makes this point clearer by showing the relationship of phase to bit value. A second diagram, called a constellation or phase-state diagram, shows the same relationship by illustrating only the phases. PSK is not susceptible to the noise degradation that affects ASK, nor to the bandwidth limitations of FSK. This means that smaller variations in the signal can be detected reliably by the receiver. Therefore, instead of utilizing only two variations of a signal, each representing one bit, we can use four variations and let each phase shift represent two bits (see Figure 5.32).

Figure 5.32   *4-PSK*

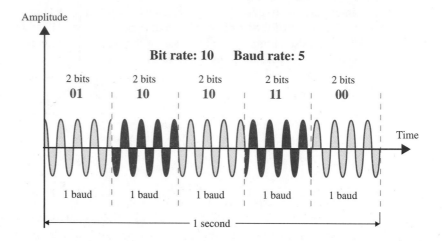

The constellation diagram for the signal in Figure 5.32 is given in Figure 5.33. A phase of 0 degrees now represents 00; 90 degrees represents 01; 180 degrees represents 10; and 270 degrees represents 11. This technique is called 4-PSK or Q-PSK. The pair of bits represented by each phase is called a dibit. We can transmit data two times as fast using 4-PSK as we can using 2-PSK.

Figure 5.33   *4-PSK characteristics*

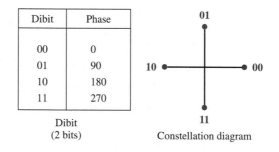

We can extend this idea to 8-PSK. Instead of 90 degrees, we now vary the signal by shifts of 45 degrees. With 8 different phases, each shift can represent three bits (one tribit) at a time. (As you can see, the relationship of number of bits per shift to number of phases is a power of two. When we have four possible phases, we can send two bits at a time—2^2 equals 4. When we have eight possible phases, we can send three bits at a time—2^3 equals 8). Figure 5.34 shows the relationships between the phase shifts and the tribits each one represents. 8-PSK is three times faster than 2-PSK.

Figure 5.34 *8-PSK characteristics*

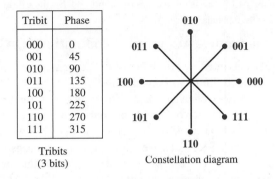

Tribit	Phase
000	0
001	45
010	90
011	135
100	180
101	225
110	270
111	315

Tribits
(3 bits)

Constellation diagram

Bandwidth for PSK

The minimum bandwidth required for PSK transmission is the same as that required for ASK transmission—and for the same reasons. As we have seen, the maximum bit rate in PSK transmission, however, is potentially much greater than that of ASK. So while the maximum baud rates of ASK and PSK are the same for a given bandwidth, PSK bit rates using the same bandwidth can be two or more times greater (see Figure 5.35).

Figure 5.35 *Bandwidth for PSK*

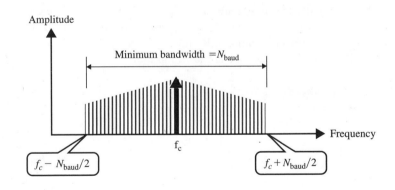

Amplitude

Minimum bandwidth $= N_{baud}$

Frequency

f_c

$f_c - N_{baud}/2$

$f_c + N_{baud}/2$

Example 5.11

Find the bandwidth for a 4-PSK signal transmitting at 2000 bps. Transmission is in half-duplex mode.

Solution

For 4-PSK the baud rate is half of the bit rate. The baud rate is therefore 1000. A PSK signal requires a bandwidth equal to its baud rate. Therefore, the bandwidth is 1000 Hz.

Example 5.12

Given a bandwidth of 5000 Hz for an 8-PSK signal, what are the baud rate and bit rate?

Solution

For PSK the baud rate is the same as the bandwidth, which means the baud rate is 5000. But in 8-PSK the bit rate is three times the baud rate. So the bit rate is 15,000 bps.

Quadrature Amplitude Modulation (QAM)

PSK is limited by the ability of the equipment to distinguish small differences in phase. This factor limits its potential bit rate.

So far, we have been altering only one of the three characteristics of a sine wave at a time to achieve our encoding, but what if we alter two? Bandwidth limitations make combinations of FSK with other changes practically useless. But why not combine ASK and PSK? Then we could have *x* variations in phase and *y* variations in amplitude, giving us *x* times *y* possible variations and the corresponding number of bits per variation. Quadrature amplitude modulation (QAM) does just that. The term *quadrature* is derived from the restrictions required for minimum performance and is related to trigonometry.

> Quadrature amplitude modulation (QAM) means combining ASK and PSK in such a way that we have maximum contrast between each bit, dibit, tribit, quadbit, and so on.

Possible variations of QAM are numerous. Theoretically any measurable number of changes in amplitude can be combined with any measurable number of changes in phase. Figure 5.36 shows two possible configurations, 4-QAM and 8-QAM. In both cases, the number of amplitude shifts is fewer than the number of phase shifts. Because amplitude changes are susceptible to noise and require greater shift differences than do phase changes, the number of phase shifts used by a QAM system is always larger than the number of amplitude shifts. The time-domain plot corresponding to the 8-QAM signal in Figure 5.36 is shown in Figure 5.37.

Figure 5.36   *4-QAM and 8-QAM constellations*

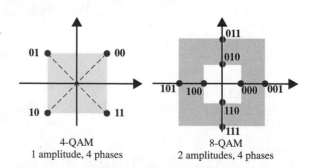

4-QAM
1 amplitude, 4 phases

8-QAM
2 amplitudes, 4 phases

Other geometric relationships besides concentric circles are also possible. Three popular 16-QAM configurations are shown in Figure 5.38. The first example, three amplitudes and 12 phases, handles noise best because of a greater ratio of phase shift to amplitude. It is the ITU-T recommendation. The second example, four amplitudes and

Figure 5.37 *Time domain for an 8-QAM signal*

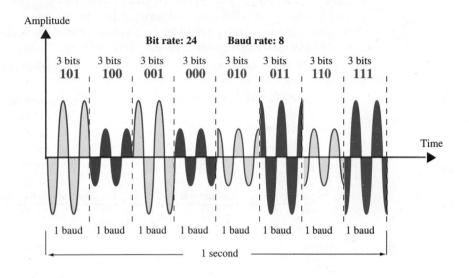

Figure 5.38 *16-QAM constellations*

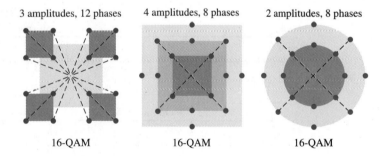

eight phases, is the OSI recommendation. If you examine the graph carefully, you will notice that although it is based on concentric circles, not every intersection of phase and amplitude is utilized. In fact, 4 times 8 should allow for 32 possible variations. But by using only half of those possibilities, the measurable differences between shifts are increased and greater signal readability is ensured. In addition, several QAM designs link specific amplitudes with specific phases. This means that even with the noise problems associated with amplitude shifting, the meaning of a shift can be recovered from phase information. In general, therefore, a second advantage of QAM encoding over ASK encoding is its lower susceptibility to noise.

Bandwidth for QAM

The minimum bandwidth required for QAM transmission is the same as that required for ASK and PSK transmission. QAM has the same advantages as PSK over ASK.

Bit/Baud Comparison

Assuming that an FSK signal over voice-grade phone lines can send 1200 bits per second, it has a bit rate of 1200. Each frequency shift represents a single bit; so it requires 1200 signal elements to send 1200 bits. Its baud rate, therefore, is also 1200. Each signal variation in an 8-QAM system, however, represents three bits. So a bit rate of 1200, using 8-QAM, has a baud rate of only 400. As Figure 5.39 shows, a dibit system has a baud rate of one-half the bit rate. A tribit system has a baud rate of one-third the bit rate. And a quadbit system has a baud rate of one-fourth the bit rate.

Figure 5.39   *Bit and baud*

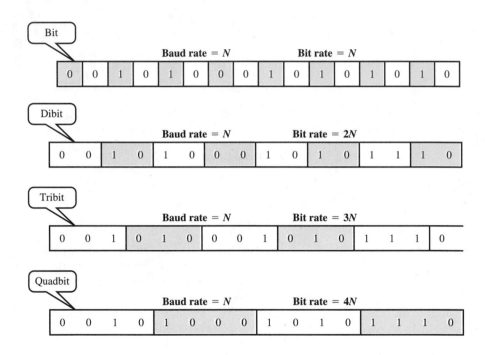

Table 5.1 shows the comparative bit and baud rates for the various methods of digital-to-analog encoding.

Table 5.1   *Bit and baud rate comparison*

Encoding	Units	Bits/Baud	Baud Rate	Bit Rate
ASK, FSK, 2-PSK	Bit	1	N	N
4-PSK, 4-QAM	Dibit	2	N	2N
8-PSK, 8-QAM	Tribit	3	N	3N
16-QAM	Quadbit	4	N	4N
32-QAM	Pentabit	5	N	5N
64-QAM	Hexabit	6	N	6N
128-QAM	Septabit	7	N	7N
256-QAM	Octabit	8	N	8N

Example 5.13

A constellation diagram consists of eight equally spaced points on a circle. If the bit rate is 4800 bps, what is the baud rate?

Solution

The constellation indicates 8-PSK encoding with the points 45 degrees apart. Since $2^3 = 8$, three bits are transmitted with each signal element. Therefore, the baud rate is

$$4800/3 = 1600 \text{ baud}$$

Example 5.14

Compute the bit rate for a 1000 baud 16-QAM signal.

Solution

A 16-QAM signal means that there are four bits per signal element since $2^4 = 16$. Thus,

$$(1000)(4) = 4000 \text{ bps}$$

Example 5.15

Compute the baud rate for a 72,000 bps 64-QAM signal.

Solution

A 64-QAM signal means that there are six bits per signal element since $2^6 = 64$. Thus,

$$72,000/6 = 12,000 \text{ baud}$$

5.4   ANALOG-TO-ANALOG ENCODING

Analog-to-analog encoding is the representation of analog information by an analog signal. Radio, that familiar utility, is an example of an analog-to-analog communication. Figure 5.40 shows the relationship between the analog information, the analog-to-analog conversion hardware, and the resultant analog signal.

Analog-to-analog encoding can be accomplished in three ways: amplitude modulation (AM), frequency modulation (FM), and phase modulation (PM). See Figure 5.41.

Figure 5.40   *Analog-to-analog encoding*

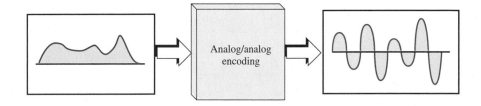

Figure 5.41   *Types of analog-to-analog encoding*

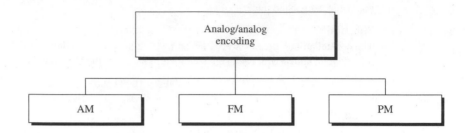

Amplitude Modulation (AM)

In AM transmission, the carrier signal is modulated so that its amplitude varies with the changing amplitudes of the modulating signal. The frequency and phase of the carrier remain the same; only the amplitude changes to follow variations in the information. Figure 5.42 shows how this concept works. The modulating signal becomes an envelope to the carrier.

Figure 5.42   *Amplitude modulation*

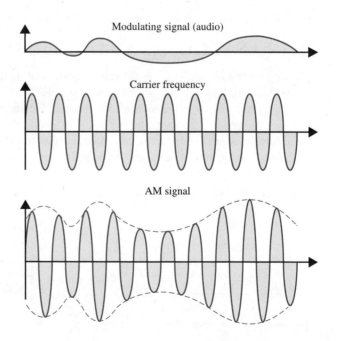

The total bandwidth required for AM can be determined from the bandwidth of the audio signal: $BW_t = 2 * BW_m$.

AM Bandwidth

The bandwidth of an AM signal is equal to twice the bandwidth of the modulating signal and covers a range centered around the carrier frequency (see Figure 5.43). The shaded portion of the graph is the frequency spectrum of the signal.

Figure 5.43   *AM bandwidth*

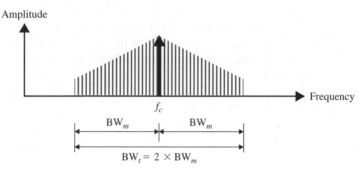

BW_m = Bandwidth of the modulating signal (audio)
BW_t = Total bandwidth (radio)
f_c = Frequency of the carrier

The bandwidth of an audio signal (speech and music) is usually 5 KHz. Therefore, an AM radio station needs a minimum bandwidth of 10 KHz. In fact, the Federal Communications Commission (FCC) allows 10 KHz for each AM station.

AM stations are allowed carrier frequencies anywhere between 530 and 1700 KHz (1.7 MHz). However, each station's carrier frequency must be separated from those on either side of it by at least 10 KHz (one AM bandwidth) to avoid interference. If one station uses a carrier frequency of 1100 KHz, the next station's carrier frequency cannot be lower than 1110 KHz (see Figure 5.44).

Figure 5.44   *AM band allocation*

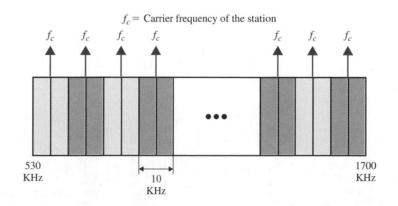

Example 5.16

We have an audio signal with a bandwidth of 4 KHz. What is the bandwidth needed if we encode the signal using AM? Ignore FCC regulations, for now.

Solution

An AM signal requires twice the bandwidth of the original signal:

$$BW = 2 \ (4) \ KHz = 8 \ KHz$$

Frequency Modulation (FM)

In FM transmission, the frequency of the carrier signal is modulated to follow the changing voltage level (amplitude) of the modulating signal. The peak amplitude and phase of the carrier signal remain constant, but as the amplitude of the information signal changes, the frequency of the carrier changes proportionately. Figure 5.45 shows the relationships of the modulating signal, the carrier signal, and the resultant FM signal.

FM Bandwidth

The bandwidth of an FM signal is equal to 10 times the bandwidth of the modulating signal and, like AM bandwidths, covers a range centered around the carrier frequency.

Figure 5.45   *Frequency modulation*

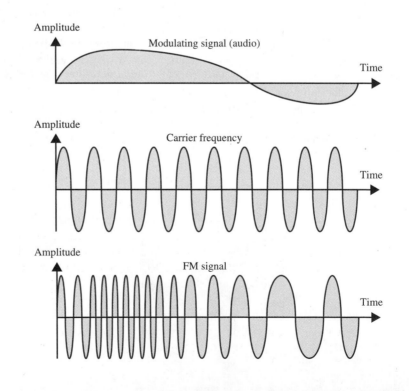

Figure 5.46   *FM bandwidth*

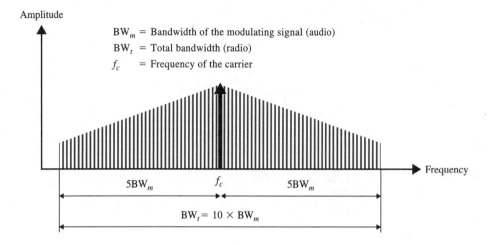

Figure 5.46 shows both the bandwidth, and, in the shaded portion, the frequency spectrum of an FM signal.

> The total bandwidth required for FM can be determined from the bandwidth of the audio signal: $BW_t = 10 * BW_m$.

The bandwidth of an audio signal (speech and music) broadcast in stereo is almost 15 KHz. Each FM radio station, therefore, needs a minimum bandwidth of 150 KHz. The FCC allows 200 KHz (0.2 MHz) for each station to provide some room for guard bands.

> The bandwidth of a stereo audio signal is usually 15 KHz. Therefore, an FM station needs at least a bandwidth of 150 KHz. The FCC requires the minimum bandwidth to be at least 200 KHz (0.2 MHz).

FM stations are allowed carrier frequencies anywhere between 88 and 108 MHz. Stations must be separated by at least 200 KHz to keep their bandwidths from overlapping. To create even more privacy, the FCC requires that in a given area, only alternate bandwidth allocations may be used. The others remain unused to prevent any possibility of two stations interfering with each other. Given 88 to 108 MHz as a range, there are 100 potential FM bandwidths in an area, of which 50 can operate at any one time. Figure 5.47 illustrates this concept.

Example 5.17

We have an audio signal with a bandwidth of 4 MHz. What is the bandwidth needed if we encode the signal using FM? Ignore FCC regulations, for now.

Figure 5.47 *FM band allocation*

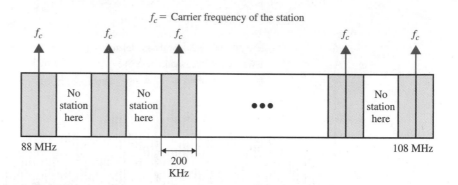

Solution

An FM signal requires 10 times the bandwidth of the original signal:

$$BW = 10 \ (4) \ MHz = 40 \ MHz$$

Phase Modulation (PM)

To make the hardware more simple, phase modulation (PM) is used in some systems as an alternative to frequency modulation. In PM transmission, the phase of the carrier signal is modulated to follow the changing voltage level (amplitude) of the modulating signal. The peak amplitude and frequency of the carrier signal remain constant, but as the amplitude of the information signal changes, the phase of the carrier changes proportionately. The analysis and the final result (modulated signal) are similar to those of frequency modulation.

5.5   SUMMARY

- Encoding means transforming information into signals.
- There are four types of encoding:
  - a. Digital-to-digital (digital information, digital signal).
  - b. Analog-to-digital (analog information, digital signal).
  - c. Digital-to-analog (digital information, analog signal).
  - d. Analog-to-analog (analog information, analog signal).
- Categories of digital-to-digital encoding include the following:
  - a. Unipolar—one voltage level is used.
  - b. Polar—two voltage levels are used. Variations of polar encoding include the following:

        NRZ (non-return to zero)
        NRZ-L (non-return to zero, level)
        NRZ-I (non-return to zero, invert)

RZ (return to zero)

Biphase: Manchester and Differential Manchester

c. Bipolar—ones are represented by alternating positive and negative voltages:

AMI (alternate mark inversion)

B8ZS (bipolar 8-zero substitution)

HDB3 (high-density bipolar 3)

■ Analog-to-digital encoding relies on PCM (pulse code modulation).

■ PCM involves sampling, quantizing each sample to a set number of bits, and then assigning voltage levels to the bits.

■ The Nyquist theorem says that the sampling rate must be twice the highest frequency component in the original signal.

■ Digital-to-analog encoding can be accomplished using the following:

a. Amplitude shift keying (ASK)—the amplitude of the carrier signal varies.

b. Frequency shift keying (FSK)—the frequency of the carrier signal varies.

c. Phase shift keying (PSK)—the phase of the carrier signal varies.

d. Quadrature amplitude modulation (QAM)—both the phase and amplitude of the carrier signal vary.

■ QAM enables a higher data transmission rate than other digital-to-analog methods.

■ Baud rate and bit rate are not synonymous. Bit rate is the number of bits transmitted per second. Baud rate is the number of signal units transmitted per second. One signal unit can represent one or more bits.

■ The minimum required bandwidth for ASK and PSK is the baud rate.

■ The minimum required bandwidth (BW) for FSK modulation is BW $= f_{c1} - f_{c0} + N_{baud}$ where f_{c1} is the frequency representing a 1 bit, f_{c0} is the frequency representing a 0 bit, and N_{baud} is the baud rate.

■ Analog-to-analog encoding can be implemented using the following:

a. Amplitude modulation (AM).

b. Frequency modulation (FM).

c. Phase modulation (PM).

■ In AM the amplitude of the carrier wave is a function of the amplitude of the modulating wave.

■ In FM the frequency of the carrier wave is a function of the amplitude of the modulating wave.

■ In AM radio, the bandwidth of the modulated signal must be twice the bandwidth of the modulating signal.

■ In FM radio, the bandwidth of the modulated signal must be 10 times the bandwidth of the modulating signal.

■ In PM the phase of the carrier signal is a function of the amplitude of the modulating signal.

5.6 PRACTICE SET

Multiple Choice

1. ASK, PSK, FSK, and QAM are examples of _____ encoding.
   a. digital-to-digital
   b. digital-to-analog
   c. analog-to-analog
   d. analog-to-digital

2. Unipolar, bipolar, and polar encoding are types of _____ encoding.
   a. digital-to-digital
   b. digital-to-analog
   c. analog-to-analog
   d. analog-to-digital

3. PCM is an example of _____ encoding.
   a. digital-to-digital
   b. digital-to-analog
   c. analog-to-analog
   d. analog-to-digital

4. AM and FM are examples of _____ encoding.
   a. digital-to-digital
   b. digital-to-analog
   c. analog-to-analog
   d. analog-to-digital

5. In QAM, both phase and _____ of a carrier frequency are varied.
   a. amplitude
   b. frequency
   c. bit rate
   d. baud rate

6. Which of the following is most affected by noise?
   a. PSK
   b. ASK
   c. FSK
   d. QAM

7. If the frequency spectrum of a signal has a bandwidth of 500 Hz with the highest frequency at 600 Hz, what should be the sampling rate according to the Nyquist theorem?
   a. 200 samples/sec
   b. 500 samples/sec

   c. 1000 samples/sec

   d. 1200 samples/sec

8. If the baud rate is 400 for a 4-PSK signal, the bit rate is _____ bps.

   a. 100

   b. 400

   c. 800

   d. 1600

9. If the bit rate for an ASK signal is 1200 bps, the baud rate is _____.

   a. 300

   b. 400

   c. 600

   d. 1200

10. If the bit rate for an FSK signal is 1200 bps, the baud rate is _____.

   a. 300

   b. 400

   c. 600

   d. 1200

11. If the bit rate for a QAM signal is 3000 bps and a signal element is represented by a tribit, what is the baud rate?

   a. 300

   b. 400

   c. 1000

   d. 1200

12. If the baud rate for a QAM signal is 3000 and a signal element is represented by a tribit, what is the bit rate?

   a. 300

   b. 400

   c. 1000

   d. 9000

13. If the baud rate for a QAM signal is 1800 and the bit rate is 9000, how many bits are there per signal element?

   a. 3

   b. 4

   c. 5

   d. 6

14. In 16-QAM, there are 16 _____.

   a. combinations of phase and amplitude

   b. amplitudes

   c. phases

   d. bits per second

15. Which modulation technique involves tribits, eight different phase shifts, and one amplitude?
    a. FSK
    b. 8-PSK
    c. ASK
    d. 4-PSK

16. The Nyquist theorem specifies the minimum sampling rate to be_____.
    a. equal to the lowest frequency of a signal
    b. equal to the highest frequency of a signal
    c. twice the bandwidth of a signal
    d. twice the highest frequency of a signal

17. Given an AM radio signal with a bandwidth of 10 KHz and the highest frequency component at 705 KHz, what is the frequency of the carrier signal?
    a. 700 KHz
    b. 705 KHz
    c. 710 KHz
    d. cannot be determined from given information

18. One factor in the accuracy of a reconstructed PCM signal is the _____.
    a. signal bandwidth
    b. carrier frequency
    c. number of bits used for quantization
    d. baud rate

19. Which encoding type always has a nonzero average amplitude?
    a. unipolar
    b. polar
    c. bipolar
    d. all of the above

20. Which of the following encoding methods does not provide for synchronization?
    a. NRZ-L
    b. RZ
    c. B8ZS
    d. HDB3

21. Which encoding method uses alternating positive and negative values for 1s?
    a. NRZ-I
    b. RZ
    c. Manchester
    d. AMI

22. Deliberate violations of alternate mark inversion are used in which type of digital-to-digital encoding?

    a. AMI

    b. B8ZS

    c. RZ

    d. Manchester

23. A modulated signal is formed by _____.

    a. changing the modulating signal by the carrier wave

    b. changing the carrier wave by the modulating signal

    c. quantization of the source data

    d. sampling at the Nyquist frequency

24. If FCC regulations are followed, the carrier frequencies of adjacent AM radio stations are _____ apart.

    a. 5 KHz

    b. 10 KHz

    c. 200 KHz

    d. 530 KHz

25. If FCC regulations are followed, _____ potential FM stations are theoretically possible in a given area.

    a. 50

    b. 100

    c. 133

    d. 150

26. In PCM, an analog-to- _____ conversion occurs.

    a. analog

    b. digital

    c. QAM

    d. differential

27. If the maximum value of a PCM signal is 31 and the minimum value is −31, how many bits were used for coding?

    a. 4

    b. 5

    c. 6

    d. 7

28. When an ASK signal is decomposed, the result is _____.

    a. always one sine wave

    b. always two sine waves

    c. an infinite number of sine waves

    d. none of the above

29. RZ encoding involves _____ levels of signal amplitude.

   a. 1

   b. 3

   c. 4

   d. 5

30. Which quantization level results in a more faithful reproduction of the signal?

   a. 2

   b. 8

   c. 16

   d. 32

31. Which encoding technique attempts to solve the loss of synchronization due to long strings of 0s?

   a. B8ZS

   b. HDB3

   c. AMI

   d. a and b

Exercises

1. Draw a 16-QAM constellation of your own choosing. Use four amplitudes and eight different phases.

2. Encode 10100100 using ASK with the maximum amplitude equal to 1.

3. Match the following to either ASK, PSK, FSK, or QAM. There may be more than one answer.

   a. Voltage is either 10 volts or 1 volt.

   b. The carrier changes phase from 0 to 180 degrees, and vice versa.

   c. High susceptibility to noise.

   d. Phase and amplitude are varied.

   e. Two frequencies are used.

   f. On-off keying.

   g. Eight phase changes, tribits.

   h. Eight phase changes, two amplitudes, quadbits.

4. What is the advantage of QAM over ASK or PSK?

5. How do the three categories of digital-to-digital encoding differ?

6. What is the major disadvantage in using NRZ encoding? How do RZ encoding and biphase encoding attempt to solve the problem?

7. Draw the time-domain plot for the bit string 010001100101 using RZ, Manchester, and Differential Manchester encoding.

8. How many amplitude values are there for each of the following methods?

   a. Unipolar

   b. NRZ-L

    c. NRZ-I

    d. RZ

    e. Manchester

    f. Differential Manchester

9. Compare and contrast RZ and bipolar AMI.

10. How does AM differ from ASK?

11. How does FM differ from FSK?

12. A signal has values from -127 to $+127$. Using PCM with a quantization level of 8, what is the bit sequence for a sample with a value of:

    a. 120

    b. 20

    c. -80

13. What is the minimum number of samples for PCM encoding if the frequency ranges from 1000 to 4000 Hz?

14. What is the difference between bit rate and baud rate? Give an example where both are the same. Give an example where they are different.

15. Calculate the baud rate for the given bit rate and type of encoding:

    a. 2000 bps, FSK

    b. 4000 bps, ASK

    c. 6000 bps, 2-PSK

    d. 6000 bps, 4-PSK

    e. 6000 bps, 8-PSK

    f. 4000 bps, 4-QAM

    g. 6000 bps, 16-QAM

    h. 36,000 bps, 64-QAM

16. Calculate the baud rate for the given bit rate and bit combination:

    a. 2000 bps, dibit

    b. 6000 bps, tribit

    c. 6000 bps, quadbit

    d. 6000 bps, bit

17. Calculate the bit rate for the given baud rate and type of encoding.

    a. 1000 baud, FSK

    b. 1000 baud, ASK

    c. 1000 baud, 8-PSK

    d. 1000 baud, 16-QAM

18. Draw the wave form for 010011110 in each of the following methods:

    a. Unipolar

    b. NRZ-L and NRZ-I

    c. RZ

d. Manchester

e. Differential Manchester

19. Draw the wave form for 110000000001010 in each of the following methods:

    a. AMI

    b. B8ZS

    c. HD3B

20. Using the Nyquist theorem, calculate the sampling rate for the following analog signals:

    a. An analog signal with bandwidth 2000 Hz.

    b. An analog signal with frequencies from 2000 to 6000 Hz.

    c. A signal with a horizontal line as the time-domain representation.

    d. A signal with a vertical line as the time-domain representation.

21. Calculate the bandwidth required for each of the following AM stations. Do not worry about FCC rules.

    a. Modulating signal with a bandwidth of 4 KHz.

    b. Modulating signal with a bandwidth of 8 KHz.

    c. Modulating signal with frequencies of 2000 to 3000 Hz.

22. Calculate the bandwidth required for each of the following FM stations. Do not worry about FCC rules.

    a. Modulating signal with a bandwidth of 12 KHz.

    b. Modulating signal with a bandwidth of 8 KHz.

    c. Modulating signal with frequencies of 2000 to 3000 Hz.

23. What is the voltage pattern if the following bits are encoded using B8ZS? 10010000000000011100101 ⇨

24. Draw the constellation diagram for the following:

    a. ASK encoding, amplitude of 1 and 3.

    b. 2-PSK encoding, amplitude of 1 at 0 and 180 degrees.

25. Data from a source ranges in value between −1.0 and 1.0. What do the data points 0.91, −0.25, 0.56, and 0.71 transform to if 8-bit quantization is used?

CHAPTER 6

TRANSMISSION OF DIGITAL DATA: INTERFACES AND MODEMS

Once we have encoded our information into a format that can be transmitted, the next step is to investigate the transmission process itself. Information-processing equipment such as PCs generate encoded signals but ordinarily require assistance to transmit those signals over a communication link. For example, a PC generates a digital signal but needs an additional device to modulate a carrier frequency before it is sent over a telephone line. How do we relay encoded data from the generating device to the next device in the process? The answer is a bundle of wires, a sort of minicommunication link, called an interface.

Because an interface links two devices not necessarily made by the same manufacturer, its characteristics must be defined and standards must be established. Characteristics of an interface include its mechanical specifications (how many wires are used to transport the signal); its electrical specifications (the frequency, amplitude, and phase of the expected signal); and its functional specifications (if multiple wires are used, what does each one do?). These characteristics are all described by several popular standards and are incorporated in the physical layer of the OSI model.

6.1   DIGITAL DATA TRANSMISSION

Of primary concern when considering the transmission of data from one device to another is the wiring. And of primary concern when considering the wiring is the data stream. Do we send one bit at a time, or do we group bits into larger groups and, if so, how? The transmission of binary data across a link can be accomplished either in parallel mode or serial mode. In parallel mode, multiple bits are sent with each clock pulse. In serial mode, one bit is sent with each clock pulse. While there is only one way to send parallel data, there are two subclasses of serial transmission: synchronous and asynchronous (see Figure 6.1).

Figure 6.1   *Data transmission*

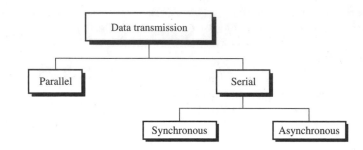

Parallel Transmission

Binary data, consisting of 1s and 0s, may be organized into groups of n bits each. Computers produce and consume data in groups of bits much as we conceive of and use spoken language in the form of words rather than letters. By grouping, we can send data n bits at a time instead of one. This is called parallel transmission.

The mechanism for parallel transmission is a conceptually simple one: use n wires to send n bits at one time. That way each bit has its own wire, and all n bits of one group can be transmitted with each clock pulse from one device to another. Figure 6.2 shows how parallel transmission works for $n = 8$. Typically the eight wires are bundled in a cable with a connector at each end.

Figure 6.2   *Parallel transmission*

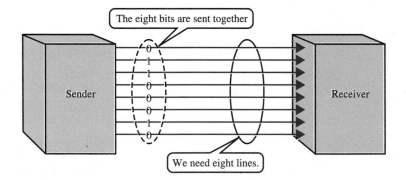

The advantage of parallel transmission is speed. All else being equal, parallel transmission can increase the transfer speed by a factor of n over serial transmission. But there is a significant disadvantage: cost. Parallel transmission requires n communication lines (wires in the example) just to transmit the data stream. Because this is expensive, parallel transmission is usually limited to short distances, up to a maximum of say 25 feet.

Serial Transmission

In serial transmission one bit follows another, so we need only one communication channel rather than n to transmit data between two communicating devices (see Figure 6.3).

Figure 6.3 *Serial transmission*

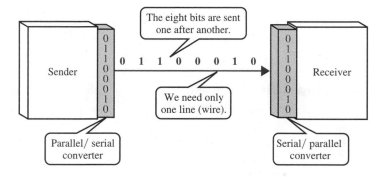

The advantage of serial over parallel transmission is that with only one communication channel, serial transmission reduces the cost of transmission over parallel by roughly a factor of n.

Since communication within devices is parallel, conversion devices are required at the interface between the sender and the line (parallel-to-serial) and between the line and the receiver (serial-to-parallel).

Serial transmission occurs in one of two ways: asynchronous or synchronous.

Asynchronous Transmission

Asynchronous transmission is so named because the timing of a signal is unimportant. Instead, information is received and translated by agreed-upon patterns. As long as those patterns are followed, the receiving device can retrieve the information without regard to the rhythm in which it is sent. Patterns are based on grouping the bit stream into bytes. Each group, usually eight bits, is sent along the link as a unit. The sending system handles each group independently, relaying it to the link whenever ready, without regard to a timer.

Without a synchronizing pulse, the receiver cannot use timing to predict when the next group will arrive. To alert the receiver to the arrival of a new group, therefore, an extra bit is added to the beginning of each byte. This bit, usually a 0, is called the start bit. To let the receiver know that the byte is finished, one or more additional bits are appended to the end of the byte. These bits, usually 1s, are called stop bits. By this method, each byte is increased in size to at least 10 bits, of which 8 are information and 2 or more are signals to the receiver. In addition, the transmission of each byte may then be followed by a gap of varying duration. This gap can be represented either by an idle channel or by a stream of additional stop bits.

> In asynchronous transmission we send one start bit (0) at the beginning and one or more stop bits (1s) at the end of each byte. There may be a gap between each byte.

The start and stop bits and the gap alert the receiver to the beginning and end of each byte and allow it to synchronize with the data stream. This mechanism is called asynchronous because, at the byte level, sender and receiver do not have to be synchronized. But within each byte, the receiver must still be synchronized with the incoming bit stream. That is, some synchronization is required, but only for the duration of a single byte. The receiving device resynchronizes at the onset of each new byte. When the receiver detects a start bit, it sets a timer and begins counting bits as they come in. After *n* bits the receiver looks for a stop bit. As soon as it detects the stop bit, it ignores any received pulses until it detects the next start bit.

> Asynchronous here means "asynchronous at the byte level," but the bits are still synchronized; their durations are the same.

Figure 6.4 is a schematic illustration of asynchronous transmission. In this example, the start bits are 0s, the stop bits are 1s, and the gap is represented by an idle line rather than by additional stop bits.

Figure 6.4 *Asynchronous transmission*

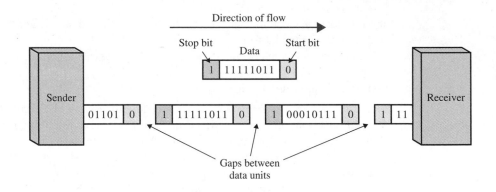

The addition of stop and start bits and the insertion of gaps into the bit stream make asynchronous transmission slower than forms of transmission that can operate without the addition of control information. But it is cheap and effective, two advantages that make it an attractive choice for situations like low-speed communication. For example, the connection of a terminal to a computer is a natural application for asynchronous transmission. A user types only one character at a time, types extremely slowly in data processing terms, and leaves unpredictable gaps of time between each character.

Synchronous Transmission

In synchronous transmission, the bit stream is combined into longer "frames," which may contain multiple bytes. Each byte, however, is introduced onto the transmission link without a gap between it and the next one. It is left to the receiver to separate the bit stream into bytes for decoding purposes. In other words, data are transmitted as an unbroken string of 1s and 0s, and the receiver separates that string into the bytes, or characters, it needs to reconstruct the information.

> In synchronous transmission we send bits one after another without start/stop bits or gaps. It is the responsibility of the receiver to group the bits.

Figure 6.5 gives a schematic illustration of synchronous transmission. We have drawn in the divisions between bytes. In reality, those divisions do not exist; the sender puts its data onto the line as one long string. If the sender wishes to send data in separate bursts, the gaps between bursts must be filled with a special sequence of 0s and 1s that means *idle*. The receiver counts the bits as they arrive and groups them in eight-bit units.

Figure 6.5 *Synchronous transmission*

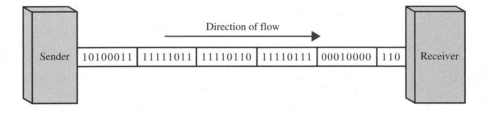

Without gaps and start/stop bits, there is no built-in mechanism to help the receiving device adjust its bit synchronization in midstream. Timing becomes very important, therefore, because the accuracy of the received information is completely dependent on the ability of the receiving device to keep an accurate count of the bits as they come in.

The advantage of synchronous transmission is speed. With no extra bits or gaps to introduce at the sending end and remove at the receiving end and, by extension, with fewer bits to move across the link, synchronous transmission is faster than asynchronous transmission. For this reason, it is more useful for high-speed applications like the transmission of data from one computer to another. Byte synchronization is accomplished in the data link layer.

6.2 DTE-DCE INTERFACE

At this point we must clarify two terms important to computer networking: *data terminal equipment* (*DTE*) and *data circuit-terminating equipment* (*DCE*). There are usually four basic functional units involved in the communication of data: a DTE and DCE on one end and a DCE and DTE on the other end, as shown in Figure 6.6. The DTE generates the data and passes them, along with any necessary control characters, to a DCE. The DCE does the job of converting the signal to a format appropriate to the transmission medium and introducing it onto the network link. When the signal arrives at the receiving end, this process is reversed.

Figure 6.6   *DTEs and DCEs*

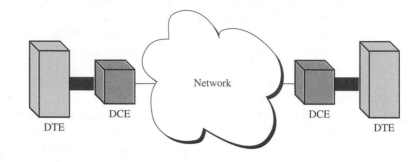

Data Terminal Equipment (DTE)

Data terminal equipment (DTE) includes any unit that functions either as a source of or as a destination for binary digital data. At the physical layer, it can be a terminal, microcomputer, computer, printer, fax machine, or any other device that generates or consumes digital data. DTEs do not often communicate directly with one another; they generate and consume information but need an intermediary to be able to communicate. Think of a DTE as operating the way your brain does when you talk. Let's say you have an idea that you want to communicate to a friend. Your brain creates the idea but cannot transmit that idea to your friend's brain by itself. Unfortunately or fortunately, we are not a species of mind readers. Instead, your brain passes the idea to your vocal chords and mouth, which convert it to sound waves that can travel through the air or over a telephone line to your friend's ear and from there to his or her brain, where it is converted back into information. In this model, your brain and your friend's brain are DTEs. Your vocal chords and mouth are your DCE. His or her ear is also a DCE. The air or telephone wire is your transmission medium.

A DTE is any device that is a source of or destination for binary digital data.

Data Circuit-Terminating Equipment (DCE)

Data circuit-terminating equipment (DCE) includes any functional unit that transmits or receives data in the form of an analog or digital signal through a network. At the physical layer, a DCE takes data generated by a DTE, converts them to an appropriate signal, and then introduces the signal onto the telecommunication link. Commonly used DCEs at this layer include modems (modulator/demodulators, discussed in Section 6.4). In any network, a DTE generates digital data and passes it to a DCE; the DCE converts the data to a form acceptable to the transmission medium and sends the converted signal to another DCE on the network. The second DCE takes the signal off the line, converts it to a form usable by its DTE, and delivers it. To make this communication possible, both the sending and receiving DCEs must use the same encoding method (e.g., FSK), much the way that if you want to communicate to someone who understands only Japanese, you must speak Japanese. The two DTEs do not need to be coordinated with each other, but each of them must be coordinated with its own DCE and the DCEs must be coordinated so that data translation occurs without loss of integrity.

A DCE is any device that transmits or receives data in the form of an analog or digital signal through a network.

Standards

Over the years, many standards have been developed to define the connection between a DTE and a DCE (see Figure 6.7). Though their solutions differ, each standard provides a model for the mechanical, electrical, and functional characteristics of the connection.

Figure 6.7   *DTE-DCE interface*

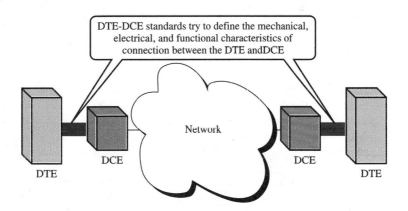

Of the organizations involved in DTE-DCE interface standards, the most active are the Electronic Industries Association (EIA) and the International Telecommunication Union–Telecommunication Standards Committee (ITU-T). The EIA standards are called, appropriately enough, EIA-232, EIA-442, EIA-449, and so on. The ITU-T standards are called the V series and the X series.

The EIA and the ITU-T have been involved in developing DTE-DCE interface standards. The EIA standards are called EIA-232, EIA-442, EIA-449, and so on. The ITU-T standards are called the V series and the X series.

EIA-232 Interface

One important interface standard developed by the EIA is the EIA-232, which defines the mechanical, electrical, and functional characteristics of the interface between a

DTE and a DCE. Originally issued in 1962 as the RS-232 standard (recommended standard), the EIA-232 has been revised several times. The most recent version, EIA-232-D, defines not only the type of connectors to be used but also the specific cable and plugs and the functionality of each pin.

> EIA-232 (previously called RS-232) defines the mechanical, electrical, and functional characteristics of the interface between a DTE and a DCE.

Mechanical Specification

The mechanical specification of the EIA-232 standard defines the interface as a 25-wire cable with a male and a female DB-25 pin connector attached to either end. The length of the cable may not exceed 15 meters (about 50 feet).

A DB-25 connector is a plug with 25 pins or receptacles, each of which is attached to a single wire with a specific function. With this design, the EIA has created the possibility of 25 separate interactions between a DTE and a DCE. Fewer are actually used in current practice, but the standard allows for future inclusion of functionality.

The EIA-232 calls for a 25-wire cable terminated at one end by a male connector and at the other end by a female connector. The term *male connector* refers to a plug with each wire in the cable connecting to a pin. The term *female connector* refers to a receptacle with each wire in the cable connecting to a metal tube, or sheath. In the DB-25 connector, these pins and tubes are arranged in two rows, with 13 on the top and 12 on the bottom.

Electrical Specification

The electrical specification of the standard defines the voltage levels and the type of signal to be transmitted in either direction between the DTE and the DCE. EIA-232 states that all data must be transmitted as logical 1s and 0s (called mark and space) using non-return to zero, level (NRZ-L) encoding, with 0 defined as a positive voltage and 1 defined as a negative voltage.

Sending the Data   The electrical specification for sending data is shown in Figure 6.8. Rather than defining a single range bounded by highest and lowest amplitudes, EIA-232 defines two distinct ranges, one for positive voltages and one for negative. A receiver recognizes and accepts as an intentional signal any voltage that falls within these ranges, but no voltages that fall outside the ranges. To be recognized as data, the amplitude of a signal must fall between 3 and 15 volts or between −3 and −15 volts. By allowing valid signals to fall within two 12-volt ranges, EIA-232 makes it unlikely that degradation of a signal by noise will affect its recognizability. In other words, as long as a pulse falls within one of the acceptable ranges, the precision of that pulse is unimportant.

Figure 6.8 shows a square wave degraded by noise into a curve. The amplitude of the fourth bit is lower than intended (compared to that of the second bit), and rather than staying at one single voltage, it covers a range of many voltages. If the receiver were looking only for a fixed voltage, the degradation of this pulse would have made it unrecoverable. The bit would also have been unrecoverable if the receiver were looking only for pulses that held a single voltage for their entire duration.

Figure 6.8   *Electrical specification for sending data in EIA-232*

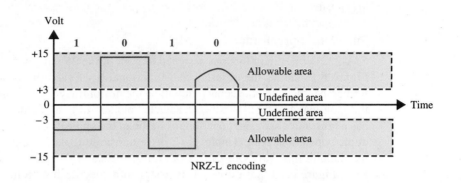

Control and Timing

Only 4 wires out of the 25 available in an EIA-232 interface are used for data functions. The remaining 21 are reserved for functions like control, timing, grounding, and testing. The electrical specifications for these other wires are similar to those governing data transmission, but simpler. Any of the other functions is considered ON if it transmits a voltage of at least +3; and OFF if it transmits a voltage with a value less than −3 volts.

The electrical specification of EIA-232 defines that signals other than data must be sent using OFF ⇨ less than −3 volts and ON ⇨ greater than +3 volts

Figure 6.9 shows one of these signals. The specification for control signals is conceptually reversed from that for data transmission. A positive voltage means ON and a negative voltage means OFF. Also note that OFF is still signified by the transmission of a specific voltage range. An absence of voltage on one of these wires while the system is running means that something is not working properly, and not that the line is turned off.

Figure 6.9   *Electrical specification for control signals in EIA-232*

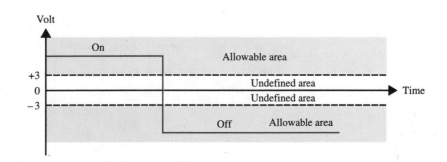

A final important function of the electrical specification is the definition of bit rate. EIA-232 allows for a maximum bit rate of 20 Kbps, although in practice this often is exceeded.

Functional Specification

EIA-232 defines the functions assigned to each of the 25 pins in the DB-25 connector. Figure 6.10 shows the ordering and functionality of each pin of a male connector. Remember that a female connector will be the mirror image of the male, so that pin 1 in the plug matches tube 1 in the receptacle, and so on. Each communications function has a mirror or answering function for traffic in the opposite direction, to allow for full-duplex operation. For example, pin 2 is for transmitting data, while pin 3 is for receiving data. In this way both parties can transmit data at the same time. As you can see from Figure 6.10, not every pin is assigned a specific function. Pins 9 and 10 are reserved for future use. Pin 11 is as yet unassigned.

Figure 6.10   *Functions of pins in EIA-232*

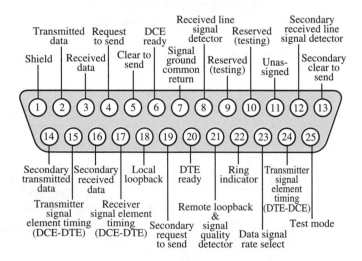

An Example

This example, Figure 6.11, demonstrates the functioning of EIA-232 in synchronous full-duplex mode over a leased line using only the primary channel. The DCEs here are modems, and the DTEs are computers. There are five distinct steps, from preparation to clearing. This is a full-duplex model, so both computer/modem systems can transmit data concurrently. In terms of the EIA model, however, one system is still classified as the initiator and the other as the responder

Figure 6.11   *Synchronous full-duplex transmission*

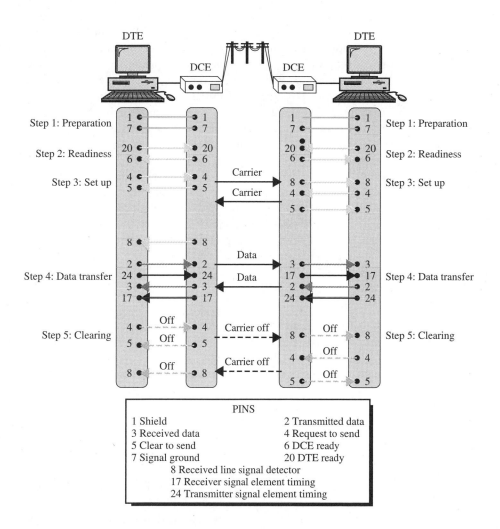

Step 1 shows the preparation of the interfaces for transmission. The two grounding circuits, 1 (shield) and 7 (signal ground), are active between both the sending computer/modem combination (left) and between the receiving computer/modem combination (right).

Step 2 ensures that all four devices are ready for transmission. First the sending DTE activates pin 20 and sends a DTE ready message to its DCE. The DCE answers by activating pin 6 and returning a DCE ready message. This same sequence is performed by the remote computer and modem.

Step 3 sets up the physical connection between the sending and receiving modems. This step can be thought of as the *on* switch for transmission. It is the first step that involves the network. First the sending DTE activates pin 4 and sends its DCE a request-to-send message. The DCE transmits a carrier signal to the idle receiving modem. When the receiving modem detects the carrier signal, it activates pin 8, the received line signal detector, telling its computer that a transmission is about to begin. After transmitting the carrier signal, the sending DCE activates pin 5 sending its DTE a clear-to-send message. The remote computer and modem perform the same step.

Step 4 is the data transfer procedure. The initiating computer transfers its data stream to its modem over circuit 2, accompanied by the timing pulse of circuit 24. The modem converts the digital data to an analog signal and sends it out over the network. The responding modem retrieves the signal, converts it back into digital data and passes it along to its computer via circuit 3, accompanied by the timing pulse of circuit 17. At the same time, however, the responding computer is transferring digital data of its own to its modem over its circuit 2, accompanied by the timing pulse of its circuit 24. The responding modem converts the response data into an analog signal, which it then sends out over the network on its own carrier signal. The initiating modem retrieves the signal, converts it to digital data, and transmits it to the initiating computer along its circuit 3, accompanied by the timing pulse of its circuit 17.

Once both sides have completed their transmissions, both computers deactivate their request-to-send circuits; the modems turn off their carrier signals, their received line signal detectors (there is no longer any signal to detect), and their clear-to-send circuits (Step 5).

Null Modem

Suppose you need to connect two DTEs in the same building, for example, two workstations, or a terminal to a workstation. Modems are not needed to connect two compatible digital devices directly; the transmission never needs to cross analog lines, such as telephone lines, and therefore does not need to be modulated. But you do need an interface to handle the exchange (readiness establishment, data transfer, receipt, etc.), just as an EIA-232 DTE-DCE cable does.

The solution, provided by the EIA standard, is called a null modem. A null modem provides the DTE-DCE/DCE-DTE interface without the DCEs. But why use a null modem? If all you need is the interface, why not just use a standard EIA-232 cable? To understand the problem, examine Figure 6.12. Part *a* shows a connection using a telephone network. The two DTEs are exchanging information through DCEs. Each DTE sends its data through pin 2 and the DCE receives it on pin 2; and each DTE receives data through pin 3 that has been forwarded by the DCE using its own pin 3. As you can see, the EIA-232 cable connects DTE pin 2 to DCE pin 2 and DCE pin 3 to DTE pin 3. Traffic using pin 2 is always outgoing from the DTEs. Traffic using pin 3 is always incoming to the DTEs. A DCE recognizes the direction of a signal and passes it along to the appropriate circuit.

Part *b* of the figure shows what happens when we use the same connections between two DTEs. Without DCEs to switch the signals to or from the appropriate pins, both DTEs are attempting to transmit over the same pin 2 wire—and to receive over the same pin 3 wire. The DTEs are transmitting to each other's transmit pins, not to their receive pins. The receive circuit (3) is void because it has been isolated completely from the transmission. The transmit circuit (2) therefore ends up full of collision noise and signals that can never be received by either DTE. No data can get through from one device to another.

Figure 6.12 *Using regular data pin connections with and without DCEs*

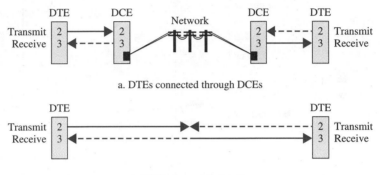

a. DTEs connected through DCEs

b. DTEs connected directly

Crossing Connections   For transmission to occur, the wires must be crossed so that pin 2 of the first DTE connects to pin 3 of the second DTE; and pin 2 of the second DTE connects to pin 3 of the first. These two pins are the most important. Several other pins, however, have similar problems and their wires also need reconnection.

A null modem is an EIA-232 interface that completes the necessary circuits to fool the DTEs at either end into believing that they have DCEs and a network between them. Because its purpose is to make connections, a null modem can be either a length of cable or a device, or you can make one yourself using a standard EIA-232 cable and a breakout box that allows you to cross-connect wires in any way you desire. Of these options, the cable is the most commonly used and the most convenient (see Figure 6.13).

Other Differences   Null modems have up to 25 wires. Of these 25, the most important are those needed for DTE-to-DTE transmission, and are shown in Figure 6.13. Note that whereas an EIA-232 DTE-DCE interface cable has a female connector at the DTE end and a male connector at the DCE end, a null modem has female connectors at both ends to allow it to connect to the EIA-232 DTE ports, which are male.

Figure 6.13   *Null modem pin connections*

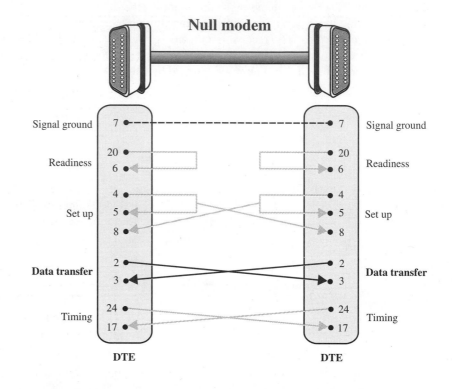

6.3   OTHER INTERFACE STANDARDS

Both data rate and cable length (signal distance capability) are restricted by EIA-232; data rate to 20 Kbps and cable length to 50 feet (15 meters). To meet the needs of users who require more speed and/or distance, the EIA and the ITU-T have introduced additional interface standards: EIA-449, EIA-530, and X.21.

EIA-449

The mechanical specifications of EIA-449 define a combination of two connectors: one with 37 pins (DB-37) and one with 9 pins (DB-9), for a combined 46 pins (see Figure 6.14).

The functional specifications of the EIA-449 give the DB-37 pins properties similar to those of the DB-25. The major functional difference between the 25- and 37-pin connectors is that all functions relating to the secondary channel have been removed from DB-37. Because the secondary channel is seldom used, EIA-449 separates those functions out and puts them in the second, 9-pin connector (DB-9). In this way, a second channel is available to systems that need it.

Figure 6.14   *DB-37 and DB-9 connectors*

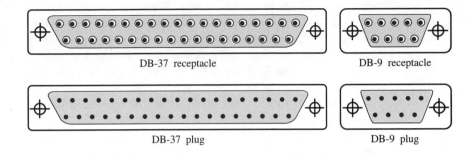

DB-37 receptacle   DB-9 receptacle

DB-37 plug   DB-9 plug

Pin Functions

To maintain compatibility with EIA-232, EIA-449 defines two categories of pins to be
used in exchanging data, control, and timing information (see Table 6.1).

Table 6.1   *DB-37 pins*

Pin	Function	Category	Pin	Function	Category
1	Shield		20	Receive Common	II
2	Signal rate indicator		21	Unassigned	I
3	Unassigned		22	Send data	I
4	Send data	I	23	Send timing	I
5	Send timing	I	24	Receive data	I
6	Receive data	I	25	Request to send	I
7	Request to send	I	26	Receive timing	I
8	Receive timing	I	27	Clear to send	I
9	Clear to send	I	28	Terminal in service	II
10	Local loopback	II	29	Data mode	I
11	Data mode	I	30	Terminal ready	I
12	Terminal ready	I	31	Receive ready	I
13	Receive ready	I	32	Select standby	II
14	Remote loopback	II	33	Signal quality	
15	Incoming call		34	New signal	II
16	Select frequency	II	35	Terminal timing	I
17	Terminal timing	I	36	Standby indicator	II
18	Test mode	II	37	Send common	II
19	Signal ground				

Category I Pins

Category I includes those pins whose functions are compatible with those of EIA-232 (although most have been renamed). For each Category I pin, EIA-449 defines two pins, one in the first column and one in the second column. For example, both pins 4 and 22 are called send data. These two pins have the equivalent functionality of pin 2 in EIA-232. Both pins 5 and 23 are called send timing. And both pins 6 and 24 are called receive data. Even more interesting, these pairs of pins are vertically adjacent to one another in the connector, with the pin from the second column occupying the position essentially below its counterpart from the first column. (Number the DB-37 connector based on the numbering of the DB-25 connector to see these relationships.) This structure is what gives EIA-449 its power. How the pins relate will become clear later in this section, when we discuss the two alternate methods of signaling defined in the electrical specifications.

Table 6.2 lists the pin functions of the DB-9 connector and shows their relationships to the EIA-232 (DB-25) equivalents.

Table 6.2   *DB-9 pins*

Pin	Function	EIA-232 Equivalent
1	Shield	1
2	Secondary receive ready	
3	Secondary send data	14
4	Secondary receive data	16
5	Signal ground	7
6	Receive common	12
7	Secondary request to send	19
8	Secondary clear to send	13
9	Send common	

Category II Pins

Category II pins are those that have no equivalent in EIA-232 or have been redefined. The numbers and functions of these new pins are as follows:

- **Local loopback.** Pin 10 is used for local loopback testing.
- **Remote loopback.** Pin 14 is used for remote loopback testing.
- **Select frequency.** Pin 16 is used to choose between two different frequency rates.
- **Receive common.** Pin 20 provides a common signal return line for unbalanced circuits from the DCE to the DTE.
- **Terminal in service.** Pin 28 indicates to the DCE whether or not the DTE is operational.
- **Select standby.** Pin 32 allows the DTE to request the use of standby equipment in the event of failure.

- **New signal.** Pin 34 is available for multiple point applications where a primary DTE controls several secondary DTEs. When activated, pin 34 indicates that one DTE has finished its data exchange and a new one is about to start.

- **Standby indicator.** Pin 36 provides the confirmation signal from the DCE in response to select standby (pin 32).

- **Send common.** Pin 37 provides a common signal return line for unbalanced circuits from the DTE to the DCE.

Electrical Specifications: RS-423 and RS-422

EIA-449 uses two other standards to define its electrical specifications: RS-423 (for unbalanced circuits) and RS-422 (for balanced circuits).

RS-423: Unbalanced Mode

RS-423 is an unbalanced circuit specification, meaning that it defines only one line for propagating a signal. All signals in this standard use a common return (or ground) to complete the circuit. Figure 6.15 gives a conceptual view of this type of circuit as well as the specifications for the standard. In unbalanced-circuit mode, EIA-449 calls for the use of only the first pin of each pair of Category I pins and all Category II pins.

Figure 6.15 *RS-423: Unbalanced mode*

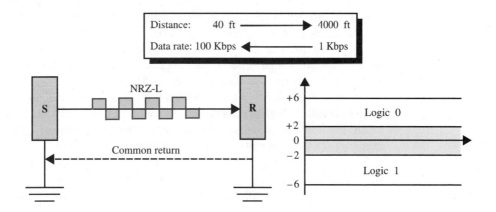

RS-422: Balanced Mode

RS-422 is a balanced circuit specification, meaning that it defines two lines for the propagation of each signal. Signals again use a common return (or ground) for the return of the signal. Figure 6.16 gives a conceptual view of and the specifications for this standard. In balanced mode, EIA-449 utilizes both pins in each Category I but does not use the Category II pins. As you can see from the electrical specifications for this standard, the ratio of data rate to distance is much higher than that of the unbalanced standard or of EIA-232: 10 Mbps for transmissions of 40 feet.

Figure 6.16   *RS-422: Balanced mode*

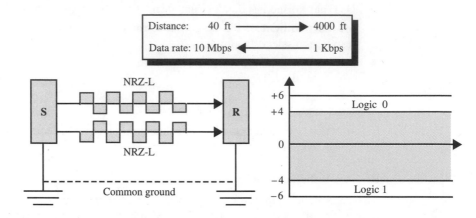

In balanced mode, two lines carry the same transmission. They do not, however, carry identical signals. The signal on one line is the complement of the signal on the other. When plotted, the complement looks like a mirror image of the original signal (see Figure 6.16). Instead of listening to either actual signal, the receiver detects the differences between the two. This mechanism makes a balanced circuit less susceptible to noise than an unbalanced circuit, and improves performance.

As the complementary signals arrive at the receiver, they are put through a subtracter (a differential amplifier). This mechanism subtracts the second signal from the first before interpretation. Because the two signals complement each other, the result of this subtraction is a doubling of the value of the first signal. For example, if at a given moment the first signal has a voltage of 5, the second signal will have a voltage of −5. The result of subtraction, therefore, is 5 − (−5), which equals 10.

If noise is added to the transmission, it impacts both signals in the same way (positive noise affects both signals positively; negative noise affects both negatively). As a result, the noise is eliminated during the subtraction process (see Figure 6.17). For example, say that two volts of noise are introduced at the point where the first signal is at 5 volts and its complement is at −5 volts. The addition distorts the first signal to 7 volts, and the second to −3 volts. 7 − (−3) still equals 10. It is this ability to neutralize the effects of noise that allows the superior data rates of balanced transmission.

EIA-530

EIA-449 provides much better functionality than EIA-232. However, it requires a DB-37 connector that the industry has been reluctant to embrace because of the amount of investment already put into the DB-25. To encourage acceptance of the new standard, therefore, the EIA developed a version of EIA-449 that uses DB-25 pins: EIA-530.

The pin functions of EIA-530 are essentially those of EIA-449 Category I plus three pins from Category II (the loopback circuits). Of the EIA-232 pins, some have been omitted, including ring indicator, signal quality detector, and data signal rate selector. EIA-530 does not support a secondary circuit.

Figure 6.17   *Canceling of noise using balanced mode*

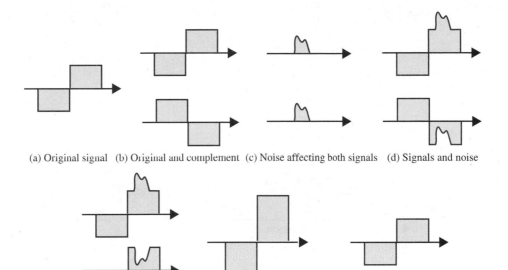

(a) Original signal   (b) Original and complement   (c) Noise affecting both signals   (d) Signals and noise

(e) After negation of second signal   (f) After adding   (g) After rescaling

X.21

X.21 is an interface standard designed by the ITU-T to address many of the problems existing in the EIA interfaces and, at the same time, paves the way for all-digital communication.

Using Data Circuits for Control

A large proportion of the circuits in the EIA interfaces are used for control. These circuits are necessary because the standards implement control functions as separate signals. With a separate line, control information is represented only by positive and negative voltages. But, if control signals are encoded using meaningful control characters from a system such as ASCII, they can be transmitted over data lines.

For this reason, X.21 eliminates most of the control circuits of the EIA standards and instead directs their traffic over the data circuits. To make this consolidation of functionality possible, both the DTE and the DCE must have added circuit logic that enables them to transform the control codes into bit streams that can be sent over the data line. Both also need additional logic to discriminate between control information and data upon receipt.

This design allows X.21 not only to use fewer pins but also to be used in digital telecommunications where control information is sent from device to device over a network rather than just between a DTE and a DCE. As digital technology emerges, more and more control information must be handled, including dialing, redialing, hold, and so on. X.21 is useful both as an interface to connect digital computers to analog devices such as modems and as a connector between digital computers and digital interfaces such as ISDN and X.25, described in Chapter 15 and 16.

X.21 is designed to work with balanced circuits at 64 Kbps, a rate that is becoming the industry standard.

Pin Functions

Figure 6.18 shows the connector specified by X.21, the DB-15. As the name indicates, the DB-15 is a 15-pin connector.

Figure 6.18   *DB-15 connector*

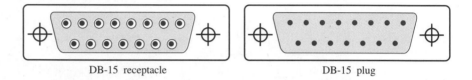

DB-15 receptacle   DB-15 plug

- **Byte timing.** Another advantage offered by X.21 is that of timing lines to control byte synchronization in addition to the bit synchronization provided by the EIA standards. By adding a byte timing pulse (pins 7 and 14), X.21 improves the overall synchronization of transmissions.
- **Control and indication.** Pins 3 and 5 of the DB-15 connector are used for the initial handshake, or agreement to begin transmitting. Pin 3 is the equivalent of request to send. Pin 5 is the equivalent of clear to send. Table 6.3 lists the functions for each pin.

Table 6.3   *DB-15 pins*

Pin	Function	Pin	Function
1	Shield	9	Transmit data or control
2	Transmit data or control	10	Control
3	Control	11	Receive data or control
4	Receive data or control	12	Indication
5	Indication	13	Signal element timing
6	Signal element timing	14	Byte timing
7	Byte timing	15	Reserved
8	Signal ground		

6.4   MODEMS

The most familiar type of DCE is a modem. Anyone who has surfed the Internet, logged on to an office computer from home, or filed a news story from a word processor over a phone line has used a modem. The external or internal modem associated with your personal computer is what converts the digital signal generated by the computer into an analog signal to be carried by a public access phone line. It is also the device that converts the analog signals received over a phone line into digital signals usable by your computer.

The term *modem* is a composite word that refers to the two functional entities that make up the device: a signal *mo*dulator and a signal *dem*odulator. The relationship of the two parts is shown in Figure 6.19.

Modem stands for modulator/demodulator.

Figure 6.19 *Modem concept*

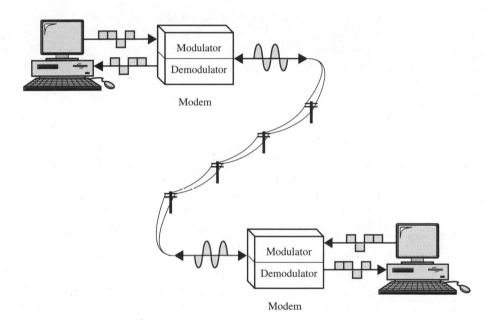

A modulator converts a digital signal into an analog signal. A demodulator converts an analog signal into a digital signal. While a demodulator resembles an analog-to-digital encoder, it is not in fact an encoder of any kind. It does not sample a signal to create a digital facsimile; it merely reverses the process of modulation.

A modulator converts a digital signal to an analog signal. A demodulator converts an analog signal to a digital signal.

Both modulators and demodulators, however, do use the same techniques as digital-to-analog encoders: modulators to further encode a signal, and demodulators to decode it. A modulator treats a digital signal as a series of 1s and 0s, and so can transform it into a completely analog signal by using the digital-to-analog mechanisms of ASK, FSK, PSK, and QAM.

Figure 6.19 shows the relationship of modems to a communication link. The two PCs at the ends are the DTEs; the modems are the DCEs. The DTE creates a digital signal and relays it to the modem via an interface (like the EIA-232, as discussed before). The modulated signal is received by the demodulation function of the second modem. The demodulator takes the ASK, FSK, PSK, or QAM signal and decodes it into whatever format its computer can accept. It then relays the resulting digital signal to the receiving computer via an interface. Each DCE must be compatible with both its own DTE and with other DCEs. A modem must use the same type of encoding (such as NRZ-L), the same voltage levels to mean the same things, and the same timing conventions as its DTE. A modem must also be able to communicate with other modems.

Transmission Rate

You may have heard modems described as high-speed or low-speed to indicate how many bits per second a specific device is capable of transmitting or receiving. But before talking about different commercial modems and their data rates, we need to examine the limitations on the transmission rate of the medium itself.

Bandwidth

We defined the concept of bandwidth at the end of Chapter 4. Now we can apply that concept to physical media to see its effect on transmission. The data rate of a link depends on the type of encoding used, the duration of the signal, the size of the voltages used, and the physical properties of the transmission medium. Of these, the last imposes the greatest limitations. One way to increase the speed of data transmission is to increase the speed (frequency) of the signal carrying it. Theoretically, the faster the signal, the faster the data rate. But increasing the speed of a signal means increasing the number of changes per second (baud rate), and every line has an inherent limitation on the number of such changes it can accommodate. In other words, every line, based on its electrical qualities, can accept only a certain range of signal changes per second. If the signal is too slow, it cannot overcome the capacitance of the line. If it is too fast, it can be impeded by the inductance of the line. So we can say that every line has an upper limit and a lower limit on the frequencies of the signals it can carry. This limited range is called the bandwidth.

> Every line has an upper limit and a lower limit on the frequencies of the signals it can carry. This limited range is called the bandwidth.

Traditional telephone lines can carry frequencies between 300 Hz and 3300 Hz, giving them a bandwidth of 3000 Hz. All of this range is used for transmitting voice, where a great deal of interference and distortion can be accepted without loss of intelligibility. As we have seen, however, data signals require a higher degree of accuracy to ensure integrity. For safety's sake, therefore, the edges of this range are not used for data communication. In general, we can say that the signal bandwidth must be smaller than the cable bandwidth. The effective bandwidth of a telephone line being used for data transmission is 2400 Hz, covering the range from 600 Hz to 3000 Hz. Note that today some telephone lines are capable of handling more bandwidth than traditional lines. However, modem design is still based on traditional capability (see Figure 6.20).

Figure 6.20 *Telephone line bandwidth*

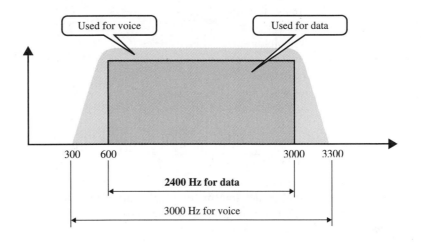

A telephone line has a bandwidth of almost 3000 Hz.

Modem Speed

As we have seen, each type of analog encoding manipulates the signal in a different way: ASK manipulates amplitude; FSK manipulates frequency; PSK manipulates phase; and QAM manipulates both phase and amplitude.

ASK   As you will recall from Chapter 5, the bandwidth required for ASK transmission is equal to the baud rate of the signal. Assuming that the entire link is being used by one signal, as it would be for simplex or half-duplex transmission, the maximum baud rate for ASK encoding is equal to the entire bandwidth of the transmission medium. Because the effective bandwidth of a telephone line is 2400 Hz, the maximum baud rate is also 2400. And, because the baud rate and bit rate are the same in ASK encoding, the maximum bit rate is also 2400 (see Figure 6.21).

Figure 6.21 *Baud rate for half-duplex ASK*

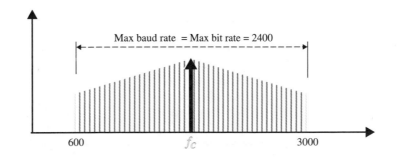

Figure 6.22   *Baud rate for full-duplex ASK*

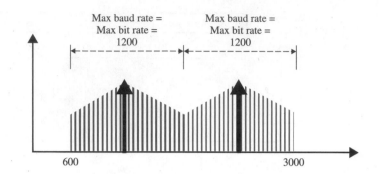

For full-duplex transmission, only half of the total bandwidth can be used in either direction. Therefore, the maximum speed for ASK transmission in full-duplex mode is 1200 bps. Figure 6.22 shows this relationship. The total available bandwidth is 2400 Hz; each direction therefore has an available 1200 Hz centered around its own carrier frequency. (Note: some modem specifications indicate half-duplex by the abbreviation *HDX*, and full-duplex by the abbreviation *FDX*.)

Although ASK's bit rate equals that of more popular types of encoding, its noise problems make it impractical for use in a modem.

Although ASK has a good bit rate, it is not used today because of noise.

FSK   As you will recall from Chapter 5, the bandwidth required for FSK transmission is equal to the baud rate of the signal plus the frequency shift. Assuming that the entire link is being used by one signal, as it would for simplex or half-duplex transmission, the maximum baud rate for FSK encoding is equal to the entire bandwidth of the transmission medium minus the frequency shift. Because the effective bandwidth of a telephone line is 2400 Hz, the maximum baud rate is therefore 2400 minus the frequency shift. And, because the baud rate and bit rate are the same in FSK encoding, the maximum bit rate is also 2400 minus the frequency shift (see Figure 6.23).

Figure 6.23   *Baud rate for half-duplex FSK*

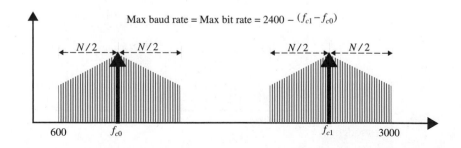

Figure 6.24   *Baud rate for full-duplex FSK*

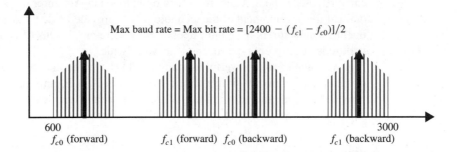

$$\text{Max baud rate} = \text{Max bit rate} = [2400 - (f_{c1} - f_{c0})]/2$$

600   3000

f_{c0} (forward) f_{c1} (forward) f_{c0} (backward) f_{c1} (backward)

For full-duplex transmission, only half of the total bandwidth of the link can be used for either direction. Therefore, the maximum theoretical rate for FSK in full-duplex mode is half of the total bandwidth minus half the frequency shift. Full-duplex FSK partitions are shown in Figure 6.24.

PSK and QAM   As you recall, the minimum bandwidth required for PSK or QAM transmission is the same as that required for ASK transmission but the bit rate can be greater depending on the number of bits that can be represented by each signal unit.

Comparison   Table 6.4 summarizes the maximum bit rate over standard twisted-wire telephone lines for each of the encoding mechanisms examined above. These figures assume a traditional two-wire line. If four-wire lines are used, the data rates for full-duplex transmission can be doubled. In that case, two wires can be used for sending and two for receiving the data, thereby doubling the available bandwidth. However, these numbers are theoretical and cannot always be achieved with available technology.

Table 6.4   *Theoretical bit rates for modems*

Encoding	Half-Duplex	Full-Duplex
ASK, FSK, 2-PSK	2400	1200
4-PSK, 4-QAM	4800	2400
8-PSK, 8-QAM	7200	3600
16-QAM	9600	4800
32-QAM	12,000	6000
64-QAM	14,400	7200
128-QAM	16,800	8400
256-QAM	19,200	9600

Modem Standards

In this section we will introduce two modem standards: Bell modems and ITU-T modems.

Bell Modems

The first commercial modems were produced by the Bell Telephone Company in the early 1970s. As the first and, for a long time, lone manufacturer in the marketplace, Bell defined the development of the technology and provided a de facto standard that subsequent manufacturers have built upon. Today there are dozens of companies producing hundreds of different types of modems worldwide.

As complex and powerful as many models have become, they all evolved from the original and relatively simple first models from Bell. Examining those first modems provides us with an understanding of the basic characteristics of modems. Figure 6.25 shows the specifications of the major Bell modems.

Figure 6.25 *Bell modems*

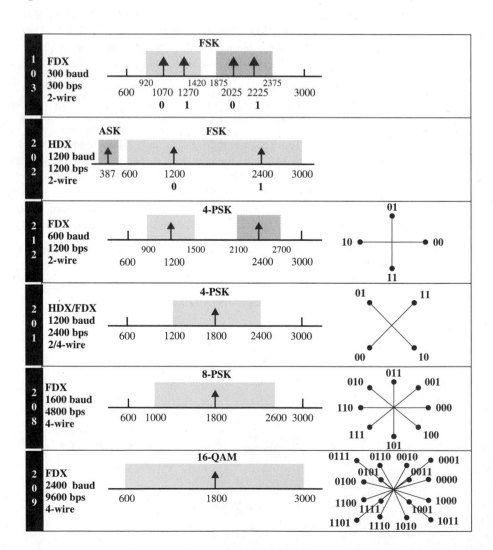

103/113 Series   One of the earliest commercially available modem series was the Bell 103/113. The Bell 103/113 series modems operate in full-duplex mode over two-wire switched telephone lines. Transmission is asynchronous, using FSK encoding. Session originator frequencies are 1070 Hz = 0 and 1270 Hz = 1. Answerer frequencies are 2025 Hz = 0 and 2225 Hz = 1. The data rate is 300 bps. The 113 series is a variation of the 103 series with additional testing features.

202 Series   The Bell 202 series modems operate in half-duplex mode over two-wire switched telephone lines. Transmission is asynchronous, using FSK encoding. Because the 202 series is half-duplex, only one pair of transmission frequencies is used: 1200 Hz = 0, and 2400 Hz = 1.

Note that the 202 series includes a secondary transmission frequency operating in either direction at 387 Hz, using ASK encoding, with a data rate of only 5 bps. This channel is used by the receiving device to tell the sender that it is connected and to send interruption messages calling for a halt to transmission (flow control) or asking for data to be resent (error control).

212 Series   The Bell 212 series modems have two speeds. The option of a second speed allows for compatibility with a wider number of systems. Both speeds operate in full-duplex mode over switched telephone lines. The slower speed, 300 bps, uses FSK encoding for asynchronous transmission, just like the 103/113 series. The higher speed, 1200 bps, can operate in either asynchronous or synchronous mode, and uses 4-PSK encoding. While the 1200 bps is the same data rate as that achieved by the 202 series, the 212 series achieves that rate in full-duplex rather than half-duplex mode.

Note that by moving from FSK to PSK encoding, the designers have dramatically increased the efficiency of transmission.

In series 202, two frequencies are used to send different bits in one direction. In series 212, two frequencies represent two different directions of transmission. The encoding is done by varying the phase on either frequency, with each of four phase shifts representing two bits.

201 Series   The 201 series modems operate in either half-duplex mode over two-wire switched lines or full-duplex mode over four-wire leased lines. The entire bandwidth of a two-wire line is dedicated to a single direction of transmission. Four-wire lines allow for two completely separate channels, one in each direction, to be processed through a single modem on each end.

Transmission is synchronous, using 4-PSK encoding, which means that only one frequency is needed for transmission over each pair of wires. Splitting the two directions of transmission into two physically separate lines allows each direction to use the entire bandwidth of the line. This means that with essentially the same technology, the data rate is doubled to 2400 bps (or 1200 baud) in both half and full-duplex modes (2400 bps is still half the theoretical maximum data rate for 4-PSK encoding over two-wire phone lines).

208 Series   The 208 series modems operate in full-duplex mode over four-wire leased lines. Transmission is synchronous, using 8-PSK encoding. Like the 201 series, the 208 series modems achieve full-duplex status by doubling the number of wires used and dedicating the equivalent of an entire line to each direction of transmission.

The difference here is that the encoding/decoding technology is now able to distinguish between eight different phase shifts. This modem has a baud rate of 1600. At three bits per baud (8-PSK creates tribits), that rate translates to a bit rate of 4800 bps.

209 series The 209 series modems operate in full-duplex mode over four-wire leased lines. Transmission is synchronous, using 16-QAM encoding. These modems achieve full-duplex status by doubling the number of wires so that each direction of transmission has a channel to itself. This series, however, allows for use of the entire bandwidth of each channel. And, because each shift represents a quadbit, with 16-QAM, the data rate is 9600 bps.

ITU-T Modem Standards

Today, many of the most popular modems available are based on standards published by the ITU-T. For our purposes, these modems can be divided into two groups: those that are essentially equivalent to Bell series modems and those that are not.

Those ITU-T modems that are Bell series compatible are listed in Table 6.5 with their Bell equivalents.

Table 6.5 *ITU-T/Bell compatibility*

ITU-T	Bell	Baud Rate	Bit Rate	Modulation
V.21	103	300	300	FSK
V.22	212	600	1200	4-PSK
V.23	202	1200	1200	FSK
V.26	201	1200	2400	4-PSK
V.27	208	1600	4800	8-PSK
V.29	209	2400	9600	16-QAM

The ITU-T modems that do not have equivalents in the Bell series are described below. Their characteristics are given in Figure 6.26.

V.22bis The term *bis* indicates that this modem is the second generation of the V.22 series (*bis* is Latin for twice). The V.22bis is a two-speed modem, meaning that it can operate at either 1200 or 2400 bps. Which speed is used depends on the speed of the DCE at the other end of the exchange. When a V.22bis receives data from a 2400 bps modem, it operates in 2400 bps mode for compatibility.

In 1200 bps mode, the V.22bis uses 4-DPSK (dibit) encoding at a transmission rate of 600 baud. DPSK stands for differential phase shift keying, which means that the modulation symbol changes phase according to the bit pattern and the previous phase. Bits are represented by relative changes of phase rather than by absolute values. The rules for representing each of the four bit patterns are as follows:

00 ⇨	90	degree phase change
01 ⇨	0	degree phase change
11 ⇨	270	degree phase change
10 ⇨	180	degree phase change

Figure 6.26   *ITU-T modem standards*

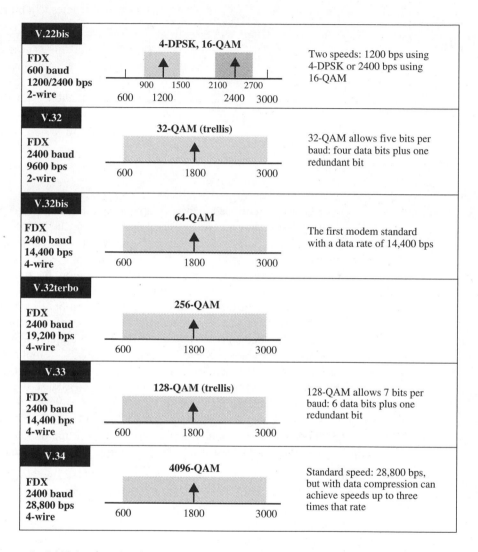

In 2400 bps mode, the V.22bis uses 16-QAM (quadbit). The two least significant digits in each quadbit are modulated using the same differential scheme described above for 1200 bps transmission. The two most significant digits are modulated based on the constellation diagram shown in Figure 6.27.

V.32   The V.32 is an enhanced version of the V.29 (see Table 6.5) that uses a combined modulation and encoding technique called trellis-coded modulation. Trellis is essentially QAM plus a redundant bit. The data stream is divided into four-bit sections. Instead of a quadbit, however, a quintbit (five-bit pattern) is transmitted. The value of the extra bit is calculated from the values of the data bits.

Figure 6.27   *V.22bis 16-QAM constellation*

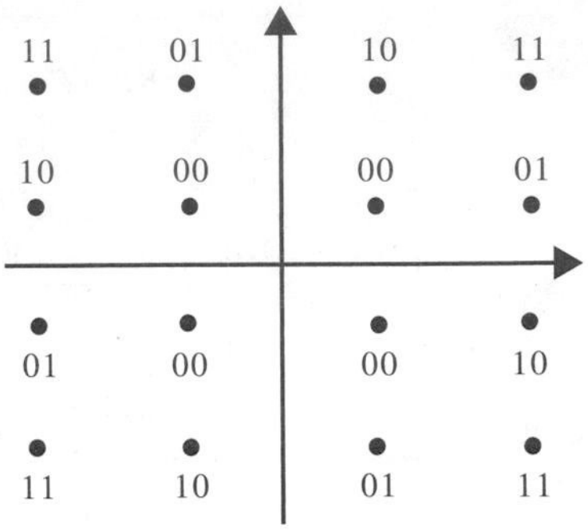

In any QAM system, the receiver compares each received signal point to all valid points in the constellation and selects the point closest as the intended bit value. A signal distorted by transmission noise can arrive closer in value to an adjacent point than to the intended point, resulting in a misidentification of the point and an error in the received data. The closer the points are in the constellation, the more likely that transmission noise can result in a signal's being misidentified. By adding a redundant bit to each quadbit, trellis-coded modulation increases the amount of information used to identify each bit pattern and thereby reduces the number of possible matches. For this reason, a trellis-encoded signal is much less likely than a plain QAM signal to be misread when distorted by noise. Some manufacturers of V.32-compliant modems use the trellis facility to provide functions such as error detection or error correction.

V.32 calls for 32-QAM with a baud rate of 2400. Because only four bits of each quintbit represent data, the resulting speed is $4 \times 2400 = 9600$ bps. The constellation diagram is shown in Figure 6.28.

V.32 modems can be used with two-wire switched line in what is called pseudo-duplex mode. Pseudo-duplex is based on a technique called echo cancellation.

V.32bis   The V.32bis modem was the first of the ITU-T standards to support 14,400 bps transmission. The V.32bis uses 64-QAM transmission (six bits per baud) at a rate of 2400 baud ($2400 \times 6 = 14,400$ bps).

An additional enhancement provided by the V.32bis is the inclusion of an automatic fall-back and fall-forward feature that enables the modem to adjust its speed upward or downward depending on the quality of the line or signal.

V.32terbo   The V.32terbo is an enhanced version of the V.32bis (*terbo* is a pun on the word *ter* which is Latin for third). It uses 256-QAM to provide a bit rate of 19,200 bps.

V.33   The V.33 is also based on the V.32. This modem, however, uses trellis-coded modulation based on 128-QAM at 2400 baud. Each signal change represents a pattern of seven bits: six data bits and one redundant bit. Six bits of data per change (baud) give it a speed of $6 \times 2400 = 14,400$ bps. The constellation diagram for this scheme is shown in Figure 6.29.

Figure 6.28 *V.32 constellation*

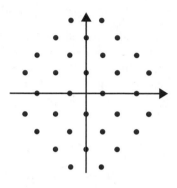

Figure 6.29 *V.33 constellation*

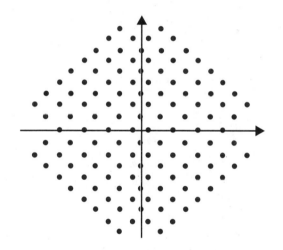

V.34 This modem provides a bit rate of 28,800 bps, earning it the nickname V.fast. It achieves this rate by representing 12 bits with each signal change. In addition, the V.34 is designed to provide data compression. With data compression, the V.34 can achieve data rates as fast as two to three times its normal speed.

Intelligent Modems

The purpose of a modem is to modulate and demodulate a signal. Many of today's modems, however, do more. In particular, a class of modems called intelligent modems contain software to support a number of additional functions, such as automatic answering and dialing.

Intelligent modems were first introduced by Hayes Microcomputer Products, Inc. More recently, other manufacturers have come out with what are referred to as Hayes-compatible modems.

Instructions in the Hayes and Hayes-compatible modems are called AT commands (the AT is short for attention). The AT command format is:

AT command [parameter] command [parameter]...

Each command starts with the letters AT followed by one or more commands, each of which can take one or more parameters. For example, to have the modem dial (408) 864-8902, the command is `TD4088648902`.

A few sample commands are given in Table 6.6. However, this list represents only a small subset of the available commands.

Table 6.6. *AT commands*

Command	Meaning	Parameters
A	Put modem in answer mode	
B	Use V.22bis at 1200 bps	
D	Dial the number	The number to dial
E	Enable/disable echo printing	0 or 1
H	Put modem on/off hook	0 or 1
L	Adjust speaker volume	n
P	Use pulse dialing	
T	Use tone dialing	

6.5   SUMMARY

■ Digital transmission can be either parallel or serial in mode.

■ In parallel transmission, a group of bits is sent simultaneously, with each bit on a separate line.

■ In serial transmission, there is only one line and the bits are sent sequentially.

■ Serial transmission can be either synchronous or asynchronous.

■ In asynchronous serial transmission each byte (group of eight bits) is framed with a start bit and a stop bit. There may be a variable-length gap between each byte.

■ In synchronous serial transmission, bits are sent in a continuous stream without start and stop bits and without gaps between bytes. Regrouping the bits into meaningful bytes is the responsibility of the receiver.

■ A DTE (data terminal equipment) is a source or destination for binary digital data.

■ A DCE (data circuit-terminating equipment) receives data from a DTE and changes it into a form appropriate for network transmission. It can also perform the reverse transformation.

■ A DTE-DCE interface is defined by its mechanical, electrical, and functional characteristics.

■ The EIA-232 standard defines a widely used DTE-DCE interface that consists of a 25-pin connector (DB-25), each pin having a specific function. The functions can be categorized as ground, data, control, timing, reserved, and unassigned.

■ The EIA-449 standard provides better data rate and distance capability than the EIA-232 standard.

■ EIA-449 specifies a 37-pin connector (DB-37) used by the primary channel; the secondary channel has its own 9-pin connector.

■ DB-37 pins are divided into Category I (pins compatible with EIA-232) and Category II (new pins not compatible with EIA-232).

■ The electrical specifications of EIA-449 are defined by standards RS-423 and RS-422.

■ RS-422 is a balanced circuit with two lines for signal propagation. Signal degradation from noise is less a problem with RS-422 than with RS-423.

■ X.21 eliminates many of the control pins of interfaces by sending control information over data pins.

■ A null modem connects two close, compatible DTEs that do not require networks or modulation.

■ A modem is a DCE that modulates and demodulates signals.

■ A modem changes digital signals to analog signals using ASK, FSK, PSK, or QAM modulation.

■ The physical properties of a transmission line limit the frequencies of signals it can transmit.

■ A regular telephone line uses frequencies between 600 Hz and 3000 Hz for data communication. This requires a bandwidth of 2400 Hz.

■ ASK modulation is especially susceptible to noise.

■ Because it uses two carrier frequencies, FSK modulation requires more bandwidth than ASK and PSK.

■ PSK and QAM modulation have two advantages over ASK:

  a. They are not as susceptible to noise.

  b. Each signal change can represent more than one bit.

■ The most popular modems today have surpassed the capabilities of the older Bell modems and are based on standards (the V series) defined by the ITU-T.

■ Trellis coding is a technique that uses redundancy to provide a lower error rate.

■ An intelligent modem contains software to perform functions in addition to modulation and demodulation.

6.6   PRACTICE SET

Multiple Choice

1. In _____ transmission, bits are transmitted simultaneously, each across its own wire.
   a. asynchronous serial
   b. synchronous serial
   c. parallel
   d. a and b

2. In _____ transmission, bits are transmitted over a single wire, one at a time.
   a. asynchronous serial
   b. synchronous serial
   c. parallel
   d. a and b

3. In _____ transmission, a start bit and a stop bit frame a character byte.
   a. asynchronous serial
   b. synchronous serial
   c. parallel
   d. a and b

4. In asynchronous transmission, the gap time between bytes is _____.
   a. fixed
   b. variable
   c. a function of the data rate
   d. zero

5. Synchronous transmission does not have _____.
   a. a start bit
   b. a stop bit
   c. gaps between bytes
   d. all of the above

6. A _____ is a device that is a source of or destination for binary digital data.
   a. data terminal equipment
   b. data transmission equipment
   c. digital terminal encoder
   d. digital transmission equipment

7. A _____ is a device that transmits or receives data in the form of an analog or digital signal through a network.
   a. digital connecting equipment
   b. data circuit-terminating equipment

    c. data converting equipment

    d. digital communication equipment

8. EIA-232 defines _____ characteristics of the DTE-DCE interface.

    a. mechanical

    b. electrical

    c. functional

    d. all of the above

9. The encoding method specified in the EIA-232 standard is _____.

    a. NRZ-I

    b. NRZ-L

    c. Manchester

    d. Differential Manchester

10. The EIA-232 standard specifies that 0 must be _____ volts.

    a. greater than −15

    b. less than −15

    c. between −3 and −15

    d. between 3 and 15

11. The EIA-232 interface has _____ pins.

    a. 20

    b. 24

    c. 25

    d. 30

12. Data are sent over pin _____ of the EIA-232 interface.

    a. 2

    b. 3

    c. 4

    d. all of the above

13. The majority (13) of the pins of the EIA-232 interface are used for _____ purposes.

    a. control

    b. timing

    c. data

    d. testing

14. In the EIA-232 standard what does −12 V on a data pin represent?

    a. 1

    b. 0

    c. undefined

    d. either a 1 or 0 depending on the coding scheme

15. Which of the following pins are needed prior to data transmission?

    a. request to send (4) and clear to send (5)

    b. received line signal detector (8)

    c. DTE ready (20) and DCE ready (6)

    d. all of the above

16. Which pin is needed for local loopback testing?

    a. local loopback (18)

    b. remote loopback and signal quality detector (21)

    c. test mode (25)

    d. a and c

17. Which pin is needed for remote loopback testing?

    a. remote loopback and signal quality detector (21)

    b. local loopback (18)

    c. test mode (25)

    d. a and c

18. Which pin is currently not in use?

    a. 9

    b. 10

    c. 11

    d. all of the above

19. Which pin is used by the secondary channel?

    a. 12

    b. 13

    c. 19

    d. all of the above

20. A maximum cable length of 50 feet is specified in standard _____.

    a. EIA-449

    b. EIA-232

    c. RS-423

    d. RS-422

21. A cable range of 40 feet to _____ feet is possible according to the EIA-449 standard.

    a. 50

    b. 500

    c. 4000

    d. 5000

22. The maximum data rate for RS-422 is _____ times that of the maximum RS-423 data rate.

    a. 0.1

    b. 10

    c. 100

    d. 500

23. In the RS-422 circuit, if noise changes a voltage from 10 V to 12 V, its complement would have a value of _____ V.

    a. −2

    b. −8

    c. −10

    d. −12

24. If 0.5 V of noise corrupts a bit on an RS-422 circuit, _____ volts will be added to the complementary bit.

    a. −1.0

    b. −0.5

    c. 0.5

    d. 1.0

25. X.21 eliminates many of the _____ pins found in EIA standards.

    a. data

    b. timing

    c. control

    d. ground

26. X.21 uses a _____ connector.

    a. DB-15

    b. DB-25

    c. DB-37

    d. DB-9

27. Control information (other than handshaking) in X.21 is mostly sent through the _____ pins.

    a. data

    b. timing

    c. control

    d. ground

28. A null modem connects the data transmit pin (2) of one DTE to the _____.

    a. data receive pin (3) of the same DTE

    b. data receive pin (3) of the other DTE

    c. data transmit pin (2) of the other DTE

    d. signal ground of the other DTE

29. If you have two close, compatible DTEs that can communicate data that do not need to be modulated, a good interface would be _____.

    a. a null modem

    b. an EIA-232 cable

    c. a DB-45 connector

    d. a transceiver

30. Given a transmission line with *H* as the highest frequency and *L* as the lowest frequency, the bandwidth of the line is _____.
    a. *H*
    b. *L*
    c. *H − L*
    d. *L − H*

31. For a telephone line, the bandwidth for voice is usually _____ the bandwidth for data.
    a. equivalent to
    b. less than
    c. greater than
    d. twice

32. For a given bit rate, the minimum bandwidth for ASK is _____ the minimum bandwidth for FSK.
    a. equivalent to
    b. less than
    c. greater than
    d. twice

33. As the bit rate of an FSK signal increases, the bandwidth _____.
    a. decreases
    b. increases
    c. remains the same
    d. doubles

34. For FSK, as the difference between the two carrier frequencies increases, the bandwidth _____.
    a. decreases
    b. increases
    c. remains the same
    d. halves

35. Which of the following modulation techniques are used by modems?
    a. 16-QAM
    b. FSK
    c. 8-PSK
    d. all of the above

36. 2-PSK usually requires _____ FSK for the same data rate.
    a. more bandwidth than
    b. less bandwidth than
    c. the same bandwidth as
    d. an order of magnitude more bandwidth

37. Which of the following modems uses FSK modulation?
    a. Bell 103
    b. Bell 201
    c. Bell 212
    d. all of the above

38. Which ITU-T modem standard uses trellis coding?
    a. V.32
    b. V.33
    c. V.34
    d. a and b

39. In trellis coding the number of data bits is _____ the number of transmitted bits.
    a. equal to
    b. less than
    c. more than
    d. double that of

40. For the V.22 bis standard, at its lower speed, if we are currently in the third quadrant and the next dibit is 11, there is a _____ -degree phase change.
    a. 0
    b. 90
    c. 180
    d. 270

41. What is the object of trellis coding?
    a. to narrow the bandwidth
    b. to simplify encoding
    c. to increase the data rate
    d. to reduce the error rate

42. In _____ modulation, the phase change is a function of the current bit pattern as well as the phase of the previous bit pattern.
    a. FSK
    b. PSK
    c. DPSK
    d. ASK

43. The bit rate always equals the baud rate in which type of signal?
    a. FSK
    b. QAM
    c. 4-PSK
    d. All of the above

44. A modulator converts a _____ signal to a(n) _____ signal.
    a. digital; analog
    b. analog; digital

    c. PSK; FSK

    d. FSK; PSK

45. The signal between two modems is always _____.

    a. digital

    b. analog

    c. PSK

    d. QAM

Exercises

1. If we want to transmit 1000 ASCII (see Appendix A) characters using asynchronous transmission, what is the minimum number of extra bits needed? What is the efficiency in percentage?

2. The transmission of characters from the terminal to the host computer is asynchronous. Explain why.

3. What does the mechanical specification of EIA-232 describe?

4. What does the electrical specification of EIA-232 describe?

5. What does the functional specification of EIA-232 describe?

6. The ASCII (see Appendix A) letter A is sent using EIA-232 interface standards and synchronous transmission. Draw a plot of the transmission (amplitude versus time), assuming a bit rate of 10 bps.

7. What is the difference between a primary and secondary channel?

8. Why are there pairs of send data, send timing, and receive data pins in the DB-37 connector?

9. What is the difference between a balanced circuit and an unbalanced circuit?

10. What is the relationship between the data rate and the distance that the data can reliably travel on an EIA interface?

11. Draw the time-domain graph for the bit pattern 10110110 as it would appear on an RS-422 circuit. Assume a 1 is 5 volts and a 0 is −5 volts. Draw the complement also.

12. Using the data in the preceding problem, assume that the first and last bits are corrupted by 1 volt of noise. Draw both lines and draw the difference of the complement from the signal.

13. According to the EIA-449 standard, what is the difference between Category I and Category II pins?

14. How does the X.21 standard handle control signals?

15. How does a demodulator differ from an analog-to-digital converter?

16. Why are modems needed for telephone communications?

17. In a two-wire telephone line, why does full-duplex transmission have half the bit rate of half-duplex transmission?

18. FSK is a good choice for low-speed modems. Explain why it is not suitable for high-speed modems.

19. Explain the difference in transmission capacity when a four-wire line is used instead of a two-wire line.

20. The minimum bandwidth of an ASK signal could be equal to the bit rate. Explain why this is impossible for FSK.

CHAPTER 7

TRANSMISSION MEDIA

As discussed in Chapter 4, computers and other telecommunication devices use signals to represent data. These signals are transmitted from one device to another in the form of electromagnetic energy. Electromagnetic signals can travel through a vacuum, through air, or through other transmission media.

Electromagnetic energy, a combination of electrical and magnetic fields vibrating in relation to each other, includes power, voice, radio waves, infrared light, visible light, ultraviolet light, and X, gamma, and cosmic rays. Each of these constitutes a portion of the electromagnetic spectrum (see Figure 7.1). Not all portions of the spectrum are currently usable for telecommunications, however, and media to harness those that are usable are limited to a few types. Voice-band frequencies are generally transmitted as current over metal cables, such as twisted-pair, or coaxial cable. Radio frequencies can travel through air or space, but require specific transmitting and receiving mechanisms. Visible light, the last type of electromagnetic energy currently used for communications, is harnessed using fiber-optic cable.

Figure 7.1 *Electromagnetic spectrum*

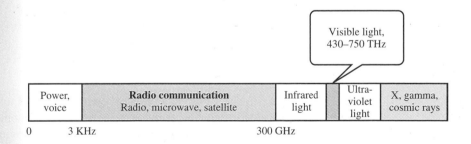

Transmission media can be divided into two broad categories: guided and unguided (see Figure 7.2).

Figure 7.2   *Classes of transmission media*

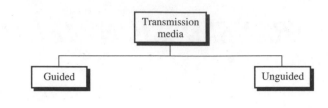

7.1   GUIDED MEDIA

Guided media, which are those that provide a conduit from one device to another, include twisted-pair cable, coaxial cable, and fiber-optic cable (see Figure 7.3). A signal traveling along any of these media is directed and contained by the physical limits of the medium. Twisted-pair and coaxial cable use metallic (copper) conductors that accept and transport signals in the form of electrical current. Optical fiber is a glass or plastic cable that accepts and transports signals in the form of light.

Figure 7.3   *Categories of guided media*

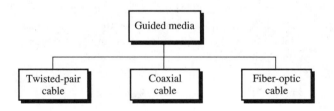

Twisted-Pair Cable

Twisted-pair cable comes in two forms: unshielded and shielded.

Unshielded Twisted-Pair (UTP) Cable

Unshielded twisted-pair (UTP) cable is the most common type of telecommunication medium in use today. Although most familiar from its use in telephone systems, its frequency range is suitable for transmitting both data and voice (see Figure 7.4). A twisted pair consists of two conductors (usually copper), each with its own colored plastic insulation. The plastic insulation is color-banded for identification (see Figure 7.5). Colors are used both to identify the specific conductors in a cable and to indicate which wires belong in pairs and how they relate to other pairs in a larger bundle.

In the past, two parallel flat wires were used for communication. However, electromagnetic interference from devices such as a motor can create noise over those wires. If the two wires are parallel, the wire closest to the source of the noise gets more interfer-

Figure 7.4   *Frequency range for twisted-pair cable*

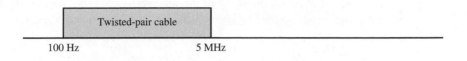

Figure 7.5   *Twisted-pair cable*

A twisted pair consists of two conductors each surrounded by an insulating material.

ence and ends up with a higher voltage level than the wire farther away, which results in an uneven load and a damaged signal (see Figure 7.6).

Figure 7.6   *Effect of noise on parallel lines*

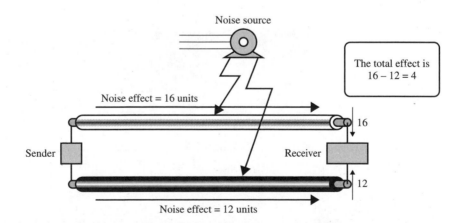

If, however, the two wires are twisted around each other at regular intervals (between 2 and 12 twists per foot), each wire is the closer to the noise source for half the time and the farther away for the other half. With twisting, therefore, the cumulative effect of the interference is equal on both wires (examine Figure 7.7). Each section of wire has a "load" of 4 when it is on the top of the twist, and 3 when it is on the bottom. The total effect of the noise at the receiver is therefore 0 (14–14). Twisting does not always eliminate the impact of noise, but does significantly reduce it.

Figure 7.7   *Effect of noise on twisted-pair lines*

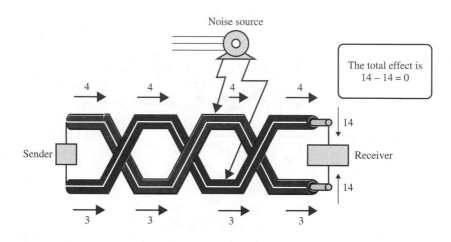

Advantages of UTP are cost and ease of use. UTP is cheap, flexible, and easy to install. Higher grades of UTP are used in many LAN technologies, including Ethernet and Token Ring. Figure 7.8 shows a cable containing five unshielded twisted pairs.

Figure 7.8   *Cable with 5 unshielded twisted pairs of wires*

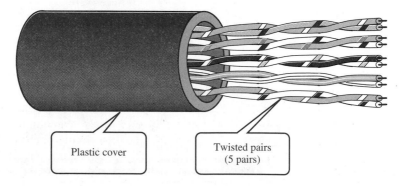

The Electronic Industries Association (EIA) has developed standards to grade UTP cables by quality. Categories are determined by cable quality, with 1 as lowest and 5 as highest. The optimal choice for any use is the cable with the minimal quality necessary to do the desired job safely and effectively. Each EIA category is suitable for certain uses and not for others:

- **Category 1.** The basic twisted-pair cabling used in telephone systems. This level of quality is fine for voice but inadequate for all but low-speed data communication.
- **Category 2**. The next higher grade, suitable for voice and for digital data transmission of up to 4 Mbps.
- **Category 3.** Required to have at least three twists per foot and can be used for data transmission of up to 10 Mbps. It is now the standard cable for most telephone systems.
- **Category 4.** Must also have at least three twists per foot as well as other conditions to bring the possible transmission rate to 16 Mbps.
- **Category 5.** Used for data transmission up to 100 Mbps.

UTP Connectors   UTP is most commonly connected to network devices via a type of snap-in plug like that used with telephone jacks. Connectors are either male (the plug) or female (the receptacle). Male connectors snap into female connectors and have a repressible tab (called a key) that locks them in place. Each wire in a cable is attached to one conductor (or pin) in the connector. The most frequently used of these plugs is an RJ45 connector with eight conductors, one for each wire of four twisted pairs (see Figure 7.9).

Figure 7.9   *UTP connection*

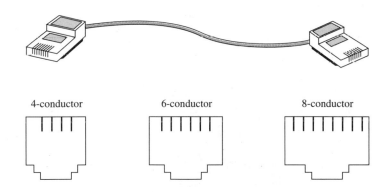

4-conductor   6-conductor   8-conductor

Shielded Twisted-Pair (STP) Cable

Shielded twisted-pair (STP) cable has a metal foil or braided-mesh covering that encases each pair of insulated conductors (see Figure 7.10). The metal casing prevents the penetration of electromagnetic noise. It also can eliminate a phenomenon called crosstalk, which is the undesired effect of one circuit (or channel) on another circuit (or channel). It occurs when one line (acting as a kind of receiving antenna) picks up some of the signals traveling down another line (acting as a kind of sending antenna). This effect can be experienced during telephone conversations when one can hear other conversations in the background. Shielding each pair of a twisted-pair cable can eliminate most of the effects of crosstalk.

STP has the same quality considerations as UTP. STP also uses the same connectors as UTP, but the shield must be connected to a ground. Materials and manufacturing requirements make STP more expensive than UTP but less susceptible to noise.

Figure 7.10   *Shielded twisted-pair cable*

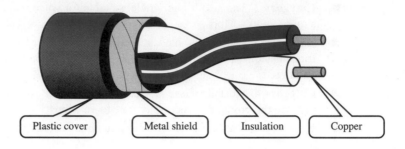

| Plastic cover | Metal shield | Insulation | Copper |

Coaxial Cable

Coaxial cable (or *coax*) carries signals of higher frequency ranges than twisted-pair cable (see Figure 7.11), in part because the two media are constructed quite differently. Instead of having two wires, coax has a central core conductor of solid or stranded wire (usually copper) enclosed in an insulating sheath, which is, in turn, encased in an outer conductor of metal foil, braid, or a combination of the two (also usually copper). The outer metallic wrapping serves both as a shield against noise and as the second conductor, which completes the circuit. This outer conductor is also enclosed in an insulating sheath, and the whole cable is protected by a plastic cover (see Figure 7.12).

Figure 7.11   *Frequency range of coaxial cable*

| Coaxial cable |

100 KHz   500 MHz

Figure 7.12   *Coaxial cable*

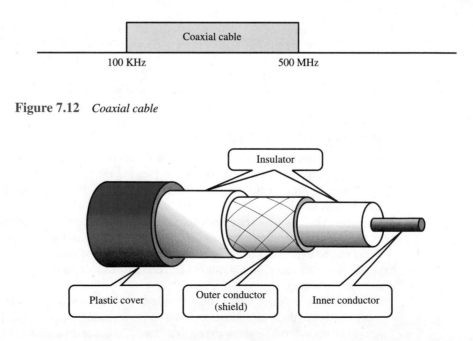

| Insulator |

| Plastic cover | Outer conductor (shield) | Inner conductor |

Coaxial Cable Standards

Different coaxial cable designs are categorized by their radio government (RG) ratings. Each RG number denotes a unique set of physical specifications, including the wire gauge of the inner conductor, the thickness and type of the inner insulator, the construction of the shield, and the size and type of the outer casing.

Each cable defined by RG ratings is adapted for a specialized function. The following are a few of the common ones:

- **RG-8**. Used in Thick Ethernet.
- **RG-9**. Used in Thick Ethernet.
- **RG-11**. Used in Thick Ethernet.
- **RG-58**. Used in Thin Ethernet.
- **RG-59**. Used for TV.

Coaxial Cable Connectors

Over the years, a number of connectors have been designed for use with coaxial cable, usually by manufacturers seeking specific solutions to specific product requirements. A few of the most widely used connector designs have become standardized. The most common of these is called a barrel connector because of its shape. Of the barrel connectors, the most popular is the bayonet network connector (BNC), which pushes on and locks into place with a half turn. Other types of barrel connectors either screw together, and thus require more effort to install, or push on without locking, which is less secure. Generally, a cable terminates in a male connector that plugs or screws onto a corresponding female connector attached to the device. All coaxial connectors have a single pin protruding from the center of the male connector that slides into a ferrule in the female connector. Coaxial connectors are familiar from cable TV and VCR hookups, which employ both threaded and slip-on styles.

Two other commonly used types of connectors are T-connectors and terminators. A T-connector (used in Thin Ethernet) allows a secondary cable or cables to branch off from a main line. A cable running from a computer, for example, can branch to connect several terminals. Terminators are required for bus topologies where one main cable acts as a backbone with branches to several devices but does not itself terminate in a device. If the main cable is left unterminated, any signal transmitted over the line echoes back and interferes with the original signal. A terminator absorbs the wave at the end, and eliminates echo-back.

Optical Fiber

Up until this point, we have discussed conductive (metal) cables that transmit signals in the form of current. Optical fiber, on the other hand, is made of glass or plastic and transmits signals in the form of light. To understand optical fiber, we first need to explore several aspects of the nature of light.

The Nature of Light

Light is a form of electromagnetic energy. It travels at its fastest in a vacuum: 300,000 kilometers/second (approximately 186,000 miles/second). The speed of light depends on the density of the medium through which it is traveling (the higher the density, the slower the speed).

Light, a form of electromagnetic energy, travels at 300,000 kilometers/second or approximately 186,000 miles/second, in a vacuum. This speed decreases as the medium through which the light travels becomes denser.

Refraction   Light travels in a straight line as long as it is moving through a single uniform substance. If a ray of light traveling through one substance suddenly enters another (more or less dense) substance, its speed changes abruptly, causing the ray to change direction. This change is called refraction. A straw sticking out of a glass of water appears bent, or even broken, because the light by which we see it changes direction as it moves from the air to the water.

The direction in which a light ray is refracted depends on the change in density encountered. A beam of light moving from a less dense into a more dense medium is bent toward the vertical axis (examine Figure 7.13). The two angles made by the beam of light in relation to the vertical axis are called I, for incident, and R, for refracted. In Figure 7.13*a,* the beam travels from a less dense medium into a more dense medium. In this case, angle R is smaller than angle I. In Figure 7.13*b,* however, the beam travels from a more dense medium into a less dense medium. In this case, the value of I is smaller than the value of R. In other words, when light travels into a more dense medium, the angle of incidence is greater than the angle of refraction; and when light travels into a less dense medium, the angle of incidence is less than the angle of refraction.

Figure 7.13   *Refraction*

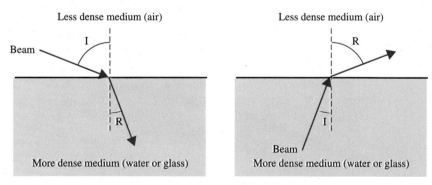

a. From less dense to more dense medium   b. From more dense to less dense medium

Fiber-optic technology takes advantage of the properties shown in Figure 7.13*b* to control the propagation of light through the fiber channel.

Critical Angle   Now examine Figure 7.14. Once again we have a beam of light moving from a more dense into a less dense medium. In this example, however, we gradually increase the angle of incidence measured from the vertical. As the angle of

Figure 7.14   *Critical angle*

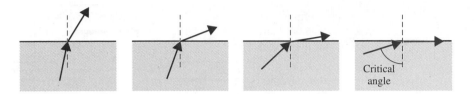

incidence increases, so does the angle of refraction. It, too, moves away from the vertical and closer and closer to the horizontal.

At some point in this process, the change in the incident angle results in a refracted angle of 90 degrees, with the refracted beam now lying along the horizontal. The incident angle at this point is known as the critical angle.

Reflection   When the angle of incidence becomes greater than the critical angle, a new phenomenon occurs called reflection (or, more accurately, complete reflection, because some aspects of reflection always coexist with refraction). Light no longer passes into the less dense medium at all In this case, the angle of incidence is always equal to the angle of reflection (see Figure 7.15).

Figure 7.15   *Reflection*

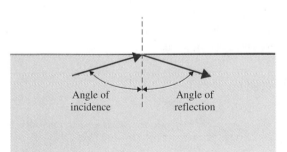

Optical fibers use reflection to guide light through a channel. A glass or plastic core is surrounded by a cladding of less dense glass or plastic. The difference in density of the two materials must be such that a beam of light moving through the core is reflected off the cladding instead of being refracted into it. Information is encoded onto a beam of light as a series of on-off flashes that represent 1 and 0 bits.

Propagation Modes

Current technology supports two modes for propagating light along optical channels, each requiring fiber with different physical characteristics: multimode and single-mode. Multimode, in turn, can be implemented in two forms: step-index or graded-index (see Figure 7.16).

Figure 7.16 *Propagation modes*

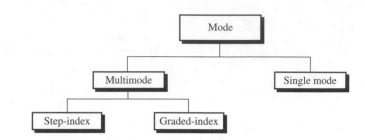

Multimode Multimode is so named because multiple beams from a light source move through the core in different paths. How these beams move within the cable depends on the structure of the core.

In step-index multimode, the density of the core remains constant from the center to the edges. A beam of light moves through this constant density in a straight line until it reaches the interface of the core and the cladding. At the interface there is an abrupt change to a lower density that alters the angle of the beam's motion. The term *step-index* refers to the suddenness of this change.

Figure 7.17 shows various beams (or rays) traveling through a step-index fiber. Some beams in the middle travel in straight lines through the core and reach the destination without reflecting or refracting. Some beams strike the interface of the core and cladding at an angle smaller than the critical angle; these beams penetrate the cladding and are lost. Still others hit the edge of the core at angles greater than the critical angle and reflect back into the core and off the other side, bouncing back and forth down the channel until they reach the destination.

Figure 7.17 *Multimode step-index*

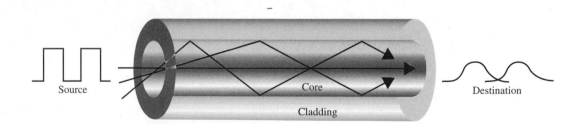

Every beam reflects off the interface at an angle equal to its angle of incidence. The greater the angle of incidence, the wider the angle of reflection. A beam with a smaller angle of incidence will require more bounces to travel the same distance than a beam with a larger angle of incidence. Consequently, the beam with the smaller incident angle must travel farther to reach the destination. This difference in path length means that different beams arrive at the destination at different times. As these different beams are recombined at the receiver, they result in a signal that is no longer an exact replica of the signal that was transmitted. Such a signal has been distorted by propagation delays. This distortion limits the available data rate and makes multimode step-index cable inadequate for certain precise applications.

A second type of fiber, called graded-index, decreases this distortion of the signal through the cable. The word *index* here refers to the index of refraction. As we saw above, index of refraction is related to density. A graded-index fiber, therefore, is one with varying densities. Density is highest at the center of the core and decreases gradually to its lowest at the edge. Figure 7.18 shows the impact of this variable density on the propagation of light beams.

Figure 7.18   *Multimode graded-index*

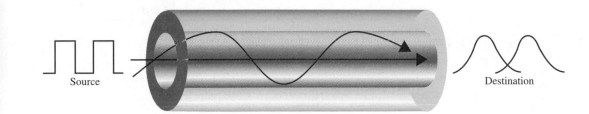

The signal is introduced at the center of the core. From this point, only the horizontal beam moves in a straight line through the constant density at the center. Beams at other angles move through a series of constantly changing densities. Each density difference causes each beam to refract into a curve. In addition, varying the refraction varies the distance each beam travels in a given period of time, resulting in different beams intersecting at regular intervals. Careful placement of the receiver at one of these intersections allows the signal to be reconstructed with far greater precision.

Single Mode   Single mode uses step-index fiber and a highly focused source of light that limits beams to a small range of angles, all close to the horizontal. The fiber itself is manufactured with a much smaller diameter than that of multimode fibers, and with substantially lower density (index of refraction). The decrease in density results in a critical angle that is close enough to 90 degrees to make the propagation of beams almost horizontal. In this case, propagation of different beams is almost identical and delays are negligible. All of the beams arrive at the destination "together" and can be recombined without distortion to the signal (see Figure 7.19).

Figure 7.19   *Single mode*

Fiber Sizes

Optical fibers are defined by the ratio of the diameter of their core to the diameter of their cladding, both expressed in microns (micrometers). The common sizes are shown in Table 7.1. The last size listed is used only for single mode.

Table 7.1 *Fiber types*

Fiber Type	Core (microns)	Cladding (microns)
62.5/125	62.5	125
50/125	50	125
100/140	100	140
8.3/125	8.3	125

Cable Composition

Figure 7.20 shows the composition of a typical fiber-optic cable. A core is surrounded by cladding, forming the fiber. In most cases, the fiber is covered by a buffer layer that protects it from moisture. Finally, the entire cable is encased in an outer jacket.

Figure 7.20 *Fiber construction*

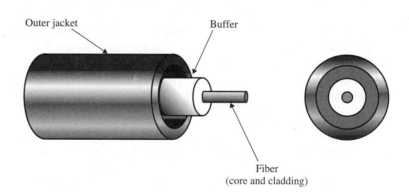

Outer jacket

Buffer

Fiber
(core and cladding)

Both core and cladding can be made of either glass or plastic but must be of different densities. In addition the inner core must be ultrapure and completely regular in size and shape. Chemical differences in material, and even small variations in the size or shape of the channel, alter the angle of reflection and distort the signal. Some applications can handle a certain amount of distortion and their cables can be made more cheaply, but others depend on complete uniformity.

The outer jacket (or sheath) can be made of several materials, including Teflon coating, plastic coating, fibrous plastic, metal tubing, and metal mesh. Each of these jacketing materials has its own purpose. Plastics are lightweight and inexpensive but do not provide structural strength and can emit fumes when burned. Metal tubing provides strength but raises cost. Teflon is lightweight and can be used in open air, but it is expensive and does not increase cable strength. The choice of the material depends on where the cable is to be installed.

Light Sources for Optical Cable

As we have seen, the purpose of fiber-optic cable is to contain and direct a beam of light from source to target. For transmission to occur, the sending device must be equipped with a light source and the receiving device with a photosensitive cell (called a photodiode) capable of translating the received light into current usable by a computer. The light source can be either a light-emitting diode (LED) or an injection laser diode (ILD). LEDs are the cheaper source, but they provide unfocused light that strikes the boundaries of the channel at uncontrollable angles and diffuses over distance. For this reason, LEDs are limited to short-distance use.

Lasers, on the other hand, can be focused to a very narrow range allowing control over the angle of incidence. Laser signals preserve the character of the signal over considerable distances.

Fiber-Optic Connectors

Connectors for fiber-optic cable must be as precise as the cable itself. With metallic media, connections are not required to be exact as long as both conductors are in physical contact. With optical fiber, on the other hand, any misalignment of one segment of core either with another segment or with a photodiode results in the signal reflecting back toward the sender, and any difference in the size of two connected channels results in a change in the angle of the signal. In addition, the connection must be complete yet not overly tight. A gap between two cores results in a dissipated signal; an overly tight connection can compress the two cores and alter the angle of reflection.

Given these constraints, manufacturers have developed several connectors that are both precise and easy to use. All of the popular connectors are barrel shaped and come in male and female versions. The cable is equipped with a male connector that locks or threads into a female connector attached to the device to be connected.

Advantages of Optical Fiber

The major advantages offered by fiber-optic cable over twisted pair and coaxial cable are noise resistance, less signal attenuation, and higher bandwidth.

■ **Noise resistance.** Because fiber-optic transmission uses light rather than electricity, noise is not a factor. External light, the only possible interference, is blocked from the channel by the outer jacket.

■ **Less signal attenuation.** Fiber-optic transmission distance is significantly greater than that of other guided media. A signal can run for miles without requiring regeneration.

■ **Higher bandwidth.** Fiber-optic cable can support dramatically higher bandwidths (and hence data rates) than either twisted-pair or coaxial cable. Currently, data rates and bandwidth utilization over fiber-optic cable are limited not by the medium but by the signal generation and reception technology available.

Disadvantages of Optical Fiber

The main disadvantages of fiber optics are cost, installation/maintenance, and fragility.

- **Cost.** Fiber-optic cable is expensive. Because any impurities or imperfections in the core can throw off the signal, manufacturing must be painstakingly precise. Also, a laser light source can cost thousands of dollars, compared to hundreds of dollars for electrical signal generators.

- **Installation/maintenance.** Any roughness or cracking in the core of an optical cable diffuses light and alters the signal. All splices must be polished and precisely fused. All connections must be perfectly aligned and matched for core size, and must provide a completely light-tight seal. Metallic media connections, on the other hand, can be made by cutting and crimping using relatively unsophisticated tools.

- **Fragility.** Glass fiber is more easily broken than wire, making it less useful for applications where hardware portability is required.

As manufacturing techniques have improved and costs come down, high data rates and immunity to noise have made fiber optics increasingly popular. Many experts are predicting that by the end of the century optical fiber will be the medium used for all fixed-location applications.

7.2 UNGUIDED MEDIA

Unguided, or wireless, media transport electromagnetic waves without using a physical conductor. Instead, signals are broadcast either through air (or, in a few cases, water), and thus are available to anyone who has a device capable of receiving them.

Radio Frequency Allocation

The section of the electromagnetic spectrum defined as radio communication is divided into eight ranges, called bands, each regulated by governmental authorities. These bands are rated from very low frequency (VLF) to extremely high frequency (EHF). Figure 7.21 shows all eight bands and their acronyms.

Propagation of Radio Waves

Types of Propagation

Radio transmission utilizes five different types of propagation: surface, tropospheric, ionospheric, line-of-sight, and space (see Figure 7.22).

Radio technology considers the earth as surrounded by two layers of atmosphere: the troposphere and the ionosphere. The troposphere is the portion of the atmosphere extending outward approximately 30 miles from the earth's surface (in radio terminology, the troposphere includes the high-altitude layer called the stratosphere) and contains what we generally think of as air. Clouds, wind, temperature variations, and weather in general occur in the troposphere, as does jet plane travel. The ionosphere is

Figure 7.21 *Radio communication band*

VLF	Very low frequency	VHF	Very high frequency
LF	Low frequency	UHF	Ultra high frequency
MF	Middle frequency	SHF	Super high frequency
HF	High frequency	EHF	Extremely high frequency

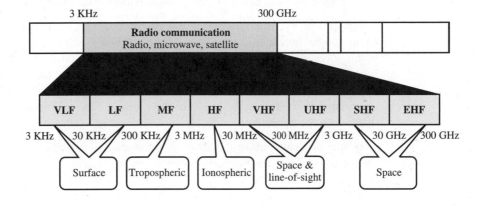

Figure 7.22 *Types of propagation*

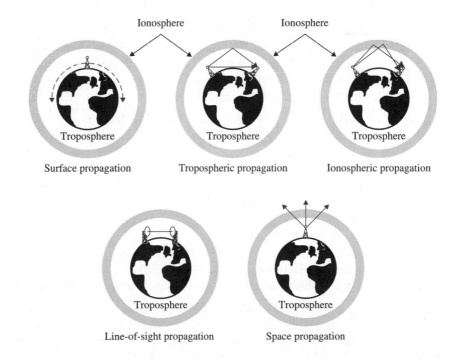

the layer of atmosphere above the troposphere but below space. It is beyond what we think of as atmosphere, and contains free electrically charged particles (hence the name).

Surface Propagation   In surface propagation, radio waves travel through the lowest portion of the atmosphere, hugging the earth. At the lowest frequencies, signals emanate in all directions from the transmitting antenna and follow the curvature of the planet. Distance depends on the amount of power in the signal: the greater the power, the greater the distance. Surface propagation can also take place in seawater.

Tropospheric Propagation   Tropospheric propagation can work two ways. Either a signal can be directed in a straight line from antenna to antenna (line-of-sight), or it can be broadcast at an angle into the upper layers of the troposphere where it is reflected back down to the earth's surface. The first method requires that the placement of the receiver and the transmitter be within line-of-sight distances, limited by the curvature of the earth in relation to the height of the antennas. The second method allows greater distances to be covered.

Ionospheric Propagation   In ionospheric propagation, higher-frequency radio waves radiate upward into the ionosphere where they are reflected back to earth. The density difference between the troposphere, and the ionosphere causes each radio wave to speed up and change direction, bending back to earth. This type of transmission allows for greater distances to be covered with lower power output.

Line-of-Sight Propagation   In line-of-sight propagation, very high frequency signals are transmitted in straight lines directly from antenna to antenna. Antennas must be directional, facing each other, and either tall enough or close enough together not to be affected by the curvature of the earth. Line-of-sight propagation is tricky because radio transmissions cannot be completely focused. Waves emanate upward and downward as well as forward, and can reflect off the surface of the earth or parts of the atmosphere. Reflected waves that arrive at the receiving antenna later than the direct portion of the transmission can corrupt the received signal.

Space Propagation   Space propagation utilizes satellite relays in place of atmospheric refraction. A broadcast signal is received by an orbiting satellite, which rebroadcasts the signal to the intended receiver back on the earth. Satellite transmission is basically line-of-sight with an intermediary (the satellite). The distance of the satellite from the earth makes it the equivalent of a super-high gain antenna and dramatically increases the distance coverable by a signal.

Propagation of Specific Signals

The type of propagation used in radio transmission depends on the frequency (speed) of the signal. Each frequency travels through a specific layer of the atmosphere and is most efficiently transmitted and received by technologies adapted to that layer.

VLF   Very low frequency (VLF) waves are propagated as surface waves, usually through air but sometimes through seawater. VLF waves do not suffer much attenuation in transmission but are susceptible to the high levels of atmospheric noise (heat and electricity) active at low altitudes. VLF waves are used mostly for long-range radio navigation and for submarine communication (see Figure 7.23).

Figure 7.23   *Frequency range for VLF*

LF   Similar to VLF, low frequency (LF) waves are also propagated as surface waves. LF waves are used for long-range radio navigation and for radio beacons or navigational locators (see Figure 7.24). Attenuation is greater during the daytime, when absorption of waves by natural obstacles increases.

Figure 7.24   *Frequency range for LF*

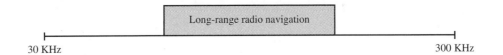

MF   Middle frequency (MF) signals are propagated in the troposphere. These frequencies are absorbed by the ionosphere. The distance they can cover is therefore limited by the angle needed to reflect the signal within the troposphere without entering the ionosphere. Absorption increases during the daytime, but most MF transmissions rely on line-of-sight antennas to increase control and avoid the absorption problem altogether. Uses for MF transmissions include AM radio, maritime radio, radio direction finding (RDF), and emergency frequencies (see Figure 7.25).

Figure 7.25   *Frequency range for MF*

HF   High-frequency (HF) signals use ionospheric propagation. These frequencies move into the ionosphere, where the density difference reflects them back to earth. Uses for HF signals include amateur radio (ham radio), citizen's band (CB) radio, international broadcasting, military communication, long-distance aircraft and ship communication, telephone, telegraph, and facsimile (see Figure 7.26).

Figure 7.26   *Frequency range for HF*

VHF   Most very high frequency (VHF) waves use line-of-sight propagation. Uses for VHF include VHF television, FM radio, aircraft AM radio, and aircraft navigational aid (see Figure 7.27).

Figure 7.27   *Frequency range for VHF*

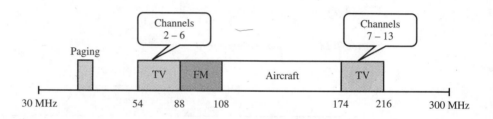

UHF   Ultrahigh frequency (UHF) waves always use line-of-sight propagation. Uses for UHF include UHF television, mobile telephone, cellular radio, paging, and microwave links (see Figure 7.28). Note that microwave communication begins at 1 GHz in the UHF band and continues into the SHF and EHF bands.

Figure 7.28   *Frequency range for UHF*

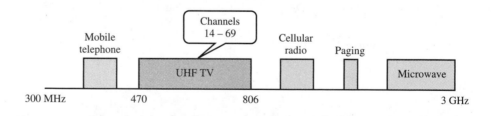

SHF   Superhigh frequency (SHF) waves are transmitted using mostly line-of-sight and some space propagation. Uses for SHF include terrestrial and satellite microwave, and radar communication (see Figure 7.29).

EHF   Extremely high frequency (EHF) waves use space propagation. Uses for EHF are predominantly scientific and include radar, satellite, and experimental communications (see Figure 7.30).

Figure 7.29   *Frequency range for SHF*

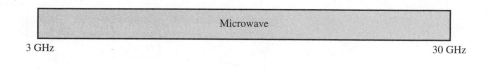

3 GHz   30 GHz

Figure 7.30   *Frequency range for EHF*

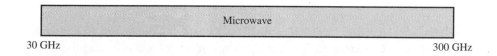

30 GHz   300 GHz

Terrestrial Microwave

Microwaves do not follow the curvature of the earth and therefore require line-of-sight transmission and reception equipment. The distance coverable by a line-of-sight signal depends to a large extent on the height of the antenna: the taller the antennas, the longer the sight distance. Height allows the signal to travel farther without being stopped by the curvature of the planet and raises the signal above many surface obstacles, such as low hills and tall buildings that would otherwise block transmission. Typically, antennas are mounted on towers that are in turn often mounted on hills or mountains.

Microwave signals propagate in one direction at a time, which means that two frequencies are necessary for two-way communication such as a telephone conversation. One frequency is reserved for transmission in one direction and the other for transmission in the other. Each frequency requires its own transmitter and receiver. Today, both pieces of equipment usually are combined in a single piece of equipment called a transceiver, which allows a single antenna to serve both frequencies and functions.

Repeaters

To increase the distance served by terrestrial microwave, a system of repeaters can be installed with each antenna. A signal received by one antenna can be converted back into transmittable form and relayed to the next antenna (see Figure 7.31). The distance required between repeaters varies with the frequency of the signal and the environment in which the antennas are found. A repeater may broadcast the regenerated signal either at the original frequency or at a new frequency, depending on the system.

Terrestrial microwave with repeaters provides the basis for most contemporary telephone systems worldwide.

Antennas

Two types of antennas are used for terrestrial microwave communications: parabolic dish and horn.

A parabolic dish is based on the geometry of a parabola: every line parallel to the line of symmetry (line of sight) reflects off the curve at angles such that they intersect

Figure 7.31   *Terrestrial microwave*

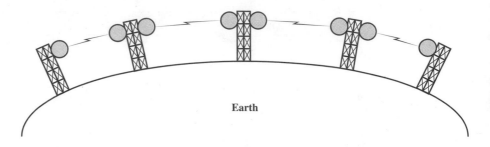

in a common point called the focus (see Figure 7.32). The parabolic dish works like a funnel, catching a wide range of waves and directing them to a common point. In this way, more of the signal is recovered than would be possible with a single-point receiver.

Figure 7.32   *Parabolic dish antenna*

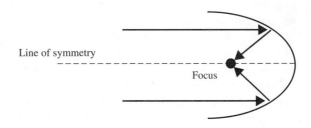

Outgoing transmissions are broadcast through a horn aimed at the dish. The microwaves hit the dish and are deflected outward in a reversal of the receipt path.

A horn antenna looks like a gigantic scoop. Outgoing transmissions are broadcast up a stem (resembling a handle) and deflected outward in a series of narrow parallel beams by the curved head (see Figure 7.33). Received transmissions are collected by the scooped shape of the horn, in a manner similar to the parabolic dish, and are deflected down into the stem.

Satellite Communication

Satellite transmission is much like line-of-sight microwave transmission in which one of the stations is a satellite orbiting the earth. The principle is the same as terrestrial microwave, with a satellite acting as a supertall antenna and repeater (see Figure 7.34). Although in satellite transmission signals must still travel in straight lines, the limitations imposed on distance by the curvature of the earth are reduced. In this way, satellite relays allow microwave signals to span continents and oceans with a single bounce.

Satellite microwave can provide transmission capability to and from any location on earth, no matter how remote. This advantage makes high-quality communication

Figure 7.33   *Horn antenna*

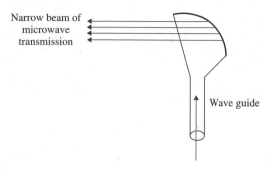

Narrow beam of microwave transmission

Wave guide

Figure 7.34   *Satellite communication*

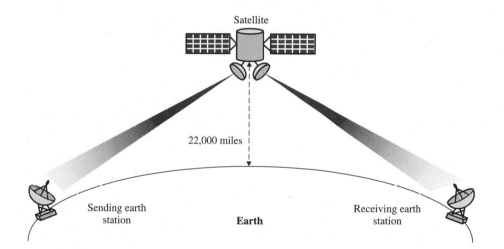

Satellite

22,000 miles

Sending earth station

Earth

Receiving earth station

available to undeveloped parts of the world without requiring a huge investment in ground-based infrastructure. Satellites themselves are extremely expensive, of course, but leasing time or frequencies on one can be relatively cheap.

Geosynchronous Satellites

Line-of-sight propagation requires that the sending and receiving antennas be locked onto each other's location at all times (one antenna must have the other in sight). For this reason, a satellite that moves faster or slower than the earth's rotation is useful only for short periods of time (just as a stopped clock is accurate twice a day). To ensure constant communication, the satellite must move at the same speed as the earth so that it seems to remain fixed above a certain spot. Such satellites are called geosynchronous.

Because orbital speed is based on distance from the planet, only one orbit can be geosynchronous. This orbit occurs at the equatorial plane and is approximately 22,000 miles from the surface of the earth.

But one geosynchronous satellite cannot cover the whole earth. One satellite in orbit has line-of-sight contact with a vast number of stations, but the curvature of the earth still keeps much of the planet out of sight. It takes a minimum of three satellites equidistant from each other in geosynchronous orbit to provide full global transmission. Figure 7.35 shows three satellites, each 120 degrees from another in geosynchronous orbit around the equator. The view is from the North Pole.

Figure 7.35   *Satellites in geosynchronous orbit*

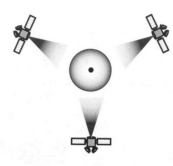

Frequency Bands for Satellite Communication

The frequencies reserved for satellite microwave communication are in the gigahertz (GHz) range. Each satellite sends and receives over two different bands. Transmission from the earth to the satellite is called uplink. Transmission from the satellite to the earth is called downlink. Table 7.2 gives the band names and frequencies for each range.

Table 7.2   *Satellite frequency bands*

Band	Downlink	Uplink
C	03.7–04.2 GHz	05.925–06.425 GHz
Ku	11.7–12.2 GHz	14.000–14.500 GHz
Ka	17.7–21.0 GHz	27.500–31.000 GHz

Cellular Telephony

Cellular telephony is designed to provide stable communications connections between two moving devices or between one mobile unit and one stationary (land) unit. A service provider must be able to locate and track a caller, assign a channel to the call, and transfer the signal from channel to channel as the caller moves out of the range of one channel and into the range of another.

To make this tracking possible, each cellular service area is divided into small regions called cells. Each cell contains an antenna and is controlled by a small office, called the cell office. Each cell office is, in turn, controlled by a switching office called a mobile telephone switching office (MTSO). The MTSO coordinates communication between all of the cell offices and the telephone central office. It is a computerized center that is responsible for connecting calls as well as recording call information and billing (see Figure 7.36).

Figure 7.36   *Cellular system*

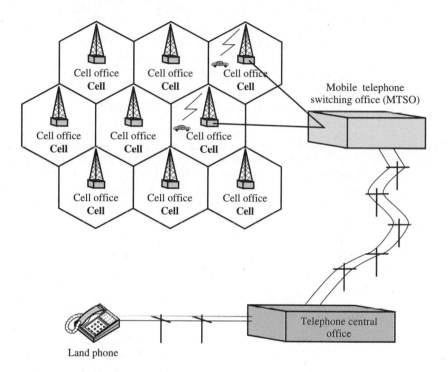

Cell size is not fixed and can be increased or decreased depending on the population of the area. The typical radius of a cell is 1 to 12 miles. High-density areas require more, geographically smaller cells to meet traffic demands than do lower density areas. Once determined, cell size is optimized to prevent the interference of adjacent cell signals. The transmission power of each cell is kept low to prevent its signal from interfering with those of other cells.

Cellular Bands

Traditional cellular transmission is analog. To maximize noise immunity, frequency modulation (FM) is used for communication between the mobile telephone itself and the cell office. The FCC has assigned two bands for cellular use (see Figure 7.37). The band between 824 and 849 MHz carries those communications that initiate from mobile phones. The band between 869 and 894 MHz carries those communications that initiate from land phones. Carrier frequencies are spaced every 30 KHz, allowing each band to support up to 833 carriers. However, two carriers are required for full-duplex communication, which doubles the required width of each channel to 60 KHz and leaves only 416 channels available for each band.

Figure 7.37   *Cellular bands*

Each band is, therefore divided into 416 FM channels (for a total of 832 channels). Of these, some are reserved for control and setup data rather than voice communication. In addition, to prevent interference, channels are distributed among the cells in such a way that adjacent cells do not use the same channels. This restriction means that each cell normally has access to only 40 channels.

Transmitting

To place a call from a mobile phone, the caller enters a code of 7 or 10 digits (a phone number) and presses the send button. The mobile phone then scans the band, seeking a setup channel with a strong signal, then sends the data (phone number) to the closest cell office using that channel. The cell office relays the data to the MTSO. The MTSO sends the data on to the telephone central office. If the called party is available, a connection is made and the result is relayed back to the MTSO. At this point, the MTSO assigns an unused voice channel to the call and a connection is established. The mobile phone automatically adjusts its tuning to the new channel and voice communication can begin.

Receiving

When a land phone places a call to a mobile phone, the telephone central office sends the number to the MTSO. The MTSO searches for the location of the mobile phone by sending query signals to each cell in a process called paging. Once the mobile phone is found, the MTSO transmits a ringing signal and, when the mobile phone is answered, assigns a voice channel to the call, allowing voice communication to begin.

Handoff

It may happen that, during a conversation, the mobile phone moves from one cell to another. When it does, the signal may become weak. To solve this problem, the MTSO monitors the level of the signal every few seconds. If the strength of the signal diminishes, the MTSO seeks a new cell that can accommodate the communication better. The MTSO then changes the channel carrying the call (hands the signal off from the old channel to a new one). Handoffs are performed so smoothly that most of the time they are not observed by the users.

Digital

Analog (FM) based cellular services are based on a standard called analog circuit switched cellular (ACSC). To transmit digital data using an ACSC service requires a modem with a maximum speed of 9600 to 19,200 bps.

Since 1993, however, several service providers have been moving to a cellular data standard called cellular digital packet data (CDPD). CDPD provides low-speed digital service over the existing cellular network. It is based on the OSI model.

To use the existing digital services, such as 56K switched service, CDPD uses what is called a trisector. A trisector is a combination of three cells each using 19.2 Kbps, for a total of 57.6 (which can be accommodated on a 56K switched line by eliminating some overhead). Under this scheme, the United States is divided into 12,000 trisectors. For every 60 trisectors, there is one router.

Integration with Satellites and PCs

Cellular telephony is moving fast toward integrating the existing system with satellite communication. This integration will make it possible to have mobile communication between any two points on the globe. Another goal is to combine cellular telephony and personal computer communication under a scheme called mobile personal communication to enable people to use small, mobile personal computers to send and receive data, voice, image, and video.

7.3   PERFORMANCE

When evaluating the suitability of a particular medium to a specific application, five factors should be kept in mind: cost, speed, attenuation, electromagnetic interference, and security.

- **Cost.** The cost of the materials, plus installation.
- **Speed.** The maximum number of bits per second that a medium can transmit reliably. Among other factors, speed varies with frequency (higher frequencies can transport more bits per second), with the physical size of the medium and/or transmission equipment, and with the conditioning of the conductor.
- **Attenuation.** The tendency of an electromagnetic signal to become weak or distorted over distance. During transmission, the signal's energy can become absorbed or dissipated by the medium itself. For example, a wire's resistance can leach energy from a signal and emit it in the form of heat.
- **Electromagnetic interference** (**EMI**). The susceptibility of the medium to external electromagnetic energy inadvertently introduced onto a link that interferes with the intelligibility of a signal. Familiar effects of EMI are static (audio) and snow (visual).
- **Security.** Protection against eavesdropping. How easy is it for an unauthorized device to listen in on the link? Some media, like broadcast radio and unshielded twisted-pair cable, are easily intercepted. Others, like fiber-optic cable, are more secure.

Table 7.3 compares the various media based on the qualities listed above.

Table 7.3 *Transmission media performance*

Medium	Cost	Speed	Attenuation	EMI	Security
UTP	Low	1–100 Mbps	High	High	Low
STP	Moderate	1–150 Mbps	High	Moderate	Low
Coax	Moderate	1 Mbps–1 Gbps	Moderate	Moderate	Low
Optical fiber	High	10 Mbps–2 Gbps	Low	Low	High
Radio	Moderate	1–10 Mbps	Low–high	High	Low
Microwave	High	1 Mbps–10 Gbps	Variable	High	Moderate
Satellite	High	1 Mbps–10 Gbps	Variable	High	Moderate
Cellular	High	9.6–19.2 Kbps	Low	Moderate	Low

7.4   SUMMARY

■ Signals travel from transmitter to receiver via a path. This path, called the medium, can be guided or unguided.

■ A guided medium is contained within physical boundaries, while an unguided medium is boundless.

■ The most popular types of guided media are the following:

   a. Twisted-pair cable (metallic).

   b. Coaxial cable (metallic).

   c. Optical fiber (glass or plastic).

■ Twisted-pair cable consists of two insulated copper wires twisted together. Twisting allows each wire to have approximately the same noise environment.

■ Shielded twisted-pair cable consists of insulated twisted pairs encased in a metal foil or braided-mesh covering.

■ Coaxial cable consists of the following layers (starting from the center):

   a. A metallic rod-shaped inner conductor.

   b. An insulator covering the rod.

   c. A metallic outer conductor (shield).

   d. An insulator covering the shield.

   e. A plastic cover.

■ Both twisted-pair cable and coaxial cable transmit data in the form of an electric current.

■ Fiber-optic cables are composed of a glass or plastic inner core surrounded by cladding, all encased in an outside jacket.

■ Fiber-optic cables carry data signals in the form of light. The signal is propagated along the inner core by reflection.

■ Fiber-optic transmission is becoming increasingly popular due to its noise resistance, low attenuation, and high bandwidth capabilities.

- In fiber optics, signal propagation can be multimode (multiple beams from a light source) or single mode (essentially one beam from a light source).

- In multimode step-index propagation, the core density is constant and the light beam changes direction suddenly at the interface between the core and cladding.

- In multimode graded-index propagation, the core density decreases with distance from the center. This causes a curving of the light beams.

- Radio waves can be used to transmit data. These waves use unguided media and are usually propagated through the air.

- Regulatory authorities have divided up and defined the uses for the electromagnetic spectrum dealing with radio communication.

- Radio wave propagation is dependent on frequency. There are five propagation types:

  a. Surface propagation.

  b. Tropospheric propagation.

  c. Ionospheric propagation.

  d. Line-of-sight propagation.

  e. Space propagation.

- VLF and LF waves use surface propagation. These waves follow the contour of the earth.

- MF waves are propagated in the troposphere, either through direct line-of-sight propagation from transmitter to receiver or through reflection, with the ionosphere as the upper bound.

- HF waves travel to the ionosphere where they are reflected back to a receiver in the troposphere.

- VHF and UHF waves use line-of-sight propagation; the transmitter and receiver must have a clear path between them; no tall buildings or hills are allowed in the line of sight.

- VHF, UHF, SHF, and EHF waves can be propagated into space and received by satellites.

- Terrestrial microwaves use line-of-sight propagation for data transmission.

- Repeaters are used to increase the distance a microwave can travel.

- The parabolic dish antenna and the horn antenna are used for transmission and reception.

- Satellite communication uses a satellite in geosynchronous orbit to relay signals. A system of three correctly spaced satellites can cover most of the earth.

- Geosynchronous orbit occurs at the equatorial plane and approximately 22,000 miles above the earth.

- Cellular telephony provides mobile communication.

- The cellular system consists of mobile phones, cells, MTSOs, and the telephone central office.

7.5   PRACTICE SET

Multiple Choice

1. Transmission media are usually categorized as _____.
   a. fixed or unfixed
   b. guided or unguided
   c. determinate or indeterminate
   d. metallic or nonmetallic

2. _____ cable consists of an inner copper core and a second conducting outer sheath.
   a. Twisted-pair
   b. Coaxial
   c. Fiber-optic
   d. Shielded twisted-pair

3. In fiber optics, the signal source is _____ waves.
   a. light
   b. radio
   c. infrared
   d. very low frequency

4. At the lower end of the electromagnetic spectrum we have _____.
   a. radio waves
   b. power and voice
   c. ultraviolet light
   d. infrared light

5. _____ are the highest frequency electromagnetic waves in use for data communications.
   a. Visible light waves
   b. Cosmic rays
   c. Radio waves
   d. Gamma rays

6. Smoke signals are an example of communication through _____.
   a. a guided medium
   b. an unguided medium
   c. a refractive medium
   d. a small or large medium

7. Which of the following primarily uses guided media?
   a. cellular telephone system
   b. local telephone system

   c. satellite communications

   d. radio broadcasting

 8. Which of the following is not a guided medium?

   a. twisted-pair cable

   b. coaxial cable

   c. fiber-optic cable

   d. atmosphere

 9. In an environment with many high-voltage devices, the best transmission medium
     would be _____.

   a. twisted-pair cable

   b. coaxial cable

   c. optical fiber

   d. the atmosphere

10. What is the major factor that makes coaxial cable less susceptible to noise than
     twisted-pair cable?

   a. inner conductor

   b. diameter of cable

   c. outer conductor

   d. insulating material

11. The RG number gives us information about _____.

   a. twisted pairs

   b. coaxial cables

   c. optical fibers

   d. all of the above

12. In an optical fiber the inner core is _____ the cladding.

   a. more dense than

   b. less dense than

   c. the same density as

   d. another name for

13. The inner core of an optical fiber is _____ in composition.

   a. glass or plastic

   b. copper

   c. bimetallic

   d. liquid

14. When making connections in fiber optics, which of the following could contribute
     to signal distortion?

   a. inner cores of connecting fibers angularly or laterally misaligned

   b. a gap between connecting inner cores

   c. roughness of connecting fiber faces

   d. all of the above

15. Radio communication frequencies range from _____.
    a. 3 KHz to 300 KHz
    b. 300 KHz to 3 GHz
    c. 3 KHz to 300 GHz
    d. 3 KHz to 3000 GHz

16. The radio communication spectrum is divided into bands based on _____.
    a. amplitude
    b. frequency
    c. cost and hardware
    d. transmission media

17. In _____ propagation, low-frequency radio waves hug the earth.
    a. surface
    b. tropospheric
    c. ionospheric
    d. space

18. The type of propagation used in radio communication is highly dependent on the _____ of the signal.
    a. data rate
    b. frequency
    c. baud rate
    d. power

19. VLF propagation occurs in _____.
    a. the troposphere
    b. the ionosphere
    c. space
    d. all of the above

20. If a satellite is in geosynchronous orbit, it completes one orbit in _____.
    a. one hour
    b. 24 hours
    c. one month
    d. one year

21. If a satellite is in geosynchronous orbit, its distance from the sending station _____.
    a. is constant
    b. varies according to the time of day
    c. varies according to the radius of the orbit
    d. none of the above

22. Which of the following does not use line-of-sight propagation?
    a. VHF
    b. UHF

    c. SHF

    d. EHF

23. When a beam of light travels through media of two different densities, if the angle of incidence is greater than the critical angle, _____ occurs.

    a. reflection

    b. refraction

    c. incidence

    d. criticism

24. When the angle of refraction is _____ the angle of incidence, the light beam is moving from a more dense to a less dense medium.

    a. more than

    b. less than

    c. equal to

    d. none of the above

25. If the critical angle is 50 degrees and the angle of incidence is 60 degrees, the angle of reflection is _____ degrees.

    a. 10

    b. 50

    c. 60

    d. 110

26. If the angle of refraction is 90 degrees and the angle of incidence is 48 degrees, the critical angle is _____ degrees.

    a. 42

    b. 48

    c. 90

    d. 138

27. If the angle of refraction is 70 degrees and the angle of incidence is 50 degrees, the critical angle must be greater than _____ degrees.

    a. 50

    b. 60

    c. 70

    d. 120

28. In _____ propagation the beam of propagated light is almost horizontal and the low-density core has a small diameter compared to the cores of the other propagation modes.

    a. multimode step-index

    b. multimode graded-index

    c. multimode single-index

    d. single mode

29. _____ is the propagation method subject to the most distortion.
   a. Multimode step-index
   b. Multimode graded-index
   c. Multimode single-index
   d. Single mode

30. In _____ propagation, the core is of varying densities.
   a. multimode step-index
   b. multimode graded-index
   c. multimode single-index
   d. single mode

31. When we talk about unguided media, usually we are referring to _____.
   a. metallic wires
   b. nonmetallic wires
   c. the atmosphere
   d. none of the above

32. Optical fibers, unlike wire media, are highly resistant to _____.
   a. high-frequency transmission
   b. low-frequency transmission
   c. electromagnetic interference
   d. refraction

33. In cellular telephony, a service area is divided into small regions called _____.
   a. cells
   b. cell offices
   c. MTSOs
   d. relay sites

34. What determines the size of a cell?
   a. the area terrain
   b. the area population
   c. the number of MTSOs
   d. all of the above

35. The MTSO is responsible for _____.
   a. connecting the cell with the telephone central office
   b. assigning channels for transmission
   c. billing functions
   d. all of the above

36. The MTSO searches for the location of a mobile phone. This is called _____.
   a. handoff
   b. handon
   c. paging
   d. receiving

Exercises

1. Explain what crosstalk is and what is needed to reduce it.
2. Describe the components of a fiber-optic cable. Draw a picture.
3. Why should the light ray be reflective rather than refractive in fiber optics?
4. Give three advantages and disadvantages of using fiber-optic cable over metallic cable.
5. Describe the layers of the atmosphere. What types of radio communication utilize each?
6. How does ionospheric propagation work? What are the uses for this type of propagation?
7. Why is there a distance limit for terrestrial microwave? What factors do you need to calculate this limit?
8. Given that the speed of light is 186,000 miles/second, and a satellite is at geosynchronous orbit, how long would it take for a signal to go from the earth station to the satellite (minimum time)?
9. In a fiber optic cable, does the light energy from the source equal the light energy recovered at the destination? Discuss this in terms of the propagation mode.
10. A beam of light moves from one medium to another, less dense medium. The critical angle is 60 degrees. Draw the path of the light through both media when the angle of incidence is:
    a. 40 degrees.
    b. 50 degrees.
    c. 60 degrees.
    d. 70 degrees.
    e. 80 degrees.

CHAPTER 8

MULTIPLEXING

Whenever the transmission capacity of a medium linking two devices is greater than the transmission needs of the devices, the link can be shared, much as a large water pipe can carry water to several separate houses at once. Multiplexing is the set of techniques that allows the simultaneous transmission of multiple signals across a single data link.

As data- and telecommunications usage increases, so does traffic. We can accommodate this increase by continuing to add individual lines each time a new channel is needed, or we can install higher capacity links and use each to carry multiple signals. As described in Chapter 7, today's technology includes high-bandwidth media such as coaxial cable, optical fiber, and terrestrial and satellite microwaves. Each of these has a carrying capacity far in excess of that needed for the average transmission signal. If the transmission capacity of a link is greater than the transmission needs of the devices connected to it, the excess capacity is wasted. An efficient system maximizes the utilization of all facilities. In addition, the expensive technology involved often becomes cost-effective only when links are shared.

Figure 8.1 shows two possible ways of linking four pairs of devices. In Figure 8.1a, each pair has its own link. If the full capacity of each link is not being utilized, a portion of that capacity is being wasted. In Figure 8.1b, transmissions between the pairs are multiplexed; the same four pairs share the capacity of a single link.

8.1   MANY TO ONE/ONE TO MANY

In a multiplexed system, *n* devices share the capacity of one link. Figure 8.1b shows the basic format of a multiplexed system. The four devices on the left direct their transmission streams to a multiplexer (MUX) which combines them into a single stream (many to one). At the receiving end, that stream is fed into a demultiplexer (DEMUX), which separates the stream back into its component transmissions (one to many) and directs them to their intended receiving devices.

Figure 8.1   *Multiplexing versus no multiplexing*

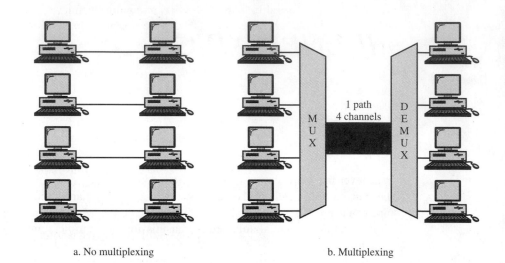

a. No multiplexing   b. Multiplexing

In Figure 8.1*b* the word *path* refers to the physical link. The word *channel* refers to a portion of a path that carries a transmission between a given pair of devices. One path can have many (*n*) channels.

8.2   TYPES OF MULTIPLEXING

Signals are multiplexed using two basic techniques: frequency-division multiplexing (FDM) and time-division multiplexing (TDM). TDM is further subdivided into synchronous TDM (usually just called TDM) and asynchronous TDM, also called statistical TDM or concentrator (see Figure 8.2).

Figure 8.2   *Categories of multiplexing*

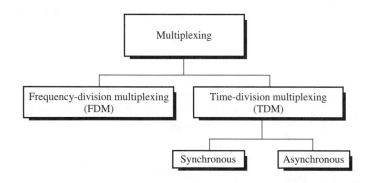

Frequency-Division Multiplexing (FDM)

Frequency-division multiplexing (FDM) is an analog technique that can be applied when the bandwidth of a link is greater than the combined bandwidths of the signals to be transmitted. In FDM, signals generated by each sending device modulate different carrier frequencies. These modulated signals are then combined into a single composite signal that can be transported by the link. Carrier frequencies are separated by enough bandwidth to accommodate the modulated signal. These bandwidth ranges are the channels through which the various signals travel. Channels must be separated by strips of unused bandwidth (guard bands) to prevent signals from overlapping. In addition, carrier frequencies must not interfere with the original data frequencies. Failure to adhere to either condition can result in unrecoverability of the original signals.

Figure 8.3 gives a conceptual view of FDM. In this illustration, the transmission path is divided into three parts, each representing a channel to carry one transmission. As an analogy, imagine a point where three narrow streets merge to form a three-lane highway. Each of the three streets corresponds to a lane of the highway. Each car merging onto the highway from one of the streets still has its own lane and can travel without interfering with cars in other lanes.

Figure 8.3   *FDM*

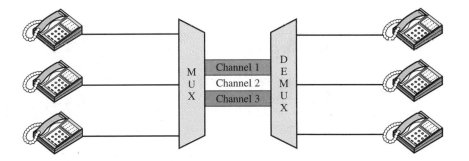

Keep in mind that although Figure 8.3 shows the path as divided spatially into separate channels, actual channel divisions are achieved by frequency rather than by space.

The FDM Process

Figure 8.4 is a conceptual time-domain illustration of the multiplexing process. FDM is an analog process and we show it here using telephones as the input and output devices. Each telephone generates a signal of a similar frequency range. Inside the multiplexer, these similar signals are modulated onto different carrier frequencies (f_1, f_2, and f_3). The resulting modulated signals are then combined into a single composite signal that is sent out over a media link that has enough bandwidth to accommodate it.

Figure 8.5 is the frequency-domain illustration for the same concept. (Note that the horizontal axis of this figure denotes frequency, not time. All three carrier frequencies exist at the same time within the bandwidth.) In FDM, signals are modulated onto separate carrier frequencies (f_1, f_2, and f_3) using either AM or FM modulation. As you

Figure 8.4 *FDM multiplexing process, time-domain*

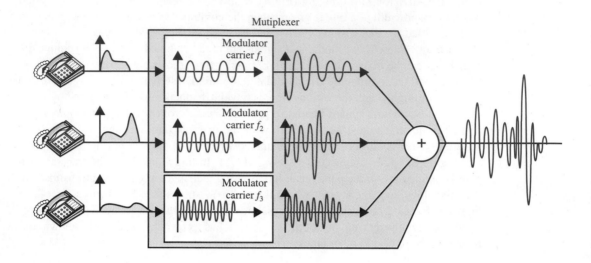

Figure 8.5 *FDM multiplexing process, frequency-domain*

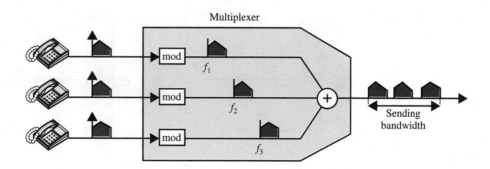

recall from Chapter 5, modulating one signal onto another results in a bandwidth of at least twice the original. To allow more efficient use of the path, the actual bandwidth can be lowered by suppressing half the band, using techniques that are beyond the scope of this book. In this illustration, the bandwidth of the resulting composite signal is more than three times the bandwidth of each input signal: three times the bandwidth to accommodate the necessary channels, plus extra bandwidth to allow for the necessary guard bands.

Demultiplexing

The demultiplexer uses a series of filters to decompose the multiplexed signal into its constituent component signals. The individual signals are then passed to a demodulator that separates them from their carriers and passes them to the waiting receivers. Figure 8.6 is a time-domain illustration of FDM multiplexing, again using three tele-

Figure 8.6 *FDM demultiplexing process, time-domain*

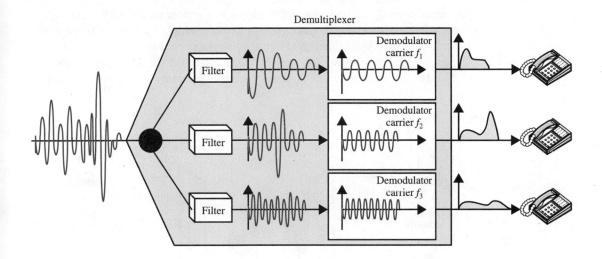

Figure 8.7 *FDM demultiplexing, frequency-domain*

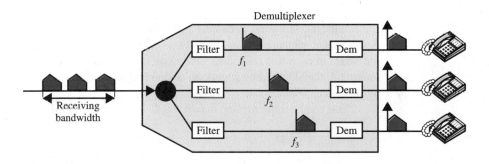

phones as the communication devices. The frequency-domain of the same example is shown in Figure 8.7.

Example: Cable Television

A familiar application of FDM is cable television. The coaxial cable used in a cable television system has a bandwidth of approximately 500 MHz. An individual television channel requires about 6 MHz of bandwidth for transmission. The coaxial cable, therefore, can carry many multiplexed channels (theoretically 83 channels, but actually fewer to allow for guard bands). A demultiplexer at your television allows you to select which of those channels you wish to receive.

Today, a new and more efficient method is being developed to implement FDM over fiber-optic cable. Called wavelength division multiplexing (WDM), it uses essentially the same concepts as FDM but incorporates the range of frequencies in the visible light spectrum.

Time-Division Multiplexing (TDM)

Time-division multiplexing (TDM) is a digital process that can be applied when the data rate capacity of the transmission medium is greater than the data rate required by the sending and receiving devices. In such a case, multiple transmissions can occupy a single link by subdividing them and interleaving the portions.

Figure 8.8 gives a conceptual view of TDM. Note that the same link is used as in the FDM; here, however, the link is shown sectioned by time rather than frequency.

Figure 8.8   *TDM*

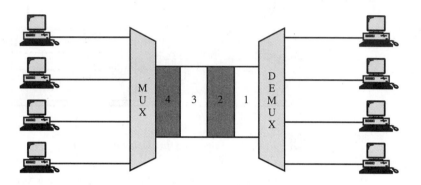

In the TDM figure, portions of signals 1, 2, 3, and 4 occupy the link sequentially. As an analogy, imagine a ski lift that serves several runs. Each run has its own line and the skiers in each line take turns getting on the lift. As each chair reaches the top of the mountain, the skier riding it gets off and skis down the run for which he or she waited in line.

TDM can be implemented in two ways: synchronous TDM and asynchronous TDM.

Synchronous TDM

In time-division multiplexing, the term *synchronous* has a different meaning from that used in other areas of telecommunications. Here synchronous means that the multiplexer allocates exactly the same time slot to each device at all times, whether or not a device has anything to transmit. Time slot A, for example, is assigned to device A alone and cannot be used by any other device. Each time its allocated time slot comes up, a device has the opportunity to send a portion of its data. If a device is unable to transmit or does not have data to send, its time slot remains empty.

Frames   Time slots are grouped into frames. A frame consists of one complete cycle of time slots, including one or more slots dedicated to each sending device, plus framing bits (see Figure 8.12). In a system with *n* input lines, each frame has at least *n* slots, with each slot allocated to carry data from a specific input line. If all the input devices sharing a link are transmitting at the same data rate, each device has one time slot per frame. However, it is possible to accommodate varying data rates. A transmission with two slots per frame will arrive twice as quickly as one with one slot per frame. The time slots dedicated to a given device occupy the same location in each frame and constitute that device's channel. In Figure 8.9, we show five input lines multiplexed onto a single path using synchronous TDM. In this example, all of the inputs have the same data rate, so the number of time slots in each frame is equal to the number of input lines.

Figure 8.9 *Synchronous TDM*

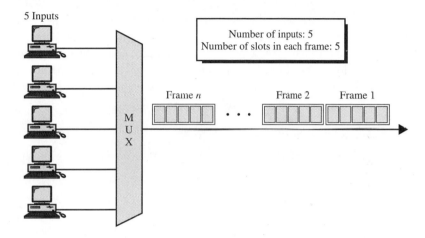

Interleaving Synchronous TDM can be compared to a very fast rotating switch. As the switch opens in front of a device, that device has the opportunity to send a specified amount (*x* bits) of data onto the path. The switch moves from device to device at a constant rate and in a fixed order. This process is called interleaving.

Interleaving can be done by bit, by byte, or by any other data unit. In other words, the multiplexer can take one byte from each device, then another byte from each device, and so on. In a given system, the interleaved units will always be of the same size.

Figure 8.10 shows interleaving and frame building. In the example, we interleave the various transmissions by character (equal to one byte each), but the concept is the

Figure 8.10 *Synchronous TDM, multiplexing process*

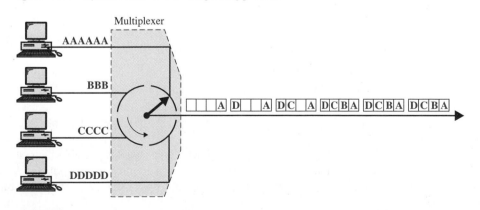

same for data units of any length. As you can see, each device is sending a different message. The multiplexer interleaves the different messages and forms them into frames before putting them onto the link.

At the receiver, the demultiplexer decomposes each frame by discarding the framing bits and extracting each character in turn. As a character is removed from a frame, it is passed to the appropriate receiving device (see Figure 8.11).

Figure 8.10 and Figure 8.11 also point out the major weakness of synchronous TDM. By assigning each time slot to a specific input line, we end up with empty slots whenever not all the lines are active. In Figure 8.10, only the first three frames are completely filled. The last three frames have a collective six empty slots. Having 6 empty slots out of 24 means that a quarter of the capacity of the link is being wasted.

Figure 8.11 *Synchronous TDM, demultiplexing process*

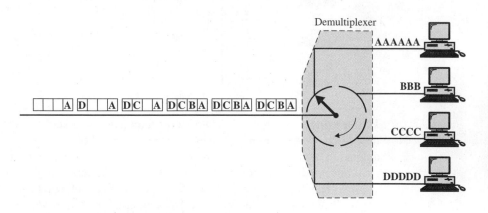

Framing Bits   Because the time slot order in a synchronous TDM system does not vary from frame to frame, very little overhead information needs to be included in each frame. The order of receipt tells the demultiplexer where to direct each time slot, so no addressing is necessary. Various factors, however, can cause timing inconsistencies. For this reason, one or more synchronization bits are usually added to the beginning of each frame. These bits, called framing bits, follow a pattern, frame to frame, that allows the demultiplexer to synchronize with the incoming stream so that it can separate the time slots accurately. In most cases, this synchronization information consists of one bit per frame, alternating between 0 and 1 (01010101010), as shown in Figure 8.12.

Synchronous TDM Example   Imagine that we have four input sources on a synchronous TDM link, where transmissions are interleaved by character. If each source is creating 250 characters per second, and each frame is carrying 1 character from each source, the transmission path must be able to carry 250 frames per second (see Figure 8.13).

If we assume that each character consists of eight bits, then each frame is 33 bits long: 32 bits for the four characters plus 1 framing bit. Looking at the bit relationships, we see that each device is creating 2000 bps (250 characters with 8 bits per character),

Figure 8.12   *Framing bits*

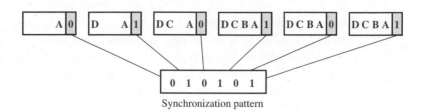

Figure 8.13   *Data rate calculation for frames*

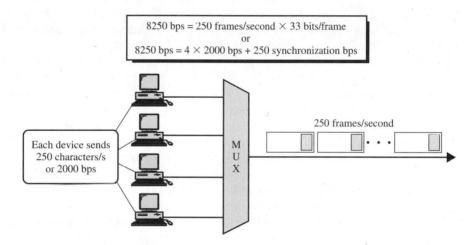

but the line is carrying 8250 bps (250 frames with 33 bits per frame): 8000 bits of data and 250 bits of overhead.

Bit Stuffing   As noted above, it is possible to connect devices of different data rates to a synchronous TDM. For example, device A uses one time slot, while the faster device B uses two. The number of slots in a frame and the input lines to which they are assigned remains fixed throughout a given system; but devices of different data rates may control different numbers of those slots. But remember that time slot length is fixed. For this technique to work, therefore, the different data rates must be integer multiples of each other. For example, we can accommodate a device that is five times faster than the other devices by giving it five slots to one for each of the other devices. We cannot, however, accommodate a device that is five and a half times faster by this method, because we cannot introduce half a time slot into a frame.

When the speeds are not integer multiples of each other, they can be made to behave as if they were, by a technique called bit stuffing. In bit stuffing, the multiplexer adds extra bits to a device's source stream to force the speed relationships among the various devices into integer multiples of each other. For example, if we have one device with a bit rate of 2.75 times that of the other devices, we can add enough bits to raise the rate to 3 times that of the others. The extra bits are then discarded by the demultiplexer.

Asynchronous TDM

As we saw in the previous section, synchronous TDM does not guarantee that the full capacity of a link is used. In fact, it is more likely that only a portion of the time slots is in use at a given instant. Because the time slots are preassigned and fixed, whenever a connected device is not transmitting the corresponding slot is empty and that much of the path is wasted. For example, imagine that we have multiplexed the output of 20 identical computers onto a single line. Using synchronous TDM, the speed of that line must be at least 20 times the speed of each input line. But what if only 10 computers are in use at a time? Half of the capacity of the line is wasted.

Asynchronous time-division multiplexing, or statistical time-division multiplexing, is designed to avoid this type of waste. As with the term *synchronous*, the term *asynchronous* means something different in multiplexing than it means in other areas of data communications. Here it means flexible or not fixed.

Like synchronous TDM, asynchronous TDM allows a number of lower speed input lines to be multiplexed to a single higher speed line. Unlike synchronous TDM, however, in asynchronous TDM the total speed of the input lines can be greater than the capacity of the path. In a synchronous system, if we have n input lines, the frame contains a fixed number of at least n time slots. In an asynchronous system, if we have n input lines, the frame contains no more than m slots, with m less than n (see Figure 8.14). In this way, asynchronous TDM supports the same number of input lines as synchronous TDM with a lower capacity link. Or, given the same link, asynchronous TDM can support more devices than synchronous TDM.

The number of time slots in an asynchronous TDM frame (m) is based on a statistical analysis of the number of input lines that are likely to be transmitting at any given

Figure 8.14   *Asynchronous TDM*

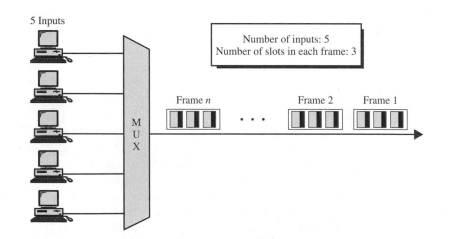

time. Rather than being preassigned, each slot is available to any of the attached input lines that has data to send. The multiplexer scans the input lines, accepts portions of data until a frame is filled, and then sends the frame across the link. If there are not enough data to fill all the slots in a frame, the frame is transmitted only partially filled; thus full link capacity may not be used 100 percent of the time. But the ability to allocate time slots dynamically, coupled with the lower ratio of time slots to input lines, greatly reduces the likelihood and degree of waste.

Figure 8.15 shows a system where five computers are sharing a data link using asynchronous TDM. In this example, the frame size is three slots. The figure shows how the multiplexer handles three levels of traffic. In the first case, only three of the five computers have data to send (the average scenario for this system, as indicated by the fact that a frame size of three slots was chosen). In the second case, four lines are sending data, one more than the number of slots per frame. In the third case (statistically

Figure 8.15 *Examples of asynchronous TDM frames*

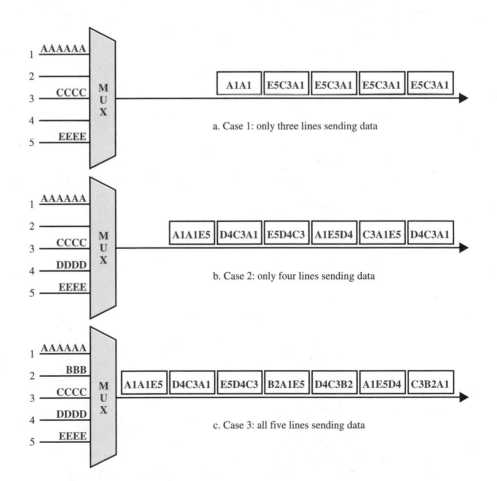

rare), all lines are sending data. In each case, the multiplexer scans the devices in order, from 1 to 5, filling time slots as it encounters data to be sent.

In the first case, the three active input lines correspond to the three slots in each frame. For the first four frames, the input is symmetrically distributed among all the communicating devices. By the fifth frame, however, devices 3 and 5 have completed their transmissions, but device 1 still has two characters to go. The multiplexer picks up the A from device 1, scans down the line without finding another transmission, and returns to device 1 to pick up the last A. There being no data to fill the final slot, the multiplexer then transmits the fifth frame with only two slots filled. In a synchronous TDM system, six frames of five time slots each would have been required to transmit all of the data—a total of 30 time slots. But only 14 of those slots would have been filled, leaving the line unused for more than half the elapsed time. With the asynchronous system shown here, only one frame is transmitted partially empty. During the rest of the transmission time, the entire capacity of the link is active.

In the second case, there is one more active input line than there are slots in each frame. This time, as the multiplexer scans from 1 to 5, it fills up a frame before all of the lines have been checked. The first frame, therefore, carries data from devices 1, 3, and 4, but not 5. The multiplexer continues its scan where it left off, putting the first portion of device 5's transmission into the first slot of the next frame, then moving back to the top of the line and putting the second portion of device 1's data into the second slot, and so on. As you can see, when the number of active senders does not equal the number of slots in a frame, the time slots are not filled symmetrically. Device 1, in this example, controls the first slot in the first frame, the second slot in the second frame, and so on.

In the third case, the frames are filled as above, but here all five input lines are active. In this example, device 1 controls the first slot in the first frame, the third slot in the second frame, and no slots at all in the third frame.

In cases 2 and 3, if the speed of the line is equal to three of the input lines, then the data to be transmitted will arrive faster than the multiplexer can put it on the link. In that case, a buffer is needed to store data until the multiplexer is ready for it.

Addressing and Overhead   Cases 2 and 3 in the above example illustrate a major weakness of asynchronous TDM: How does the demultiplexer know which slot belongs to which output line? In synchronous TDM, the device to which the data in a time slot belong is indicated by the position of the time slot in the frame. But in asynchronous TDM, data from a given device might be in the first slot of one frame and in the third of the next. In the absence of fixed positional relationships, each time slot must carry an address telling the demultiplexer how to direct the data. This address, for local use only, is attached by the multiplexer and discarded by the demultiplexer once it has been read. In Figure 8.15, the address is specified by a digit.

Adding address bits to each time slot increases the overhead of an asynchronous system and somewhat limits its potential efficiency. To limit their impact, addresses usually consist of only a small number of bits and can be made even shorter by appending a full address only to the first portion of a transmission, with abbreviated versions to identify subsequent portions.

The need for addressing makes asynchronous TDM inefficient for bit or byte interleaving. Imagine bit interleaving with each bit carrying an address: one bit of data plus, say, three bits of address. All of a sudden it takes four bits to transport one bit of data. Even if the link is kept full, only a quarter of the capacity is used to transport data; the rest is overhead. For this reason, asynchronous TDM is efficient only when the size of the time slots is kept relatively large.

Variable-Length Time Slots   Asynchronous TDM can accommodate traffic of varying data rates by varying the length of the time slots. Stations transmitting at a faster data rate can be given a longer slot. Managing variable-length fields requires that control bits be appended to the beginning of each time slot to indicate the length of the coming data portion. These extra bits also increase the overhead of the system and, again, are efficient only with larger time slots.

Inverse Multiplexing

As its name implies, inverse multiplexing is the opposite of multiplexing. Inverse multiplexing takes the data stream from one high-speed line and breaks it into portions that can be sent across several lower speed lines simultaneously, with no loss in the collective data rate (see Figure 8.16).

Figure 8.16   *Multiplexing and inverse multiplexing*

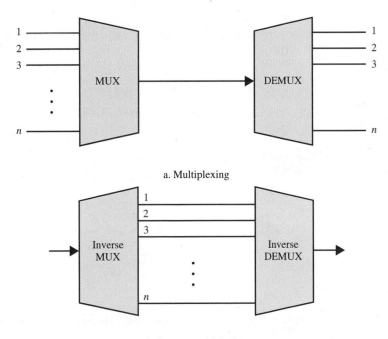

a. Multiplexing

b. Inverse multiplexing

Why do we need inverse multiplexing? Think of an organization that wants to send data, voice, and video, each of which requires a different data rate. To send voice, it may need a 64 Kbps link. To send data, it may need a 128 Kbps link. And to send video, it may need a 1.544 Mbps link. To accommodate all of these needs, the organization has two options. It can lease a 1.544 Mbps channel from a common carrier (the telephone company) and use the full capacity only sometimes, which is not an efficient use of the facility. Or it can lease several separate channels of lower data rates. Using an agreement called bandwidth on demand, the organization can use any of these channels whenever and however it needs them. Voice transmissions can be sent intact over any of the channels. Data or video signals can be broken up and sent over two or more lines. In other words, the data and video signals can be inversely multiplexed over multiple lines.

8.3 MULTIPLEXING APPLICATION: THE TELEPHONE SYSTEM

Multiplexing has long been an essential tool of the telephone industry. A look at some telephone company basics can help us understand the application of both FDM and TDM in the field. Of course, different parts of the world use different systems. We will concentrate only on the system used in North America.

The North American telephone system includes many common carriers that offer local and long-distance services to subscribers. These carriers include local companies, such as Pacific Bell, and long-distance providers, such as AT&T, MCI, and Sprint.

For the purposes of this discussion, we will think of these various carriers as a single entity called the telephone network, and the line connecting a subscriber to that network as a *service line* (see Figure 8.17).

Figure 8.17 *Telephone network*

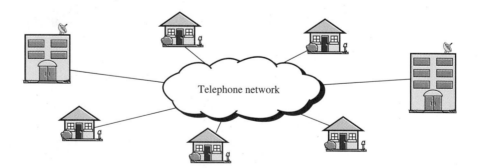

Common Carrier Services and Hierarchies

Telephone companies began by providing their subscribers with analog services that used analog networks. Later technology allowed the introduction of digital services and networks. Today, North American providers are in the process of changing even their service lines from analog to digital. It is anticipated that soon the entire network will be digital. For now, however, both types of services are available and both FDM and TDM are in use (see Figure 8.18).

Figure 8.18 *Categories of telephone services*

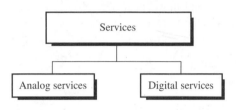

Analog Services

Of the many analog services available to subscribers, two are particularly relevant to our discussion here: switched services and leased services (see Figure 8.19).

Figure 8.19 *Categories of analog services*

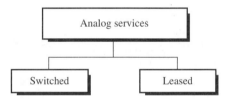

Analog Switched Service

Analog switched service is the familiar dial-up service most often encountered when using a home telephone. It uses two-wire (or, for specialized uses, four-wire) twisted-pair cable to connect the subscriber's handset to the network via an exchange. This connection is called the local loop. The network it joins is sometimes referred to as a public switched telephone network (PSTN).

The signal on a local loop is analog, and the bandwidth is usually between 0 and 4000 Hz. (For more information on telephone bandwidth, refer back to Chapter 7.)

With switched lines, when the caller dials a number, the call is conveyed to a switch, or series of switches, at the exchange. The appropriate switches are then activated to link the caller's line to that of the person being called. The switch connects the two lines for the duration of the call (see Figure 8.20).

Analog Leased Service

A leased service offers customers the opportunity to lease a line, sometimes called a dedicated line, that is permanently connected to another customer. Although the connection still passes through the switches in the telephone network, subscribers experience it as a single line because the switch is always closed; no dialing is needed (see Figure 8.21).

Figure 8.20   *Analog switched service*

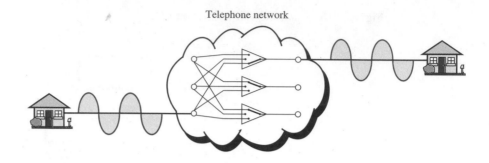

Figure 8.21   *Analog leased service*

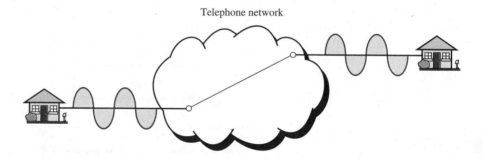

Conditioned Lines   Telephone carriers also offer a service called conditioning. Conditioning means improving the quality of a line by lessening attenuation, signal distortion, or delay distortion. Conditioned lines are analog, but their quality makes them usable for digital data communication if they are connected to modems.

The Analog Hierarchy

To maximize the efficiency of their infrastructure, telephone companies have traditionally multiplexed signals from lower bandwidth lines onto higher bandwidth lines. In this way many switched or leased lines can be combined into fewer but bigger channels. For analog lines, FDM is used.

One of these hierarchical systems used by AT&T, is made up of groups, supergroups, master groups, and jumbo groups (see Figure 8.22).

In this hierarchy, 12 voice channels are multiplexed onto a higher bandwidth line to create a group. (To conserve bandwidth, AT&T uses modulation techniques that suppress the carrier and the lower sidebands of each signal, and recover them upon demultiplexing.) A group has 48 KHz of bandwidth and supports 12 voice channels.

At the next level, up to five groups can be multiplexed to create a composite signal called a supergroup. A supergroup has a bandwidth of 240 KHz and supports up to

Figure 8.22   *Analog hierarchy*

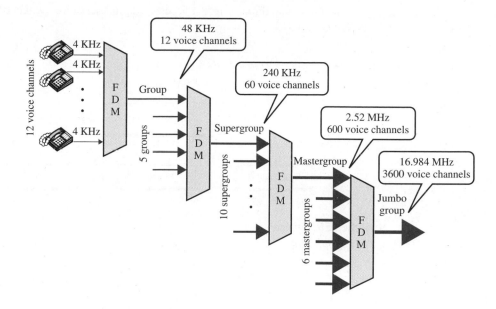

60 voice channels. Supergroups can be made up of either five groups or 60 independent voice channels.

At the next level, 10 supergroups are multiplexed to create a master group. A master group must have 2.40 MHz of bandwidth, but the need for guard bands between the channels increases the necessary bandwidth to 2.52 MHz. Master groups support up to 600 voice channels.

Finally, six master groups can be combined into a jumbo group. A jumbo group must have 15.12 MHz (6×2.52 MHz), but is augmented to 16.984 MHz to allow for guard bands between the master groups.

There are many variations of this hierarchy in the telecommunications industry (the ITU-T has approved a different system for use in Europe). However, because this analog hierarchy will be replaced by digital services in the near future, we will limit our discussion to the system above.

Digital Services

Recently telephone companies began offering digital services to their subscribers. One advantage is that digital services are less sensitive than analog services to noise and other forms of interference. A telephone line acts like an antenna and will pick up noise during both analog and digital transmission. In analog transmissions, both signal and noise are analog and cannot be easily separated. In digital transmission, on the other hand, the signal is digital but the interference is still analog. The signal can therefore be easily distinguished and separated. Another advantage to digital transmission is its lower cost. Because it needs to differentiate between only two or three levels of voltage instead of a continuous range of values, digital transmission equipment uses less expensive electronics than does the corresponding analog equipment.

We will examine three different types of digital services: switched/56, DDS, and DS (see Figure 8.23).

Figure 8.23   *Categories of digital services*

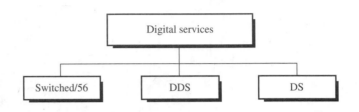

Switched/56 Service

Switched/56 is the digital version of an analog switched line. It is a switched digital service that allows data rates of up to 56 Kbps. To communicate through this service, both parties must subscribe. A caller with normal telephone service cannot connect to a telephone or computer with switched/56 even if using a modem. On the whole, digital and analog services represent two completely different domains for the telephone companies.

Because the line in a switched/56 service is already digital, subscribers do not need modems to transmit digital data. They do, however, need another device called a digital service unit (DSU). This device changes the rate of the digital data created by the subscriber's device to 56 Kbps and encodes it in the format used by the service provider (see Figure 8.24). The DSU is often included in the dialing process (DSU with dial pad).

Figure 8.24   *Switched/56 service*

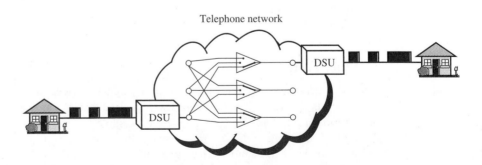

Ironically, a DSU is more expensive than a modem. So why would a subscriber elect to pay for the switched/56 service and DSU? Because the digital line has better speed, better quality, and less susceptibility to noise than an equivalent analog line.

Bandwidth on Demand   Switched/56 supports bandwidth on demand, allowing subscribers to obtain higher speeds by using more than one line (see the section on Inverse Multiplexing, above). This option allows switched/56 to support video conferencing, fast facsimile, multimedia, and fast data transfer, among other features.

Digital Data Service (DDS)

Digital data service (DDS) is the digital version of an analog leased line; it is a digital leased line.

The maximum speed available over DDS is 56 Kbps (the same as switched/56). However, a subscriber can choose among five actual rates: 2.4, 4.8, 9.6, 19.2, or 56 Kbps. Once the speed is chosen by the subscriber, it is set by the telephone company and must be observed.

Like switched/56, DDS requires the use of a DSU. The DSU for this service is cheaper than that required for switched/56, however, because it does not need a dial pad (see Figure 8.25).

Figure 8.25   *DDS service*

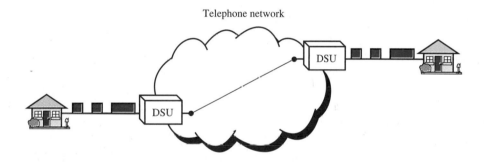

Digital Signal (DS) Service

After offering switched/56 and DDS services, the telephone companies saw a need to develop a hierarchy of digital services much like that used for analog services. The next step was digital signal (DS) service. DS is a hierarchy of digital signals. Figure 8.26 shows the data rates supported by each level.

- A DS-0 service resembles DDS. It is a single digital channel of 64 Kbps.
- DS-1 is a 1.544 Mbps service; 1.544 Mbps is 24 times 64 Kbps plus 8 Kbps of overhead. It can be used as a single service for 1.544 Mbps transmissions, or it can be used to multiplex 24 DS-0 channels or to carry any other combination desired by the user that can fit within its 1.544 Mbps capacity.
- DS-2 is a 6.312 Mbps service; 6.312 Mbps is 96 times 64 Kbps plus 168 Kbps of overhead. It can be used as a single service for 6.312 Mbps transmissions, or it can also be used to multiplex four DS-1 channels, 96 DS-0 channels, or a combination of these service types.

Figure 8.26 *DS hierarchy*

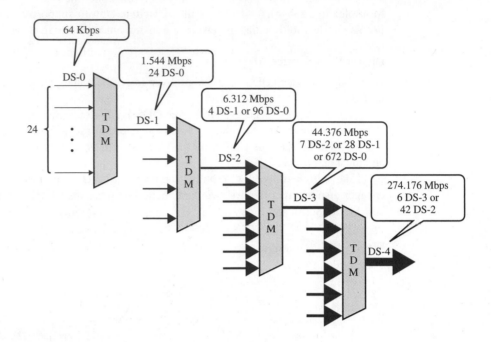

- DS-3 is a 44.376 Mbps service; 44.376 Mbps is 672 times 64 Kbps plus 1.368 Mbps of overhead. It can be used as a single service for 44.376 Mbps transmissions, or it can be used to multiplex seven DS-2 channels, 28 DS-1 channels, 672 DS-0 channels, or a combination of these service types.
- DS-4 is a 274.176 Mbps service; 274.176 is 4032 times 64 Kbps plus 16.128 Mbps of overhead. It can be used to multiplex six DS-3 channels, 42 DS-2 channels, 168 DS-1 channels, 4032 DS-0 channels, or a combination of these service types.

T Lines

DS-0, DS-1, and so on are the names of services. To implement those services, the telephone companies use T lines (T-1 to T-4). These are lines whose capacities are precisely matched to the data rates of the DS-1 to DS-4 services (see Table 8.1).

Table 8.1 *DS and T line rates*

Service	Line	Rate (Mbps)	Voice Channels
DS-1	T-1	1.544	24
DS-2	T-2	6.312	96
DS-3	T-3	44.376	672
DS-4	T-4	274.176	4032

T-1 is used to implement DS-1, T-2 is used to implement DS-2, and so on. As you can see from Table 8.1, DS-0 is not actually offered as a service, but it has been defined as a basis for reference purposes. Telephone companies believe that customers needing the level of service that would be found in DS-0 can substitute DDS.

T Lines for Analog Transmission   T lines are digital lines designed for the transmission of digital data, voice, or audio signals. However, they can also be used for analog transmission (regular telephone connections), provided the analog signals are sampled first, then time-division multiplexed.

The possibility of using T lines as analog carriers opened up a new generation of services for the telephone companies. Earlier, when an organization wanted 24 separate telephone lines, it needed to run 24 twisted-pair cables from the company to the central exchange. (Remember those old movies showing a busy executive with 10 telephones lined up on his desk? Or the old office telephones with a big fat cable running from them? Those cables contained a bundle of separate lines.) Today, that same organization can combine the 24 lines into one T-1 line and run only the T-1 line to the exchange. Figure 8.27 shows how 24 voice channels can be multiplexed onto one T-1 line. (Refer back to Chapter 5 for PCM encoding.)

Figure 8.27   *T-1 line for multiplexing telephone lines*

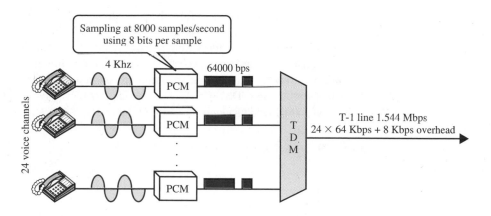

The T-1 Frame   As noted above, DS-1 requires 8 Kbps of overhead. To understand how this overhead is calculated, we must examine the format of a 24-voice-channel frame.

The frame used on a T-1 line is usually 193 bits divided into 24 slots of 8 bits each plus 1 extra bit for synchronization ($24 \times 8 + 1 = 193$); see Figure 8.28. In other words, each slot contains 1 signal segment from each channel; 24 segments are interleaved in one frame. If a T-1 line carries 8000 frames, the data rate is 1.544 Mbps ($193 \times 8000 = 1.544$ Mbps)—the capacity of the line.

Fractional T Lines   Many subscribers may not need the entire capacity of a T line. To accommodate these customers, the telephone companies have developed fractional

Figure 8.28   *T-1 frame structure*

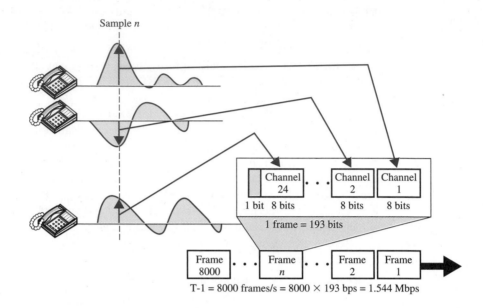

T services, which allow several subscribers to share one line by multiplexing their transmissions.

For example, a small business may need only one-fourth of the capacity of a T-1 line. If four businesses that size have offices in the same building, they can share a T-1 line. To do so, they direct their transmissions through a device called a data service unit/channel service unit (DSU/CSU). This device lets them divide the capacity of the line into four interleaved channels (see Figure 8.29).

Figure 8.29   *Fractional T-1 line*

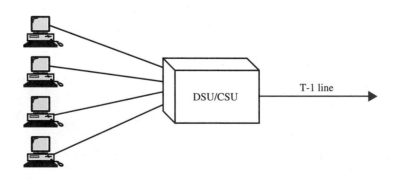

E Lines

Europeans use a version of T lines called E lines. The two systems are conceptually identical, but their capacities differ. Table 8.2 shows the E lines and their capacities.

Table 8.2   *E line rates*

Line	Rate (Mbps)	Voice Channels
E-1	2.048	30
E-2	8.448	120
E-3	34.368	480
E-4	139.264	1920

Other Multiplexing Services

We have discussed multiplexing over physical cable, but multiplexing is equally vital to the efficient use of both terrestrial and satellite microwave transmission. Today telephone service providers are introducing other powerful services, such as ISDN, SONET, and ATM, which also depend on multiplexing. These services will be discussed in Chapters 15 through 19.

8.4   SUMMARY

- Multiplexing is the simultaneous transmission of multiple signals across a single data link.
- Two types of multiplexing are frequency-division multiplexing (FDM) and time-division multiplexing (TDM).
- In FDM, each signal modulates a different carrier frequency. The modulated carriers are combined to form a new signal that is then sent across the link.
- In FDM, multiplexers modulate and combine signals while demultiplexers decompose and demodulate.
- In FDM, guard bands keep the modulated signals from overlapping and interfering with one another.
- In TDM, digital signals from *n* devices are interleaved with one another, forming a frame of data (bits, bytes, or any other data unit).
- TDM can be classified as either synchronous or asynchronous (statistical).
- In synchronous TDM, each frame contains at least one time slot dedicated to each device. The order in which each device sends its data to the frame is unvarying. If a device has no data to send, its time slot is sent empty.
- In synchronous TDM, a bit may be added to the beginning of each frame for synchronization.
- In asynchronous TDM, the time slot order of a frame depends on which devices have data to send at that time.
- Asynchronous TDM adds device addresses to each time slot.

- Inverse multiplexing splits a data stream from one high-speed line onto multiple lower speed lines.
- Telephone services can be analog or digital.
- Analog switched service requires dialing, switching, and a temporary dedicated link.
- Analog leased service is a permanent dedicated link between two customers. No dialing is necessary.
- Telephone companies use multiplexing to combine voice channels into successively larger groups for more efficient transmission.
- Switched/56 service is the digital equivalent of an analog switched line. It requires a digital service unit (DSU) to ensure a 56 Kbps data rate.
- Digital data service (DDS) is the digital equivalent of an analog leased line. DDS also requires a DSU.
- Digital system (DS) is a hierarchy of TDM signals.
- T lines (T-1 to T-4) are the implementation of DS services. A T-1 line consists of 24 voice channels.
- Fractional T service allows several subscribers to share one line by multiplexing their signals.
- T lines are used in North America. The European standard defines a variation called E lines.

8.5   PRACTICE SET

Multiple Choice

1. The sharing of a medium and its path by two or more devices is called _____.
   a. modulation
   b. encoding
   c. line discipline
   d. multiplexing
2. Which multiplexing technique transmits analog signals?
   a. FDM
   b. synchronous TDM
   c. asynchronous TDM
   d. b and c
3. Which multiplexing technique transmits digital signals?
   a. FDM
   b. synchronous TDM
   c. asynchronous TDM
   d. b and c

4. Which multiplexing technique shifts each signal to a different carrier frequency?

   a. FDM

   b. synchronous TDM

   c. asynchronous TDM

   d. none of the above

5. Which of the following is necessary for multiplexing?

   a. high-capacity data links

   b. parallel transmission

   c. QAM

   d. modems

6. Multiplexing involves _____.

   a. one path and one channel

   b. one path and multiple channels

   c. multiple paths and one channel

   d. multiple paths and multiple channels

7. In synchronous TDM, for n signal sources, each frame contains at least _____ slots.

   a. n

   b. $n + 1$

   c. $n - 1$

   d. 0 to n

8. In asynchronous TDM, for n signal sources, each frame contains m slots, where m is usually _____ n.

   a. less than

   b. greater than

   c. equal to

   d. 1 less than

9. In asynchronous TDM, the transmission rate of the multiplexed path is usually _____ the sum of the transmission rates of the signal sources.

   a. greater than

   b. less than

   c. equal to

   d. 1 less than

10. Which type of multiplexing has multiple paths?

    a. FDM

    b. asynchronous TDM

    c. synchronous TDM

    d. inverse multiplexing

11. Which type of telephone service is least expensive?

    a. analog switched line

    b. analog leased line

    c. switched/56 service

    d. DDS service

12. Which type of analog telephone service requires dialing?

    a. analog switched line

    b. analog leased line

    c. switched/56 service

    d. DDS service

13. Which type of analog telephone service provides a dedicated line between two customers?

    a. analog switched line

    b. analog leased line

    c. switched/56 service

    d. all of the above

14. Switched service means that connections between subscribers must involve _____.

    a. modems

    b. dedicated lines

    c. dialing

    d. leased lines

15. Leased service means that connections between subscribers must involve _____.

    a. modems

    b. dedicated lines

    c. dialing

    d. phase shifts

16. To decrease attenuation and distortion of a signal a line can be _____.

    a. multiplexed

    b. grounded

    c. extended

    d. conditioned

17. In switched/56 service, the 56 stands for _____.

    a. the number of dedicated lines possible per connection

    b. the data rate in Kbps

    c. the number of microseconds to make a connection

    d. the resistance of the line in ohms

18. A digital service unit (DSU) is needed in _____.

    a. DDS service

    b. switched/56 service

    c. analog leased service

    d. a and b

19. Which telephone service offers the subscriber a choice of transmission speeds?

    a. analog switched service

    b. analog leased service

    c. switched/56 service

    d. DDS service

20. In AT&T's FDM hierarchy, the bandwidth of each group type can be found by multiplying _____ and adding extra bandwidth for guard bands.

    a. the number of voice channels by 4000 Hz

    b. the sampling rate by 4000 Hz

    c. the number of voice channels by 8 bits/sample

    d. the sampling rate by 8 bits/sample

21. DS-0 through DS-4 are _____ while T-1 through T-4 are _____.

    a. services, multiplexers

    b. services, signals

    c. services, lines

    d. multiplexers, signals

22. In a T-1 line, _____ interleaving occurs.

    a. bit

    b. byte

    c. DS-0

    d. switch

23. Guard bands increase the bandwidth for _____.

    a. FDM

    b. synchronous TDM

    c. asynchronous TDM

    d. all of the above

Exercises

1. Given the following information, find the minimum bandwidth for the path:

    FDM multiplexing.

    Five devices, each requiring 4000 Hz.

    200 Hz guard band for each device.

2. Given the following information, find the maximum bandwidth for each signal source:

    FDM multiplexing.

    Total available bandwidth = 7900 Hz.

    Three signal sources.

    A 200 Hz guard band for each device.

3. Four signals are multiplexed together. We take one measurement n of the multiplexed signal. For FDM what does n represent? For TDM what does n represent?

4. Five signal sources are multiplexed together using synchronous TDM. Each source produces 100 characters per second. Assume that there is byte interleaving and that each frame requires one bit for synchronization. What is the frame rate? What is the bit rate on the path?

5. In asynchronous TDM, how is the number of slots per frame derived?

6. Draw the synchronous TDM frames showing the character data given the following information:

   Four signal sources

   Source 1 message: T E G

   Source 2 message: A

   Source 3 message:

   Source 4 message: E F I L

7. Do the previous problem assuming asynchronous TDM and a frame size of three characters.

8. Why is the number of slots for asynchronous TDM less than the number of slots for synchronous TDM?

9. What is the time duration for a T-1 frame?

10. The T-2 line offers a 6.312 Mbps service. Why is this number not 4 * 1.544 Mbps?

11. Name three ways in which digital services are superior to analog services.

12. How does a DSU differ from a modem?

13. How does slot size affect synchronous TDM? Asynchronous TDM?

14. Assume there is a small town of 500 households, each with one telephone. If every phone connection is point-to-point (a dedicated line) how many total lines are necessary? How can multiplexing help?

15. The bandwidth for analog switched service is usually between 0 to 4000 Hz. Why?

16. In Figure 8.27 the sampling rate is 8000 samples per second. Why?

17. How does an analog signal get converted to a digital signal for a T-1 line?

18. If a single mode optical fiber can transmit at 2 Gbps, how many telephone channels can one cable carry?

19. A DS-0 signal has a data rate of 64 Kbps. Where does this number come from?

20. Calculate the overhead (in bits) per voice channel for each T line. What is the percentage of overhead per voice channel?

CHAPTER 9

ERROR DETECTION AND CORRECTION

Networks must be able to transfer data from one device to another with complete accuracy. A system that cannot guarantee that the data received by one device are identical to the data transmitted by another device is essentially useless. Yet anytime data are transmitted from source to destination, they can become corrupted in passage. In fact, it is more likely that some part of a message will be altered in transit than that the entire contents will arrive intact. Many factors, including line noise, can alter or wipe out one or more bits of a given data unit. Reliable systems must have a mechanism for detecting and correcting such errors.

> Data can be corrupted during transmission. For reliable communication, errors must be detected and corrected.

Error detection and correction are used either at the data link layer or the transport layer of the OSI model.

9.1 TYPES OF ERRORS

Whenever an electromagnetic signal flows from one point to another, it is subject to unpredictable interference from heat, magnetism, and other forms of electricity. This interference can change the shape or timing of the signal. If the signal is carrying encoded binary data, such changes can alter the meaning of the data, changing 0 to 1 or 1 to 0. Bits can be changed singly or in clumps. For example, a 0.01 second burst of impulse noise on a transmission with a data rate of 1200 bps might change 12 bits of information. Other circumstances can alter just one bit of a data unit, or the first and third bits but not the second. These errors, though seemingly less significant, can make the data just as unreadable as wiping out 12 bits. So it is important to understand all three types of errors and how to detect them. These types are usually referred to as single-bit, multiple-bit, and burst errors. Of the three, a single-bit error is the most likely to occur and a burst error the least likely (see Figure 9.1).

Figure 9.1   *Types of errors*

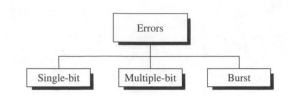

Single-Bit Error

The term *single-bit error* means that only one bit of a given data unit (such as a byte, character, data unit, or packet) is changed from 1 to 0 or from 0 to 1.

> A single-bit error is when only one bit in the data unit has changed.

Figure 9.2 shows the effect of a single-bit error on a data unit. To understand the impact of the change, imagine that each group of eight bits is an ASCII character with a 0 bit appended to the end. In the example, 00000010 (ASCII *STX)* was sent, meaning *start of text*, but 00001010 (ASCII *LF*) was received, meaning *line feed*. For more information about ASCII code, see Appendix A.)

Figure 9.2   *Single-bit error*

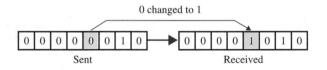

Multiple-Bit Error

The term *multiple-bit error* means that two or more nonconsecutive bits in a data unit have changed from 1 to 0 or from 0 to 1.

> A multiple-bit error is when two or more nonconsecutive bits in the data unit have changed.

Figure 9.3 shows the effect of a multiple-bit error on a byte of data. In this example, if we read the bit pattern as an ASCII character, 01000010 (ASCII *B*) was sent, but 00001010 (ASCII *LF*) meaning *line feed,* was received.

Figure 9.3   *Multiple-bit error*

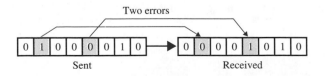

Burst Error

The term *burst error* means that two or more consecutive bits in the data unit have changed from 1 to 0 or from 0 to 1.

> A burst error means that two or more consecutive bits in the data unit have changed.

Figure 9.4 shows the effect of a burst error on a data unit. In this case, 0100010001000011 was sent, but 0101101101000011 was received.

Figure 9.4   *Burst error*

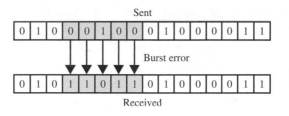

9.2   DETECTION

Even if we know what types of errors can occur, will we recognize one when we see it? If we have a copy of the intended transmission for comparison, of course we will. But what if we don't have a copy of the original? Then we will have no way of knowing we have received an error until we have decoded the transmission and failed to make sense of it. For a machine to check for errors this way would be slow, costly, and of questionable value. We don't need a system where computers decode whatever comes in, then sit around trying to decide if the sender really meant to use the word *glbrshnif* in the middle of an array of weather statistics. What we need is a mechanism that is simple and completely objective.

Redundancy

One mechanism that would satisfy these requirements would be to send every data unit twice. The receiving device would then be able to do a bit for bit comparison between the two versions of the data. Any discrepancy would indicate an error, and an appropriate correction mechanism could be set in place. This system would be completely accurate (the odds of errors being introduced onto exactly the same bits in both sets of data are infinitesimally small), but it would also be insupportably slow. Not only would the transmission time double, but the time it takes to compare every unit bit by bit must be added.

The concept of including extra information in the transmission solely for the purposes of comparison is a good one. But instead of repeating the entire data stream, a shorter group of bits may be appended to the end of each unit. This technique is called redundancy because the extra bits are redundant to the information; they are discarded as soon as the accuracy of the transmission has been determined.

Error detection uses the concept of redundancy, which means adding extra bits for detecting errors at the destination.

Figure 9.5 shows the process of using redundant bits to check the accuracy of a data unit. Once the data stream has been generated, it passes through a device that analyzes it and adds on an appropriately coded redundancy check. The data unit, now enlarged by several bits (in this illustration, seven), travels over the link to the receiver. The receiver puts the entire stream through a checking function. If the received bit stream passes the checking criteria, the data portion of the data unit is accepted and the redundant bits are discarded.

Figure 9.5   *Redundancy*

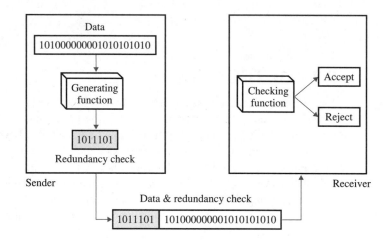

Four types of redundancy checks are used in data communications: vertical redundancy check (VRC) (also called parity check), longitudinal redundancy check (LRC), cyclical redundancy check (CRC), and checksum. The first three, VRC, LRC, and CRC, are implemented in the physical layer for use in the data link layer. The fourth, checksum, is used primarily by networks, including the Internet, and is implemented in the transport layer (see Figure 9.6).

Vertical Redundancy Check (VRC)

The most common and least expensive mechanism for error detection is the vertical redundancy check (VRC), often called a parity check. In this technique, a redundant bit, called a parity bit, is appended to every data unit so that the total number of 1s in

Figure 9.6   *Detection methods*

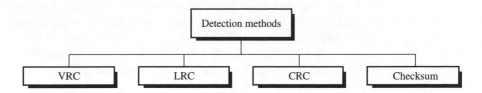

the unit (including the parity bit) becomes either even (if the system is checking for even parity) or odd (if the system is checking for odd parity). Both the sending and receiving systems must use the same type of parity so that if an even-parity unit is transmitted and an odd-parity unit is received, the receiver knows that the data unit has been damaged along the way and does not accept it.

Suppose we want to transmit the binary data unit 1100001 [ASCII *a* (97)]; see Figure 9.7. Adding together the number of 1s gives us 3, an odd number. Before transmitting, we pass the data unit through a parity generator. The parity generator counts the 1s and appends the appropriate parity bit to the end. If we are using an even-parity check, the parity generator adds on a 1 parity bit (11100001): the total number of 1s is now four, an even number. The system now transmits the entire expanded unit across the network link. When it reaches its destination, the receiver puts all eight bits through an even-parity checking function. If the receiver sees 11100001, it counts four 1s, an even number, and the data unit passes. But what if the data unit has been damaged in transit? What if, instead of 11100001, the receiver sees 11100101? Then, when the even-parity checker counts the 1s, it gets 5, an odd number. The receiver knows that an error has been introduced into the data somewhere and therefore rejects the whole unit.

In vertical redundancy check (VRC) a parity bit is added to every data unit so that the total number of 1s (including the parity bit) becomes even for even-parity check or odd for odd-parity check.

Figure 9.7   *Even parity VRC concept*

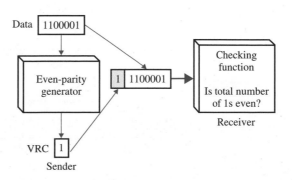

Reliability

VRC can detect all single-bit errors. It can also detect multiple-bit and burst errors as long as the total number of bits changed is odd (1, 3, 5, etc.). Let's say we have an even-parity data unit where the total number of 1s, including the parity bit, is 6: 1000111011. If any three bits change value, the resulting parity will be odd and the damage will be detected: 1*111*111011:9, 0*11*0111011:7, 1*1*000*1*0011:5—all odd. The VRC checker would return a result of 1 and the data unit would be rejected. The same holds true for any odd number of errors.

Suppose, however, that two bits of the data unit are changed: 1*11*0111011:8, 1*1*00011011:6, 1000011010:4. In each case the number of 1s in the data unit is still even. The VRC checker will add them and return a parity of 0 even though the data unit contains two errors. VRC cannot detect errors where the total number of bits changed is even. If any two bits change in transmission, the changes cancel each other and the data unit will pass a parity check even though the data unit is damaged. The same holds true for any even number of errors.

> VRC can detect all single-bit errors. It can detect multiple-bit or burst errors only if the total number of errors is odd.

Longitudinal Redundancy Check (LRC)

Longitudinal redundancy check (LRC) is VRC in two dimensions. To increase the likelihood of detecting multiple-bit and burst errors, we need to increase the complexity of the checks we run on the data by looking at each bit twice.

LRC error detection groups a predetermined number of data units, each already containing a VRC parity bit, together into a block. The corresponding bits of each data unit (all the first bits, all the second bits, etc.) are passed through a generator to find the parity of each position. Each position then gets its own parity bit. The parity bits of all the positions are then assembled into a new data unit, which is added to the end of the data block (see Figure 9.8). As the data block reaches the receiver, it passes through an LRC checker. The total parity, including VRC bits and LRC bits, must match the parity expected—either all even or all odd depending on the convention used. The receiver drops off the LRC and VRC bits and accepts the data. If any of the values are wrong, the receiver knows that some part of the block was damaged in transit and therefore rejects the entire block.

Figure 9.8   *LRC*

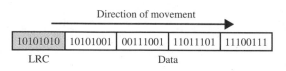

Direction of movement

| 10101010 | 10101001 | 00111001 | 11011101 | 11100111 |

LRC   Data

In longitudinal redundancy check (LRC), a redundant unit is added after a number of data units. The bits in the redundant unit are calculated from the corresponding bits in the data units using VRC.

Figure 9.9 shows how the LRC is calculated. The least significant bits are added together and their parity found (even or odd, depending on the LRC). Then the second bits are added and their parity found, and so on. The final bit of the LRC is both the parity bit for the LRC data unit itself and the parity bit for all the VRC parity bits in the block.

Figure 9.9 not only illustrates the logic of LRC but also shows how the vertical and longitudinal redundancy checks got their names. When both processes were developed, computer instructions and data were all input on punched cards, on which all characters were printed vertically.

Figure 9.9   *VRC and LRC*

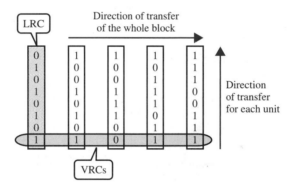

Reliability

LRC enormously increases the likelihood of detecting multiple-bit and burst errors. There is, however, one pattern of errors that remains elusive. If two bits in one data unit are damaged and two bits *in exactly the same positions* in another data unit are also damaged, the LRC checker will not detect an error. Consider, for example, two data units: 11110000 and 11000011. If the first and last bits in each of them are changed, making the data units read *0*111000*1* and *0*100001*0*, the longitudinal parity of the first position (now 0 + 0) is still even and the longitudinal parity of the last position (now 1 + 0) is still odd. The combined errors of these two data units leave both the longitudinal and the vertical parities unchanged. With no parity differences, an LRC checker will not pick up the damage. This logic holds true for any even number of errors in corresponding positions in any even number of data units.

Cyclic Redundancy Check (CRC)

The third and most powerful of the redundancy checking techniques is the cyclic redundancy check (CRC). Unlike VRC and LRC which are based on addition, CRC is based on binary division. In CRC, instead of adding bits together to achieve a desired parity, a sequence of redundant bits, called the CRC or the CRC remainder, is appended to the end of a data unit so that the resulting data unit becomes exactly divisible by a second, predetermined binary number. At its destination, the incoming data unit is divided by the same number. If at this step there is no remainder, the data unit is assumed to be intact and is therefore accepted. A remainder indicates that the data unit has been damaged in transit and therefore must be rejected.

The redundancy bits used by CRC are derived by dividing the data unit by the predetermined divisor; the remainder is the CRC. To be valid, a CRC must have two qualities: it must have exactly one less bit than the divisor, and appending it to the end of the data string must make the resulting bit sequence exactly divisible by the divisor.

Both the theory and the application of CRC error detection are straightforward. The only complexity is in deriving the CRC. In order to clarify this process, we will start with an overview and add complexity as we go. Figure 9.10 provides an outline of the three basic steps.

Figure 9.10   *CRC generator and checker*

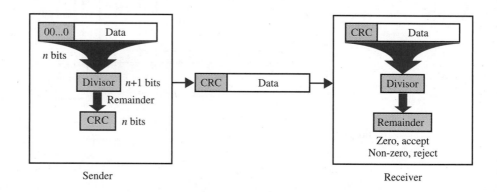

First, a string of *n* 0s is appended to the end of the data unit. The number *n* is one less than the number of bits in the predetermined divisor, which is *n* + 1 bits.

Second, the newly elongated data unit is divided by the divisor using a process called binary division. The remainder resulting from this division is the CRC.

Third, the CRC of *n* bits derived in step 2 replaces the appended 0s at the end of the data unit. If the derived remainder has fewer than *n* bits, the missing, leftmost, bits are presumed to be 0s. If the division process has not yielded a remainder at all—that is, if the original data unit is already divisible by the divisor—then *n* 0s take the place of a remainder as the CRC. The resulting bit pattern is exactly divisible by the divisor.

The data unit arrives at the receiver data first, followed by the CRC. The receiver treats the whole string as a unit and divides it by the same divisor that was used to find the CRC remainder.

If the string arrives without error, the CRC checker yields a remainder of zero and the data unit passes. If the string has been changed in transit, the division yields a non-zero remainder and the data unit does not pass.

Reliability

CRC will detect all possible errors except those that change the bit value of a block of code by exactly the value of the divisor. Even with the four-bit divisor used above, the odds of this happening are low. Popular CRC divisors, however, use 13, 17, and 33 bits, bringing the likelihood of an undetected error almost to zero.

The CRC Generator

A CRC generator uses modulo-2 division. Figure 9.11 shows this process. In the first step, the four-bit divisor is subtracted from the first four bits of the dividend. Each bit of the divisor is subtracted from the corresponding bit of the dividend without disturbing the next higher bit. In our example, the divisor, 1101, is subtracted from the first four bits of the dividend, 1001, yielding 100 (the leading 0 of the remainder is dropped off).

Figure 9.11 *Binary division*

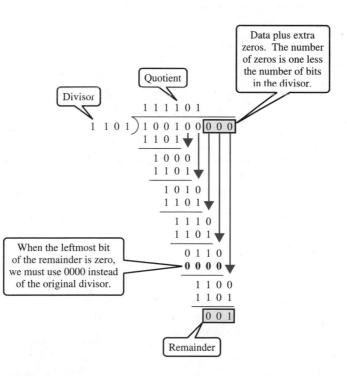

The next unused bit from the dividend is then pulled down to make the number of bits in the remainder equal to the number of bits in the divisor. The next step, therefore, is $1000 - 1101$, which yields 101, and so on.

In binary division, the divisor always begins with a 1; the divisor is subtracted from a portion of the previous dividend/remainder that is equal to it in length; the divisor can only be subtracted from a dividend/remainder whose leftmost bit is 1. Anytime the leftmost bit of the dividend/remainder is 0, a string of 0s, of the same length as the divisor, replaces the divisor in that step of the process. For example, if the divisor is four bits long, it is replaced by four 0s. (Remember, we are dealing with bit patterns, not with quantitative values; 0000 is not the same as 0.) This restriction means that, at any step, the leftmost subtraction will be either $0 - 0$, or $1 - 1$, both of which equal 0. So, after subtraction, the leftmost bit of the remainder will always be a leading zero, which is dropped off (just as it would be in decimal division), and the next unused bit of the dividend is pulled down to fill out the remainder. Note that only the first bit of the remainder is dropped—if the second bit is also 0, it is retained, and the dividend/remainder for the next step will begin with 0. This process repeats until the entire dividend has been used.

Polynomials

The CRC generator (the divisor) is most often represented not as a string of 1s and 0s, but as an algebraic polynomial (see Figure 9.12). The polynomial format is useful for two reasons: It is short, and it can be used to prove the concept mathematically (which is beyond the scope of this book).

Figure 9.12   *A polynomial*

$$x^7 + x^5 + x^2 + x + 1$$

The relationship of a polynomial to its corresponding binary representation is shown in Figure 9.13. The standard polynomials used by popular protocols for CRC generation are shown in Figure 9.14. The numbers 12, 16, and 32 refer to the size of the CRC remainder. The CRC divisors are 13, 17, and 33 bits, respectively.

Figure 9.13   *A polynomial representing a divisor*

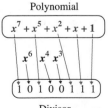

Figure 9.14 *Standard polynomials*

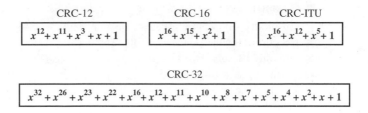

CRC-12

$$x^{12} + x^{11} + x^3 + x + 1$$

CRC-16

$$x^{16} + x^{15} + x^2 + 1$$

CRC-ITU

$$x^{16} + x^{12} + x^5 + 1$$

CRC-32

$$x^{32} + x^{26} + x^{23} + x^{22} + x^{16} + x^{12} + x^{11} + x^{10} + x^8 + x^7 + x^5 + x^4 + x^2 + x + 1$$

Checksum

The error detection method used by the higher layer protocols is called checksum. Like VRC, LRC, and CRC, checksum is based on the concept of redundancy.

Checksum Generator

In the sender, the checksum generator subdivides the data unit into equal segments of n bits (usually 16). These segments are added together using one's complement arithmetic (see Appendix D) in such a way that the total is also n bits long. That total (sum) is then complemented and appended to the end of the original data unit as redundancy bits, called the checksum field. The extended data unit is transmitted across the network. So if the sum of the data segment is T, the checksum will be $-T$ (see Figure 9.15 and Figure 9.16).

Figure 9.15 *Checksum*

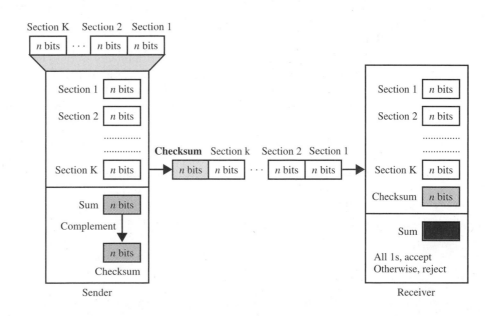

To create the checksum the sender does the following:

- The unit is divided into k sections, each of n bits.
- Sections 1 and 2 are added together using one's complement.
- Section 3 is added to the result of the previous step.
- Section 4 is added to the result of the previous step.
- The process repeats until section k is added to the result of the previous step.
- The final result is complemented to make the checksum.

Figure 9.16 *Data unit and checksum*

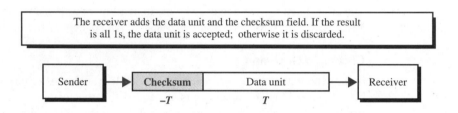

Checksum Checker

The receiver subdivides the data unit as above (the last segment will be the checksum field) and adds all segments together. If the extended data unit is intact the total value found by adding the data segments and the checksum field should be zero (T plus $-T$ is zero). If the result is not zero, the packet contains an error and the receiver rejects it. The actual result of the addition will be n 1s if the data unit is undamaged. In one's complement representation, a number made up of all 1s has the value -0 (see Appendix D).

Reliability

Checksum detects all errors involving odd numbers of bits, as well as most errors involving even numbers of bits. However, if one or more bits of a segment are damaged and the corresponding bit or bits of opposite value in a second segment are also damaged, the sums of those columns will not change and the receiver will not detect a problem. If the last digit of one segment is a 0 and it gets changed to a 1 in transit, then the last 1 in another segment must be changed to a 0 if the error is to go undetected. In LRC, two 0s could both change to 1s without altering the parity because carries were discarded. Checksum retains all carries; so, although two 0s becoming 1s would not alter the value of their own column, they would change the value of the next higher column. But anytime a bit inversion is balanced by an opposite bit inversion in the corresponding digit of another data segment, the error is invisible.

9.3   ERROR CORRECTION

The mechanisms that we have covered up to this point detect errors but do not correct them. Error correction can be handled in two ways. In one, when an error is discovered, the receiver can have the sender retransmit the entire data unit. In the other, a receiver can use an error-correcting code, which automatically corrects certain errors.

In theory, it is possible to correct any binary code errors automatically. Error-correcting codes, however, are more sophisticated than error-detection codes and require more redundancy bits. The number of bits required to correct a multiple-bit or burst error is so high that in most cases it is inefficient to do so. For this reason, most error correction is limited to one-, two-, or three-bit errors.

Single-Bit Error Correction

The concept underlying error correction can be most easily understood by examining the simplest case: single-bit errors.

As we saw earlier, single-bit errors can be detected by the addition of a redundant (parity) bit to the data unit (VRC). A single additional bit can detect single-bit errors in any sequence of bits because it must distinguish between only two conditions: error or no error. A bit has two states (0 and 1). These two states are sufficient for this level of detection.

But what if we want to correct as well as detect single-bit errors? Two states are enough to detect an error but not to correct it. An error occurs when the receiver reads a 1 bit as a 0, or a 0 bit as a 1. To correct the error, the receiver simply reverses the value of the altered bit. To do so, however, it must know which bit is in error. The secret of error correction, therefore, is to locate the invalid bit or bits.

For example, to correct a single-bit error in an ASCII character, the error correction code must determine which of the seven bits has changed. In this case, we have to distinguish between eight different states: no error, error in position 1, error in position 2, and so on, up to error in position 7. To do so requires enough redundancy bits to show all eight states.

At first glance, it looks like a three-bit redundancy code should be adequate because three bits can show eight different states (000 to 111) and can therefore indicate the locations of eight different possibilities. But what if an error occurs in the redundancy bits themselves? Seven bits of data (the ASCII character) plus three bits of redundancy equals 10 bits. Three bits, however, can identify only eight possibilities. Additional bits are necessary to cover all possible error locations.

Redundancy Bits

To calculate the number of redundancy bits (r) required to correct a given number of data bits (m), we must find a relationship between m and r. Figure 9.17 shows m bits of data with r bits of redundancy added to it. The length of the resulting code is $m + r$.

Figure 9.17 *Data and redundancy bits*

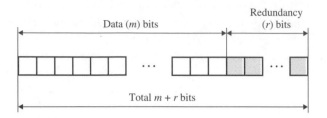

If the total number of bits in a transmittable unit is $m + r$, then r must be able to indicate at least $m + r + 1$ different states. Of these, one state means no error and $m + r$ states indicate the location of an error in each of the $m + r$ positions.

So, $m + r + 1$ states must be discoverable by r bits; and r bits can indicate 2^r different states. 2^r, therefore, must be equal to or greater than $m + r + 1$:

$$2^r \geq m + r + 1$$

The value of r can be determined by plugging in the value of m (the original length of the data unit to be transmitted). For example, if the value of m is 7 (as in a seven-bit ASCII code), the smallest r value that can satisfy this equation is 4:

$$2^4 \geq 7 + 4 + 1$$

Table 9.1 shows some possible m values and the corresponding r values.

Table 9.1 *Relationship between data and redundancy bits*

Number of Data Bits (m)	Number of Redundancy Bits (r)	Total Bits (m + r)
1	2	3
2	3	5
3	3	6
4	3	7
5	4	9
6	4	10
7	4	11

Hamming Code

So far, we have examined the number of bits required to cover all of the possible single-bit error states in a transmission. But how do we manipulate those bits to discover which state has occurred? A technique developed by R. W. Hamming provides a practical solution.

Positioning the Redundancy Bits

The Hamming code can be applied to data units of any length and uses the relationship between data and redundancy bits discussed above. For example, a seven-bit ASCII code requires four redundancy bits that can be added to the end of the data unit or interspersed with the original data bits. In Figure 9.18, these bits are placed in positions 1, 2, 4, and 8 (the positions in an 11-bit sequence that are powers of 2). For clarity in the examples below, we refer to these bits as r_1, r_2, r_4, and r_8.

Figure 9.18   *Positions of redundancy bits in Hamming code*

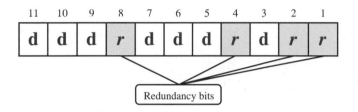

In the Hamming code, each r bit is the VRC bit for one combination of data bits; r_2 is the VRC bit for another combination of data bits, and so on. The combinations used to calculate each of the four r values for a seven-bit data sequence are as follows:

$$r_1: \text{bits } 1, 3, 5, 7, 9, 11$$

$$r_2: \text{bits } 2, 3, 6, 7, 10, 11$$

$$r_4: \text{bits } 4, 5, 6, 7$$

$$r_8: \text{bits } 8, 9, 10, 11$$

Each data bit may be included in more than one VRC calculation. In the sequences above, for example, each of the original data bits is included in at least two sets, while the r bits are included in only one.

To see the pattern behind this strategy, look at the binary representation of each bit position. The r_1 bit is calculated using all bit positions whose binary representation includes a 1 in the rightmost position. The r_2 bit is calculated using all bit positions with a 1 in the second position, and so on (see Figure 9.19).

Calculating the *r* Values

Figure 9.20 shows a Hamming code implementation for an ASCII character. In the first step, we fill in each bit of the original character in its appropriate position in the 11-bit unit. In the subsequent steps, we calculate the even parities for the various bit combinations. The parity value for each combination is the value of the corresponding r bit. For example, the value of r_1 is calculated to provide even parity for a combination of bits 3, 5, 7, 9, and 11. The value of r_2 is calculated to provide even parity with bits 3, 6, 7, 10, and 11, and so on. The final 11-bit code is sent through the transmission line.

Figure 9.19   *Redundancy bits calculation*

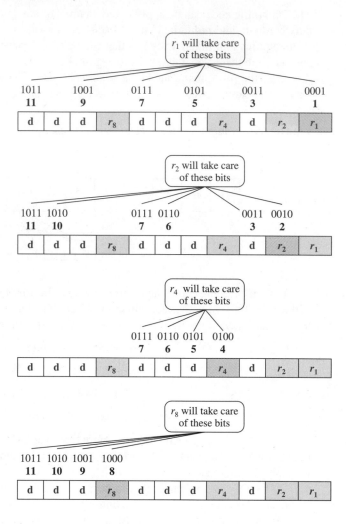

Error Detection and Correction

Now imagine that by the time the above transmission is received, the number 7 bit has been changed from 1 to 0 (see Figure 9.21).

The receiver takes the transmission and recalculates four new VRCs using the same sets of bits used by the sender plus the relevant parity (r) bit for each set (see Figure 9.22). Then it assembles the new parity values into a binary number in order of r position (r_8, r_4, r_2, r_1) In our example, this step gives us the binary number 0111 (7 in decimal), which is the precise location of the bit in error.

Once the bit is identified, the receiver can reverse its value and correct the error.

Figure 9.20   *Example of redundancy bit calculation*

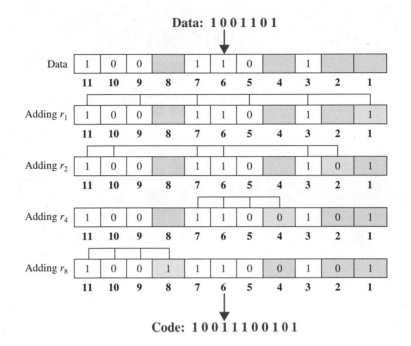

Figure 9.21   *Single-bit error*

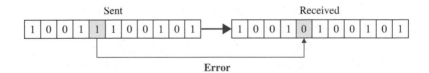

Multiple-Bit Error Correction

Redundancy bits calculated on overlapping sets of data bits can also be used to correct multiple-bit errors. The number of redundancy bits required to make these corrections, however, is dramatically higher than that required for single-bit errors. To correct double-bit errors, for example, we must take into consideration that the two bits can be a combination of any two bits in the entire sequence. Three-bit correction means any three bits in the entire sequence, and so on. So the simple strategy used by the Hamming code to correct single-bit errors must be redesigned to be applicable for multiple-bit correction. We leave the details of these more sophisticated schemes to advanced books on error handling.

Figure 9.22   *Error detection using Hamming code*

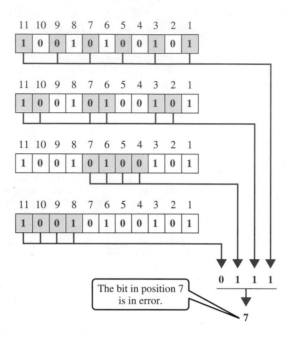

9.4   SUMMARY

- Transmission errors are usually detected at the physical layer of the OSI model.
- Transmission errors are usually corrected at the data link layer of the OSI model.
- Errors can be categorized as follows:
  - a. Single-bit: one bit error per data unit.
  - b. Multiple-bit: two or more nonconsecutive bit errors per data unit.
  - c. Burst: two or more consecutive bit errors per data unit.
- Redundancy is the concept of sending extra bits for use in error detection.
- Four common methods of error detection are the following:
  - a. Vertical redundancy check (VRC).
  - b. Longitudinal redundancy check (LRC).
  - c. Cyclic redundancy check (CRC).
  - d. Checksum.
- In VRC an extra bit (parity bit) is added to the data unit.
- VRC can detect only an odd number of errors; it cannot detect an even number of errors.
- In LRC a redundant data unit follows *n* data units. The bits are determined by calculating the VRC of each bit of the data units.

■ CRC, the most powerful of redundancy checking techniques, is based on binary division.

■ Checksum is used by the higher layer protocols (TCP/IP) for error detection.

■ To calculate a checksum:

   a. Divide the data into sections.

   b. Add the sections together using one's complement arithmetic.

   c. Take the complement of the final sum; this is the checksum.

■ At the receiver, when using the checksum method, the data and checksum should add up to −0 if there are no errors present.

■ The Hamming code is a single-bit error correction method using redundant bits. These bits are a function of the length of the data bits.

■ In the Hamming code, for a data unit of m bits, use the formula $2^r \geq m + r + 1$ to determine r, the number of redundant bits needed.

9.5   PRACTICE SET

Multiple Choice

1. Error detection is usually used in the _____ layer of the OSI model.

   a. transport

   b. data link

   c. network

   d. a and b

2. Which error detection method consists of a parity bit for each data unit as well as an entire data unit of parity bits?

   a. VRC

   b. LRC

   c. CRC

   d. checksum

3. Which error detection method uses one's complement arithmetic?

   a. VRC

   b. LRC

   c. CRC

   d. checksum

4. Which error detection method consists of just one redundant bit per data unit?

   a. VRC

   b. LRC

   c. CRC

   d. checksum

5. Which error detection method involves polynomials?

   a. VRC

   b. LRC

   c. CRC

   d. checksum

6. Which of the following best describes a single bit error?

   a. A single bit is inverted.

   b. A single bit is inverted per data unit.

   c. A single bit is inverted per transmission.

   d. any of the above

7. If the ASCII character G is sent and the character D is received, what type of error is this?

   a. single-bit

   b. multiple-bit

   c. burst

   d. recoverable

8. If the ASCII character H is sent and the character I is received, what type of error is this?

   a. single-bit

   b. multiple-bit

   c. burst

   d. recoverable

9. In cyclic redundancy checking what is the CRC?

   a. the divisor

   b. the quotient

   c. the dividend

   d. the remainder

10. In cyclic redundancy checking, the divisor is _____ the CRC.

   a. the same size as

   b. one bit less than

   c. one bit more than

   d. two bits more than

11. If the data unit is 111111, the divisor 1010, and the remainder 110, what is the dividend at the receiver?

   a. 111111011

   b. 111111110

   c. 1010110

   d. 110111111

12. If the data unit is 111111 and the divisor 1010, what is the dividend at the transmitter?
    a. 111111000
    b. 1111110000
    c. 111111
    d. 1111111010

13. If odd parity is used for ASCII error detection, the number of 0s per eight-bit symbol is _____.
    a. even
    b. odd
    c. indeterminate
    d. 42

14. The sum of the checksum and data at the receiver is _____ if there are no errors.
    a. −0
    b. +0
    c. the complement of the checksum
    d. the complement of the data

15. The Hamming code is a method of _____.
    a. error detection
    b. error correction
    c. error encapsulation
    d. a and b

16. In CRC there is no error if the remainder at the receiver is _____.
    a. equal to the remainder at the sender
    b. zero
    c. nonzero
    d. the quotient at the sender

17. In CRC the quotient at the sender _____.
    a. becomes the dividend at the receiver
    b. becomes the divisor at the receiver
    c. is discarded
    d. is the remainder

Exercises

1. Explain the concept of redundancy in error detection.
2. Is there any advantage of even parity over odd parity?
3. What is the maximum effect of a 2 ms burst of noise on data transmitted at
    a. 1500 bps?
    b. 12,000 bps?
    c. 96,000 bps?

Generalize about transmission speed and burst errors.

4. Assuming even parity, find the parity bit for each of the following data units:

   a. 1001011

   b. 0001100

   c. 1000000

   d. 1110111

5. Assuming odd parity, find the parity bit for each of the data units in the preceding problem.

6. Assuming even parity and using VRC and LRC, find the redundant data unit for the following data units. Data units are separated by a hyphen.

   10011001-01101111 ⇨ direction of data

7. Find the checksum for the following bit sequence. Assume a 16-bit segment size.

   1001001110010011

   1001100001001101

8. Given a 10-bit sequence 1010011110 and a divisor 1011, find the CRC. Check your answer.

9. Given a remainder of 111, a data unit of 10110011, and a divisor of 1001, is there an error in the data unit?

10. A line transmitting at 9600 bps is hit by a 0.01 second electrical disturbance. What is the maximum number of bits that could be in error?

11. Find the minimum number of redundancy bits needed for data bits of the following sizes:

    a. 12

    b. 16

    c. 24

    d. 64

12. Construct the Hamming code for the bit sequence 10011101.

CHAPTER 10

DATA LINK CONTROL

Up to this point, we have been examining the structure and transmission of signals across media links. But unless accurately received by a second device, a signal transmitted over a wire is just so much wasted electricity. With transmission alone we can put a signal onto a line, but we have no way of controlling which of several devices attached to that line will receive it, no way of knowing if the intended receiver is ready and able to receive it, and no way of keeping a second device on the line from transmitting at the same time and thereby destroying our signal. In the physical layer of the OSI model, we have transmission but we do not yet have communication.

Communication requires at least two devices working together, one to send and one to receive. Even such a basic arrangement requires a great deal of coordination for an intelligible exchange to occur. For example, in half-duplex transmission, it is essential that only one device transmit at a time. If both ends of the link put signals on the line simultaneously, they collide, leaving nothing on the line but noise. The coordination of half-duplex transmission is part of a procedure called line discipline, which is one of the functions included in the second layer of the OSI model, the data link layer.

In addition to line discipline, the most important functions in the data link layer are flow control and error control (see Figure 10.1). Collectively, these functions are known as data link control.

Figure 10.1   *Data link layer*

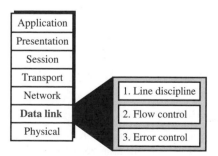

- Line discipline answers the question, Who should send now? It is important for the coordination of the linked systems.

- Flow control coordinates how much data can be sent in some time interval (essentially the rate of transfer). It also provides the receiver's acknowledgment of frames received intact, and so is linked to error control.

- Error control really means error correction. It allows the receiver to inform the sender of any frames lost or damaged in transmission, and coordinates the retransmission of those frames by the sender (see Figure 10.2).

Figure 10.2   *Data link layer functions*

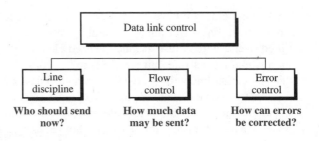

10.1   LINE DISCIPLINE

Whatever the system, no device in it should be allowed to transmit until that device has evidence that the intended receiver is able to receive and is prepared to accept the transmission. What if the receiving device does not expect a transmission, is busy, or is out of commission? With no way to determine the status of the intended receiver, the transmitting device may waste its time sending data to a nonfunctioning receiver or may interfere with signals already on the link. The line discipline functions of the data link layer oversee the establishment of links, and the right of a particular device to transmit at a given time.

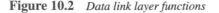

Line discipline answers the question, Who should send now?

Line discipline can be done in two ways: enquiry/acknowledgment (ENQ/ACK) and poll/select. The first method is used in peer-to-peer communication; the second method is used in primary-secondary communication (see Figure 10.3).

ENQ/ACK

Enquiry/acknowledgment (ENQ/ACK) is used primarily in systems where there is no question of the wrong receiver getting the transmission, that is, when there is a dedicated link between two devices so that the only device capable of receiving the transmission is the intended one.

Figure 10.3   *Line discipline categories*

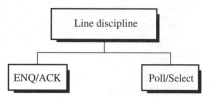

ENQ/ACK coordinates which device may start a transmission and whether or not the intended recipient is ready and enabled. Using ENQ/ACK, a session can be initiated by either station on a link as long as both are of equal rank—a printer, for example, cannot initiate communication with a CPU (see Figure 10.4).

Figure 10.4   *Line discipline concept: ENQ/ACK*

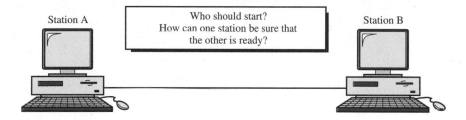

In both half-duplex and full-duplex transmission, the initiating device establishes the session. In half-duplex, the initiator then sends its data while the responder waits. The responder may take over the link when the initiator is finished or has requested a response. In full-duplex, both devices can transmit simultaneously once the session has been established.

How It Works   The initiator first transmits a frame called an enquiry (ENQ) asking if the receiver is available to receive data. The receiver must answer either with an acknowledge (ACK) frame if it is ready to receive, or with a negative acknowledge (NAK) frame if it is not. By requiring a response even if the answer is negative, ENQ/ACK lets the initiator know that its enquiry was in fact received even if the receiver is currently unable to accept a transmission. If neither an ACK nor a NAK is received within a specified time limit, the initiator assumes that the ENQ frame was lost in transit, disconnects, and sends a replacement. An initiating system ordinarily makes three such attempts to establish a link before giving up.

If the response to the ENQ is negative and three attempts have failed, the initiator disconnects and begins the process again at another time. If the response is positive, the initiator is free to send its data. Once all of its data have been transmitted, the sending system finishes with an end of transmission (EOT) frame. This process is illustrated in Figure 10.5.

Figure 10.5 *ENQ/ACK line discipline*

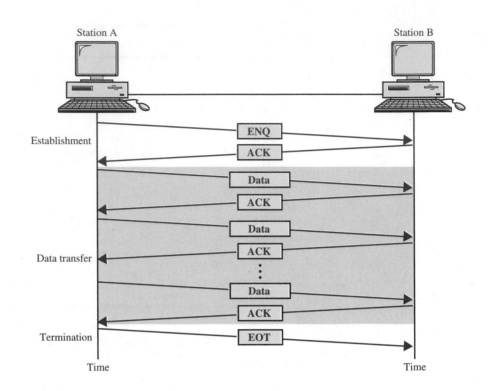

Poll/Select

The poll/select method of line discipline works with topologies where one device is designated as primary and the other devices are secondary. Multipoint systems must coordinate several nodes, not just two. The question to be determined in these cases, therefore, is more than just, Are you ready? It is also, Which of the several nodes has the right to use the channel?

How It Works Whenever a multipoint link consists of a primary device and multiple secondary devices using a single transmission line, all exchanges must be made through the primary device even when the ultimate destination is a secondary device. (Although the illustrations that follow show a bus topology, the concepts are the same for any multipoint configuration.) The primary device controls the link; the secondary devices follow its instructions. It is up to the primary to determine which device is allowed to use the channel at a given time (see Figure 10.6). The primary, therefore, is always the initiator of a session. If the primary wants to receive data, it asks the secondaries if they have anything to send; this function is called polling. If the primary wants to send data, it tells the target secondary to get ready to receive; this function is called selecting.

Addresses For point-to-point configurations, identification is unimportant; any transmission put onto the link by one device can be intended only for the other. For the pri-

Figure 10.6   *Multipoint line discipline*

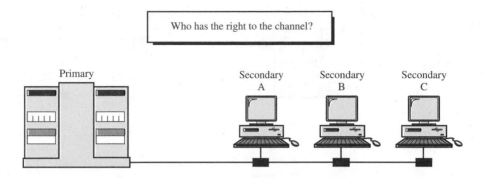

mary device in a multipoint topology to be able to identify and communicate with a specific secondary device, however, there must be a naming convention. To transmit data in a multipoint situation without being able to specify the recipient would be equivalent to mailing a letter in a blank envelope. The post office could deliver it to anyone it chooses; you would have no control over who would receive it. For this reason, every device on a link has a name or address that can be used for identification.

Poll/select protocols identify each frame as being either to or from a specific device on the link. Each secondary device has an address that differentiates it from the others. In any transmission, that address will appear in a specified portion of each frame, called an address field or header depending on the protocol. If the transmission comes from the primary device, the address indicates the recipient of the data. If the transmission comes from a secondary device, the address indicates the originator of the data. We will discuss addressing further when we discuss specific protocols in Chapter 12.

Select   The select mode is used whenever the primary device has something to send. Remember that the primary controls the link. If the primary is not either sending or receiving data, it knows the link is available. If it has something to send, it sends it. What it does not know, however, is whether the target device is prepared to receive (usually, *prepared to receive* means *on*). So the primary must alert the secondary to the upcoming transmission and wait for an acknowledgment of the secondary's ready status. Before sending data, the primary creates and transmits a select (SEL) frame, one field of which includes the address of the intended secondary. Multipoint topologies use a single link for several devices, which means that any frame on the link is available to every device. As a frame makes its way down the link, each of the secondary devices checks the address field. Only when a device recognizes its own address does it open the frame and read the data. In the case of a SEL frame, the enclosed data consist of an alert that data are forthcoming.

If the secondary is awake and running, it returns an ACK frame to the primary. The primary then sends one or more data frames, each addressed to the intended secondary. Figure 10.7 illustrates this procedure.

Poll   The polling function is used by the primary device to solicit transmissions from the secondary devices. As noted above, the secondaries are not allowed to transmit data

Figure 10.7   *Multipoint select*

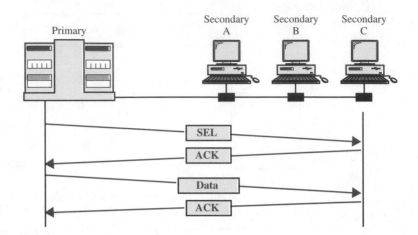

Figure 10.8   *Multipoint poll*

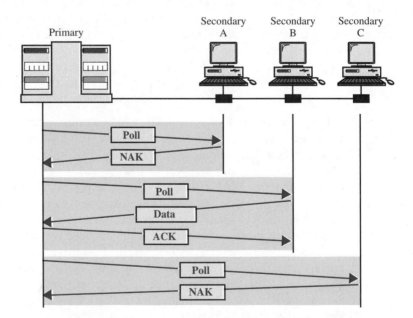

unless asked (don't call us—we'll call you). By keeping all control with the primary, the multipoint system guarantees that only one transmission can occur at a time, thereby ensuring against signal collisions without requiring elaborate precedence protocols. When the primary is ready to receive data, it must ask each device in turn if it has anything to send. When the first secondary is approached, it responds either with a NAK frame if it has nothing to send or with data (in the form of a data frame) if it does.

If the response is negative (a NAK frame), the primary then polls the next secondary in the same way until it finds one with data to send. When the response is positive (a data frame), the primary reads the frame and returns an acknowledgment (ACK frame) verifying its receipt. The secondary may send several data frames one after the other, or it may be required to wait for an ACK before sending each one, depending on the protocol being used.

There are two possibilities for terminating the exchange: either the secondary sends all its data, finishing with an end of transmission (EOT) frame, or the primary says "Time's up." Which of these occurs depends on the protocol and the length of the message. Once a secondary has finished transmitting, the primary can poll the remaining devices (see Figure 10.8).

10.2   FLOW CONTROL

The second aspect of data link control, following line discipline, is flow control. In most protocols flow control is a set of procedures that tell the sender how much data it can transmit before it must wait for an acknowledgment from the receiver. Two issues are at stake:

■   The flow of data must not be allowed to overwhelm the receiver. Any receiving device has a limited speed at which it can process incoming data, and a limited amount of memory, in which to store incoming data. The receiving device must be able to inform the sending device before those limits are reached and to request that the transmitting device send fewer frames or stop temporarily. Incoming data must be checked and processed before they can be used. The rate of such processing is often slower than the rate of transmission. For this reason, each receiving device has a block of memory, called a buffer, reserved for storing incoming data until they are processed. If the buffer begins to fill up, the receiver must be able to tell the sender to halt transmission until it is once again able to receive.

■   As frames come in, they are acknowledged, either frame by frame or several frames at a time. If a frame arrives damaged, the receiver sends an error message (a NAK frame).

> Flow control refers to a set of procedures used to restrict the amount of data the sender can send before waiting for acknowledgment.

Two methods have been developed to control the flow of data across communications links: stop-and-wait and sliding window (see Figure 10.9).

Stop-and-Wait

In a stop-and-wait method of flow control, the sender waits for an acknowledgment after every frame it sends (see Figure 10.10). Only when an acknowledgment has been received is the next frame sent. This process of alternately sending and waiting repeats until the sender transmits an end of transmission (EOT) frame. Stop-and-wait can be

Figure 10.9   *Categories of flow control*

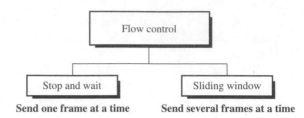

compared to a picky executive giving dictation: she says a word, her assistant says "OK," she says another word, her assistant says "OK," and so on.

In the stop-and-wait method of flow control, the sender sends one frame and waits for an acknowledgment before sending the next frame.

Figure 10.10   *Stop-and-wait*

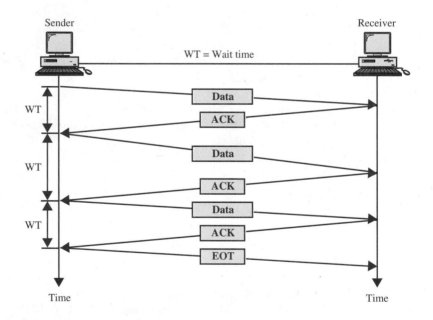

The advantage of stop-and-wait is simplicity: each frame is checked and acknowledged before the next frame is sent. The disadvantage is inefficiency: stop-and-wait is slow. Each frame must travel all the way to the receiver and an acknowledgment must travel all the way back before the next frame can be sent. In other words, each frame is alone on the line. Each frame sent and received uses the entire time needed to traverse the link. If the distance between devices is long, the time spent waiting for ACKs between each frame can add significantly to the total transmission time.

Sliding Window

In the sliding window method of flow control, the sender can transmit several frames before needing an acknowledgment. Frames can be sent one right after another, meaning that the link can carry several frames at once and its capacity can be used efficiently. The receiver acknowledges only some of the frames, using a single ACK to confirm the receipt of multiple data frames.

> In the sliding window method of flow control, several frames can be in transit at a time.

The word *window* in the term *sliding window* refers to an extra buffer, created by both the sender and the receiver. This window can hold frames at either end and provides the upper limit on the number of frames that can be transmitted before requiring an acknowledgment. Frames may be acknowledged at any point without waiting for the window to fill up and may be transmitted as long as the window is not yet full. To keep track of which frames have been transmitted and which received, sliding window introduces an identification scheme based on the size of the window. The frames are numbered modulo–n, which means they are numbered from 0 to $n-1$. For example, if $n=8$, the frames are numbered 0, 1, 2, 3, 4, 5, 6, 7, 0, 1, 2, 3, 4, 5, 6, 7, 0, 1,… The size of the window is $n-1$ (in this case, 7). In other words, the window cannot cover the whole module (8 frames); it covers one frame less. The reason for this will be discussed at the end of this section.

When the receiver sends an ACK, it includes the number of the next frame it expects to receive. In other words, to acknowledge the receipt of a string of frames ending in frame 4, the receiver sends an ACK containing the number 5. When the sender sees an ACK with the number 5, it knows that all frames up through number 4 have been received.

The window can hold $n-1$ frames at either end; therefore, a maximum of $n-1$ frames may be sent before an acknowledgment is required. Figure 10.11 shows the relationship of a window to the main buffer.

Figure 10.11 *Sliding window*

Sender Window

At the beginning of a transmission, the sender's window contains $n-1$ frames. As frames are sent out, the left boundary of the window moves inward, shrinking the size of the window. Given a window of size w, if three frames have been transmitted since the last acknowledgment, then the number of frames left in the window is $w - 3$. Once an ACK arrives, the window expands to allow in a number of new frames equal to the number of frames acknowledged by that ACK. Figure 10.12 shows a sender sliding window of size 7.

Figure 10.12   *Sender sliding window*

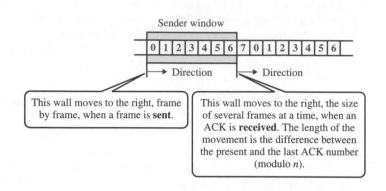

Given a window of size 7, as shown in Figure 10.12, if frames 0 through 4 have been sent and no acknowledgment has been received, the sender's window contains two frames (numbers 5 and 6). Now, if an ACK numbered 4 is received, four frames (0 through 3) are known to have arrived undamaged and the sender's window expands to include the next four frames in its buffer. At this point the sender's window contains six frames (numbers 5, 6, 7, 0, 1, 2). If the received ACK had been numbered 2, the sender's window would have expanded by only two frames, to contain a total of four.

> Conceptually, the sliding window of the sender shrinks from the left when frames of data are sent. The sliding window of the sender expands to the right when acknowledgments are received.

Receiver Window

At the beginning of transmission, the receiver window contains not $n-1$ frames but $n-1$ spaces for frames. As new frames come in, the size of the receiver window shrinks. The receiver window therefore represents not the number of frames received but the number of frames that may still be received before an ACK must be sent. Given a window of size w, if three frames are received without an acknowledgment being returned, the number of spaces in the window is $w-3$. As soon as an acknowledgment is sent, the window expands to include places for a number of frames equal to the number of frames acknowledged. Figure 10.13 shows a receiving window of size 7. In the figure, the window contains space for seven frames, meaning that seven frames may be received before an ACK must be sent. With the arrival of the first frame, the receiving window shrinks, moving the boundary from space 0 to 1. The window has shrunk by one, so the receiver may now accept six frames before it is required to send an ACK. If frames 0 through 3 have arrived but not been acknowledged, the window will contain three frame spaces.

As each ACK is sent out, the receiving window expands to include as many new placeholders as newly acknowledged frames. The window expands to include a number

Figure 10.13   *Receiver sliding window*

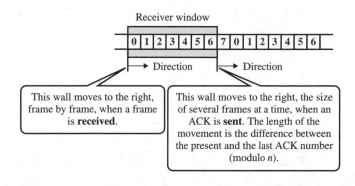

Conceptually, the sliding window of the receiver shrinks from the left when frames of data are received. The sliding window of the receiver expands to the right when acknowledgments are sent.

of new frame spaces equal to the number of the most recently acknowledged frame minus the number of the previously acknowledged frame. In a seven-frame window, if the prior ACK was for frame 2 and the current ACK is for frame 5, the window expands by three (5–2). If the prior ACK was for frame 3 and the current ACK is for frame 1, the window expands by six (1+8–3).

An Example

Figure 10.14 shows a sample transmission that uses sliding window flow control with a window of seven frames. In this example, all frames arrive undamaged. As we will see in the next section, if errors are found in received frames, or if one or more frames are lost in transit, the process will become more complex.

At the beginning of the transmission, both sender and receiver windows are fully expanded to include seven frames (seven transmittable frames in the sender window, seven placeholder frames in the receiver window). The frames within the windows are numbered 0 through 7, and are part of a larger data buffer, 13 of which are shown here.

More about Window Size

In the sliding window method of flow control, the size of the window is one less than the modulo range so that there is no ambiguity in the acknowledgment of the received frames. Assume that the frame sequence numbers are modulo 8 and the window size is also 8. Now imagine that frame 0 is sent and ACK 1 is received. The sender expands its window and sends frames 1, 2, 3, 4, 5, 6, 7, and 0. If it now receives an ACK 1 again, it is not sure if this is a duplicate of the previous ACK 1 (duplicated by the network) or a new ACK 1 confirming the most recently sent eight frames. But if the window size is 7 (instead of 8), this scenario could not happen.

Figure 10.14   *Example of sliding window*

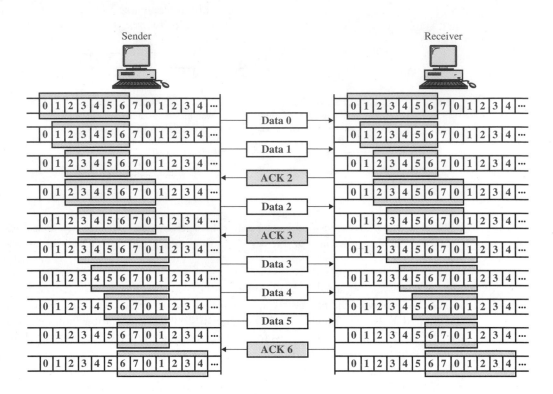

10.3   ERROR CONTROL

In the data link layer, the term *error control* refers primarily to methods of error detection and retransmission.

Automatic Repeat Request (ARQ)

Error correction in the data link layer is implemented simply: anytime an error is detected in an exchange, a negative acknowledgment (NAK) is returned and the specified frames are retransmitted. This process is called automatic repeat request (ARQ).

> Error control in the data link layer is based on automatic repeat request (ARQ), which means retransmission of data in three cases: damaged frame, lost frame, and lost acknowledgment.

It sometimes happens that a frame is so damaged by noise during transmission that the receiver does not recognize it as a frame at all. In those cases, ARQ allows us to say that the frame has been lost. A second function of ARQ is the automatic retransmission of lost frames, including lost ACK and NAK frames (where the loss is detected by the sender instead of the receiver).

ARQ error control is implemented in the data link layer as an adjunct to flow control. In fact, stop-and-wait flow control is usually implemented as stop-and-wait ARQ and sliding window is usually implemented as one of two variants of sliding window ARQ, called go-back-*n* or selective-reject (see Figure 10.15).

Figure 10.15   *Categories of error control*

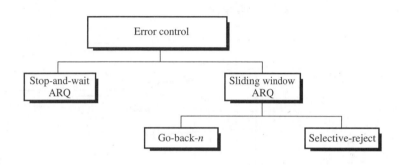

Stop-and-Wait ARQ

Stop-and-wait ARQ is a form of stop-and-wait flow control extended to include re-transmission of data in case of lost or damaged frames. For retransmission to work, four features are added to the basic flow control mechanism:

- The sending device keeps a copy of the last frame transmitted until it receives an acknowledgment for that frame. Keeping a copy allows the sender to retransmit lost or damaged frames until they are received correctly.

- For identification purposes, both data frames and ACK frames are numbered alternately 0 and 1. A data 1 frame is acknowledged by an ACK 1 frame, indicating that the receiver has gotten data 1 and is now expecting data 0. This numbering allows for identification of data frames in case of duplicate transmission (important in the case of lost acknowledgments, as we will see below).

- If an error is discovered in a data frame, indicating that it has been corrupted in transit, a NAK frame is returned. NAK frames, which are not numbered, tell the sender to retransmit the last frame sent. Stop-and-wait ARQ requires that the sender wait until it receives an acknowledgment for the last frame transmitted before it transmits the next one. When the sending device receives a NAK, it re-sends the frame transmitted after the last acknowledgment, regardless of number.

- The sending device is equipped with a timer. If an expected acknowledgment is not received within an allotted time period, the sender assumes that the last data frame was lost in transit and sends it again.

Damaged Frames

When a frame is discovered by the receiver to contain an error, it returns a NAK frame and the sender retransmits the last frame. For example, in Figure 10.16, the sender transmits a data frame: data 1. The receiver returns an ACK 1, indicating that data 1 arrived

Figure 10.16   *Stop-and-wait ARQ, damaged frame*

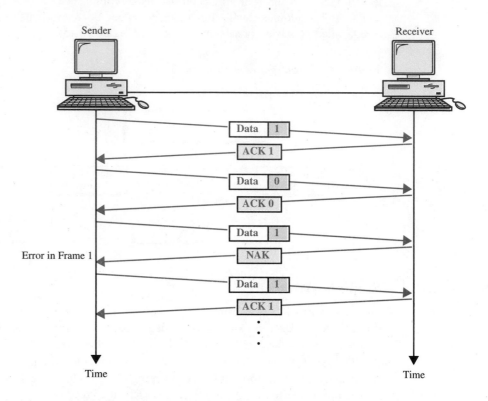

undamaged and it is now expecting data 0. The sender transmits its next frame: data 0. It arrives undamaged, and the receiver returns ACK 0. The sender transmits its next frame: data 1. The receiver discovers an error in data 1 and returns a NAK. The sender retransmits data 1. This time data 1 arrives intact, and the receiver returns ACK 1.

Lost Frame

Any of the three frame types can be lost in transit.

Lost Data Frame   Figure 10.17 shows how stop-and-wait ARQ handles the loss of a data frame. As noted above, the sender is equipped with a timer that starts every time a data frame is transmitted. If the frame never makes it to the receiver, the receiver can never acknowledge it, positively or negatively. The sending device waits for an ACK or NAK frame until its timer goes off, at which point it tries again. It retransmits the last data frame, restarts its timer, and waits for an acknowledgment.

Lost Acknowledgment   In this case, the data frame has made it to the receiver and been found to be either acceptable or not acceptable. But the ACK or NAK frame returned by the receiver is lost in transit. The sending device waits until its timer goes off, then retransmits the data frame. The receiver checks the number of the new data frame. If the lost frame was a NAK, the receiver accepts the new copy and returns the appropriate ACK (assuming the copy arrives undamaged). If the lost frame was an

Figure 10.17 *Stop-and-wait ARQ, lost data frame*

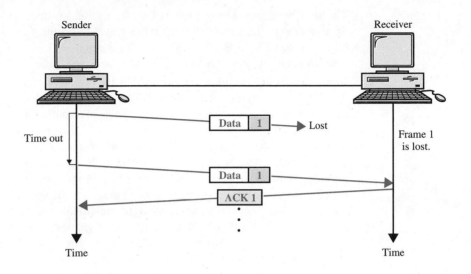

Figure 10.18 *Stop-and-wait ARQ, lost ACK frame*

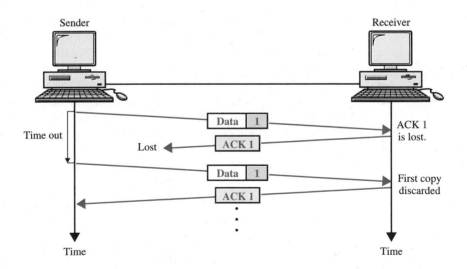

ACK, the receiver recognizes the new copy as a duplicate, acknowledges its receipt, then discards it and waits for the next frame (see Figure 10.18).

Sliding Window ARQ

Among the several popular mechanisms for continuous transmission error control, two protocols are the most popular: go-back-*n* ARQ and selective-reject ARQ, both based on sliding window flow control. To extend sliding window to cover retransmission of lost or damaged frames, three features are added to the basic flow control mechanism:

- The sending device keeps copies of all transmitted frames until they have been acknowledged. If frames 0 through 6 have been transmitted, and the last acknowledgment was for frame 2 (expecting 3), the sender keeps copies of frames 3 through 6 until it knows that they have been received undamaged.

- In addition to ACK frames, the receiver has the option of returning a NAK frame if the data have been received damaged. The NAK frame tells the sender to retransmit a damaged frame. Because sliding window is a continuous transmission mechanism (as opposed to stop-and-wait), both ACK and NAK frames must be numbered for identification. ACK frames, you will recall, carry the number of the next frame expected. NAK frames, on the other hand, carry the number of the damaged frame itself. In both cases, the message to the sender is the number of the frame that the receiver expects next. Note that data frames that are received without errors do not have to be acknowledged individually. If the last ACK was numbered 3, an ACK 6 acknowledges the receipt of frames 3 and 4 as well as frame 5. Every damaged frame, however, must be acknowledged. If data frames 4 and 5 are received damaged, both NAK 4 and NAK 5 must be returned. However, a NAK 4 tells the sender that all frames received before data 4 have arrived intact.

- Like stop-and-wait ARQ, the sending device in sliding window ARQ is equipped with a timer to enable it to handle lost acknowledgments. In sliding window ARQ, $n-1$ frames (the size of the window) may be sent before an acknowledgment must be received. If $n-1$ frames are awaiting acknowledgment, the sender starts a timer and waits before sending any more. If the allotted time has run out with no acknowledgment, the sender assumes that the frames were not received and retransmits one or all of the frames depending on the protocol. Note that as with stop-and-wait ARQ, the sender here has no way of knowing whether the lost frames are data, ACK, or NAK frames. By retransmitting the data frames two possibilities are covered: lost data and lost NAK. If the lost frame was an ACK frame, the receiver can recognize the redundancy by the number on the frame and discard the redundant data.

Go-Back-*n* ARQ

In this sliding window go-back-*n* ARQ method, if one frame is lost or damaged, all frames sent since the last frame acknowledged are retransmitted.

Damaged Frame   What if frames 0, 1, 2, and 3 have been transmitted, but the first acknowledgment received is a NAK 3? Remember that a NAK means two things: (1) a positive acknowledgment of all frames received prior to the damaged frame, and (2) a negative acknowledgment of the frame indicated. If the first acknowledgment is a NAK 3, it means that data frames 0, 1, and 2 were all received in good shape. Only frame 3 must be resent.

What if frames 0 through 4 have been transmitted before a NAK is received for frame 2? As soon as the receiver discovers an error, it stops accepting subsequent frames until the damaged frame has been replaced correctly. In the scenario above, data 2 arrives damaged and so is discarded, as are data 3 and data 4 whether or not they have arrived intact. Data 0 and data 1, which were received before the damaged frame, have already been accepted, a fact indicated to the sender by the NAK 2 frame. The retransmission therefore consists of frames 2, 3, and 4.

Figure 10.19 gives an example where six frames have been transmitted before an error is discovered in frame 3. In this case, an ACK 3 has been returned, telling the sender that frames 0, 1, and 2 have all been accepted. In the figure, the ACK 3 is sent before data 3 has arrived. Data 3 is discovered to be damaged, so a NAK 3 is sent immediately and frames 4 and 5 are discarded as they come in. The sending device retransmits all three frames (3, 4, and 5) sent since the last acknowledgment, and the process continues. The receiver continues to discard frames 4 and 5 (as well as any subsequent frames) until it receives a good data 3.

Figure 10.19 *Go-back-*n, *damaged data frame*

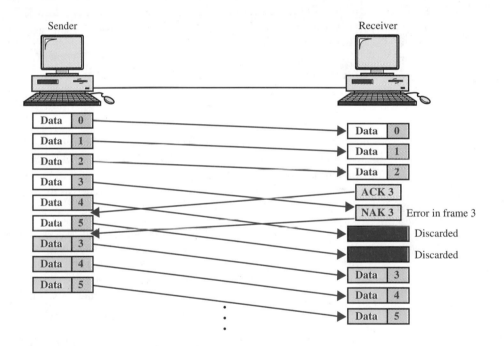

Lost Data Frame Sliding window protocols require that data frames be transmitted sequentially. If one or more frames are so noise corrupted that they become lost in transit, the next frame to arrive at the receiver will be out of sequence. The receiver checks the identifying number on each frame, discovers that one or more have been skipped, and returns a NAK for the first missing frame. A NAK frame does not indicate whether the frame has been lost or damaged, just that it needs to be resent. The sending device then retransmits the frame indicated by the NAK, as well as any frames that it had transmitted after the lost one.

In Figure 10.20, data 0 and data 1 arrive intact but data 2 is lost. The next frame to arrive at the receiver is data 3. The receiver is expecting data 2 and so considers data 3

Figure 10.20 *Go-back-*n, *lost data frame*

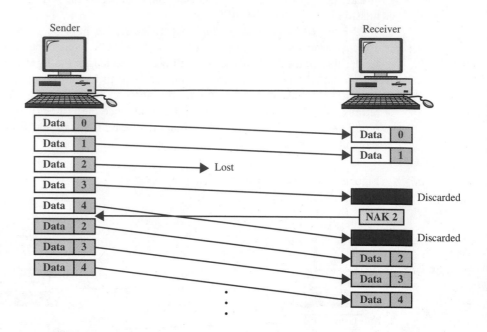

to be an error, discards it, and returns a NAK 2, indicating that 0 and 1 have been accepted but 2 is in error (in this case lost). In this example, because the sender has transmitted data 4 before receiving the NAK 2, data 4 arrives at the destination out of sequence and is therefore discarded. Once the sender receives the NAK 2, it retransmits all three pending frames (2, 3, and 4).

Lost Acknowledgment   The sender is not expecting to receive an ACK frame for every data frame it sends. It cannot use the absence of sequential ACK numbers to identify lost ACK or NAK frames. Instead, it uses a timer. The sending device can send as many frames as the window allows before waiting for an acknowledgment. Once that limit has been reached or the sender has no more frames to send, it must wait. If the ACK (or, especially, if the NAK) sent by the receiver has been lost, the sender could wait forever. To avoid tying up both devices, the sender is equipped with a timer that begins counting whenever the window capacity is reached. If an acknowledgment has not been received within the time limit, the sender retransmits every frame transmitted since the last ACK.

Figure 10.21 shows a situation in which the sender has transmitted all of its frames and is waiting for an acknowledgment that has been lost along the way. The sender waits a predetermined amount of time, then retransmits the unacknowledged frames. The receiver recognizes that the new transmission is a repeat of an earlier one, sends another ACK, and discards the redundant data.

Figure 10.21   *Go-back-*n, *lost ACK*

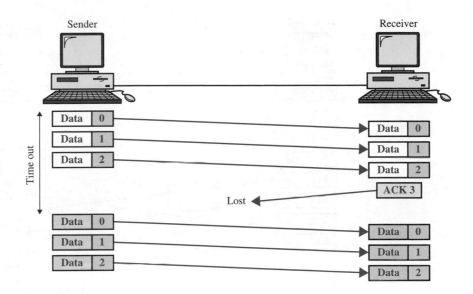

Selective-Reject ARQ

In selective-reject ARQ, only the specific damaged or lost frame is retransmitted. If a frame is corrupted in transit, a NAK is returned and the frame is resent out of sequence. The receiving device must be able to sort the frames it has and insert the corrected frame into its proper place in the sequence. To make such selectivity possible, a selective-reject ARQ system differs from a go-back-*n* ARQ system in the following ways:

- The receiving device must contain sorting logic to enable it to reorder frames received out of sequence. It must also be able to store frames received after a NAK has been sent until the damaged frame has been replaced.

- The sending device must contain a searching mechanism that allows it to find and select only the requested frame for retransmission.

- A buffer in the receiver must keep all previously received frames on hold until all retransmissions have been sorted and any duplicate frames have been identified and discarded.

- To aid selectivity, ACK numbers, like NAK numbers, must refer to the frame received (or lost) instead of the next frame expected.

- This complexity requires a smaller window size than is needed by the go-back-*n* method if it is to work efficiently. It is recommended that the window size be less than or equal to $(n+1)/2$, where $n-1$ is the go-back-*n* window size.

Damaged Frames   Figure 10.22 shows a situation in which a frame is received in error. As you can see, frames 0 and 1 are received but not acknowledged. Data 2 arrives and is found to contain an error, so a NAK 2 is returned. Like NAK frames in go-back-*n* error correction, a NAK here acknowledges both the intact receipt of any previously unacknowledged data frames and indicates an error in the current frame. In the figure,

Figure 10.22   *Selective-reject, damaged data frame*

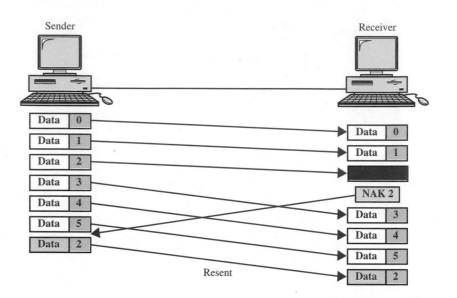

NAK 2 tells the sender that data 0 and data 1 have been accepted, but that data 2 must be resent. Unlike the receiver in a go-back-*n* system, however, the receiver in a selective-reject system continues to accept new frames while waiting for an error to be corrected. However, because an ACK implies the successful receipt not only of the specific frame indicated but of all previous frames, frames received after the error frame cannot be acknowledged until the corrected frame has been received. In the figure, the receiver accepts data 3, 4, and 5 while waiting for a new copy of data 2. When the new data 2 arrives, an ACK 5 can be returned, acknowledging the new data 2 and the original frames 3, 4, and 5. Quite a bit of logic is required by the receiver to sort out-of-sequence retransmissions and to keep track of which frames are still missing and which have yet to be acknowledged.

Lost Frames   Although frames can be accepted out of sequence, they cannot be acknowledged out of sequence. If a frame is lost, the next frame will arrive out of sequence. When the receiver tries to reorder the existing frames to include it, it will discover the discrepancy and return a NAK. Of course, the receiver will recognize the omission only if other frames follow. If the lost frame was the last of the transmission, the receiver does nothing and the sender treats the silence like a lost acknowledgment.

Lost Acknowledgment   Lost ACK and NAK frames are treated by selective-reject ARQ just as they are by go-back-*n* ARQ. When the sending device reaches either the capacity of its window or the end of its transmission, it sets a timer. If no acknowledgment arrives in the time allotted, the sender retransmits all of the frames that remain unacknowledged. In most cases, the receiver will recognize any duplications and discard them.

Comparison between Go-Back-*n* and Selective-Reject

Although retransmitting only specific damaged or lost frames may seem more efficient than resending undamaged frames as well, it is in fact less so. Because of the complexity of the sorting and storage required by the receiver, and the extra logic needed by the sender to select specific frames for retransmission, selective-reject ARQ is expensive and not often used. In other words, selective-reject gives better performance, but in practice it is usually discarded in favor of go-back-*n* for simplicity of implementation.

10.4   SUMMARY

- The second layer in the OSI model, the data link layer has three main functions: line discipline, flow control, and error control.
- Line discipline establishes the status of a device (sender or receiver) on a link.
- ENQ/ACK is a line discipline method used in point-to-point connections.
- The receiving device using ENQ/ACK line discipline responds with an acknowledge (ACK) if it is ready to receive data, or a negative acknowledge (NAK) if it is not ready.
- Poll/select is a line discipline method. The primary device always initiates communication with either a poll or select (SEL) frame.
- A poll frame is sent to the secondary device by the primary to determine if the secondary has data to send. The secondary can respond by sending a NAK (no data to send) or a data frame.
- A SEL frame is sent from the primary device to the secondary device to tell the secondary to prepare to receive data. The secondary responds with an ACK or a NAK.
- Flow control is regulation of data transmission so that the receiver buffer does not become overwhelmed by data.
- There are two main methods of flow control:
  a. stop-and-wait
  b. sliding window
- In stop-and-wait flow control each frame must be acknowledged by the receiver before the next frame can be sent.
- In sliding window flow control, the sending of data is constrained by an imaginary window that expands and contracts according to the acknowledgments received by the sender. Likewise, the receiving of data is constrained by an imaginary window that expands and contracts according to the data received.
- Error control, or how to handle lost or damaged data or acknowledgments, is simply the retransmission of data.
- Retransmission of data is initiated by automatic repeat request (ARQ).
- Three types of errors require ARQ: a damaged frame, a lost frame, and a lost acknowledgment.

- The method used to handle error control depends on the method used for flow control.
- For stop-and-wait flow control, stop-and-wait ARQ is used.
- For sliding window flow control, go-back-*n* or selective-reject ARQ is used.
- In stop-and-wait ARQ the unacknowledged frame is retransmitted.
- In go-back-*n* ARQ, retransmission begins with the last unacknowledged frame even if subsequent frames have arrived correctly. Duplicate frames are discarded.
- In selective-reject ARQ, only the unacknowledged frame is retransmitted.

10.5   PRACTICE SET

Multiple Choice

1. The secondary device in a multipoint configuration sends data in response to _____.
   a. an ACK
   b. an ENQ
   c. a poll
   d. a SEL

2. In sliding window flow control, if the window size is 63, what is the range of sequence numbers?
   a. 0 to 63
   b. 0 to 64
   c. 1 to 63
   d. 1 to 64

3. In sliding window flow control, the frames to the left of the receiver window are frames _____.
   a. received but not acknowledged
   b. received and acknowledged
   c. not received
   d. not sent

4. Regulation of the rate of transmission of data frames is known as _____.
   a. line discipline
   b. flow control
   c. data rate control
   d. switch control

5. _____ decides the role (sender or receiver) of a device on a network.
   a. Line connection
   b. Link connection

   c. Line discipline

   d. Link decision

6. The retransmission of damaged or lost frames in the data link layer is known as
   _____.

   a. error control

   b. error conditioning

   c. line discipline

   d. flow control

7. When a primary device wants to send data to a secondary device, it needs to first
   send _____ frame.

   a. an ACK

   b. a poll

   c. a SEL

   d. an ENQ

8. When a secondary device is ready to send data, it must wait for _____ frame.

   a. an ACK

   b. a poll

   c. a SEL

   d. an ENQ

9. In a peer-to-peer system, when one device wants to send data to another device, it
   first sends _____ frame.

   a. an ACK

   b. a poll

   c. a SEL

   d. an ENQ

10. Flow control is needed to prevent _____.

   a. bit errors

   b. overflow of the sender buffer

   c. overflow of the receiver buffer

   d. collision between sender and receiver

11. In go-back-n ARQ, if frames 4, 5, and 6 are received successfully, the receiver may
    send an ACK _____ to the sender.

   a. 5

   b. 6

   c. 7

   d. any of the above

12. For a sliding window of buffer size n, there can be a maximum of _____ frames
    sent but unacknowledged.

   a. 0

   b. $n - 1$

  c. n

  d. $n + 1$

13. An ACK 3 in sliding window flow control (window size of 8) means that frame _____ is next expected by the receiver.

  a. 2

  b. 3

  c. 4

  d. 8

14. In stop-and-wait ARQ, if data 1 has an error, the receiver sends a _____ frame.

  a. NAK 0

  b. NAK 1

  c. NAK 2

  d. NAK

15. In _____ ARQ, when a NAK is received, all frames sent since the last frame acknowledged are retransmitted.

  a. stop-and-wait

  b. go-back-n

  c. selective-reject

  d. a and b

16. In _____ ARQ, if a NAK is received, only the specific damaged or lost frame is retransmitted.

  a. stop-and-wait

  b. go-back-n

  c. selective-reject

  d. a and b

17. ARQ stands for _____.

  a. automatic repeat quantization

  b. automatic repeat request

  c. automatic retransmission request

  d. acknowledge repeat request

Exercises

1. Why and where is flow control needed? What are some of the parameters to be considered?

2. In stop-and-wait flow control, define and discuss the handling of

  a. A damaged frame.

  b. A lost frame.

3. In stop-and-wait ARQ, what happens if a NAK is lost in transit? Why is there no need for NAKs to be numbered?

4. Which sliding window ARQ is more popular? Why?

5. When are frames discarded in the three ARQ methods?

6. Draw the sender and receiver windows for a system using go-back-*n* ARQ given the following:

    a. Frame 0 is sent; frame 0 is acknowledged.

    b. Frames 1 and 2 are sent; frames 1 and 2 are acknowledged.

    c. Frames 3, 4, and 5 are sent; NAK 4 is received.

    d. Frames 4, 5, 6, and 7 are sent; frames 4 through 7 are acknowledged.

7. Repeat problem 6 using selective-reject ARQ.

8. What can the receiver send in response to each of the following?

    a. a poll

    b. a select

9. What does the number on a NAK frame mean for:

    a. Stop-and-wait ARQ?

    b. Go-back-*n* ARQ?

    c. Selective-reject ARQ?

10. What does the number on an ACK frame mean for:

    a. Stop-and-wait ARQ?

    b. Go-back-*n* ARQ?

    c. Selective-reject ARQ?

11. ACK 7 has been received by the sender in a sliding window system. Now frames 7, 0, 1, 2, and 3 are sent. For each of the following separate scenarios, discuss the significance of the receiving of:

    a. An ACK 1.

    b. An ACK 4.

    c. An ACK 3.

    d. A NAK 1.

    e. A NAK 3.

    f. A NAK 7.

CHAPTER 11

DATA LINK PROTOCOLS

In general, the word *protocol* refers to a set of rules or conventions for executing a particular task. In data communications, *protocol* is used in a narrower sense to mean the set of rules or specifications used to implement one or more layers of the OSI model. We have already encountered the EIA 232-D interface, which is a protocol used at the physical layer in the OSI model.

A protocol in data communications is the set of rules, or specifications used to implement one or more layers of the OSI model.

Data link protocols are sets of specifications used to implement the data link layer. To this end, they contain rules for line discipline, flow control, and error handling, among others.

A data link protocol is a set of specifications used to implement the data link layer.

Data link protocols can be divided into two subgroups: asynchronous protocols and synchronous protocols (see Figure 11.1). Asynchronous protocols treat each character in a bit stream independently. Synchronous protocols take the whole bit stream and chop it into characters of equal size.

Figure 11.1 *Data link protocol categories*

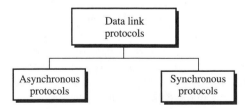

11.1   ASYNCHRONOUS PROTOCOLS

A number of asynchronous data link protocols have been developed over the last several decades, some of which are shown in Figure 11.2. Today, these protocols are employed mainly in modems. Due to its inherent slowness (stemming from the required additions of start and stop bits and extended spaces between frames), asynchronous transmission at this level is being replaced by higher-speed synchronous mechanisms.

Figure 11.2   *Asynchronous protocols*

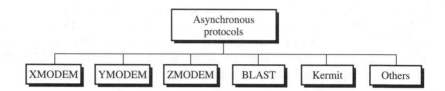

Asynchronous protocols are not complex and are inexpensive to implement. As discussed in Chapter 6, in asynchronous transmission a data unit is transmitted with no timing coordination between sender and receiver. A receiver does not need to know exactly when a data unit is sent; it only needs to recognize the beginning and the end of the unit. This is accomplished by using extra bits (start and stop bits) to frame the data unit.

> Asynchronous protocols, used primarily in modems, feature start and stop bits and variable-length gaps between characters.

A variety of asynchronous data link layer protocols have been developed; we will discuss only a few of them.

XMODEM

In 1979 Ward Christiansen designed a file transfer protocol for telephone-line communication between PCs. This protocol, now known as XMODEM, is a half-duplex stop-and-wait ARQ protocol. The frame with its fields is shown in Figure 11.3.

The first field is a one-byte start of header (SOH). The second field is a two-byte header. The first header byte, sequence number, carries the frame number. The second header byte is used to check the validity of the sequence number. The fixed data field holds 128 bytes of data (binary, ASCII, Boolean, text, etc.). The last field, CRC, checks for errors in the data field only.

In this protocol, transmission begins with the sending of a NAK frame from the receiver to the sender. Each time the sender sends a frame, it must wait for an acknowledgment (ACK) before the next frame can be sent. If instead a NAK is received, the previously sent frame is sent again. A frame can also be resent if a response is not

Figure 11.3   *XMODEM frame*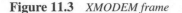

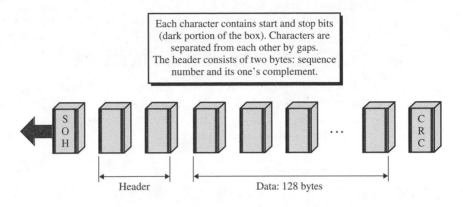

> Each character contains start and stop bits (dark portion of the box). Characters are separated from each other by gaps. The header consists of two bytes: sequence number and its one's complement.

Header

Data: 128 bytes

received by the sender after a specified amount of time. Besides a NAK or an ACK, the sender can receive a cancel signal (CAN), which aborts the transmission.

YMODEM

YMODEM is a protocol similar to XMODEM, with the following major differences:

- The data unit is 1024 bytes.
- Two CANs are sent to abort a transmission.
- ITU-T CRC-16 is used for error checking.
- Multiple files can be sent simultaneously.

ZMODEM

ZMODEM is a newer protocol combining features of both XMODEM and YMODEM.

BLAST

Blocked asynchronous transmission (BLAST) is more powerful than XMODEM. It is full-duplex with sliding window flow control. It allows the transfer of data and binary files.

Kermit

Kermit, designed at Columbia University, is currently the most widely used asynchronous protocol. This file transfer protocol is similar in operation to XMODEM, with the sender waiting for a NAK before it starts transmission. Kermit allows the transmission of control characters as text using two steps. First, the control character, which is used as text, is transformed to a printable character by adding a fixed number to its ASCII code representation. Second, the # character is added to the front of the transformed character. In this way, a control character used as text is sent as two characters. When the receiver encounters a # character, it knows that this must be dropped and that the next character is a control character. If the sender wants to send a # character, it will send two of them.

11.2   SYNCHRONOUS PROTOCOLS

The speed of synchronous transmission makes it the better choice, over asynchronous transmission, for both LAN, MAN, and WAN technology. Protocols governing synchronous transmission can be divided into two classes: character-oriented protocols and bit-oriented protocols (see Figure 11.4).

Figure 11.4   *Synchronous protocols*

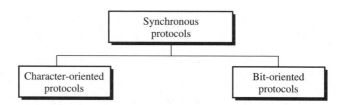

Character-oriented protocols (also called byte-oriented protocols) interpret a transmission frame or packet as a succession of characters, each usually composed of one byte (eight bits). All control information is in the form of an existing character encoding system (e.g., ASCII characters).

Bit-oriented protocols interpret a transmission frame or packet as a succession of individual bits, made meaningful by their placement in the frame and by their juxtaposition with other bits. Control information in a bit-oriented protocol can be one or multiple bits depending on the information embodied in the pattern.

> In a character-oriented protocol the frame or packet is interpreted as a series of characters. In a bit-oriented protocol the frame or packet is interpreted as a series of bits.

11.3   CHARACTER-ORIENTED PROTOCOLS

For reasons we will examine later in this section, character-oriented protocols are not as efficient as bit-oriented protocols and therefore are now seldom used. They are, however, easy to comprehend and employ the same logic and organization as the bit-oriented protocols. An understanding of character-oriented protocols provides an essential foundation for an examination of bit-oriented protocols.

In all data link protocols, control information is inserted into the data stream either as separate control frames or as additions to existing data frames. In character-oriented protocols, this information is in the form of code words taken from existing character sets such as ASCII or EBCDIC. These multibit characters carry information about line discipline, flow control, and error control. Of the several existing character-oriented protocols, the best known is IBM's binary synchronous communication (BSC).

Binary Synchronous Communication (BSC)

Binary synchronous communication (BSC) is a popular character-oriented data link protocol developed by IBM in 1964. Usable in both point-to-point and multipoint configurations, it supports half-duplex transmission using stop-and-wait ARQ flow control and error correction. BSC does not support full-duplex transmission or sliding window protocol.

> A popular character-oriented data link protocol is binary synchronous communication (BSC), which specifies half-duplex transmission with stop-and-wait ARQ. It was developed by IBM.

Control Characters

Table 11.1 is a list of standard control characters used in a BSC frame. Note that the character ACK is not used in this protocol. Remember that BSC uses stop-and-wait ARQ; acknowledgments must be either ACK 0 or ACK 1 to specify alternating data frames.

Table 11.1 *Control characters for BSC*

Character	ASCII Code	Function
ACK 0	DLE and 0	Good even frame received or ready to receive
ACK 1	DLE and 1	Good odd frame received
DLE	DLE	Data transparency marker
ENQ	ENQ	Request for a response
EOT	EOT	Sender terminating
ETB	ETB	End of transmission block; ACK required
ETX	ETX	End of text in a message
ITB	US	End of intermediate block in a multiblock transmission
NAK	NAK	Bad frame received or nothing to send
NUL	NULL	Filler character
RVI	DLE and <	Urgent message from receiver
SOH	SOH	Header information begins
STX	STX	Text begins
SYN	SYN	Alerts receiver to incoming frame
TTD	STX and ENQ	Sender is pausing but not relinquishing the line
WACK	DLE and ;	Good frame received but not ready to receive more

ASCII Codes

The characters in Table 11.1 are represented differently in different coding systems, and not all of them are available in every system. Whatever the system, not all control characters can be represented by a single character. Often they must be represented by two or three characters. The ASCII codes are also shown in Table 11.1. For a complete list of the ASCII code, see Appendix A.

BSC Frames

The BSC protocol divides a transmission into frames. If a frame is used strictly for control purposes, it is called a control frame. Control frames are used to exchange information between communicating devices, for example, to establish the initial connection, to control the flow of the transmission, to request error corrections, and to disconnect the devices at the close of a session. If a frame contains part or all of the message data itself, it is called a data frame. Data frames are used to transmit information, but may also contain control information applicable to that information (see Figure 11.5).

Figure 11.5   *BSC frames*

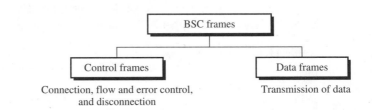

Data Frames

Figure 11.6 shows the format of a simple data frame. The arrow shows the direction of transmission. The frame begins with two or more synchronization (SYN) characters. These characters alert the receiver to the arrival of a new frame and provide a bit pattern used by the receiving device to synchronize its timing with that of the sending device. From Appendix A, you will discover that the ASCII code for SYN is 0010110. The leading (eighth) bit of the byte is usually filled out by an additional 0. Two SYN characters together look like this: 0001011000010110.

After the two synchronization characters comes a start of text (STX) character. This character signals to the receiver that the control information is ending and the next byte will be data. Data or text can consist of varying numbers of characters. An end of text (ETX) character indicates the transition between text and more control characters.

Finally, one or two characters called the block check count (BCC) are included for error detection. A BCC field can be a one-character longitudinal redundancy check (LRC) or a two-character cyclic redundancy check (CRC).

Header Fields   A frame as simple as the one described above is seldom useful. Usually we need to include the address of the receiving device, the address of the sending device, and the identifying number of the frame (0 or 1) for stop-and-wait ARQ (see Figure 11.7). This information is included in a special field called a header which begins with a start of header (SOH) character. The header comes after the SYNs and

Figure 11.6   *A simple BSC data frame*

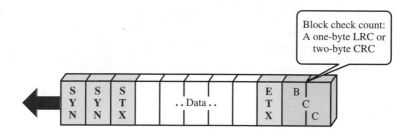

Figure 11.7   *A BSC frame with a header*

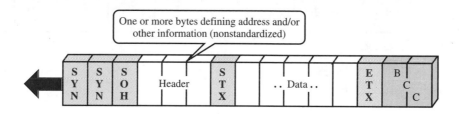

before the STX character; everything received after the SOH field but before the STX character is header information.

Multiblock Frames   The probability of an error in the block of text increases with the length of the frame. The more bits in a frame, the greater the likelihood that one of them will be corrupted in transit, and the greater the likelihood that changes in several bits will cancel each other out and make detection difficult. For this reason, text in a message is often divided between several blocks. Each block, except the last one, starts with an STX character and ends with an intermediate text block (ITB). The last block starts with an STX but ends with an ETX. Immediately after each ITB or ETX, a BCC field is sent. In that way, the receiver can check each block separately for errors, thereby increasing the likelihood of detection. If any block contains an error, however, the entire frame must be retransmitted. After the ETX has been reached and the last BCC checked, the receiver sends a single acknowledgment for the entire frame. Figure 11.8 shows the structure of a multiblock frame; the example includes two blocks, but actual frames can have more than two.

Multiframe Transmission   In the examples explored above, a single frame carries an entire message. After each frame, the message is complete and control of the line passes to the secondary device (half-duplex mode). Some messages, however, may be too long to fit into the format of a single frame. In such cases, the sender can split the message not only among blocks but among frames. Several frames can carry continuations of a single message. To let the receiver know that the end of the frame is not the end of the transmission, the ETX character in all frames but the last one is replaced by

Figure 11.8 *A multiblock frame*

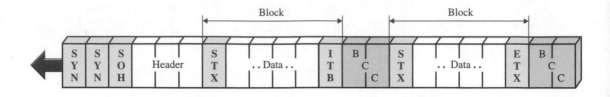

Figure 11.9 *Multiframe transmission*

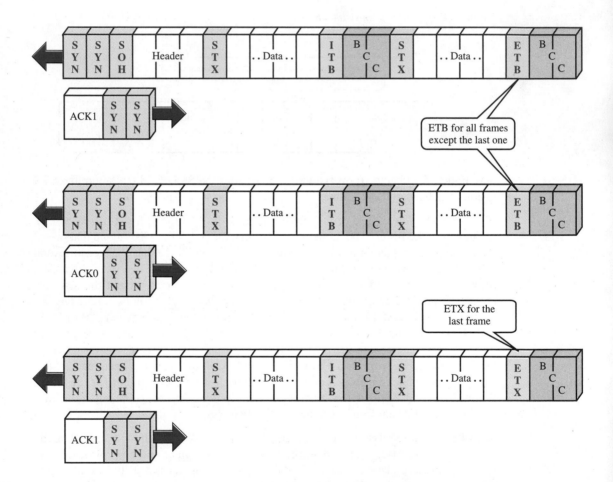

an end of transmission block (ETB). The receiver must acknowledge each frame separately but cannot take over control of the link until it sees the ETX in the last frame (see Figure 11.9).

Control Frames

A control frame should not be confused with a control character. A control frame is used by one device to send commands to, or solicit information from, another device. A control frame contains control characters but no data; it carries information specific to the functioning of the data link layer itself. Figure 11.10 shows the basic format of a BSC control frame.

Figure 11.10   *BSC control frame*

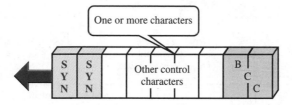

Control frames serve three purposes: establishing connections, maintaining flow and error control during data transmission, and terminating connections (see Figure 11.11).

Data Transparency

BSC was originally designed to transport only textual messages (words or figures composed of alphanumeric characters). Today, however, a user is just as likely to want to send binary sequences that contain nontextual information and commands, like programs and graphics. Unfortunately, messages of this sort can create problems for BSC transmission. If the text field of a transmission includes an eight-bit pattern that looks like a BSC control character, the receiver interprets it as one, destroying the sense of the message. For example, a receiver seeing the bit pattern 0000011 reads it as an ETX character. As we learned from the control frames above, whenever a receiver finds an ETX, it expects the next two bytes to be the BCC and begins an error check. But the pattern 0000011 here is intended as data and not as control information. Confusion between control information and data is called a lack of data transparency.

For a protocol to be useful, it must be transparent—it must be able to carry any combination of bits as data without their being confused with control information.

> Data transparency in data communication means we should be able to send any combination of bits as data.

Data transparency in BSC is achieved by a process called byte stuffing. It involves two activities: defining the transparent text region with data link escape (DLE) characters and preceding any DLE character within the transparent region by an extra DLE character.

To define the transparent region, we insert one DLE character just before the STX character at the beginning of the text field and another just before the ETX (or ITB or ETB) character at the end of the text field. The first DLE tells the receiver that the text

Figure 11.11   *Control frames*

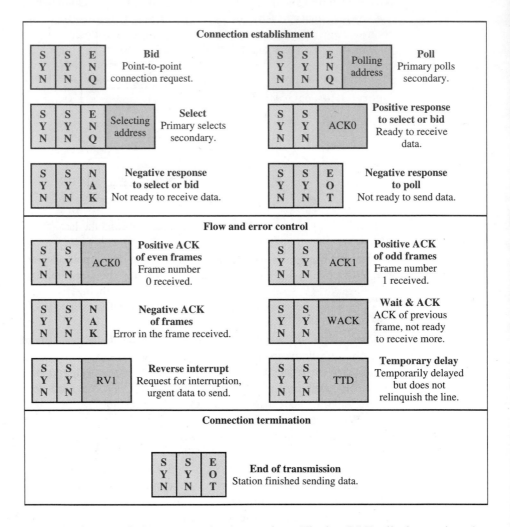

may contain control characters and to ignore them. The last DLE tells the receiver that the transparent region has ended.

Problems may still arise if the transparent region contains a DLE character as text. In that case, we insert an additional DLE just before each DLE within the text. Figure 11.12 shows an example of a transparent frame.

11.4   BIT-ORIENTED PROTOCOLS

In character-oriented protocols, bits are grouped into predefined patterns forming characters. By comparison, bit-oriented protocols can pack more information into shorter frames and avoid the transparency problems of character-oriented protocols.

Figure 11.12   *Byte stuffing*

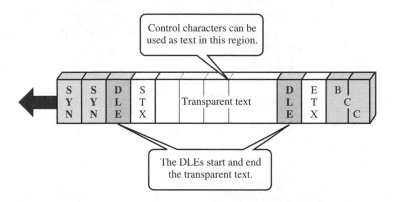

Figure 11.13   *Bit-oriented protocols*

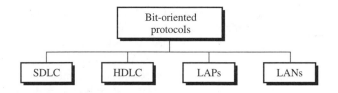

Given the advantages of bit-oriented protocols and the lack of any preexisting coding system (like ASCII) to tie them to, it is no wonder that over the last two decades many different bit-oriented protocols have been developed, all vying to become the standard (see Figure 11.13). Most of these offerings have been proprietary, designed by manufacturers to support their own products. One of them, HDLC, is the design of the ISO and has become the basis for all bit-oriented protocols in use today.

In 1975, IBM pioneered the development of bit-oriented protocols with synchronous data link control (SDLC), and lobbied the ISO to make SDLC the standard. In 1979, the ISO answered with high-level data link control (HDLC), which was based on SDLC. Adoption of HDLC by the ISO committees led to its adoption and extension by other organizations. The ITU-T was one of the first organizations to embrace HDLC. Since 1981, ITU-T has developed a series of protocols called link access protocols (LAPs: LAPB, LAPD, LAPM, LAPX, etc.), all based on HDLC. Other protocols (such as frame relay, PPP, etc.) developed by both ITU-T and ANSI also derive from HDLC, as do most LANs' access control protocols. In short, all bit-oriented protocols in use today either derive from or are sources for HDLC. Through HDLC, therefore, we have a basis for understanding the others.

All bit-oriented protocols are related to high-level data link control (HDLC), a bit-oriented protocol published by ISO. HDLC supports both half-duplex and full-duplex modes in point-to-point and multipoint configurations.

HDLC

HDLC is a bit-oriented data link protocol designed to support both half-duplex and full-duplex communication over point-to-point and multipoint links. Systems using HDLC can be characterized by their station types, their configurations, and their response modes.

Station Types

HDLC differentiates between three different types of stations: primary, secondary, and combined.

A primary station in HDLC functions in the same way as the primary devices in the discussions of flow control in Chapter 10. The primary is the device in either a point-to-point or multipoint line configuration that has complete control of the link. The primary sends commands to the secondaries. A primary issues commands, a secondary issues responses. An example of the relation of a primary to a secondary is that of computer to terminal.

A combined station can both command and respond. A combined station is one of a set of connected peer devices programmed to behave either as a primary or as a secondary depending on the nature and direction of the transmission.

> Stations in HDLC are of three types: primary, secondary, and combined. A primary station sends commands. A secondary station sends responses. A combined station sends commands and responses.

Configurations

The word *configuration* refers to the relationship of hardware devices on a link. Devices may be organized as primary and secondary or as peers. Peer devices must be able to act as both primary or secondary, depending on the mode selected for the exchange (see the section Modes of Communication. Primary, secondary, and combined stations can be configured in three ways: unbalanced, symmetrical, and balanced (see Figure 11.14). Any of these configurations can support both half-duplex and full-duplex transmission.

An unbalanced configuration (also called a master/slave configuration) is one in which one device is primary and the others are secondary. Unbalanced configurations can be point-to-point if only two devices are involved; more often they are multipoint, with one computer controlling several peripherals. An example of an unbalanced configuration is a computer and one or more terminals.

A symmetrical configuration is one in which each physical station on a link consists of two logical stations, one a primary and the other a secondary. Separate lines link the primary aspect of one physical station to the secondary aspect of another physical station. A symmetrical configuration behaves like an unbalanced configuration except that control of the link can shift between the two stations.

A balanced configuration is one in which both stations in a point-to-point topology are of the combined type. The stations are linked by a single line that can be controlled by either station.

Figure 11.14 *HDLC configurations*

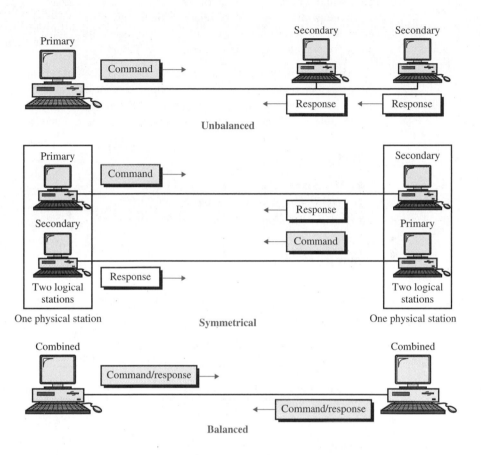

HDLC does not support balanced multipoint. This necessitated the invention of media access protocols for LANs.

Modes of Communication

A mode in HDLC is the relationship between two devices involved in an exchange; the mode describes who controls the link. Exchanges over unbalanced configurations are always conducted in normal response mode. Exchanges over symmetrical or balanced configurations can be set to a specific mode using a frame designed to deliver the command (discussed in the section on U-frames). HDLC supports three modes of communication between stations: normal response mode (NRM), asynchronous response mode (ARM), and asynchronous balanced mode (ABM).

NRM Normal response mode (NRM) refers to the standard primary–secondary relationship. In this mode, a secondary device must have permission from the primary device before transmitting. Once permission has been granted, the secondary may initiate a response transmission of one or more frames containing data.

ARM   In asynchronous response mode (ARM), a secondary may initiate a transmission without permission from the primary whenever the channel is idle. ARM does not alter the primary–secondary relationship in any other way. All transmissions from a secondary (even to another secondary on the same link) must still be made to the primary for relay to a final destination.

ABM   In asynchronous balanced mode (ABM), all stations are equal and therefore only combined stations connected in point-to-point are used. Either combined station may initiate transmission with the other combined station without permission.

Figure 11.15 shows the relationships between these modes and station types.

Modes:

■   Normal response mode (NRM)
■   Asynchronous response mode (ARM)
■   Asynchronous balanced mode (ABM)

Figure 11.15   *HDLC modes*

	NRM	ARM	ABM
Station type	Primary & secondary	Primary & secondary	Combined
Initiator	Primary	Either	Any

Frames

To provide the flexibility necessary to support all of the options possible in the modes and configurations described above, HDLC defines three types of frames: information frames (*I-frames*), supervisory frames (*S-frames*), and unnumbered frames (*U-frames*); see Figure 11.16. Each type of frame works as an envelope for the transmission of a different type of message. I-frames are used to transport user data and control information relating to user data. S-frames are used only to transport control information, primarily data link layer flow and error controls. U-frames are reserved for system management. Information carried by U-frames is intended for managing the link itself.

Each frame in HDLC may contain up to six fields: a beginning flag field, an address field, a control field, an information field, a frame check sequence (FCS) field, and an ending flag field. In multiple frame transmissions, the ending flag of one frame can double as the beginning flag of the next frame.

Flag Field

The flag field of an HDLC frame is an eight-bit sequence with a bit pattern 01111110 that identifies both the beginning and end of a frame and serves as a synchronization

Figure 11.16 *HDLC frame types*

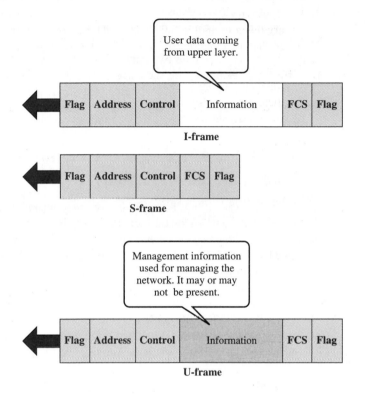

I-frame

S-frame

U-frame

Figure 11.17 *HDLC flag field*

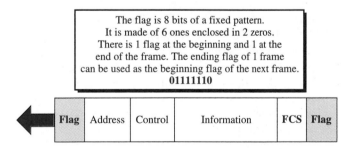

pattern for the receiver. Figure 11.17 shows the placement of the two flag fields in an I-frame.

The flag field is the closest that HDLC comes to a control character that might be misread by a receiver. The flag field is also, therefore, HDLC's only potential cause of transparency problems. Once a station finds a flag on the line, determines that the frame is addressed to it, and begins reading the transmission, it is watching for the next flag that signifies the end of the frame. It is always possible that a bit sequence, whether control information or data, might contain the pattern 01111110. If that were to happen in the data, for example, the receiver would find it and assume that the end of the frame had been reached (with disastrous results).

To guarantee that a flag does not appear inadvertently anywhere else in the frame, HDLC uses a process called bit stuffing. Every time a sender wants to transmit a bit sequence having more than five consecutive 1s, it inserts (stuffs) one redundant 0 after the fifth 1. For example, the sequence 011111111000 becomes 0111110111000. This extra 0 is inserted regardless of whether the sixth bit is another 1 or not. Its presence tells the receiver that the current sequence is not a flag. Once the receiver has seen the stuffed 0, it is dropped from the data and the original bit stream is restored.

> Bit stuffing is the process of adding one extra 0 whenever there are five consecutive 1s in the data so that the receiver does not mistake the data for a flag.

With three exceptions, bit stuffing is required whenever five 1s occur consecutively. The exceptions are when the bit sequence really is a flag, when the transmission is being aborted, when the channel is being put into idle. The flowchart in Figure 11.18 shows the process the receiver follows to identify and discard a stuffed bit. As the receiver reads the incoming bits, it counts 1s. When it finds five consecutive 1s after a 0, it checks the next (seventh) bit. If the seventh bit is a 0, the receiver recognizes it as a stuffed bit, discards it, and resets its counter. If the seventh bit is a 1, the receiver checks the eighth bit. If the eighth bit is a 0, the sequence is recognized as a flag and treated accordingly. If the eighth bit is another 1, the receiver continues counting. A total of 7 to 14 consecutive 1s indicates an abort. A total of 15 or more 1s indicates an idle channel.

Address Field

The second field of an HDLC frame contains the address of the secondary station that is either the originator or destination of the frame (or the station acting as secondary in the case of combined stations). If a primary station creates a frame, it contains a *to* address. If a secondary creates the frame, it contains a *from* address. An address field can be one byte or several bytes long, depending on the needs of the network. One byte can identify up to 128 stations (because one bit is used for another purpose). Larger networks require multiple-byte address fields. Figure 11.19 shows the address field in relation to the rest of the frame.

If the address field is only one byte, the last bit is always a 1. If the address is more than one byte, all bytes but the last one will end with 0; only the last will end with 1. Ending each intermediate byte with 0 indicates to the receiver that there are more address bytes to come.

Control Field

The control field is a one- or two-byte segment of the frame used for flow management. We will limit our discussion to the one-byte case. The two-byte case is similar.

Control fields differ depending on frame type. If the first bit of the control field is 0, the frame is an I-frame. If the first bit is a 1 and the second bit is 0, it is an S-frame. If both the first and second bits are 1s, it is a U-frame. The control fields of all three types of frames contain a bit called the poll/final (P/F) bit (discussed below).

Figure 11.18   *Bit stuffing in HDLC*

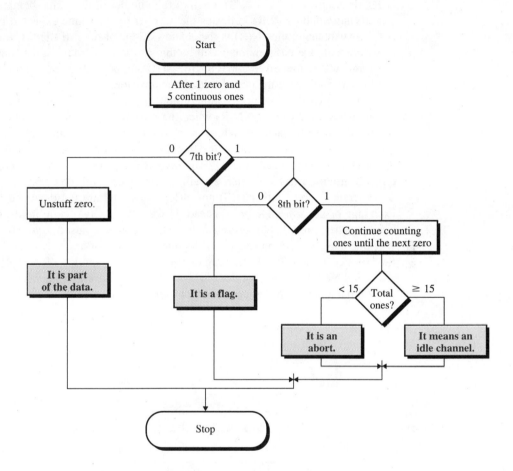

Figure 11.19   *HDLC address field*

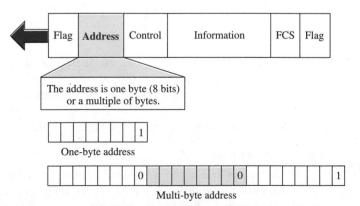

An I-frame contains two 3-bit flow and error control sequences, called N(S) and N(R), flanking the P/F bit. N(S) specifies the number of the frame being sent (its own identifying number). N(R) indicates the number of the frame expected in return in a two-way exchange; thus N(R) is the acknowledgment field. If the last frame received was error-free, the N(R) number will be that of the next frame in the sequence. If the last frame was not received correctly, the N(R) number will be the number of the damaged frame, indicating the need for its retransmission.

The control field of an S-frame contains an N(R) field but not an N(S) field. S-frames are used to return N(R) when the receiver does not have data of its own to send. Otherwise the acknowledgment is contained in the control field of an I-frame (above). S-frames do not transmit data and so do not require N(S) fields to identify them. The two bits preceding the P/F bit in an S-frame are used to carry coded flow and error control information, which we will discuss later in this chapter.

U-frames have neither N(S) nor N(R) fields, and are not designed for user data exchange or acknowledgment. Instead, U-frames have two code fields, one two bits and the other three, flanking the P/F bit. These codes are used to identify the type of U-frame and its function (e.g., establishing the mode of an exchange). If the control field of a U-frame is two bytes long instead of one, the modes NRM, ARM, and ABM are called NRME, ARME, and ABME, the *E* standing for *extended.* The control fields of all three types of frames are shown in Figure 11.20.

Figure 11.20   *HDLC control field*

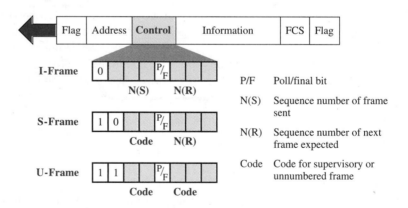

The P/F field is a single bit with a dual purpose. It has meaning only when it is set (bit = 1) and can mean poll or final. It means poll when the frame is sent by a primary station to a secondary (when the address field contains the address of the receiver). It means final when the frame is sent by a secondary to a primary (when the address field contains the address of the sender); see Figure 11.21.

Information Field

The information field contains the user's data in an I-frame, and network management information in a U-frame (see Figure 11.22). Its length can vary from one network to another but is always fixed within each network. An S-frame has no information field.

Figure 11.21   *Use of P/F bit*

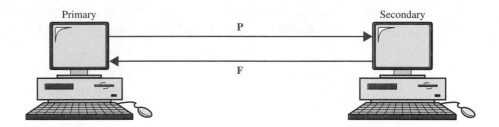

Figure 11.22   *Information field in HDLC*

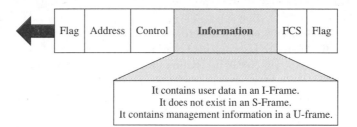

As we have seen in several cases above, it is often possible to include flow, error, and other control information in an I-frame that also contains data. For example, in a two-way exchange of data (either half- or full-duplex), station 2 can acknowledge receipt of data from station 1 in the control field of its own data frame rather than sending a separate frame just for the acknowledgment. Combining data to be sent with control information this way is called piggybacking.

> Piggybacking means combining data to be sent and acknowledgment of the frame received in one single frame.

FCS Field

The frame check sequence (FCS) is HDLC's error detection field. It can contain either a two- or four-byte CRC (see Figure 11.23).

More about Frames

Of the three frames used by HDLC, the I-frame is the most straightforward. I-frames are designed for user information transport and piggybacked acknowledgments and nothing else. For this reason the range of variation in I-frames is small—all differences relate either to the data (content and CRC), to the identifying number of the frame, or to the acknowledgment of received frames (ACK or NAK).

S-frames and U-frames, however, contain subfields within their control fields. As we saw in our discussion of control fields, these subfields carry codes that alter the

Figure 11.23   *Frame check sequence (FCS) field in HDLC*

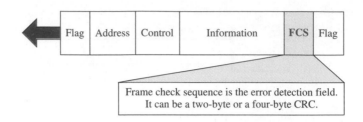

| Flag | Address | Control | Information | FCS | Flag |

Frame check sequence is the error detection field.
It can be a two-byte or a four-byte CRC.

meaning of the frame. For example, an S-frame coded for selective-reject (SREJ) cannot be used in the same context as an S-frame coded for receive ready (RR). In this section, we will examine the different types of and uses for S- and U-frames.

S-frames

Supervisory frames are used for acknowledgment, flow control, and error control whenever piggybacking that information onto an I-frame is either impossible or inappropriate (when the station either has no data of its own to send, or needs to send a command or response other than an acknowledgment). S-frames do not have information fields, yet each one carries messages to the receiving station. These messages are based on the type of the S-frame and the context of the transmission. The type of each S-frame is determined by a two-bit code set into its control field just before the P/F bit. There are four types of S-frames: receive ready (RR), receive not ready (RNR), reject (REJ), and selective-reject (SREJ); see Figure 11.24.

Figure 11.24   *S-frame control field in HDLC*

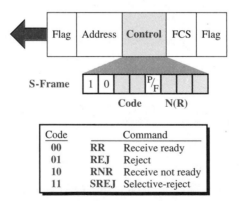

| Flag | Address | **Control** | FCS | Flag |

S-Frame | 1 | 0 | | | P/F | | | |

Code   N(R)

Code	Command	
00	RR	Receive ready
01	REJ	Reject
10	RNR	Receive not ready
11	SREJ	Selective-reject

Receive Ready   An S-frame containing the code for RR (00) can be used in four possible ways, each having a different significance.

- **ACK.** RR is used by a receiving station to return a positive acknowledgment of a received I-frame when the receiver has no data of its own to send (no I-frame on which to piggyback the acknowledgment). In this case, the N(R) field of the control frame contains the sequence number of the next frame expected by the receiver. An N(R) field can have from one to three bits. Three bits allow an S-frame to acknowledge up to eight frames.
- **Poll.** When transmitted by the primary (or acting primary in a combined station) with the P/F bit (now functioning as the P bit) set, RR asks the secondary if it has anything to send.
- **Negative response to poll.** When sent by a secondary with the P/F bit (now functioning as the F bit) set, RR tells the primary that the secondary has nothing to send. If the secondary does have data to transmit, it responds to the poll with an I-frame, not an S-frame.
- **Positive response to select.** When a secondary is able to receive a transmission from the primary, it returns an RR frame with the P/F (used as F) bit set to 1. (For a description of selection, see RNR, below.)

Receive Not Ready   RNR frames can be used in three different ways:
- **ACK.** RNR returned by a receiver to a sending station acknowledges receipt of all frames up to, but not including, the one indicated in the N(R) field but requests that no more frames be sent until an RR frame is issued.
- **Select.** When a primary wishes to transmit data to a specific secondary, it alerts the secondary by sending an RNR frame with the P/F (used as P) bit set. The RNR code tells the secondary not to send data of its own, that the frame is a select and not a poll.
- **Negative response to select.** When a selected secondary is unable to receive data, it returns an RNR frame with the P/F (used as F) bit set.

Reject   A third type of S-frame is reject (REJ). REJ is the negative acknowledgment returned by a receiver in a go-back-*n* ARQ error correction system when the receiver has no data on which to piggyback the response. In an REJ frame, the N(R) field contains the number of the damaged frame to indicate that the frame and all that follow it need to be retransmitted.

Selective Reject   A selective-reject (SREJ) frame is a negative acknowledgment in a selective-reject ARQ system. It is sent by the receiver to the sender to indicate that a specific frame (the number in the N(R) field) has been received damaged and must be resent.

Figure 11.25 shows the use of the P/F bit in polling and selecting.

U-frames

Unnumbered frames are used to exchange session management and control information between connected devices. Unlike S-frames, U-frames contain an information field, but one used for system management information not user data. As with S-frames, however, much of the information carried by U-frames is contained in codes included in the control field. U-frame codes are divided into two sections, a two-bit prefix before the P/F bit and a three-bit suffix after the P/F bit. Together, these two segments (five

Figure 11.25 *Use of P/F bit in polling and selecting*

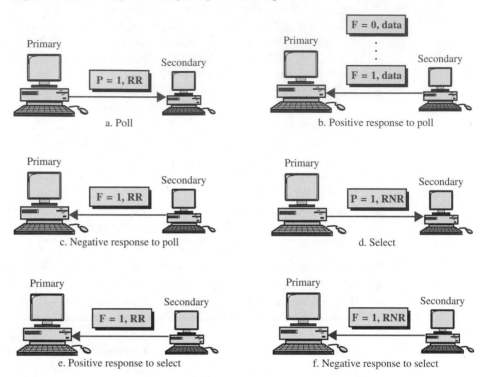

a. Poll

b. Positive response to poll

c. Negative response to poll

d. Select

e. Positive response to select

f. Negative response to select

bits) can be used to create up to 32 different types of U-frames. Some of the more common combinations are shown in Figure 11.26.

The U-frame commands and responses listed in Table 11.2 can be divided into five basic functional categories: mode setting, unnumbered-exchange, disconnection, initialization, and miscellaneous.

Mode Setting   Mode-setting commands are sent by the primary station, or by a combined station wishing to control an exchange, to establish the mode of the session. A mode-setting U-frame tells the receiving station what format the transmission will take. For example, if a combined station wishes to establish a temporary primary-to-secondary relationship with another station, it sends a U-frame containing the code 00 001 (for set normal response mode). The addressed station understands that it is being selected to receive a transmission (as if from a primary) and adjusts itself accordingly (see Table 11.2).

Unnumbered-Exchange   Unnumbered-exchange codes are used to send or solicit specific pieces of data link information between devices. The unnumbered poll (UP) code (00 100) is transmitted by the primary station on a link (or the combined station acting as a primary) to establish the send/receive status of the addressed station in an unnumbered exchange. The unnumbered information (UI) code (00 000) is used for the transmission of specific pieces of information such as time/date for synchronization. UI frames can be sent either as commands (e.g., a list of parameters for the coming

Figure 11.26 *U-frame control field in HDLC*

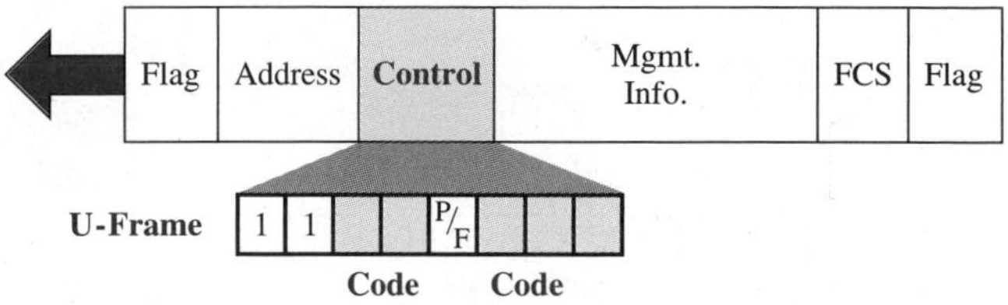

Code		Command	Response
00	001	SNRM	
11	011	SNRME	
11	000	SARM	DM
11	010	SARME	
11	100	SABM	
11	110	SABME	
00	000	UI	UI
00	110		UA
00	010	DISC	RD
10	000	SIM	RIM
00	100	UP	
11	001	RSET	
11	101	XID	XID
10	001		FRMR

Table 11.2 *U-frame control command and response*

Command/ response	Meaning
SNRM	Set normal response mode
SNRME	Set normal response mode (extended)
SARM	Set asynchronous response mode
SARME	Set asynchronous response mode (extended)
SABM	Set asynchronous balanced mode
SABME	Set asynchronous balanced mode (extended)
UP	Unnumbered poll
UI	Unnumbered information
UA	Unnumbered acknowledgment
RD	Request disconnect
DISC	Disconnect
DM	Disconnect mode
RIM	Request information mode
SIM	Set initialization mode
RSET	Reset
	(continued)

Table 11.2   *U-frame control command and response   (Concluded)*

Command/response	Meaning
XID	Exchange ID
FRMR	Frame reject

transmission) or as responses (e.g., a description of the capzabilities of the addressed station to receive data). The unnumbered acknowledgment (UA) code (00 110) is returned by the addressed station in answer to an unnumbered poll, to acknowledge one of the unnumbered request frames (e.g., RD: request disconnect), or to accept a set-mode command (see Table 11.2).

Disconnection   There are three disconnect codes, one a command from the acting primary or combined station, the other two responses from the receiving station. The first of these, disconnect (DISC, 00 010), is sent by the first station to the second to terminate the connection. The second, request disconnect (RD, 00 010), is a request by the second station to the first that a DISC be issued. The third, disconnect mode (DM, 11 000), is transmitted by the addressed station to the initiating station as a negative response to a mode setting command (see Table 11.2).

Initialization Mode   The code 10 000, used as a command (first system to second system), means set initialization mode (SIM). SIM prepares the addressed station to initialize its data link control functions. The SIM command is then followed by UI frames containing, for example, a new program or a new parameter set. The same code, 10 000, used as a response (second system to first system), means request initialization mode (RIM) and solicits a SIM command from the first station. It is used to respond to a mode setting command when the second station cannot act upon the command without first receiving a SIM (see Table 11.2).

Miscellaneous   Of the final three commands, the first two—reset (RSET, 11 001) and exchange ID (XID, 11 101)—are commands from the initiating system to the addressed system. The third, frame reject (FRMR, 10 001) is a response sent from the addressed system to the initiating system.

RSET tells the second station the first station is resetting its send sequence numbering and instructs the second system to do likewise. It is usually issued in response to an FRMR.

XID requests an exchange of identifying data from the second station (What is your address?).

FRMR tells the first system that a U-frame received by the second system contains a syntax error (This doesn't look like an HDLC frame!). It is returned by the addressed system when, for example, a frame is identified as an S-frame but contains an information field (see Table 11.2).

Example 1: Poll/Response

In Figure 11.27, the primary device (the mainframe) on a multipoint link polls the secondary device (A), with an S-frame containing the codes for poll. The flag field is first, followed by the address of the secondary being polled, in this case A. The third field,

Figure 11.27   *Example of polling using HDLC*

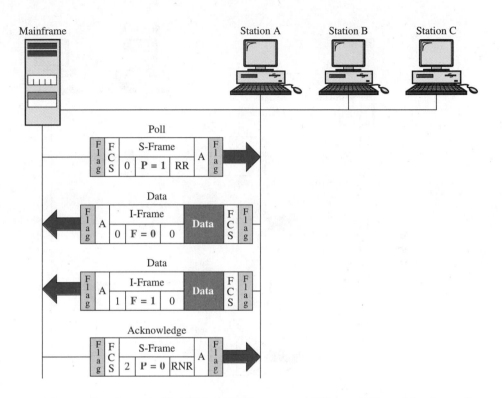

control, contains the code identifying the frame as an S-frame followed by the codes indicating the RR (receive ready) status of the sender, the P/F bit set to poll, and an N(R) = 0 field. After the control field, comes the error detection code (FCS) and the ending flag field.

Station A has data to send, so it responds with two I-frames numbered 0 and 1. The second of these has the P/F bit set for *final* to indicate the end of the data. The primary acknowledges both frames at once with an S-frame containing the number 2 in its N(R) field to tell station A that frames 0 and 1 have been received, and that if A sends additional frames, the primary expects number 2 to arrive next.

Example 2: Select/Response

This example uses the same multipoint configuration to show a primary device selecting a secondary device, station B, to receive a transmission (see Figure 11.28).

First, the primary sends out an S-frame addressed to station B that contains the codes for select. The select frame is identical to the poll frame in the previous example, except that the RR status in the control field has been changed to RNR, telling the secondary to be ready but not to send. Station B responds with another S-frame, addressed from B, that contains the code for RR as well as the final bit set, to indicate that the station is ready to receive and that this frame is the last.

Figure 11.28 *Example of selecting using HDLC*

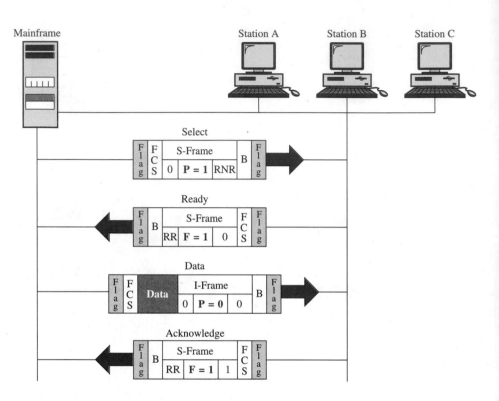

The primary sends an I-frame containing its data. The frame is addressed to B, the N(S) field identifies it as frame number 0, the P bit is not set to indicate that the frame is not a poll, and the N(R) field indicates that if an I-frame is returned, it is expected also to be number 0. Station B responds with an RR frame with a dual purpose: the set final bit tells the primary that B does not have anything to send, and the 1 in the N(R) field acknowledges the receipt of frame 0 and indicates that B next expects to receive frame 1.

Example 3: Peer Devices

The example in Figure 11.29 shows an exchange in asynchronous balanced mode (ABM) using piggybacked acknowledgments. The two stations are of equal status and are connected by a point-to-point link.

Station A issues a U-frame containing the code for SABM to establish a link in asynchronous balanced mode. The P bit is set to indicate that station A expects to control the session and to transmit first. Station B accepts the request by returning a U-frame containing the code for UA, with the F bit set. By agreeing to transmit in asynchronous balanced mode, both stations are now of combined type, rather than primary-secondary, so the P/F bit is no longer valid and can be ignored in the frames that follow.

Station A begins the exchange of information with an I-frame numbered 0 followed by another I-frame numbered 1. Station B piggybacks its acknowledgment of

Figure 11.29 *Example of peer-to-peer communication using HDLC*

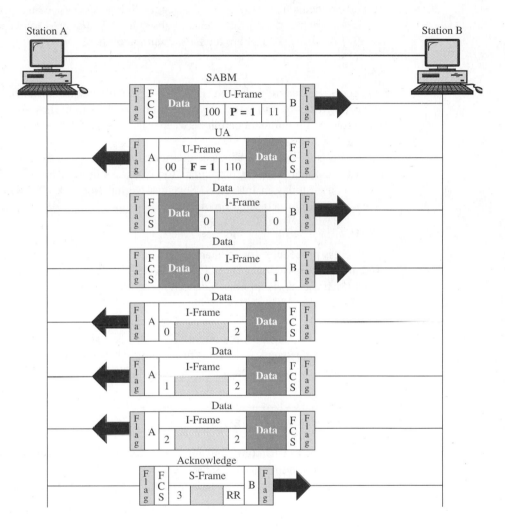

both frames onto an I-frame of its own. Station B's first I-frame is also numbered 0 (N(S) field) and contains a 2 in its N(R) field, acknowledging the receipt of A's frames 1 and 0 and indicating that it expects frame 2 to arrive next. Station B transmits its second and third I-frames (numbers 1 and 2) before accepting further frames from station A. Its N(R) information, therefore, has not changed: B frames 1 and 2 indicate that station B is still expecting A frame 2 to arrive next.

Station A has sent all of its data. Therefore, it cannot piggyback an acknowledgment onto an I-frame and sends an S-frame instead. The RR code indicates that A is still ready to receive. The number 3 in the N(R) field tells B that frames 0, 1, and 2 have all been accepted and that A is now expecting frame number 3.

Link Access Procedures

Several protocols under the general category link access procedure (LAP) have been developed. Each of these protocols is a subset of HDLC tailored for a specific purpose. LAPB, LAPD, and LAPM are the most common of these.

LAPB

Link access procedure, balanced (LAPB) is a simplified subset of HDLC used only for connecting a station to a network. It therefore provides only those basic control functions required for communication between a DTE and a DCE (e.g., it does not include poll and select characters).

LAPB is used only in balanced configurations of two devices, where both devices are of the combined type. Communication is always in asynchronous balanced mode. LAPB is used today in Integrated Services Digital Network (ISDN) on B channels. (See Chapter 15 for a discussion of ISDN.)

LAPD

Link access procedure, for D channel (LAPD) is another simplified subset of HDLC used in Integrated Services Digital Network (ISDN). It is used for out-of-band (control) signaling. It uses asynchronous balanced mode (ABM).

LAPM

Link access procedure, for modems (LAPM) is a simplified subset of HDLC for modems. It is designed to do asynchronous-synchronous conversion, error detection, and retransmission. It has been developed to apply HDLC features to modems.

11.5   SUMMARY

- A protocol in data communication is a group of specifications used to implement one or more layers of the OSI model.
- Data link protocols can be classified as synchronous or asynchronous.
- Asynchronous protocols such as XMODEM, YMODEM, ZMODEM, BLAST, and Kermit are used in file transfer.
- Synchronous protocols can be classified into two groups:
  a. Character-oriented protocols.
  b. Bit-oriented protocols.
- In character-oriented protocols, the frame is interpreted as a series of characters.
- In bit-oriented protocols, each bit or group of bits can have meaning.
- Binary synchronous communication (BSC) is the most well-known character-oriented protocol.
- BSC operates in half-duplex mode using stop-and-wait ARQ in a point-to-point or multipoint link configuration.

- There are two types of BSC frames:
  a. Control frames.
  b. Data frames.
- Control frames perform these functions:
  a. Make a connection.
  b. Control flow and error.
  c. Sever a connection.
- A bit pattern that resembles a BSC control character in the data field must not be recognized as a control character; it must be made transparent.
- Data transparency in BSC is achieved by a process called byte stuffing.
- Byte stuffing involves
  a. Demarcation of the transparent region.
  b. Addition of DLE (in the transparent region) before every DLE character.
- All bit-oriented protocols are related to high-level data link control (HDLC).
- HDLC operates in half- or full-duplex mode in a point-to-point or multipoint link configuration.
- HDLC stations are categorized as follows:
  a. Primary station—sends commands.
  b. Secondary station—sends responses.
  c. Combined station—sends commands and responses.
- HDLC stations are configured as follows:
  a. Unbalanced—one primary, one or more secondaries.
  b. Symmetrical—two physical stations, each capable of switching from primary to secondary.
  c. Balanced—two combined stations, each of equal status.
- HDLC stations communicate in one of three modes:
  a. Normal response mode (NRM)—the secondary station needs permission to transmit.
  b. Asynchronous response mode (ARM)—the secondary station does not need permission to transmit.
  c. Asynchronous balanced mode (ABM)—either combined station may initiate transmission.
- HDLC protocol defines three types of frames:
  a. Information frame (I-frame)—for data transmission and control.
  b. Supervisory frame (S-frame)—for control.
  c. Unnumbered frame (U-frame)—for control and management.
- HDLC handles data transparency by adding a 0 whenever there are five consecutive 1s following a 0. This is called bit stuffing.

11.6   PRACTICE SET

Multiple Choice

1. BSC stands for _____.
   a. binary synchronous control
   b. binary synchronous communication
   c. bit-oriented synchronous communication
   d. byte-oriented synchronous communication

2. A negative response to a poll in BSC is _____.
   a. NAK
   b. EOT
   c. WACK
   d. b and c

3. A negative response to a select in BSC is _____.
   a. NAK
   b. EOT
   c. WACK
   d. b and c

4. In BSC, a receiver responds with _____ if the frame received is error-free and even-numbered.
   a. an ACK
   b. an ACK 0
   c. an ACK 1
   d. a or b

5. BSC protocol uses _____ mode for data transmission.
   a. simplex
   b. half-duplex
   c. full-duplex
   d. half-simplex

6. BSC frames can be categorized as either data frames or _____ frames.
   a. transmission
   b. control
   c. communication
   d. supervisory

7. In BSC protocol, after an ETB, ETX, or ITB, a _____ field follows.
   a. DLE
   b. EOT

   c. BCC

   d. SYN

8. In BSC protocol, _____ can terminate a transmission or be a negative response to a poll.

   a. DLE

   b. ETX

   c. EOT

   d. ETB

9. Which of the following are variable-length fields in BSC?

   a. data

   b. BCC

   c. header

   d. all of the above

10. HDLC is an acronym for _____.

   a. high-duplex line communication

   b. high-level data link control

   c. half-duplex digital link combination

   d. host double level circuit

11. The address field of a frame in HDLC protocol contains the address of the _____ station.

   a. primary

   b. secondary

   c. tertiary

   d. a and b

12. HDLC is a _____ protocol.

   a. character-oriented

   b. bit-oriented

   c. byte-oriented

   d. count-oriented

13. BSC is a _____ protocol.

   a. character-oriented

   b. bit-oriented

   c. byte-oriented

   d. count-oriented

14. The HDLC _____ field defines the beginning and end of a frame.

   a. flag

   b. address

   c. control

   d. FCS

15. What is present in all HDLC control fields?
    a. P/F bit
    b. N(R)
    c. N(S)
    d. code bits

16. Frame acknowledgment, flow control, and error control are functions of the
    _____ in HDLC protocol.
    a. I-frame
    b. S-frame
    c. U-frame
    d. a and b

17. In HDLC protocol, the poll/final bit's meaning in an I-frame is dependent on
    _____.
    a. the system configuration
    b. whether the frame is a command or a response
    c. the system mode
    d. none of the above

18. The shortest frame in HDLC protocol is usually the _____ frame.
    a. information
    b. supervisory
    c. management
    d. none of the above

19. When data and acknowledgment are sent on the same frame, this is called
    _____.
    a. piggybacking
    b. backpacking
    c. piggypacking
    d. a good idea

Exercises

1. What is data transparency in BSC?
2. When would a DLE DLE pattern be seen in BSC?
3. Make the following data transparent and put it in a BSC frame:
   DLE ETX SYN DLE DLE ETX
4. What is the difference between the information fields in an HDLC I-frame and an HDLC U-frame?
5. In HDLC, what does each of the following received bit patterns represent?
   a. 011111010101010111...
   b. 01111110...
   c. 011111111111111111...

6. Show how a supervisory response frame in HDLC can simulate each of the following BSC frames.
   a. ACK 0
   b. ACK 1
   c. NAK
   d. WACK

CHAPTER 12

LOCAL AREA NETWORKS

A local area network (LAN) is a data communication system that allows a number of independent devices to communicate directly with each other in a limited geographic area.

LANs are dominated by four architectures: Ethernet, token bus, token ring, and fiber distributed data interface (FDDI). Ethernet, token bus, and token ring are standards of the IEEE and are part of its Project 802; FDDI is an ANSI standard.

The data link control portion of the LAN protocols in use today are all based on HDLC. However, each protocol has adapted HDLC to fit the specific requirements of its own technology. (For example, ring technology has different needs than star technology, as we will see later in this chapter.) Differences in the protocols are necessary to handle the differing needs of the designs.

12.1 PROJECT 802

In 1985, the Computer Society of the IEEE started a project, called Project 802, to set standards to enable intercommunication between equipment from a variety of manufacturers. Project 802 does not seek to replace any part of the OSI model. Instead, it is a way of specifying functions of the physical layer, the data link layer, and to a lesser extent the network layer to allow for interconnectivity of major LAN protocols.

In 1985, the Computer Society of IEEE developed Project 802. It covers the first two layers of the OSI model and part of the third level.

The relationship of Project 802 to the OSI model is shown in Figure 12.1. The IEEE has subdivided the data link layer into two sublayers: logical link control (LLC) and media access control (MAC).

The LLC is non-architecture-specific; that is it is the same for all IEEE-defined LANs. The MAC sublayer, on the other hand, contains a number of distinct modules; each carries proprietary information specific to the LAN product being used.

Figure 12.1   *LAN compared with the OSI model*

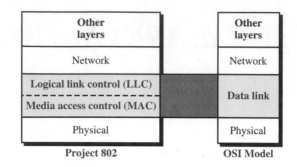

Project 802 has split the data link layer into two different sublayers: logical link control (LLC) and media access control (MAC).

In addition to the two sublayers, Project 802 contains a section governing internetworking. This section assures the compatibility of different LANs and MANs across protocols and allows data to be exchanged across otherwise incompatible networks.

The strength of Project 802 is modularity. By subdividing the functions necessary for LAN management, the designers were able to standardize those that can be generalized and to isolate those that must remain specific. Each subdivision is identified by a number: 802.1 (internetworking); 802.2 (LLC); and the MAC modules 802.3 (CSMA/CD), 802.4 (token bus), 802.5 (token ring), and others (see Figure 12.2).

Figure 12.2   *Project 802*

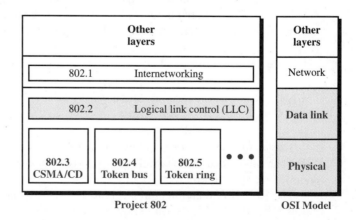

IEEE 802.1

802.1 is the section of Project 802 devoted to internetworking issues in LANs and MANs. Although not yet complete, it seeks to resolve the incompatibilities between network architectures without requiring modifications in existing addressing, access, and error recovery mechanisms, among others. Some of these issues will be discussed in Chapter 20.

> IEEE 802.1 is an internetworking standard for LANs.

LLC

In general, the IEEE Project 802 model takes the structure of an HDLC frame and divides it into two sets of functions. One set contains the end-user portions of the frame: the logical addresses, control information, and data. These functions are handled by the IEEE 802.2 logical link control (LLC) protocol. LLC is considered the upper layer of the IEEE 802 data link layer and is common to all LAN protocols.

> IEEE 802.2 logical link control (LLC) is the upper sublayer of the data link layer.

MAC

The second set of functions, the media access control (MAC) sublayer, resolves the contention for the shared media. It contains the synchronization, flag, flow, and error control specifications necessary to move information from one place to another, as well as the physical address of the next station to receive and route a packet. MAC protocols are specific to the LAN using them (Ethernet, token ring, and token bus, etc.).

> Media access control (MAC) is the lower sublayer of the data link layer.

Protocol Data Unit (PDU)

The data unit in the LLC level is called the protocol data unit (PDU). The PDU contains four fields familiar from HDLC: a destination service access point (DSAP), a source service access point (SSAP), a control field, and an information field (see Figure 12.3).

DSAP and SSAP

The DSAP and SSAP are addresses used by the LLC to identify the protocol stacks on the receiving and sending machines that are generating and using the data. The first bit of the DSAP indicates whether the frame is intended for an individual or a group. The first bit of the SSAP indicates whether the communication is a command or response PDU (see Figure 12.3).

Figure 12.3 *PDU format*

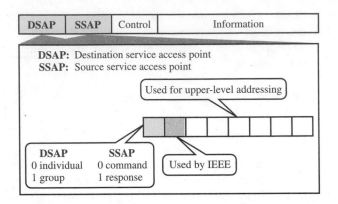

Control

The control field of the PDU is identical to the control field in HDLC. As in HDLC, PDU frames can be I-frames, S-frames, or U-frames and carry all of the codes and information that the corresponding HDLC frames carry (see Figure 12.4).

The PDU has no flag fields, no CRC, and no station address. These fields are added in the lower sublayer (the MAC layer).

Figure 12.4 *Control field in a PDU*

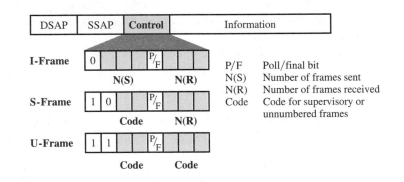

12.2 ETHERNET

IEEE 802.3 supports a LAN standard originally developed by Xerox and later extended by a joint venture between Digital Equipment Corporation, Intel Corporation, and Xerox. This was called Ethernet.

802.3 defines two categories: baseband and broadband, as shown in Figure 12.5. The word *base* specifies a digital signal (in this case, Manchester encoding). The word *broad* specifies an analog signal (in this case, PSK encoding). IEEE divides the base-

Figure 12.5 *IEEE 802.3*

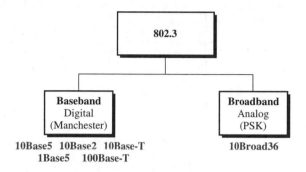

band category into five different standards: 10BASE5, 10BASE2, 10BASE-T, 1BASE5, and 100BASE-T. The first number (10, 1, or 100) indicates data rate in Mbps. The last number or letter (5, 2, 1, or T) indicates maximum cable length or the type of cable. IEEE defines only one specification for the broadband category: 10BROAD36. Again, the first number (10) indicates data rate. The last number defines the maximum cable length. However, the maximum cable length restriction can be changed using networking devices such as repeaters or bridges (see Chapter 20).

Access Method: CSMA/CD

Whenever multiple users have unregulated access to a single line, there is a danger of signals overlapping and destroying each other. Such overlaps, which turn the signals into unusable noise, are called collisions. As traffic increases on a multiple access link, so do collisions. A LAN therefore needs a mechanism to coordinate traffic, minimize the number of collisions that occur, and maximize the number of frames that are delivered successfully. The access mechanism used in an Ethernet is called carrier sense multiple access with collision detection (CSMA/CD, standardized in IEEE 802.3).

CSMA/CD is the result of an evolution from multiple access (MA) to carrier sense multiple access (CSMA), and finally, to carrier sense multiple access with collision detection (CSMA/CD). The original design was a multiple access method in which every workstation had equal access to a link. In MA, there was no provision for traffic coordination. Access to the line was open to any node at any time, with the assumption that the odds of two devices competing for access at the same time were small enough to be unimportant. Any station wishing to transmit did so, then relied on acknowledgments to verify that the transmitted frame had not been destroyed by other traffic on the line.

In a CSMA system, any workstation wishing to transmit must first listen for existing traffic on the line. A device listens by checking for a voltage. If no voltage is detected, the line is considered idle and the transmission is initiated. CSMA cuts down on the number of collisions but does not eliminate them. Collisions can still occur. If another station has transmitted too recently for its signal to have reached the listening station, the listener assumes the line is idle and introduces its own signal onto the line.

The final step is the addition of collision detection (CD). In CSMA/CD the station wishing to transmit first listens to make certain the link is free, then transmits its data, then listens again. During the data transmission, the station checks the line for the extremely high voltages that indicate a collision. If a collision is detected, the station waits a predetermined amount of time for the line to clear, then sends its data again (see Figure 12.6).

Today the terms Ethernet, CSMA/CD, and 802.3 are used interchangeably.

Figure 12.6   *Evolution of CSMA/CD*

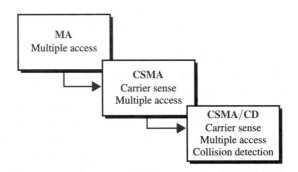

Addressing

Each station on an Ethernet network (such as a PC, workstation, or printer) has its own network interface card (NIC). The NIC usually fits inside the station and provides the station with a six-byte physical address. The number on the NIC is unique.

Electrical Specification

Signaling

The baseband systems use Manchester digital encoding (See Figure 5.8 in Chapter 5). There is one broadband system, 10BROAD36. It uses digital/analog encoding (differential PSK).

Data Rate

Ethernet LANs can support data rates between 1 and 100 Mbps.

Frame Format

IEEE 802.3 specifies one type of frame containing seven fields: preamble, SFD, DA, SA, length/type of PDU, 802.2 frame, and the CRC. Ethernet does not provide any mechanism for acknowledging received frames, making it what is known as an unreliable medium. Acknowledgments must be implemented at the higher layers. The format of the MAC frame in CSMA/CD is shown in Figure 12.7.

Figure 12.7 *802.3 MAC frame*

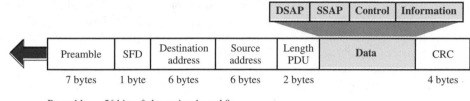

| | | | | | DSAP | SSAP | Control | Information |

Preamble	SFD	Destination address	Source address	Length PDU	Data	CRC
7 bytes	1 byte	6 bytes	6 bytes	2 bytes		4 bytes

Preamble   56 bits of alternating 1s and 0s.
SFD   Start field delimiter, flag (10101011)

- **Preamble.** The first field of the 802.3 frame contains seven bytes (56 bits) of alternating 0s and 1s that alert the receiving system to the coming frame, and enable it to synchronize its input timing. The pattern 1010101 provides only an alert and a timing pulse; it can be too easily aliased to be useful in indicating the beginning of the data stream. HDLC combined the alert, timing, and start synchronization into a single field; the flag. IEEE 802.3 divides these three functions between the preamble and the second field, the start frame delimiter (SFD).

- **Start frame delimiter (SFD).** The second field (one byte: 10101011) of the 802.3 frame signals the beginning of the frame. The SFD tells the receiver that everything that follows is data, starting with the addresses.

- **Destination address (DA).** The DA field is allotted six bytes and contains the physical address of the packet's next destination. A system's physical address is a bit pattern encoded on its network interface card (NIC). Each NIC has a unique address that distinguishes it from any other NIC. If the packet must cross from one LAN to another to reach its destination, the DA field contains the physical address of the router connecting the current LAN to the next one. When the packet reaches the target network, the DA field contains the physical address of the destination device.

- **Source address (SA).** The SA field is also allotted six bytes and contains the physical address of the last device to forward the packet. That device can be the sending station or the most recent router to receive and forward the packet.

- **Length/type of PDU.** These next two bytes indicate the number of bytes in the coming PDU. If the length of the PDU is fixed, this field can be used to indicate type, or as a base for other protocols. For example, Novell and the Internet use it to identify the network layer protocol that is using the PDU.

- **802.2 frame (PDU).** This field of the 802.3 frame contains the entire 802.2 frame as a modular, removable unit. The PDU can be anywhere from 46 to 1500 bytes long, depending on the type of frame and the length of the information field. The PDU is generated by the upper (LLC) sublayer, then linked to the 802.3 frame.

- **CRC.** The last field in the 802.3 frame contains the error detection information, in this case a CRC-32.

Implementation

Although the bulk of the IEEE Project 802 standard focuses on the data link layer of the OSI model, the 802 model also defines some of the physical specifications for each of the protocols defined in the MAC layer. In the 802.3 standard, the IEEE defines the types of cable, connections, and signals that are to be used in each of five different Ethernet implementations. All Ethernet LANs are configured as logical buses, although they may be physically implemented in bus or star topologies. Each frame is transmitted to every station on the link but read only by the station to which it is addressed.

10BASE5: Thick Ethernet

The first of the physical standards defined in the IEEE 802.3 model is called 10BASE5, thick Ethernet, or Thick-Net. The nickname derives from the size of the cable, which is roughly the size of garden hose and too stiff to bend with your hands. 10BASE5 is a bus topology LAN that uses baseband signaling and has a maximum segment length of 500 meters.

As we will see in Chapter 20, networking devices (such as repeaters and bridges) can be used to overcome the size limitation of local area networks. In thick Ethernet, a local area network can be divided into segments by connecting devices. In this case, the length of each segment is limited to 500 meters. However, to reduce collisions, the total length of the bus should not exceed 2500 meters (five segments). Also, the standard demands that each station be separated from each neighbor by 2.5 meters (200 stations per segment and 1000 stations total); see Figure 12.8.

Figure 12.8 *Ethernet segments*

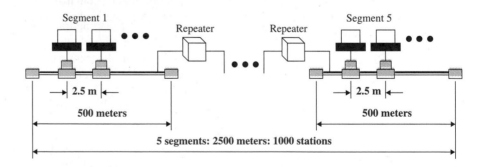

The physical connectors and cables utilized by 10BASE5 include coaxial cable, network interface cards, transceivers, and attachment unit interface (AUI) cables. The interaction of these components is illustrated in Figure 12.9.

RG-8 Cable   RG-8 cable (RG stands for radio government) is a thick coaxial cable that provides the backbone of the IEEE 802.3 standard.

Transceiver   Each station is attached by an AUI cable to an intermediary device called a medium attachment unit (MAU) or, more commonly, a transceiver (short for transmitter-receiver). The transceiver performs the CSMA/CD function of checking for

Figure 12.9 *Topology of 10BASE5*

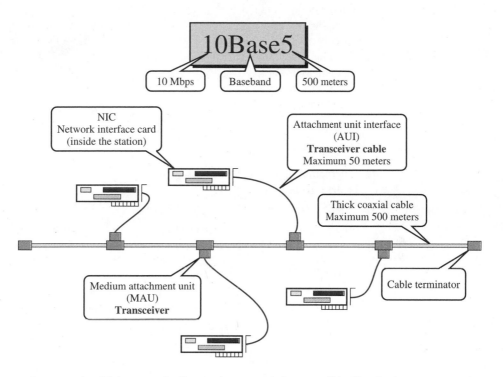

voltages and collisions on the line and may contain a small buffer. It also serves as the connector that attaches a station to the thick coaxial cable itself via a tap (see below).

AUI Cables   Each station is linked to its corresponding transceiver by an attachment unit interface (AUI). An AUI is a 15-wire cable with plugs that perform the physical layer interface functions between the station and the transceiver. Each end of an AUI terminates in a DB-15 (15-pin) connector. One connector plugs into a port on the NIC, the other into a port on the transceiver. AUIs are restricted to a maximum length of 50 meters, allowing for some flexibility in placement of stations relative to the 10BASE5 backbone cable.

Transceiver Tap   Each transceiver contains a connecting mechanism, called a tap because it allows the transceiver to tap into the line at any point. The tap is a thick cable-sized well with a metal spike in the center (see Figure 12.10). The spike is attached to wires inside the transceiver. When the cable is pressed into the well, the spike pierces the jacket and sheathing layers and makes an electrical connection between the transceiver and the cable. This kind of connector is often called a vampire tap because it bites the cable.

10BASE2: Thin Ethernet

The second Ethernet implementation defined by the IEEE 802 series is called 10BASE2 or thin Ethernet.Thin Ethernet (also called Thin-Net, Cheapnet, and thin-

Figure 12.10   *Transceiver connection in 10BASE5*

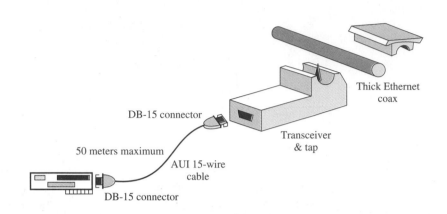

wire Ethernet) provides an inexpensive alternative to 10BASE5 Ethernet, with the same data rate. Like 10BASE5, 10BASE2 is a bus topology LAN. The advantages of thin Ethernet are reduced cost and ease of installation (the cable is lighter weight and more flexible than that used in thick Ethernet). The disadvantages are shorter range (185 meters as opposed to the 500 meters available with thick Ethernet) and smaller capacity (the thinner cable accommodates fewer stations). In many situations—such as a small number of users on a UNIX-based minicomputer, or a network of personal computers and workstations—these disadvantages are irrelevant, and the cost savings make 10BASE2 the better choice.

The physical layout of 10BASE2 is illustrated in Figure 12.11. The connectors and cables utilized are: NICs, thin coaxial cable, and BNC-T connectors. In this technology, the transceiver circuitry has moved into the NIC, and the transceiver-tap has been replaced by a connector that splices the station directly into the cable, eliminating the need for AUI cables.

NIC   The NICs in a thin Ethernet system provide all of the same functionality as those in a thick Ethernet system, plus the functions of the transceivers. That means that a 10BASE2 NIC not only provides the station with an address but also checks for voltages on the link.

Thin Coaxial Cable   The cable required to implement the 10BASE2 standard is RG-58. These cables relatively easy to install and move around (especially inside existing buildings where cabling must be pulled through the walls and ceilings).

BNC-T   The BNC-T connector is a T-shaped device with three ports: one for the NIC and one each for the input and output ends of the cable.

10BASE-T: Twisted-Pair Ethernet

The most popular standard defined in the IEEE 802.3 series is 10BASE-T, a star-topology LAN using unshielded twisted pair (UTP) cable instead of coaxial cable. It supports a data rate of 10 Mbps and has a maximum length (hub to station) of 100 meters.

Figure 12.11   *Topology of 10BASE2*

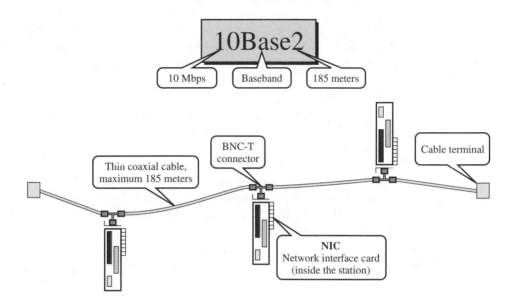

Instead of individual transceivers, 10BASE-T Ethernet places all of its networking operations in an intelligent hub with a port for each station. Stations are linked into the hub by four-pair RJ-45 cable (eight-wire unshielded twisted-pair cable) terminating at each end in a male-type connector much like a telephone jack (see Figure 12.12). The hub fans out any transmitted frame to all of its connected stations. Logic in the NIC assures that the only station to open and read a given frame is the station to which that frame is addressed.

Figure 12.12   *10BASE-T topology*

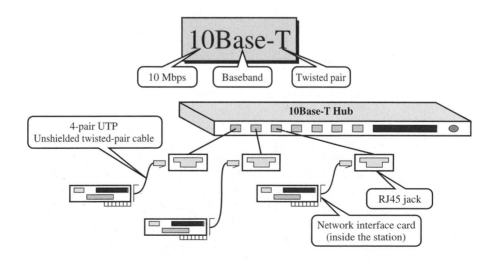

As Figure 12.12 shows, each station contains an NIC. A length of four-pair UTP of not more than 100 meters connects the NIC in the station to the appropriate port in the 10BASE-T hub.

The weight and flexibility of the cable and the convenience of the RJ-45 jack and plug make 10BASE-T the easiest of the 802.3 LANs to install and reinstall. When a station needs to be replaced, a new station can simply be plugged in.

1BASE5: StarLAN

StarLAN is an AT&T product used infrequently today because of its slow speed. At only 1 Mbps, it is 10 times slower than the three standards discussed above.

What is interesting about StarLAN is its range, which can be increased by a mechanism called daisy chaining. Like 10BASE-T, StarLAN uses twisted-pair cable to connect stations to a central intelligent hub. Unlike 10BASE-T, which requires that each station have its own dedicated cable into the hub, StarLAN allows as many as 10 stations to be linked, each to the next, in a chain in which only the lead device connects to the hub (see Figure 12.13).

Figure 12.13   *1BASE5 topology*

Figure 12.14   *Fast Ethernet categories*

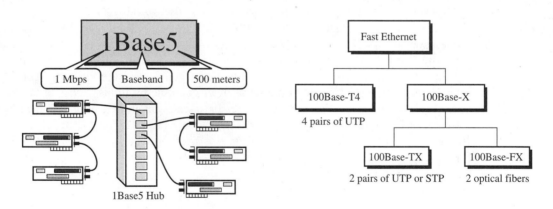

Fast Ethernet

The IEEE developed a set of specifications that provides a low-cost Ethernet, called Fast Ethernet, operating at 100 Mbps. The specification uses star topology and the same MAC protocol and frame format as 10BASE-T. The encoding system has been changed to accommodate a 100-Mbps data rate. Also, two different links between the computer and the hub are specified. One link is for transmission, the other for reception. The specification defines two different standards for physical medium: 100BASE-T4 and 100BASE-X. The first standard, 100BASE-T4 allows the use of four pairs of category 3 or category 5 UTP between a computer and the hub (two pairs for transmission and two pairs for reception). The second standard, 100BASE-X, specifies the use of two pairs of high-quality category 5 UTP, two pairs of STP (100BASE-TX), or two optical fibers (100BASE-FX); see Figure 12.14.

12.3   TOKEN BUS

Local area networks have a direct application in factory automation and process control, where the nodes are computers controlling the manufacturing process. In this type of application, real-time processing with minimum delay is needed. Processing must occur at the same speed as the objects moving along the assembly line. Ethernet (IEEE 802.3) is not a suitable protocol for this purpose because the number of collisions is not predictable and the delay in sending data from the control center to the computers along the assembly line is not a fixed value. Token ring (IEEE 802.5; see next section) is also not a suitable protocol because an assembly line resembles a bus topology and not a ring. Token bus (IEEE 802.4) combines features of Ethernet and token ring. It combines the physical configuration of Ethernet (a bus topology) and the collision-free (predictable delay) feature of token ring. Token bus is a physical bus that operates as a logical ring using tokens.

Stations are logically organized into a ring. A token is passed among stations. If a station wants to send data, it must wait and capture the token. However, like Ethernet, stations communicate via a common bus.

Token bus is limited to factory automation and process control and has no commercial application in data communication. Also the details of the operation are very involved. For these two reasons, we will not further discuss this protocol.

12.4   TOKEN RING

As mentioned above, the network access mechanism used by Ethernet (CSMA/CD) is not infallible and may result in collisions. Stations may attempt to send data multiple times before a transmission makes it onto the link. This redundancy may create delays of indeterminable length if the traffic is heavy. There is no way to predict either the occurrence of collisions or the delays produced by multiple stations attempting to capture the link at the same time.

Token ring resolves this uncertainty by requiring that stations take turns sending data. Each station may transmit only during its turn and may send only one frame during each turn. The mechanism that coordinates this rotation is called token passing. A token is a simple placeholder frame that is passed from station to station around the ring. A station may send data only when it has possession of the token.

Token ring allows each station to send one frame per turn.

Access Method: Token Passing

Token passing is illustrated in Figure 12.15. Whenever the network is unoccupied, it circulates a simple three-byte token. This token is passed from NIC to NIC in sequence until it encounters a station with data to send. That station waits for the token to enter its network board. If the token is free, the station may then send a data frame. It keeps

Figure 12.15 *Token passing*

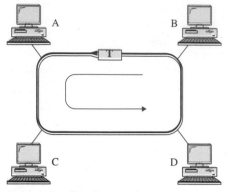

a. Token is traveling along the ring.

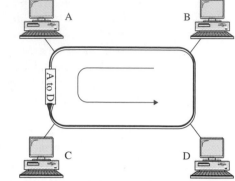

b. Station A captures the token and sends its data to D.

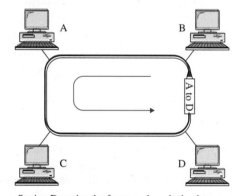

c. Station D copies the frame and sends the data back to the ring.

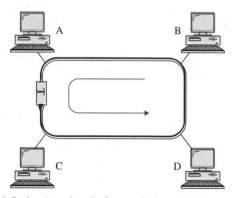

d. Station A receives the frame and releases the token.

the token and sets a bit inside its NIC as a reminder that it has done so, then sends its one data frame.

This data frame proceeds around the ring, being regenerated by each station. Each intermediate station examines the destination address, finds that the frame is addressed to another station, and relays it to its neighbor. The intended recipient recognizes its own address, copies the message, checks for errors, and changes four bits in the last byte of the frame to indicate address recognized and frame copied. The full packet then continues around the ring until it returns to the station that sent it.

The sender receives the frame and recognizes itself in the source address field. It then examines the address-recognized bits. If they are set, it knows the frame was received. The sender then discards the used data frame and releases the token back to the ring.

Priority and Reservation

Generally, once a token has been released, the next station on the ring with data to send has the right to take charge of the ring. However, in the IEEE 802.5 model another option is possible. The busy token can be reserved by a station waiting to transmit, regardless of that station's location on the ring. Each station has a priority code. As a frame passes by, a station waiting to transmit may reserve the next open token by entering its priority code in the access control (AC) field of the token or data frame (discussed later in this section). A station with a higher priority may remove a lower priority reservation and replace it with its own. Among stations of equal priority, the process is first come, first served. Through this mechanism, the station holding the reservation gets the opportunity to transmit as soon as the token is free, whether or not it comes next physically on the ring.

Time Limits

To keep traffic moving, token ring imposes a time limit on any station wanting to use the ring. A starting delimiter (the first field of either a token or data frame) must reach each station within a specified interval (usually 10 milliseconds). In other words, each station expects to receive frames within regular time intervals (it receives a frame and expects to receive the next frame within a specified period).

Monitor Stations

Several problems may occur to disrupt the operation of a token ring network. In one scenario, a station may neglect to retransmit a token or a token may be destroyed by noise, in which case there is no token on the ring and no station may send data. In another scenario, a sending station may neglect to remove its used data frame from the ring or may not release the token once its turn has ended.

To handle these occurrences, one station on the ring is designated as a monitor. The monitor sets a timer each time the token passes. If the token does not reappear in the allotted time, it is presumed to be lost and the monitor generates a new token and introduces it to the ring. The monitor guards against perpetually recirculating data frames by setting a bit in the AC field of each frame. As a frame passes, the monitor checks the status field. If the status bit has been set, it knows that the packet has already been around the ring and should have been discarded. The monitor then destroys the frame and puts a token onto the ring. If the monitor fails, a second station, designated as backup, takes over.

Addressing

Token ring uses a six-byte address, which is imprinted on the NIC card similar to Ethernet addresses.

Electrical Specification

Signaling

Token ring uses differential Manchester digital signal encoding (See Figure 5.8 in Chapter 5).

Data Rate

Token ring supports data rates of up to 16 Mbps. (The original specification was 4 Mbps.)

Frame Formats

The token ring protocol specifies three types of frames: data, token, and abort. The token and abort frames are both truncated data frames (see Figure 12.16).

Data Frame

In token ring, the data frame is the only one of the three types of frames that can carry a PDU and is the only one addressed to a specific destination rather than being available to the ring at large. The nine fields of the data frame are start delimiter (SD), access control (AC), frame control (FC), destination address (DA), source address (SA), 802.2 PDU frame, CRC, end delimiter (ED), and frame status (FS).

Figure 12.16   *Token ring frame*

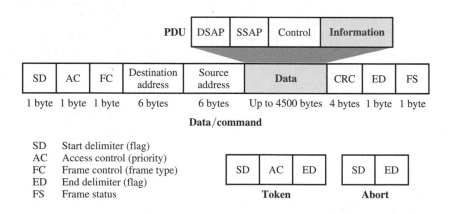

- **Start delimiter (SD).** The first field of the data/command frame, SD, is one byte long and is used to alert the receiving station to the arrival of a frame as well as to allow it to synchronize its retrieval timing. It is equivalent to the flag field in HDLC. Figure 12.17 shows the format of the SD. The J and K violations are created at the physical layer and are included in every start delimiter to ensure transparency in the data field. In this way, an SD bit pattern that appears in the data field cannot be taken for the start of a new frame. These violations are created by changing the encoding pattern for the duration of the bit. As you remember, in differential Manchester, each bit may have two transitions: one at the beginning and another at the middle. In the J violation, both transitions are canceled. In the K violation, the middle transition is canceled.

Figure 12.17 *Data frame fields*

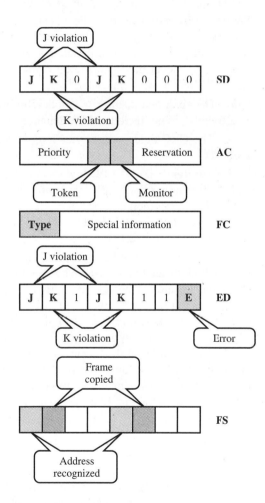

- **Access control (AC).** The AC field is one byte long and includes four subfields (see Figure 12.17). The first three bits are the priority field. The fourth bit is called the token bit and is set to indicate that the frame is a data frame rather than a token or an abort frame. The token bit is followed by a monitor bit. Finally, the last three bits are a reservation field that can be set by stations wishing to reserve access to the ring.

- **Frame control (FC).** The FC field is one byte long and contains two fields (see Figure 12.17). The first is a one-bit field used to indicate the type of information contained in the PDU (whether it is control information or data). The second uses the remaining seven bits of the byte and contains information used by the token ring logic (e.g., how to use the information in the AC field).

- **Destination address (DA).** The six-byte DA field contains the physical address of the frame's next destination. If its ultimate destination is another network, the DA is the address of the router to the next LAN on its path. If its ultimate destination is on the current LAN, the DA is the physical address of the destination station.

- **Source address (SA).** The SA field is also six bytes long and contains the physical address of the sending station. If the ultimate destination of the packet is a station on the same network as the originating station, the SA is that of the originating station. If the packet has been routed from another LAN, the SA is the physical address of the most recent router.

- **Data.** The sixth field, data, is allotted 4500 bytes and contains the PDU. A token ring frame does not include a PDU length or type field.

- **CRC.** The CRC field is four bytes long and contains a CRC-32 error detection sequence.

- **End delimiter (ED).** The ED is a second flag field of one byte and indicates the end of the sender's data and control information. Like the SD, it is changed at the physical layer to include J and K violations. These violations are necessary to ensure that a bit sequence in the data field cannot be mistaken for an ED by the receiver (see Figure 12.17).

- **Frame status (FS).** The last byte of the frame is the FS field. It can be set by the receiver to indicate that the frame has been read, or by the monitor to indicate that the frame has already been around the ring. This field is not an acknowledgment, but it does tell the sender that the receiving station has copied the frame, which can now be discarded. Figure 12.17 shows the format of an FS field. As you can see, it contains two 1-bit pieces of information: address recognized and frame copied. These bits come at the beginning of the field and are repeated in the fifth and sixth bits. This repetition is for the purpose of preventing errors and is necessary because the field contains information inserted after the frame leaves the sending station. It cannot therefore be included in the CRC and so has no error checking performed on it.

Token Frame

Because a token is really a placeholder and reservation frame, it includes only three fields: the SD, AC, and ED. The SD indicates that a frame is coming. The AC indicates that the frame is a token and includes the priority and reservation fields The ED indicates the end of the frame.

Abort Frame

An abort frame carries no information at all—just starting and ending delimiters. It can be generated either by the sender to stop its own transmission (for whatever reason), or by the monitor to purge an old transmission from the line.

Implementation

Ring

The ring in a token ring consists of a series of 150-ohm, shielded twisted-pair sections linking each station to its immediate neighbors (see Figure 12.18). Each section connects an output port on one station to an input port on the next, creating a ring with unidirectional traffic flow. The output from the final station connects to the input of the first to complete the ring. A frame is passed to each station in sequence, where it is examined, regenerated, and then sent on to the next station.

> Each station in the token ring regenerates the frame.

Figure 12.18 *Token ring*

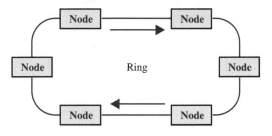

Switch

As Figure 12.18 shows, configuring the network as a ring introduces a potential problem: One disabled or disconnected node could stop the flow of traffic around the entire network. To solve this problem, each station is connected to an automatic switch. This switch can bypass an inactive station. While a station is disabled, the switch closes the ring without it. When the station comes on, a signal sent by the NIC moves the switch and brings the station into the ring (see Figure 12.19).

Each station's NIC has a pair of input and output ports combined in a nine-pin connector. A nine-wire cable connects the NIC to the switch. Of these wires, four are used for data and the remaining five are used to control the switch (to include or bypass a station).

Figure 12.19 shows the two switching modes. In the first part, connections are completed to the station, thereby inserting it into the ring. In the second part, an alternate pair of connections are completed to bypass the station.

Multistation Access Unit (MAU)

For practical purposes, individual automatic switches are combined into a hub called a multistation access unit (MAU); see Figure 12.20. One MAU can support up to eight stations. Looked at from the outside, this system looks like a star with the MAU at the middle. But, as Figure 12.20 shows, it is in fact a ring.

Figure 12.19   *Token ring switch*

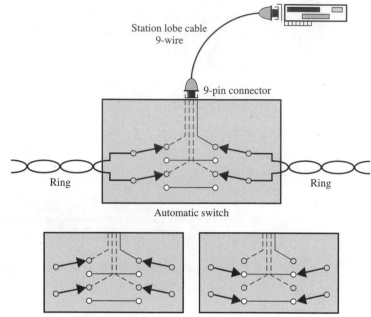

Station lobe cable
9-wire

9-pin connector

Ring

Automatic switch

Ring

Inserted mode

Bypassed mode

Figure 12.20   *MAU*

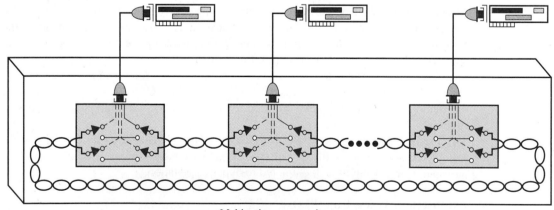

Multistation access unit
MAU

12.5   FDDI

Fiber distributed data interface (FDDI) is a local area network protocol standardized by ANSI and the ITU-U (ITU-T X.3). It supports data rates of 100 Mbps and provides a high-speed alternative to Ethernet and token ring. When FDDI was designed, speeds of 100 Mbps required fiber-optic cable. Today, however, comparable speeds are available using copper cable. The copper version of FDDI is known as CDDI.

Access Method: Token Passing

In a token ring network, a station can send only one frame each time it captures the token. In FDDI, access is limited by time. A station may send as many frames as it can within its allotted access period, with the proviso that time-sensitive frames be sent first.

To implement this access mechanism, FDDI differentiates between two types of data frames: synchronous and asynchronous. *Synchronous* here refers to information that is time sensitive, while *asynchronous* refers to information that is not. These frames are usually called S-frames and A-frames.

Each station that captures the token is required to send S-frames first. In fact, it must send its S-frames whether or not its time allotment has run out (see below). Any remaining time may then be used to send A-frames. To understand how this mechanism ensures fair and timely link access, it is necessary to understand the FDDI time registers and timers.

Time Registers

FDDI defines three time registers to control circulation of the token and distribute link-access opportunities among the nodes equitably. Each station has three registers. The registers hold time values that control the operation of the ring. These values are set when the ring is initialized and do not vary in the course of operation. The registers are called synchronous allocation (SA), target token rotation time (TTRT), and absolute maximum time (AMT).

Synchronous Allocation (SA)   The SA register indicates the length of time allowed each station for sending synchronous data. This value is different for each station and is negotiated during initialization of the ring.

Target Token Rotation Time (TTRT)   The TTRT register indicates the average time required for a token to circulate around the ring exactly once (the elapsed time between a token's arrival at a given station and its next arrival at the same station). This value is the same for all stations and is negotiated during the initialization of the ring. Because it is an average, the actual time of any rotation may be greater or less than this value.

Absolute Maximum Time (AMT)   The AMT register holds a value equal to twice the TTRT. A token may not take longer than this time to make one rotation of the ring. If it does, some station or stations are monopolizing the network and the ring must be reinitialized.

Timers

Each station contains a set of timers that enable it to compare actual timings with the values contained in the registers. Timers can be set and reset, and their values decremented at a rate set by the system clock. The two timers used by FDDI are called the token rotation timer (TRT), and token holding timer (THT).

Token Rotation Timer (TRT)   The TRT runs continuously and measures the actual time taken by the token to complete a cycle. When the token returns, the station records the time remaining on its TRT into its THT. Then the station resets its TRT based on the TTRT value. As soon as the TRT is set, it begins counting down. The time indicated by the TRT at any given point therefore is the difference between the actual time that has elapsed during the current rotation and the expected or allowed time (TTRT time). When the token completes a rotation and returns to the station, the time indicated by the TRT is equal to the amount of time remaining for that rotation (the difference between the TTRT and the actual elapsed time). That remaining time is then available to the station to send its frames.

Token Holding Timer (THT)   The THT begins running as soon as the token is received. Its function is to show how much time remains for sending asynchronous frames once the synchronous frames have been sent. Each time the station receives the token, the TRT value is copied into the THT. At that point, the THT starts its own countdown. Any waiting synchronous frames must be sent as soon as the token is received. The THT shows how much time (if any) remains for sending asynchronous frames. The station may send only as many A-frames as it has THT credit for. As long as the THT is positive, the station can send asynchronous data. Once the value of this timer reaches or falls below zero, however, the station must release the token. We may think of the THT as the station's bank account. S-frames are bills that must be paid immediately—even if the station has to go into debt to do so. A-frames are expenditures that can be put off for a while; the station needs to make them but can wait until its bank account can cover the expense.

Gaining Access

Figure 12.21 and Figure 12.22 show how FDDI access works. We have simplified this example by showing only four stations and making the following assumptions: the TTRT is 30 time units; the time required to send each frame is 1 time unit; each station is allowed to send five synchronous data units per turn (total time, five units per turn); and each station has a lot of asynchronous data to send (waiting in buffers). We also assume that the system illustrated is completely free of propagation or other delays.

The timing process is shown in Figure 12.22. At time zero, all four stations start together. Each transfers the value of the TTRT (30 time units) to its TRT and starts counting down.

Station 1 receives the token and does three things: it transfers the value in its TRT to its THT to start the THT countdown; it copies the value of the TTRT into its TRT and restarts the TRT countdown; and it sends its first S-frame. By the time it has sent all five of its allotted S-frames, its TRT and THT are at 25. Because the value of the THT is 25, the station is able to send 25 A-frames. Once these have been sent, both counters are at 0 and the station releases the token. Station 1 has held the token for 30 time units.

Figure 12.21 *FDDI operation*

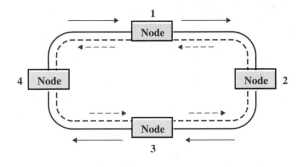

Figure 12.22 *FDDI example*

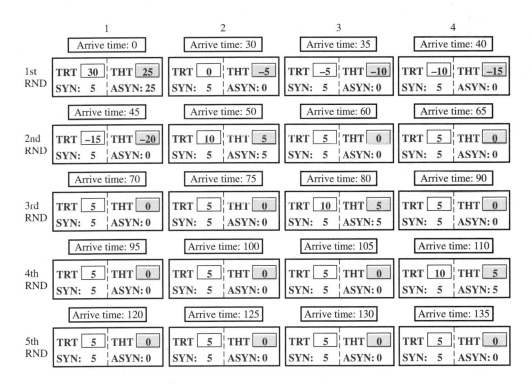

When the token arrives at station 2, its TRT, which started with the rest of the system at 30, is now zero (see arrive time in the second frame of Figure 12.22). The station must send its five S-frames, however, so it keeps the token for five time units in order to do so. When these frames have been sent, the THT is at −5. Because this value is negative, the station is deprived of the right to send any A-frames at all. Instead, it must pass on the token immediately. This process is repeated for each station.

As you follow the process step-by-step through a number of rounds, you notice that FDDI is both fair and self-adjusting. In the first round, station 1 overused its rights by sending 25 asynchronous frames. It therefore is automatically barred from sending any asynchronous data in the second round (its TRT was already at 0 by the time it released the token in the first round). By the time it receives the token for the second round, its TRT is −15. Once it sends its synchronous frames, its THT is at −20, and it must pass the token immediately.

When station 1 receives the token for round 2, it restarts its TRT at −15, and begins counting down. As we saw, it uses five units to send its S-frames, then passes the token. Station 2 uses 10 units (five S-frames plus five A-frames). Stations 3 and 4 use five units each: 30 − 5 − 10 − 5 − 5 = 5. In round 3 therefore station 1 has a total of five time units available for sending its data. Once it sends its synchronous data, those five units are used up and it must pass the token. In other words, station 1 does not have the opportunity to send asynchronous data in round 3 either.

Station 2, on the other hand, does have an opportunity to send asynchronous data in the second round. In the third round, station 3 has an opportunity to send asynchronous data.

Addressing

FDDI uses a six-byte address, which is imprinted on the NIC card similar to Ethernet addresses.

Electrical Specification

Signaling (Physical Layer)

FDDI uses a special encoding mechanism called four bits/five bits (4B/5B). In this system, each four-bit segment of data is replaced by five-bit code before being encoded in NRZ-I (refer back to Figure 5.6). The NRZ-I used here inverts on the 1 (see Figure 12.23).

Figure 12.23 *Encoding*

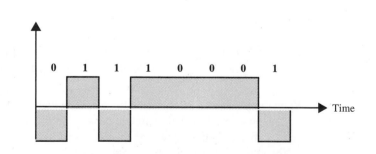

The reason for this extra encoding step is that, although NRZ-I provides adequate synchronization under average circumstances, sender and receiver may go out of synchronization anytime the data includes a long sequence of 0s. 4B/5B encoding transforms each four-bit data segment into a five-bit unit that contains no more than two consecutive 0s. Each of the 16 possible four-bit patterns is assigned a five-bit pattern to represent it. These five-bit patterns have been carefully selected so that even sequential data units cannot result in sequences of more than three 0s (none of the five-bit patterns start with more than one 0 or end with more than two 0s); see Table 12.1.

Table 12.1 *4B/5B encoding*

Data Sequence	Encoded Sequence	Data Sequence	Encoded Sequence
0000	11110	1000	10010
0001	01001	1001	10011
0010	10100	1010	10110
0011	10101	1011	10111
0100	01010	1100	11010
0101	01011	1101	11011
0110	01110	1110	11100
0111	01111	1111	11101

Five-bit codes that have not been assigned to represent a four-bit counterpart are used for control (see Table 12.2). The SD field contains the J and K codes, and the ED field contains the symbols TT. To guarantee that these control codes do not endanger synchronization or transparency, the designers specify bit patterns that can never occur in the data field. In addition, their order is controlled to limit the number of sequential bit patterns possible. A K always follows a J, and an H is never followed by an R.

Table 12.2 *4B/5B control symbols*

Control Symbol	Encoded Sequence
Q (Quiet)	00000
I (Idle)	11111
H (Halt)	00100
J (Used in start delimiter)	11000
K (Used in start delimiter)	10001
T (Used in end delimiter)	01101
S (Set)	11001
R (Reset)	00111

Data Rate
FDDI supports data rates up to 100 Mbps.

Frame Format

The FDDI standard divides transmission functions into four protocols: physical medium dependent (PMD), physical (PHY), media access control (MAC), and logical link control (LLC). These protocols correspond to the physical and data link layers of the OSI model (see Figure 12.24). In addition, the standard specifies a fifth protocol (used for station management), details of which are beyond the scope of this book.

Figure 12.24   *FDDI layers*

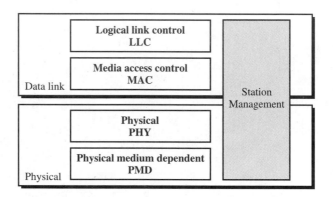

Logical Link Control

The LLC layer is similar to that defined in the IEEE 802.2 protocols.

Media Access Control

The FDDI MAC layer is almost identical to that defined for token ring. However, although the functions are similar, the FDDI MAC frame itself is different enough to warrant an independent discussion of each field (see Figure 12.25).

Each frame is preceded by 16 idle symbols (1111), for a total of 64 bits to initialize clock synchronization with the receiver.

Frame Fields   There are eight fields in the FDDI frame:

- **Start delimiter (SD).** The first byte of the field is the frame's starting flag. As in token ring, these bits are replaced in the physical layer by the control codes (violations) J and K (the five-bit sequences used to represent J and K are shown in Table 12.2).
- **Frame control (FC).** The second byte of the frame identifies the frame type.
- **Addresses.** The next two fields are the destination and source addresses. Each address consists of two to six bytes.
- **Data.** Each data frame can carry up to 4500 bytes of data.
- **CRC.** FDDI uses the standard IEEE four-byte cyclic redundancy check.
- **End delimiter (ED).** This field consists of half a byte in the data frame or a full byte in the token frame. It is changed in the physical layer with one T violation

Figure 12.25   *FDDI frame types*

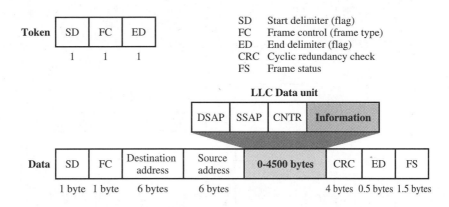

symbol in the data frame or two T symbols in the token frame. (The code for the T symbol is shown Table 12.2.)

■ **Frame status (FS).** The FDDI FS field is similar to that of token ring. It is included only in the data frame and consists of 1.5 bytes.

Implementation: Physical Medium Dependent (PMD) Layer

The physical medium dependent (PMD) layer defines the required connections and electronic components. Specific specifications for this layer depend on whether the transmission medium used is fiber-optic or copper cable.

Dual Ring

FDDI is implemented as a dual ring (see Figure 12.26). In most cases, data transmission is confined to the primary ring. The secondary ring is provided in case the primary fails.

Figure 12.26   *FDDI ring*

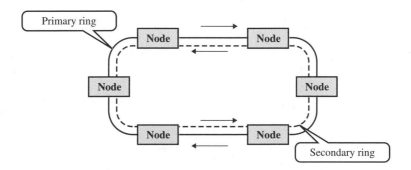

The secondary ring makes FDDI self-healing. Whenever a problem occurs on the primary ring, the secondary can be activated to complete data circuits and maintain service (see Figure 12.27).

Figure 12.27   *FDDI ring after a failure*

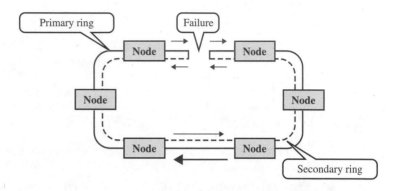

Nodes connect to one or to both rings using a media interface connector (MIC) that can be either male or female depending on the requirements of the station. Every MIC has two fiber ports that allow it to connect to both ring cables.

Nodes

FDDI defines three types of nodes: dual attachment station (DAS), single attachment station (SAS), and dual attachment concentrator (DAC); see Figure 12.28.

Figure 12.28   *Node connections*

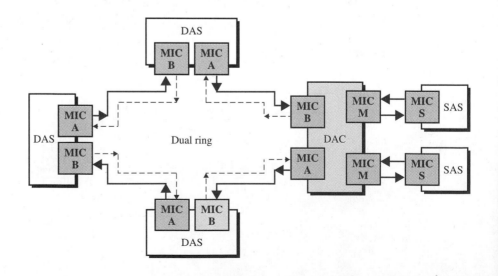

DAS   A dual attachment station (DAS) has two MICs (called MIC A and MIC B) and connects to both rings. To do so requires an expensive NIC with two inputs and two outputs. The connection to both rings gives it improved reliability and throughput. These improvements, however, are predicated on the stations remaining on. Faults are bypassed by a station's making a wrap connection from the primary ring to the secondary to switch signals from one input to another output. However, for DAS stations to make this switch, they must be active (turned on).

SAS   Most workstations, servers, and minicomputers attach to the ring in single attachment station (SAS) mode. An SAS has only one MIC (called MIC S) and therefore can connect only to one ring. Robustness is achieved by connecting SASs to intermediate nodes (DACs) rather than to the FDDI ring directly. This configuration allows each workstation to operate through a simple NIC with only one input and one output. The concentrator (DAC) provides the connection to the dual ring. Faulty stations can be turned off and bypassed to keep the ring alive (see below).

DAC   As mentioned above, a dual attachment concentrator (DAC) connects an SAS to the dual ring. It provides wrapping (diverting traffic from one ring to the other to bypass a failure) as well as control functions.

12.6   COMPARISON

Table 12.3 compares the features of the three LANs discussed above. Ethernet is good for low-level loads but collapses as the load increases due to collisions and retransmissions. Token ring and FDDI perform poorly at low-level loads but always guarantee some maximum time between transmission of two adjacent frames.

Table 12.3   *LAN comparison*

Network	Access Method	Address Length	Signaling	Data Rate	Error Control
Ethernet	CSMA/CD	6 bytes	Manchester	1, 10 Mbps	No
Token ring	Token passing	6 bytes	Differential Manchester	10–16 Mbps	Yes
FDDI	Token passing	6 bytes	4B/5B	100 Mbps	Yes

12.7   SUMMARY

- The purpose of the IEEE's Project 802 is to set up standards so that LAN equipment manufactured by different companies is compatible.
- Project 802 divides the data link layer into sublayers:
  a. Logical link control (LLC).
  b. Media access control (MAC).

- The LLC is the upper sublayer and is the same for all LANs. Its functions include flow control and error detection. Logical addresses, control information, and data from the upper layers are packaged into a packet called the protocol data unit (PDU).
- The MAC sublayer coordinates the data link tasks within a specific LAN.
- The MAC sublayer is manufacturer-specific and dependent on the LAN type.
- Three LANs specified by Project 802 are the following:
  a. Ethernet (802.3).
  b. Token bus (802.4).
  c. Token ring (802.5).
- CSMA/CD operates as follows: Any station may listen to the line to determine if the line is clear. If clear, transmission can commence. If a collision occurs, transmission stops and the process is repeated.
- The 802.3 standard defines five different physical standards:
  a. 10BASE5 (thick Ethernet).
  b. 10BASE2 (thin Ethernet).
  c. 10BASE-T (twisted-pair Ethernet).
  d. 1BASE5 (StarLAN).
  e. 100BASE-T (Fast Ethernet).
  f. 10BROAD36 (broadband Ethernet).
- Token bus (IEEE 802.4), used in factory automation and process control, combines features of Ethernet and token ring.
- Token ring (IEEE 802.5), employs token passing as its method of transmission initiation.
- Switches in token ring can be encased in a multistation access unit (MAU).
- Capture of a frame called the token in token ring entitles a station to send one frame of data.
- In token ring, a frame travels from node to node, getting regenerated at each node, until the destination is reached.
- Fiber distributed data interface (FDDI) is a LAN protocol using optical fiber as a medium, with a 100 Mbps data rate.
- FDDI consists of a primary ring for data transmission and a secondary ring that assists in failure situations.
- A media interface connector (MIC) is a device that connects the dual FDDI ring to a node.
- A dual attachment station (DAS) is a node with 2 MICs.
- A single attachment station (SAS) is a node with one MIC. An SAS must attach to the FDDI rings via a dual attachment concentrator (DAC).
- FDDI specifies protocols for the physical and data link layers.
- The FDDI data link layer consists of an LLC sublayer and an MAC sublayer. The former is similar to that specified in IEEE Project 802.2. The latter is similar to that of the token ring protocol (802.5).

- In the physical layer, FDDI uses 4B/5B encoding, a process that converts four bits to five bits.
- 4B/5B ensures that there cannot be a data sequence of more than three 0s transmitted across media in FDDI protocol. This takes care of the bit synchronization problems arising from long strings of 0s in NRZ-I encoding.
- In FDDI protocol, token possession is controlled by three time values and two timers.

12.8   PRACTICE SET

Multiple Choice

1. In CSMA/CD, the number of collisions is _____ that in MA.
   a. greater than
   b. less than
   c. equal to
   d. twice

2. In Ethernet, the source address field in the MAC frame is _____ address.
   a. the original sender's physical
   b. the previous station's physical
   c. the next destination's physical
   d. the original sender's service port

3. The counterpart to the 802.3 frame's preamble field is the _____ field on the 802.5 frame.
   a. SD
   b. AC
   c. FC
   d. FS

4. _____ uses a star topology.
   a. 10BASE5
   b. 10BASE2
   c. 10BASE-T
   d. none of the above

5. 10BASE2 uses _____ cable, while 10BASE5 uses _____.
   a. thick coaxial, thin coaxial
   b. twisted-pair, thick coaxial
   c. thin coaxial, thick coaxial
   d. fiber-optic, thin coaxial

6. 10BASE2 and 10BASE5 have different _____.
   a. signal band types
   b. fields on the 802.3 frame
   c. maximum segment lengths
   d. maximum data rates

7. _____ specifies a star topology featuring a central hub and daisy chaining.
   a. 10BASE5
   b. 10BASE2
   c. 10BASE-T
   d. 1BASE5

8. The _____ is a product of the LLC sublayer.
   a. 802.3 frame
   b. 802.5 frame
   c. PDU
   d. preamble

9. The monitor station in the _____ standard ensures that one and only one token is circulating.
   a. 802.3
   b. 802.5
   c. FDDI
   d. all of the above

10. The _____ houses the switches in token ring.
    a. NIC
    b. MAU
    c. nine-pin connector
    d. transceiver

11. What can happen at a token ring station?
    a. examination of the destination address
    b. regeneration of the frame
    c. passing of the frame to the next station
    d. all of the above

12. In token ring, where is the token when a data frame is in circulation?
    a. at the receiving station
    b. at the sending station
    c. circulating in the ring
    d. none of the above

13. In token ring, when a frame reaches its destination station, which of the following occurs?
    a. The message is copied.
    b. Four bits in the packet are changed.

c. The message is taken off the ring and replaced by the token.

d. a and b

14. Which of the following is not a transceiver function?

a. transmits and receives data

b. checks line voltages

c. addition and subtraction of headers

d. collision detection

15. Which of the following frame types is specified in the 802.5 standard?

a. token

b. abort

c. data/command

d. all of the above

16. Which Project 802 standard provides for a collision-free protocol?

a. 802.2

b. 802.3

c. 802.5

d. 802.6

17. Which LAN has the highest data rate?

a. 10BASE5

b. 10BASE-T

c. twisted-pair token ring

d. FDDI

18. Another term for CSMA/CD and the IEEE 802.3 standard is _____.

a. Ethernet

b. token ring

c. FDDI

d. token bus

19. IEEE project 802 divides the data link layer into an upper _____ sublayer and a lower _____ sublayer.

a. LLC, MAC

b. MAC, LLC

c. PDU, HDLC

d. HDLC, PDU

20. FDDI is an acronym for _____.

a. fast data delivery interface

b. fiber distributed data interface

c. fiber distributed digital interface

d. fast distributed data interface

21. In FDDI, data normally travel on _____.
    a. the primary ring
    b. the secondary ring
    c. both rings
    d. neither ring

22. What is the main purpose of the secondary ring in FDDI protocol?
    a. If the primary ring fails, the secondary takes over.
    b. If the primary ring fails, the primary makes a wrap connection with the secondary to heal the ring.
    c. The secondary alternates with the primary in transmission of data.
    d. The secondary is used to send emergency messages when the primary is busy.

23. Which type of node has two MICs and is connected to both rings?
    a. SAS
    b. DAS
    c. DAC
    d. b and c

24. Which type of node has only one MIC and can therefore connect to only one ring?
    a. SAS
    b. DAS
    c. DAC
    d. a and b

25. In which OSI layers does the FDDI protocol operate?
    a. physical
    b. data link
    c. network
    d. a and b

26. Which fields in the MAC frame of FDDI are variable?
    a. preambles
    b. address fields
    c. data fields
    d. b and c

27. Which of the following is not a legitimate 4B/5B sequence?
    a. 11100 01010
    b. 10100 01111
    c. 11100 01001
    d. 11100 00111

28. What type of encoding does FDDI use?
    a. NRZ-I
    b. NRZ-L

    c. 4B/5B

    d. a and c

29. In FDDI, if a token arrives later than the time specified in the _____ register, the ring must be reinitialized.

    a. synchronous allocation (SA)

    b. target token rotation time (TTRT)

    c. absolute maximum time (AMT)

    d. token rotation time (TRT)

30. The _____ register holds the amount of time a station has to send its synchronous data.

    a. synchronous allocation (SA)

    b. target token rotation time (TTRT)

    c. absolute maximum time (AMT)

    d. token rotation time (TRT)

31. The _____ register holds the average amount of time a token must take to finish a rotation.

    a. synchronous allocation (SA)

    b. target token rotation time (TTRT)

    c. absolute maximum time (AMT)

    d. token rotation time (TRT)

Exercises

1. Define and explain the data link layer in IEEE Project 802. Why is this layer divided into sublayers?

2. Explain CSMA/CD and its use. What part of the 802 project uses CSMA/CD?

3. Compare and contrast the SSAP and DSAP on the PDU with the source and destination address of the MAC frame.

4. Explain why there are no physical address, flag, or CRC fields in a PDU.

5. What does Project 802 have to do with the physical layer of the OSI model?

6. Contrast the IEEE project 802.3 frame with the HDLC I-frame.

7. Contrast the IEEE project 802.5 data/command frame with the HDLC I-frame.

8. What is the difference between baseband and broadband?

9. Discuss the placement of the transceiver in 10BASE5, 10BASE2, and 10BASE-T standards.

10. What is a collision?

11. A small start-up company operating on a shoestring budget needs an Ethernet LAN to handle a maximum of 10 workstations. The company will occupy two floors of an existing building. What would be a good LAN, and why?

12. What are the advantages of FDDI over a basic token ring?

13. Why is there no AC field in the 802.3 frame?

14. Explain the mechanism whereby an SAS is able to access both the primary and secondary rings.

15. How does 4B/5B encoding guarantee that there will be no sequences of four or more 0s in the data field?

16. In Figure 12.22, is reinitialization ever warranted? Why or why not?

17. Using Figure 12.22 as a basis, continue with rounds 6 to 10.

CHAPTER 13

METROPOLITAN AREA NETWORKS

A metropolitan area network (MAN) is a network designed to extend over an entire city. When local area networks (LANs) in close proximity need to exchange data, they can be connected privately using cable and routers or gateways. When LANs of a single enterprise are distributed over a larger area (such as a city or large campus), however, privately owned connecting infrastructure is impractical. Most organizations find that even if they could get permits to lay cable on public land, a better alternative is to use the services of existing utilities, such as the telephone company. These services include: distributed queue dual bus (DQDB) and switched multimegabit data services (SMDS).

13.1   IEEE 802.6

In addition to the protocols discussed in Chapter 12, another protocol in the IEEE Project 802 (802.6) is distributed queue dual bus (DQDB). Although DQDB resembles a LAN standard, it is designed to be used in MANs.

Access Method: Dual Bus

As its name implies, DQDB uses a dual bus configuration: each device in the system connects to two backbone links. Access to these links is granted not by contention (as in 802.3) or token passing (as in 802.4 and 802.5) but by a mechanism called distributed queues.

Figure 13.1 shows a DQDB topology. In this illustration, the two unidirectional buses are labeled Bus A and Bus B. Five numbered stations connect to the buses as shown. Each bus connects to the stations directly through input and output ports; no drop lines are used.

Directional Traffic

Each bus supports traffic in only one direction. The direction of traffic on one bus is the opposite of traffic on the other. In Figure 13.1, for example, where the beginning of each bus is represented by a square and the end by a triangle, Bus A traffic moves from

Figure 13.1 *DQDB buses and nodes*

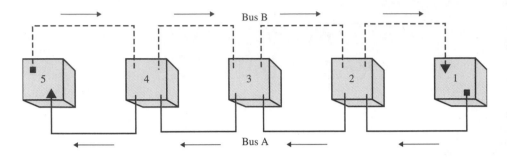

right to left. The bus itself starts at station 1 and ends at station 5. Bus B traffic moves from left to right. The bus starts at station 5 and ends at station 1.

Upstream and Downstream Stations   The relationships of the stations on a DQDB network are understood in relation to the direction of traffic flow on a bus. As Bus A is configured, stations 1 and 2 are considered to be upstream with respect to station 3, and stations 4 and 5 are considered to be downstream with respect to station 3. In the example in Figure 13.1, station 1 has no upstream stations but has four downstream stations. For this reason, station 1 is regarded as the head of Bus A. Station 5 has no downstream stations but has four upstream stations; it is regarded as the end of Bus A.

As Bus B is configured, stations 1 and 2 are considered downstream with respect to station 3, and stations 4 and 5 are considered upstream with respect to station 3. In this case, station 5 has no upstream stations but has four downstream stations. It is therefore the head of Bus B. Station 1 has no downstream stations but has four upstream stations; it is the end of Bus B.

Transmission Slots

Data travel on each bus as a steady stream of 53-byte slots. These slots are not packets; they are merely continuous streams of slots. The head of Bus A (station 1 in Figure 13.1) generates empty slots for use on Bus A. The head of Bus B (station 5) generates empty slots for use on Bus B. The data rate is dependent on the number of slots generated per second. A number of different data rates are in use today.

An empty slot travels down its bus until a transmitting station drops data into it and the intended destination station reads the data. But which bus will the source station choose to carry data to a given destination station? The source station must choose the bus for which the destination station is considered downstream This rule is intuitive. The slots in each bus travel from their head station to their end station. Within each bus, the slots are moving toward the next downstream station. If a station wants to send data, it must choose the bus whose traffic flows toward its destination.

The source station must choose the bus for which the destination station is considered downstream.

Figure 13.2*a* shows station 2 sending data to station 4. Station 2 chooses a slot on Bus A because Bus A is flowing downstream from station 2 toward station 4. The transmission process is as follows: the head station in Bus A (station 1) creates an empty slot. Station 2 drops its data into the passing slot and addresses the slot to station 4. Station 3 reads the address and passes the slot along unread. Station 4 recognizes its address. It reads the data and changes the status of the slot to "read" before passing it along to station 5, where the slot is absorbed.

Figure 13.2   *Data transmission in DQDB*

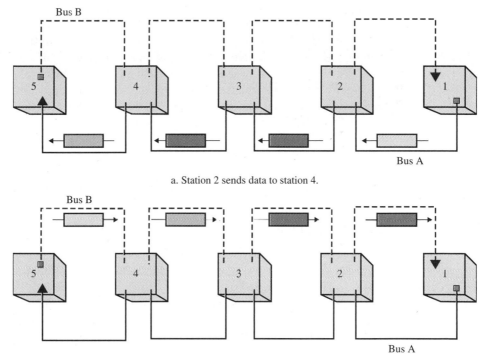

a. Station 2 sends data to station 4.

b. Station 3 sends data to station 1.

In Figure 13.2*b*, station 3 needs to send data to station 1. Station 1 is downstream from station 3 on Bus B, so Bus B is chosen to carry the data. The head of the bus (in this case, station 5) creates an empty slot and sends it down the bus. Station 4 ignores the slot (why it does so is discussed below) and passes it to station 3. Station 3 inserts its data into the slot and addresses the slot to station 1. Station 2 reads the address and relays the slot unread. Station 1 recognizes its address, reads the data, and discards the used slot. Note that because station 1 is the end of the bus, it does not set the read field, but just discards the frame once it has read the data.

Slot Reservation   To send data downstream, a station must wait for the arrival of an unoccupied slot. But what is to stop an upstream station from monopolizing the bus and occupying all the slots? Should stations near the end of a bus suffer because the upstream stations have access to empty slots before they do? This imbalance can be more than an injustice; it can degrade quality of service—particularly if the system carries time-sensitive information such as voice or video.

The solution is to require stations to make reservations for the slots they want. But if you will look at Figure 13.2 again, you will notice a problem. A station makes a reservation to keep upstream stations from using slots on the bus. But how can station 2 make a reservation on Bus A? How can it communicate its reservation upstream to station 1? The solution, of course, is for station 2 to make its reservation for Bus A on Bus B, which is carrying traffic in the other direction. Station 2 sets a reservation bit in a slot on Bus B to tell each station it passes that a station is reserving a slot on Bus A. The slot passes every station downstream from station 2 on Bus B—the same stations that are upstream from it on Bus A.

These stations must respect the reservation of a downstream station and leave slots free for the downstream station's use. How this process works is described below. For now, just remember that to send data on one bus, a station must make a reservation on the other bus. Another important aspect of the reservations process is that no station may send data without first making a reservation, even if it sees slot after slot pass by empty. Empty slots may be reserved by downstream stations. In fact, even a station that has made a reservation cannot claim just any empty slot. It must wait for the arrival of the specific slot it reserved.

> To send data on one bus, a station must use the other bus to make a reservation.

Distributed Queues

Making reservations and tracking the reservations of the other stations on a bus require that each station store two queues—one for each bus. Each station has one queue for Bus A, called queue A, and one queue for Bus B, called queue B.

A queue is a storage mechanism with first-in, first-out (FIFO) functionality. It is comparable to the waiting list at a restaurant. As patrons arrive, they sign the list. The first party on the list is seated first. Thus, a DQDB queue is essentially a waiting list of stations. Each station maintains two queues, one for each bus. Whenever a station sends a reservation request, the stations receiving that request add it to their queues. The queues are used to allocate bus access for the entire network.

Figure 13.3 gives a conceptual view of a queue. Elements are inserted from the rear and removed from the front as the queue advances.

Remember, each station keeps two queues, queue A and queue B. Figure 13.4 shows these two queues for one station.

Using a Queue for Bus Access

For clarity, let's examine queue A by itself. Station X adds itself to queue A to reserve space on Bus A. To do so, it needs to know how many of its downstream neighbors have made slot requests on Bus A already. To track these reservations, it uses virtual tokens. It adds a token at the rear of the queue each time a slot passes on Bus B with a reservation bit set. When the station needs to make a reservation for itself, it sets one of

Figure 13.3   *Queues*

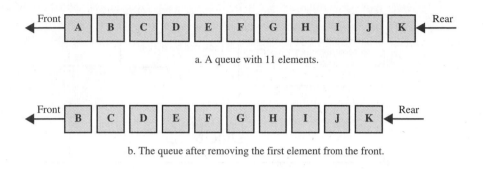

a. A queue with 11 elements.

b. The queue after removing the first element from the front.

c. The queue after inserting two elements at the rear.

Figure 13.4   *Distributed queues in a node*

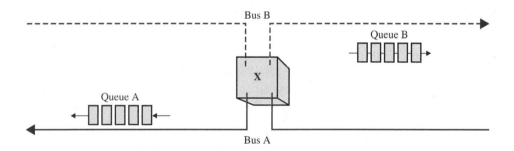

the reservation bits in a slot passing on Bus B (the slot can be occupied or not, provided a request bit is available). The station then inserts its own token into its queue A. This token, however, is of a different type from the others to indicate that it is the station's own reservation (see Figure 13.5).

Each time the station reads its queue A, it can tell how many downstream reservations have been made by counting how many tokens are in the queue. The station can also tell how many empty slots it must allow to pass before it can capture a slot for itself. The station watches the unoccupied slots passing in Bus A. For each empty slot that passes, it removes and discards one token from the front of the queue. When it sees an empty slot and finds its own token at the front of the queue, it discards the token but captures the empty slot and inserts its own data. The station knows it has satisfied the reservation requirements of the downstream stations by letting the same number of empty slots pass as there are tokens ahead of its own in its queue.

Figure 13.5   *Reservation token in a queue*

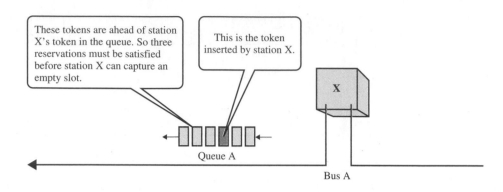

Now, referring back to Figure 13.2, let's examine the behavior of each of our original five stations with respect to Bus A.

Station 1 is responsible for slot creation. It creates empty slots continuously and releases them to Bus A. To use one of these slots to send its own data, however, it must take its place in its queue A just like any other station. If there are tokens in front of its own, station 1 releases empty slots for the downstream stations (stations 2, 3, 4, and 5) until its own token comes up. At that point, it inserts its own data into a slot and sets the slot's busy bit (to 1 for "on") before releasing the slot to the bus.

The behavior of stations 2, 3, and 4 is essentially the same as that of station 1 except that these stations do not create slots. Instead, they watch the empty slots as they pass. For each empty slot that passes, each station removes one token from its queue A until it removes its own token. At that point, it captures the next empty slot, loads data into it, sets the busy bit, and releases it back to the bus.

Station 5, on the other hand, cannot send data by Bus A (there is no station downstream from station 5 on Bus A). In fact, it does not even need a queue A, although it may contain a queue A for network compatibility in case a station is added downstream from it in the future.

The preceding description also applies to Bus B, with the difference that in Bus B station 5 creates and releases the slots and station 1 does not need a queue B.

Queue Structure

The DQDB standard states explicitly how logical queues A and B are to be used. However, the design of each queue is left to the implementors. Networks and stations can be made to simulate the operations of the queues as long as those simulations follow the stated rules.

Ring Configuration

DQDB can also be implemented as a ring. In this case, one station plays the roles of both header and end (see Figure 13.6). This topology has the advantage of being reconfigurable whenever a link or a station fails. Figure 13.6b shows the original ring reconfigured after a link failure.

Figure 13.6   *DQDB rings*

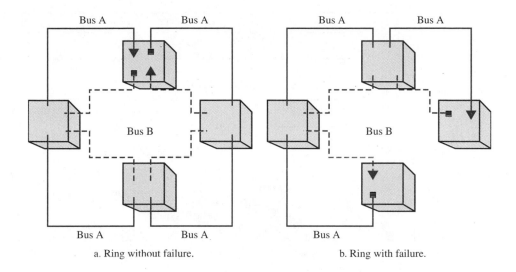

a. Ring without failure.   b. Ring with failure.

Operation: DQDB Layers

The IEEE defines both the media access control (MAC) sublayer and the physical layer for DQDB. The specifics of the MAC layer functions are complex and fall beyond the scope of this book. In general, however, the MAC layer splits the data stream coming from the upper layers (the LLC layer) into 48-byte segments and adds a 5-byte header to each segment to create slots of 53 bytes each (see Figure 13.7). Having 53 bytes makes a DQDB slot compatible with the size of a cell in Asynchronous Transfer Mode (ATM); see Chapter 18.

The DQDB Header

The five bytes of the DQDB header are distributed among five major fields: access, address, type, priority, and CRC.

Access Field   The DQDB access field is an eight-bit field that controls access to the bus. It is subdivided into five subfields:

- **Busy (B).** The B bit indicates whether or not the slot is carrying data. When set, it means the slot is occupied.

- **Slot type (ST).** The ST bit can define two types of slots, one for packet transmissions and the other for isochronous transmission.

- **Reserved (R).** The R bit is reserved.

- **Previous slot read (PSR).** The two-bit PSR field is set to 0 by the addressed station once it has read the contents of the slot.

- **Request (RQ).** The RQ field consists of three bits set by stations to make reservations for slots. The three bits can represent eight levels of priority in networks with different station levels. In networks with no priorities, the first bit is used.

Figure 13.7   *DQDB layers*

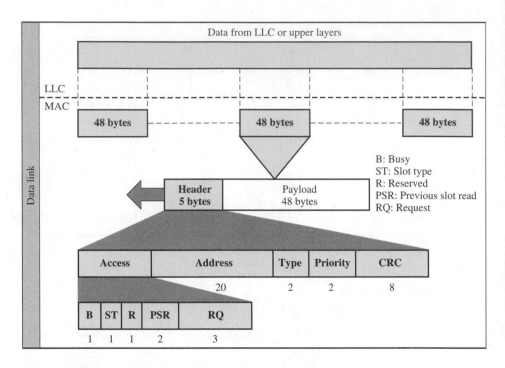

Address Field   The address field holds a 20-bit virtual channel identifier (VCI) to be used for MAN and WAN transmission. When used in a LAN, this field contains all 1s and an additional header is added to carry the MAC physical address.

Type Field   The 2-bit type field identifies the type of the payload as user data, management data, and so on.

Priority   The priority field identifies the priority of the slot in a network that uses priorities.

CRC   The CRC field carries an eight-bit cyclic redundancy check ($x^8 + x^2 + x + 1$) that is used to detect single- or multiple-bit errors and to correct single-bit errors in the header.

Implementation

Physical layer specifications are left open. The DQDB standard defines the electronic devices used to access the dual bus. Access media can be either coaxial or fiber-optic cable with a variety of data rates.

13.2 SMDS

Switched multimegabit data services (SMDS) is a service for handling high-speed communications for metropolitan area networks. It was developed to support organizations that need to exchange data between a number of LANs located in different parts of a city or large campus. Before the introduction of SMDS, making these exchanges was often difficult. One option was to subscribe to an existing telephone company service such as switched/56 or DDS (described in Chapter 8). Most LANs, however, create and consume data at 10 to 16 Mbps, whereas the data rates of the switched/56 and DDS services (56 Kbps and 64 Kbps) create insupportable delays and a resulting degradation of service.

A faster alternative is to subscribe to a DS-1 service with a leased T-1 line and data rate of 1.544 Mbps, or to a DS-3 service with a leased T-3 line and data rate of 44.736 Mbps. These options solve the data rate problem, but they are expensive. For example, consider an enterprise with three offices in three different parts of a city. To join their LANs into a MAN requires a mesh of three point-to-point connections (three T-1 or T-3 lines); see Figure 13.8.

Figure 13.8 *Connecting LANs using T-1 or T-3 lines*

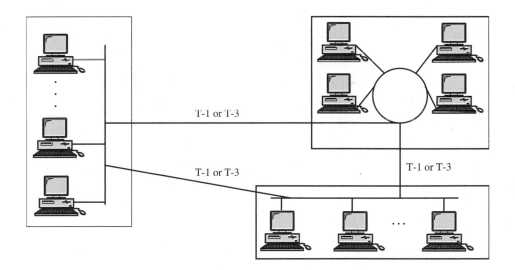

One T-1 line costs almost $1500 per month. Three T-1 lines therefore cost a company $4500 per month (or $54,000 per year)—for a data rate of only 1.544 Mbps. The cost of T-3 lines is even higher: 10 times that of the T-1 lines. T-3 lines have better data rates than T-1 lines (44.736 Mbps instead of 1.544 Mbps), but $540,000 per year is more than most companies can afford.

Of course, most companies' data traffic does not utilize a line 100 percent of the time. The lines would therefore be more affordable if they could be shared. Unfortunately, the telephone companies do not offer switched-based leases for T lines. A subscriber must lease the line either all of the time or not at all.

SMDS provides the solution. It is a packet-switched datagram service for high-speed MAN traffic (see Chapter 14). SMDS is provided by common carriers and is intended to replace switched services such as switched/56. Because SMDS is a switched network, subscribers pay only for the time they use.

Connection and Access

SMDS is described by a series of specifications developed by Bell Communications Research (Bellcore) and adopted by the telecommunications providers. Subscriber LANs link to an SMDS network through routers (see Figure 13.9).

Figure 13.9   *SMDS as a MAN: subscriber LANs linked to SMDS through routers*

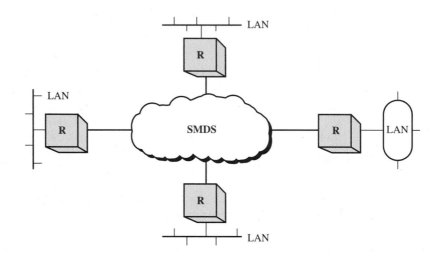

Access to SMDS is coordinated using the SMDS interface protocol (SIP) which is based on DQDB. A comprehensive discussion of SIP is beyond the scope of this book; however, we will mention a few basic points.

A customer LAN is connected by its router and a dual bus to the SMDS network (see Figure 13.10). If each customer site has only one LAN to connect to the network, the DQDB mechanism is simplified: no queues are required.

A customer site can connect multiple LANs to the SMDS network through a single DQDB. In this case, the full capability of the DQDB is required (see Figure 13.11).

The SMDS standard does not specify the implementation for the SMDS network itself. A provider can choose any technology that supports the required services at the required rate.

Today SMDS networks offer rates that differ from those provided by the DS services (DS-1 to DS-4) and therefore cannot be used for WAN traffic. It is expected, however, that in the future SMDS networks may offer services at rates as high as 600 Mbps.

Figure 13.10 *Use of DQDB in a MAN: single LAN connection to SMDS*

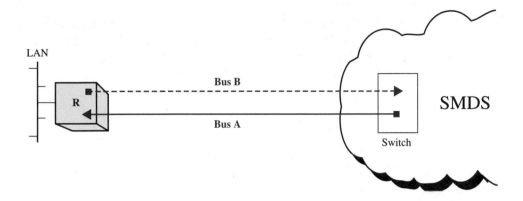

Figure 13.11 *Use of DQDB in a MAN with multiple LANs*

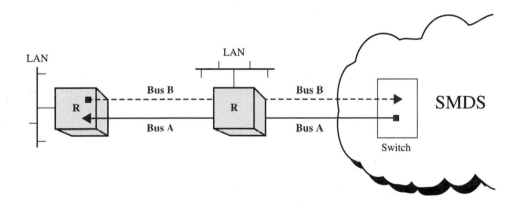

13.3 SUMMARY

- Distributed queue dual bus (DQDB) uses two unidirectional buses. The buses travel in opposite directions.

- Data transmission in DQDB occurs through capture of an empty slot and insertion of data into the slot.

- A station can transmit data only in the downstream direction. The reservation for a slot is made on the other (upstream) bus.

- Through the use of first in, first out (FIFO) queues, each station has an equal opportunity to send its data.

- DQDB operates in the physical layer and the MAC sublayer.

- DQDB can also be implemented as a ring topology.

- In the MAC sublayer, a 5-byte header is added to a 48-byte payload.
- In the physical layer, the protocols define the electronic devices, media, and data rates.
- Switched multimegabit data services (SMDS) is a packet switched datagram service used to handle high-speed communications in a MAN.
- SMDS is a good choice for users who
  a. Require a data rate greater than that of switched/56 or DDS.
  b. Do not need full-time use of a link.
- SMDS uses DQDB for media access.

13.4   PRACTICE SET

Multiple Choice

1. DQDB is an acronym for _____.
   a. distributed queue data base
   b. differential queue data bus
   c. data queue dual bus
   d. distributed queue dual bus
2. A DQDB is composed of _____.
   a. 2 one-directional buses traveling in opposite directions
   b. 1 two-directional bus
   c. 2 two-directional buses traveling in opposite directions
   d. 1 one-directional bus
3. In a DQDB with bus A and bus B, if a source station sends data via bus B, the reservation is made on _____.
   a. the bus with the closest head
   b. the less busy bus
   c. bus B
   d. bus A
4. We have a six-element queue in the order A B C D E F, with A being the first in. If two elements are removed and element G and then H are inserted, which element is at the front of the queue?
   a. C
   b. D
   c. G
   d. H
5. DQDB operates in the _____ layer.
   a. physical
   b. data link

   c. physical and data link

   d. network

6. Which bit field in the DQDB access field byte is used for station reservations?

   a. B

   b. ST

   c. PSR

   d. RQ

7. Which bit field in the DQDB access field byte is set to 0 after the slot contents are read?

   a. B

   b. ST

   c. PSR

   d. RQ

8. Which field in the DQDB header identifies the type of payload?

   a. access

   b. address

   c. type

   d. priority

9. SMDS is an acronym for _____.

   a. switched multimegabit data services

   b. switched media data services

   c. synchronous multimegabit data services

   d. synchronous media data services

10. SMDS is a service designed to handle high-speed communications in _____.

   a. a LAN

   b. a MAN

   c. a WAN

   d. all of the above

11. The SMDS interface protocol (SIP) specifies the use of _____ as a media access method between the router and SMDS.

   a. CSMA/CA

   b. CSMA/CD

   c. DQDB

   d. DBDQ

Exercises

1. There are 10 stations, numbered successively 1 through 10, connected in a DQDB. Station 1 generates the slots in Bus A; Station 10 generates slots in Bus B. Draw the system, labeling the heads, ends, buses, stations, and bus directions.

2. In Exercise 1, how many stations are upstream with respect to station 7? How many stations are downstream with respect to station 3?

3. Using Figure 13.1, match the following to stations 1, 2, 3, 4, and/or 5. There may be more than one match per problem.

   a. Generates empty slots.

   b. Doesn't need queue A.

   c. Doesn't need queue B.

   d. Needs both queues.

4. Explain how the address field in the DQDB header functions on a MAN and on a LAN.

5. Draw four token ring LANs connected to SMDS using DQDB.

CHAPTER 14

SWITCHING:
A NETWORK LAYER FUNCTION

Whenever we have multiple devices, we have the problem of how to connect them to make one-on-one communication possible. One solution is to install a point-to-point link between each pair of devices (a mesh topology) or between a central device and every other device (a star topology). These methods, however, are impractical and wasteful when applied to very large networks. The number and length of the links require too much infrastructure to be cost efficient; and the majority of those links would be idle most of the time. Imagine a network of six devices: A, B, C, D, E, and F. If device A has point-to-point links to devices B, C, D, E, and F, then whenever only A and B are connected, the links connecting A to each of the other devices are idle and wasted.

Other topologies employing multipoint connections, such as a bus, are ruled out because the distances between devices and the total number of devices increase beyond the capacities of the media and equipment.

A better solution is to use switching. A switched network consists of a series of interlinked nodes, called switches. Switches are hardware and/or software devices capable of creating temporary connections between two or more devices linked to the switch but not to each other. In a switched network, some of these nodes are connected to the communicating devices. Others are used only for routing.

Figure 14.1 shows a switched network. The communicating devices (in this example, computers) are labeled A, B, C, D, and so on, and the switches I, II, III, IV, and so on. Each switch is connected to multiple links and is used to complete the connections between them, two at a time.

Traditionally, three methods of switching have been important: circuit switching, packet switching, and message switching (see Figure 14.2). The first two are commonly used today. The third has been phased out in general communications, but still has networking applications. New switching strategies are gaining prominence, among them cell relay (ATM) and frame relay. We will discuss these technologies in Chapters 17 and 18. Understanding the older methods provides a good basis for understanding the newer ones, so we will examine older methods first.

Figure 14.1   *Switched network*

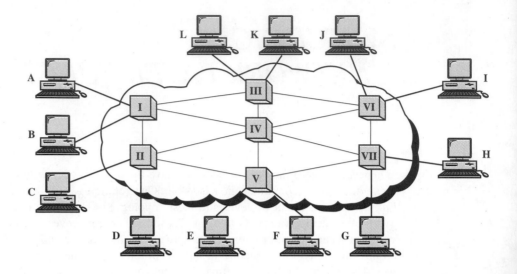

Figure 14.2   *Switching methods*

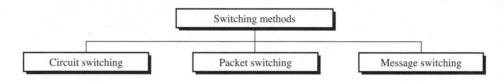

14.1   CIRCUIT SWITCHING

Circuit switching creates a direct physical connection between two devices such as phones or computers. For example, in Figure 14.3, instead of point-to-point connections between the three computers on the left (A, B, and C) to the four computers on the right (D, E, F, and G), requiring 12 links, we can use four switches to reduce the number and the total length of the links. In Figure 14.3, computer A is connected through switches I, II, and III to computer D. By moving the levers of the switches, any computer on the left can be connected to any computer on the right.

A circuit switch is a device with *n* inputs and *m* outputs that creates a temporary connection between an input link and an output link (see Figure 14.4). The number of inputs does not have to match the number of outputs.

An *n*-by-*n* folded switch can connect *n* lines in full-duplex mode. For example, it can connect *n* telephones in such a way that each phone can be connected to every other phone (see Figure 14.5).

Circuit switching today can use either of two technologies: space-division switches or time-division switches (see Figure 14.6).

Figure 14.3   *Circuit-switched network*

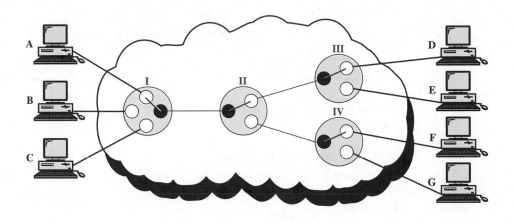

Figure 14.4   *A circuit switch*

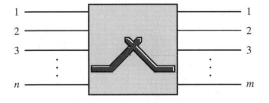

Figure 14.5   *A folded switch*

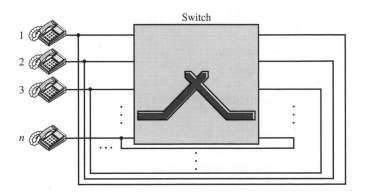

Space-Division Switches

In a space-division switch, the paths in the circuit are separated from each other spatially. This technology was originally designed for use in analog networks but is used

Figure 14.6   *Switching*

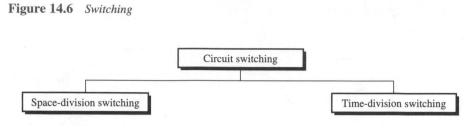

currently in both analog and digital networks. It has evolved through a long history of many designs. Today, however, the only type used is the crossbar.

Crossbar Switches

A crossbar switch connects *n* inputs to *m* outputs in a grid, using electronic micro-switches (transistors) at each crosspoint (see Figure 14.7). The major limitation of this

Figure 14.7   *Crossbar switch*

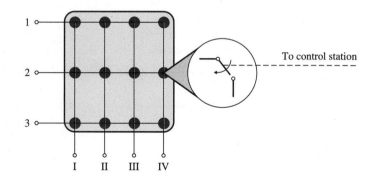

design is the number of switches required. Connecting *n* inputs by *m* outputs using a crossbar switch requires *n* × *m* crosspoints. For example, to connect 1000 inputs to 1000 outputs requires a crossbar with 1,000,000 crosspoints. This factor makes the crossbar impractical because it makes the size of the crossbar huge, and inefficient because statistics show that, in practice, fewer than 25 percent of the crosspoints are in use at a given time. The rest are idle.

Multistage Switches

The solution to the limitations of the crossbar switch is multistage switching, in which crossbar switches are combined in several stages. In multistage switching, devices are linked to switches that, in turn are linked to a hierarchy of other switches (see Figure 14.8).

The design of a multistage switch depends on the number of stages and the number of switches required (or desired) in each stage. Normally, the middle stages have fewer switches than do the first and last stages. For example, imagine that we want a multi-stage switch as in Figure 14.8 to do the job of a single 15-by-15 crossbar switch.

Figure 14.8 *Multistage switch*

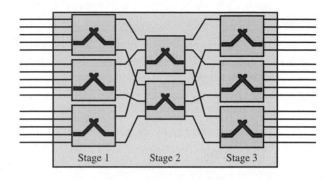

Assume that we have decided on a three-stage design that uses three switches in the first and final stages and two switches in the middle stage. Because there are three of them, each of the first-stage switches has inputs from one-third of the input devices, giving them five inputs each ($5 \times 3 = 15$).

Next, each of the first-stage switches must have an output to each of the intermediate switches. There are two intermediate switches; therefore, each first-stage switch has two outputs. Each third-stage switch must have inputs from each of the intermediate switches; two intermediate switches means two inputs. The intermediate switches must connect to all three first-stage switches and all three last-stage switches, and so must have three inputs and three outputs each.

Multiple Paths Multistage switches provide several options for connecting each pair of linked devices. Figure 14.9 shows two ways traffic can move from an input to an output using the switch designed in the example above.

In Figure 14.9*a*, a pathway is established between input line 4 and output line 9. In this instance, the path uses the lower intermediate switch and that switch's center output

Figure 14.9 *Switching path*

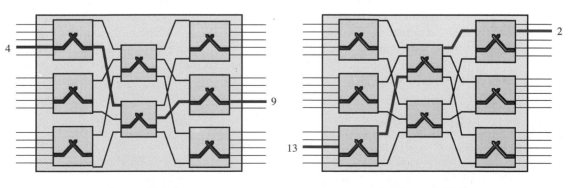

a. 4 connected to 9   b. 13 connected to 2

line to reach the last-stage switch connected to line 9. It could have used the upper intermediate switch just as easily.

Figure 14.9*b* shows a pathway between input line 13 and output line 2. What other paths could have been used to make this connection?

Blocking   Let us compare the number of crosspoints in a 15-by-15 single-stage crossbar switch with the 15-by-15 multistage switch that we described above. In the single-stage switch, we need 225 crosspoints (15×15). In the multistage switch, we need

- Three first-stage switches, each with 10 crosspoints (5×2), for a total of 30 crosspoints at the first stage.

- Two second-stage switches, each with 9 crosspoints (3×3), for a total of 18 crosspoints at the second stage.

- Three third-stage switches, each with 10 crosspoints (5×2), for a total of 30 crosspoints at the last stage.

The total number of crosspoints required by our multistage switch is 78. In this example, the multistage switch requires only 35 percent as many crosspoints as the single-stage switch.

This savings comes with a cost, however. The reduction in the number of crosspoints results in a phenomenon called blocking during periods of heavy traffic. Blocking refers to times when one input cannot be connected to an output because there is no path available between them—all of the possible intermediate switches are occupied.

In a single-stage switch blocking does not occur. Because every combination of inputs and outputs has its own switch, there is always a path. (Cases where two inputs are trying to contact the same output don't count. That path is not blocked; the output is merely busy.) In the multistage switch described in the example above, however, only two of the first five inputs can use the switch at a time; only two of the second five inputs can use the switch at a time, and so on. The small number of outputs at the middle stage further increases the restriction on the number of available links.

In large systems, such as those having 10,000 inputs and outputs, the number of stages can be increased to cut down the number of crosspoints required. As the number of stages increases, however, possible blocking increases as well. Many people have experienced blocking on public telephone systems in the wake of a natural disaster when calls being made to check on or reassure relatives far outnumber the ordinary load of the system. In those cases, it is often impossible to get a connection. Under normal circumstances, however, blocking is not usually a problem. In countries that can afford it, the number of switches between lines is calculated to make blocking unlikely. The formula for finding this number is based on statistical analysis, which is beyond the scope of this book.

Time-Division Switches

In a time-division switch, the slots are divided by time instead of space. Switching is accomplished using time-division multiplexing (TDM). TDM alone, however, is not sufficient; a device known as a time-slot interchange (TSI) must be used.

TSI

Figure 14.10 shows a system connecting four input lines (A, B, C, and D, in that order) with four output lines (W, X, Y, and Z, in that order). Imagine that each input wants to send data to one of the outputs according to the following pattern:

$$A \Rightarrow Y \qquad B \Rightarrow Z \qquad C \Rightarrow W \qquad D \Rightarrow X$$

Figure 14.10*a* shows the results of ordinary time-division multiplexing. As you can see, the desired switching is not accomplished. Data are output in the same order as they are input. Data from A go to W, from B go to X, from C go to Y, and from D go to Z.

In Figure 14.10*b,* however, we insert a device called a time-slot interchange (TSI) into the link. A TSI changes the ordering of the slots based on the desired connections. In this case, it changes the input order of A, B, C, D to C, D, A, B. Now, when the demultiplexer separates the slots, it passes them to the proper outputs.

> The main component of time-division switching is a device called a time-slot interchange (TSI).

Figure 14.10   *Time-division multiplexing, without and with a time-slot interchange (TSI)*

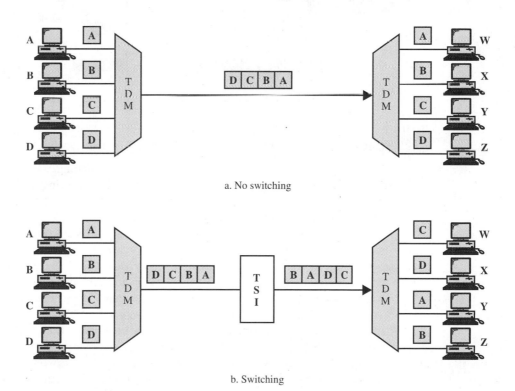

a. No switching

b. Switching

How a TSI works is shown in Figure 14.11. A TSI consists of random access memory (RAM) with several memory locations. The size of each location is the same as the size of a single time slot. The number of locations is the same as the number of inputs (in most cases, the number of inputs and outputs are equal). The RAM fills up with incoming data from time slots in the order received. Slots are then sent out in an order based on the decisions of a control unit.

Figure 14.11   *Time-slot interchange*

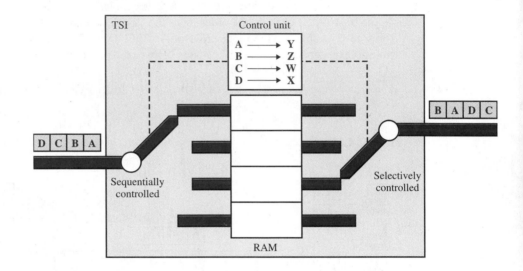

Space- and Time-Division Switching Combinations

When we compare space-division and time-division switching, some interesting facts emerge. The advantage of space-division switching is that it is instantaneous. Its disadvantage is the number of crosspoints required to make space-division switching acceptable in terms of blocking.

The advantage of time-division switching is that it needs no crosspoints. Its disadvantage is that processing each connection creates delays. Each time slot must be stored by the RAM, then retrieved and passed on.

In a third option, we combine space-division and time-division technology to take advantage of the best of both. Combining the two results in switches that are optimized both physically (the number of crosspoints) and temporally (the amount of delay). Multistage switches of this sort can be designed as time-space-time (TST), time-space-space-time (TSST), space-time-time-space (STTS), or other possible combinations.

Figure 14.12 shows a simple TST switch that consists of two time stages and one space stage, and has 12 inputs and 12 outputs. Instead of one time-division switch, it divides the inputs into three groups (of four inputs each) and directs them to three time-slot interchanges. The result in this case is that the average delay is one-third of that which would result from using one time-slot interchange to handle all 12 inputs.

Figure 14.12 *TST switch*

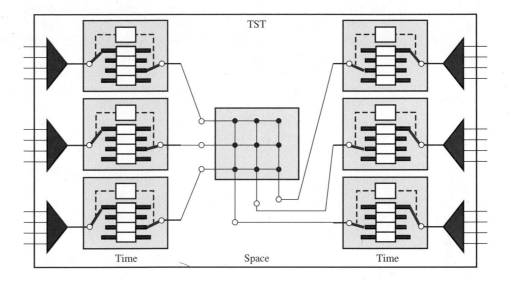

The last stage is a mirror image of the first stage. The middle stage is a space-division switch (crossbar) that connects the TSI groups together to allow connectivity between all possible input and output pairs (e.g., to connect input 3 of the first group to output 7 of the second group).

14.2 PACKET SWITCHING

Circuit switching was designed for voice communication. In a telephone conversation, for example, once a circuit is established it remains connected for the duration of the session. Circuit switching creates temporary dedicated links that are well suited to this type of communication.

Circuit switching is less well suited to data and other nonconversational transmissions. Nonvoice transmissions tend to be bursty, meaning that data come in spurts with idle gaps between them. When circuit-switched links are used for data transmission, therefore, the line is often idle and its facilities wasted. Multiplexing improves line utilization but is only minimally effective unless transmission is predictable and every user is transmitting at essentially the same rate.

A second weakness of circuit-switched connections for data transmission is in its data rate. A circuit-switched link creates the equivalent of a single cable between two devices and thereby assumes a single data rate for both devices. This assumption limits the flexibility and usefulness of a circuit-switched connection for networks interconnecting a variety of digital devices.

Third, circuit switching is inflexible. Once a circuit has been established, that circuit is the path taken by all parts of the transmission whether or not it remains the most efficient or available.

Finally, circuit switching sees all transmissions as equal. Any request is granted to whatever link is available. But often with data network transmission, we want to be able to prioritize: to say, for example, that transmission x can go anytime but transmission z is time dependent and must go immediately.

A better solution for data transmission is called packet switching. In a packet-switched network, data are transmitted in discrete units of potentially variable length blocks called packets. The maximum length of the packet is established by the network. Longer transmissions are broken-up into multiple packets. Each packet contains not only data but also a header with control information (such as priority codes and source and destination addresses). The packets are sent over the network node-to-node. At each node, the packet is stored briefly then routed according to the information in its header.

There are two popular approaches to packet switching: datagram and virtual circuit (see Figure 14.13).

Figure 14.13   *Packet switching approaches*

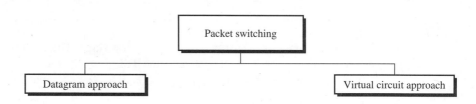

Datagram Approach

In the datagram approach to packet switching, each packet is treated independently from all others. Even when one packet represents just a piece of a multipacket transmission, the network (and network layer functions) treats it as though it existed alone. Packets in this technology are referred to as datagrams.

Figure 14.14 shows how the datagram approach can be used to deliver four packets from station A to station X. In this example, all four packets (or datagrams) belong to the same message but may go by different paths to reach their destination.

This approach can cause the datagrams of a transmission to arrive at their destination out of order. It is the responsibility of the transport layer in most protocols to reorder the datagrams before passing them on to the destination port.

The link joining each pair of nodes can contain multiple channels. Each of these channels is capable, in turn, of carrying datagrams either from several different sources or from one source simultaneously. Packets can be carried simultaneously by either TDM or FDM multiplexing (see Figure 14.15).

In Figure 14.15, devices A and B are sending datagrams to devices X and Y. Some paths use one channel while others use more than one. As you can see, the bottom link is carrying two packets of different formats in the same direction. The link on the right, however, is carrying datagrams in two directions.

Figure 14.14   *Datagram approach*

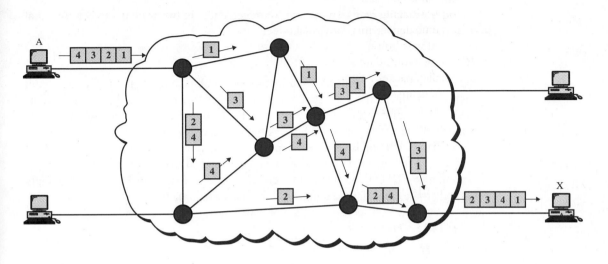

Figure 14.15   *Multiple channels in datagram approach*

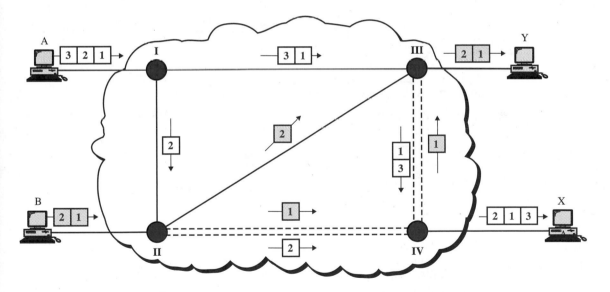

Virtual Circuit Approach

In the virtual circuit approach to packet switching, the relationship between all packets belonging to a message or session is preserved. A single route is chosen between sender and receiver at the beginning of the session. When the data are sent, all packets of the transmission travel one after another along that route.

So what is the difference between circuit switching and virtual circuits? Although circuit switching can use multiplexing at the end-user level, no multiplexing is done at the switches. However, in the virtual circuit approach we can have multiplexing at the switches.

Today, virtual circuit transmission is implemented in two formats: switched virtual circuit (SVC) and permanent virtual circuit (PVC).

SVC

The switched virtual circuit (SVC) format is comparable conceptually to dial-up circuit switching. In this method, a virtual circuit is created whenever it is needed and exists only for the duration of the specific exchange. For example, imagine that station A wants to send four packets to station X. First, A requests the establishment of a connection to X. Once the connection is in place, the packets are sent one after another and in sequential order. When the last packet has been received and, if necessary, acknowledged, the connection is released and that virtual circuit ceases to exist (see Figure 14.16). Only one single route exists for the duration of transmission, although the network could pick an alternate route in response to failure or congestion.

Figure 14.16 *Switched virtual circuit (SVC)*

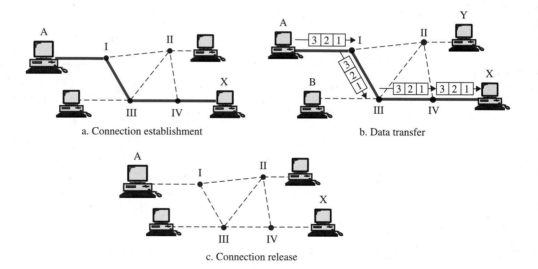

a. Connection establishment

b. Data transfer

c. Connection release

Each time that A wishes to communicate with X, a new route is established. The route may be the same each time, or it may differ in response to varying network conditions. For this reason, SVC allows virtual circuit reliability with a degree of datagram flexibility.

PVC

Permanent virtual circuits (PVC) are comparable to leased lines. In this method, the same virtual circuit is provided between two users on a continuous basis. The circuit is dedicated to the specific user. No one else can use it and, because it is always in place, it can be used without connection establishment and connection termination. Whereas two SVC users may get a different route every time they request a connection, two PVC users always get the same route.

14.3 MESSAGE SWITCHING

Message switching is best known by the descriptive term *store and forward*. In this mechanism, a node (usually a special computer with a number of disks) receives a message, stores it until the appropriate route is free, then sends it along.

Store and forward is considered a switching technique because there is no direct link between the sender and receiver of a transmission. A message is delivered to the node along one path then rerouted along another to its destination.

Note that in message switching the messages are stored and relayed from the secondary storage (disk), while in packet switching the packets are stored and forwarded from primary storage (RAM).

Message switching was common in the 1960s and 1970s. The primary uses have been to provide high-level network services (e.g., delayed delivery, broadcast) for unintelligent devices. Since such devices have been replaced, this type of switch has virtually disappeared. Also the delays inherent in the process, as well as the requirements for large capacity storage media at each node, make it unpopular for direct communication (see Figure 14.17).

Figure 14.17   *Message switching*

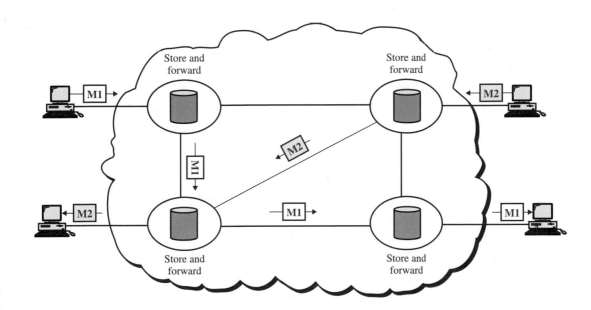

14.4 NETWORK LAYER

With switching, we have introduced the network layer of the OSI model. The network layer is responsible for establishing, managing, and terminating connections between physical networks. Protocols at this layer provide transparent routing and relaying services between networks; these services are used by protocols in the upper layers of the model.

Connection-Oriented and Connectionless Services

At the network layer, the OSI model supports two types of protocols: connection-oriented network services (CONS) and connectionless network services (CLNS).

CONS

A connection-oriented network service (CONS) establishes a virtual circuit for the transmission of data that is active for the entire transmission. All packets belonging to a single transmission are sent, in order, over the same route, thereby allowing a degree of control over the quality of service that would not otherwise be possible.

In a CONS environment, a connection must be established between both ends of a transmission (sending and receiving) before any data may be sent. At the onset of the transmission, the sending device transmits a request-to-send packet. If the receiver is available, it returns a ready-to-receive packet. This exchange alerts the receiver to expect an entire transmission rather than a single packet. No data may be transmitted until both ends have demonstrated readiness.

Once the connection has been made, a single path is chosen and maintained for the entire transmission (this characteristic is especially relevant to connection-oriented services at the transport layer). A transmission is a series of related data units traveling in one direction and is handled both by the network and the transport layers. Connections for the duration of an entire exchange are handled by the session layer. Remember that packet switching allows transmissions to be split into a number of smaller segments and sent by various routes. If a connection is established, the segments are numbered and sent in sequence by a single route, one right after the other.

Process A connection-oriented network service follows five general steps:

- Sender transmits a connection-request packet.
- Receiver acknowledges with a connection-confirm packet.
- Sender transmits data. (This step can be repeated.)
- Sender transmits a disconnect-request packet.
- Receiver acknowledges with a disconnect-confirm packet.

Advantages A CONS environment allows a protocol to include comprehensive sequence, error, and flow control. Sequential numbering allows the protocol to ensure that all packets make it to the receiver and that they are received in order. In addition, packets are identifiable and can be acknowledged or retransmitted as necessary. Numbering also allows the use of a sliding window for flow control. All segments of a transmission must be received and acknowledged before a transmission is considered complete and the virtual circuit can be discarded.

An additional advantage gained by CONS transmission is packet size. Because all packets follow the same path, less protocol control information (PCI) is needed on subsequent packets. For example, the first packet must contain explicit addressing information, but the remaining ones can use abbreviated forms to save overhead.

Disadvantages   On the down side of CONS, once a connection has been established, routing flexibility is lost. If a link becomes congested or problematic in other ways, subsequent packets are not free to take alternative routes.

Speed is also an issue. Packets must be checked and either acknowledged or retransmitted. If complete reliability is unimportant to a particular exchange, the extra time required can be wasted.

CLNS

In a connectionless network service (CLNS), each packet of a multipacket transmission is treated as an independent unit. Connectionless protocols provide no logical connection (no virtual circuit). The sender does not alert the receiver to the coming transmission, it just sends the data. The arrival of each datagram at the destination is a separate event, unexpected by the receiver, who may or may not be able to accept it.

Process   The CLNS process is simpler than that of a CONS:

■   Sender transmits data. (This step can be repeated.)

Advantages and Disadvantages   If reliability is essential, or if packets must arrive in a specific order, connectionless routing is inadequate. If accountability and reordering can be handled by upper-layer protocols (e.g., checksum at the transport layer), however, a CLNS provides advantages of speed and cost. If a particular route becomes congested or breaks down, packets can take alternate routes. The various segments of a single transmission can travel by different paths to maximize efficiency.

Besides unreliability, a second disadvantage of a CLNS is the overhead required by each packet. Because packets are not transmitted as a stream, each must carry complete PCI, which can make transmission unwieldy.

Note that transmissions can be connectionless or connection-oriented at three layers (data link, network, and transport) and can still switch between the two states depending on the protocol.

14.5   SUMMARY

■   Switching is a method by which multiple communication devices are connected to one another efficiently.

■   A switch is intermediary hardware or software that links devices together temporarily.

■   There are three fundamental switching methods: circuit switching, packet switching, and message switching

■   In circuit switching, packets from a single device travel on dedicated links to the destination. Space-division and/or time-division switches may be used.

■ In a space-division switch, each path from one device to another is spatially separated from the other.

■ A crossbar is the most common space-division switch. It connects n inputs to m outputs via $n \times m$ crosspoints.

■ Multistage switches can reduce the number of crosspoints needed, but blocking may result.

■ Blocking occurs when not every input has its own unique path to every output.

■ In a time-division switch, the inputs are divided in time, using TDM. A control unit sends the input to the correct output device.

■ Space- and time-division switches may be combined.

■ Packet switching is generally more efficient than circuit switching for nonvoice communication.

■ There are two popular approaches to packet switching: the datagram approach and the virtual circuit approach.

■ In the datagram approach, each packet (called a datagram) is treated independently from all other packets.

■ In the virtual circuit approach, all packets of a message or session follow the exact same route. Virtual circuit packet switching is implemented in two forms: switched virtual circuit (SVC) and permanent virtual circuit (PVC).

■ In circuit switching the different segments of a message follow a dedicated path, while in virtual circuit packet switching the segments follow dedicated channels.

■ In message switching (also known as store and forward), a node receives a message, stores it, and then sends it.

14.6   PRACTICE SET

Multiple Choice

1. Which type of switching uses the entire capacity of a dedicated link?
   a. circuit switching
   b. datagram packet switching
   c. virtual circuit packet switching
   d. message switching

2. The _____ is a device that connects n inputs to m outputs.
   a. crosspoint
   b. crossbar
   c. modem
   d. RAM

3. In which type of switching do all the datagrams of a message follow the same channels of a path?
   a. circuit switching
   b. datagram packet switching
   c. virtual circuit packet switching
   d. message switching

4. How many crosspoints are needed in a single-stage switch with 40 inputs and 50 outputs?
   a. 40
   b. 50
   c. 90
   d. 2000

5. In a crossbar with 1000 crosspoints, how many statistically are in use at any time?
   a. 100
   b. 250
   c. 500
   d. 1000

6. A device called _____ controls the order of delivery of slot values that are stored in RAM.
   a. a crossbar
   b. a crosspoint
   c. a TSI
   d. a transceiver

7. In _____ circuit switching, delivery of data is delayed because data must be stored and retrieved from RAM.
   a. space-division
   b. time-division
   c. virtual
   d. packet

8. In _____, each packet of a message need not follow the same path from sender to receiver.
   a. circuit switching
   b. message switching
   c. the virtual approach to packet switching
   d. the datagram approach to packet switching

9. In _____, each packet of a message follows the same path from sender to receiver.
   a. circuit switching
   b. message switching
   c. the virtual approach to packet switching
   d. the datagram approach to packet switching

10. A switched virtual circuit involves _____.
    a. connection establishment
    b. data transfer
    c. connection release
    d. all of the above
11. A permanent virtual circuit involves _____.
    a. connection establishment
    b. data transfer
    c. connection release
    d. all of the above

Exercises

1. Draw a space-division three-stage switch. There are 18 inputs and 20 outputs. Stage 1 has three switches, stage 2 has two switches, and stage 3 has four switches. How many crosspoints are needed? Compare this to a system using just one crossbar.
2. Reduce the number of stage 2 switches in the preceding problem to 1. Redo the problem.
3. Using Figure 14.12 of a TST switch system, discuss how this system is superior to
    a. A single crossbar.
    b. A single TSI.
4. Which is more efficient, circuit switching or virtual circuit switching? Why?
5. In a two-byte address field, what is the maximum number of permanent virtual circuits possible? What about a three-byte address?

CHAPTER 15

INTEGRATED SERVICES DIGITAL NETWORK (ISDN)

In Chapter 14, we introduced different types of switching, namely, circuit switching, packet switching, and message switching. A good example of a circuit-switched network is the Integrated Services Digital Network (ISDN), an evolving communications network standard that provides universal end-to-end connectivity over digital lines. ISDN services are still being introduced and are not yet available everywhere. Once ISDN is fully implemented, however, today's disparate transmission and switching services will be accessible internationally via a single set of interface standards.

As a worldwide telecommunications network standard, ISDN will pull together a wide variety of consumer services into a single access package. An ISDN allows users to send data, voice, image, facsimile, and so on over the same wires and to have ready access to digital services.

15.1 SERVICES

The purpose of the ISDN is to provide fully integrated digital services to users. These services fall into three categories: bearer services, teleservices, and supplementary services (see Figure 15.1).

Bearer Services

Bearer services provide the means to transfer information (voice, data, and video) between users without the network manipulating the content of that information. The network does not need to process the information and therefore does not change the content. Bearer services belong to the first three layers of the OSI model and are well defined in the ISDN standard. They can be provided using circuit-switched, packet-switched, frame-relay, or cell-relay networks (discussed in Chapters 14, 16, 17, and 18).

Figure 15.1 *ISDN services*

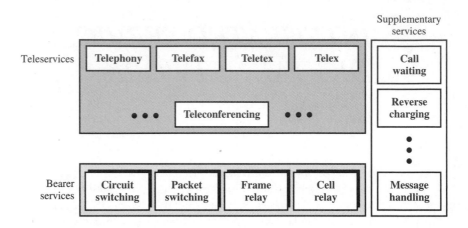

Teleservices

In teleservicing, the network may change or process the contents of the data. These services correspond to layers 4–7 of the OSI model. Teleservices rely on the facilities of the bearer services and are designed to accommodate complex user needs without the user having to be aware of the details of the process. Teleservices include telephony, teletex, telefax, videotex, telex, and teleconferencing. Although the ISDN defines these services by names, they have not yet become standards.

Supplementary Services

Supplementary services are those services that provide additional functionality to the bearer services and teleservices. Examples of these services are reverse charging, call-waiting, and message handling, all familiar from today's telephone company services.

15.2 HISTORY

The evolution of the ISDN reveals the concepts most critical to an understanding of it.

Voice Communication over Analog Networks

Initially, telecommunications networks were entirely analog and were reserved for the transmission of analog information in the form of voice. The local loops connecting the subscriber's handset to the telephone company's central office were also analog (see Figure 15.2).

Figure 15.2 *Voice communication over an analog telephone network*

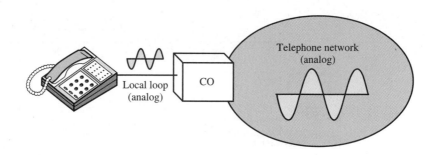

Voice and Data Communication over Analog Networks

With the advent of digital processing, subscribers needed to exchange data as well as voice. Modems were developed to allow digital exchanges over existing analog lines (see Figure 15.3).

Figure 15.3 *Voice and data communication over an analog telephone network*

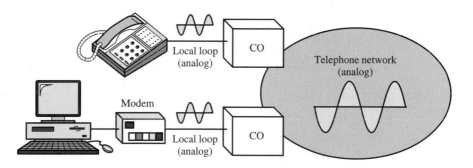

Analog and Digital Services to Subscribers

To reduce cost and improve performance, the telephone companies gradually began to add digital technologies while continuing their analog services to their customers (see Figure 15.4).

Three types of customers were identified at this time: traditional customers using their local loops only for analog purposes; customers using analog facilities to transmit digital information via modem; and customers using digital services to transmit digital information. Of these, the first group was still the most prominent and therefore most of the services offered remained analog.

Figure 15.4   *Analog and digital services over the telephone network*

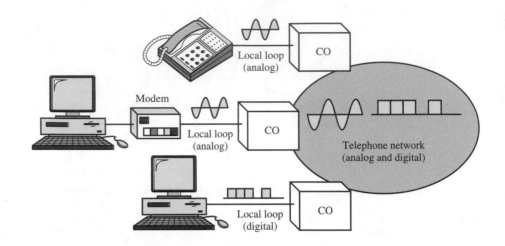

Integrated Digital Network (IDN)

Next, customers began to require access to a variety of networks, such as packet-switched networks and circuit-switched networks. To meet these needs, the telephone companies created integrated digital networks (IDNs). An IDN is a combination of networks available for different purposes (see Figure 15.5). Access to these networks is by digital pipes, which are time-multiplexed channels sharing very high-speed paths. Customers can use their local loops to transmit both voice and data to their telephone company's central office. The office then directs these calls to the appropriate digital

Figure 15.5   *IDN*

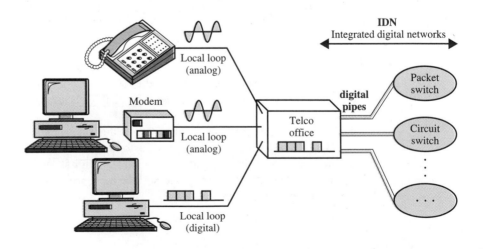

networks via the digital pipes. Notice that the majority of subscribers today continue to use analog local loops, although digital local loop services such as switched/56, DDS, and DSS are available. (These services were discussed in Chapter 8.)

Integrated Services Digital Network (ISDN)

The ISDN integrates customer services with the IDN. As we saw in the discussion of packet-switched networks in Chapter 14, fully digital services are much more efficient and flexible than analog services. To receive the maximum benefit from the integrated digital networks, the next step is to replace the analog local loops with digital subscriber loops. Voice transmissions can be digitized at the source, thereby removing the final need for analog carriers. It then becomes possible to send data, voice, image, facsimile, and so on over any digital network. With ISDN all customer services will become digital rather than analog, and the flexibility offered by the new technology will allow customer services to be made available on demand. Most important, ISDN will allow all communication connections in a home or building to occur via a single interface.

ISDN incorporates all communication connections in a home or building into a single interface.

Figure 15.6 gives a conceptual view of the connections between users and an ISDN central office. Each user is linked to the central office through a digital pipe. These pipes can be of different capacities to allow different rates of transmission and support different subscriber needs.

Figure 15.6 *ISDN*

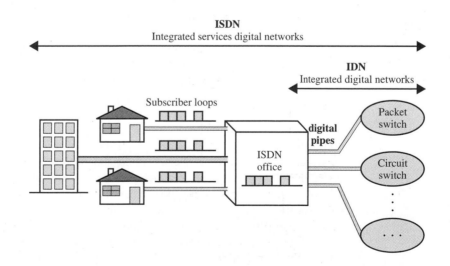

15.3   SUBSCRIBER ACCESS TO THE ISDN

To allow flexibility, digital pipes between customers and the ISDN office (the subscriber loops) are organized into multiple channels of different sizes. The ISDN standard defines three channel types, each with a different transmission rate: bearer channels, data channels, and hybrid channels (see Table 15.1).

Table 15.1   *Channel rates*

Channel	Data Rate (Kbps)
Bearer (B)	64
Data (D)	16, 64
Hybrid (H)	384, 1536, 1920

B Channels

A bearer channel (B channel) is defined at a rate of 64 Kbps. It is the basic user channel and can carry any type of digital information in full-duplex mode as long as the required transmission rate does not exceed 64 Kbps. For example, a B channel can be used to carry digital data, digitized voice, or other low-data-rate information. Several transmissions can be accommodated at once if the signals are multiplexed first. Multiplexed transmissions of this sort, however, must be destined for a single recipient. A B channel carries transmissions end-to-end. It is not designed to demultiplex a stream midway in order to separate and divert transmissions to more than one recipient.

D Channels

A data channel (D channel) can be either 16 or 64 Kbps, depending on the needs of the user. Although the name says *data*, the primary function of a D channel is to carry control signaling for the B channels.

Up to this point, the transmission protocols we have examined all use in-channel signaling. Control information (such as call establishment, ringing, call interrupt, or synchronization) is carried by the same channel that carries the message data. The ISDN separates control signals onto a channel of their own, the D channel. A D channel carries the control signaling for all of the channels in a given path, using a method called common-channel signaling.

In this mechanism, a subscriber uses the D channel to connect to the network and secure a B channel connection. The subscriber then uses the B channel to send actual data to another user. All the devices attached to a given subscriber loop use the same D channel for signaling, but each sends data over a B channel dedicated to a single exchange for the duration of the exchange. Using the D channel is similar to having a telephone operator place a call for you. You pick up the phone and tell the operator what type of call you wish to place and the number you wish to contact. The operator finds an open line appropriate for your needs, rings your party, and connects you. The D channel acts like an operator between the user and the network at the network layer.

Less common uses for the D channel include low-rate data transfer and applications such as telemetry and alarm transmission.

H Channels

Hybrid channels (H channels) are available with data rates of 384 Kbps (H0), 1536 Kbps (H11), or 1920 Kbps (H12). These rates suit H channels for high data-rate applications such as video, teleconferencing, and so on.

User Interfaces

Digital subscriber loops can currently be of two types: basic rate interface (BRI) and primary rate interface (PRI). Each type is suited to a different level of customer needs. Both include one D channel and some number of either B or H channels.

BRI

The basic rate interface (BRI) specifies a digital pipe consisting of two B channels and one 16 Kbps D channel (2B + D); see Figure 15.7.

Figure 15.7   *BRI*

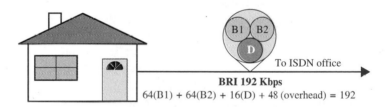

BRI 192 Kbps
64(B1) + 64(B2) + 16(D) + 48 (overhead) = 192

Two B channels of 64 Kbps each, plus one D channel of 16 Kbps, equals 144 Kbps. In addition, the BRI service itself requires 48 Kbps of operating overhead. BRI therefore requires a digital pipe of 192 Kbps. Conceptually, the BRI service is like a large pipe that contains three smaller pipes, two for the B channels and one for the D channel. The remainder of the space inside the large pipe carries the overhead bits required for its operation. In Figure 15.7, the overhead is shown by the shaded portion of the circle surrounding the B and D channels.

Remember, two B channels and one D channel are the maximum number of channels a BRI can support. However, these channels do not have to be used separately. All 192 Kbps can be used to carry a single signal (using in-channel signaling).

The BRI is designed to meet the needs of residential and small-office customers. In most cases, there is no need to replace the existing local-loop cable. The same twisted-pair local loop that delivers analog transmission can be used to handle digital transmission. Occasionally, however, some conditioning of the line is necessary.

PRI

The usual primary rate interface (PRI) specifies a digital pipe with 23 B channels and one 64 Kbps D channel (see Figure 15.8).

Figure 15.8   *PRI*

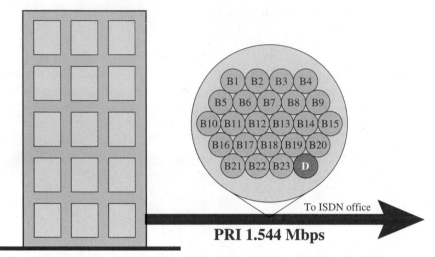

PRI 1.544 Mbps

To ISDN office

$23 \times 64(B1 - B23) + 64 (D) + 8 \text{ (overhead)} = 1544$

Twenty-three B channels of 64 Kbps each, plus one D channel of 64 Kbps equals 1.536 Mbps. In addition, the PRI service itself uses 8 Kbps of overhead. PRI therefore requires a digital pipe of 1.544 Mbps. Conceptually, the PRI service is like a large pipe containing 24 smaller pipes, 23 for the B channels and 1 for the D channel. The rest of the pipe carries the overhead bits required for its operation. In Figure 15.8, the overhead is shown by the shaded portion of the circle surrounding the B and D channels.

The 23 B channels and 1 D channel indicate the maximum number of separate channels a PRI can contain. In other words, one PRI can provide full-duplex transmission between as many as 23 source and receiving nodes. The individual transmissions are collected from their sources and multiplexed onto a single path (digital subscriber line) for sending to the ISDN office.

The 1.544 Mbps of a PRI can be divided up in many other ways to meet the requirements of a number of users. For example, a LAN using a PRI to connect it to other LANs uses all 1.544 Mbps to send one 1.544 Mbps signal. Other applications can use other combinations of the 64 Kbps B channels. At 1.544 Mbps, the capacity of the PRI digital pipe is exactly the same as the capacity of the T-1 line used to support the North American DS-1 telephone service. This similarity is not a coincidence. PRI was designed to be compatible with existing T-1 lines. In Europe, the PRI includes 30 B channels and 2 D channels, giving it a capacity of 2.048 Mbps—the capacity of an E-1 line.

For more specialized transmission needs, other channel combinations are also supported by the PRI standard. They are 3H0 + D, 4H0 + D, and H12 + D.

Functional Grouping

In the ISDN standard, the devices that enable users to access the services of the BRI or PRI are described by their functional duties and collected in functional groupings. Subscribers choose the specific devices best suited to their needs from these groupings. Remember that the ISDN defines only the functional behavior of each group. The standard does not say anything about implementation. Each functional grouping is a model that can be implemented using devices, or equipment chosen by the subscriber. Functional groupings used at the subscriber's premises include network terminations (types 1 and 2), terminal equipment (types 1 and 2), and terminal adapters.

Network Termination 1 (NT1)

A network termination 1 (NT1) device controls the physical and electrical termination of the ISDN at the user's premises and connects the user's internal system to the digital subscriber loop. These functions are comparable to those defined for the OSI physical layer (see Figure 15.9).

Figure 15.9   *Functional grouping*

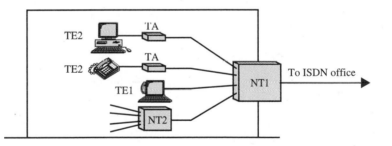

An NT1 organizes the data streams from a connected subscriber into frames that can be sent over the digital pipe, and translates the frames received from the network into a format usable by the subscriber's devices. To this end it performs the basic multiplexing functions of byte interleaving, but it is not a multiplexer. An NT1 synchronizes the data stream with the frame-building process in such a way that multiplexing occurs automatically. This mechanism is called implicit multiplexing, or multiplexing that occurs as part of another process (in this case, frame building).

The easiest way to visualize how frame building in an NT1 can result in an interleaved signal is by analogy. Imagine a manufacturing plant with two conveyor belts. One belt collects a variety of completed products from several parts of the manufacturing department and carries them to the shipping department. At the shipping department, that belt meets a conveyor belt carrying boxes, each of which is designed to hold a specific product. The conveyor belt of products meets the conveyor belt of boxes at right angles. The two belts are synchronized so that as a given product reaches the end of its belt, it falls off into the appropriate box. The ordering of the boxes and products and the timing of the two belts must be controlled to keep the synchronization accurate. Discrepancies can result in a product's landing in the wrong box or missing the boxes altogether. With adequate synchronization, however, product packaging occurs accurately without switching or other manipulation. In the same way, an NT1 synchronizes the timing of the contributing data streams to the building of the outgoing frames so that bytes are interleaved without the need for multiplexing devices.

Network Termination 2 (NT2)

A network termination 2 (NT2) device performs functions at the physical, data link, and network layers of the OSI model (layers 1, 2, and 3). NT2s provide multiplexing (layer 1), flow control (layer 2), and packetizing (layer 3). An NT2 provides intermediate signal processing between the data generating devices and an NT1. The NT1 is still required to provide a physical interface to the network. There must be a point-to-point connection between an NT2 and an NT1. NT2s are used primarily to interface between a multiuser system and an NT1 in a PRI (see Figure 15.9).

NT2s can be implemented by a variety of equipment types. For example, a private branch exchange (digital PBX) can be an NT2; it coordinates transmissions from a number of incoming links (user phone lines) and multiplexes them to make them transmittable by an NT1. A LAN also can function as an NT2.

If a PRI carries signals from multiple devices, those signals must be multiplexed in a separate process provided by the NT2 before the composite signal passes to the NT1 for transmission to the network. This multiplexing is explicit. A digital PBX is an example of an NT2 that contains explicit multiplexing functions.

Terminal Equipment 1 (TE1)

The term *terminal equipment* is used by the ISDN standard to mean the same thing as DTE in other protocols. It refers to digital subscriber equipment. Terminal equipment 1 (TE1) is any device that supports the ISDN standards. Examples of TE1s are digital telephones, integrated voice/data terminals, and digital facsimiles (see Figure 15.9).

Terminal Equipment 2 (TE2)

To provide backward compatibility with a customer's existing equipment, the ISDN standard defines a second level of terminal equipment called terminal equipment 2 (TE2). TE2 equipment is any non-ISDN device, such as a terminal, workstation, host computer or regular telephone. TE2 devices are not immediately compatible with an ISDN network but can be used with the help of another device called a terminal adapter (TA); see Figure 15.9.

Terminal Adapter (TA)

A terminal adapter (TA) converts information received in non-ISDN format from a TE2 into a format capable of being carried by the ISDN (see Figure 15.9).

Reference Points

Used here, the term *reference point* refers to the label used to identify individual interfaces between two elements of an ISDN installation. Just as the functional grouping defines the function of each type of equipment used in the ISDN, a reference point defines the functions of the connections between them. Specifically, a reference point defines how two network elements must be connected and the format of the traffic between them. We mention here only those reference points that define the interfaces between a subscriber's equipment and the network: reference points R, S, T, and U (see Figure 15.10). Other reference points define functions within the ISDN.

Figure 15.10   *Reference points*

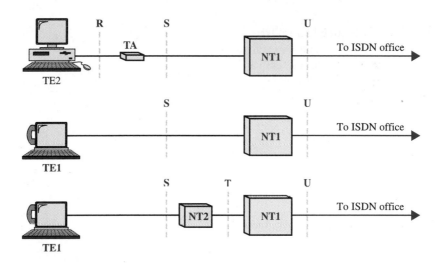

Reference point R defines the connection between a TE2 and a TA. Reference point S defines the connection between a TE1 or TA and an NT1 or NT2 (if present). Reference point T defines the interface between an NT2 and an NT1. Finally, reference point U defines the interface between an NT1 and the ISDN office. Figure 15.10 shows these reference points as they apply to three different scenarios. We will discuss the specifications for each reference point when we explore the different ISDN layers in the next section of this chapter.

15.4   THE ISDN LAYERS

It is difficult to apply the simple seven-layer architecture specified by the OSI to the ISDN. One reason is that the ISDN specifies two different channels (B and D) with different functionalities. As we saw earlier in this chapter, B channels are for user-to-user communication (information exchange). D channels are predominantly for user-to-network signaling. The subscriber uses the D channel to connect to the network, then the B channel to send information to another user. These two functions require different protocols from each other at many of the OSI layers. The ISDN also differs from the OSI standard in its management needs. A primary consideration of the ISDN is global integration. Maintaining the flexibility required to keep the network truly integrated using public services requires a great deal of management.

For these reasons, the ITU-T has devised an expanded model for the ISDN layers. Instead of a single seven-layer architecture like the OSI, the ISDN is defined in three separate planes: the user plane, the control plane, and the management plane. The user plane defines the functionality of the B channel and H channel: the user-to-user connection. The control plane defines the functionality of the D channel when used for signaling. (When used for subscriber data, the D channel is defined on the user plane.) The management plane encompasses both the user and control planes and is used for managing the whole network (see Figure 15.11).

Figure 15.11   *ISDN layers*

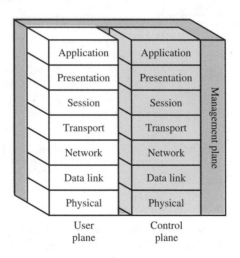

All three planes are divided into seven layers that correspond to the OSI model. The discussion of the management plane is beyond the scope of this book; the other two planes are discussed below.

Figure 15.12 shows a simplified version of the ISDN architecture for the user and control planes (B and D channels). In this figure we make a number of assumptions that enable us to simplify the model for the purposes of discussion. First of all, we assume that the subscriber uses the D channel only for signaling. When a D channel is used for data, it behaves like a B channel (discussed below). Eventually D channels will be used for services like telemetry, but the protocols that will make those services possible are still under study. For our purposes, then, the D channel is a signaling channel. Further, the D channel is used primarily for user-to-network signaling. Its functions are therefore confined to the first three layers. Layers 4 to 7, which are concerned with end-to-end user signaling, use other ISDN protocols (such as SS7).

Figure 15.12 *ISDN layers for B and D channels*

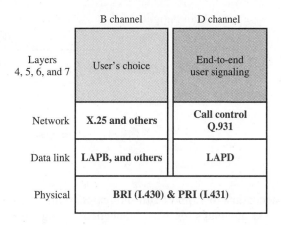

At the physical layer, the B and D channels are alike. They use either the BRI or PRI interfaces and devices discussed earlier in this chapter. At the data link layer, the B channel uses LAPB or some version of it, discussed in Chapter 11. At the network layer, the B channel has many options. B channels (and D channels acting like B channels) can connect to circuit-switched networks, packet-switched networks (X.25), frame relay networks, and ATM networks, among others. The user-plane options for layers 4 to 7 are left to the user and are not defined specifically in the ISDN. In summary, we need only discuss the physical layer shared by the B and D channels, and the second and third layers of the D channel standard.

Physical Layer

The ISDN physical layer specifications are defined by two ITU-T standards: I.430 for BRI access and I.431 for PRI access. These standards define all aspects of the BRI and PRI. Of these aspects, four are of primary importance:

- The mechanical and electrical specifications of interfaces R, S, T, and U.
- Encoding.
- Multiplexing channels to make them carriable by the BRI and PRI digital pipes.
- Power supply.

Physical Layer Specifications for BRI

As you recall, a BRI consists of two B channels and one D channel. A subscriber connects to the BRI using the R, S, and U interfaces (reference points); see Figure 15.13.

R Interface   The R interface is not defined by the ISDN. A subscriber can use any of the EIA standards (such as EIA-232, EIA-499, or EIA-530) or any of the V or X series standards (such as X.21).

S Interface   For the S interface, the ITU-T specifies the ISO standard, ISO8887. This standard calls for four-, six-, or eight-wire connections. (At least four wires are

Figure 15.13   *BRI interfaces*

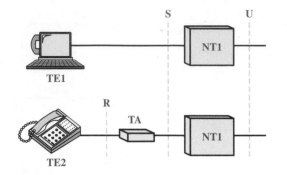

necessary to support full-duplex communication over every B or D channel.) The jacks and plugs for these connections, along with the electrical specifications for each wire, are shown in Figure 15.14.

Figure 15.14   *S interface*

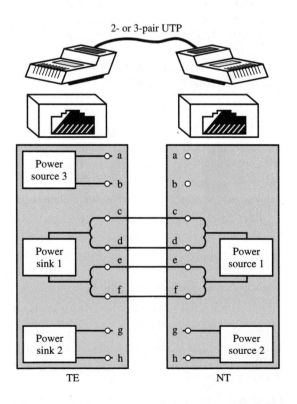

The individual wires in an S interface connection are organized according to Table 15.2. Only four of the wires are necessary for balanced transmission of data in full-duplex mode. (For a discussion of balanced transmission, see the section on the X.21 Interface in Chapter 6.) The others supply power to the NT1 and TE. The standard provides three methods for supplying power. In the first, the NT1 is the supplier. The power can come from a battery or power outlet, or it can come from the ISDN center to the NT1. In this case, only four connections are needed to connect the TE and NT1 (wires c, d, e, and f in Figure 15.14).

Table 15.2   *S interface pins*

Name	TE	NT
a	Power Source 3	Power Sink 3
b	Power Source 3	Power Sink 3
c	Transmit	Receive
d	Receive	Transmit
e	Receive	Transmit
f	Transmit	Receive
g	Power Sink 2	Power Source 2
h	Power Sink 2	Power Source 2

In the second case, the power again comes from the NT1, but two separate lines are used to relay it to the TE. In this case, six wires are used (c, d, e, f, g, and h in Figure 15.14). ISO8887 allows for another possibility: that the TE supplies the power itself and passes it to other TEs (using wires a and b). The ISDN, however, does not use this version. A two- or three-pair twisted cable is adequate to support all of the ISDN defined uses.

Encoding: U Interface   ISDN signal encoding is pseudoternary, a version of bipolar AMI with the 0 and 1 levels reversed. A 1 is encoded as no-voltage and a 0 is encoded as alternate positive and negative voltages (see Figure 15.15).

Figure 15.15   *Pseudoternary encoding*

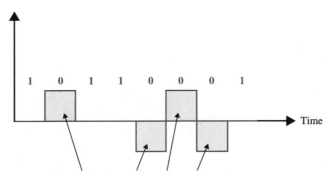

The 0s are alternately positive and negative.

lost

For the U interface (digital subscriber or local loop), the ITU-T specifies a single-pair twisted-pair cable in each direction. Encoding for this interface uses a mechanism called two binary, one quaternary (2B1Q). 2B1Q uses four voltage levels instead of two. Each level can therefore represent two bits rather than one, thereby lowering the baud rate and enabling more efficient use of the available bandwidth (see Figure 15.16). The four voltage levels represent the dibits 00, 01, 10, and 11.

Figure 15.16 *2B1Q encoding*

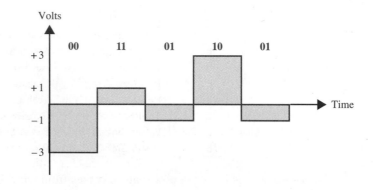

BRI Frame The format for a BRI frame is shown in Figure 15.17. Each B channel is sampled twice during each frame (eight bits per sample). The D channel is sampled four times during each frame (one bit per sample). The balance of the frame, shown in Figure 15.17 as black spaces, is reserved for overhead, the discussion of which is beyond the scope of this book. The entire frame consists of 48 bits: 32 bits for the B channels, 4 bits for the D channel, and 12 bits of overhead. (The reason that each B channel is sampled twice and the D channel four times is to create a longer frame. As we will see in Chapter 18, 48 bits makes the size of the BRI frame a precise match for the data portion of an ATM cell.)

Figure 15.17 *BRI frame*

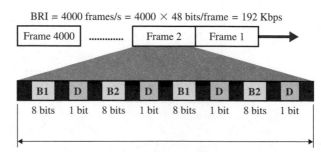

Connection and Topology   BRI services can be supported by either a bus or star topology. The main restriction governing the choice of topology for a BRI is the distance of the data devices from the NT1 (see Figure 15.18). In a point-to-point connection, each device can be as far as 1000 meters away from the NT1. In a multipoint connection, however, the maximum length of the line generally cannot be more than 200 meters. This restriction is necessary to ensure frame synchronization.

As we discussed earlier in this chapter, NT1s interleave the outputs of connected devices as part of the process of frame building. The results of this implicit multiplexing are evident in the structure of the frame. To make this implicit multiplexing possible, the frame building functions of the NT1 must be timed to coordinate precisely with the data dumps of the connected devices. If the synchronization between the frame and the devices is off, data dumped by one device can end up in a part of the frame devoted to data from another device, or to another kind of information altogether. Unavoidable propagation delays over distance can result in a shifted frame. If the distance between the first and last device on a link is great enough, data collection timing can deteriorate to the point where much of the frame becomes unusable.

To ensure frame accuracy for multipoint links, we must limit the impact of timing shifts between the data units dumped by each device. We do so by limiting the link distance between the devices. In general, that means restricting the total length of the link to 200 meters, as noted above. However, if we cluster the devices at the end of the link farthest from the NT1, we can extend the length of the link to 500 meters. Clustering the devices means that propagation delays will impact the data from all devices almost equally, allowing the relationships between the data units to remain predictable for 500 meters. If only one device is attached to a link, the NT1 does not need to distinguish between the data of different devices and greater timing distortions can be tolerated. Star topology links can be as long as 1000 meters (see Figure 15.18).

As many as eight devices can be connected to an NT1. Of these, only two can access the B channels at one time, one exchange per channel. Every device, however, can contend for access to the D channel. D channels use a mechanism like CSMA to control access. Once a device has access to the D channel, it can request a B channel. If a B channel is available, the connection is made by the D channel and the user may then send data.

Physical Layer Specifications for PRI

As you recall, the PRI consists of 23 B channels and 1 D channel. Interfaces associated with PRI usage include R, S, T, and U (see Figure 15.19).

The R and S standards are the same as those defined for the BRI. The T standard is identical to the S standard with the substitution of B8ZS encoding. The U interface is the same for both standards except that the PRI rate is 1.544 Mbps instead of 192 Kbps. 1.544 Mbps allows the PRI to be implemented using T-1 specifications (see Chapter 8).

PRI Frame   The B and D channels are time-multiplexed using synchronous TDM to create a PRI frame. The frame format is identical to that defined for T-1 lines. For convenience, we repeat the format here in Figure 15.20. Notice that the PRI frame samples each channel, including the D channel, only once per frame.

Figure 15.18   *BRI topology*

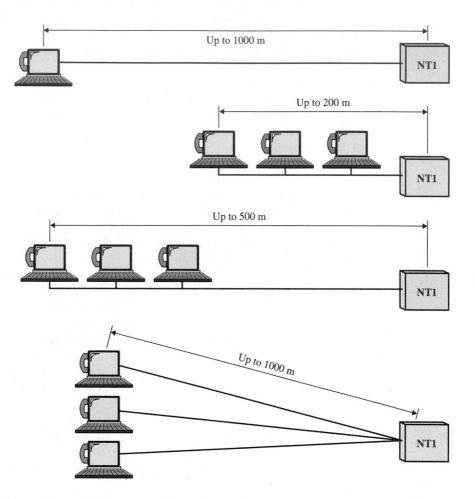

Connection and Topology   Connection and topology considerations for linking data generating devices to an NT2 can be the same as those described for the device-to-NT1 links in the BRI, or they can differ. Specific implementation depends on the application. If the NT2 is a LAN, its topology will be specified by the LAN being used; if the NT2 is a PBX, its topology will be specified by the PBX being used, and so on. The link from the NT2 to the NT1, however, must always be point-to-point.

Data Link Layer

B and D channels use different data link protocols. B channels use LAPB protocol. The D channel uses link access procedure for D channel (LAPD). LAPD is HDLC with a few modifications, two of which require explanation here. First, LAPD can be used in either unacknowledged (without sequence numbering) or acknowledged (with

Figure 15.19 *PRI interfaces*

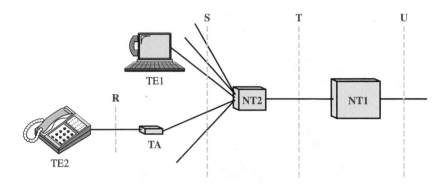

Figure 15.20 *PRI frame*

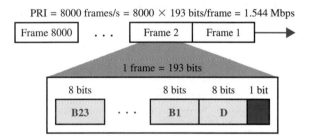

sequence numbering) formats. The unacknowledged format is used only seldomly, however, so in general practice LAPD and HDLC are alike. The second difference is addressing.

LAPD Addressing

The address field of the LAPD is two bytes long (see Figure 15.21). The first byte contains a six-bit field called a service access point identifier (SAPI); a one-bit command/response field set to 0 if the frame is a command and to 1 if the frame is a response; and a one-bit field set to 0 to indicate that the address is continued in the next byte (see HDLC, Chapter 11).

The second byte contains a seven-bit field called a terminal equipment identifier (TEI), and a one-bit field set to 1 to indicate that the address is complete.

SAPI Field The SAPI field identifies the type of upper-layer service (network layer) using the frame. It indicates the intended use of the D channel. It is a six-bit field and can therefore define up to 64 different service access points. To date, however, only four of the possible bit combinations have been assigned:

- **000000.** Call control for network layer (signaling use of D channel).
- **000001**. Call control for upper layer (end-to-end signaling), not yet in use.

- **010000.** Packet communication (data use of D channel).
- **111111**. Management.

TEI Field   The TEI field is the unique address of the TE. It consists of seven bits and can therefore identify up to 128 different TEs.

Figure 15.21   *LAPD address field*

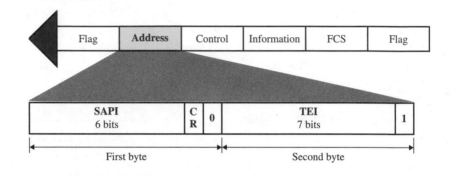

Network Layer

Once a connection has been established by the D channel, the B channel sends data using circuit switching, X.25, or other similar protocols. The network layer functions of the D channel, however, must be discussed here. These functions are defined by the ITU-T Q.931 standard.

The network-layer packet is called a message. A message is encapsulated in the information field of an LAPD I-Frame for transport across a link (see Figure 15.22).

Figure 15.22   *Network layer packet format*

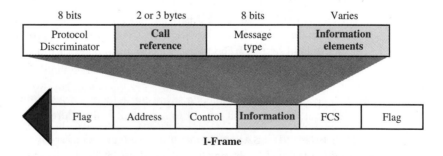

The format of the message in this layer consists of a small but variable number of fields. These fields are of four types:

- Protocol discriminator (a single one-byte field).
- Call reference (two- or three-byte field).

■ Message type (a single one-byte field).

■ Information elements (a variable number of variable-length fields).

Protocol Discriminator

The protocol discriminator field identifies the protocol in use. For Q.931, the value of this field is 00001000.

Call Reference

The call reference is the sequence number of the call. The format for this field is shown in Figure 15.23.

Figure 15.23   *Call reference field*

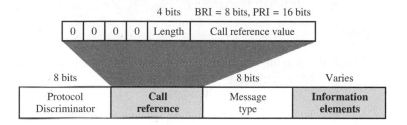

Message Type

The message type is a one-byte field that identifies the purpose of the message. There are four categories of message type: call establishment messages, call information messages, call clearing messages, and miscellaneous messages. The available messages are described below.

Call Establishment Messages   The following are call establishment messages:

■ **SETUP.** Sent by the calling user to the network or by the network to the called user to initiate a call.

■ **SETUP ACKNOWLEDGMENT.** Sent by the called user to the network or by the network to the calling user to indicate that the SETUP has been received. This message does not mean that a connection is in place (more information may be required), merely that the desired process has begun.

■ **CONNECT.** Sent by the called user to the network or by the network to the calling user to indicate acceptance of the call.

■ **CONNECT ACKNOWLEDGMENT.** Sent by the network to the called user to say that the desired connection has been awarded.

■ **PROGRESS.** Sent by the network to the called user to indicate that call establishment is in progress. This message works as a "please stand by" request in case the call establishment process needs more time.

■ **ALERTING.** Sent by the called user to the network or by the network to the calling user to indicate that the call user alert (ringing) has been initiated.

- **CALL PROCESSING.** Sent by the called user to the network or by the network to the calling user to indicate that the requested call establishment has been initiated and that no more information is needed.

Call Information Messages   The following are call information messages:

- **RESUME.** Sent by a user to the network to request that a suspended call be resumed.
- **RESUME ACKNOWLEDGMENT.** Sent by the network to the user to acknowledge a request to resume the call.
- **SUSPEND.** Sent by a user to request that the network suspend a call.
- **SUSPEND ACKNOWLEDGMENT.** Sent by the network to the user to acknowledge the requested suspension of the call.
- **SUSPEND REJECT.** Sent by the network to the user to reject the requested suspension.
- **USER INFORMATION.** Sent by a user to the network to be delivered to the remote user. This message allows the user to send information using out-of-channel signaling.

Call Clearing Messages   The following are call clearing messages:

- **DISCONNECT.** Sent by the calling user to the network or by the network to the called user to clear the end-to-end connection (termination).
- **RELEASE.** Sent by a user or network to indicate the intention to disconnect and release the channel.
- **RELEASE COMPLETE.** Sent by a user or network to show that the channel has been released.

Miscellaneous   Other messages carry information defined in the protocols of specific services. These messages are not used in routine communication and further discussion of them is beyond the scope of this book.

Information Elements

An information elements field carries specific details about the connection that are required for call establishment, for example, the addresses of the sender and receiver (discussed below), routing information, and the type of network that is desired for the B channel exchange (such as circuit-switched, X.25, ATM, or frame relay); see Figure 15.24. The details of the latter elements are complex and fall beyond the scope of this book.

Information Element Types   An information element consists of one or more bytes. A one-byte information element can be of type 1 or type 2. In type 1, the first bit is 0, the next three bits identify the information being sent, and the remaining four bits carry the specific content or attribute of the element. Type 2 elements start with a 1 bit. The remainder of the byte is reserved for the ID. In multibyte information elements, the first bit of the first byte is 0 and the remainder of the byte is the ID. The second byte defines the length of the content in bytes. The remaining bytes are content (see Figure 15.25).

Figure 15.24   *Information elements*

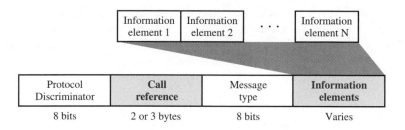

Figure 15.25   *Information element types*

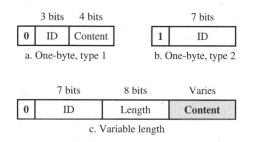

Addressing   An important type of information element is addressing. The ISDN recommends an addressing system based on the format shown in Figure 15.26.

Figure 15.26   *Addressing in ISDN*

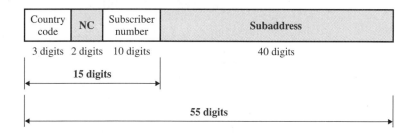

The country code consists of up to three digits. The NC field is the national code and consists of two digits. It identifies the specific network in countries with more than one ISDN network. The subscriber number is the 10-digit number familiar from national telephone numbers: a three-digit area code and a seven-digit phone number. Together these 15 digits define the access to a subscriber NT1. Often, however, a given NT1 may have multiple devices connected to it, either directly or indirectly through an NT2. In these situations, each device is identified by a subaddress. The ISDN allows up to 40 digits for a subaddress.

15.5   BROADBAND ISDN

When the ISDN was originally designed, data rates of 64 Kbps to 1.544 Mbps were sufficient to handle all existing transmission needs. As applications using the telecommunications networks advanced, however, these rates proved inadequate to support many applications. In addition, the original bandwidths proved too narrow to carry the large numbers of concurrent signals produced by a growing industry of digital service providers.

Figure 15.27 shows the bit rates required by a variety of applications. As you can see, several are beyond the capacities of both the BRI and PRI.

Figure 15.27   *Bit rates for different applications*

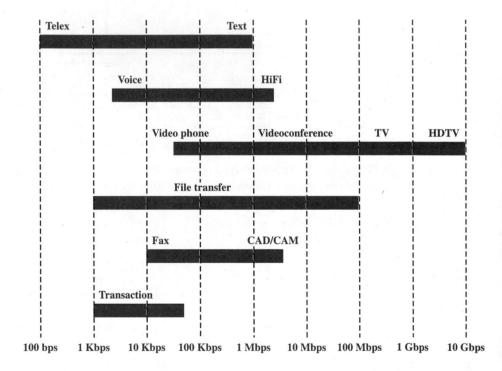

To provide for the needs of the next generation of technology, an extension of ISDN, called broadband ISDN (B-ISDN), is under study. The original ISDN is now known as narrowband ISDN (N-ISDN). B-ISDN provides subscribers to the network with data rates in the range of 600 Mbps, almost 400 times faster than the PRI rate. Technology exists to support higher rates but is not yet implemented or standardized.

As we saw earlier in this chapter, narrowband ISDN is an outcome of the logical evolution of the telephone system. Broadband ISDN, however, represents a revolution in thinking that radically alters entire aspects of communication. B-ISDN is based on a change from metal cable to fiber-optic cable at all levels of telecommunications. You have only to check the telephone wiring in your neighborhood to know that this revolution has not yet occurred on a wide basis. The majority of current research and development in the fields of telecommunications and networking, however, is devoted to bringing this revolution about.

Services

Broadband ISDN provides two types of services: interactive and distributive (see Figure 15.28).

Figure 15.28   *B-ISDN services*

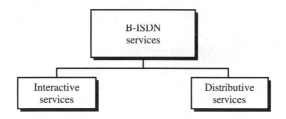

Interactive Services

Interactive services are those that require two-way exchanges between either two subscribers or between a subscriber and a service provider. These services are of three types: conversational, messaging, and retrieval.

Conversational   Conversational services are those, such as telephone calls, that support real-time exchanges (as opposed to store and forward). These real-time services can be used for telephony, video telephony, video conferencing, data transfer, and so on.

Messaging   Messaging services are store-and-forward exchanges. These services are bidirectional, meaning that all parties in an exchange can use them at the same time. The actual exchange, however, may not occur in real-time. One subscriber asking another for information may have to wait for an answer, even though both parties are available at the same time. These services include voice mail, data mail, and video mail.

Retrieval   Retrieval services are those used to retrieve information from a central source, called an information center. These services are like libraries; they must allow public access and allow users to retrieve information on demand. That is, information is not distributed unless asked for. An example of a retrieval service is a videotex that allows subscribers to select video data from an on-line library. The service is bidirectional because it requires action on the part of both the requester and the provider.

Distributive Services

Distributive services are unidirectional services sent from a provider to subscribers without the subscriber having to transmit a request each time a service is desired. These services can be without or with user control.

Without User Control   Distributive services without user control are broadcast to the user without the user's having requested them or having control over either broadcast times or content. User choice is limited to whether or not to receive the service at all. An example of this type of service is commercial TV. Programming content and times are decided by the provider alone. The user can turn on the television and change the channel but cannot request a specific program or a specific broadcast time.

With User Control   Distributive services with user control are broadcast to the user in a round-robin fashion. Services are repeated periodically to allow the user a choice of times during which to receive them. Which services are broadcast at which times, however, is the option of the provider alone. Examples of this type of service are educational broadcasting, teleadvertising, and pay TV. With pay TV, for example, a program is made available in a limited number of time slots. A user wishing to view the program must activate his or her television to receive it, but he or she has no other control.

Physical Specifications

The B-ISDN model is divided into layers that are different from those of N-ISDN. These layers are closely tied to the design of ATM. For this reason, we will postpone our discussion of them to our discussion of ATM (see Chapter 18).

Physical aspects of B-ISDN not related to ATM include access methods, functional equipment groupings, and reference points, described below.

Access Methods

B-ISDN defines three access methods designed to provide for three levels of user needs. They are symmetrical 155.520 Mbps, asymmetrical 155.520 Mbps/622.080 Mbps, and symmetrical 622.080 Mbps (see Figure 15.29).

Figure 15.29   *B-ISDN accesses*

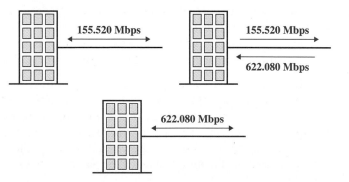

- **155.520 Mbps full-duplex.** This rate matches that of an OC-3 SONET link (see Chapter 19). It is high enough to support customers who need access to all narrowband ISDN services and to one or more regular video transmission services. This method is geared to fill the needs of most residential and many business subscribers.

- **155.520 Mbps output/622.080 Mbps input.** This method provides asymmetrical full-duplex network access. The outgoing rate is 155.520 Mbps (the same as an OC-3 SONET link), but the incoming rate is 622.080 Mbps (the same as an OC-120 SONET link). It is designed to fill the needs of businesses that require the simultaneous receipt of multiple services and video conferencing but that are not service providers and do not broadcast distributive services. The input needs of these subscribers are far greater than their output needs. Providing only one rate would either limit their receipt of services or result in wasted link capacity. The asymmetrical configuration provides for a balanced use of resources.
- **622.080 Mbps full-duplex.** This final mechanism is designed for businesses that provide and receive distributive services.

Functional Grouping

The functional groupings of equipment in the B-ISDN model are the same as those for N-ISDN. Here, however, they are called B-NT1, B-NT2, B-TE1, B-TE2, and B-TA.

Reference Points

B-ISDN also uses the same reference points as N-ISDN (R, S, T, and U). Some of these, however, are currently under scrutiny and may be redefined.

15.6 SUMMARY

- An ISDN provides digital services to users over integrated digital networks.
- Digital services fall into one of three classes:
  a. Bearer services—no network manipulation of the information contents.
  b. Teleservices—network may change or process information contents.
  c. Supplementary services—cannot stand alone; must be used with bearer or teleservices.
- A digital pipe is a high-speed path composed of time-multiplexed channels. There are three types of channels:
  a. Bearer (B)—basic user channel.
  b. Data (D)—for control of B channels, low-rate data transfer, and other applications.
  c. Hybrid (H)—high-data-rate applications.
- A BRI is a digital pipe composed of two B channels and one D channel.
- A PRI is a digital pipe composed of 23 B channels and one D channel.
- Three functional groupings of equipment enable users to access an ISDN: network terminations, terminal equipment, and terminal adapters.
- There are two types of network terminations:
  a. NT1—equipment that controls the physical and electrical termination of the ISDN at the user's premises.

  b. NT2—equipment that performs functions related to layers one through three of the OSI model.

- Terminal equipment (data sources similar to DTEs) can be classified as follows:

  a. TE1—subscriber equipment conforming to ISDN standards.

  b. TE2—subscriber equipment that does not conform to ISDN standards.

  c. TA—converts data from TE2s to ISDN format.

- A reference point defines ISDN interfaces. The reference points are:

  a. R—between a TE2 and a TA.

  b. S—between a TE or TA and an NT.

  c. T—between an NT1 and an NT2.

  d. U—between an NT1 and the ISDN office.

- ISDN architecture consists of three planes, each made up of the seven layers of the OSI model. The planes are:

  a. User plane—defines the functionality of the B and H channels.

  b. Control plane—defines the functionality of the D channel when used for signaling purposes.

  c. Management plane—encompasses the other two planes and used for network management.

- The physical layer of the user and control planes are the same.

- BRI has a data rate of 192 Kbps (4000 frames/sec, 48 bits/frame).

- PRI has a data rate of 1.544 Mbps (8000 frames/sec, 193 bits/frame).

- The distance from a TE to an NT is dependent on connection, topology, and placement of multiple TEs.

- In the data link layer, the B channel (user) uses LAPB protocol. The D channel (control) uses LAPD protocol, which is also similar to HDLC.

- In the network layer, the D channel data packet is called a message. It has four fields:

  a. Protocol discriminator—identifies the protocol used.

  b. Call reference—identifies sequence number.

  c. Message type—identifies purpose of the message.

  d. Information elements (multifield)—information about the connection.

- Broadband ISDN (B-ISDN), using fiber-optic media, fulfills the needs of users who require a higher data rate than that offered by ISDN. B-ISDN has a data rate of 600 Mbps.

- B-ISDN offers two services:

  a. Interactive—two-way services (two subscribers or a subscriber-service provider pair).

  b. Distributive—one-way service from service provider to subscriber.

- Three access methods in B-ISDN are available:

  a. 155.520 Mbps, full-duplex.

  b. 155.520 Mbps outgoing and 622.080 Mbps incoming, asymmetric full-duplex.

   c. 622.080 Mbps, full-duplex.

■   The functional grouping and reference points of B-ISDN are the same as for regular ISDN (also known as narrowband ISDN, N-ISDN).

15.7   PRACTICE SET

Multiple Choice

1. ISDN is an acronym for _____.
   a. Information Services for Digital Networks
   b. Internetwork System for Data Networks
   c. Integrated Services Digital Network
   d. Integrated Signals Digital Network

2. The _____ channel can be used for the control of B channels.
   a. BC
   b. D
   c. H
   d. C

3. The _____ channel has the lowest data rate.
   a. B
   b. C
   c. D
   d. H

4. The _____ channel is used for applications requiring a transmission rate greater than 64Kbps.
   a. B
   b. C
   c. D
   d. H

5. The _____ channel can be used for telemetry and alarms.
   a. B
   b. C
   c. D
   d. H

6. The normal user interface to an ISDN is PRI or _____.
   a. bit rate interface
   b. basic rate interface
   c. byte rate interface
   d. broad rate interface

7. The BRI is composed of _____.
   a. two B channels
   b. one H channel
   c. one D channel
   d. a and c

8. The overhead using BRI is _____ percent of the total data rate.
   a. 10
   b. 20
   c. 25
   d. 30

9. PRI consists of _____ channels.
   a. 23
   b. 24
   c. 64
   d. 65

10. Equipment that controls the physical and electrical termination of the ISDN at the user's premises is called _____.
    a. NT1
    b. NT2
    c. NT3
    d. NT4

11. Equipment that performs functions related to the OSI model's layers 1, 2, and 3 is called _____.
    a. NT1
    b. NT2
    c. NT3
    d. NT4

12. The ISDN equivalent of DTE is _____.
    a. TE1
    b. TE2
    c. TE3
    d. TE4

13. _____ is a group of non-ISDN equipment.
    a. TE1
    b. TE2
    c. TEx
    d. T3

14. A _____ converts information from non-ISDN format to ISDN format.
    a. TE1
    b. TE2

   c. TEx

   d. TA

15. Reference point R is the specification for connecting TE2 and _____.

   a. TE1

   b. NT1

   c. NT2

   d. TA

16. Reference point U is the specification for connecting the ISDN office with _____.

   a. NT1

   b. NT2

   c. TE1

   d. TE2

17. Reference point _____ is the specification for connecting NT1 with NT2.

   a. R

   b. S

   c. T

   d. U

18. Which ISDN plane is associated with signaling and the D channel?

   a. user

   b. control

   c. management

   d. supervisory

19. Which ISDN plane is associated with the B channels and the transmission of user information?

   a. user

   b. control

   c. management

   d. supervisory

20. Each PRI frame lasts _____ microseconds.

   a. 1

   b. 1.544

   c. 125

   d. 193

21. In ISDN _____, the network can change or process the contents of the data.

   a. bearer services

   b. teleservices

   c. supplementary services

   d. none of the above

22. In ISDN _____, the network does not change or process the contents of the data.
    a. bearer services
    b. teleservices
    c. supplementary services
    d. none of the above

23. In B-ISDN, the general class of service between subscriber and service provider or between two subscribers is _____ services.
    a. interactive
    b. distributive
    c. conversational
    d. messaging

24. In B-ISDN, when you obtain information from a public center in B-ISDN, you are using _____ services.
    a. conversational
    b. messaging
    c. retrieval
    d. distributive

25. In _____ services, all transmission is real-time between the two entities.
    a. conversational
    b. messaging
    c. retrieval
    d. distributive

26. When you store and forward messages in B-ISDN, you are using _____ services.
    a. conversational
    b. messaging
    c. retrieval
    d. distributive

27. Commercial TV is an example of _____.
    a. messaging services
    b. conversational services
    c. distributive services without user control
    d. distributive services with user control

28. Which B-ISDN access method is designed for customers who need to receive distributive services but do not provide distributive services to others?
    a. 155.520 Mbps full-duplex
    b. 155.520 and 622.080 Mbps asymmetrical full-duplex
    c. 622.080 Mbps full-duplex
    d. 400 Mbps full-duplex

Exercises

1. Why is the R interface standard not defined by ISDN?
2. Draw the time-domain graph of the bit sequence 0010 0101 1101 at the S interface for BRI. Do the same for the U interface.
3. Why is the T interface not needed for BRI?
4. Compare and contrast 2B1Q encoding with ASK.
5. Why can a device be 1000 meters away from an NT1 in a star topology, but a maximum of only 200 meters in a multipoint bus connection for BRI?
6. Why is there a need for B-ISDN?

CHAPTER 16

X.25

The packet switching protocol most widely used today is called X.25. Developed by the ITU-T in 1976, X.25 has been revised several times.

According to the formal definition given in the ITU-T standard X.25 is an interface between data terminal equipment and data circuit terminating equipment for terminal operation at the packet mode on public data networks. Informally, we can say that X.25 is a packet switching protocol used in a wide area network.

X.25 is a packet switching protocol used in a wide area network.

X.25 defines how a packet-mode terminal can be connected to a packet network for the exchange of data. It describes the procedures necessary for establishing, maintaining, and terminating connections (such as connection establishment, data exchange, acknowledgment, flow control, and data control). It also describes a set of services, called facilities, to provide functions such as reverse charge, call direct, and delay control.

X.25 is what is known as a subscriber network interface (SNI) protocol. It defines how the user's DTE communicates with the network and how packets are sent over that network using DCEs. It uses a virtual circuit approach to packet switching (SVC and PVC) rather than a datagram approach, and uses asynchronous (statistical) TDM to multiplex packets.

Figure 16.1 gives a conceptual overview of X.25. Although X.25 is an end-to-end protocol, the actual movement of packets through the network is invisible to it. It sees the network as a cloud through which each packet passes on its way to the receiving DCE.

16.1   X.25 LAYERS

The X.25 protocol is organized into three layers: the physical layer; the link access procedure, balanced layer; and the packet layer protocol layer. These layers define functions at the physical, data link, and network layers of the OSI model. Figure 16.2 shows the relationship between the X.25 layers and the OSI layers.

Figure 16.1   *X.25*

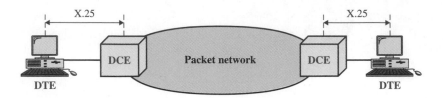

Figure 16.2   *X.25 layers in relation to the OSI layers*

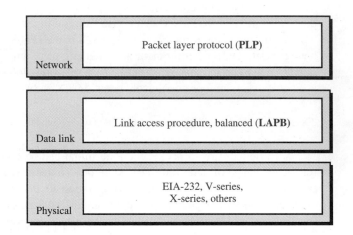

Physical Layer

At the physical layer, X.25 specifies a protocol called X.21 (or X.21bis) which has been specifically defined for X.25 by the ITU-T. X.21, however, is close enough to other physical layer protocols, such as EIA-232, that X.25 is able to support them as well. (See Chapter 6 for a discussion of these interface protocols.)

Data Link Layer

X.25 provides data link controls using a bit-oriented protocol called link access procedure, balanced (LAPB) which is a subset of HDLC (see Chapter 11).

Network Layer

The network layer in X.25 is called the packet layer protocol (PLP). This layer is responsible for establishing the connection, transferring the data, and terminating the connection. User and system data are passed down from the upper layers. At the PLP, a header containing control information is added to transform the data into a PLP packet.

PLP packets are in turn passed to the LAPB layer, where they are encapsulated into LAPB information frames and passed to the physical layer to be sent through the network (see Figure 16.3).

X.25 requires error detection and correction in both the data link and the network layers.

Figure 16.3   *Encapsulation of PLP packet*

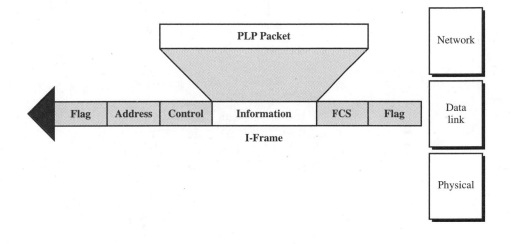

16.2   PACKET LAYER PROTOCOL

There are two types of PLP packets: information packets (I-packets) and control packets (C-packets). The formats of the two types of packets are essentially the same except that the information packet contains user data coming from the upper layers. The control packet does not contain user data; however, it may contain an information field necessary for the operation of the network.

In the network layer, X.25 uses two types of PLP packets: information packets (I-packets) and control packets (C-packets).

Information Packets

Information packets are used to transmit user data. Figure 16.4*a* shows the structure of an information packet. The general format is simple: a header and a user data field. The header, however, is complex and requires discussion here. There are two formats for information packets: short and long. The primary purpose of the long format is to support facilities with long delays, such as satellites. Information packets are differentiated from control packets by the last bit in the header. If this bit is set to 0, the packet is an information packet.

Figure 16.4 *PLP packets*

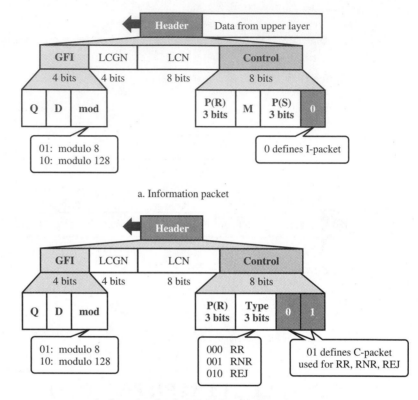

a. Information packet

b. Control packet for RR, RNR, and REJ

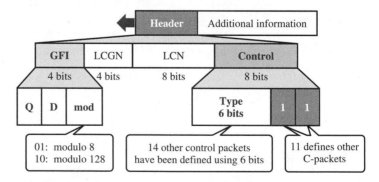

c. Control packet for other control purposes

The fields in the header are described as follows:

■   **General format identifier (GFI) field.** The GFI is a four-bit field. The first bit, called the Q bit, is not defined in the standard, but it can allow the user to define two types of data. For example, if the upper layer (transport layer) uses two different protocols, the Q bit can be set to show from which of these protocols the data are coming. The D bit is used in packet sequencing, which is described on p. 417. The next two bits are called modulo bits. They indicate the length of the header. If these bits are 01, the header is short. If these bits are 10, the header is long.

■ **Virtual circuit identification fields**. The logical channel group number (LCGN) is a 4-bit field that, together with the 8-bit logical channel number (LCN), make up a 12-bit number that identifies the virtual circuit chosen for a given transmission.

■ **Control field.** The control field consists of four sections, as shown in Figure 16.4*a*. P(S) and P(R) carry the packet sequence numbers for flow and error control. P(S) stands for *packet send* and indicates the number of the packet being sent. This number is assigned by the sending DTE to outgoing packets to be used for sliding-window ARQ. P(R) stands for *packet receive* and is the number of the next packet expected by the receiver. This field is used to piggyback acknowledgments to information packets when both parties have data to send. In the short header, both the P(S) and P(R) fields are three bits long. Three bits limit the size of the window to eight packets (referred to as modulo 8). In the long header, each field contains seven bits. Seven bits allow the window size to be as large as 128 packets (referred to as modulo 128). The M bit is used in packet sequencing. The last bit in this field defines the packet as an I-packet.

Control Packets

There are essentially two categories of control packets. The first category is used for flow and error control. The second category is used for connection, termination, and management control.

Category I

The control packets in Category I consist of only a header. In these packets, the last two header bits are set to 01 (see Figure 16.4*b)*. The general format of the header is essentially the same as in the information packet. The only difference is in the control field. These packets are used solely for flow and error control; they do not carry data and therefore do not have a P(S) field. Instead, they contain a new field, the type field. The type field carries a code number that describes the purpose of the packet.

These packets can be of three types: receive ready (RR), receive not ready (RNR), and reject (REJ). They are described as follows with the code numbers used to identify them in the packet:

■ **RR (000).** Receive ready (RR) means that the station is ready to receive more packets. It also acknowledges the receipt of a data packet by indicating the number of the next packet expected in the P(R) field.

■ **RNR (001).** Receive not ready (RNR) means that the station cannot accept packets at this time. The other party must stop sending packets as soon as this packet is received.

■ **REJ (010).** Reject (REJ) means that there was an error in the packet identified by the P(R) field. The other party must resend all packets including and following the packet indicated (go-back-*n* error recovery).

Category II

The control packets in Category II may carry information in addition to the header. However, the information is only for control and does not contain user data. In these packets the last two header bits are set to 11 (see Figure 16.4c). The general format of the header is essentially the same as in the information packet. The only difference is in the control field. However, the D bit in these packets has a slightly different significance from the D bit in an information packet. When set (1), it means that the sender requires confirmation from the remote DTE. When not set (0), it means that the sender needs confirmation only from the local (the sender's own) DCE.

The type field in these control packets is six bits long and can be used to specify up to 64 different functions. As of this writing, however, only a handful of the possible codes have been assigned meanings. Table 16.1 shows some of these types. Packet formats for the various types are shown in Figure 16.5. The functions of each type are described below.

Table 16.1   *Control packet type*

DTE to DCE	DCE to DTE	Code
Call request	Incoming call	000010
Call accepted	Call connected	000011
Clear request	Clear indication	000100
Clear confirm	Clear confirm	000101
Interrupt	Interrupt	001000
Interrupt confirm	Interrupt confirm	001001
Reset request	Reset indication	000110
Reset confirm	Reset confirm	000111
Restart request	Restart indication	111110
Restart confirmation	Restart confirmation	111111
Registration request		111100
	Registration confirm	111101

Call Request/Incoming Call   The call request and incoming call packets are used to request the establishment of a connection between two DTEs. Call request goes from the local DTE to the local DCE. Incoming call goes from the remote DCE to the remote DTE (see Figure 16.6). In addition to the header, each of these packets includes fields specifying the length of the address, the addresses of the DTEs, the length of any facilities, facilities, and optional information such as log-on codes and database access information.

Facilities are optional services that can be included on a contractual or per call basis. Facilities are made available by agreement between the users and network providers. Contractual options can include such services as incoming calls barred, outgoing calls barred, flow control parameter negotiation, fast select acceptance, and D-bit modification. Per call options can include flow control negotiation, fast select, and reverse charging.

Figure 16.5   *Control packet formats*

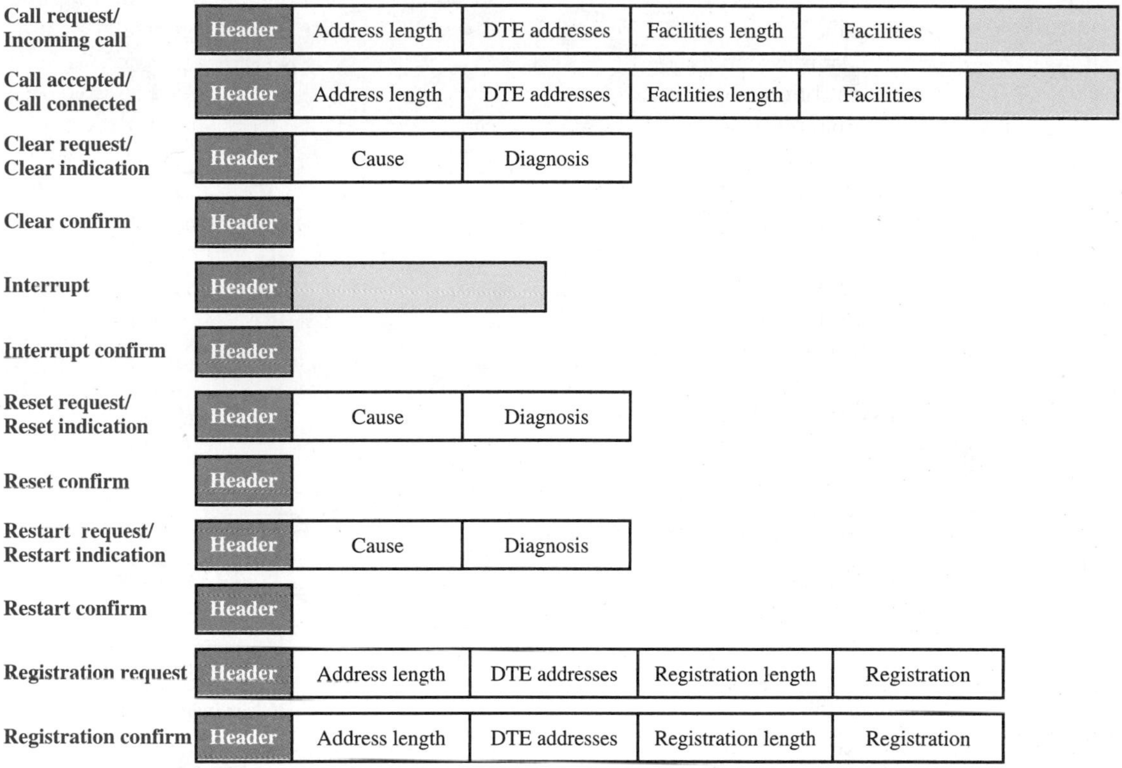

Call request/ Incoming call	Header	Address length	DTE addresses	Facilities length	Facilities	
Call accepted/ Call connected	Header	Address length	DTE addresses	Facilities length	Facilities	
Clear request/ Clear indication	Header	Cause	Diagnosis			
Clear confirm	Header					
Interrupt	Header					
Interrupt confirm	Header					
Reset request/ Reset indication	Header	Cause	Diagnosis			
Reset confirm	Header					
Restart request/ Restart indication	Header	Cause	Diagnosis			
Restart confirm	Header					
Registration request	Header	Address length	DTE addresses	Registration length	Registration	
Registration confirm	Header	Address length	DTE addresses	Registration length	Registration	

Call Accepted/Call Connected   The call accepted and call connected packets indicate the acceptance of the requested connection by the called system. They are sent in response to the call request and incoming call packets. Call accepted is sent by the remote (called) DTE to the remote DCE. Call connected is sent by the local (calling) DCE to the local DTE (see Figure 16.6).

Clear Request/Clear Indication   The clear request and clear indication packets are used at the end of an exchange to disconnect (clear) the connection. Either DTE or DCE can initiate the clearing (see Figure 16.7). These packets also can be used by a remote DTE to respond negatively to an incoming Call packet when it is unable to accept the requested connection.

Clear Confirm   The clear confirm packet is sent in response to the clear indication packet described above (see Figure 16.7).

Interrupt   The interrupt packet is used under unusual circumstances to break into an exchange and get attention. It can be sent by either of the DTEs or DCEs involved in the exchange and acts as an alert. For example, imagine that a DTE waits a long time without receiving either a positive or negative acknowledgment from the remote DCE.

Figure 16.6   *Connection establishment*

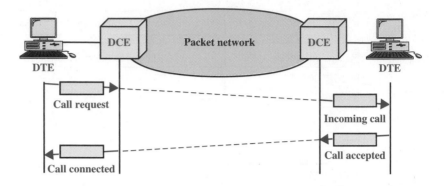

Figure 16.7   *Clearing*

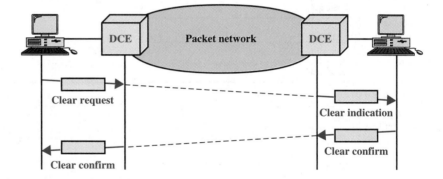

Its window has reached the end. It cannot send more packets and it cannot quit. It sends an interrupt message to get attention.

Interrupt Confirm   The interrupt confirm packet confirms the receipt of the interrupt packet described above.

Reset Request/Reset Indication   The reset request and reset indication packets are used to reset the sequence numbers in an exchange over a particular virtual circuit. Reset packets are used when a connection has been damaged to the point where the virtual circuit must be reinitialized. The virtual circuit remains active, but the transmission begins again from a predetermined point; all packets from that point on are renumbered, starting from 0.

Reset Confirm   The reset confirm packet confirms the reset process.

Restart Request/Restart Indication   The restart request and restart indication packets restart all virtual circuits created by a DTE. This process is different from the reset process. Reset packets activate a new set of sequence numbers on an existing virtual circuit. Restart packets start up a new virtual circuit. Restart terminates and reestablishes a call by establishing a new virtual circuit for transmission. Any packets on the original pathway are lost and new packets are renumbered starting with 0. An analogy to this process is a phone call where the connection becomes so bad that you hang up and dial again.

Restart Confirm   The restart confirm packet confirms the restart request.

Registration Request   The registration request packet allows on-line registration of new users to the network.

Registration Confirm   The registration confirm packet confirms a registration.

Complete Packet Sequence

The maximum length of the data field in an information packet varies from network to network, based in part on the limitations of the hardware, and is left to the discretion of system designers to determine. This flexibility means that an information packet that has to cross several networks to reach its destination may be too large or too small to be compatible with one or more of those networks and therefore must be resized in transit to accommodate the difference. In addition, a given message might be too long to fit within a single packet at the point of origin.

It is therefore important to be able to break up a long message among multiple packets but still keep those packets identifiable as a single contiguous transmission. The X.25 mechanism is the complete packet sequence.

A complete packet sequence involves the use of two types of packets: A packets and B packets. An A packet is one in which the data field is full and at least one additional packet is needed to carry the remainder of the message. An A packet is identified by a 1 in the More (M) field and by a 0 in the data terminal (D) field. The 1 in the M field means that more packets are to follow in the sequence. The D field tells the receiver whether or not an acknowledgment is required for that packet. (The 0 in the D field means that no acknowledgment is expected.) Any A packet must always be followed by at least one other packet and do not require acknowledgment.

B packets can either stand alone or act as the final packet in a multipacket sequence. The data field of a B packet does not have to be completely full. B packets always have a 1 in the D field to indicate that an acknowledgment is required. A complete packet sequence consists of one B packet following zero or more A packets. If all of a message's data fits into the data field of a single information packet, then the complete packet sequence consists of one B packet. If it takes two packets to carry the data, then the complete packet sequence consists of an A packet and a B packet. If it takes three packets to carry the data, then the complete packet sequence consists of two A packets and a B packet, and so on.

If, during transmission, the sequence crosses into a network that requires smaller packets, the data carried by each packet can be distributed among additional A packets without losing the integrity of the message. In the same way, when the sequence crosses into a network that uses longer packets, the data fields of the A and B packets can be combined into fewer A packets or even into a single B packet. For example, a transmission can begin as one long B packet. In the next network it can subdivided into three shorter packets; two As and a B. In the next network it can be recombined into one A packet and one B packet, and so on. Such transformations occur without jeopardizing the integrity of the message.

In long transmissions, the sender may want to receive acknowledgments more often than just at the end of the entire sequence. In this case, the complete packet sequence can be divided into subsequences of one or more A packets and a B packet (see Figure 16.8). When a transmission includes only one B packet, the M bit of that packet is set to 0 to indicate that it is the last packet in the sequence. To identify a B packet as a subsequence B packet rather than a complete-sequence B packet, the M bit is set to 1, meaning that more packets are to come.

Examine Figure 16.8. Packets 1 to 8 have the M bit set to 1 to indicate that more packets are to follow. Packets 1, 2, 4, 5, 7 and 8 have the D bit set to 0 to indicate that they do not require acknowledgment; they are A packets. Packets 3, 6, and 9 have the D bit set to 1. These packets do require acknowledgment, so they are B packets. In this example, every third frame is a B packet. Packets 3 and 6 are B packets with the M bit set to 1, which makes them subsequence B packets. B packet 9, however, has the M bit set to 0. It is the final packet of the complete packet sequence.

In summary, if the D bit is set to 1, the packet requires an acknowledgment from the final destination. If the D bit is set to 0, no acknowledgment is needed. If the M bit is set to 1, more packets are to follow. If the M bit is 0 that packet is the last one of the message. Complete packet sequences consist of one B packet following 0 to n A packets. Long transmissions may consist of several complete packet sequences (subsequences) strung together.

Figure 16.8   *Sequence and subsequence*

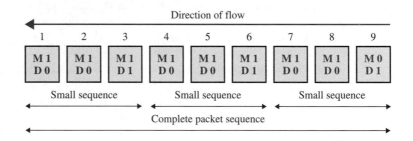

Virtual Channel ID Numbers

X.25 allows up to 4096 (2^{12}) multiplexed channels to be identified between each DTE and DCE. ID numbers are assigned to each channel to identify which packet belongs to which channel. These numbers are not permanent, but are allocated dynamically as the channels are assigned and used only for the duration of the specific exchange. In addition, the calling and called hosts use different numbers to identify a virtual circuit. Figure 16.9 shows how these numbers are allocated.

Figure 16.9   *Virtual channel ID numbers*

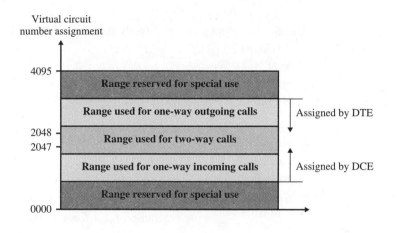

16.3   SUMMARY

- X.25 is the packet switching protocol used in ISDN.
- X.25 defines the procedures for data transmission between a DTE and a DCE.
- X.25 protocol specifies three layers that correspond to the OSI model: the physical layer, the link access procedure, balanced (LAPB) layer and the packet level protocol (PLP) layer. The latter two layers perform both flow and error control.
- The network layer of X.25 is called the packet layer protocol (PLP). This layer handles connection establishment and termination, data transfer, and packet creation protocols.
- There are two types of PLP packets: information and control.
- X.25 specifies protocols to handle resizing of messages.
- Up to 4096 channels may be multiplexed at the PLP level.

16.4   PRACTICE SET

Multiple Choice

1. X.25 protocol uses _____ for end-to-end transmission.
   a. message switching
   b. circuit switching
   c. the datagram approach
   d. the virtual circuit approach
2. The X.25 protocol operates in the _____ of the OSI model.
   a. physical layer

    b. data link layer

    c. network layer

    d. all of the above

3. The physical layer protocol directly specified for the X.25 protocol is _____.

    a. RS-232

    b. X.21

    c. DB-15

    d. DB-37

4. The PLP packet is a product of the _____ layer in the X.25 standard.

    a. physical

    b. data link

    c. network

    d. transport

5. The PLP _____ is used to transport data from the upper layers in the X.25 standard.

    a. S-packet

    b. I-packet

    c. C-packet

    d. P-packet

6. When no data need to be sent but an acknowledgment is necessary, the PLP _____ is used.

    a. S-packet

    b. I-packet

    c. C-packet

    d. P-packet

7. In the X.25 standard, the PLP _____ is used for connection establishment, connection release, and other control purposes.

    a. S-packet

    b. I-packet

    c. C-packet

    d. P-packet

8. In the X.25 standard, if the _____ bit is set to 1, the receiver requires acknowledgment prior to the end of a complete packet sequence.

    a. Q

    b. D

    c. M

    d. P

9. If the _____ bit in X.25 standard is set to 1, it means that there is more than one packet.

    a. Q

    b. D

   c. M

   d. P

10. The _____ bit in the X.25 standard allows the user to distinguish between two possible types of protocol that the data might follow.

   a. Q

   b. D

   c. M

   d. P

11. X.25 protocol requires error checking at the _____ layer.

   a. physical

   b. data link

   c. network

   d. b and c

Exercises

1. Why are there two types of headers for the I-packet in the X.25 standard?
2. What distinguishes the PLP packet types of the X.25 standard from each other?
3. What does the X.25 provide in the area of error control/detection?
4. X.25 allows up to 4096 multiplexed channels between a DTE and a DCE. Where does this number come from?

CHAPTER 17

FRAME RELAY

X.25 provides extensive error checking and flow control. Packets are checked for accuracy at each station (node) to which they are routed. Each station keeps the copy of the original frame until it receives confirmation from the next station that the frame has arrived intact. Such station-to-station checking is implemented at the data link layer of the OSI model.

But X.25 does not stop there. It also checks for errors from source to receiver at the network layer. The source keeps a copy of the original packet until it receives confirmation from the final destination. Much of the traffic on an X.25 network is devoted to error checking to ensure complete reliability of service.

Figure 17.1 shows the traffic required to transmit one packet from source to receiver. The white boxes show the data and data link acknowledgments. The shaded boxes show the network layer confirmation and acknowledgments. Only one-fourth of this traffic is message data; the rest is reliability. Such extensive traffic was necessary at the time X.25 was introduced because transmission media were more error prone then than they are today.

Unfortunately, all this overhead eats up bandwidth that cannot therefore be used for message data. If bandwidth is limited, the data rate of the transmission, which is proportional to the available channel width, is severely reduced. In addition, the requirement that each station keep a copy of the frame in its storage while it waits for acknowledgment results in another traffic bottleneck and further reductions in speed.

Improvements in traditional transmission media and a greater use of fiber-optic cable, which is far less susceptible to noise than metallic cable, have decreased the probability of transmission error to a point where this level of caution is not only unnecessary but counterproductive as well.

Frame relay does not provide error checking or require acknowledgment in the data link layer. Instead, all error checking is left to the protocols at the network and transport layers, which use the services of frame relay. (Frame relay operates at only the physical and data link layers.) Many data link layer operations are eliminated while others are combined. Instead of the complex situation shown in Figure 17.1, we now have the simplified transmission shown in Figure 17.2.

Figure 17.1   *X.25 traffic*

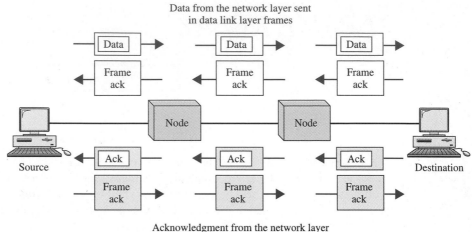

Figure 17.2   *Frame relay traffic*

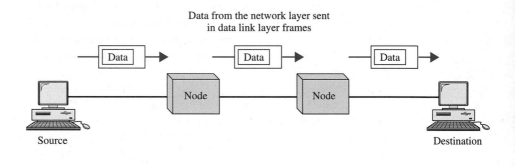

17.1   FRAME RELAY LAYERS

Figure 17.3 shows the frame relay layers in relation to the conventional layers of a packet switching network. Frame relay has only 1.5 layers whereas X.25 has 3 layers. Frame relay eliminates all of the network layer functions and a portion of the conventional data link layer functions.

Physical Layer

No specific protocol is defined for the physical layer in frame relay. Instead, it is left to the implementer to use whatever is available. Frame relay supports any of the protocols recognized by ANSI.

Figure 17.3 *Frame relay layers*

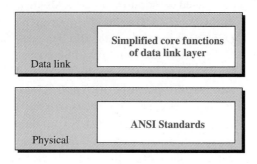

Frame relay operates only at the physical and data link layers.

Data Link Layer

At the data link layer, frame relay employs a simplified version of HDLC. The simpler version is used because HDLC provides extensive error and flow control fields that are not needed in frame relay.

Figure 17.4 shows the format of a frame relay frame. The frame is similar to that of HDLC. In fact, the flag, FCS, and information fields are the same. The address and control fields, however, have been combined into a single field. This field, though still labeled as an address field, is actually the data link connection identifier (DLCI). The DLCI (address) field consists of two or more bytes divided among a combination of address fields and control functions. Frame relay provides more congestion control

Figure 17.4 *Frame relay frame*

C/R: Command/response   BECN: Backward explicit congestion notification
EA: Extended address   DE: Discard eligibility
FECN: Forward explicit congestion notification   DLCI: Data link connection identifier

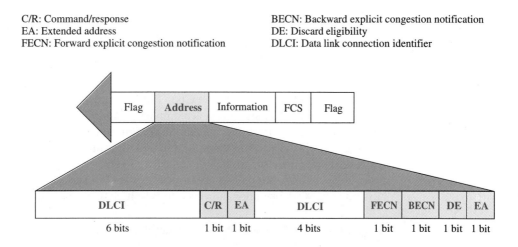

than error control. Congestion functions are implemented in three one-bit fields in the second byte of the address field.

The detailed descriptions of the fields are as follows:

- **Addressing (DLCI) fields.** The first six bits of the first byte make up part 1 of the DLCI. The second part of the DLCI uses the first four bits of the second byte. These bits are part of the 16-bit data link connection identifier defined by the standard. The function of the DLCI is discussed in section 17.2, Frame Relay Operation.
- **Command/Response (C/R).** The C/R bit is provided to allow upper layers to identify a frame as either a command or a response.
- **Extended address (EA).** The EA bit tells whether or not the current byte is the final byte of the address. EA 0 means that another address byte is to follow. EA 1 means that the current byte is the final one. In a two-byte address, the EA is 0 in the first byte and 1 in the second byte. If an application requires additional addressing bits, the EA field in the second byte is also 0 and a third byte is added that includes a seven-bit address field and an EA field of 1.
- **Forward explicit congestion notification (FECN).** The FECN bit can be set by any routing node to indicate that traffic is congested in the direction in which the frame is traveling. It informs the destination that congestion may cause the present or future frames to arrive late. The use of this facility is discussed on p. 429.
- **Backward explicit congestion notification (BECN).** The BECN bit is set to indicate a congestion problem in the direction opposite to the one in which the frame is traveling. It informs the receiver that data sent back to the sender may be delayed by congestion. The use of this facility is also discussed on p. 429.
- **Discard eligibility (DE).** The DE bit indicates the priority level of the frame. In emergency situations, nodes may have to discard frames to relieve bottlenecks and keep the network from collapsing due to overload. When set (DE 1), this bit tells the network not to discard this frame as long as there are other frames in the stream with priorities of 0.

17.2   FRAME RELAY OPERATION

Frame relay transmission is based on permanent virtual circuit (PVC) connections. Virtual circuits in other standards are implemented by the network layer. Frame relay uses data link connection identifiers (DLCIs). The DLCI identifies a permanent virtual circuit that is set up when the system is put in place. All traffic between two given stations takes the same path (hence the appellation *permanent virtual circuit*).

Figure 17.5 shows a network where stations are connected directly to a frame relay network. In practice, this situation is unusual. Stations are more likely to connect to a frame relay network through another type of network or service. It is helpful to our discussion of network operation, however, to base it on this simplified model.

Frame relay uses the permanent virtual circuit (PVC) approach.

Figure 17.5   *Frame relay network*

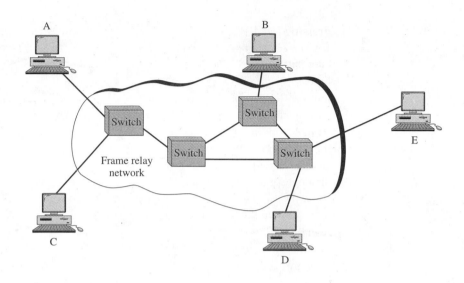

Relay

Using the model shown in Figure 17.5, we can visualize a series of paths between stations. Figure 17.6 shows some possible PVCs and DLCI combinations. A 10-bit DLCI can identify up to 1024 different permanent virtual circuits. A third address byte increases that number.

An examination of these figures brings to light a significant aspect of frame relay. The use of PVCs means that routing information is included in the destination information. The path from point A to point D always passes through the same nodes. Thus, if the network knows the destination, it knows the route. By relying on permanent virtual circuits, the functions of routing and switching, traditionally handled by the network layer, can be handled by the data link layer. Instead of requiring both a network layer address and a data link layer address, therefore, frame relay satisfies both functions with the DLCI.

In fact, that is where we get the name *frame relay*. Packet switching occurs at the network layer where the transmission unit is the packet. Frame relay (frame switching) occurs at the data link layer where the transmission unit is the frame.

Switching

Switches in the frame relay network have only two functions. When a frame is received, the switch checks it for errors using the FCS field, which is a CRC. If the frame is intact, the switch then compares the DLCI to an entry in a switching table. The table tells the switch which outgoing port corresponds to that DLCI and therefore to the correct PVC (see Figure 17.7). The switch then sends the frame out through that port. If an error is found in the frame, the switch discards it.

Figure 17.6   *Frame relay addresses*

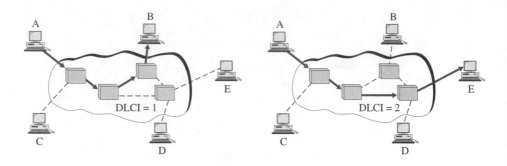

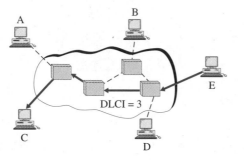

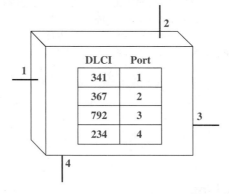

Figure 17.7   *Frame relay switch*

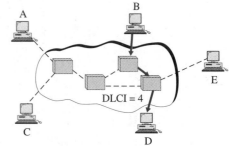

What happens when a frame is discarded? How does the sender find out? Frame relay leaves that communication to the sender's transport layer functions. The sender does not need to know where or when a frame is discarded or lost, only that a frame has not arrived at its destination. At the receiver, the transport layer checks the integrity of the transmission. If something is missing, it requests that segment's retransmission. The job of a switch in frame relay, therefore, is to check but not to correct errors, and to route frames along predetermined paths.

A switch in frame relay uses a table associating a DLCI number to a port number.

Congestion Control

An issue in frame relay is congestion control. Because the standard eliminates flow control, the switches and destination can become congested with data. Congestion not only delays traffic but, when heavy enough, can cause a node to fail altogether. Frame relay does not solve this problem but does provide ways to lessen the probability of its occurrence.

Anytime a switch in a permanent virtual circuit encounters congestion, it warns its downstream switches and destination by turning on the FECN bit (setting it to 1). This bit tells downstream devices that congestion has begun and that they may expect some frames to be discarded.

The receiver, in turn, can set the BECN bit to warn upstream switches and the sender that the link is congested, and to send frames more slowly. However, this option cannot be used unless the channel is either full- or half-duplex and the receiver is sending its own data or acknowledgments to the sender. Most of the time, the sender (the only device in a position to take steps to avoid congestion) will remain unnotified. It will continue to send frames, unaware of any problem as the congestion becomes more and more dense.

17.3 IMPLEMENTATION

Frame relay can be implemented in a variety of ways. The most likely, however, is to use it as a WAN backbone to connect a number of LANs using T-1 links. To do so requires the addition of interface devices called frame relay assembler/disassemblers (FRADs). This simple device assembles and disassembles packets coming from other protocols to allow them to be carried by frame relay frames (see Figure 17.8).

A frame relay network is most often used as the backbone of a wide area network (WAN).

Figure 17.8   *Frame relay implementation*

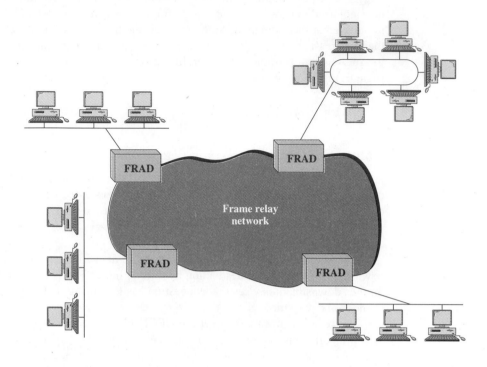

17.4   SUMMARY

- Frame relay eliminates the extensive error checking necessary in X.25 protocol.
- Frame relay operates in the physical and data link layers of the OSI model. No protocol is specified for the physical layer; the choice is up to the user.
- In the data link layer, frame relay uses a simplified version of HDLC protocol.
- Frame relay uses permanent virtual circuits (PVCs). The PVC link is identified through the data link connection identifier (DLCI) in the address field of the data link frame.
- In frame relay, routing and switching are functions of the data link layer. Frames, not packets, are switched.
- A switch in frame relay performs error checking and routing. Error correction is left to the other protocols at the higher layers.
- Flow control is handled through setting the backwards explicit congestion notification (BECN) and/or forward explicit congestion notification (FECN) bits in the address field of the frame.

17.5   PRACTICE SET

Multiple Choice

1. Frame relay requires error checking at the _____ layer.
   a. physical
   b. data link
   c. network
   d. none of the above

2. Frame relay operates in the _____.
   a. physical layer
   b. data link layer
   c. physical and data link layers
   d. physical, data link, and network layers

3. In the data link layer, frame relay uses _____.
   a. BSC protocol
   b. a simplified HDLC protocol
   c. LAPB
   d. any ANSI standard protocol

4. Which bit in the address field in frame relay is set to one to signify the last address byte?
   a. discard eligibility (DE)
   b. extended address (EA)
   c. command/response (C/R)
   d. forward explicit congestion notification (FECN)

5. Which bit in the address field in frame relay determines whether or not a frame may be eliminated in emergency cases?
   a. discard eligibility (DE)
   b. extended address (EA)
   c. command/response (C/R)
   d. forward explicit congestion notification (FECN)

6. In Figure 17.6, what is the minimum number of bytes that the address field needs to handle all the DLCIs?
   a. 1
   b. 2
   c. 3
   d. 4

7. Routing and switching in frame relay is performed by the _____ layer.
   a. physical
   b. data link

  c. network
  d. b and c
8. Which field contains the permanent virtual circuit address in frame relay?
  a. EA
  b. FECN/BECN
  c. DE
  d. DLCI
9. Which of the following is a switch function in frame relay?
  a. error checking
  b. error correction
  c. line discipline
  d. a and b
10. Which of the following is a switch function in frame relay?
  a. data regeneration
  b. broadcasting
  c. collision detection
  d. routing

Exercises

1. How is flow control handled in frame relay?
2. How are frame relay assemblers/dissemblers (FRADs) used in a frame relay backbone?
3. Name some advantages of frame relay over X.25.
4. What is the advantage of X.25 over frame relay?
5. How does a packet get retransmitted in frame relay?

CHAPTER 18

ATM

Asynchronous Transfer Mode (ATM) is the cell relay protocol designed by the ATM Forum and adopted by the ITU-T. To date, only some aspects of the protocol have been standardized. When complete, the combination of ATM and B-ISDN will allow high-speed interconnection of all the world's networks. In fact, ATM can be thought of as the "highway" for the information superhighway.

18.1   DESIGN GOALS

Among the challenges faced by the designers of ATM, six stand out. First and foremost is the need for a transmission system to optimize the use of high data-rate transmission media, in particular optical fiber. In addition to offering ultrawide bandwidths, newer transmission media and equipment are dramatically less susceptible to noise degradation. A technology is needed to take advantage of both factors and thereby maximize data rates.

Second is the need for a system that can interface with existing systems, such as the various packet networks, and to provide wide area interconnectivity between them without lowering their effectiveness or requiring their replacement. ATM is potentially as effective a LAN and short-haul mechanism as it is a WAN mechanism. Its proponents hope that it will eventually replace the existing systems. Until that happens, however, the protocol provides mechanisms for mapping the packets and frames of other systems onto ATM cells.

Third is the need for a design that can be implemented inexpensively so that cost would not be a barrier to adoption. If ATM is to become the backbone of international communications, as intended, it must be available at low cost to every user who wants it.

Fourth, the new system must be able to work with and support the existing telecommunications hierarchies (local loops, local providers, long-distance carriers, etc.).

Fifth, the new system must be connection-oriented to ensure accurate and predictable delivery.

And last but not least, one objective is to move as many of the functions to hardware as possible (for speed) and eliminate as many software functions as possible (again for speed).

Before discussing the solutions to these design requirements, it is useful to examine some of the problems associated with existing systems.

> In ATM, some software functions have moved to hardware; this can increase the data rate.

Packet Networks

Data communications today are based on packet switching and packet networks. As explained in Chapter 14, a packet is a combination of data and overhead bits that can be passed through the network as a self-contained unit. The overhead bits, in the form of a header and trailer, act as an envelope that provide identification and addressing information as well as the data required for routing, flow control, error control, and so on.

Different protocols use packets of varying size and intricacy. As networks become more complex, the information that must be carried in the header becomes more extensive. The result is larger and larger headers relative to the size of the data unit. In response, some protocols have enlarged the size of the data unit to make header use more efficient (sending more data with the same size header). Unfortunately, large data fields create waste. If the data unit is small, much of the field goes unused. To improve utilization, some protocols provide variable packet sizes to users. We now have packets that can be as long as 65,545 bytes sharing long-haul links with packets of fewer than 200 bytes.

Mixed Network Traffic

As you can imagine, the variety of packet sizes makes traffic unpredictable. Switches, multiplexers, and routers must incorporate elaborate software systems to manage the various sizes of packets. A great deal of header information must be read, and each bit counted and evaluated to ensure the integrity of every packet. Internetworking among the different packet networks is slow and expensive at best, and impossible at worst.

Another problem is that of providing consistent data-rate delivery when packet sizes are unpredictable and can vary so dramatically. To get the most out of broadband technology, traffic must be time-domain multiplexed onto shared paths. Imagine the results of multiplexing packets from two networks with different requirements (and packet designs) onto one link (see Figure 18.1). What happens when line 1 uses long packets (usually data packets) while line 2 uses very small packets (the norm for audio and video information)?

If line 1's gigantic packet X arrives at the multiplexer even a moment earlier than line 2's packets, the multiplexer puts packet X onto the new path first. After all, even if line 2's packets have priority, the multiplexer has no way of knowing to wait for them, and processes the packet that has arrived. Packet A must therefore wait for the entire X bit stream to move into place before it can follow. The sheer size of X creates an unfair delay for packet A. The same imbalance can affect all of the packets from line 2. As an analogy, imagine yourself in a car arriving at a crossroads just after

Figure 18.1 *Multiplexing using different packet sizes*

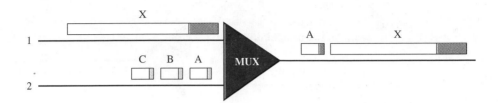

a parade has arrived from the opposite direction. The parade takes the same outbound road that you need to take but, because it arrived just before you did, it is already beginning its turn when you get there. You have to wait for the entire parade to turn onto the road before you can follow. Now imagine that you had been following another car that made the turn before the parade. You will now arrive at your shared destination separated by a huge gap of time.

Because audio and video packets ordinarily are small, mixing them with conventional data traffic often creates unacceptable delays of this type and makes shared packet links unusable for audio and video information. Traffic must travel over different paths, much the same way that automobile and train traffic do. But to fully utilize broad bandwidth links, we need to be able to send all kinds of traffic over the same links.

Cell Networks

Many of the problems associated with packet internetworking are solved by adopting a concept called cell networking. A cell is small data unit of fixed size. In a cell network, which uses the cell as the basic unit of data exchange, all data are loaded into identical cells that can be transmitted with complete predictability and uniformity. As packets of different sizes and formats reach the cell network from a tributary network, they are split into multiple small data units of equal length and loaded into cells. The cells are then multiplexed with other cells and routed through the cell network. Because each cell is the same size and all are small, the problems associated with multiplexing different sized packets are avoided.

> A cell network uses the cell as the basic unit of data exchange. A cell is defined as a small, fixed-sized block of information.

Advantages of Cells

Figure 18.2 shows the multiplexer from Figure 18.1 with the two lines sending cells instead of packets. Packet X has been segmented into three cells: X, Y, and Z. Only the first cell from line 1 gets put on the link before the first cell from line 2. The cells from the two lines are interleaved so that none suffers a long delay.

A second advantage of this same scenario is that the high speed of the links coupled with the small size of the cells means that, despite interleaving, cells from each line arrive at their respective destinations in an approximation of a continuous stream

Figure 18.2   *Multiplexing using cells*

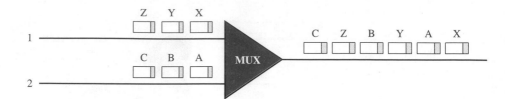

(much as a movie appears to your brain to be continuous action when in fact it is really a series of separate still photos). In this way, a cell network can handle real-time transmissions, such as a phone call, without the parties being aware of the segmentation or multiplexing at all.

In addition, the predictability conferred by fixed cell size allows switches and terminals to treat each cell as a unit rather than as a bit stream. In other words, to a cell network the smallest unit is a cell, not a bit. This distinction makes network operation not only more efficient but also cheaper. Switching and multiplexing can be implemented in hardware rather than software, resulting in devices that are less expensive both to produce and to maintain.

Routing in Cell Networks

Of course, cells are useful only if we can use them to move information from one point to another efficiently and with minimal delays. For this reason, the cell routing strategy is as important as the cell itself.

Virtual Circuits   Cell networks are based on virtual circuit routing. All cells belonging to a single message follow the same path and remain in their original order until they reach their destination. The reasoning behind this requirement is that when cells are routed by different paths, they may arrive out of order and with uneven and unpredictable delays. The erratic quality of a connectionless delivery of this sort makes it unsuitable for on-line video or audio transmission. In addition, connectionless services require more overhead information (complete addressing, flow and error control data appended to every packet). The resulting header lengths negate the advantages of small, uniform cells.

Switching   The efficiency of a cell network is linked to its simplicity. Just as a cell is an extremely streamlined packet, the strategy for routing those cells must be equally simple.

The concepts behind cell switching are most easily examined if we limit our sample network to two parameters. First, we assume that we are using a baseband technique. Second, we assume that the link between any two devices consists of only one channel. In reality, of course, networks are far more complex.

Examine the sample cell network in Figure 18.3. The boxes numbered I, II, III, IV, V, VI, and VII represent switches. Each switch has several ports (interfaces) numbered 1, 2, 3, and so on. Now assume that device A wants to send a message to device B. The message consists of a number of cells, and the route chosen for them is A to I to III to

Figure 18.3   *Cell switching*

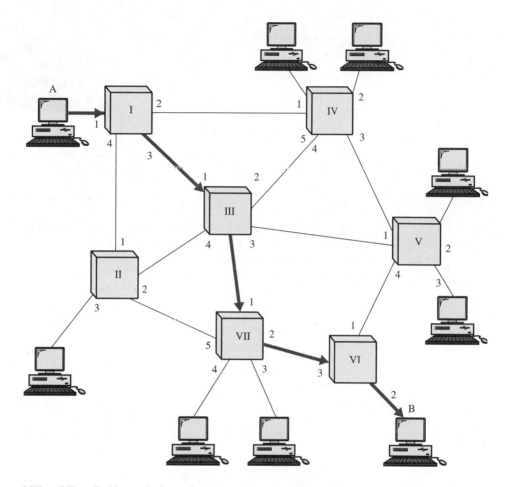

VII to VI to B (the technique for choosing a route is discussed on p. 438). Each cell must carry information identifying this route, and this information must be contained in the smallest possible format. In cell networking, route identification is contained in a brief header field called the virtual path identifier (VPI); see Figure 18.4.

Each switch in the network contains a list of numbers that identify paths to every other switch in the network. These numbers are specific to each switch. A single path may be identified by a different number at each switch. Each switch chooses its own ID numbers for each path. This independence allows VPIs to be kept short: each switch needs enough ID numbers to accommodate only the paths it serves. If every path in the network had a unique identifier, the numbers would have to be much longer, and would increase the size of the header. Independence also makes reconfiguration easier. The VPI in the header is valid for only one link. Each switch replaces the arriving VPI with its own outgoing VPI. Device A inserts into the header the VPI that it uses to refer to the path to device B. Each node, therefore, also has a table to show which VPI coming from which port matches each of its own outgoing VPIs.

Figure 18.4   *VPI*

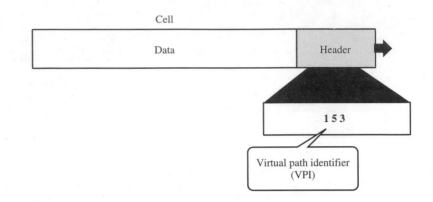

The path itself is constant for the duration of the exchange, but the numbers identifying it change from link to link. VPIs can be assigned by a network manager to create permanent identifiers, or they can be allocated dynamically during the signaling process at the beginning of a transmission.

Now, let's examine the mechanism by which a cell arrives at a switch and is given a new VPI. Figure 18.5 uses switch I from Figure 18.3 as an example.

Figure 18.5   *Switching using VPI*

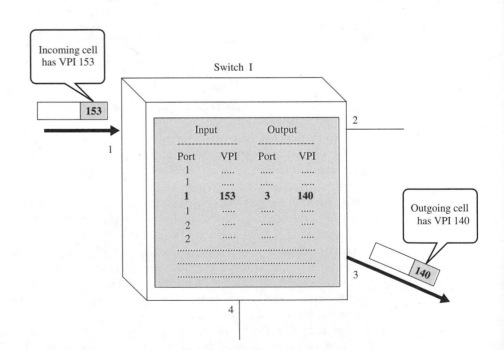

A cell with a VPI of 153 arrives at the switch through port 1. To route the cell, the switch needs to determine which of its exit ports corresponds to a VPI of 153 from port 1. It does so by comparing what it knows about the incoming cell to information stored in its switching table. This table stores four pieces of information at each row: arrival port number, incoming VPI, corresponding outgoing port number, and the new VPI. In the figure, the cell has arrived by port 1. The switch finds the port 1 entry with VPI 153 and discovers that the combination corresponds to output port 3 and VPI 140. It changes the VPI in the header to 140 and sends the cell out through port 3.

The same mechanism can be applied to switches handling traffic for multiple channels on each path. In this case, the cell header must contain two identifiers: the VPI, and a virtual channel identifier (VCI); see Figure 18.6. The combination of entry port number and VPI tells the switch through which port to route the cell. The combination of VPI and VCI tells the switch over which of the possible channels serviced by that port the cell should be directed.

Figure 18.6 *VPI and VCI*

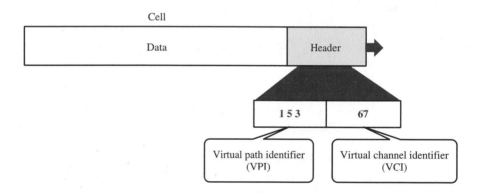

Figure 18.7 shows switch I's table augmented to reflect this additional information.

Additional Advantages of ATM

ATM is an asynchronous transmission mode that uses cells of only 53 bytes each. In this case, asynchronous means that each cell travels independently without being tied to others. However, as we have mentioned, transmission is connection-oriented. The cells may be self-contained, but all cells of a single message travel sequentially by a single path.

In addition, although individual cells may be delayed in transmission, the fact that they take the same path means that a delay affects all cells of a message equally. And the small size of each cell means that such delays are likely to be short. If a cell is delayed, the delay is distributed among the entire cell stream and appears to the receiver merely as if the message left the sender a little later than it did. The system can compensate for such delays either by having the sender produce the data slightly earlier than expected or by increasing the data rate so that the cells arrive faster than they can

Figure 18.7   *Switching using VPI and VCI*

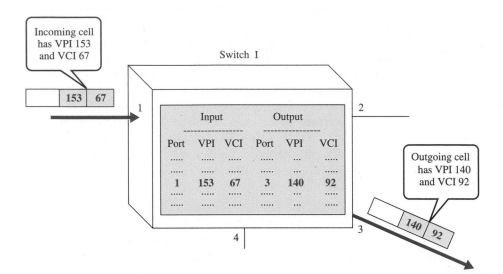

be consumed. (Data rates can be controlled by adding or removing dummy bits to or from cells, as well as by changing the bandwidth allocated for transmission.)

In the term *asynchronous transfer mode (ATM)*, *asynchronous* means that the cells are independent of each other with potentially different gaps between them. The cells are transmitted only when there is data.

A third distinction of ATM is that it provides automatic error correction rather than relying on retransmission. As mentioned in Chapter 17, today's transmission media are less susceptible to errors than earlier technologies. In addition, smaller cell sizes offer fewer possibilities for introduction of errors. It has been shown that, in general, an error in an ATM cell affects only a single bit. Single-bit errors can be corrected easily at the receiver by the inclusion of an error code that contains sufficient redundancy to allow the original bit-pattern to be reconstructed. Automatic error correction is possible with packets of any type. However, the number of redundancy bits required for automatic correction increases with the size of the packet. The process, therefore, is efficient only when applied to cell networks.

Finally, there are no complex flow or congestion control mechanisms in ATM as in other wide area network protocols.

18.2   ATM TOPOLOGY

Although much of ATM is still under study, the basic topology has been mapped out. At this point, ATM is intended to be a hierarchy of networks connected by associated interfaces. The two most important of these interfaces are the user network interface

(UNI) and the network-to-network interface (NNI). A UNI is the interface between a user and the wide area ATM network. An NNI is the interface between two wide area ATM networks (between two B-ISDN nodes); see Figure 18.8.

Figure 18.8   *ATM interfaces*

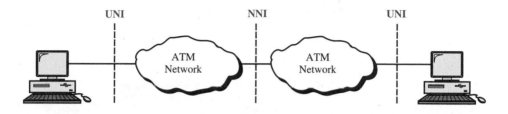

In addition, we can have ATM switches that are used outside of the public ATM network, such as ATM LANs or an ATM backbone connecting the networks of a campus. To connect these private switches to the public network, we need a second type of UNI. A UNI that connects a user or service to an ATM switch is called a private UNI. A UNI that connects a user or service to a public ATM network is called a public UNI (see Figure 18.9). Note that the terms *private* and *public* in this context do not describe ownership. They merely indicate whether the interface is located inside or outside the user's premises.

Figure 18.9   *Public and private UNIs*

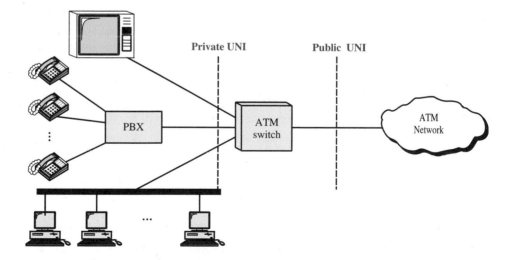

18.3   ATM PROTOCOL ARCHITECTURE

The ATM standard defines a series of layers not analogous to those of the OSI model. They are, from top to bottom, the application adaptation layer, the ATM layer, and the physical layer (see Figure 18.10).

Figure 18.10   *ATM layers*

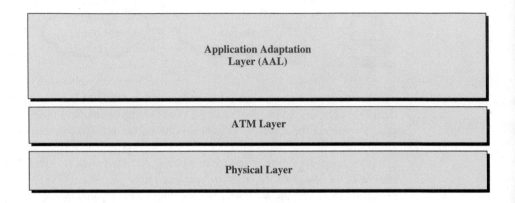

Application Adaptation Layer (AAL)

The application adaptation layer (AAL) allows existing networks (such as packet networks) to connect to ATM facilities. AAL protocols accept transmissions from upper-layer services (e.g., packet data) and map them into fixed-sized ATM cells. These transmissions can be of any type (voice, data, audio, video) and can be of variable or fixed rates. At the receiver, this process is reversed—segments are reassembled into their original formats and passed to the receiving service.

The AAL layer reformats data from other protocols, acting like a gateway (see Chapter 20) in internetworking.

Data Types

Instead of one protocol for all types of data, however, the ATM standard divides the AAL layer into categories, each supporting the requirements of a different type of application. In defining these categories, the ATM designers identified four types of data streams: constant bit-rate data, variable bit-rate data, connection-oriented packet data, and connectionless packet data.

- **Constant bit-rate data** refers to applications that generate and consume bits at a constant rate. In this type of application, transmission delays must be minimal and transmission must simulate real-time. Examples of constant bit-rate applications include real time voice (telephone calls) and real time video (television).

- **Variable bit-rate data** refers to applications that generate and consume bits at variable rates. In this type of application, the bit rate varies from section to section of the transmission, but within established parameters. Examples of variable bit-rate applications include compressed voice, data, and video.

- **Connection-oriented packet data** refers to conventional packet applications (such as X.25 and the TCP protocol of TCP/IP) that use virtual circuits.

- **Connectionless packet data** refers to applications that use a datagram approach to routing (such as the IP protocol in TCP/IP).

The ITU-T recognized the need for an additional category, one that cuts across all of the above data types but is adapted for point-to-point rather than multipoint or inter-network transmissions. The sublayer designed to meet the needs of this type of transmission is called the simple and efficient adaptation layer (SEAL).

The AAL categories designed to support each of these types of data have been called AAL1, AAL2, AAL3, AAL4, and AAL5, respectively. More recently however, it has been decided that there is too much overlap between AAL3 and AAL4 to justify their remaining separate, so they have been combined into a single category, AAL3/4. AAL2, though still a part of the ATM design, may also be dropped and its functions combined with those of another category.

Convergence and Segmentation

In addition to dividing the AAL by category, the ITU-T also divides it by function. As a result, each of the AAL categories is actually two layers: the convergence sublayer (CS), and the segmentation and reassembly sublayer (SAR); see Figure 18.11. The duties of these two sublayers vary and will be described as we describe each AAL category.

Figure 18.11 *AAL types*

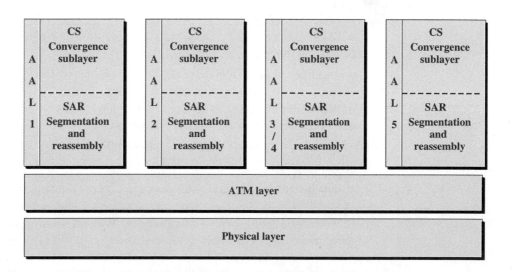

AAL1

AAL1 supports applications that transfer information at constant bit rates, such as video and voice, and allows ATM to connect existing digital telephone networks such as DS-3 or E-1.

Convergence Sublayer   The convergence sublayer divides the bit stream into 47-byte segments and passes them to the SAR sublayer below.

Segmentation and Reassembly   Figure 18.12 shows the format of an AAL1 data unit at the SAR layer. As you can see, this layer accepts a 47-byte payload from the CS and adds a one-byte header. The result is a 48-byte data unit that is then passed to the ATM layer, where it is encapsulated in a cell.

Figure 18.12   *AAL1*

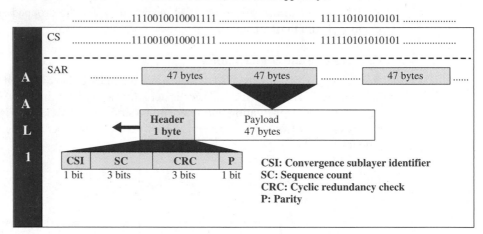

The header at this layer consists of four fields:

- **Convergence sublayer identifier (CSI).** The one-bit CSI field will be used for signaling purposes that are not yet clearly defined.
- **Sequence count (SC).** The three-bit SC field is a modulo 8 sequence number to be used for ordering and identifying the cells for end-to-end error and flow control.
- **Cyclic redundancy check (CRC).** The three-bit CRC field is calculated over the first four bits using the four-bit divisor $x^3 + x + 1$. Three bits may look like too much redundancy. However, they are intended not only to detect a single- or multiple-bit error, but also to correct several single-bit errors. In non-real-time applications, an error in a cell is inconsequential (the cell can be retransmitted). In real-time applications, however, retransmission is not an option. With no retransmission, the quality of the received data deteriorates. With one missing cell, you might hear a click during a telephone call or see a black dot on your video monitor; large numbers of missing cells can destroy intelligibility. Automatic correction of single-bit header

errors dramatically reduces the number of cells that are missing and is therefore a boon to quality of service.

■ **Parity (P).** The one-bit P field is a standard parity bit calculated based on the first seven bits of the header. A parity bit can detect an odd number of errors but not an even number of errors. This feature can be used for error correction of the first four bits. If one single bit is in error, both the CRC and the P bit will detect it. In this case, the CRC corrects the bit and the cell is accepted. However, if there are two bits in error, the CRC will detect them and the P bit will not. In this case, the CRC correction is invalid and the cell is discarded.

AAL2

AAL2 is intended to support variable bit-rate applications. For example, in a news broadcast, when the news anchor's face is on the screen, there is a minimum amount of change. Compare this to news footage of a basketball game where there is a huge amount of change. In the first case, the data can be sent at a lower data rate, while in the second case the data can be transferred at a higher data rate. How AAL2 will do so has not yet been explicitly defined.

Convergence Sublayer   The format for reordering the received bit stream and adding overhead is not defined here. Different applications may use different formats.

Segmentation and Reassembly   Figure 18.13 shows the format of an AAL2 data unit at the SAR layer. Functions at this layer accept a 45-byte payload from the CS and add a one-byte header and two-byte trailer. The result is a 48-byte data unit that is then passed to the ATM layer, where it is encapsulated in a cell.

Figure 18.13   *AAL2*

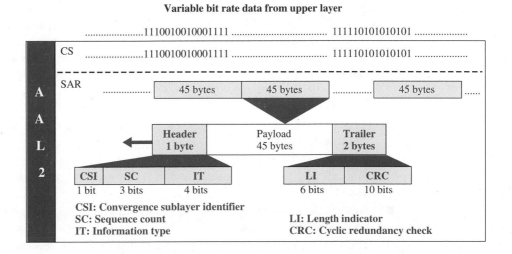

The overhead at this layer consists of three fields in the header and two fields in the trailer:

- **Convergence sublayer identifier (CSI)**. The one-bit CSI field will be used for signaling purposes that are not yet clearly defined.
- **Sequence count (SC).** The three-bit SC field is a modulo 8 sequence number to be used for ordering and identifying the cells for end-to-end error and flow control.
- **Information type (IT).** The IT bits identify the data segment as falling at the beginning, middle, or end of the message.
- **Length indicator (LI).** The first six bits of the trailer are used with the final segment of a message (when the IT in the header indicates the end of the message) to indicate how much of the final cell is data and how much is padding. If the original bit stream is not divisible by 45, dummy bits are added to the last segment to make up the difference. This field indicates where in the segment those bits start.
- **CRC.** The last 10 bits of the trailer are a CRC for the entire data unit. The can also be used to correct single-bit errors in the data unit.

AAL3/4

Initially, AAL3 was intended to support connection-oriented data services and AAL4 to support connectionless services. As they evolved, however, it became evident that the fundamental issues of the two protocols were the same. They have therefore been combined into a single format called AAL3/4.

Convergence Sublayer   The convergence sublayer accepts a data packet of no more than 65,535 ($2^{16} - 1$) bytes from an upper layer service (such as SMDS or frame relay) and adds a header and trailer (see Figure 18.14). The header and trailer indicate the beginning and end of the message (for reassembly purposes), as well as how much of the final frame is data and how much is padding. Because packets vary in length, padding may be required to ensure that segments are of the same size, and that the final control fields fall where the receiver expects to find them. Once the header, trailer, and padding are in place, the CS passes the message in 44-byte segments to the SAR layer.

It is important to note that the CS header and trailer are added to the beginning and end of the original packet, not to every segment. The middle segments are passed to the SAR layer without added overhead. In this way, ATM retains the integrity of the original packets and keeps the ratio of overhead to data bytes low. The AAL3/4 CS header and trailer fields are as follows:

- **Type (T).** The one-byte T field is a holdover from the previous version of AAL3 and is set to 0 in this format.
- **Begin tag (BT).** The one-byte BT field serves as a beginning flag. It identifies the first cell of a segmented packet and provides synchronization for the receiving clock.
- **Buffer allocation (BA).** The two-byte BA field tells the receiver what size buffer is needed for the coming data.
- **Pad (PAD).** As mentioned above, padding is added when necessary to fill out the final cell(s) in a segmented packet. Total padding for a packet can be between 0

and 43 bytes and is added to the last or the last two segments. There are three possible padding scenarios:

a. When the number of data bytes in the final segment is exactly 40, no padding is required (the 4-byte trailer is added to the 40-byte segment to make it 44 bytes).

b. When the number of data bytes in the final segment is less than 40 (0 to 39), we add padding bytes (40 to 1) to bring the total to 40.

c. When the number of data bytes available for the final segment is between 41 and 43, we add padding bytes (43 to 41) to bring the total to 84. The first 44 bytes make a complete segment. The next 40 bytes and the trailer make the last segment.

■ **Alignment (AL).** The one-byte AL field is included to make the rest of the trailer four bytes long.

■ **Ending Tag (ET).** The one-byte ET field serves as an ending flag for synchronization.

■ **Length (L).** The two-byte L field indicates the length of the data unit.

Segment and Reassembly   Figure 18.14 shows the format of an AAL3/4 data unit. Functions at this layer accept a 44-byte payload from the CS and add a 2-byte header

Figure 18.14   *AAL3/4*

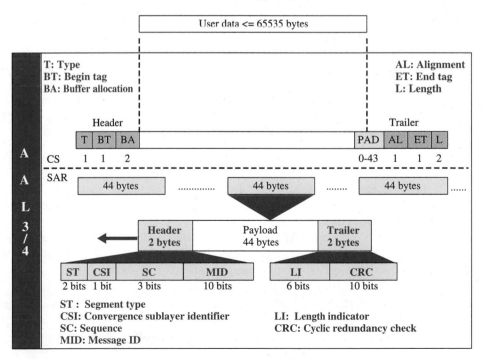

and a 2-byte trailer. The result is a 48-byte data unit that is passed to the ATM layer for inclusion in a cell.

The header and the trailer at this sublayer consists of six fields:

- **Segment type (ST).** The two-bit ST identifier tells whether the segment belongs to the beginning, middle, or end of a message, or is a single-segment message.
- **Convergence sublayer identifier (CSI).** The one-bit CSI field will be used for signaling purposes that are not yet clearly defined.
- **Sequence count (SC).** The three-bit SC field is a modulo 8 sequence number to be used for ordering and identifying the cells for end-to-end error and flow control.
- **Multiplexing identification (MID).** The 10-bit MID field identifies cells coming from different data flows and multiplexed on the same virtual connection.
- **Length indicator (LI).** The first six bits of the trailer are used in conjunction with the ST to indicate how much of the last segment is message and how much is padding. The LI field is used only in frames identified by the ST as being the last in the message (end of packet).
- **CRC.** The last 10 bits of the trailer are a CRC for the entire data unit.

AAL5

AAL3/4 provides comprehensive sequencing and error control mechanisms that are not necessary to every application. When transmissions are not routed through multiple nodes or multiplexed with other transmissions, sequencing and elaborate error correction mechanisms are an unnecessary overhead. ATM backbones and LANs that use point-to-point links are examples of applications that are more efficient without them. For these applications, the designers of ATM have provided a fifth AAL sublayer called the simple and efficient adaptation layer (SEAL). AAL5 assumes that all cells belonging to a single message travel sequentially, and that the rest of the functions usually provided by the CS and SAR headers are already included in the upper layers of the sending application. AAL5 therefore provides no addressing, sequencing, or other header information either at the CS or SAR. Instead, only a pad and a four-field trailer are added at the CS.

Convergence Sublayer   The convergence sublayer accepts a data packet of no more than 65,535 bytes from an upper layer service and adds an 8-byte trailer as well as any padding required to ensure that the position of the trailer falls where the receiving equipment expects it (at the last 8 bytes of the last data unit); see Figure 18.15. Once the padding and trailer are in place, the CS passes the message in 48-byte segments to the SAR layer.

As with AAL3/4, the padding and trailer are added to the end of the entire message, not to each segment. Segments therefore consist of 48 bytes of data or, in the case of the last segment, 40 bytes of data and 8 of overhead (trailer). Fields added at the end of the message include the following:

- **Pad (PAD).** The total padding for a packet can be between 0 and 47 bytes. The rules for padding are the same as those described above for AAL3/4, with the difference that body segments must equal 48 bytes rather than 44.

- **User-to-user ID (UU).** Use of the one-byte UU field is left to the discretion of the user.
- **Type (T).** The one-byte T field is reserved but not yet defined.
- **Length (L).** The two-byte L field indicates how much of the message is data and how much padding.
- **CRC.** The last four bytes are an error check for the entire data unit.

Figure 18.15 *AAL5*

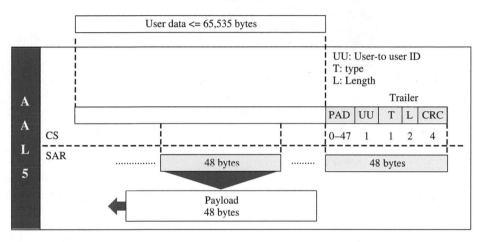

Segmentation and Reassembly No header or trailer is defined for the SAR level. Instead it passes the message in 48-byte segments directly to the ATM layer.

ATM Layer

The ATM layer provides routing, traffic management, switching, and multiplexing services. It processes outgoing traffic by accepting 48-byte segments from the AAL sublayers and transforming them into 53-byte cells by the addition of a 5-byte header (see Figure 18.16).

Header Format

ATM uses two formats for this header, one for user network interface (UNI) cells and another for network-to-network interface (NNI) cells. Figure 18.17 shows these headers in the byte-by-byte format preferred by the ITU-T (each row represents a byte).

- **Generic flow control (GFC).** The four-bit GFC field provides flow control at the UNI level. The ITU-T has determined that this level of flow control is not necessary at the NNI level. In the NNI header, therefore, these bits are added to the VPI. The longer VPI allows more virtual paths to be defined at the NNI level. The format for this additional VPI has not yet been determined.

Figure 18.16 *ATM layer*

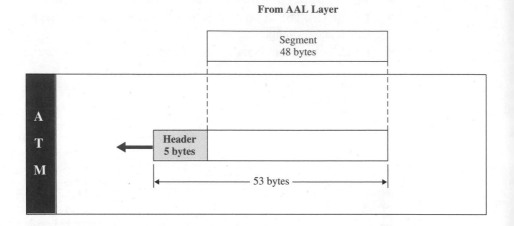

Figure 18.17 *ATM headers*

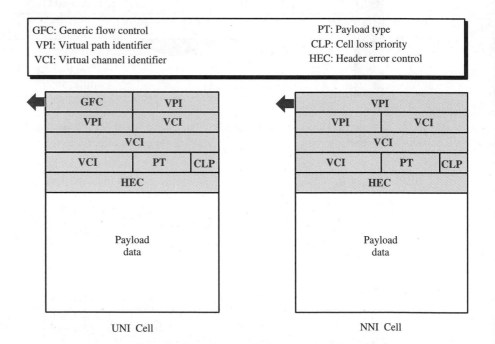

- **Virtual path identifier (VPI).** The VPI is an 8-bit field in a UNI cell and a 12-bit field in an NNI cell (see above).
- **Virtual channel identifier (VCI).** The VCI is a 16-bit field in both frames.

■ **Payload type (PT).** In the three-bit PT field, the first bit defines the payload as user data or managerial information. The interpretation of the last two bits depends on the first bit (see Figure 18.18).

Figure 18.18 *PT fields*

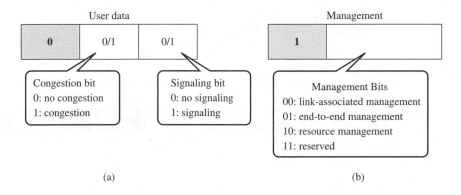

(a)   (b)

■ **Cell loss priority (CLP).** The one-bit CLP field is provided for congestion control. When links become congested, low-priority cells may be discarded to protect the quality of service for higher priority cells. This bit indicates to a switch which cells may be dropped and which must be retained. A cell with its CLP bit set to 1 must be retained as long as there are cells with a CLP of 0. This ability to distinguish priority is useful in many circumstances. For example, suppose a user is assigned a bit rate of x bits per second but is unable to create data that fast. He or she can insert dummy cells into the data stream to raise the bit rate artificially. These dummy cells will show a priority of 0 to indicate that they can be discarded without consequence to the actual data. A second scenario is that of a user who has been assigned one data rate but decides to transmit at a higher one. In this case, the network can set this field to 0 in some cells to indicate that they must be dropped if the link becomes overloaded.

■ **Header error correction (HEC).** The HEC is a code computed for the first four bytes of the header. It is a CRC of $x^8 + x^2 + x + 1$ that is used to correct single-bit errors and a large class of multiple-bit errors.

ATM Switches

Switches in ATM provide both switching and multiplexing. Switching is based on a switching table (discussed earlier in this chapter) that is implemented in hardware for permanent virtual circuit (PVC) networking or stored in RAM for switched virtual circuit (SVC) networking.

Switches can be designed to provide either virtual path (VP) switching using VPIs, or both virtual path switching and virtual channel switching. The latter combination is called virtual path and channel (VPC) switching and uses both VPIs and VCIs.

Figure 18.19 gives a conceptual view of VP switching. Note that, although the VPs in the figure cross each other, the channels within each VP remain with that VP rather than passing into another.

Figure 18.19   *VP switching*

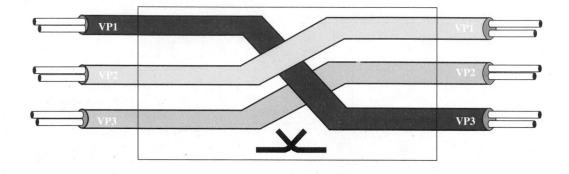

Figure 18.20 gives a conceptual view of VPC switching. In this type of switching, a channel from one VP may pass into another VP.

Figure 18.20   *VPC switching*

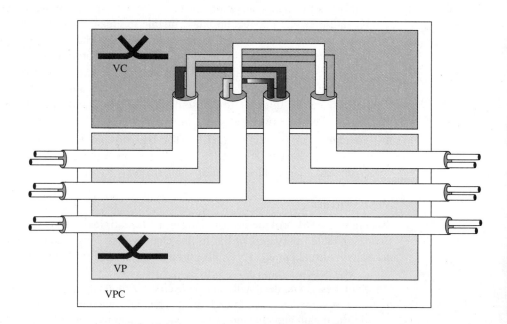
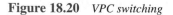

Physical Layer

The physical layer defines the transmission medium, bit transmission, encoding, and electrical to optical transformation. It provides convergence with physical transport protocols, such as SONET (described in Chapter 19) and T-3, as well as the mechanisms for transforming the flow of cells into a flow of bits.

The ATM Forum has left most of the specifications for this level to the implementor. For example, the transport medium can be twisted-pair, coaxial, or fiber-optic cable (although the speed necessary to support B-ISDN is unlikely to be achieved with twisted-pair cable).

18.4   SUMMARY

- Asynchronous Transfer Mode (ATM) is the cell relay protocol designed by the ATM Forum and adopted by the ITU-T.
- The ATM data packet is called a cell and is composed of 53 bytes (5 bytes of header and 48 bytes of payload). Because each cell is the same size and all are relatively small, delay and other problems associated with multiplexing different sized packets are avoided.
- A cell network is based on permanent virtual circuit (PVC) routing.
- A virtual path identifier (VPI) specifies the path a cell should take.
- A virtual channel identifier (VCI) specifies the channel a cell should take.
- ATM can handle or minimize the severity of:
  a. Out-of-sequence packets.
  b. Delay time between packets of a message.
  c. Bit errors.
- A user network interface (UNI) is the interface between a user and the wide area ATM network.
- A network-to-network interface (NNI) is the interface between two wide area ATM networks.
- The ATM standard defines three layers:
  a. Application adaptation layer (AAL)—accepts transmissions from upper layer services and maps them into ATM cells.
  b. ATM layer—provides routing, traffic management, switching, and multiplexing services.
  c. Physical layer—defines the transmission medium, bit transmission, encoding, and electrical to optical transformation.
- The AAL is divided into two sublayers:
  a. Convergence sublayer (CS)—adds overhead and manipulates the data stream at the sending station; performs the opposite function at the receiving station.
  b. Segmentation and reassembly (SAR)—at the sending station, segments the bit stream into same-sized packets; adds headers and trailers; performs the opposite function at the receiving station.

- There are four different AALs, each for a specific data type:
  a. AAL1—constant bit-rate stream.
  b. AAL2—variable bit-rate stream.
  c. AAL3/4—conventional packet switching (virtual circuit approach or datagram approach).
  d. AAL5—packets requiring no information from the SAR layer.
- In the ATM layer, a 5-byte header is added to each 48-byte segment.
- Switches in ATM provide both switching and multiplexing.
- There are two types of switching:
  a. Virtual path (VP) switching—channels within each VP remain with the VP.
  b. Virtual path and channel (VPC) switching—a channel from one VP may pass into another VP.

18.5   PRACTICE SET

Multiple Choice

1. ATM can use _____ as a transmission medium.
   a. twisted-pair cable
   b. coaxial cable
   c. fiber-optic cable
   d. all of the above
2. In data communications, ATM is an acronym for _____.
   a. Automated teller machine
   b. Automatic Transmission Model
   c. Asynchronous Telecommunication Method
   d. Asynchronous Transfer Mode
3. Because ATM _____, which means that cells follow the same path, the cells do not usually arrive out of order.
   a. is asynchronous
   b. is multiplexed
   c. is a network
   d. uses virtual circuit routing
4. The _____ interface lies between an ATM switch and a wide area ATM network.
   a. NNI
   b. public UNI
   c. private UNI
   d. switched UNI
5. The _____ interface lies between two wide area ATM networks.
   a. NNI

    b. public UNI

    c. private UNI

    d. switched UNI

6. The _____ interface lies between the user and an ATM switch.

    a. NNI

    b. public UNI

    c. private UNI

    d. switched UNI

7. Which layer in ATM protocol reformats the data received from other networks?

    a. physical

    b. ATM

    c. application adaptation

    d. data adaptation

8. Which layer in ATM protocol has a 53-byte cell as an end product?

    a. physical

    b. ATM

    c. application adaptation

    d. cell transformation

9. Which AAL type can best process a data stream having a nonconstant bit rate?

    a. AAL1

    b. AAL2

    c. AAL3/4

    d. AAL5

10. Which AAL type is designed to support a data stream that has a constant bit rate?

    a. AAL1

    b. AAL2

    c. AAL3/4

    d. AAL5

11. Which AAL type is designed to support conventional packet switching that uses the virtual circuit approach?

    a. AAL1

    b. AAL2

    c. AAL3/4

    d. AAL5

12. Which AAL type is designed to support SEAL?

    a. AAL1

    b. AAL2

    c. AAL3/4

    d. AAL5

13. The end product of the SAR is a data packet that is _____.
   a. variable in length
   b. 48 bytes long
   c. 44 to 48 bytes long
   d. greater than 48 bytes long

14. In the SAR sublayer of _____, 1 byte of header is added to 47 bytes of data.
   a. AAL1
   b. AAL2
   c. AAL3/4
   d. AAL5

15. In the SAR sublayer of _____, 1 byte of header and 2 bytes of trailer are added to a 45-byte payload.
   a. AAL1
   b. AAL2
   c. AAL3/4
   d. AAL5

16. In the SAR sublayer of _____, the payload is 48 bytes and there is no added header or trailer.
   a. AAL1
   b. AAL2
   c. AAL3/4
   d. AAL5

17. A _____ field on a UNI cell header is used for connection purposes.
   a. VPI (virtual path identifier)
   b. VCI (virtual channel identifier)
   c. CLP (cell loss priority)
   d. GFC (generic flow constant)

18. A _____ field on a cell header in the ATM layer determines whether a cell can be dropped.
   a. VPI (virtual path identifier)
   b. VCI (virtual channel identifier)
   c. CLP (cell loss priority)
   d. GFC (generic flow constant)

Exercises

1. Why should a cell network use a permanent virtual circuit routing strategy?
2. Why is multiplexing more efficient if all the data units are the same size?
3. Discuss the relationship between delay length, data unit size, and real-time audio and video transmission.
4. Discuss the different methods of error detection in each of the AAL types.

5. Which AAL type has no header added to its SAR layer and why is this so?

6. If an application uses AAL5 and there are 47,787 bytes of data coming in to the CS sublayer, how many data units get passed from the SAR to the ATM layer? How many PAD bytes are necessary?

7. If an application uses AAL3/4 and there are 47,787 bytes of data coming in to the CS sublayer, how many data units get passed from the SAR to the ATM layer? How many PAD bytes are necessary?

CHAPTER 19

SONET/SDH

The high bandwidths of fiber-optic cable suit it to today's highest data-rate technologies (such as video conferencing) and to carrying large numbers of lower-rate technologies at the same time. For this reason, the importance of fiber optics grows in conjunction with the development of technologies requiring high data rates or wide bandwidths for transmission. With their prominence came a need for standardization. Without standards, internetworking among the existing proprietary systems is impossible. The United States (ANSI) and Europe (ITU-T) have responded by defining standards that, though independent, are fundamentally similar and ultimately compatible. The ANSI standard is called the Synchronous Optical Network (SONET). The ITU-T standard is called the Synchronous Digital Hierarchy (SDH). These two standards are nearly identical.

SONET was developed by ANSI. SDH was developed by ITU-T.

Among the concerns addressed by the designers of SONET and SDH, three are of particular interest to us. First, SONET/SDH is a synchronous network. A single clock is used to handle the timing of transmissions and equipment across the entire network. Networkwide synchronization adds a level of predictability to the system. This predictability, coupled with a powerful frame design, enables individual channels to be switched without first demultiplexing the entire signal, thereby streamlining transmission, improving speed, and reducing cost.

Second, SONET/SDH contains recommendations for the standardization of fiber-optic transmission system (FOTS) equipment sold by different manufacturers. Third, the SONET/SDH physical specifications and frame design include mechanisms that allow it to carry signals from incompatible tributary systems (particularly asynchronous services such as DS-0 and DS-1). It is this flexibility that gives SONET a reputation for universal connectivity.

It is important to emphasize that SONET is a multiplexed transport mechanism (no switching) and as such can be the carrier for broadband services, particularly ATM and B-ISDN.

19.1   SYNCHRONOUS TRANSPORT SIGNALS

As the first step in its flexibility, SONET defines a hierarchy of signaling levels called synchronous transport signals (STSs). Each STS level (STS-1 to STS-192) supports a certain data rate, specified in megabits per second (see Table 19.1). The physical links defined to carry each level of STS are called optical carriers (OCs). OC levels describe the conceptual and physical specifications of the links required to support each level of signaling. Actual implementation of those specifications is left up to the manufacturers. Currently, the most popular implementations are OC-1, OC-3, OC-12, and OC-48.

Table 19.1   *SONET/SDH rates*

STS	OC	Rate (Mbps)	STM
STS-1	OC-1	51.840	
STS-3	OC-3	155.520	STM-1
STS-9	OC-9	466.560	STM-3
STS-12	OC-12	622.080	STM-4
STS-18	OC-18	933.120	STM-6
STS-24	OC-24	1244.160	STM-8
STS-36	OC-36	1866.230	STM-12
STS-48	OC-48	2488.320	STM-16
STS-96	OC-96	4976.640	STM-32
STS-192	OC-192	9953.280	STM-64

A glance through Table 19.1 reveals some interesting points. First, the lowest level in this hierarchy has a data rate of 51.840 Mbps, which is greater than that of the DS-3 service and T-3 line (44.736 Mbps). That means that the lowest SONET level supports greater bit rates than the highest T level. (T-3 is the highest common electrical line commercially available today, although T-4 is defined.) In fact, the STS-1 is designed to accommodate data rates equivalent to those of the DS-3. The difference in capacity is provided to handle the overhead needs of the optical system.

Second, the STS-3 rate is exactly three times the STS-1 rate; and the STS-9 rate is exactly half the STS-18 rate. These relationships mean that 18 STS-1 channels can be multiplexed into one STS-18, six STS-3 channels can be multiplexed into one STS-18, and so on. As you can see, the concept of hierarchy here is similar to that for DS signals and T lines (see Chapter 8).

SDH specifies a similar system called synchronous transport module (STM). STM is intended to be compatible with existing European hierarchies, such as E lines, and with STS levels. To this end, the lowest STM level, STM-1, is defined at 155.520 Mbps, which is exactly equal to STS-3.

19.2 PHYSICAL CONFIGURATION

Figure 19.1 shows the devices used in a SONET transmission system and some possible ways of arranging and linking those devices.

SONET Devices

SONET transmission relies on three basic devices: STS multiplexers, regenerators, and add/drop multiplexers. STS multiplexers mark the beginning and end points of a SONET link. They provide the interface between a tributary network and the SONET. The devices between them can be of any number and configuration required by the system. Regenerators extend the length of the links possible between generator and receiver. Add/drop multiplexers allow insertion and extraction of SONET paths.

■ **STS Multiplexer.** An STS multiplexer has a double function. It converts electronic signals to optical signals. At the same time, it multiplexes the incoming signals to create a single STS signal (STS-1, STS-3, etc.).

■ **Regenerator.** An STS regenerator is a repeater (see Chapter 20) that takes a received optical signal and regenerates it. Regenerators in this system, however, add a function to those of physical layer repeaters. A SONET regenerator replaces some of the existing overhead information (header information) with new information. These devices function at the data link layer.

■ **Add/drop multiplexer.** An add/drop multiplexer can add signals coming from different sources into a given path, or remove a desired signal from a path and redirect it without demultiplexing the entire signal. Instead of relying on timing and bit positions, add/drop multiplexers use header information such as addresses and pointers (described later in this section) to identify individual streams.

Figure 19.1 *A SONET system*

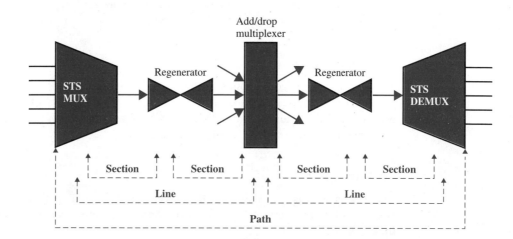

In the simple configuration shown by the figure, a number of incoming electronic signals are fed into an STS multiplexer, where they are combined into a single optical signal. The optical signal is transmitted to a regenerator, where it is recreated without noise it has picked up in transit. The regenerated signals from a number of sources are then fed into an add/drop multiplexer. The add/drop multiplexer reorganizes these signals, if necessary, and sends them out as directed by information in the data frames. These remultiplexed signals are sent to another regenerator, and from there to the receiving STS multiplexer, where they are returned to a format usable by the receiving links.

Sections, Lines, and Paths

As you can see from Figure 19.1, the various levels of SONET connections are called sections, lines, and paths. A section is the optical link connecting two neighbor devices: multiplexer to multiplexer, multiplexer to regenerator, or regenerator to regenerator. A line is the portion of the network between two multiplexers: STS multiplexer to add/drop multiplexer, two add/drop multiplexers, or two STS multiplexers. A path is the end-to-end portion of the network between two STS multiplexers. In a simple SONET of two STS multiplexers linked directly to each other, the section, line, and path are the same.

19.3 SONET LAYERS

The SONET standard includes four functional layers: the photonic layer, the section layer, the line layer, and the path layer. These layers are usually thought to correspond only to the first layer (physical) of the OSI model. In fact, they correspond to both the physical and the data link layers (see Figure 19.2). The headers added to the frame at the various layers are discussed later in this chapter.

> SONET defines four layers. The photonic layer is the lowest and performs physical layer activities. The section, line, and path layers correspond to the OSI model's data link layer.

Photonic Layer

The photonic layer corresponds to the physical layer of the OSI model. It includes physical specifications for the optical fiber channel, the sensitivity of the receiver, multiplexing functions, and so on. SONET uses NRZ encoding with the presence of light representing 1 and the absence of light representing 0.

Section Layer

The section layer is responsible for the movement of a signal across a physical section. It handles framing, scrambling, and error control. Section layer overhead is added to the frame at this layer.

Figure 19.2   *SONET layers*

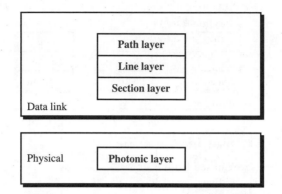

Line Layer

The line layer is responsible for the movement of a signal across a physical line. Line layer overhead is added to the frame at this layer. STS multiplexers and add/drop multiplexers provide line layer functions.

Path Layer

The path layer is responsible for the movement of a signal from its optical source to its optical destination. At the optical source, the signal is changed from an electronic form into an optical form, multiplexed with other signals, and encapsulated in a frame. At the optical destination, the received frame is demultiplexed, and the individual optical signals are changed back into their electronic forms. Path layer overhead is added at this layer. STS multiplexers provide path layer functions.

Device-Layer Relationships

Figure 19.3 shows the relationship between the devices used in SONET transmission and the four layers of the standard. As you can see, an STS multiplexer is a four-layer device. An add/drop multiplexer is a three-layer device. A regenerator is a two-layer device.

19.4   THE SONET FRAME

Data received from an electronic interface, such as a T-1 line, is encapsulated in a frame at the path layer and overhead is added. Additional overhead is added, first at the line layer and then at the section layer. Finally, the frame is passed to the photonic layer, where it is transformed into an optical signal (see Figure 19.4).

Note, however, that SONET overhead is not added as headers and trailers as we have seen in other protocols. Instead, SONET inserts overhead at a variety of locations

Figure 19.3   *Device-layer relationship in SONET*

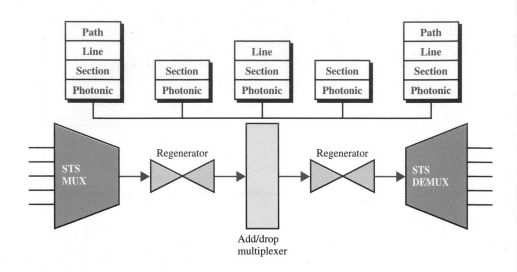

Figure 19.4   *Data encapsulation in SONET*

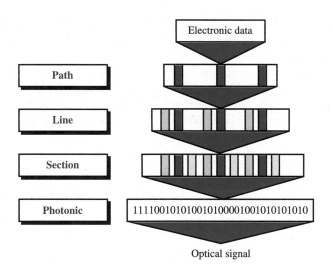

in the middle of the frame. The locations and meanings of these insertions are discussed below.

Frame Format

The basic format of an STS-1 frame at the photonic layer is shown in Figure 19.5. Each frame contains 6480 bits (810 octets). STS-1 therefore transmits at a rate of 51.840 Mbps.

Figure 19.5 *STS-1 frame*

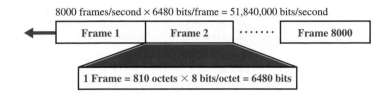

Figure 19.6 *STS-1 frame overheads*

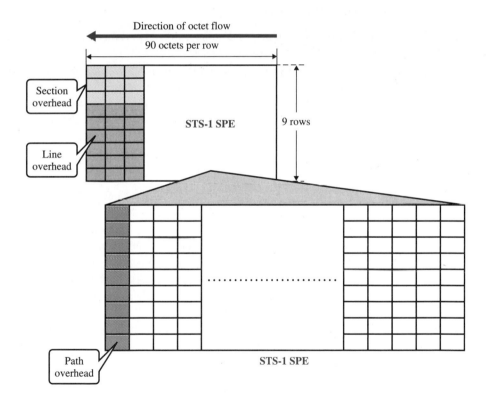

SONET uses a matrix of nine rows of 90 octets each, for a total of 810 octets (see Figure 19.6).

The first three columns of the frame are used for section and line overhead, divided vertically. The upper three rows of the first three columns are used for section overhead. The lower six are line overhead. The rest of the frame is called the synchronous payload envelope (SPE). It contains user data and details about charges and payment required for transmission (if any). One column of the SPE, however, is used for path overhead (usually the first). Path overhead includes end-to-end tracking information.

Figure 19.7 *STS-1 frame: section overhead*

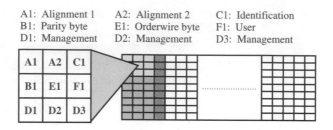

A1: Alignment 1   A2: Alignment 2   C1: Identification
B1: Parity byte   E1: Orderwire byte   F1: User
D1: Management   D2: Management   D3: Management

Section Overhead

Section overhead consists of nine octets. The labels, functions, and organization of these octets are shown in Figure 19.7.

■ **Alignment bytes (A1 and A2).** Bytes A1 and A2 are used for framing and synchronization, and are called alignment bytes. These bytes alert a receiver that a frame is arriving, and give the receiver a predetermined bit pattern on which to synchronize. The bit patterns for these two bytes in both hexadecimal and binary form are as follows:

A1 ➪ F6 ➪ 11110110
A2 ➪ 28 ➪ 00101000

■ **Identification byte (C1).** Byte C1 carries a unique identifier for the STS-1 frame. This byte is necessary when multiple STS-1s are multiplexed to create a higher rate STS (STS-3, STS-9, STS-12, etc.). Information in this byte allows the various signals to be easily recognized upon demultiplexing.

■ **Parity byte (B1).** Byte B1 is for bit interleaved parity (BIP-8). Its value is based on the section header of the previous STS-1, and it is inserted in the current STS-1. It functions as a longitudinal redundancy check.

■ **Orderwire byte (E1).** Byte E1 is the orderwire byte. Orderwire bytes in consecutive frames form a channel of 64 Kbps (8000 frames per second times 8 bits per frame). This channel is used for communication between regenerators, or by terminals and regenerators.

■ **User's byte (F1).** The F1 bytes in consecutive frames form a 64 Kbps channel that is reserved for user needs at the section level.

■ **Management bytes (D1, D2, and D3).** Bytes D1, D2, and D3 together form a 192 Kbps channel ($3 \times 8000 \times 8$) called the data communication channel. This channel is required for operation, administration, and maintenance (OAM) signaling.

Line Overhead

Line overhead consists of 18 bytes. The labels, functions, and arrangement of these bytes are shown in Figure 19.8.

Figure 19.8 *STS-1 frame: line overhead*

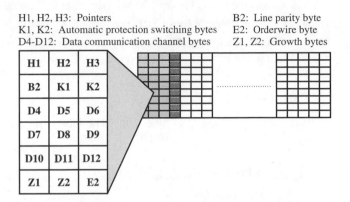

H1, H2, H3: Pointers
K1, K2: Automatic protection switching bytes
D4-D12: Data communication channel bytes

B2: Line parity byte
E2: Orderwire byte
Z1, Z2: Growth bytes

- **Pointer bytes (H1, H2, and H3).** Bytes H1, H2, and H3 are pointers. They identify the location of the payload in the frame when the payload starts somewhere other than at the beginning of the STS envelope (see Figure 19.9). Pointers are essential in several situations. SONET is a synchronous protocol. Frames are built by matching the timing of the data input to the network frame functions. For this reason, data collected from asynchronous network inputs may not be synchronized with the SPE and may end up occupying two frames. Pointers enable SONET to accommodate such framing discrepancies. In these cases, bytes H1, H2, and H3 together form a pointer to the beginning byte of the payload. Other, more complex, uses for pointers also exist; a discussion of them is beyond the scope of this book.

Figure 19.9 *Payload pointers*

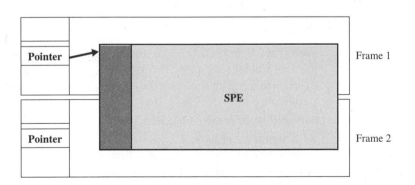

- **Line parity byte (B2).** Byte B2 is for bit interleaved parity, like byte B1, but calculated for the line header.
- **Automatic protection switching bytes (K1 and K2).** The K1 and K2 bytes in consecutive frames form a 128 Kbps channel used for automatic detection of problems in line-terminating equipment (e.g., multiplexers).

- **Data communication channel bytes (D4 to D12).** The line-overhead D bytes (D4 to D12) in consecutive frames form a 576 Kbps channel that provides the same service as the D1-D3 bytes (OAM), but at the line rather than the section level.
- **Growth bytes (Z1 and Z2).** The Z1 and Z2 bytes are reserved for future use.
- **Orderwire byte (E2).** The E2 bytes in consecutive frames form a 64 Kbps channel that provides the same functions as the E1 orderwire byte, but at the line level.

Path Overhead

Path overhead consists of nine bytes. The labels, functions, and arrangement of these bytes are shown in Figure 19.10.

Figure 19.10 *STS-1 frame: path overhead*

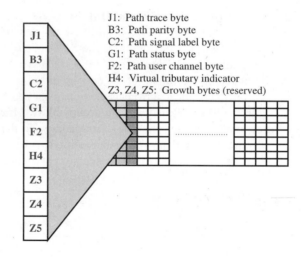

- **Path trace byte (J1).** The J1 bytes in consecutive frames form a 64 Kbps channel used for tracking the path. The J1 byte sends a continuous 64-bit string to verify the connection. The choice of the string is left to the application program.
- **Path parity byte (B3).** Byte B3 is for bit interleaved parity, like bytes B1 and B2, but calculated for the path header.
- **Path signal label byte (C2).** Byte C2 is the path identification byte. It is used to identify different protocols used at higher levels (such as FDDI or SMDS).
- **Path status byte (G1).** Byte G1 is sent by the receiver to communicate its status to the sender.
- **Path user channel byte (F2).** The F2 bytes in consecutive frames, like the F1 bytes, form a 64 Kbps channel that is reserved for user needs, but at the path level.

- **Virtual tributary indicator (H4).** Byte H4 is the multiframe indicator. It indicates payloads that cannot fit into a single frame. Virtual tributaries are discussed on p. 470.
- **Growth bytes (Z3, Z4, and Z5).** Bytes Z3, Z4, and Z5 are reserved for future use.

Virtual Tributaries

SONET is designed to carry broadband payloads. Current digital hierarchy rates (DS-1 to DS-3), however, are lower than STS-1. To make SONET backward compatible with the current hierarchy, its frame design includes a system of virtual tributaries (VTs) (see Figure 19.11). A virtual tributary is a partial payload that can be inserted into an STS-1 and combined with other partial payloads to fill out the frame. Instead of using all 86 payload columns of an STS-1 frame for data from one source, we can subdivide the SPE and call each component a VT.

Figure 19.11 *Virtual tributaries*

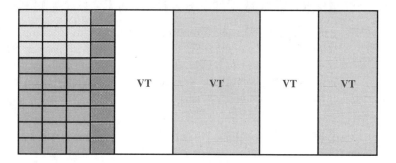

Types of VTs

Four types of VTs have been defined to accommodate existing digital hierarchies (see Figure 19.12). Notice that the number of columns allowed for each type of VT can be determined by doubling the type identification number (VT1.5 gets three columns, VT2 gets four columns, etc.).

- **VT1.5.** VT1.5 accommodates the U.S. DS-1 service (1.544 Mbps).
- **VT2.** VT2 accommodates the European CEPT-1 service (2.048 Mbps).
- **VT3.** VT3 accommodates the DS-1C service (fractional DS-1, 3.152 Mbps).
- **VT6.** VT6 accommodates the DS-2 service (6.312 Mbps).

When two or more tributaries are inserted into a single STS-1 frame, they are interleaved column by column. SONET provides mechanisms for identifying each VT and separating them without demultiplexing the entire stream. Discussion of these mechanisms and the control issues behind them are beyond the scope of this book.

Figure 19.12 *VT types*

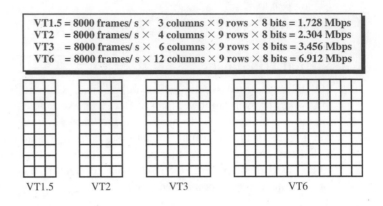

$$VT1.5 = 8000\ frames/s \times\ \ 3\ columns \times 9\ rows \times 8\ bits = 1.728\ Mbps$$
$$VT2\ \ \ = 8000\ frames/s \times\ \ 4\ columns \times 9\ rows \times 8\ bits = 2.304\ Mbps$$
$$VT3\ \ \ = 8000\ frames/s \times\ \ 6\ columns \times 9\ rows \times 8\ bits = 3.456\ Mbps$$
$$VT6\ \ \ = 8000\ frames/s \times 12\ columns \times 9\ rows \times 8\ bits = 6.912\ Mbps$$

VT1.5   VT2   VT3   VT6

19.5 MULTIPLEXING STS FRAMES

Lower rate STSs can be multiplexed to make them compatible with higher rate systems. For example, three STS-1s can be combined into one STS-3. Four STS-3s can be multiplexed into one STS-12, and so on. The general format for an STS-n made up of lower rate STSs is shown in Figure 19.13. Remember, however, that in actual practice these frames are interleaved.

Figure 19.13 *STS-*n

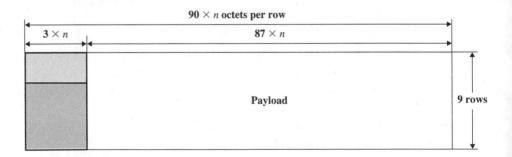

$90 \times n$ **octets per row**

$3 \times n$ $87 \times n$

Payload   9 rows

Figure 19.14 shows how three STS-1s are multiplexed into a single STS-3. To create an STS-12 out of lower rate services, we could multiplex either 12 STS-1s or four STS-3s.

ATM Convergence to SONET/SDH

The most important physical carrier for ATM is projected to be SONET's STS-3 service (STM-1 in Europe's SDH). Because ATM provides multiplexing, the entire pay-

Figure 19.14 *STS multiplexing*

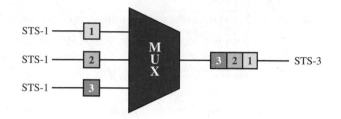

Figure 19.15 *ATM in an STS-3 envelope*

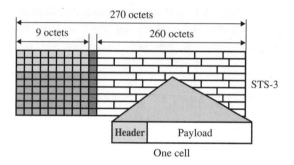

load of the STS-3 can be used for cell transport without the additional overhead required by other systems. One possible mapping of ATM to an STS-3 envelope is shown in Figure 19.15.

Each row of the frame (envelope) consists of 270 octets (3×90). Of these, nine octets are used for section and line overhead, and one octet is used for path overhead. The remaining 260 octets can carry close to five cells ($5 \times 53 = 265$). The fifth frame in the first row must be split between the first and second rows. Other rows may have partial cells at both ends.

19.6   SUMMARY

- Synchronous Optical Network (SONET) is a standard developed by ANSI for fiber-optic networks.
- SONET has defined a hierarchy of signals (similar to the DS hierarchy) called synchronous transport signals (STS).
- Optical carrier (OC) levels are the implementation of STSs.
- SONET defines four layers. The photonic layer is the lowest and performs physical layer activities.

- SONET's section, line, and path layers correspond to the OSI model's data link layer. Each of these layers is responsible for signal transfer across a specific portion of the transmission path.
- A SONET system can use the following equipment:
  a. STS multiplexer—combines several optical signals to make an STS signal.
  b. Regenerator—removes noise from an optical signal.
  c. Add/drop multiplexer—adds STS signals from different paths and removes STS signals from a path.
- A frame at the photonic layer for STS-1 consists of 6480 bits. There are 8000 frames/second.
- Overhead and data (payload) in a STS-1 are arranged in a matrix configuration (9 rows of 90 octets).
- SONET is backward compatible with the current DS hierarchy through the virtual tributary (VT) concept. VTs are a partial payload consisting of an m by n block of octets. An STS payload can be a combination of several VTs.
- STSs can be multiplexed to get a new STS with a higher data rate.

19.7   PRACTICE SET

Multiple Choice

1. SONET is a standard for _____ networks.
   a. twisted-pair cable
   b. coaxial cable
   c. Ethernet
   d. fiber-optic cable
2. SONET is an acronym for _____ network.
   a. synchronous optical
   b. standard optical
   c. symmetrical open
   d. standard open
3. In a SONET system, _____ removes noise from a signal and can also add or remove headers.
   a. an STS multiplier
   b. a regenerator
   c. an add/drop multiplexer
   d. a repeater
4. In a SONET system, _____ can remove signals from a path.
   a. an STS multiplier
   b. a regenerator

c. an add/drop multiplexer

d. a repeater

5. The optical link between any two SONET devices is called _____.

   a. a section

   b. a line

   c. a path

   d. none of the above

6. The optical link between an STS multiplexer and a regenerator is called _____.

   a. a section

   b. a line

   c. a path

   d. none of the above

7. The optical link between an STS multiplexer and an add/drop multiplexer is called _____.

   a. a section

   b. a line

   c. a path

   d. none of the above

8. SONET's _____ layer corresponds to the OSI model's physical layer.

   a. path

   b. line

   c. section

   d. photonic

9. SONET's _____ layer performs framing, scrambling, and error handling.

   a. path

   b. line

   c. section

   d. photonic

10. SONET's _____ layer transfers a signal across a physical line.

   a. path

   b. line

   c. section

   d. photonic

11. SONET's _____ layer transfers data from its optical source to its optical destination.

   a. path

   b. line

   c. section

   d. photonic

12. Which of the following SONET layers corresponds to the OSI's data link layer?
    a. path
    b. line
    c. section
    d. all of the above

13. An STS multiplexer operates in _____ layers: _____.
    a. four; path, line, section, and photonic
    b. two; section and photonic
    c. three; line, section, and photonic
    d. two; photonic and path

14. An add/drop multiplexer operates in _____ layers: _____.
    a. four; path, line, section, and photonic
    b. two; section and photonic
    c. three; line, section, and photonic
    d. two; photonic and path

15. A regenerator operates in _____ layers: _____.
    a. four; path, line, section, and photonic
    b. two; section and photonic
    c. three; line, section, and photonic
    d. two; photonic and path

16. In an STS-1 frame, the first three columns contain _____.
    a. section and line overhead
    b. user data
    c. section, line, and path overhead
    d. path overhead

17. The synchronous payload envelope (SPE) of an STS-1 frame contains _____.
    a. pointers
    b. user data
    c. path overhead
    d. b and c

18. A parity byte exists for an STS-1 frame's _____.
    a. section overhead
    b. line overhead
    c. path overhead
    d. all of the above

19. Which overhead contains the pointers to the payload?
    a. section
    b. line
    c. path
    d. a and b

20. What is the maximum number of VT1.5s that STS-1 can accommodate?

    a. 3

    b. 9

    c. 28

    d. 29

21. What is the maximum number of VT2s that STS-1 can accommodate?

    a. 4

    b. 21

    c. 22

    d. 23

Exercises

1. How is an STS multiplexer different from an add/drop multiplexer since both can add signals together?

2. What is the relationship between STS levels and OC levels?

3. What is the purpose of the pointer in the line overhead?

4. Compare the STS hierarchy with the DS hierarchy.

5. Draw a SONET network using all of the following devices. Label all lines, sections and paths.

    a. Three STS multiplexers.

    b. Two add/drop multiplexers.

    c. Five regencrators.

CHAPTER 20

NETWORKING AND INTERNETWORKING DEVICES

Two or more devices connected for the purpose of sharing data or resources are stations on a network. Putting together a network is often more complicated than simply plugging cable into a hub. A local area network (LAN) may need to cover more distance than its media can handle effectively. Or the number of stations may be too great for efficient frame delivery or management of the network, and the network may need to be subdivided. In the first case, a device called a repeater or regenerator is inserted into the network to increase the coverable distance. In the second, a device called a bridge is inserted for traffic management.

When two or more separate networks are connected for exchanging data or resources, they become an internetwork (or internet). Linking a number of LANs into an internet requires additional internetworking devices called routers and gateways. These devices are designed to overcome obstacles to interconnection without disrupting the independent functioning of the networks.

An internet is an interconnection of individual networks. To create an internet, we need internetworking devices called routers and gateways.

Note: Do not confuse the term *internet* (lowercase *i*) with *the Internet* (uppercase *I*). The first is a generic term used to mean an interconnection of networks. The second is the name of a specific worldwide network.

An internet is different from the Internet.

As mentioned above, networking and internetworking devices are divided into four categories: repeaters, bridges, routers, and gateways (see Figure 20.1).

Each of these four device types interacts with protocols at different layers of the OSI model. Repeaters act only upon the electrical components of a signal, and are therefore active only at the physical layer. Bridges utilize addressing protocols, and can affect the flow control of a single LAN; they are most active at the data link layer. Routers provide links between two separate but same-type LANs, and are most active at the network layer. Finally, gateways provide translation services between incompatible

Figure 20.1 *Connecting devices*

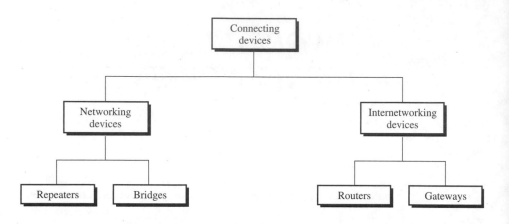

Figure 20.2 *Connecting devices and the OSI model*

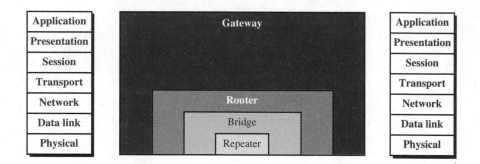

LANs or applications, and are active in all of the layers. Each of these internetworking devices also operates in all of the layers below the one in which it is most active (see Figure 20.2).

20.1 REPEATERS

A repeater (or regenerator) is an electronic device that operates on only the physical layer of the OSI model (see Figure 20.3). Signals that carry information within a network can travel a fixed distance before attenuation (weakening of the signal due to friction) or interference from noise endangers the integrity of the data. A repeater installed on a link receives the signal before it becomes too weak or corrupted, regenerates the original bit pattern, and puts the refreshed copy back onto the link. In effect, the signal, with the corruption removed, is transmitted a second time from a location closer to the destination.

Figure 20.3 *A repeater in the OSI model*

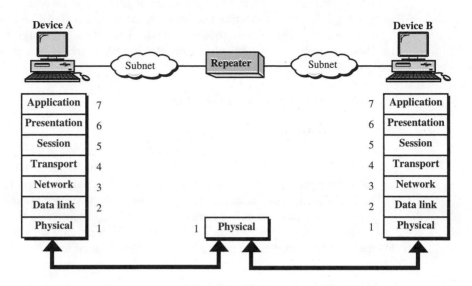

A repeater allows us to extend only the physical length of a network. The repeater does not change the functionality of the network in any way (see Figure 20.4). The two sections connected by the repeater in Figure 20.4 are, in reality, one network. If station A sends a frame to station B, all stations (including C and D) will receive the frame, just as they would without the repeater. The repeater does not have the intelligence to keep the frame from passing to the right side when it is meant for a station on the left. The difference is that, with the repeater, stations C and D receive a truer copy of the frame than would otherwise have been possible.

Figure 20.4 *A repeater*

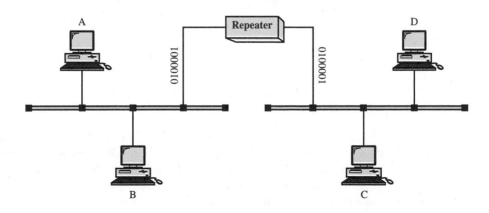

Not an Amplifier

It is tempting to compare a repeater to an amplifier, but the comparison is inaccurate. An amplifier cannot discriminate between the intended signal and noise; it amplifies equally everything fed into it. A repeater does not amplify the signal; it regenerates it. When it receives a weakened or corrupted signal, it creates a copy bit for bit, at the original strength.

A repeater is a regenerator, not an amplifier.

The location of a repeater on a link is vital. A repeater must be placed so that a signal reaches it before any noise changes the meaning of any of its bits. A little noise can alter the precision of a bit's voltage without destroying its identity (see Figure 20.5). If the corrupted bit travels much farther, however, accumulated noise can change its meaning completely. At that point, the original voltage becomes unrecoverable and the error can be corrected only by retransmission. A repeater placed on the line before the legibility of the signal becomes lost can still read the signal well enough to determine the intended voltages and replicate them in their original form.

Figure 20.5   *Function of a repeater*

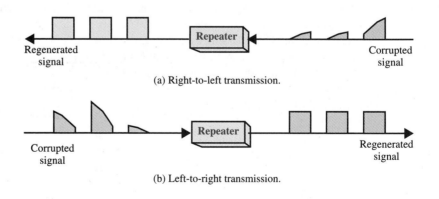

(a) Right-to-left transmission.

(b) Left-to-right transmission.

20.2   BRIDGES

Bridges operate in both the physical and the data link layers of the OSI model (see Figure 20.6). Bridges divide a large network into smaller segments (see Figure 20.7). They can also relay frames between two originally separate segments of one type. Unlike repeaters, however, bridges contain logic that allows them to keep the traffic for each segment separate. Bridges are repeaters that are smart enough to relay a frame only to the side of the segment containing the intended recipient. In this way, they filter traffic,

Figure 20.6   *A bridge in the OSI model*

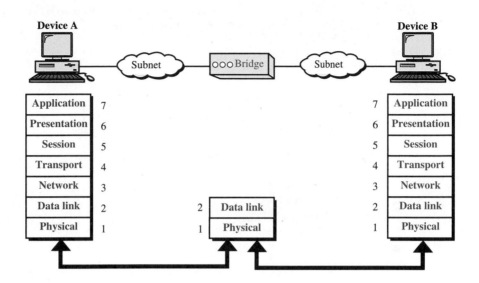

Figure 20.7   *A bridge*

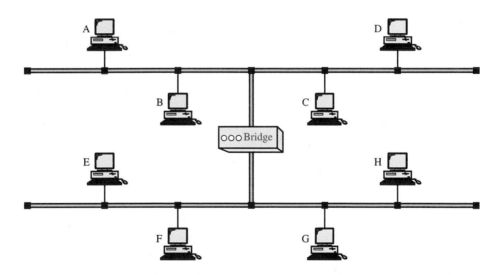

a fact that makes them useful for controlling congestion and isolating problem links. Bridges can also provide security through this partitioning of traffic.

Bridges do not modify the structure or contents of a packet in any way and can therefore be used only between segments that use the same protocol.

A bridge operates at the data link layer, giving it access to the physical addresses of all stations connected to it. When a frame enters a bridge, the bridge not only regenerates the signal but checks the address of the destination and forwards the new copy only to the segment to which the address belongs. As a bridge encounters a packet, it reads the address contained in the frame, and compares that address with a table of all the stations on both segments. When it finds a match, it discovers to which segment the station belongs and relays the packet only to that segment.

Figure 20.8 *Function of a bridge*

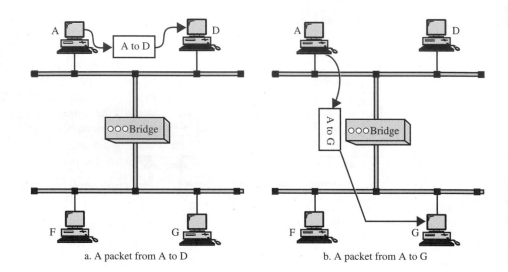

a. A packet from A to D   b. A packet from A to G

For example, Figure 20.8*a* shows two segments joined by a bridge. A packet from station A addressed to station D arrives at the bridge. Station A is on the same segment as station D; therefore, the packet is blocked from crossing into the lower segment. Instead the packet is relayed to the entire upper segment and received by station D.

In Figure 20.8*b*, a packet generated by station A is intended for station G. The bridge allows the packet to cross and relays it to the entire lower segment, where it is received by station G.

Types of Bridges

To select between segments, a bridge must have a look-up table that contains the physical addresses of every station connected to it. The table indicates to which segment each station belongs. How this table is generated and how many segments are connected by a single bridge determine the type and cost of the bridge. There are three types of bridges: simple, learning, and multiport.

Simple Bridges

Simple bridges are the most primitive and least expensive type of bridge. A simple bridge links two segments and contains a table that lists the addresses of all the stations included in each of them. What makes it primitive is that these addresses must be entered manually. Before a simple bridge can be used, an operator must sit down and program the addresses of every station. Whenever a new station is added, the table must be modified. If a station is removed, the newly invalid address must be deleted. The logic included in a simple bridge, therefore, is of the pass/no pass variety, a configuration that makes a simple bridge straightforward and inexpensive to manufacture. Installation and maintenance of simple bridges are time-consuming and potentially more trouble than the cost savings are worth.

Learning Bridges

A learning bridge builds its table of station addresses on its own, as it performs its bridge functions. When the learning bridge is first installed, its table is empty. As it encounters each packet, it looks at both the destination and the source addresses. It checks the destination to decide where to send the packet. If it does not yet recognize the destination address, it relays the packet to all of the stations on both segments. It uses the source address to build its table. As it reads the source address, it notes which side the packet came from and associates that address with the segment to which it belongs. For example, if the bridge in Figure 20.8 is a learning bridge, then when station A sends its packet to station G, the bridge learns that packets coming from A are coming from the upper segment, and that station A must be located in the upper segment. Now, whenever the bridge encounters packets addressed to A, it knows to relay them only to the upper segment.

With the first packet transmitted by each station, the bridge learns the segment associated with that station. Eventually it has a complete table of station addresses and their respective segment stored in its memory.

By continuing this process even after the table is complete, a learning bridge is also self-updating. Suppose the person at station A trades offices with the person at station G, and they both take their computers (including their NICs) with them. All of a sudden, the stored segment locations for both stations are wrong. But because the bridge is constantly checking the source address of received packets, it notices that packets from station A are now coming from the lower segment, and that packets from station G are coming from the upper segment and updates its table accordingly.

The logic required to achieve this kind of automation makes a learning bridge more expensive than a simple bridge. For most applications, however, the convenience is worth the cost.

Multiport Bridges

A multiport bridge can be either simple or learning, and is used to interconnect more than two same-type segments.

20.3   ROUTERS

Repeaters and bridges are simple hardware devices capable of executing specific tasks. Routers are more sophisticated. They have access to network layer addresses and contain software that enables them to determine which of several possible paths between those addresses is the best for a particular transmission. Routers operate in the physical, data link, and network layers of the OSI model (see Figure 20.9).

Figure 20.9   *A router in the OSI model*

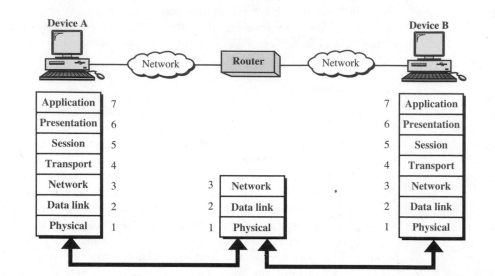

Routers relay packets among multiple interconnected networks. They route packets from one network to any of a number of potential destination networks on an internet. Figure 20.10 shows a possible internetwork of five networks. A packet sent from a station on one network to a station on a neighboring network goes first to the jointly held router, which switches it over to the destination network. If there is no one router connected to both the sending and receiving networks, the sending router transfers the

Figure 20.10   *Routers in an internet*

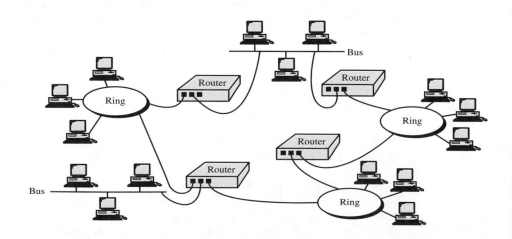

packet across one of its connected networks to the next router in the direction of the ultimate destination. That router forwards the packet to the next router on the path, and so on, until the destination is reached.

Routers act like stations on a network. But unlike most stations, which are members of only one network, routers have addresses on, and links to, two or more networks at the same time. In their simplest function they receive packets from one connected network and pass them to a second, connected, network. However, if a received packet is addressed to a node on a network of which the router is not a member, the router is capable of determining which of its connected networks is the best next relay point for the packet. Once a router has identified the best route for a packet to travel, it passes the packet along the appropriate network to another router. That router checks the destination address, finds what it considers the best route for the packet, and passes it to the destination network (if that network is a neighbor), or across a neighboring network to the next router on the chosen path.

Routing Concepts

As we have seen, the job of routers is to forward packets through an internetwork of compatible networks. Imagine, for example, that we want to move a packet from network A to network C via router (network) B. Often, however, more than one pathway exists between the point of origin and the point of destination. For example, the packet could reach network C by going through router D instead of router B, or possibly even going directly from A to C. Whenever there are multiple options, the router chooses the pathway.

Least-Cost Routing

But which path does it choose? The decision is based on efficiency: which of the available pathways is the cheapest or, in networking terminology, the shortest. A value is assigned to each link; the length of a particular route is equal to the total of the values of the component links. The term *shortest*, in this context, can mean either of two things depending on the protocol. In some cases, shortest means the route requiring the smallest number of relays, or hops; for example, a direct link from A to D would be considered shorter than the route A-B-C-D even if the actual distance covered by the latter is the same or less. In other cases, shortest means fastest, cheapest, most reliable, most secure, or best of any other quality that can make one particular link (or combination of links) more attractive than another. Usually, shortest means a combination of all of these.

> In routing the term *shortest* can mean the combination of many factors including shortest, cheapest, fastest, most reliable, and so on.

When shortest means the pathway requiring the smallest number of relays, it is called hop-count routing, in which every link is considered to be of equal length and given the value 1. Equal link values make hop-count routing simple: one-hop routes are always equal to 1, two-hop routes are always equal to 2, and so on. Routes need updating only when a link becomes unavailable. In that case, the value of the link becomes infinite and an alternate is found. Hop-count algorithms usually limit the routes known by a single router to those within fifteen hops. For transmissions with special requirements (e.g., military transmissions that require highly secure lines) a particular hop-count algorithm may be customized. In such cases, some links will be given a value of 1, while others will have higher values and will be avoided. Novell, AppleTalk, OSI, and TCP/IP protocols all use hop count as the basis for their routing algorithms.

Other protocols factor a number of qualities relevant to the functioning of a link before assigning a value to a link. These qualities can include speed, traffic congestion, and link medium (telephone line, satellite transmission, etc.). When all relevant factors for a particular link are combined, a number that represents the value or length of the link is issued. This number represents an assessment of efficiency, not a physical distance; thus, it is called the symbolic length of the link.

> We can combine all of the factors affecting a link into one number and call that number the symbolic length of the link.

In some protocols, each link in a network is assigned a length based on whatever qualities are considered important to that network. If the link between two routers is half-duplex or full-duplex (has two-way traffic), the length of the link in one direction might be different from the length of the link in the other direction. The physical distance that the signal has to travel is not changed, but other factors, such as traffic load or quality of the cable, may differ. As with hop-count routing, the decision of which route is best is based on shortest distance, calculated by totaling the lengths of every link used by a given path. In hop-count routing all three-hop paths have a total length of 3 and are considered longer than two-hop paths. When different links are assigned different lengths, however, the total length of a three-hop link may turn out to be shorter than that of a two-hop link.

Distributed Routing

In some routing protocols, once a pathway to a destination has been selected, the router sends all packets for that destination along that one route. Other routing protocols employ a technique called distributed routing, by which a router may select a new route for each packet (even packets belonging to the same transmission) in response to changes in the relative lengths of the links. Given a transmission from network A to network D, a router may send the first packet by way of network B, the second packet by way of network C, and the third packet by way of network Q, depending on which route is most efficient at the moment.

Packet Lifetime

Once a router has decided on a pathway, it passes the packet to the next router on that path and forgets about it. The next router, however, may choose the same pathway or may decide that a different pathway is shorter and relay the packet to the next router in that direction. This handing-off of responsibility allows each router to contain minimal logic, keeps the amount of control information that must be contained in the frame to a minimum, and allows for route adjustment based on up-to-the-minute appraisals of each link. It also creates the potential for a packet's getting stuck in a never ending loop or bounce in which a packet is passed around from router to router without ever actually reaching its destination.

Loops and bouncing can occur when a router updates its routing table, then relays a packet based on new pathways before the receiving router has updated its own vector. For example, A believes that the shortest route to C is through B, and relays a packet accordingly. Before B receives the packet, it learns that its link to C has been disabled. B updates its vector and finds that the current shortest route from itself to C is through A. A has not yet received the information about the B-C link and still believes the best route to C to be through B. The packet is relayed back to B. B relays it back to A, and so on. Problems of this sort are more likely on systems using distance vector algorithms than on those using link state algorithms. (The former send update packages more frequently than the latter; see Routing Algorithms below.)

The problem created by looping and bouncing is not primarily one of lost packets—the data link functions of the transmission's originator and receiver report lost frames and replace them with new copies. The problem is that processing eternally looping packets uses network resources and increases congestion. Looping packets must be identified and destroyed to free the links for legitimate traffic.

The solution is an added packet field called packet lifetime. As it is generated, each packet is marked with a lifetime, usually the number of hops that are allowed before a packet is considered lost and, accordingly, destroyed. Each router to encounter the packet subtracts 1 from the total before passing it on. When the lifetime total reaches 0, the packet is destroyed.

20.4   GATEWAYS

Gateways potentially operate in all seven layers of the OSI model (see Figure 20.11). A gateway is a protocol converter. A router by itself transfers, accepts, and relays packets only across networks using similar protocols. A gateway, on the other hand, can accept a packet formatted for one protocol (e.g., AppleTalk) and convert it to a packet formatted for another protocol (e.g., TCP/IP) before forwarding it.

A gateway is generally software installed within a router. The gateway understands the protocols used by each network linked into the router and is therefore able to translate from one to another. In some cases, the only modifications necessary are the header and trailer of the packet. In other cases, the gateway must adjust the data rate, size, and format as well. Figure 20.12 shows a gateway connecting an SNA network (IBM) to a NetWare network (Novell).

20.5   ROUTING ALGORITHMS

As explained earlier, in routing the pathway with the lowest cost is considered the best. As long as the cost of each link is known, a router can find the optimal combination for any transmission. Several algorithms exist for making these calculations. The most popular are distance vector routing and link state routing.

Figure 20.11   *A gateway in the OSI model*

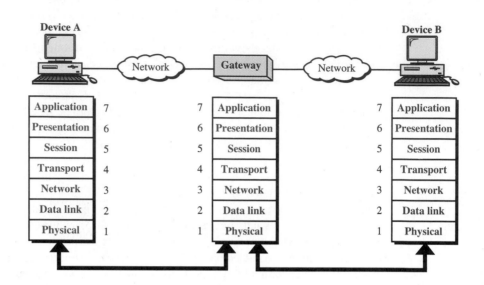

Figure 20.12   *A gateway*

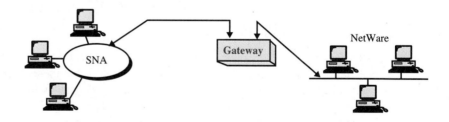

Two common methods are used to calculate the shortest path between two routers: distance vector routing and link state routing.

Distance Vector Routing

In distance vector routing each router periodically shares its knowledge about the entire network with its neighbors. The three keys to understanding how this algorithm works are as follows:

1. **Knowledge about the whole network.** Each router shares its knowledge about the entire network. It sends all of its collected knowledge about the network to its neighbors. At the outset, a router's knowledge of the network may be sparse. How much it knows, however, is unimportant: it sends whatever it has.

2. **Routing only to neighbors.** Each router periodically sends its knowledge about the network only to those routers to which it has direct links. It sends whatever

knowledge it has about the whole network through all of its ports. This information is received and kept by each neighboring router and used to update that router's own information about the network.

3. **Information sharing at regular intervals.** For example, every 30 seconds, each router sends its information about the whole network to its neighbors. This sharing occurs whether or not the network has changed since the last time information was exchanged.

> In distance vector routing, each router periodically shares its knowledge about the entire network with its neighbors.

Sharing Information

To understand how distance vector routing works, examine the internet shown in Figure 20.13. In this example, the ovals represent local area networks (LANs). The number inside each cloud is that LAN's network ID. These LANs can be of any type (Ethernet, token ring, FDDI, etc.). The LANs are connected by routers (or gateways), represented by the boxes labeled A, B, C, D, E, and F.

Figure 20.13   *Example of an internet*

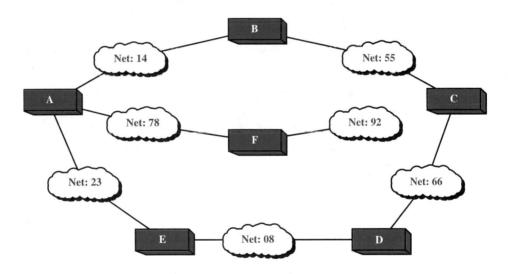

Distance vector routing simplifies the routing process by assuming a cost of 1 unit for every link. In this way, the efficiency of transmission is a function only of the number of links required to reach a destination. Distance vector routing, therefore, is based not on cost but on hop count.

Figure 20.14 shows the first step in the algorithm. The boxes indicate the relationships of the routers in Figure 20.13 to their neighbors. As you can see, each router sends its information about the internetwork only to its immediate neighbors. How, then, do non-neighboring routers learn about each other and share knowledge?

Figure 20.14   *The concept of distance vector routing*

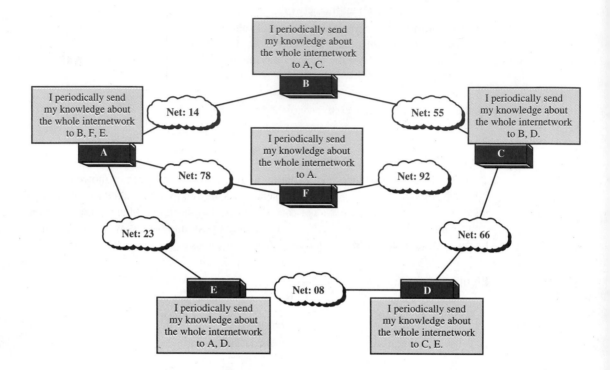

A router sends its knowledge to its neighbors. The neighbors add this knowledge to their own knowledge and send the whole table to their own neighbors. In this way, the first router gets its own information back plus new information about its neighbor's other neighbors. Each of these neighbors adds its knowledge and sends the updated table on to its own neighbors (to neighbors of neighbors of neighbors of the original router), and so on. Eventually, every router knows about every other router in the network.

Routing Table

Now let's examine how each router gets its initial knowledge about the whole network (internetwork) and how it uses shared information to update that knowledge.

Creating the Table   At start-up, a router's knowledge of the internetwork is sparse. All it knows is that it is connected to some number of LANs (two or more). Because a router is a station on each of those LANs, it also knows the ID of each station. In most systems, a station port ID and a network ID share the same prefix. So a router can discover to which networks it is connected by examining its own logical addresses (remember, a router has as many logical addresses as it has connected ports). This information is enough for it to construct its original routing table (see Figure 20.15).

A routing table has columns for at least three types of information (some protocols require more): the network ID, the cost, and the ID of the next router. The network ID is

Figure 20.15 *Distance Vector routing table*

Network ID	Cost	Next Router
· · · · · · · · · ·	· · · · · · ·	· · · · · · · · · ·
· · · · · · · · · ·	· · · · · · ·	· · · · · · · · · ·
· · · · · · · · · ·	· · · · · · ·	· · · · · · · · · ·
· · · · · · · · · ·	· · · · · · ·	· · · · · · · · · ·
· · · · · · · · · ·	· · · · · · ·	· · · · · · · · · ·

the final destination of the packet. The cost is the number of hops a packet must make to get there. And the next router is the router to which a packet must be delivered on its way to a particular destination. The table tells a router that it costs *x* to reach network Y via router Z.

The original routing tables for our sample internetwork are shown in Figure 20.16. At this point, the third column is empty because the only destination networks identified are those attached to the current router. No multiple-hop destinations and therefore no next routers have been identified. These basic tables are sent out to neighbors (as shown in the figure by arrows). For example, A sends its routing table to routers B, F, and E. B sends its routing table to routers C and A, and so on.

Figure 20.16 *Routing table distribution in distance vector routing*

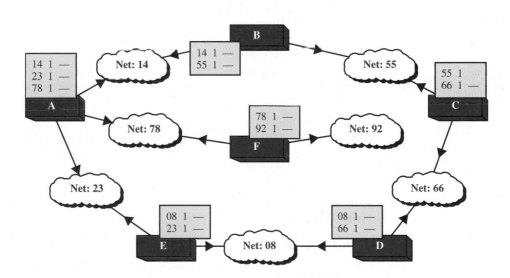

Updating the Table When A receives a routing table from B, it uses the information to update its own table (see Figure 20.17). It says to itself: "B has sent me a table that shows how its packets can get to networks 55 and 14. I know that B is my neighbor, so my packets can reach B in one hop. So, if I add one hop to all of the costs shown in B's table, the sum will be my cost for reaching those other networks." Therefore, A adjusts

Figure 20.17   *Updating routing table for router A*

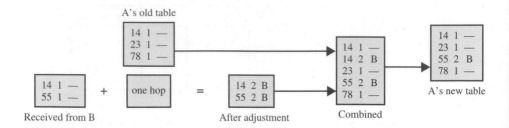

A's old table

14	1	—
23	1	—
78	1	—

| 14 | 1 | — |
| 55 | 1 | — |

Received from B

+

one hop

=

| 14 | 2 | B |
| 55 | 2 | B |

After adjustment

14	1	—
14	2	B
23	1	—
55	2	B
78	1	—

Combined

14	1	—
23	1	—
55	2	B
78	1	—

A's new table

the information shown in B's table by adding one to each listed cost. It then combines this table with its own to create a new, more comprehensive table.

This combined table may contain duplicate data for some network destinations. Router A therefore finds and purges any duplications, and keeps whichever version shows the lowest cost. For example, as Figure 20.17 shows, router A can send a packet to network 14 in two ways. The first, which uses no next router, costs one hop. The second, via router B, requires two hops (A to B, then B to 14). The first option has the lower cost; it is kept and the second entry is dropped. This selection process is the reason for the cost column: the cost serves as a weighting that allows the router to differentiate between various routes to the same destination.

Now, suppose that while A and B are exchanging tables, router C receives a copy of D's routing table. C follows the same process as A and updates its table (see Figure 20.18).

Figure 20.19 shows the routing situation in our sample internetwork after A and C have updated their tables once.

If, at this point, router F receives a copy of A's new table, it updates its own (see Figure 20.20).

Figure 20.21 shows the internetwork after these first steps. Routers A, C, and F all have improved routing tables.

The process continues until, after a certain number of table exchanges, each router's table shows the optimal path and hop count to each of the networks on the internetwork (see Figure 20.22).

If you examine Figure 20.22, you see that this simple procedure results in complete consistency among the routing tables. Imagine that router A receives a packet addressed to network 66. A looks at its table and sees that 66 is three hops away and that a packet destined for 66 first must be delivered to router E. Router A relays the packet to router E and forgets about it. A's duty is limited to delivering the packet to the next station on its route (one hop), in this case, router E. Router E takes it from there.

Router E now examines its own table and sees that to deliver a packet to network 66 requires two hops, the next of which is to router D. It therefore relays the packet to D and its responsibility ends. Router D receives the packet, looks at its own table, and finds that it is connected directly to network 66 (one hop, no next router). Network 66 delivers the packet to its final destination.

Figure 20.18 *Updating routing table for router C*

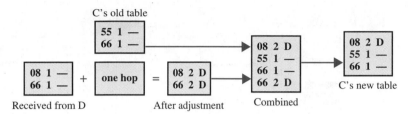

Figure 20.19 *Updated routing tables*

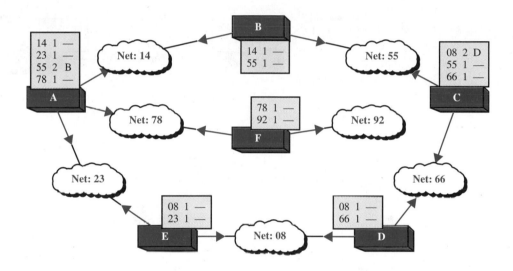

Figure 20.20 *Updating routing table for router F*

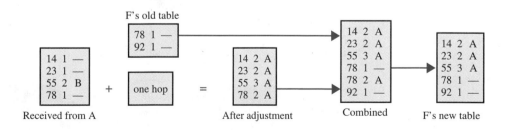

Figure 20.21 *New updated routing tables*

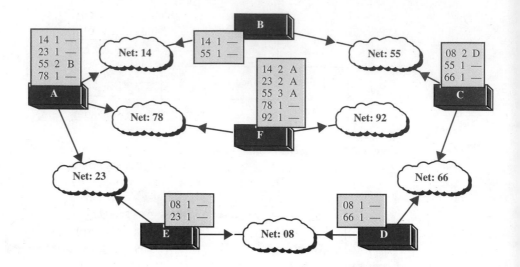

Figure 20.22 *Final routing tables*

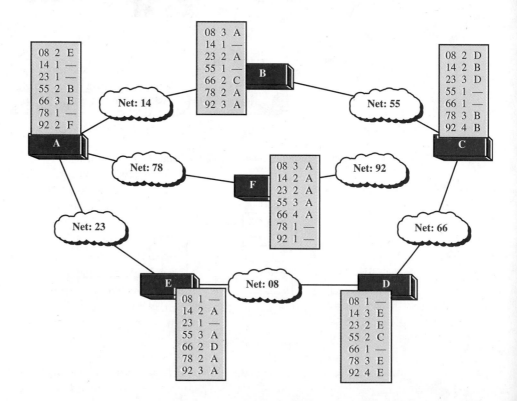

Link State Routing

The keys to understanding link state routing are different from those in distance vector routing. In link state routing, each router shares its knowledge of its neighborhood with every other router in the network. The following are true of link state routing:

In link state routing, each router shares its knowledge of its neighborhood with all routers in the internetwork.

1. **Knowledge about the neighborhood.** Instead of sending its entire routing table, a router sends information about its neighborhood only.
2. **To all routers.** Each router sends this information to every other router on the internetwork, not just to its neighbors. It does so by a process called flooding. Flooding means that a router sends its information to all of its neighbors (through all of its output ports). Each neighbor sends the packet to all of its neighbors, and so on. Every router that receives the packet sends copies to all of its neighbors. Finally, every router (without exception) receives a copy of the same information.
3. **Information sharing at regular intervals.** Each router sends out information about the neighbors periodically. However, the interval in link state routing is normally much longer than the one in distance vector routing (e.g., 30 minutes versus 30 seconds).

Information Sharing

Let's examine the link state routing process using the same internetwork we used for distance vector routing (see Figure 20.13).

The first step in link state routing is information sharing (see Figure 20.23). Each router sends its knowledge about its neighborhood to every other router in the internetwork.

Packet Cost   Both distance vector and link state routing are lowest cost algorithms. In distance vector routing, cost refers to hop count. In link state routing, cost is a weighted value based on a variety of factors such as security levels, traffic, or the state of the link. The cost from router A to network 14, therefore, might be different from the cost from A to 23.

In determining a route, the cost of a hop is applied to each packet as it leaves a router and enters a network. (Remember, cost is just a weighting and should not be confused with the transmission fees paid by the sender or receiver.) This cost is an outbound cost, meaning that it is applied when a packet leaves the router. Two factors govern how cost is applied to packets in determining a route:

■   Cost is applied only by routers and not by any other stations on a network. Remember, the link from one router to the next is a network, not a point-to-point cable. In many topologies (such as ring and bus), every station on the network examines the header of every packet that passes. If cost was added by every station, instead of by routers alone, it would accumulate unpredictably (the number of stations in a network can change for a variety of reasons, many of them unpredictable).

■   Cost is applied as a packet leaves the router rather than as it enters. Most networks are broadcast networks. When a packet is in the network, every station, including

Figure 20.23   *Concept of link state routing*

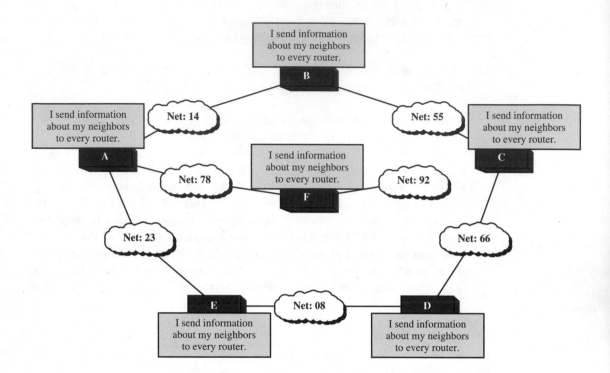

the router, can pick it up. Therefore, we cannot assign any cost to a packet when it goes from a network to a router.

Figure 20.24 shows our sample internet as it appears to the link state routing algorithm. The costs shown are arbitrary; in actual practice they would reflect attributes of each network.

Link State Packet   When a router floods the network with information about its neighborhood, it is said to be advertising. The basis of this advertising is a short packet called a link state packet (LSP); see Figure 20.25. An LSP usually contains four fields: the ID of the advertiser, the ID of the destination network affected, the cost, and the ID of the neighbor router.

Getting Information about Neighbors   A router gets its information about its neighbors by periodically sending them a short greeting packet. If the neighbor responds to the greeting as expected, it is assumed to be alive and functioning. If it does not, a change is assumed to have occurred and the sending router then alerts the rest of the network in its next LSP. These greeting packets are small enough that they do not occupy network resources to any significant degree (unlike the routing tables used by distance vector routing).

Initialization   Imagine that all routers in our sample network come up at the same time. Each router sends a greeting packet to its neighbors to find out the state of each

Figure 20.24   *Cost in link state routing*

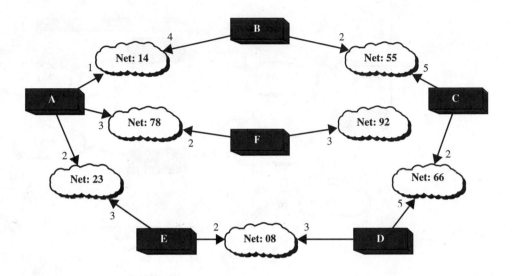

Figure 20.25   *Link state packet*

Advertiser	Network	Cost	Neighbor
....	......	....	....
....	......	....	....
....	......	....	....

link. It then prepares an LSP based on the results of these greetings and floods the network with it. Figure 20.26 shows this process for router A.

The same steps are performed by every router in the network as each comes up. Figure 20.27 shows router B's process.

Link State Database   Every router receives every LSP and puts the information into a link state database. Figure 20.28 shows the database for our sample network.

Because every router receives the same LSPs, every router builds the same database. It stores this database on its disk, and uses it to calculate its routing table. If a router is added to or deleted from the system, the whole database must be shared to create fast updating.

> In link state routing, every router has exactly the same link state database.

The Dijkstra Algorithm

To calculate its routing table, each router applies an algorithm called the Dijkstra algorithm to its link state database. The Dijkstra algorithm calculates the shortest path between two points on a network using a graph made up of nodes and arcs. Nodes are

Figure 20.26   *Flooding of A's LSP*

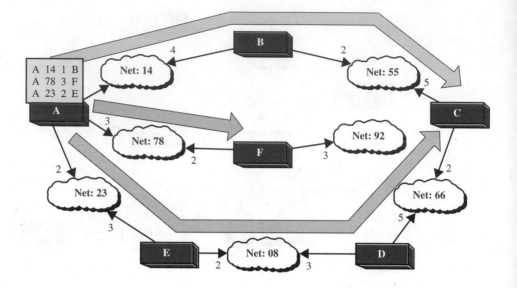

Figure 20.27   *Flooding of B's LSP*

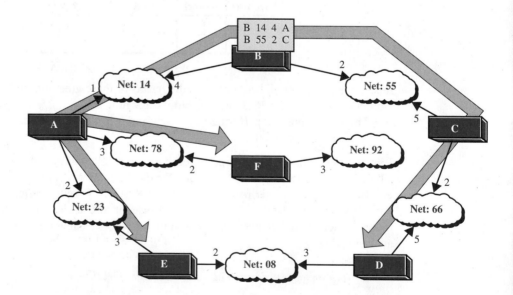

of two types: networks and routers. Arcs are the connections between a router and a network (router-to-network and network-to-router). Cost is applied only to the arc from router to network. The cost of the arc from network-to-router is always zero (see Figure 20.29).

Figure 20.28   *Link state database*

Advertiser	Network	Cost	Neighbor
A	14	1	B
A	78	3	F
A	23	2	E
B	14	4	A
B	55	2	C
C	55	5	B
C	66	2	D
D	66	5	C
D	08	3	E
E	23	3	A
E	08	2	D
F	78	2	A
F	92	3	–

Figure 20.29   *Costs in the Dijkstra algorithm*

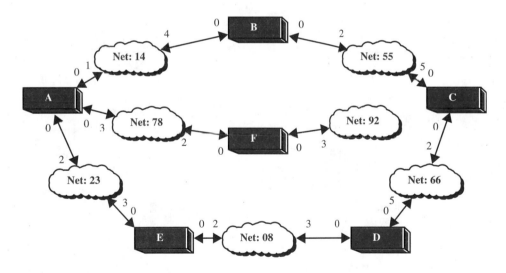

Shortest Path Tree   The Dijkstra algorithm follows four steps to discover what is called the shortest path tree (routing table) for each router:

■   The algorithm begins to build the tree by identifying its root. The root of each router's tree is itself. The algorithm then attaches all nodes that can be reached from that root—in other words, all of the other neighbor nodes. Nodes and arcs are temporary at this step.

Figure 20.30   *Shortest path calculation, part 1*

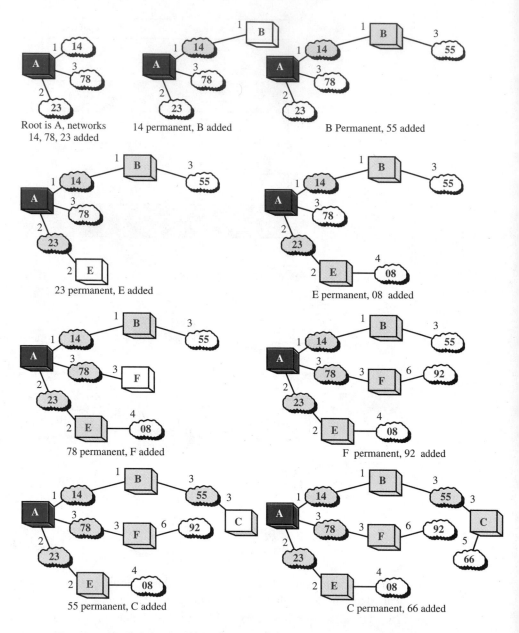

- The algorithm compares the tree's temporary arcs and identifies the arc with the lowest cumulative cost. This arc and the node that it connects to are now a permanent part of the shortest path tree.

Figure 20.31   *Shortest path calculation, part 2*

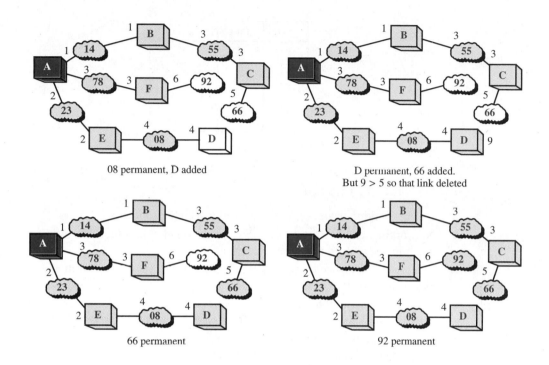

08 permanent, D added

D permanent, 66 added.
But 9 > 5 so that link deleted

66 permanent

92 permanent

- The algorithm examines the database and identifies every node that can be reached from its chosen node. These nodes and their arcs are added temporarily to the tree.
- The last two steps are repeated until every node in the network has become a permanent part of the tree. The only permanent arcs are those that represent the shortest (lowest cost) route to every node.

Figure 20.30 shows the steps of the Dijkstra algorithm applied by node A of our sample internet. The cost number next to each node represents the cumulative cost from the root node, not the cost of the individual arc. The second and third steps are repeated until four more nodes have become permanent.

Figure 20.31 shows the completion of the shortest path tree for router A.

Routing Table   Each router now uses the shortest path tree to construct its routing table. Each router uses the same algorithm and the same link state database to calculate its own shortest path tree and routing table: these are different for each router. Figure 20.32 shows the table developed by router A.

In link state routing, the link state database is the same for all routers, but the shortest path trees and the routing tables are different for each router.

Figure 20.32   *Link state routing table for router A*

Net	Cost	Next router
08	4	E
14	1	—
23	2	—
55	3	B
66	5	B
78	3	—
92	6	F

20.6   SUMMARY

- Internetworking devices connect networks to create an internet.
- Networking and internetworking devices are divided into four categories: repeaters, bridges, routers, and gateways.
- A repeater is a device that operates in the physical layer of the OSI model. Its purpose is regeneration of the signal.
- Bridges operate in the physical and data link layers of the OSI model. They have access to station addresses and can forward or filter a packet in a network.
- Routers operate in the physical, data link, and network layers of the OSI model. They decide the path a packet should take.
- Gateways operate in all seven layers of the OSI model. They convert one protocol to another and can therefore connect two dissimilar networks.
- There are two methods to calculate the shortest path between two routers: distance vector routing and link state routing.
- In distance vector routing, each router periodically shares its own knowledge about the network with its immediate neighbor routers.
- In distance vector routing, each router has a table with information about networks (ID, cost, and the router to access the particular network).
- In link state routing each router creates its own link state packet (LSP). Every other router receives this LSP through the flooding process. All routers therefore have the same information; this is compiled into the link state database. From this common database, each router finds its own shortest paths to the other routers by using the Dijkstra algorithm.
- A cost is assigned to a packet when it leaves the router in link state routing.
- In link state routing, every router has its own unique routing table.

20.7 PRACTICE SET

Multiple Choice

1. Which of the following is not an internetworking device?
   a. bridge
   b. gateway
   c. router
   d. all of them are

2. Which of the following uses the greatest number of layers in the OSI model?
   a. bridge
   b. repeater
   c. router
   d. gateway

3. A bridge forwards or filters a packet by comparing the information in its address table to the packet's _____.
   a. layer 2 source address
   b. source node's physical address
   c. layer 2 destination address
   d. layer 3 destination address

4. A simple bridge does which of the following?
   a. filters a data packet
   b. forwards a data packet
   c. extends LANs
   d. all of the above

5. Which of the following are bridge types?
   a. simple, complex, learning
   b. simple, learning, multiport
   c. simple, complex, multiport
   d. spanning, contract, suspension

6. The shortest path in routing can refer to _____.
   a. the least expensive path
   b. the least distant path
   c. the path with the smallest number of hops
   d. any or a combination of the above

7. Which routing algorithm requires more traffic between routers for setup and updating?
   a. distance vector
   b. link state

   c. Dijkstra

   d. vector link

8. In distance vector routing each router receives vectors from _____.

   a. every router in the network

   b. every router less than two units away

   c. a table stored by the software

   d. its neighbors only

9. If there are five routers and six networks in an internetwork using link state routing, how many routing tables are there?

   a. 1

   b. 5

   c. 6

   d. 11

10. If there are five routers and six networks in an internetwork, how many link state databases are there?

   a. 1

   b. 5

   c. 6

   d. 11

11. In link state routing, flooding allows changes to be recorded by _____.

   a. all routers

   b. neighbor routers only

   c. some routers

   d. all networks

12. In an LSP, the advertiser is _____.

   a. a router

   b. a network

   c. a data packet

   d. none of the above

13. Which of the following can be handled by a gateway?

   a. protocol conversion

   b. packet resizing

   c. data encapsulation

   d. a and b

14. Gateways function in which OSI layers?

   a. the lower three

   b. the upper four

   c. all seven

   d. all but the physical layer

15. Repeaters function in the _____ layer.
    a. physical
    b. data link
    c. network
    d. a and b

16. Bridges function in the _____ layer.
    a. physical
    b. data link
    c. network
    d. a and b

17. A repeater takes a weakened or corrupted signal and _____ it.
    a. amplifies
    b. regenerates
    c. resamples
    d. reroutes

18. A bridge has access to the _____ address of a station on the same network.
    a. physical
    b. network
    c. service access point
    d. all of the above

19. What type of bridge must have its address table entered manually?
    a. simple
    b. learning
    c. multiport
    d. b and c

20. Which type of bridge builds and updates its tables from address information on packets?
    a. simple
    b. learning
    c. a and b
    d. none of the above

21. Routers function in the _____ layers.
    a. physical and data link
    b. physical, data link, and network
    c. data link and network
    d. network and transport

22. In which routing method do all the routers have a common database?
    a. distance vector
    b. link state

   c. link vector

   d. none of the above

23. A packet traveling from one token ring network to another token ring network uses the services of a _____. (Each network is an independent network.)

   a. simple bridge

   b. repeater

   c. router

   d. learning bridge

Exercises

1. How is a repeater different from an amplifier?

2. Describe the functions of the four connecting devices mentioned in this chapter. Rank them according to their complexity and give the OSI layers in which they operate.

3. A token ring of 30 stations is connected to a second token ring of 30 stations by a bridge. Discuss why the network administrator used this configuration instead of just one large 60-station token ring.

4. Assume three token ring LANs are connected by one bridge. What happens if a fault occurs on one of the rings? What happens if the bridge fails?

5. What is the LSP database, and how is it created?

6. Describe some of the factors that need to be considered in connecting networks.

7. Starting with Figure 20.21, update router E with A's new table and then with D's original table.

8. In Figure 20.21, what contribution to router A does router F's table make? (That is, how does router A's table change when it receives router F's table?)

9. Starting with Figure 20.22, assume router D fails. Draw the final configuration.

10. Complete the link state routing algorithm example based on Figure 20.24. Find the shortest path trees and routing tables for nodes B, C, D, E, and F in the same way it was done for node A. Show all of the details.

CHAPTER 21

TRANSPORT LAYER

The transport layer is the core of the OSI model. Protocols at this layer oversee the delivery of data from an application program on one device to an application program on another device. More important, they act as a liaison between the upper-layer protocols (session, presentation, and application) and the services provided by the lower layers (network, data link, and physical). The upper layers can use the services of the transport layer to interact with the network without ever having to interact directly with or even be aware of the existence of the lower layers. To make this separation possible, the transport layer itself is independent of the physical network.

To better understand the role of the transport layer, it is helpful to visualize an internet made up of a variety of different physical networks such as the LANs, MANs, and WANs shown in Figure 21.1. These networks are connected to enable the transport of data from a computer on one network to a computer on another network. As a transmission moves from network to network, the data may be encapsulated in different types and lengths of packets. One network's network or data link functions may chop it into smaller segments to fit a more restricted packet or frame size, while another network's peer functions may link several segments together in a single large packet. The data may even share a frame with other, nonrelated data segments. No matter what transformations they must go through on the way, however, the data must arrive at their destination in their original form.

The upper-layer protocols are kept unaware of the intricacy of the physical networks, so that only one set of upper-layer software has to be developed. To the upper layers, the individual physical networks are a simple homogeneous cloud that somehow takes data and delivers it to its destination safe and sound. For example, even if an Ethernet in the internet is replaced by a token ring, the upper layers remain unaware of it. To them, the internet is a single and essentially unchanging network. The transport layer provides this transparency.

Examples of transport layer protocols are transmission control protocol (TCP) and user datagram protocol (UDP), both of which will be discussed in Chapter 23.

Figure 21.1 *An internetwork*

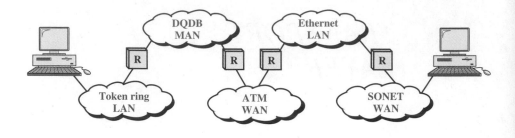

21.1 DUTIES OF THE TRANSPORT LAYER

Transport layer services are implemented by a transport protocol used between two transport entities (see Figure 21.2).

Figure 21.2 *Transport layer concept*

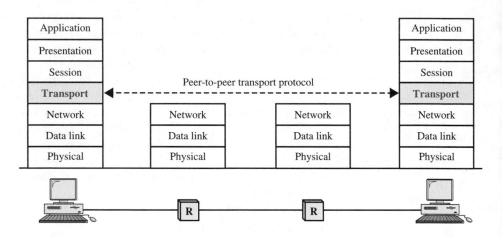

The services provided are similar to those of the data link layer. The data link layer, however, is designed to provide its services within a single network, while the transport layer provides these services across an internetwork made of many networks. The data link layer controls the physical layer, while the transport layer controls all three of the lower layers (see Figure 21.3).

The services provided by transport layer protocols can be divided into five broad categories: end-to-end delivery, addressing, reliable delivery, flow control, and multiplexing (see Figure 21.4).

End-to-End Delivery

The network layer oversees the end-to-end delivery of individual packets but does not see any relationship between those packets, even those belonging to a single message.

Figure 21.3   *Transport layer compared with data link layer*

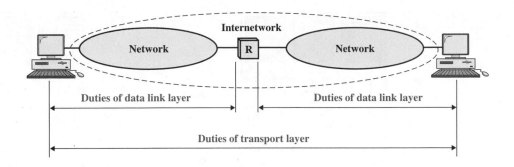

Figure 21.4   *Transport layer duties*

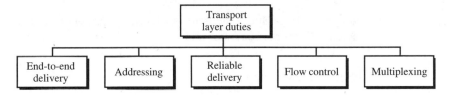

It treats each as an independent entity. The transport layer, on the other hand, makes sure that the entire message (not just a single packet) arrives intact. Thus, it oversees the end-to-end (source-to-destination) delivery of an entire message.

Addressing

The transport layer interacts with the functions of the session layer. However, many protocols (or protocol stacks, meaning groups of protocols that interact at different levels) combine session, presentation, and application level protocols into a single package, called an application. In these cases, delivery to the session layer functions is effectively delivery to the application. So communication occurs not just from end machine to end machine but from end application to end application. Data generated by an application on one machine must be received not just by the other machine but by the correct application on that other machine.

In most cases, therefore, we end up with communication between many-to-many entities, called service points (see Figure 21.5). But how does the network identify which service point on one host is communicating with which service point on the other host?

To ensure accurate delivery from service point to service point, we need another level of addressing in addition to those at the data link and network levels. Data link level protocols need to know which two computers within a network are communicating. Network level protocols need to know which two computers within an internet are

Figure 21.5 *Service points*

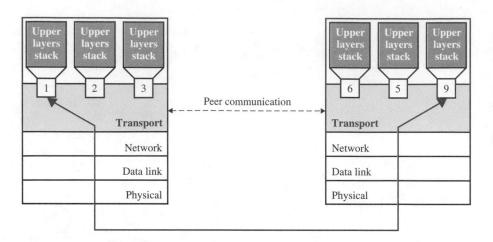

communicating. But at the transport level, the protocol needs to know which upper-layer protocols are communicating.

Reliable Delivery

At the transport layer, reliable delivery has four aspects: error control, sequence control, loss control, and duplication control (see Figure 21.6).

Figure 21.6 *Aspects of reliable delivery*

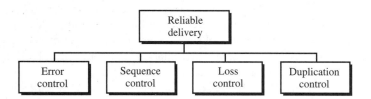

Error Control

When transferring data, the primary goal of reliability is error control. As we said earlier, data must be delivered to their destination exactly as they originated from the source. The realities of physical data transport are that, while 100 percent error-free delivery is probably impossible, transport layer protocols are designed to come as close as possible.

Mechanisms for error handling at this layer are based on error detection and retransmission with the error handling usually performed using algorithms implemented in software, such as checksum (see Chapter 9, Error Detection and Correction).

But if we already have error handling at the data link layer, why do we need it at the transport layer? Data link layer functions guarantee error-free delivery node-to-node for each link. However, node-to-node reliability does not ensure end-to-end reliability. Figure 21.7 shows a situation where an error is introduced that cannot be caught by data link layer error controls.

Figure 21.7   *Transport and data link error control*

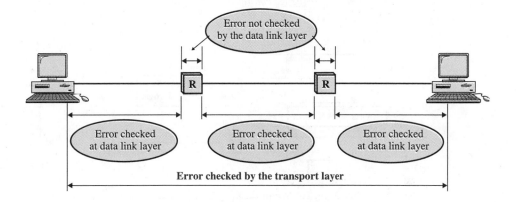

In Figure 21.7, the data link layer ensures that packets passing between each network are error free. But an error is introduced as the packet is processed inside one of the routers. This error will not be caught by the data link functions of the next link because those functions just check to see that no errors have been introduced between the beginning and end of that link. The transport layer must therefore do its own checking end-to-end to make sure that the packet has arrived as intended by the source.

Sequence Control

The second aspect of reliability implemented at the transport layer is sequence control. On the sending end, the transport layer is responsible for ensuring that data units received from the upper layers are usable by the lower layers. On the receiving end, it is responsible for ensuring that the various pieces of a transmission arrive in the order intended.

Segmentation and Concatenation   When the size of the data unit received from the upper layer is too long for the network layer datagram or data link layer frame to handle, the transport protocol divides it into smaller, usable blocks. The dividing process is called segmentation. When, on the other hand, the size of the data units belonging to a single session are so small that several can fit together into a single datagram or frame, the transport protocol combines them into a single data unit. The combining process is called concatenation.

Sequence Numbers   Most transport layer services add a sequence number at the end of each segment. If a longer data unit has been segmented, the numbers indicate the order for reassembly. If several shorter units have been concatenated, the numbers indicate the end of each subunit and allow them to be separated accurately at the destination. In addition, each segment carries a field that indicates whether it is the final segment of a transmission or a middle segment with more still to come.

Imagine a situation in which a bank customer sends a message to the bank instructing it to first transfer $5000 from a checking account to a savings account and then to transfer the balance of the checking account to the checking account of another customer. Imagine what would happen if the two parts of the message were received out of order (see Figure 21.8).

Figure 21.8   *Sequence control*

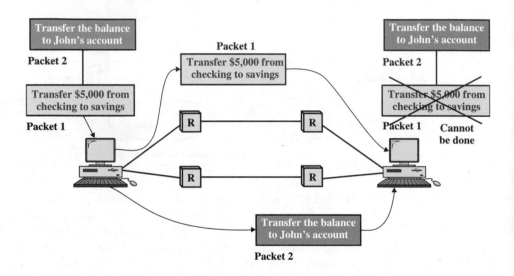

From the sender's and receiver's points of view, it is not important in what order pieces of a transmission travel. What is important is that they are properly reassembled at the destination—just as, for example, you don't care how the pieces of your car got to the assembly plant but you do want them put together properly by the time the car is delivered to you.

Loss Control

The third aspect of reliability covered by the transport layer is loss control. The transport layer ensures that all pieces of a transmission arrive at the destination, not just some of them. When data have been segmented for delivery, some segments may be lost in transit (see Figure 21.9). Sequence numbers allow the receiver's transport layer protocol to identify any missing segments and request redelivery.

Duplication Control

The fourth aspect of reliability covered by the transport layer is duplication control. Transport layer functions must guarantee that no pieces of data arrive at the receiving system duplicated. Just as they allow identification of lost packets, sequence numbers allow the receiver to identify and discard duplicate segments.

Duplication may seem like a trivial problem, but it can have major consequences. Imagine that bank customer A sends a message instructing the bank to

Figure 21.9 *Loss control*

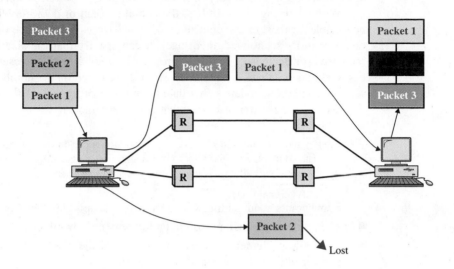

Figure 21.10 *Duplication control*

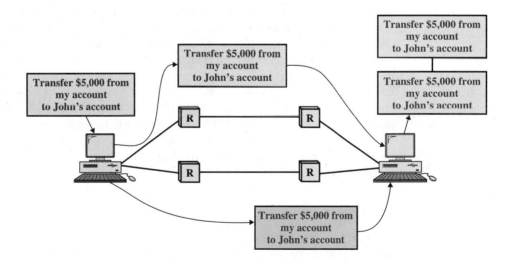

transfer $5000 from his account to customer B. What happens if this message is duplicated? See Figure 21.10.

Flow Control

Like the data link layer, the transport layer is responsible for flow control. However, flow control at this layer is performed end-to-end rather than across a single link.

Transport layer flow control also uses a sliding window protocol. However, the window at the transport layer can vary in size to accommodate buffer occupancy.

With a varying-size window, the actual amount of data the window can hold is negotiable. In most cases, control of window size is the province of the receiver. The receiver, in its acknowledgment packet, can specify that the size of the window be increased (or decreased, but most protocols do not allow decreases in size). In most cases, sliding windows at the transport layer are based on the number of bytes that the receiver can accommodate rather than the number of frames. A pair of communicating entities will use a buffer of x bytes that may accommodate y frames.

> A sliding window is used to make data transmission more efficient as well as to control the flow of data so that the receiver does not become overcrowded. Sliding windows used at the transport layer are usually byte oriented rather than frame oriented.

Some points about sliding windows at the transport layer are as follows:

- The sender does not have to send a full window's worth of data.
- An acknowledgment can expand the size of the window based on the sequence number of the acknowledged data segment.
- The size of the window can be increased or decreased by the receiver.
- The receiver can send an acknowledgment anytime it wants to.

To accommodate the variability in size, transport layer sliding windows use three pointers (which act as virtual walls) to identify the buffer (see Figure 21.11). The left wall moves to the right when acknowledgments are received. The middle wall moves to the right as data are sent. The right wall moves to the right or left to fix the size of the window. If acknowledgments are received and the size of the window is not changed, this third wall moves to the right to keep the size of the window constant (because the left wall has moved to the right). For example, if five bytes are acknowledged and the size of the window is not changed, then the left wall has moved to the right five bytes, shrinking the window, so the right wall must move to the right five bytes for the size of the window to remain constant. If 5 bytes are acknowledged but the receiver also increases the size of the window by 10 bytes, the right wall must move 15 bytes to the right to accommodate the new size.

Multiplexing

To improve transmission efficiency, the transport layer has the option of multiplexing. Multiplexing at this layer occurs two ways: upward, meaning that many transport layers use the same network connection, or downward, meaning that one transport layer uses many network connections.

Upward

The transport layer uses virtual circuits based on the services of the lower three layers. Normally, the underlying networks charge for each virtual circuit connection. To make more cost-effective use of an established circuit, the transport layer can send several

Figure 21.11 *Sliding window*

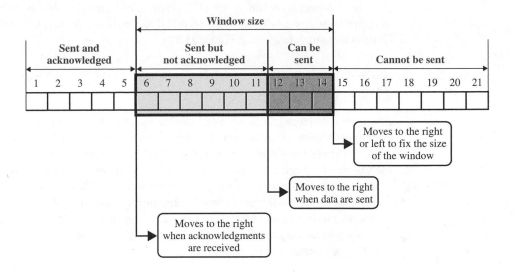

Figure 21.12 *Multiplexing*

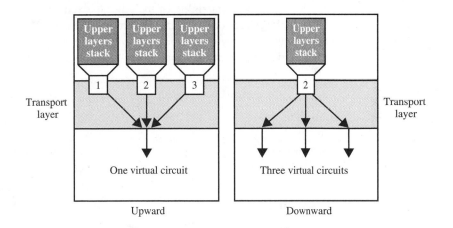

transmissions bound for the same destination along the same path by multiplexing (see Figure 21.12).

Downward

Downward multiplexing allows the transport layer to split a single transmission among a number of different paths to improve throughput (speed of delivery). This option is useful when the underlying networks have low or slow capacity. For example, some network layer protocols have restrictions on the size of packet sequence numbers that can be handled. X.25 uses a three-bit numbering code, so sequence numbers are restricted to the range of 0 to 7 (only eight packets may be sent before acknowledgment is required). In this case, throughput can be unacceptably low. To counteract this problem, the transport layer can opt to use more than one virtual circuit at the network layer to improve throughput. By sending several data segments at once, the speed of delivery is made that much faster (see Figure 21.12).

21.2   CONNECTION

End-to-end delivery can be accomplished in either of two modes: connection-oriented or connectionless. Of these two, the connection-oriented mode is the more commonly used. A connection-oriented protocol establishes a virtual circuit or pathway through the internet between the sender and receiver. All of the packets belonging to a message are then sent over this same path. Using a single pathway for the entire message facilitates the acknowledgment process and retransmission of damaged or lost frames. Connection-oriented services, therefore, are generally considered reliable.

Connection-oriented transmission has three stages: connection establishment, data transfer, and connection termination.

Connection Establishment

Before either communicating device can send data to the other, the initiating device must first determine the availability of the other to exchange data and a pathway must be found through the network by which the data can be sent. This step is called connection establishment (see Figure 21.13). Connection establishment requires three actions in what is called a three-way handshake:

Figure 21.13   *Connection establishment*

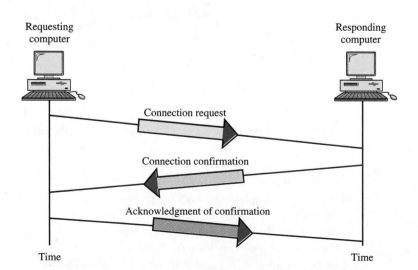

- The computer requesting the connection sends a connection request packet to the intended receiver.
- The responding computer returns a confirmation packet to the requesting computer.
- The requesting computer returns a packet acknowledging the confirmation.

Connection Termination

Once all of the data have been transferred, the connection must be terminated (see Figure 21.14).

Figure 21.14   *Connection termination*

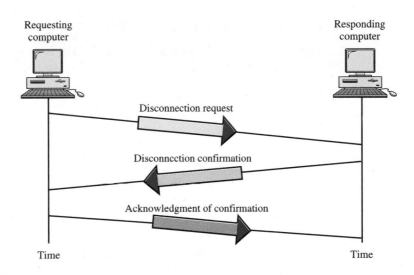

- Connection termination also requires a three-way handshake:
- The requesting computer sends a disconnection request packet.
- The responding computer confirms the disconnection request.
- The requesting computer acknowledges the confirmation.

21.3   THE OSI TRANSPORT PROTOCOL

As an example, let's examine how the transport layer is implemented using the OSI model.

Transport Classes

To avoid redundant services, the OSI defines five types of transport classes:

- **TP0.** Simple class.
- **TP1.** Basic error recovery class.

- **TP2.** Multiplexing class.
- **TP3.** Error recovery and multiplexing class.
- **TP4.** Error detection and recovery class.

Which class is used depends on the type of service required by the upper layers. The transport layer tries to match these requests to the available networking services:

- TP0 and TP2 are used with perfect network layers. A perfect network layer is one in which the number of packets that are lost or damaged is almost zero.
- TP1 and TP3 are used with residual-error network layers. A residual-error network layer is one in which some percentage of errors are never corrected.
- TP4 is used with unreliable network layers. TP4 provides fully reliable, full-duplex, connection-oriented services similar to TCP in the TCP/IP protocol suite.

Transport Protocol Data Unit (TPDU)

The format of a transport protocol data unit (TPDU) is shown in Figure 21.15. Each TPDU consists of four general fields: length, fixed parameters, variable parameters, and data.

Figure 21.15 *TPDU*

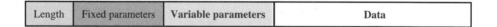

Length	Fixed parameters	Variable parameters	Data

Length The length field occupies the first byte and indicates the total number of bytes (excluding the length field itself) in the TPDU.

Fixed Parameters The fixed parameters field contains parameters, or control fields, that are commonly present in all transport layer packets. It consists of five parts: code, source reference, destination reference, sequence number, and credit allocation.

- **Code**. The code identifies the type of the data unit, for example, CR for connection request or DT for data. The following codes are recognized by the ISO and ITU-T:

  CR: Connection request
  CC: Connection confirm
  DR: Disconnect request
  DC: Disconnect confirm
  DT: Data
  ED: Expedited data
  AK: Data acknowledge
  EA: Expedited data acknowledge
  RJ: Reject
  ER: Error

- **Source and destination reference**. The source and destination reference fields contain the addresses of the original sender and the ultimate destination of the packet.

■ **Sequence number**. As a transmission is divided into smaller packets for transport, each segment is given a number that identifies its place in the sequence. Sequence numbers are used for acknowledgment, flow control, and reordering of packets at the destination.

■ **Credit allocation**. Credit allocation enables a receiving station to tell the sender how many more data units may be sent before the sender must wait for an acknowledgment. It allows the receiver to supersede existing sliding window or flow control restrictions, and to change the allocation at any time based on its processing needs. Credit allocation separates flow control from acknowledgments and means that the sender and receiver need not have the same sliding window size. For example, a remote station may return an AK 3 and a credit 7. This combination tells the sender that units 0 to 2 have been received successfully, that the next unit expected is number 3, and that seven more units may be sent before the sender must wait for another acknowledgment.

Variable Parameters   The variable parameters section of a TPDU contains parameters that occur infrequently. These control codes are used mostly for management (e.g., testing the reliability of a router).

Data   The data section of a TPDU may contain regular data or expedited data coming from the upper layers. Expedited data consist of a high-priority message that must be handled out of sequence. An urgent request (such as an interrupt command to a remote log-in) can supersede the incoming queue of the receiver and be processed ahead of packets that have been received before it.

Connection-Oriented and Connectionless Services

The OSI model supports both connection-oriented and connectionless transport services. Of these two, the connection-oriented mode is the more commonly used.

Connection-Oriented Transport Services

Connection-oriented transport services (COTS) first create a virtual circuit between two remote entities. To this end, COTS makes four different kinds of services available to the upper layers: T-CONNECT, T-DATA, T-EXPEDITED-DATA, and T-DISCONNECT (T stands for transfer). The relationship of these services to the upper and lower layers of the OSI model is illustrated in Figure 21.16.

The upper-layer user of COTS first uses the T-CONNECT service to set up a full-duplex transport connection with a peer function on a remote device. During the establishment of the transport connection, the users can negotiate the quality of services (QOS) desired and decide between normal and expedited data transfer modes.

Once the connection has been established, the two peers can transfer data using the services of either T-DATA or T-EXPEDITED-DATA. T-DATA provides nonconfirmed service but is still reliable. Successfully delivered packets are not acknowledged. If a failure occurs, however, the transport service provider notifies the sender of the failure so that corrections can be made. The amount of user data that can be carried by a T-DATA TPDU is restricted to a size negotiated by the two parties making the exchange.

Figure 21.16   *Transport layer protocols in the OSI model*

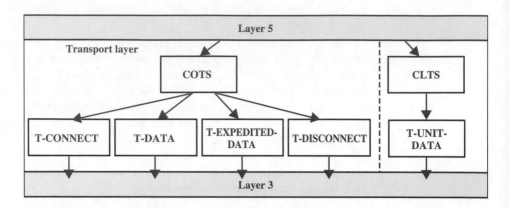

If the T-EXPEDITED-DATA service is used, the amount of expedited data that can be carried is limited (by common agreement) to 16 octets (bytes).

Either the user or the transport service provider may employ the T-DISCONNECT service to terminate a transport connection at any time during the data transfer. The T-DISCONNECT is destructive. Any data still in transit when it is invoked may be lost. T-DISCONNECT can also be used by the transport service provider or the called user to reject a connection request.

Connectionless Transport Services

Connectionless transport services (CLTS) provide only one kind of service to the upper layers: T-UNIT-DATA.

T-UNIT-DATA provides a single freestanding data unit for all transmissions. Each unit contains all of the protocol control information necessary for delivery but contains no provision for sequencing or flow control.

21.4   SUMMARY

- The transport layer, by hiding all of the manipulations necessary to move a message from source to destination, makes data transmission transparent to the upper layers.

- The data link and transport layers perform many of the same duties. The data link layer functions in a single network, while the transport layer operates across an internet.

- The transport layer needs port or service-point addresses.

- Reliable delivery requires error control, sequence control, loss control, and duplication control.

- Flow control at the transport level is handled by a three-walled sliding window.

- Multiplexing can be downward or upward in the transport layer.

- Connection establishment and termination are both accomplished through three-way handshakes.
- The transport layer is responsible for end-to-end delivery, segmentation, and concatenation.
- The transport layer supports two service types:
    a. Connection-oriented transport services (COTS).
    b. Connectionless transport services (CLTS).
- The transport protocol data unit (TPDU) format consists of four fields:
    a. Length.
    b. Fixed parameters.
    c. Variable parameters.
    d. Data.
- The five types of transport classes are based on the reliability of the lower layers. Class TP4 is similar to TCP in the TCP/IP suite.

21.5   PRACTICE SET

Multiple Choice

1. The transport layer performs the same types of functions as the _____ layer.
    a. session
    b. network
    c. data link
    d. physical

2. End-to-end delivery is the movement of a message from _____.
    a. one station to the next station
    b. one network to the next network
    c. source to destination
    d. none of the above

3. What type of addressing is specifically used by the transport layer?
    a. station addresses
    b. network addresses
    c. application program port addresses
    d. dialog addresses

4. Error control is needed at the transport layer because of potential errors occurring _____.
    a. from transmission line noise
    b. in routers
    c. from out-of-sequence delivery
    d. from packet losses

5. Making sure that data segments arrive in the correct order is _____ control.
   a. error
   b. sequence
   c. loss
   d. duplication

6. Making sure that all the data packets of a message are delivered to the destination is _____ control.
   a. error
   b. sequence
   c. loss
   d. duplication

7. If two identical data packets arrive at a destination, then _____ control is not functioning.
   a. error
   b. sequence
   c. loss
   d. duplication

8. The window size is originally 16. If 10 bytes are acknowledged and the window size is increased to 32, how many bytes should the right wall move?
   a. 10
   b. 26
   c. 32
   d. 42

9. The left wall is at the beginning of byte L; the middle wall is at the beginning of byte M; and the right wall is at the beginning of byte R. What is the window size?
   a. $L + R$
   b. $L - R$
   c. $R - L$
   d. $R - L + 1$

10. Using the same designations (L, M, and R) as in the previous problem, what is the expression for the maximum number of bytes that the sender can send?
    a. $M - L$
    b. $M + L$
    c. $R - M$
    d. $R - M + 1$

11. Which transport class should be used with a perfect network layer?
    a. TP0 and TP2
    b. TP1 and TP3
    c. TP0, TP1, and TP3
    d. TP0, TP1, TP2, TP3, and TP4

12. Which transport class should be used with a residual-error network layer?
    a. TP0 and TP2
    b. TP1 and TP3
    c. TP1, TP3, and TP4
    d. TP0, TP1, TP2, TP3, and TP4

13. In _____ services, connections must be established and terminated.
    a. connectionless
    b. connection-oriented
    c. segmentation
    d. none of the above

14. In _____ services, no connection establishment is needed.
    a. connectionless
    b. connection-oriented
    c. segmentation
    d. none of the above

15. In the transport layer, _____ is a connectionless service.
    a. CONS
    b. CLNS
    c. COTS
    d. CLTS

16. A virtual circuit is associated with a _____ service.
    a. connectionless
    b. connection-oriented
    c. segmentation
    d. none of the above

17. In _____ services, packets of a single transmission travel from source to destination via different paths.
    a. connectionless
    b. connection-oriented
    c. segmentation
    d. none of the above

Exercises

1. Many of the duties of the transport layer (e.g. flow control and reliable delivery) are also handled by the data link layer. Is this a duplication of effort? Why or why not?

2. Compare the sliding window walls of the sender in the data link layer versus those in the transport layer.

3. In the sending of the transport layer sliding window,
   a. When is the middle wall at the same location as the left wall?
   b. When is the middle wall at the same location as the right wall?
4. Starting with Figure 21.11, draw the walls after each sequential event.
   a. Three bytes are sent.
   b. Eight bytes are acknowledged; window size increased by 2.
   c. Nine bytes are sent.
5. What are the three phases a connection-oriented transport service goes through?

CHAPTER 22

UPPER
OSI LAYERS

The upper layers of the OSI model—the session layer, the presentation layer, and the application layer—are considered the user layers. They are implemented primarily in software. In most protocols (such as TCP/IP and Novell), the services of these layers are implemented as a single unit called an application. For this reason, we cover them together in one chapter.

22.1   SESSION LAYER

The fifth layer of the OSI model is the session layer. The session layer establishes, maintains, and synchronizes dialogs between communicating upper layers (communication may be between either users or applications). The session layer provides a user interface to the transport layer and is therefore the first layer with which a user interacts directly (e.g., to select the level of synchronization or control needed for a transmission). The session layer also handles upper-level problems such as inadequate disk space or lack of paper for the printer. Although the session layer is described as a user layer, it is often implemented within the operating system as system software.

The concept behind the session layer is illustrated in Figure 22.1. The session layer manages the back-and-forth nature of the exchange. Imagine that we need a system to manage interactions between application programs. Within this system, user application programs must be able to communicate and exchange files or transactions with a host application program. How do we coordinate the activities of each user application program with those of the host? Do we allow each application program to transfer a file or transaction at any time? Do we provide periodic checkpoints to allow the application programs to back up their work and recover from processing? Should the process be full- or half-duplex? If half-duplex, how do we control the direction of flow? These and other issues are the responsibility of the session layer.

Figure 22.1   *Session layer dialog*

Services of the session layer:

- To coordinate connection and disconnection of dialogs between applications.
- To provide synchronization points for data exchange.
- To coordinate who sends when.
- To ensure that the data exchange is complete before the session closes (a graceful close).

Session and Transport Interaction

The concept of a graceful close illustrates an important difference between the behavior of the transport layer and that of the session layer. The transport layer can make an abrupt disconnection. The session layer, on the other hand, has an obligation to the user and cannot disconnect until the session can be brought to a graceful conclusion.

Imagine you are trying to get cash from the automated teller machine (ATM) at your bank. You are involved in a session made up of many different half-duplex information exchanges. First, you insert your ATM card into the machine and, in response to prompts, enter your PIN number, type of the transaction, and the amount of cash that you want. Then you wait while the computer checks the validity of your card, PIN number, and balance. Once all of these factors have been verified, the computer updates your balance by the amount you are withdrawing and sends a command to the ATM to give you your cash.

But assume that, just then, something goes wrong with the network and the message to give you your money does not reach the machine. Your account has been debited by the amount of your intended withdrawal, but you do not receive any cash. Fortunately, the session layer is handling the problem behind the scenes. First of all, it does not allow the transaction to close until all of the steps have been completed. It must update the account, but it leaves the update pending until it receives a confirmation from the ATM that the money has been delivered. The transport layer quits after the delivery of the message to the machine to give you your money. The session layer cannot finish until it receives confirmation that the transaction has actually been completed. It can continue the session with another transport layer connection.

The transport layer is allowed to do "some" of the job; but the session layer must do "all or none."

Session-to-Transport Communication

For any of these services to work, the session layer must communicate with the transport layer. This communication can be of three types: one-to-one, many-to-one, and one-to many. Figure 22.2 illustrates each type.

Figure 22.2 *Session-to-transport layer communication*

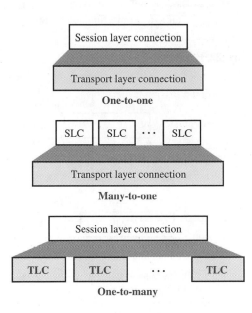

Synchronization Points

As we have seen, the transport layer is responsible for delivering a transmission with complete reliability. But what if an error is introduced after the transmission has been delivered to the destination process but before it can be used (due, perhaps, to a bug in the processing software)? The session layer provides a mechanism, called synchronization points, for recovering data that have been delivered but mishandled.

To control the flow of information and allow recovery from software or operator errors, the session layer allows reference points to be introduced into the data. Depending on the type of service being used, these points may call for user acknowledgment or may just provide a go-back facility for data recovery.

Two types of synchronization points may be used: major and minor. Major synchronization points divide an exchange into a series of dialogs. Generally, each major synchronization point must be acknowledged before the session can continue. If an error occurs, data can be recovered only up to the last major point. A session layer activity can be a single dialog or several dialogs separated by major synchronization points.

Minor synchronization points are inserted into the middle of dialogs and may or may not require confirmation, depending on the application. They are primarily security blankets. If an error occurs, the control flow can go back one or more minor synchronization points within a dialog to recover the data. The two types of synchronization points are shown in Figure 22.3.

> The major synchronization points must be confirmed. If there is an error, the flow can go back only to the last major synchronization point. The minor synchronization points do not need to be confirmed; they are only security blankets. If there is an error, the control flow can go back one or more minor synchronization points and resend the data.

Figure 22.3 *Synchronization points*

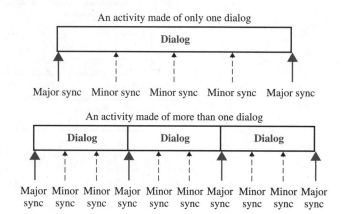

Imagine that a consumer database is being transferred from one location to another. The transfer takes three hours. Assume that after one hour and 20 minutes, a failure occurs and communication is interrupted. When communication resumes, the system can go back to the last major synchronization point and resend the data from that point.

Session Protocol Data Unit

The session layer supports 36 different types of session protocol data units (SPDUs). Fortunately, all of them follow the same general format (see Figure 22.4). The fields are as follows:

■ **SPDU identifier (SI).** The SPDU identifier indicates the type of the data unit.

■ **Length indicator (LI).** The length indicator gives the length of the SPDU parameter field.

■ **Parameter group information/parameter information (PGI/PI).** The parameter group information/parameter information field includes control information and quality of service specifications.

Figure 22.4 *SPDU*

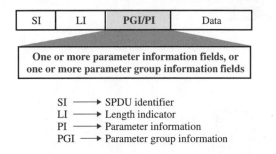

22.2 PRESENTATION LAYER

The sixth layer in the OSI model is the presentation layer. The functions performed in this layer include translation, encryption/decryption, authentication, and compression (see Figure 22.5).

Figure 22.5 *Presentation layer functions*

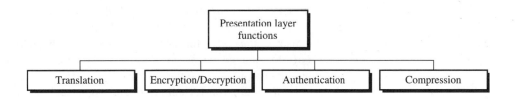

Translation

The internal representation of a piece of information might vary enormously from one machine to the other. For example, one computer may store a character string in the form of ASCII code, while another may store the same character string in the form of EBCDIC code (see Appendix A). If a piece of information is sent by one computer in ASCII format and is interpreted by the other computer in EBCDIC, the result will be gibberish. The presentation layer is responsible for solving this problem.

The problem can be solved either directly or indirectly. In the direct method (we assume simplex transmission; the half-duplex and full-duplex cases are almost the same), ASCII code is translated into EBCDIC code at the receiver. In the indirect

Figure 22.6   *Direct and indirect methods of translation*

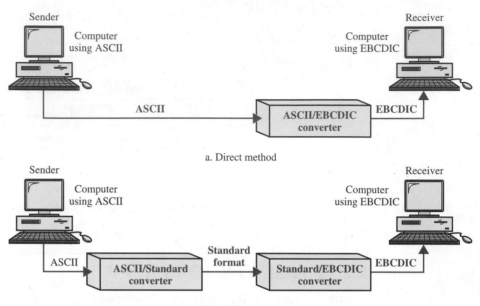

a. Direct method

b. Indirect method

method, ASCII code is translated to a standard format at the sender and translated into EBCDIC at the receiver (see Figure 22.6).

The direct method is not acceptable in most cases. If a computer is communicating with several other computers, it may need several conversion tables.

The indirect method is recommended by the OSI. The recommended model is called abstract syntax notation 1 (ASN.1). This model not only takes care of the translation problem but also handles other formatting problems such as the diverse nature of data (text, program, etc.) and the diversity in data storage (one computer may store data in one format, another computer in another format).

ASN.1 provides a mechanism for defining data types (such as integer, real, bits, strings, etc.) in an implementation-independent format. ASN.1 uses the concept of objects. An object is defined as an information entity with type and value that can be easily translated from one representation to another.

As an analogy, imagine that you want to order a glass of club soda in a country whose language has no word for club soda. Instead of continuing to order club soda and getting no response, you identify the physical elements of club soda and look up the words *carbonated* and *water* in your dictionary. Club soda is a culturally specific concept. Carbonated water, however, is an abstract description that can be translated into any number of languages. ASN.1 is the OSI equivalent to defining club soda by its component elements, carbonation and water.

Encryption/Decryption

To carry sensitive information, such as military or financial data, a system must be able to assure privacy. Microwave, satellite, and other wireless media, however, cannot be protected from the unauthorized reception (or interception) of transmissions. Even cable systems cannot always prevent unauthorized access. Cables pass through out-of-the-way areas (such as basements) that provide opportunities for malicious access to the cable and illegal reception of information.

It is unlikely that any system can completely prevent unauthorized access to transmission media. A more practical way to protect information is to alter it so that only an authorized receiver can understand it. Data tampering is not a new issue, nor is it unique to the computer era. In fact, efforts to make information unreadable by unauthorized receivers date from Julius Caesar (100–44 BC). The method used today is called the encryption and decryption of information. Encryption means that the sender transforms the original information to another form and sends the resulting unintelligible message out over the network. Decryption reverses the encryption process in order to transform the message back to its original form.

Figure 22.7 shows the basic encryption/decryption process. The sender uses an encryption algorithm and a key to transform the plaintext (as the original message is called) into a ciphertext (as the encrypted message is called). The receiver uses a decryption algorithm and a key to transform the ciphertext back to the original plaintext.

Figure 22.7   *Concept of encryption and decryption*

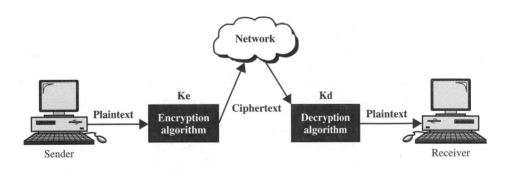

Encryption and decryption methods fall into two categories: conventional and public key (see Figure 22.8).

Conventional Methods

In conventional encryption methods, the encryption key (Ke) is known only to the sender and the decryption key (Kd) is known only to the receiver. Neither is public.

The conventional methods started a long time ago. In the beginning, encryption was achieved by what is called monoalphabetic substitution: In this type of encryption (sometimes called Caesar Cipher because it was used by Julius Caesar), each character is replaced by another character.

Figure 22.8   *Encryption/decryption methods*

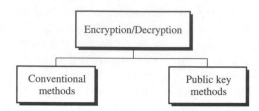

The safer form of character substitution is polyalphabetic substitution. Here again, we substitute one character for another. In this method, however, the same plaintext character is replaced by different ciphertext characters; substitution depends not only on the identity of the character but also on the position of the character in the text. For example, each of the three occurrences of the character O in the message GOOD MORNING would be replaced by a different cipher character.

An even better method is transpositional encryption. In this method, the characters retain their plaintext form but their positions are changed to create the ciphertext. This type of encryption is most efficiently accomplished by organizing the text into a two dimensional table, then interchanging the columns according to a key. For example, we can organize the plaintext into a six-column table and then reorganize the columns according to a key that indicates which column is transposed with which other column.

Most of the above methods are obsolete. The conventional encryption methods used today are based on bits, not characters. In bit-level techniques, data are first divided into blocks of bits, then altered by substitution, transposition, swapping, exclusive-or, circular shifting, and so on.

DES   One interesting example of bit-level encryption is the data encryption standard (DES). DES was designed by IBM and adopted by the U.S. government as the standard encryption method for nonmilitary and nonclassified use. The algorithm takes a 64-bit plaintext and 56-bit key. The text is put through 19 different and very complex procedures to create a 64-bit ciphertext.

Figure 22.9 shows a schematic diagram of DES. The first and the last two steps are relatively simple. However, steps 2 through 17 are complex, each requiring substeps that are combinations of transposition, substitution, swapping, exclusive-or, and circular shift. Although steps 2 through 17 are the same, each uses a different key derived from the original key. Additional complexity is achieved by having each step use the output of the previous step as input.

Public Key Methods

In conventional encryption/decryption methods, the decryption algorithm is always the inverse of the encryption algorithm and uses the same key. Anyone who knows the encryption algorithm and key can deduce the decryption algorithm and key. For this reason, security can be assured only if the entire process is kept secret. In cases where there are many senders and one receiver, however, this level of secrecy can be inconvenient. For example, imagine that a bank wants to give customers access to their

Figure 22.9 *DES*

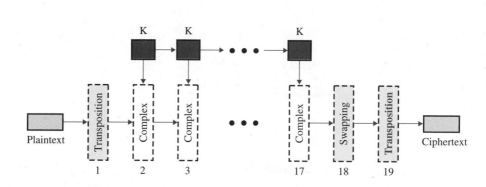

accounts. To limit each customer's access to only his or her own account using conventional encryption, the bank would have to create millions of encryption algorithms and keys. This solution is impractical, particularly with old customers leaving and new customers joining the bank all the time. On the other hand, if the bank were to give the same encryption algorithm and key to every customer, it could not guarantee the privacy of any customer.

The solution is public key encryption. In this method, every user has the same encryption algorithm and key. The decryption algorithm and key, however, are kept secret. Anyone can encrypt information, but only an authorized receiver can decrypt it. The decryption algorithm is designed in such a way that it is not the inverse of the encryption algorithm. The encryption and decryption algorithms use completely different functions, and knowing one does not enable a user to know the other. In addition, the keys are different. Even with the encryption algorithm and encryption key, an intruder still will be unable to decipher the code (at least not easily).

Figure 22.10 illustrates the idea of using public keys for customer access to bank services. The encryption algorithm and key are publicly announced. Every customer can use them. The decryption algorithm and key are kept secret and used only by the bank.

RSA Encryption   One public key encryption technique is called RSA (for Rivest, Shamir, and Adleman). Figure 22.11 shows a simplified form of the RSA algorithm, which is based on number theory.

In this example, the letter F is encrypted as number 41 using the following procedure:

- Encode character F to 6 (F is the 6th character in the alphabet).
- Choose two prime numbers (we chose 7 and 17).
- Subtract 1 from each prime and multiply the two results: $(7 - 1) \times (17 - 1) = 96$.
- Choose a number that is relatively prime with 96 (we chose 5). This number is the Ke (Ke = 5).
- Multiply the two original numbers (17×7 gives us 119).
- Calculate $6^{Ke} \% \ 119$ (modulo division), which is 41.

Now the encrypted text (41) is sent along the network. Note that even if an intruder knows the whole encryption procedure and the Ke (5), he or she cannot decipher the original character F easily because the procedure is not reversible.

Figure 22.10   *Public key encryption*

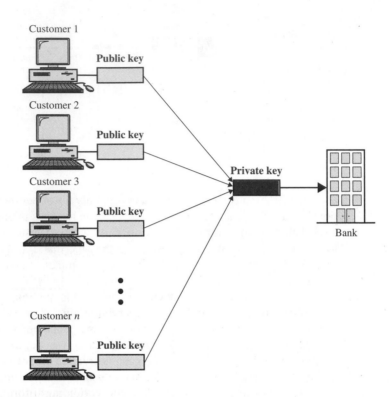

At the receiver, the number 41 is decrypted as F using a different procedure and a different key as follows:

- Subtract 1 from each prime and multiply the two results: $(7 - 1) \times (17 - 1) = 96$.
- Multiply the two original numbers $(17 \times 7$ gives us 119).
- Find a number, Kd, such that when we divide (Kd × Ke) by 96 the remainder is 1. We did and came up with 77 (Kd = 77).
- Calculate the $41^{Kd}\%$ 119 (modulo division), which is 6.
- Decode 6 as F.

It may appear that anyone with the public Ke (5) and the number 119 could find the secret Ke (77) by trial and error. However, if the private key is a large number and another very large number is chosen in place of 119, it is extremely difficult and time-consuming to do so.

Authentication

Authentication means verifying the identity of a sender. In other words, an authentication technique tries to verify that a message is coming from an authentic sender and not from an imposter. Although many methods have been developed for authentication, we

Figure 22.11   *RSA encryption and decryption*

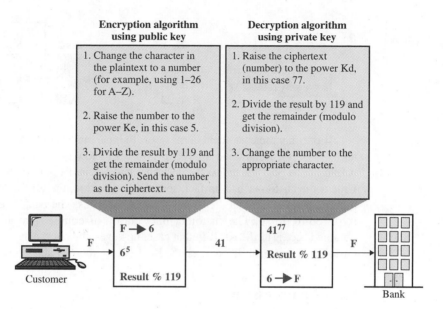

introduce only a method called digital signature, which is based on public key encryption/decryption.

The concept of a digital signature is similar to that of signing transaction documents when you do business with a bank. To withdraw large amounts of money from your bank, you go to the bank and fill out a withdrawal form. The bank requires that you sign the form and keeps the signed form on record. The signature is required in case there is any question later about authorization for the withdrawal. If, for example, you say later that you never withdrew money in that amount, the bank can show you your signature (or show it to a judge in court), proving that you did.

In network transactions you cannot personally sign the request for withdrawal. You can, however, create the equivalent of an electronic or digital signature by the way you send data.

Digital signatures add another level of encryption and decryption to the process discussed above. This time, however, a private (secret) encryption key is developed and kept by the customer while the corresponding private decryption key is kept and used by the bank. In this case, the customer uses one public and one private key (Ke) for encryption and the bank uses one private and one public key (Kd) for decryption.

Figure 22.12 shows how a digital signature works. The customer encrypts the plaintext (P) using a secret key (Ks-1, chosen and kept by the customer) and creates the first level of ciphertext (C1). The first ciphertext is encrypted again using the public key (Kp-1) to create the second ciphertext (C2). C2 is sent through the network and received by the bank. The bank uses the secret key (Ks-2) to decipher C2 into C1. It then uses the public key (Kp-2) to decipher C1 into the original plaintext. Before it does so, however, it copies C1 and stores it in a separate file.

Figure 22.12 *Signature authentication*

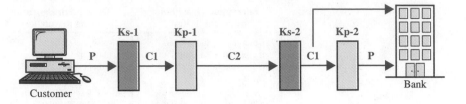

If one day the customer claims never to have made such a transaction, the bank can take C1 out of its file and apply Kp-2 to it to show that it creates P. This decryption would not be possible unless the customer had originally applied Ks-1 to P to create C1. Unless the customer had, in fact, sent the transaction, the C1 could not exist. The customer cannot claim that the bank created C1 because the bank does not have the Ks-1 required to do so. The customer may claim, of course, that an unauthorized user obtained access to the Ks-1. In that case, however, the court can point out that it was the customer's responsibility to keep the Ks-1 secret, thereby absolving the bank of liability.

Data Compression

Until we have very fast transmission media, we need to somehow speed up the transfer of data. Data compression tries to use methods to send data by reducing the number of bits. Data compression becomes particularly important when we try to send multimedia (text, audio, video) information.

The methods used to compress data are generally divided into two broad categories: lossless and lossy (see Figure 22.13).

Figure 22.13 *Data compression methods*

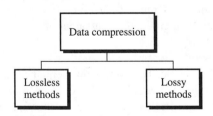

Lossless Compression

In lossless compression, the compressing and decompressing algorithms are usually the inverse of each other. In other words, after decompressing, we will get the exact data as they were before compressing. Nothing is lost. The following are some of the techniques used in lossless compression.

Run Length Compression   When data contain strings of repeated symbols (such as bits, characters, etc), the strings can be replaced by a special marker, followed by the repeated symbol, followed by the number of occurrences. For example, in Figure 22.14, the symbol # is the marker. The symbol being repeated (the run symbol) follows the marker. After the run symbol, the number of occurrences (length) is shown by a two-digit number. This method can be used in audio (silence is a run of 0s) and video (run of a picture element having the same brightness and color).

Figure 22.14   *Run length encoding*

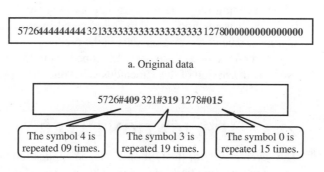

a. Original data

b. Compressed data

Statistical Compression   Another example of lossless compression is statistical compression. This method uses short codes for frequent symbols and long codes for infrequent symbols. In this way, the length of the total data is reduced tremendously. The three common encoding systems using this principle are Morse code, Huffman coding, and Lempel-Ziv coding.

■   **Morse code.** Morse code uses variable-length combinations of mark (dash) and space (dot) to encode data. It uses one-symbol codes to represent the most frequent characters and five-symbol codes for the least frequent characters. For example, it uses a dot (.) to represent the character E and three dashes and a dot (--.-) to represent character Q.

■   **Huffman coding.** Huffman encoding (see Appendix G) uses variable-length codes (a string of 0s and 1s) to encode a set of symbols.

■   **Lempel-Ziv coding.** Lempel-Ziv coding looks for repeated strings or words and stores them in variables. It then replaces occurrences of that string with a pointer to that variable. For example, the words *the*, *then*, *and*, and even some strings such as *-in* and *-tion*, are repeated many times. Each of these words or strings can be stored in separate variables and then pointers can point to them. A pointer (address) requires only a few bits, but a word may need tens of bits. This method is used in UNIX.

Relative Compression   Another way of reducing the number of bits is a method called relative or differential encoding. This is extremely useful if we are sending, for example, video. Commercial TVs send 30 frames of 0s and 1s every second. However, usually there is little difference between consecutive frames. So, instead of sending the second frame, we send only the difference between the frames. The small differences can be encoded into small streams of bits and sent after the first frame.

Lossy Compression

If the decompressed information need not be an exact replica of the original information but something very close, we can use a lossy compression method. For example, in video transmission, if an image does not have sharp discontinuities, after transformation to a mathematical expression, most of the information is contained in the first few terms. Sending only these terms may allow us to reproduce the frame with enough accuracy. The methods developed are called lossy compression methods because we will lose some of the original data in the process.

Several methods have been developed using lossy compression techniques. However, the discussion of these methods is beyond the scope of this book.

22.3   APPLICATION LAYER

The seventh layer of the OSI model is the application layer. The application layer contains whatever functions are required by the user—for example, electronic mail and airline reservations—and as such, no standardization in general is possible. However, the ITU-T has recognized that there are several common applications for which standardization is possible. We will examine five of them here: the message handling system (MHS), file transfer access and management (FTAM), virtual terminal (VT), directory system (DS) and common management information protocol (CMIP).

Message Handling System (MHS)

MHS is the OSI protocol that underlies electronic mail and store-and-forward handling. It is derived from the ITU-T X.400 series. MHS is the system used to send any message (including copies of data or files) that can be delivered in a store-and-forward manner. Store-and-forward delivery means that, instead of opening an active channel between the sender and receiver, the protocol provides a delivery service that forwards the message when a link becomes available. In most information-sharing protocols, both the sender and receiver must be able to participate in the exchange concurrently. In a store-and-forward system, the sender passes the message to a delivery system. The delivery system may not be able to transmit the message immediately, in which case it stores the message until conditions change. When the message is delivered, it is stored in the recipient's mailbox until called for.

The regular postal system provides a good analogy to the OSI model's message handling system: A sender composes and addresses a letter and deposits it in a mailbox for collection. The postal carrier collects the letter and passes it to a postal office. The postal service routes the letter through the necessary intervening post offices to the office that serves the address of the recipient. Another postal carrier delivers the letter to the mailbox of the recipient. Finally, the recipient checks his or her mailbox and finds the letter.

Similarly, in an electronic mail system, the user deposits an electronic message with an electronic mail delivery system. The delivery system cooperates with other systems to transfer the message to the mailbox of the intended receiver.

The Structure of the MHS

The structure of the OSI message handling system is shown in Figure 22.15. Each user communicates with a program or process called a user agent (UA). The UA is unique for each user (each user receives a copy of the program or process). An example of a UA is the electronic mail program associated with a specific operating system that allows a user to type and edit messages.

Figure 22.15   *MHS*

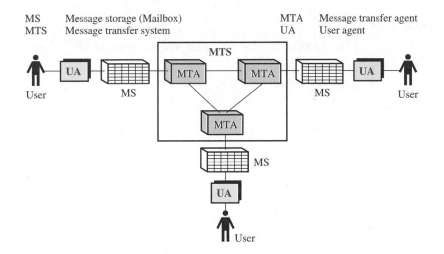

Each user has message storage (MS) which consists of disk space in a mail storage system and is usually referred to as a mailbox. Message storage can be used for storing, sending, or receiving messages.

The message storage communicates with a series of processes called message transfer agents (MTA). MTAs are like the different departments of a post office. The combined MTAs make up the message transfer system (MTS).

Message Format

The MHS standard defines the format of a message (see Figure 22.16). The body of the message corresponds to the material (like a letter) that goes inside the envelope of a conventional mailing. Every message can include the address (name) of the sender, the address (name) of the recipient, the subject of the message, and a list of anyone other than the primary recipient who is to receive a copy.

Figure 22.16 *Message format in MHS*

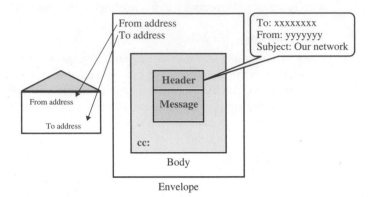

File Transfer, Access, and Management (FTAM)

The FTAM protocol is used to transfer (copy); access (read, write, or modify); and manage (control) files.

Files are stored differently in different systems. In a UNIX environment, a file is a sequence of characters (bytes). In an IBM VMS environment, on the other hand, a file is a collection of records. The organization of a file depends on the operating system of the host.

Virtual Files and Filestores

To allow the interaction of different file systems, FTAM uses the concept of virtual files and virtual filestores. A virtual filestore is a non-implementation-specific model for files and databases that can be used as an intermediary for file transfer, access, and management. The concept of filestore for files is similar to that behind ASN.1 (described earlier in this chapter as part of the presentation layer) for data.

FTAM is based on asymmetrical access of a virtual file. By asymmetrical, we mean that each transaction requires an initiator and a responder. The initiator requests the transfer of, access to, or management of a file from the responder. The responder creates a virtual file model of its actual file and allows the initiator to use the virtual model rather than the real file (see Figure 22.17). Because the model is software, it can be designed to be independent of hardware and operating system constraints. The model also creates a secure separation between the file that the initiator is allowed access to and others in the same real storage.

Attribute and Content

The creation of a virtual filestore is based on two aspects of the file in question: attributes and content. The attributes of a file are a set of properties or security measures used to control either the contents or access. FTAM distinguishes between two different types of attributes: per-content and per-access. Per-content attributes are those

Figure 22.17   *Virtual file storage*

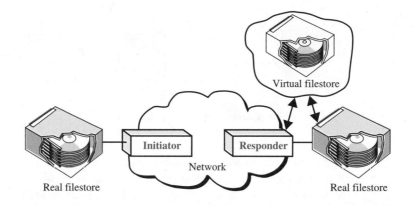

related to the contents of the file. Per-access attributes are security measures that control access to the file.

Virtual Terminal (VT)

One of the most important applications defined in the OSI model is the virtual terminal (VT).

Remote Access

Ordinarily, access to a host (such as a minicomputer, workstation, or mainframe) is gained through a terminal. Terminals are physically linked to the host. This physical connection is referred to as local access (see Figure 22.18). Each host contains software (called a terminal driver) designed to provide an interface with the specific terminal types usually attached to it. For example, an IBM computer is designed to communicate with IBM terminals, DEC computers are designed to communicate with DEC terminals, and so on.

One of the attractions of networks, however, is the ability to log on to a host to which your terminal is not directly linked. The user's terminal is connected to a local

Figure 22.18   *Local access*

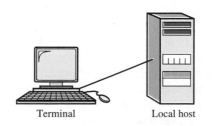

Figure 22.19 *Remote access*

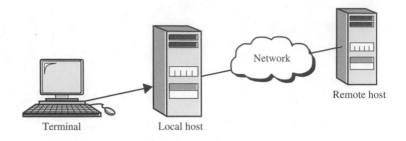

Terminal   Local host   Remote host

host, which is in turn connected through a network to a remote host (see Figure 22.19). If the terminal and remote host are of the same type (both IBM, for example), then the network merely acts as an extra-long local link. Problems arise, however, when a terminal of one type wishes to be connected (remotely or locally) to a host of another type. A machine designed to communicate with every type of terminal in the world would require hundreds of terminal drivers. The challenge to the designers of the OSI model was to create a mechanism that would allow any terminal to have access to any computer despite hardware incompatibility.

Virtual Terminal

The problem is solved by a construct called a virtual terminal (VT). A virtual terminal is an imaginary terminal (a software model of a terminal) with a set of standard characteristics that every host understands. It is a software version of a physical terminal.

A terminal that wishes to communicate with a remote host communicates to its local host. The local host contains VT software that translates the request or data received from the actual terminal into the intermediary format used by the virtual terminal. The reformatted data travel over the network to the remote host. The remote host passes the transmission to its own VT software, which transforms it from its VT format into the format used by the remote host's own terminals. The remote host, therefore, receives the input as if from a local host (the virtual terminal). After processing the request, the remote host can return a response following the same procedure in reverse (see Figure 22.20).

Directory Services (DS)

The OSI directory service is designed according to the ITU-T X.500 standard. A directory is a global source of information about many different objects. An OSI directory service is an application program used to represent and locate objects (such as people, organizations, logical groups, programs, and files) contained in an OSI directory. The type of information that a directory holds varies according to the type of the object.

To the user of a directory service, all of this information appears to be stored in a single database, located in a single host. In fact, such an arrangement would be supremely impractical. A directory is a distributed database, with each host holding only a part. The access mechanism, however, is structured so that users know of only

Figure 22.20 *Virtual terminal*

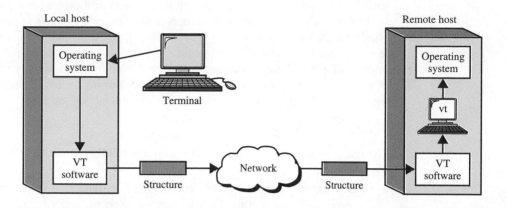

one entry port from which all information may be retrieved. (Note that the user of a directory service can be either a person or an application.)

DIB

The information contained in the directory is called the directory information base (DIB). It is stored as a set of entries, each describing one object. An entry may consist of several parts, each of which describes a different attribute of the object. For example, an entry about the ISO might include a short description of the purpose of the organization, a mailing address, phone number, and so on.

The entire structure is organized as a tree with different levels of generality at each branch.

DUAs and DSAs

Users gain access to the DS through a mechanism called a directory user agent (DUA). The DUA communicates with one or more entities called directory system agents (DSAs) contained within the directory system itself.

The DUA passes a request for information to a DSA. If the DSA knows the whereabouts of the information sought, it either fills the request or passes it on to another DSA with the necessary access, and so on. The requested information is retrieved and passed back through the successive DSAs to the DUA.

If a DSA does not know how to fill a request, it has three options: it can forward the request to a DSA with access to a different level of the tree; it can broadcast the request and wait for a response; or it can return a report of failure to the DUA.

Common Management Information Protocol (CMIP)

The ISO and the ITU-T, working together, have developed a series of services for the management of an OSI system. The most important OSI management services are called the common management information services (CMIS). The protocol for implementing those services is called the common management information protocol (CMIP).

All CMIP management occurs by monitoring and manipulating communication between OSI entities called managed objects. A managed object is a network resource such as a workstation, a switch, routing hardware or software, queuing programs, and so on. CMIP allows two OSI management-service users to perform actions on managed objects (including changing their status for efficiency or testing purposes), and to collect data about the status of those objects. By keeping logs of collected data (e.g., the number of bytes of data processed by a router over specified periods of time) and by changing the settings of a managed object and monitoring the response, a user can evaluate the performance of a system and identify problems as they arise.

CMIS

The common management information services (CMIS) have been designed to fulfill five objectives:

- **Fault management.** Services are included to detect, isolate, and correct any abnormal operation of the OSI environment. Specific tasks include diagnostic testing, fault tracing, and, when possible, fault correction.
- **Accounting management.** Services are included to track user costs and charges and, if necessary, to place limits on the use of managed objects.
- **Configuration and name management.** Services are included for initializing and closing down managed objects, for reconfiguring an open system, and for associating names with objects or sets of objects. CMIS allows a user to ensure the continuous operation of communications services in a changing environment.
- **Performance management.** Services are provided to allow users to evaluate the behavior of managed objects and the effectiveness of networking functions.
- **Security management.** Services are provided to evaluate the effectiveness and operability of network security measures.

CMISE

The specific services provided by CMIS are called common management information service elements (CMISEs). These service elements fall into three categories: management association services, management notification services, and management operation services.

Management Association Services

Management association services establish application associations to allow CMIS users to communicate. CMIS includes three association service elements. M-INITIAL-IZE is used to establish an association with a peer CMISE service. M-TERMINATE is used to obtain normal termination of an association. M-ABORT is used to obtain an abrupt release from an association.

Management Notification Services

Management notification services are used to convey notifications of managed object events. M-EVENT-REPORT is used to report managed object events to a service user.

A report can be about any event the CMISE user chooses to collect and includes a time stamp of the occurrence.

Management Operation Services

Management operation services include six services used to convey management information about system operations to a CMISE user:

■ **M-GET.** M-GET requests the retrieval of management information from a peer CMISE user.

■ **M-CANCEL-GET.** M-CANCEL-GET requests cancellation of a previous M-GET request.

■ **M-SET.** M-SET requests the modification of specific attribute values of a managed object.

■ **M-ACTION.** M-ACTION requests another user to perform an action on a managed object.

■ **M-CREATE.** M-CREATE requests another user to create a representation of an instance of a managed object and the associated management information values.

■ **M-DELETE.** M-DELETE requests a peer user to delete an instance of a managed object (the opposite of M-CREATE).

22.4 SUMMARY

■ The session layer establishes, maintains, and synchronizes dialogs between nodes.

■ Flow and error control in the session layer use synchronization points, which are reference points introduced into the data.

■ The presentation layer handles translation, encryption, authentication, and compression.

■ Encryption renders a message (plaintext) unintelligible to unauthorized personnel.

■ Decryption transforms an intentionally unintelligible message (ciphertext) into meaningful information.

■ Encryption/decryption methods can be broadly classified into the conventional methods and the public key methods.

■ In conventional encryption, the encrypting algorithm is known by everyone but the key is secret except to the sender and receiver.

■ One of the commonly used conventional encryption methods is DES.

■ In public key encryption both the encrypting algorithm and the encryption key are known to everyone but the decryption key is known only to the receiver.

■ One of the commonly used public key encryption methods is the RSA algorithm.

■ Digital signature is one of the authentication methods used today.

■ Five standard application protocols are the following:

a. Mail handling system (MHS)—the protocol for electronic mail and store-and-forward handling.

b. File transfer, access, and management (FTAM)—transfers, accesses, and manages files. FTAM uses virtual files.

c. Virtual terminal (VT)—allows dissimilar terminals or machines to communicate with one another.

d. Directory service (DS)—an application program that creates a directory to find OSI objects.

e. Common management information protocol (CMIP)—implements an OSI management service called CMIS.

22.5   PRACTICE SET

Multiple Choice

1. Encryption and decryption are functions of the _____ layer.
   a. transport
   b. session
   c. presentation
   d. application

2. Which of the following describes a user agent?
   a. a process that a user communicates with
   b. the person that is sending the message
   c. the storage facility for a spooled message
   d. the operating system used by MHS

3. Which of the following is true about FTAM?
   a. The filestore is a collection of files.
   b. Attributes and contents define a file.
   c. It was developed as a method to handle different file mechanisms on different operating systems.
   d. All of the above.

4. The _____ layer is responsible for dialog establishment, maintenance, synchronization, and termination.
   a. transport
   b. session
   c. presentation
   d. application

5. The _____ layer can disconnect a session abruptly, while the _____ layer provides for graceful closure.
   a. session; presentation
   b. session; application

   c. session; transport

   d. transport; session

6. _____ points provide a method to recover data that has been delivered but not yet used.

   a. Segmentation

   b. Concatenation

   c. Translation

   d. Synchronization

7. Which of the following are presentation layer functions?

   a. encryption of data

   b. compression of data

   c. translation of data

   d. all of the above

8. A _____ is an application program that can represent and locate objects in a directory.

   a. MHS

   b. FTAM

   c. DS

   d. CMIP

9. The _____ uses a store-and-forward method for mail delivery.

   a. MHS

   b. FTAM

   c. DS

   d. CMIP

10. The protocol to define services that manage a system based on the OSI model is called _____.

   a. MHS

   b. FTAM

   c. DS

   d. CMIP

11. A protocol that is concerned with file transfer, management, and access is _____.

   a. MHS

   b. FTAM

   c. DS

   d. CMIP

12. In MHS, the UA is _____.

   a. the user

   b. a program

      c. disk space for storage

      d. the transmission media

13. In the conventional method of encryption and decryption, which key is publicly known?

      a. Ke only

      b. Kd only

      c. Ke and Kd

      d. none

14. In the public key method of encryption and decryption, which key is publicly known?

      a. Ke only

      b. Kd only

      c. Ke and Kd

      d. none

15. In the public key method of encryption and decryption, only the receiver has possession of the _____.

      a. Ke

      b. Kd

      c. Ke and Kd

      d. none of the above

16. The main problem in conventional encryption is maintenance of the secrecy of the _____.

      a. encryption algorithm

      b. key

      c. ciphertext

      d. decryption algorithm

Exercises

1. Compare and contrast a graceful close with a T-DISCONNECT.

2. Why is the concept of the virtual terminal needed?

CHAPTER 23

TCP/IP

The transmission control protocol/internetworking protocol (TCP/IP) is a set of protocols, or a protocol suite, that defines how all transmissions are exchanged across the Internet. Named after its two most popular protocols, TCP/IP has been in active use for almost 20 years and has demonstrated its effectiveness on a worldwide scale.

23.1 OVERVIEW OF TCP/IP

In 1969, a project was funded by the Advanced Research Project Agency (ARPA), an arm of the U.S. Department of Defense. ARPA established a packet-switching network of computers linked by point-to-point leased lines called ARPANET that provided a basis for early research into networking. The conventions developed by ARPA to specify how individual computers could communicate across that network became TCP/IP.

As networking possibilities grew to include other types of links and devices, ARPA adapted TCP/IP to the demands of the new technology. As involvement in TCP/IP grew, the scope of ARPANET expanded until it became the backbone of an internetwork today referred to as the Internet.

TCP/IP and the Internet

TCP/IP and the concept of internetworking developed together, each shaping the growth of the other. Before moving more deeply into the protocols, therefore, we need to understand how TCP/IP relates to the physical entity of any internet it serves.

An internet under TCP/IP operates like a single network connecting many computers of any size and type. Internally, an internet (or, more specifically, the Internet) is an interconnection of independent physical networks (such as LANs) linked together by internetworking devices. Figure 23.1 shows the topology of a possible internet. In this example, the letters A, B, C, and so on represent hosts. A host in TCP/IP is a computer. The solid circles in the figure, numbered 1, 2, 3, and so on, are routers or gateways. The larger ovals containing roman numerals (I, II, III, etc.) represent separate physical networks.

Figure 23.1   *An internet according to TCP/IP*

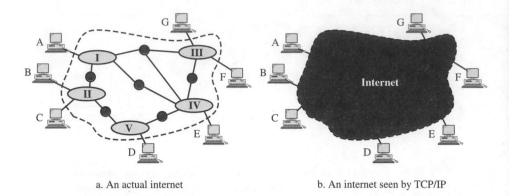

a. An actual internet   b. An internet seen by TCP/IP

To TCP/IP, the same internet appears quite differently (see again Figure 23.1). TCP/IP considers all interconnected physical networks to be one huge network. It considers all of the hosts to be connected to this larger logical network rather than to their individual physical networks.

TCP/IP and OSI

TCP was developed before OSI. Therefore, the layers in the TCP/IP protocol do not match exactly with those in the OSI model. The TCP/IP protocol is made of five layers: physical, data link, network, transport, and application. The application layer in TCP/IP can be equated with the combination of session, presentation, and application layers of the OSI model.

At the transport layer, TCP/IP defines two protocols: TCP and UDP. At the network layer, the main protocol defined by TCP/IP is IP, although there are some other protocols that support data movement in this layer.

At the physical and data link layers, TCP/IP does not define any specific protocol. It supports all of the standard and proprietary protocols discussed earlier in this book. A network in a TCP/IP internetwork can be a local area network (LAN), a metropolitan area network (MAN), or a wide area network (WAN); see Figure 23.2.

Encapsulation

Figure 23.2 also shows the encapsulation of data units at different layers of the TCP/IP protocol suite. The data unit created at the application layer is called a message. TCP or UDP creates a data unit that is called either a segment or a user datagram. The IP layer in turn will create a data unit called a datagram. The movement of the datagram across the Internet is the responsibility of the TCP/IP protocol. However, to be able to move physically from one network to another, the datagram must be encapsulated in a frame in the data link layer of the underlying network and finally transmitted as signals along the transmission media.

Figure 23.2 *TCP/IP and OSI model*

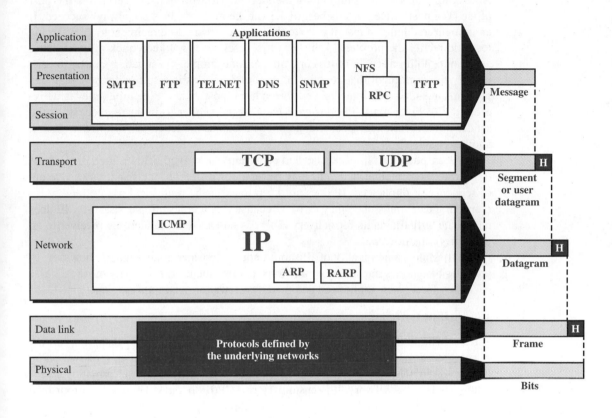

23.2   NETWORK LAYER

At the network layer (or, more accurately, the internetwork layer), TCP/IP supports the internetwork protocol (IP). IP, in turn, contains three supporting protocols: ARP, RARP, and ICMP. Each of these protocols is described in detail later in this chapter.

Internetwork Protocol (IP)

IP is the transmission mechanism used by the TCP/IP protocols. It is an unreliable and connectionless datagram protocol—a best-effort delivery service. The term *best-effort* means that IP provides no error checking or tracking. IP assumes the unreliability of the underlying layers and does its best to get a transmission through to its destination, but with no guarantees. As we have seen in previous chapters, transmissions along physical networks can be destroyed for a number of reasons. Noise can cause bit errors during transmission across a medium; a congested router may discard a datagram if it is unable to relay it before a time limit runs out; routing quirks can end in looping and the ultimate destruction of a datagram; and disabled links may leave no usable path to the destination.

If reliability is important, IP must be paired with a reliable protocol such as TCP. An example of a more commonly understood best-effort delivery service is the post office. The post office does its best to deliver the mail but does not always succeed. If an unregistered letter is lost, it is up to the sender or would-be recipient to discover the loss and rectify the problem. The post office itself does not keep track of every letter and cannot notify a sender of loss or damage. An example of a situation similar to pairing IP with a protocol that contains reliability functions is a self-addressed, stamped postcard included in a letter mailed through the post office. When the letter is delivered, the receiver mails the postcard back to the sender to indicate success. If the sender never receives the postcard, he or she assumes the letter was lost and sends out another copy.

IP transports data in packets called datagrams (described below), each of which is transported separately. Datagrams may travel along different routes and may arrive out of sequence or duplicated. IP does not keep track of the routes and has no facility for reordering datagrams once they arrive. Because it is a connectionless service, IP does not create virtual circuits for delivery. There is no call setup to alert the receiver to an incoming transmission.

The limited functionality of IP should not be considered a weakness, however. IP provides bare-bones transmission functions that free the user to add only those facilities necessary for a given application and thereby allows for maximum efficiency.

Datagram

Packets in the IP layer are called datagrams. Figure 23.3 shows the IP datagram format. A datagram is a variable-length packet (up to 65,536 bytes) consisting of two parts: header and data. The header can be from 20 to 60 bytes and contains information essential to routing and delivery. It is customary in TCP/IP to show the header in four-byte sections. A brief description of each field is in order.

- **Version.** The first field defines the version number of the IP. The current version is 4 (IPv4), with a binary value of 0100.

- **Header length (HLEN).** The HLEN field defines the length of the header in multiples of four bytes. The four bits can represent a number between 0 and 15, which, when multiplied by 4, gives a maximum of 60 bytes.

- **Service type.** The service type field defines how the datagram should be handled. It includes bits that define the priority of the datagram. It also contains bits that specify the type of service the sender desires such as the level of throughput, reliability, and delay.

- **Total length.** The total length field defines the total length of the IP datagram. It is a two-byte field (16 bits) and can define up to 65,536 bytes.

- **Identification.** The identification field is used in fragmentation. A datagram, when passing through different networks, may be divided into fragments to match the network frame size. When this happens, each fragment is identified with a sequence number in this field.

- **Flags.** The bits in the flags field deal with fragmentation (the datagram can or cannot be fragmented; can be the first, middle, or last fragment; etc.).

Figure 23.3 *IP datagram*

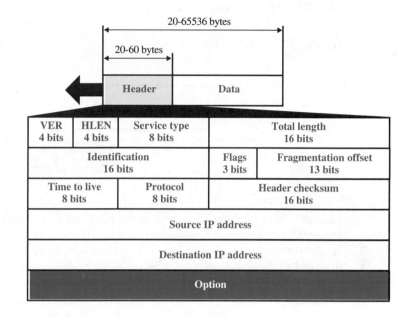

- **Fragmentation offset.** The fragmentation offsct is a pointer that shows the offset of the data in the original datagram (if it is fragmented).

- **Time to live.** The time to live field defines the number of hops a datagram can travel before it is discarded. The source host, when it creates the datagram, scts this field to an initial value. Then, as the datagram travels through the Internet, router by router, each router decrements this value by 1. If this value becomes 0 before the datagram reaches its final destination, the datagram is discarded. This prevents a datagram from going back and forth forever between routers.

- **Protocol.** The protocol field defines which upper-layer protocol data are encapsulated in the datagram (TCP, UDP, ICMP, etc.).

- **Source address.** The source address field is a four-byte (32-bit) Internet address. It identifies the original source of the datagram.

- **Destination address.** The destination address field is a four-byte (32-bit) Internet address. It identifies the final destination of the datagram.

- **Options.** The options field gives more functionality to the IP datagram. It can carry fields that control routing, timing, management, and alignment.

Addressing

In addition to the physical addresses (contained on NICs) that identify individual devices, the Internet requires an additional addressing convention: an address that identifies the connection of a host to its network.

Each Internet address consists of four bytes (32 bits), defining three fields: class type, netid, and hostid. These parts are of varying lengths, depending on the class of the address (see Figure 23.4).

Figure 23.4 *Internet address*

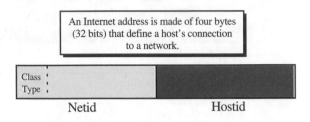

Classes To accommodate the vast numbers of addresses required for global interconnectivity, the class type fields vary in length. There are currently five different field-length patterns in use, each defining a class of address. The different classes are designed to cover the needs of different types of organizations. For example, class A addresses are numerically the lowest. They use only one byte to identify class type and netid, and leave three bytes available for hostid numbers. This division means that class A networks can accommodate far more hosts than can class B or class C networks, which provide two- and one-byte fields, respectively. Currently both class A and class B are full. Addresses are available in class C only.

Class D is reserved for multicast addresses. Multicasting allows copies of a datagram to be passed to a select group of hosts rather than to an individual host. It is similar to broadcasting, but, where broadcasting requires that a packet be passed to all possible destinations, multicasting allows transmission to a selected subset. Class E addresses are reserved for future use. Figure 23.5 shows the structure of each class of IP address.

Figure 23.5 *Internet classes*

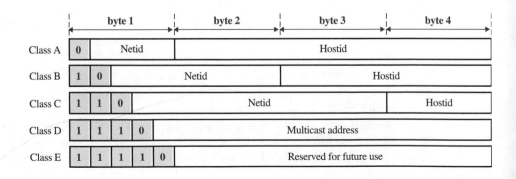

Figure 23.6   *IP addresses in decimal notation*

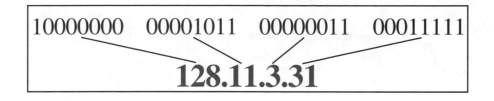

Figure 23.7   *Class ranges of Internet addresses*

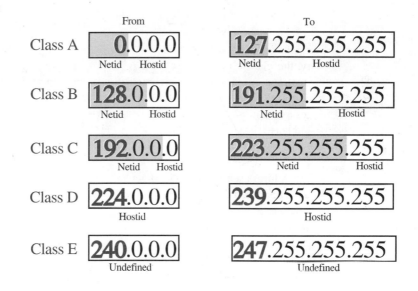

To make the 32-bit form shorter and easier to read, Internet addresses are usually written in decimal form with decimal points separating the bytes. Figure 23.6 shows the bit pattern and decimal formats of a possible address.

Looking at the first byte of an address in decimal form allows us to determine at a glance to which class a particular address belongs (see Figure 23.7).

Nodes with More Than One Address   As we have said, an internet address defines the node's connection to its network. It follows, therefore, that any device connected to more than one network (e.g., any router) must have more than one internet address. In fact, a device has a different address for each network connected to it.

A Sample Internet   An internet address specifies both the network to which a host belongs (netid) and the host itself (hostid). Figure 23.8 gives an example of an internet made up of LANs (two Ethernets and a token ring are illustrated). The addresses are all class B. Routers are indicated by circles containing Rs. Gateways are indicated by boxes containing Gs. Each has a separate address for each of its connected networks. One other computer is shown with addresses on two networks. The figure also shows the network addresses in boldface. A network address is the netid with the hostid part set to 0s. The three network addresses in the figure are 129.8.0.0, 165.3.0.0, and 145.42.0.0.

Figure 23.8   *Network and hosts addresses in an internet*

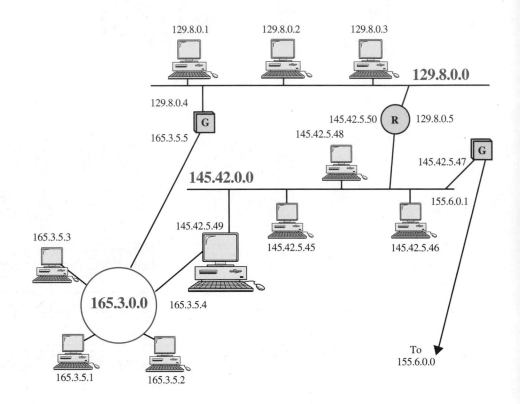

Other Protocols in the Network Layer

TCP/IP supports three more protocols in the network layer: ARP, RARP, and ICMP.

Address Resolution Protocol (ARP)

The address resolution protocol (ARP) is used to associate an IP address with the physical address. On a typical physical network, such as a LAN, each device on a link is identified by a physical or station address usually imprinted on the network interface card (NIC).

Physical addresses have local jurisdiction and can be changed easily. For example, if the NIC on a particular machine fails, the physical address changes. The IP addresses, on the other hand, have universal jurisdiction and cannot be changed. ARP is used to find the physical address of the node when its Internet address is known.

Anytime a host, or a router, needs to find the physical address of another host on its network, it formats an ARP query packet that includes the IP address and broadcasts it over the network (see Figure 23.9). Every host on the network receives and processes the ARP packet, but only the intended recipient recognizes its internet address and sends back its physical address. The host holding the datagram adds the address of the target host both to its cache memory and to the datagram header, then sends the datagram on its way.

Figure 23.9 *ARP*

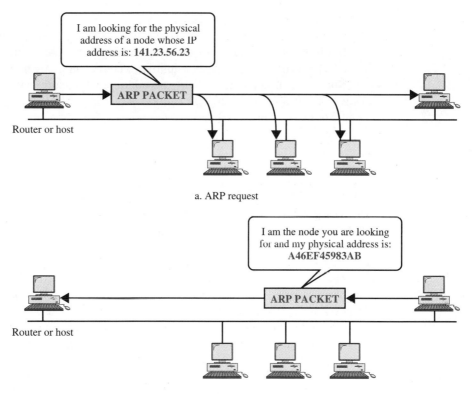

a. ARP request

b. ARP response

Reverse Address Resolution Protocol (RARP)

The reverse address resolution protocol (RARP) allows a host to discover its internet address when it knows only its physical address. The question here is, Why do we need RARP? A host is supposed to have its internet address stored on its hard disk!

Answer: True, true. But what if the host is a diskless computer? Or what if the computer is being connected to the network for the first time (when it is being booted)? Or what if you get a new computer but decide to keep the old NIC?

RARP works much like ARP. The host wishing to retrieve its internet address broadcasts an RARP query packet that contains its physical address to every host on its physical network. A server on the network recognizes the RARP packet and returns the host's internet address.

Internet Control Message Protocol (ICMP)

The internet control message protocol (ICMP) is a mechanism used by hosts and gateways to send notification of datagram problems back to the sender.

As we saw above, IP is essentially an unreliable and connectionless protocol. ICMP, however, allows IP to inform a sender if a datagram is undeliverable. A datagram travels from gateway to gateway until it reaches one that can deliver it to its final destination. If a gateway is unable to route or deliver the datagram because of unusual conditions (disabled links, or the device is on fire) or because of network congestion, ICMP allows it to inform the original source.

ICMP uses echo test/reply to test whether a destination is reachable and responding. It also handles both control and error messages, but its sole function is to report problems, not correct them. Responsibility for correction lies with the sender.

Note that a datagram carries only the addresses of the original sender and the final destination. It does not know the addresses of the previous router(s) that passed it along. For this reason, ICMP can send messages only to the source, not to an intermediate router.

23.3   TRANSPORT LAYER

The transport layer is represented in TCP/IP by two protocols: TCP and UDP. Of these, UDP is the simpler; it provides nonsequenced transport functionality when reliability and security are less important than size and speed. Most applications, however, require reliable end-to-end delivery and so make use of TCP.

The IP delivers a datagram from a source host to a destination host, making it a host-to-host protocol. Today's operating systems, however, support multiuser and multiprocessing environments. An executing program is called a process. A host receiving a datagram may be running several different concurrent processes, any one of which is a possible destination for the transmission. In fact, although we have been talking about hosts sending messages to other hosts over a network, it is actually a source process that is sending a message to a destination process.

The transport protocols of the TCP/IP suite define a set of conceptual connections to individual processes called protocol ports or, more simply, ports. A protocol port is a destination point (usually a buffer) for storing data for use by a particular process. The interface between processes and their corresponding ports is provided by the operating system of the host.

The IP is a host-to-host protocol, meaning that it can deliver a packet from one physical device to another. TCP/IP's transport level protocols are port-to-port protocols that work on top of the IP protocols to deliver the packet from the originating port to the IP services at the start of a transmission, and from the IP services to the destination port at the end (see Figure 23.10).

Each port is defined by a positive integer address carried in the header of a transport layer packet. An IP datagram uses the host's 32-bit internet address. A frame at the

Figure 23.10   *Port-to-port addresses*

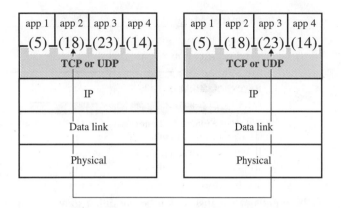

transport level uses the process port address of 16 bits, enough to allow the support of up to 65,536 (00000 to 65535) ports.

User Datagram Protocol (UDP)

The user datagram protocol (UDP) is the simpler of the two standard TCP/IP transport protocols. It is an end-to-end transport level protocol that adds only port addresses, checksum error control, and length information to the data from the upper layer. The packet produced by the UDP is called a user datagram (see Figure 23.11). A brief description of fields is in order.

- **Source port address.** The source port address is the address of the application program that has created the message.
- **Destination port address.** The destination port address is the address of the application program that will receive the message.
- **Total length.** The total length field defines the total length of the user datagram in bytes.
- **Checksum.** The checksum is a 16-bit field used in error detection.

   UDP provides only the basic functions needed for end-to-end delivery of a transmission. It does not provide any sequencing or reordering functions, and cannot specify the damaged packet when reporting an error (for which it must be paired with ICMP). UDP can discover that an error has occurred; ICMP can then inform the sender that a user datagram has been damaged and discarded. Neither, however, has the ability to specify which packet has been lost. UDP contains only a checksum; it does not contain an ID or sequencing number for a particular data segment.

Transmission Control Protocol (TCP)

The transmission control protocol (TCP) provides full transport layer services to applications. TCP is a reliable stream transport port-to-port protocol. The term *stream,* in this context, means connection-oriented: a connection must be established between

Figure 23.11 *UDP datagram format*

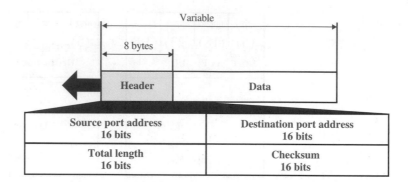

both ends of a transmission before either may transmit data. By creating this connection, TCP generates a virtual circuit between sender and receiver that is active for the duration of a transmission. (Connections for the duration of an entire exchange are different, and are handled by session functions in individual applications.) TCP begins each transmission by alerting the receiver that more datagrams are on their way (connection establishment) and ends each transmission with a connection termination. In this way, the receiver knows to expect the entire transmission rather than a single packet.

IP and UDP treat multiple datagrams belonging to a single transmission as entirely separate units, unrelated to each other. The arrival of each datagram at the destination is therefore a separate event, unexpected by the receiver. TCP, on the other hand, is responsible for the reliable delivery of the entire stream of bits contained in the data unit originally generated by the sending application. Reliability is ensured by provision for error detection and retransmission of damaged frames; all segments must be received and acknowledged before the transmission is considered complete and the virtual circuit is discarded.

At the sending end of each transmission, TCP divides long transmissions into smaller data units and packages each into a frame called a segment. Each segment includes a sequencing number for reordering after receipt, together with an acknowledgment ID number and a window-size field for sliding window ARQ. Segments are carried across network links inside of IP datagrams. At the receiving end, TCP collects each datagram as it comes in and reorders the transmission based on sequence numbers.

The TCP Segment

The scope of the services provided by TCP requires that the segment header be extensive (see Figure 23.12). A comparison of the TCP segment format with that of a UDP user datagram shows the differences between the two protocols. TCP provides a comprehensive range of reliability functions but sacrifices speed (connections must be established, acknowledgments waited for, etc.). Because of its smaller frame size, UDP is much faster than TCP, but at the expense of reliability. A brief description of each field is in order.

Figure 23.12   *TCP segment format*

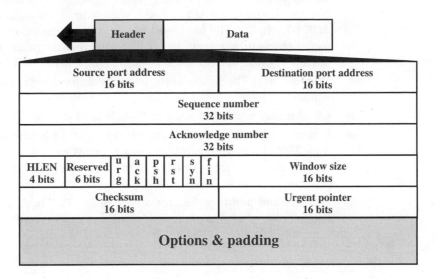

- **Source port address.** The source port address defines the application program in the source computer.

- **Destination port address.** The destination port address defines the application program in the destination computer.

- **Sequence number.** A stream of data from the application program may be divided into two or more TCP segments. The sequence number field shows the position of the data in the original data stream.

- **Acknowledgment number.** The 32-bit acknowledgment number is used to acknowledge the receipt of data from the other communicating device. This number is valid only if the ACK bit in the control field (explained later) is set. In this case, it defines the byte sequence number that is next expected.

- **Header length (HLEN).** The four-bit HLEN field indicates the number of 32-bit (four-byte) words in the TCP header. The four bits can define a number up to 15. This is multiplied by 4 to give the total number of bytes in the header. Therefore, the size of the header can be a maximum of 60 bytes (4 × 15). Since the minimum required size of the header is 20 bytes, 40 bytes are thus available for the options section.

- **Reserved.** A six-bit field is reserved for future use.

- **Control.** Each bit of the six-bit control field functions individually and independently. A bit can either define the use of a segment or serve as a validity check for other fields. The urgent bit, when set, validates the urgent pointer field. Both this bit and the pointer indicate that the data in the segment are urgent. The ACK bit, when set, validates the acknowledgment number field. Both are used together and have different functions, depending on the segment type. The PSH bit is used to inform the sender that a higher throughput is needed. If possible, data must be pushed through paths with higher throughput.The reset bit is used to reset the connection when there is confusion in the sequence numbers. The SYN bit is used for sequence number synchronization in three types of segments: connection request, connection confirmation (with the ACK bit set), and confirmation acknowledgment (with the ACK bit set). The FIN bit is used in connection termination in three types of segments: termination request, termination confirmation (with the ACK bit set), and acknowledgment of termination confirmation (with the ACK bit set).

■ **Window size.** The window is a 16-bit field that defines the size of the sliding window.

■ **Checksum.** The checksum is a 16-bit field used in error detection.

■ **Urgent pointer.** This is the last required field in the header. Its value is valid only if the URG bit in the control field is set. In this case, the sender is informing the receiver that there are urgent data in the data portion of the segment. This pointer defines the end of urgent data and the start of normal data.

■ **Options and padding**. The remainder of the TCP header defines the optional fields. They are used to convey additional information to the receiver or for alignment purposes.

23.4   APPLICATION LAYER

The application layer in TCP/IP is equivalent to the combined session, presentation, and application layers in the OSI model. There are many protocols defined at this layer, of which we cover only a few of the most popular.

Before discussing specific protocols at the application level, we need to understand the concept of client-server at this level. One of the benefits of networks is the ability to distribute processing responsibilities. When a program at one location enlists the services of a program running at another site, the system is called client-server. An application program, in the role of client, issues a request for services to a second application program, in the role of server, which provides the requested service. All of the application programs in the TCP/IP protocol use the client-server paradigm (see Figure 23.13).

Figure 23.13   *The concept of client-server*

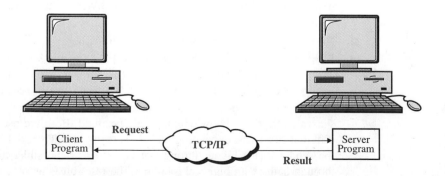

Domain Name System (DNS)

A good example of a TCP/IP client-server application is the domain name system (DNS). Up to this point, the identification systems we have examined have all been designed with machines and software in mind, and so have used bit patterns and numbers. But the actual users of the Internet are people, and people prefer names to numbers. DNS identifies each host on the Internet with a unique name that identifies it as unambiguously as its IP address. Given the domain name, a program can obtain the IP address associated with it by engaging the services of a name server in a client-server session.

To create names that are unique, and at the same time decentralized and easy to change, the TCP/IP designers have chosen a hierarchical system made up of a number of labels separated by dots (e.g., chal.atc.fhda.edu). A host can have any number of identifying labels to make its name unique as long as the length of the label does not exceed 63 characters.

DNS is implemented using a tree in which each node represents one possible label. The right-most label in the name corresponds to the level of the tree closest to the root (here called the lowest), and the left-most label to the level farthest from the root (the highest). The tree is divided into three different domains: generic, country, and reverse (see Figure 23.14).

Generic Domain

The generic domain (also called the organization domain), divides registered hosts according to their generic behavior. Generic domain names, read left to right, start with the most specific information given about the host (e.g., the name of the workstation) and become more and more general with each label until they reach the rightmost label, which describes the broadest affiliation of the named host: the nature of the organization (e.g., com for commercial).

Looking at the tree, we see that the first level of the generic domain convention allows seven possible three-character labels describing organization type:

- **com.** Commercial organization.
- **edu.** Educational institution.
- **gov.** Government institution.
- **int.** International organization.
- **mil.** Military group.
- **net.** Network support center.
- **org.** Organizations other than those listed above.

Each domain name corresponds to a particular IP address. To find the address, the resolution application begins searching with the first-level label (the organization). As a match is found, a pointer leads to the next level and finally to the associated IP address.

Country Domain

The country domain convention follows the same format as generic domain but uses two-character country abbreviations (e.g., us for U.S.A.) in place of the three-character organizational abbreviations at the first level. Second-level labels can be organizational,

Figure 23.14   *Domain name system*

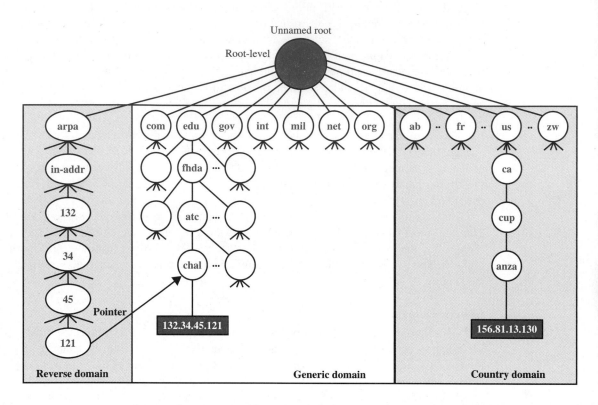

or they can be more specific national designations. The United States, for example, uses state abbreviations as a subdivision of us (e.g., ca.us).

Figure 23.14 also shows the country domain version of the generic address. The address anza.cup.ca.us translates to DeAnza College in Cupertino in California in the United States.

Reverse Domain

When you have the IP address but need the domain name, you use the reverse domain functions of the DNS (see Figure 23.14).

To use reverse domain, you give the server the IP address. DNS appends arpa.inaddr at the beginning. However, for example, 132.34.45.121 becomes arpa.inaddr.132.34.45.121. The system then starts from the top of the tree (arpa) and searches until it finds the number. Once the number is found, a pointer leads it to the associated domain name.

TELNET

A second important and extremely popular TCP/IP application is TELNET, which is TCP/IP's client-server process for remote login.

Remote login allows a user at one site to gain access to a computer at another site (see Figure 23.15). As you can imagine, this brings up issues of security. TELNET protects the server against unlawful access by requiring would-be users to supply login and password identifiers.

Figure 23.15   *Local versus remote login*

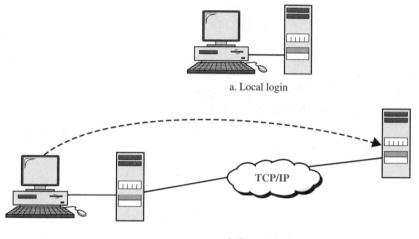

a. Local login

b. Remote login

To use TELNET, a user invokes a TELNET client at his own site and establishes a connection with a TELNET server at the remote site. TELNET then relays the keystrokes from the user's keyboard to the remote computer as if they had been typed at the remote computer. TELNET also carries the output of the remote computer back to the user's screen. (Note that the user's hardware is communicating with software in the remote server.)

Virtual Terminals

To bring about homogeneity between the user and the remote server, TELNET provides translation services between the two machines.

The TELNET client transforms the output from the actual terminal to standard code. The information in the standard code is sent to the TELNET server in the remote host. The TELNET server will transform this information into characters accepted by the remote host. In this process, the remote host is fooled into thinking that a terminal is locally connected to it. In other words, a virtual terminal (VT) is connected to the remote host. Figure 23.16 illustrates the process. The concept of virtual terminals makes a complex process, if not simple, at least straightforward, and relieves one of the great potential impediments to true universal connectivity: that of connecting multiple incompatible terminals to a single remote server.

Figure 23.16   *TELNET*

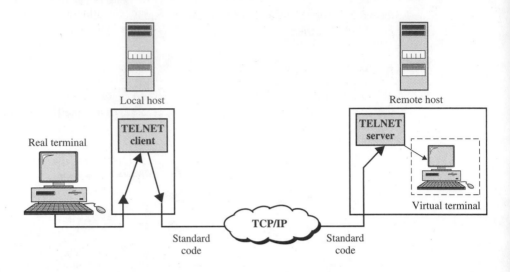

File Transfer Protocols

Two application programs are used to transfer files from a server to a client host: trivial file transfer protocol (TFTP) and file transfer protocol (FTP).

Trivial File Transfer Protocol (TFTP)

The trivial file transfer protocol (TFTP) is the simpler of the two file transfer protocols, and is intended for applications that do not require complex interaction between client and server. TFTP allows a local host to obtain files from a remote host but does not provide security or reliability (see Figure 23.17). By restricting its services this way, TFTP is simpler to use and smaller to store than FTP.

TFTP does not require the reliability of a connection-oriented base protocol such as TCP and instead uses the fundamental packet delivery services offered by UDP.

Figure 23.17   *TFTP*

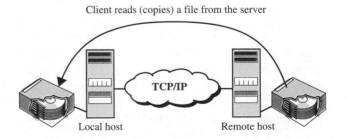

TFTP does, however, include some basic connection and error detection/retransmission features to ensure that the file requested does indeed arrive.

Because of TFTP's simplicity and small size, specific applications can be encoded into read-only memory, making it useful for hosts that lack the disk capacity to store more elaborate file transfer protocols.

File Transfer Protocol (FTP)

The file transfer protocol (FTP) is the standard mechanism provided by TCP/IP for copying a file from one host to another. FTP messages are encapsulated in TCP, and are both reliable and secure. FTP uses the TELNET protocol and requires the user to supply login and password identifiers before transferring files.

FTP differs from other client-server applications in that it establishes two connections (virtual circuits) between the hosts (see Figure 23.18). One connection is used for data transfer, the other for control information.

Figure 23.18   *FTP*

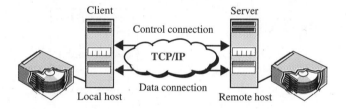

The control connection, as it is called, is used for commands, replies, and process updates. It uses minimize delay type of service (TOS), and remains on for the entire period of the exchange. While the data transfer is occurring across the data connection, the control connection is issuing such reassurances to the user interface as file transfer beginning, expected duration x minutes, data transfer complete, and x bytes transferred successfully (see Figure 23.19).

Figure 23.19   *Client and server in FTP*

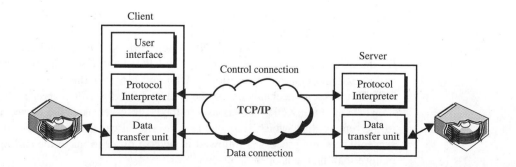

File Access Using NFS and RPC

Network File System (NFS)

The network file system (NFS) is a file access protocol. FTP and TFTP transfer entire files from a server to the client host. A file access service, on the other hand, makes file systems on a remote machine visible, as though they were on your own machine but without actually transferring the files. NFS allows you to edit a file on another machine exactly as you would if it were on your own machine. It even allows you to transfer files from the server to a third host not directly connected to either of you.

Remote Procedure Call (RPC)

NFS works by invoking the services of a second protocol called remote procedure call (RPC). Figure 23.20 shows a local procedure call (in this case, a C program calling the open function to access a disk).

Figure 23.20   *Concept of local procedure call*

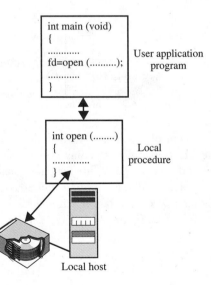

Local host

    RPC transfers the procedure call to another machine. Using RPC, local procedure calls are mapped onto appropriate RPC function calls. Figure 23.21 illustrates the process: a program issues a call to the NFS client process. The NFS client formats the call for the RPC client and passes it along. The RPC client transforms the data to a format called external data representation (XDR) and provides the interface with the actual TCP/IP transport mechanisms. At the remote host, the RPC server retrieves the call, translates it out of XDR, and passes it to the NFS server. The NFS server relays the call to the remote disk, which responds as if to a local call and opens the file to the NFS server. The same process is followed in reverse order to make the calling application believe that the file is open on its own host.

Figure 23.21   *Concept of remote procedure call*

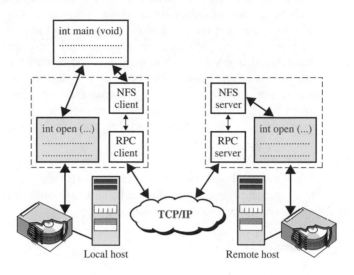

Electronic Mail: SMTP

One of the most familiar network services is electronic mail. The TCP/IP protocol that supports electronic mail on the Internet is called simple mail transfer protocol (SMTP).

What Is Electronic Mail?

Electronic mail is a widely used network service. It is a system for sending messages or files to other computer users based on mailbox addresses rather than a direct host-to-host exchange, and supports mail exchange between users on the same or different computers. Unlike other client-server applications, e-mail allows users to send anything from short notes to extensive files without worrying about the current availability of the receiving host. Some e-mail uses are as follows:

- Send a single message to one or many recipients.
- Send messages that include text, voice, video, or graphics.
- Send messages to users on networks outside the Internet.
- Send messages calling for a response from a computer program rather than a user.

E-mail design echoes the postal system. Addresses are used to identify both the recipient and sender of a message (return address). Messages that cannot be delivered within a specified amount of time are returned to the sender. Every user on the network has a private mailbox. Received mail is stored in the mailbox until the recipient removes or discards it.

What makes electronic mail different from other message transfer services provided by the Internet is a mechanism called spooling, which allows a user to send mail even if a network is currently disconnected or the receiving machine is not operational. When a message is sent, a copy is placed in a storage facility called a spool. A spool resembles a queue with some fundamental differences. Messages in a queue are processed on a first-come, first-served basis. Messages in a spool are processed on a first-come, first-*searched* basis. Once in the spool, a message is searched every 30 seconds by a client process running in the background. The background client looks for new messages and not-yet-sent old messages and attempts delivery. If the client process is unable to deliver a message, it marks the message with the time of the attempted delivery, leaves it in the spool, and repeats the attempt at a later time. If all attempts at delivery fail, the message may be deemed undeliverable after several days and returned to the mailbox of the sender. A message is considered delivered only when both client and server agree that the recipient has seen and disposed of it. Until then copies are kept in both the sending spool and the receiving mailbox.

Electronic Mail Addresses

Electronic mail addresses consist of two parts (see Figure 23.22). The first part is the mailbox identifying name followed by an @ symbol and the domain name of the destination (e.g., Rocco@somecompany.org).

Figure 23.22   *Electronic mail addresses*

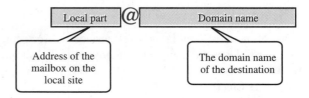

At sites using protocols other than TCP/IP, the formats may differ. For example, you may see a mail address that looks like xxxx%yyyy@zzzz.

Aliases   It is possible to forward messages to more than one recipient at a time by including several mailing addresses. However, in situations where frequent messages are sent to the same group of people, this process can become tedious and time-wasting. Many systems provide a solution called electronic mailing lists or mailbox groups. An e-mail facility called mail alias expansion allows one name (called an alias) to refer to an entirely different name or even to multiple recipients. For example, the accounting department of a company might need to send frequent reports to the managers of all departments as well as the executive board. They can set up an electronic mailing list under an alias (e.g., bigwigs) that includes the e-mail addresses of everyone receiving those reports. When a report is distributed, the sender puts the alias as the recipient, but all members of the mailing list receive the transmission.

Another advantage of aliases is that one person can have several mail names, including first and last names, maiden names, married names, nicknames, and job titles. Aliases are stored in a database accessed by an alias expansion program. Once a message has been sent to the spooler, the mail interface program passes the recipient name to the alias expander, which checks it against aliases stored in its database. If a match is found, the existing recipient address is mapped to its official address (or all of the indi-

Figure 23.23   *Two-directional electronic mail*

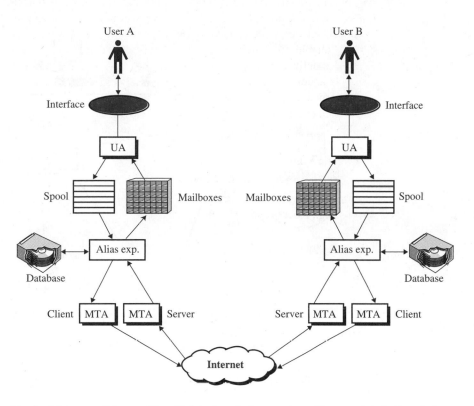

vidual addresses of the mailing list) before being sent on. If no match is found, it may mean that no alias exists or that the alias is not stored locally and will be found by the recipient system.

Figure 23.23 illustrates the process of sending and receiving e-mail as described above. The box labeled UA is the user agent. The user agent supports the user interface and provides an interface to the internals of the system. A user agent is like a good secretary—it goes to the mailbox to retrieve your incoming messages, mails your outgoing messages, and hands you the means to write messages (in this case, a word processor rather than pencil and paper). The boxes labeled MTA are the mail transfer agents, which serve as the mail system's interface with the network. SMTP defines the specifications for each of these processes using TCP/IP.

Simple Network Management Protocol (SNMP)

The simple network management protocol (SNMP) provides a set of fundamental operations for monitoring and maintaining an internet.

Agents and Management Information Bases (MIBs)

SNMP uses the concept of manager and managed devices. Every host or router can be a managed device. A few hosts are managers (see Figure 23.24). To aid in monitoring,

Figure 23.24   *SNMP*

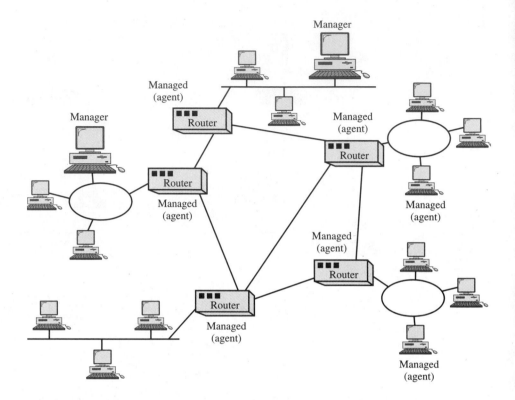

every managed device contains a combination of hardware and software called an agent, which acts as a bookkeeper for the host and can be accessed by a manager.

Inside of each agent is a management information base (MIB). The MIB is a list of the variables that the protocol supports and tracks (see Figure 23.25). A variable is a performance record of an agent (e.g., the number of bytes that have come in and gone out of the host over a given time period). Managers can check variables to see if the numbers look healthy. They can also set the value of a variable to change or monitor its behavior. Management on TCP/IP internetworks is accomplished by setting and checking these variables.

To monitor the network, the management software polls the agents looking for problems. Alternatively, when an agent is in trouble (e.g., a board burns out), rather than wait to be polled and tested, it issues a trap (like an S.O.S.). If the management software is listening, the trap gets read. Intelligent management software can fix the problem automatically or page the system administrator.

Security and Reliability

SNMP is a simple request/response protocol built upon UDP. As such, it provides little reliability and no security. Because most monitoring and maintenance is done using single datagrams, the level of reliability available through UDP usually is sufficient.

Figure 23.25   *Use of variables in network management*

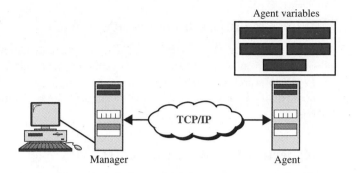

The lack of security, however, raises problems for the management of confidential systems. In 1993, a version of SNMP called SNMPv2 was proposed. The new protocol does provide security and rectifies other weaknesses of SNMP. It is, however, less a set of operations than a framework upon which applications can be built. As such, it is more difficult to implement, though more powerful, than SNMP.

Gopher

Gopher was developed at the University of Minnesota (home of the Golden Gophers). It is a menu-driven application program that can navigate through the Internet and find a requested document. By selecting an item from a menu, a user can retrieve information or go to another menu. Gopher hides computer boundaries completely, and makes information on a large set of computers appear to be part of a single, integrated set of menus.

Gopher is a client-server application program using multiple servers. Gopher uses the concept of bookmarks to allow a user to record the location of information for future use.

Archie

Archie, short for archives, is an automated title-search application program that finds all files having a given name. Archie has a database that associates all file names in the Internet with the names of the hosts. Many hosts have Archie databases all over the world. The one in the United States is archie.internic.net, which can be accessed through TELNET.

Veronica

Veronica is also an automated title-search application program. It uses a worldwide index to computerized archives. Veronica uses the services of gopher. It searches gopher menus all over the world to find a file. You can even use conditional expression to narrow down the search. For example, Programming, "NOT FORTRAN" can find all files whose title contains the word *programming* but not the word *FORTRAN*.

Wide Area Information Service (WAIS)

Wide Area Information Service (WAIS) is a content-search service that finds the name of a file given some information about the contents. Of course, it is very difficult for WAIS to search the contents of all the files in the world. Therefore, the database has been divided into different sources. The user must limit the search to a particular source.

Hypertext Transfer Protocol (HTTP)

The hypertext transfer protocol (HTTP) is an advanced file-retrieving application program that can access distributed and linked documents on the World Wide Web. It can access linked textual documents called hypertext or linked documents containing images, graphics, and sounds called hypermedia.

Messages in HTTP are divided into two broad categories: request and response. So far only three request packets and one type of response packet have been defined.

The request command is sent from the client to the server. The response command is sent from the server to the client. The get-request command is used to retrieve information from the server. The head-request command is used by the client to receive just header information, not data. The post-request command is sent by the client to the server for passing information to the server. It is usually used for sending mail, news, bulletin boards, and so on (see Figure 23.26).

Figure 23.26   *HTTP commands*

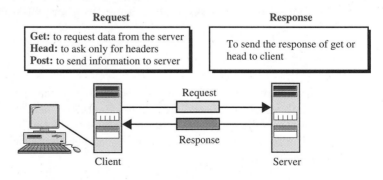

23.5   WORLD WIDE WEB (WWW)

The World Wide Web is a repository of information spread all over the world and linked together (see Figure 23.27).

Figure 23.27   *World Wide Web*

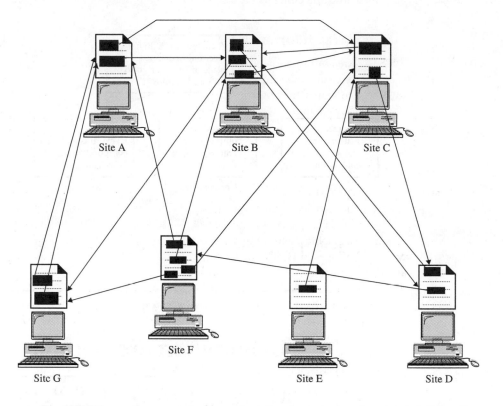

The WWW uses the concept of hypertext. In a hypertext environment, information is stored in a set of documents. The documents are linked together using the concept of pointers. An item can be associated with another document using these pointers. The reader who is browsing through a document can move to other documents by choosing (clicking) the items that are linked to other documents. Figure 23.28 shows the concept of hypertext.

A hypertext available on the Web is called a page. The main page for an organization or an individual is known as a homepage.

Information about one specific subject can be undistributed or distributed. In the first case, the whole information may consist of one or more Web pages on the same server. In the second case, the information is made of many pages distributed on different servers.

Uniform Resource Locator (URL)

If a client needs to access a Web page, it needs an address. To facilitate the access of documents distributed all over the world, WWW uses the concept of locators. The uniform resource locator (URL) is a standard for specifying any kind of information on the

Figure 23.28   *Hypertext*

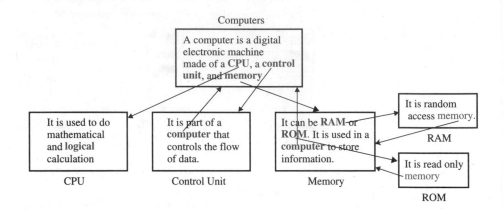

Computers

A computer is a digital electronic machine made of a **CPU**, a **control unit**, and **memory**.

It is used to do mathematical and **logical** calculation

CPU

It is part of a **computer** that controls the flow of data.

Control Unit

It can be **RAM** or **ROM**. It is used in a **computer** to store information.

Memory

It is random access memory.

RAM

It is read only memory

ROM

Figure 23.29   *URL*

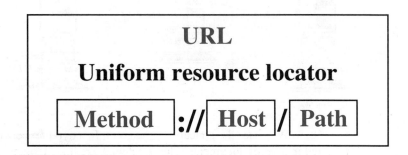

URL
Uniform resource locator

| Method | :// | Host | / | Path |

Internet. URL defines only three things: method, host computer, and pathname (see Figure 23.29).

Method

The method is the protocol used to retrieve the document. There are several different protocols that can retrieve a document, among them gopher, FTP, HTTP, news, and TELNET.

Host

The host is the computer at which the information is located. However, the name of the computer can be an alias. Today, Web pages are usually stored in computers given alias names that usually begin with www.

Path

Path is the pathname of the file where the information is located. Note that the path can contain slashes that separate directories from subdirectories and files in the UNIX operating system.

Browser Architecture

There are many commercial browsers that interpret and display a Web document. Almost all of them use the same architecture. The browser is usually is made of three parts: controller, client programs, and interpreters. The controller gets input from the keyboard or the mouse and uses the client program to access the document. After the document has been accessed, the controller uses one of the interpreters to display the document on the screen. The client program can be one of the methods (protocols) described before such as HTTP, FTP, gopher, or TELNET. The interpreter can be HTML, CGI, or Java, depending on the type of document (see Figure 23.30).

Figure 23.30 *Architecture of a browser*

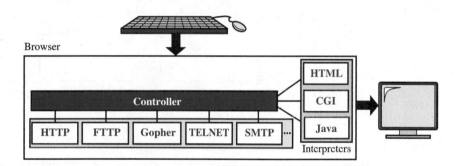

Documents in the World Wide Web can be grouped into three broad categories. The category is based on the time when the contents of the document are determined (see Figure 23.31).

Figure 23.31 *Categories of WWW documents*

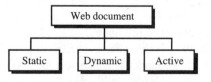

Static Documents

Static documents are fixed-content documents that are created and stored in a server. The client can only get a copy of it; in other words, the contents of the file are determined when it is created, not when it is used. Of course, the contents can be changed in the server, but the user cannot change it. When a client accesses the document, a copy of the document is sent. The user can then use a browsing program to display the document (see Figure 23.32).

Figure 23.32   *Accessing a static document*

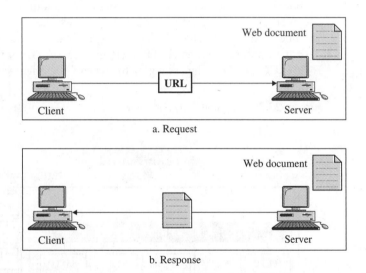

a. Request

b. Response

HTML   Hypertext markup language (HTML) is a markup language for writing Web pages. It is called a markup language because the only thing it does is let the browsers format the Web pages. The idea came from the book publishing industry. Before a book goes for its final printing, a copy editor reads the manuscript and puts a lot of marks on it. These marks tell the designer how to format the text. For example, if the copy editor wants part of a line to be printed in boldface, he or she draws a wavy line under that part; if the copy editor wants a part of the line to be in italics, he or she draws a straight line under it.

Let us explain the idea with an example. In HTML, to make a part of the text to be displayed boldface, we must include the beginning and ending boldface markup tag in the text, as shown in Figure 23.33.

The two marks, <B> and </B>, are instructions for the browser. When the browser sees these two marks, it knows that the text must be boldface (see Figure 23.34).

A markup language like HTML allows us to embed formatting instructions in the file itself. The instructions are stored with the text. In this way, any browser can read the instructions and format the text according to the workstation being used. One might ask why we do not use the formatting capabilities of word processors and create text that is already formatted and save this formatted text. The answer is that different word pro-

Figure 23.33 *Example of tags*

<B> This is the text that must be boldfaced.</B>

Figure 23.34 *Effect of <B> tags*

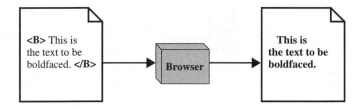

cessors use different techniques or procedures for formatting the text. For example, imagine that a user creates formatted text using a Macintosh computer and stores it in a Web page. A user who is using an IBM computer is not able to receive the Web page because the two computers are using different formatting procedures.

Using HTML lets us use only ASCII characters for both the main text and formatting instructions. In this way, every computer can receive the whole document as an ASCII document. The main text can be used as the data, and the formatting instructions can be used by the browser to format the data.

Dynamic Documents

Dynamic documents do not exist in a predefined format. Instead, a dynamic document is created by a Web server whenever a browser requests the document. When a request arrives, the Web server runs an application program that creates the dynamic document. The server returns the output of the program as a response to the browser that requested the document. Because a fresh document is created for each request, the contents of a dynamic document can vary from one request to another. A very simple example is getting the time and date from the server. Time and date are types of information that are dynamic. They change from moment to moment. The client can request that the server run a program such as the date program in UNIX and send the result of the program to the client (see Figure 23.35).

CGI Common gateway interface (CGI) is a standard for building dynamic Web documents. It is a model in the sense that it defines the type of language to be used in preparing the document. Today, most of the CGI programs have been created using shell scripts in UNIX. Note that the browser in the client machine does not have to know anything about running the script. The script is run at the server site.

Figure 23.35   *Accessing a dynamic document*

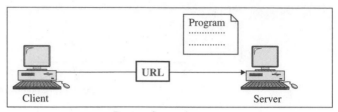

a. Request for running a program

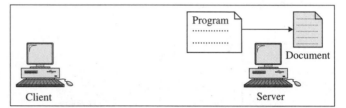

b. Running the program and creating the document

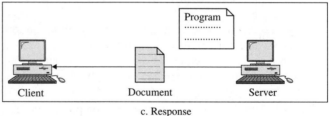

c. Response

Active Documents

Dynamic documents are produced when they are called. However, they are produced at the server site, not the client site. For many applications, we need the program to be run at the client site. These are called active documents. For example, imagine we want to run a program that creates animated graphics on the screen. The program definitely needs to be run at the client site, where the animation must take place. In this case, the program is created, compiled, and stored at the server site. However, when the client needs it, it requests a copy. A copy of the program, in binary form, is sent to the client. The interpreter at the client site is responsible for running the program (see Figure 23.36).

Java   To enable the use of active documents, Sun Microsystems, Incorporated has defined a technology and a language called Java. Java is a combination of three components: programming language, runtime environment, and a class library. The programming language is used to create programs at the server site. It is an object-oriented language that has many similarities to C++. The runtime environment component is used at the client site to run the program in binary form. The class library is a collection of predefined objects to make object-oriented programming easier.

Figure 23.36 *Accessing an active document*

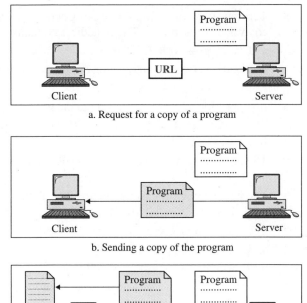

a. Request for a copy of a program

b. Sending a copy of the program

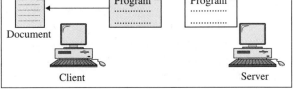

c. Running the program and creating the document

Java uses the term *applet* to define an active document program. The term distinguishes active programs from regular programs.

23.6 SUMMARY

- Transmission control protocol/internetworking protocol (TCP/IP) is a set of rules and procedures that governs the exchange of messages in an internetwork.

- TCP/IP was originally developed as a protocol for networks that wanted to be connected to ARPANET, a U.S. Department of Defense project. ARPANET is now known as the Internet.

- TCP/IP is a five-layer protocol suite whose bottom four layers match the OSI model fairly closely. The highest level, the applications layer, corresponds to OSI's top three layers.

- The internetwork protocol (IP) is defined at the network layer. IP is unreliable and connectionless.

- The IP packet, called the datagram, consists of a variable header and a variable data field.

- An internet address (better known as the IP address) uniquely defines the connection of a host to its network. A host with more than one IP address is a multi-homed host.
- The four-byte IP address is usually written n1.n2.n3.n4, nx being the decimal equivalent of each byte. The IP address contains three pieces of information:
  a. Class type—A, B, C, D, or E.
  b. Netid—network identification number.
  c. Hostid—host address.
- If the hostid is 0, we are referring to the whole physical network.
- The address resolution protocol (ARP) finds the physical address of a device if its IP address is known.
- The reverse address resolution protocol (RARP) will find a host's IP address from its physical address.
- The internet control message protocol (ICMP) handles control and error messages in the IP layer.
- There are two protocols at the transport level:
  a. User datagram protocol (UDP).
  b. Transmission control protocol (TCP).
- A protocol port is a source or destination point of an executing program in the application layer.
- UDP is unreliable and connectionless. UDP communication is port-to-port. The UDP packet is called a user datagram.
- TCP is reliable and connection-oriented. TCP communication is also port-to-port. The packet is called a segment.
- In a client-server system, an application program (the client) requests services from another application program (the server).
- The domain name system (DNS) was devised to provide user-friendly names for hosts.
- Given a domain name, the IP address can be found. Given the IP address, the domain name can be found.
- TELNET, a remote login application, is a client-server application using TCP/IP.
- The trivial file transfer protocol (TFTP) uses UDP for file transfer.
- The file transfer protocol (FTP) uses two TCP/IP connections (one for control and one for data) for file transfer.
- The network file system (NFS) is an application available on TCP/IP that allows file access and manipulation on a remote system. RPC and XDR work in conjunction with NFS.
- The simple mail transfer protocol (SMTP) is the electronic mail application available on TCP/IP. SMTP provides alias capabilities and a spool based on the first come, first searched concept.
- The simple network management protocol (SNMP) is an application on TCP/IP used to monitor and manage hosts on a network. An SNMP manager checks

variable values on a managed host. It can change these values to effect a desired outcome.

- Gopher is a menu-driven file retrieval method. The user sorts through menus to find the files needed.

- Archie is an automated title-search application program.

- Veronica, using the services of gopher, is an automated retrieval application program that uses conditional expressions in the search field.

- The wide area information service (WAIS) is an application program that searches file contents for key words. It returns the file names of successful finds.

- The hypertext transfer protocol (HTTP) is an advanced application program that links files on the World Wide Web.

- The World Wide Web (WWW) consists of information repositories located all over the world that are linked together.

- Hypertext and hypermedia are documents linked to each other through the concept of pointers.

- The uniform resource locator (URL) requires a method, a host computer, and a pathname to locate information on the WWW.

- Browsers interpret and display a Web document.

- In a static document, the contents are fixed and stored in a server. No changes in the server document can be made by the client.

- The hypertext markup language (IITML) is a language used to create static Web pages.

- A dynamic Web document is created by a server at a browser request.

- The common gateway interface (CGI) is a standard for building dynamic Web documents.

- An active document is a copy of a program retrieved by the client and run at the client site.

- Java is a technology and a language that enables the running of an active document.

23.7   PRACTICE SET

Multiple Choice

1. Which OSI layer corresponds to the TCP-UDP layer?
   a. physical
   b. data link
   c. network
   d. transport

2. Which OSI layer corresponds to the IP layer?
   a. physical
   b. data link

   c. network

   d. transport

3. Which OSI layers correspond to TCP/IP's application layer?

   a. application

   b. presentation

   c. session

   d. all of the above

4. The _____ is a user-friendly unique name of a station on an internet.

   a. domain name

   b. internet address

   c. station address

   d. physical address

5. The _____ consists of a set of labels separated by periods.

   a. domain name

   b. internet address

   c. station address

   d. physical address

6. Which of the following is true about the IP address?

   a. It's divided into exactly two classes.

   b. It contains a fixed-length hostid.

   c. It was established as a user-friendly interface.

   d. It is 32 bits long.

7. What is the major benefit of the DNS?

   a. Routers can use it to interpret addresses.

   b. It provides ease of addressing to humans.

   c. It can interact with the server.

   d. It creates a hierarchical structure that segments a network.

8. Which IP address class has few hosts per network?

   a. A

   b. B

   c. C

   d. D

9. What does the data link layer look for as it sends a frame from one link to another?

   a. hostid

   b. IP address

   c. domain name

   d. station address

10. The purpose of ARP on a network is to find the _____ given the _____.

   a. Internet address, domain name

   b. Internet address, netid

    c. Internet address, station address

    d. station address, Internet address

11. Which of the following apply to UDP?

    a. unreliable and connectionless

    b. contains destination and source port addresses

    c. reports certain errors

    d. all of the above

12. Which of the following apply to both UDP and TCP?

    a. transport layer protocols

    b. port-to-port communication

    c. uses services of IP layer

    d. all of the above

13. Which of the following is involved in NFS?

    a. RPC

    b. DNS

    c. FTP

    d. a and b

14. Which of the following is a class A network address?

    a. 128.4.5.6

    b. 127.4.5.0

    c. 127.0.0.0

    d. 127.8.0.0

15. Which of the following is a class B host address?

    a. 230.0.0.0

    b. 130.4.5.6

    c. 230.4.5.9

    d. 30.4.5.6

16. The data unit in the TCP/IP application layer is called a _____.

    a. message

    b. segment

    c. datagram

    d. frame

17. The data unit in the TCP/IP data link layer is called a _____.

    a. message

    b. segment

    c. datagram

    d. frame

18. The data unit in the TCP/IP IP layer is called a _____.

    a. message

    b. segment

    c. datagram

    d. frame

19. The data unit from the transport layer that uses UDP is called a _____.

    a. user datagram

    b. message

    c. segment

    d. frame

20. TCP/IP's _____ layer corresponds to the OSI model's top three layers.

    a. application

    b. presentation

    c. session

    d. transport

21. When a host knows its physical address but not its IP address, it can use _____.

    a. ICMP

    b. IGMP

    c. ARP

    d. RARP

22. This transport layer protocol is connectionless.

    a. UDP

    b. TCP

    c. FTP

    d. NVT

23. This transport layer protocol requires acknowledgment.

    a. UDP

    b. TCP

    c. FTP

    d. NVT

24. Both transport layer protocols have _____.

    a. source and destination port address fields

    b. a sequence number field

    c. an acknowledgment number field

    d. a and c

25. Which of the following is an example of a client-server model?

    a. DNS

    b. FTP

    c. TELNET

    d. all of the above

26. Which application allows a user to log in to a remote computer?

    a. DNS

    b. FTP

c. TELNET

d. RPC

27. Which application allows a user to access and change remote files without actual transfer?

a. DNS

b. FTP

c. NFS

d. TELNET

28. DNS can obtain the _____ of a host if its domain name is known, and vice versa.

a. station address

b. IP address

c. port address

d. checksum

29. In DNS, the first-level classification in the _____ domain is based on the organization type of the host's network.

a. reverse

b. generic

c. country

d. group

30. Use the _____ domain functions to find the domain name if the IP address is known.

a. reverse

b. generic

c. country

d. group

31. Which file transfer protocol uses UDP?

a. FTP

b. TFTP

c. TELNET

d. NFS

32. Which file transfer protocol uses TCP and establishes two virtual circuits between the local and remote server?

a. FTP

b. TFTP

c. TELNET

d. NFS

33. Which TCP/IP protocol monitors and maintains an internet?

a. MIB

b. SNMP

    c. CMIS

    d. CMIP

34. Which file retrieval method uses conditional expressions in its search field?

    a. Archie

    b. Veronica

    c. WAIS

    d. HTTP

35. Which file retrieval method searches the contents of a file for requested information?

    a. Archie

    b. Veronica

    c. WAIS

    d. HTTP

36. Which file retrieval method uses hypermedia?

    a. Archie

    b. Veronica

    c. WAIS

    d. HTTP

37. Hypertext documents are linked through _____.

    a. DNS

    b. TELNET

    c. pointers

    d. homepages

38. What does the URL need to access a document?

    a. pathname

    b. host computer

    c. retrieval method

    d. all of the above

39. Which of the following is not a retrieval method?

    a. gopher

    b. Archie

    c. HTTP

    d. HTML

40. Which of the following is not an interpreter?

    a. HTTP

    b. HTML

    c. CGI

    d. Java

41. What are the components of a browser?

    a. retrieval method, host computer, pathname

    b. controller, client program, interpreter

   c. hypertext, hypermedia, HTML

   d. all of the above

42. Which type of Web document is run at the client site?

   a. static

   b. dynamic

   c. active

   d. all of the above

43. Which type of Web document is created at the server site only when requested by a client?

   a. static

   b. dynamic

   c. active

   d. all of the above

44. Which type of Web document is fixed-content and is created and stored at the server site?

   a. static

   b. dynamic

   c. active

   d. all of the above

45. _____ is used to build dynamic Web documents.

   a. HTML

   b. CGI

   c. Java

   d. all of the above

46. Shell scripts are involved in _____ documents.

   a. active

   b. static

   c. passive

   d. dynamic

47. _____ is used to enable the use of active documents.

   a. HTML

   b. CGI

   c. Java

   d. all of the above

48. Java is _____.

   a. a programming language

   b. a runtime environment

   c. a class library

   d. all of the above

49. An applet is _____ document application program.

    a. a static

    b. an active

    c. a passive

    d. a dynamic

Exercises

1. Physical, port, and IP addresses are used in data communications. In a TCP/IP environment, what layers are they associated with?

2. Both the DNS and the IP address identify a host computer. Are both identifications necessary? Why or why not?

3. What is encapsulation?

4. Define the term *reliable* as used in data communications and relate it to TCP.

5. Define the term *connection-oriented* as used in data communications and relate it to TCP.

6. Draw two Ethernet LANs connected by a gateway. Each LAN has three hosts. One LAN is class B and one is class C. Choose appropriate internet addresses. How many connections must the gateway have?

7. What is the difference between a physical address and a logical address?

8. Order the following ARP events correctly.

    a. Host in possession of IP address sends station address.

    b. Transmission of data to correct host.

    c. IP address is broadcast.

    d. IP address and station address stored in cache memory.

9. What are the advantages of using UDP over TCP?

10. Why is the domain name reversed when searching for the IP address?

11. Discuss the two connections between client and server that are needed in FTP.

12. How does a manager using SNMP make changes on the network it is managing? Include a discussion of the role of variables.

13. Show by calculation how many networks (not hosts) each IP address class (A, B, and C only) can have.

14. Show by calculation how many hosts per network each IP address class (A, B, and C only) can have.

15. Write the binary form of the following internet addresses:

    a. 124.34.6.9

    b. 23.67.6.3

    c. 0.23.56.0

    d. 12.34.67.125

16. Find the class of the following host addresses:
    a. 121.56.3.67
    b. 193.23.56.23
    c. 231.23.67.123
    d. 142.23.56.23
17. Find the network address of each host address in the preceding problem.
18. Draw an internet with the following specifications. Show all of the hosts, their addresses, and connections. The address selection is up to you.
    a. One token ring network with four hosts (Class A).
    b. One Ethernet with four hosts (Class C).
    c. The token ring is connected to the Ethernet by a gateway.

APPENDIX A

ASCII AND EBCDIC CODES

In this appendix, we will give a brief description of two codes used to encode text: ASCII and EBCDIC. ASCII is the code used in most microcomputers, minicomputers, and mainframes. EBCDIC is used in IBM's mainframe computers.

A.1 ASCII

The American Standard Code for Information Interchange (ASCII) is the most commonly used code for encoding printable and nonprintable (control) characters.

ASCII uses seven bits to encode each character. It can therefore represent up to 128 characters. Table A.1 lists the ASCII characters and shows their codes in both binary and hexadecimal form. The table divides the codes into two parts, listed along the top and left side of the table. The vertical headings give the first part of the code (left-hand digits). The horizontal headings give the second part of the code (right-hand digits). The first row and column are the hexadecimal codes. The second row and column are the binary codes. To find the appropriate code for a given character, locate the character in the table, then find the corresponding first and second parts. For example, the ASCII code (in binary) for the character M is found by moving to the left (100) and then to the top (1101). The code is therefore 1001101. The same code in hexadecimal is 4D. The definitions of some control characters are as follows:

ACK: acknowledgment	ENQ: enquiry	NUL: null
BEL: bell	EOT: end of transmission	RS: record separator
BS: backspace	ESC: escape	SI: shift in
CAN: cancel	ETB: end of transmission	SO: shift out
CR: carriage return	ETX: end of text	SOH: start of header
DC1: device control	FF: form feed	SP: space
DC2: device control	FS: file separator	STX: start of text
DC3: device control	GS: group separator	SUB: substitute
DC4: device control	HT: horizontal tab	SYN: synchronous idle
DLE: data link escape	LF: line feed	US: unit separator
EM: end of medium	NAK: negative ACK	VT: vertical tab

APPENDIX A   ASCII AND EBCDIC CODES

Table A.1   *ASCII code*

Left \ Right		0	1	2	3	4	5	6	7	8	9	A	B	C	D	E	F
		0000	0001	0010	0011	0100	0101	0110	0111	1000	1001	1010	1011	1100	1101	1110	1111
0	000	NULL	SOH	STX	ETX	EOT	ENQ	ACK	BEL	BS	HT	LF	VT	FF	CR	SO	SI
1	001	DLE	DC1	DC2	DC3	DC4	NAK	SYN	ETB	CAN	EM	SUB	ESC	FS	GS	RS	US
2	010	SP	!	"	#	$	%	&	'	(	)	*	+	,	-	.	/
3	011	0	1	2	3	4	5	6	7	8	9	:	;	<	=	>	?
4	100	@	A	B	C	D	E	F	G	H	I	J	K	L	M	N	O
5	101	P	Q	R	S	T	U	V	W	X	Y	Z	[	\	]	^	_
6	110	`	a	b	c	d	e	f	g	h	i	j	k	l	m	n	o
7	111	p	q	r	s	t	u	v	w	x	y	z	{	|	}	~	DEL

A.2   EBCDIC

The Extended Binary Coded Decimal Interchange Code (EBCDIC) is used mostly by IBM mainframe computers. Table A.2 shows the EBCDIC code.

The EBCDIC is an eight-bit code. It can therefore code up to 256 characters. However, not all of the possible combinations have been assigned symbols yet. To find a binary or hexadecimal code, locate the character in the table; move to the left to find the first half of the code; then move to the top to find the second half of the code. For example, the binary code for the character M in EBCIDIC is 11010100. The same code in hexadecimal is D4. Only the symbols not defined before are as follows:

BYP: bypass
CC: unit backspace
DEL: delete
DS: digit select
IFS: interchange file separator
IGS: interchange group separator
IL: idle
IRS: interchange record separator
IUS: interchange unit separator

LC: lower case
NL: new line
PF: punch off
PN: punch on
RES: restore
SM: start message
SMM: repeat
SOS: start of significance
UC: upper case

Table A.2   *EBCDIC code*

Left \ Right		0	1	2	3	4	5	6	7	8	9	A	B	C	D	E	F
		0000	0001	0010	0011	0100	0101	0110	0111	1000	1001	1010	1011	1100	1101	1110	1111
0	0000	NUL	SOH	STX	ETX	PF	HT	LC	DEL			SMM	VT	FF	CR	SO	SI
1	0001	DLE	DC1	DC2	DC3	RES	NL	BS	IL	CAN	EM	CC		IFS	IGS	IRS	IUS
2	0010	DS	SOS	FS		BYP	LF	ETB	ESC			SM			ENQ	ACK	BEL
3	0011			SYN		PN	RS	UC	EOT					DC4	NAK		SUB
4	0100	SP											.	<	(	+	|
5	0101	&										!	$	*	)	;	
6	0110	-	/									|		%	_	>	?
7	0111										\	:	#	@	'	=	"
8	1000		a	b	c	d	e	f	g	h	i						
9	1001		j	k	l	m	n	o	p	q	r						
A	1010		~	s	t	u	v	w	x	y	z						
B	1011																
C	1100	{	A	B	C	D	E	F	G	H	I						
D	1101	}	J	K	L	M	N	O	P	Q	R						
E	1110	\		S	T	U	V	W	X	Y	Z						
F	1111	0	1	2	3	4	5	6	7	8	9						

APPENDIX B

NUMBERING SYSTEMS AND TRANSFORMATION

Today's computers make use of four numbering systems: decimal, binary, octal, and hexadecimal. Each has advantages for different levels of digital processing. In the first section of this appendix, we describe each of the four systems. In the second section, we show how a number in one system can be transformed into another.

B.1 NUMBERING SYSTEMS

All of the numbering systems examined here are positional, meaning that the position of a symbol in relation to other symbols determines its value. Within a number, each symbol is called a digit (decimal digit, binary digit, octal digit, or hexadecimal digit). For example, the decimal number 798 has three decimal digits. Digits are arranged in order of ascending value, moving from the lowest value on the right to the highest on the left. For this reason, the leftmost digit is referred to as the most significant and the rightmost as the least significant digit (see Figure B.1). For example, in the decimal number 1234, the most significant digit is the 1 and the least significant is the 4.

Figure B.1 *Digit positions and their significance*

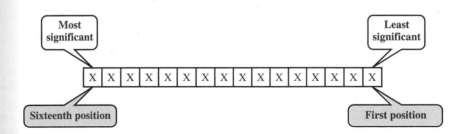

595

Decimal Numbers

The decimal system is the one most familiar to us in everyday life. All of our terms for indicating countable quantities are based on it, and, in fact, when we speak of other numbering systems, we tend to refer to their quantities by their decimal equivalents. Also called base 10, the name decimal is derived from the Latin stem *deci,* meaning ten. The decimal system uses 10 symbols to represent quantitative values: 0, 1, 2, 3, 4, 5, 6, 7, 8, and 9.

Decimal numbers use 10 symbols: 0, 1, 2, 3, 4, 5, 6, 7, 8, and 9.

Counting in Base 10

Figure B.2 shows counting in the decimal system. In the first line, we use symbols 0 through 9 to count from no objects to nine objects. Once we have counted to nine, we have used every available symbol. To continue counting, we must reuse the symbols starting with 0. To show that we have already used each symbol once, we insert a 1 at the second position (to the left of the 0), giving us the compound symbol *10.* The 1 in the second position equals 10; the 0 in the first position equals 0: 10 plus 0 equals 10. Thus, 11 is 10 plus 1. Each time we run through the symbol set, we advance the digit in the second position by one. When we reach 99, we have exhausted the available symbols in both the first and the second positions. At this point, we insert a 1 in the third position, and so on.

Figure B.2   *Counting in base 10*

0	1	2	3	4	5	6	7	8	9				
10	11	12	13	14	15	16	17	18	19	20	21	... 99	
100	101	102	103	104	105	106	107	108	109	110	111	112	... 999

Weight and Value

But how does symbol placement relate to value? All of these number systems are weighted systems. Each digit has a weight based on its position in the number. The weight of a position is the base raised to the power that the position represents. As you move from right to left in a number, each position represents one power higher than the previous position. The value of the digit in the least significant position is the value of the symbol times the base number raised to the 0th power (1); the value of the next digit is equal to the value of the symbol times the base number raised to the 1st power; and so on.

In the decimal system, each weight equals 10 raised to the power of its position. The weight of the first position, therefore, is 10^0, which, as noted above, equals 1. So the value of a digit in the first position is equal to the value of the digit times 1. The weight of the second position is 10^1, which equals 10. The value of a digit in the second position, therefore, is equal to the value of the digit times 10. The weight of the third position is 10^2. The value of a digit in the third position is equal to the value of the digit times 100 (see Table B.1).

Table B.1 *Decimal weights*

Position	Fifth	Fourth	Third	Second	First
Weight	10^4 (10,000)	10^3 (1,000)	10^2 (100)	10^1 (10)	10^0 (1)

The value of the number as a whole is the sum of each digit times its weight. Figure B.3 shows the weightings of the decimal number 4567.

Figure B.3 *Example of a decimal number*

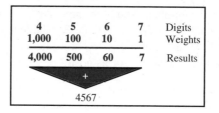

Binary Numbers

The binary number system provides the basis for all computer operations. Computers work by manipulating electrical current on and off. The binary system uses two symbols, *0* and *1*, so it corresponds naturally to a two-state device, such as a switch, with 0 to represent the off state and 1 to represent the on state. Also called base 2, the word *binary* derives from the Latin stem *bi,* meaning two.

> Binary numbers use two symbols: 0 and 1.

Counting in Base 2

The structure of the binary system is identical to that of the decimal system except that, with only two symbols, we are forced to reuse those symbols more often. Figure B.4 demonstrates counting in base 2. Here, we use the symbols 0 and 1 to count from no objects to one object. After counting one object, we have used all of the available symbols and must start again with 0. To show that we have already used the set of symbols once, we insert a 1 at the second position (to the left of the 0), giving us the compound symbol 10. This time the 1 in the second position means one *2,* however, rather than one *10.*

We continue counting until we have counted three objects (0, 1, 10, 11). At this point, we again run out of symbols, this time in both the first and second positions. Once again, we start over with 0, this time inserting 1 in the third position to show that we have run through the symbol set twice and are on our third iteration, and so on.

Figure B.4 *Counting in base 2*

0	1						
10	11						
100	101	110	111				
1000	1001	1010	1011	1100	1101	1110	1111
10000	10001	10010	10011	10100	10101	10110	10111 ... 11111

Weight and Value

The binary system is also a weighted system. Each digit has a weight based on its position in the number. Weight in the binary system is two raised to the power represented by a position, as shown in Table B.2. Note that the value of the weightings is shown in decimal terms next to the weight itself. The value of a specific digit is equal to its face value times the weight of its position.

Table B.2 *Binary weights*

Position	Fifth	Fourth	Third	Second	First
Weight	2^4 (16)	2^3 (8)	2^2 (4)	2^1 (2)	2^0 (1)

To calculate the value of a number, multiply each digit by the weight of its position, and then add together the results. Figure B.5 demonstrates the weighting of the binary number 1101. As you can see, 1101 is the binary equivalent of decimal 13.

Figure B.5 *Example of a binary number*

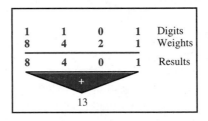

Octal Numbers

The octal number system is used by computer programmers to represent binary numbers in a compact form. Also called base 8, the term *octal* derives from the Greek stem *octa,* meaning *eight*. Eight is a power of two (2^3) and therefore can be used to model binary concepts. The octal system uses eight symbols to represent quantitative values: 0, 1, 2, 3, 4, 5, 6, and 7.

Octal numbers use eight symbols: 0, 1, 2, 3, 4, 5, 6, and 7.

Counting in Base 8

The octal system also functions like the decimal system but is grouped by 8s rather than by 10s (see Figure B.6). This time, we use the symbols 0 through 7 to count from no objects to seven objects. Once we reach 7, we have used all of the available symbols. To continue counting, we must reuse the same eight symbols. Again, we start with the symbol 0. To indicate that we have used the set of symbols once already, we insert a 1 at the second position (to the left of the 0) giving us the compound symbol 10 (0, 1, 2, 3, 4, 5, 6, 7, 10). In base 8, the 1 in the second position stands for one iteration of eight. The symbol 10, therefore, is the octal equivalent of the decimal symbol 8. The symbol 11 is the equivalent of decimal 9 ($1 \times 8 + 1$), and so on.

We continue counting in this fashion until we reach octal 17 (equal to decimal 15). At this point, we again run out of symbols and must start over again with 0. We advance the digit in the second position to 2 to indicate that we now have used the entire symbol set twice. This process continues until we have used the entire symbol set in both the first and second positions (77). At this point we insert a 1 in the third position, and so on.

Figure B.6   *Counting in base 8*

0	1	2	3	4	5	6	7					
10	11	12	13	14	15	16	17	20	...	77		
100	101	102	103	104	105	106	107	107	110	111	...	777

Weight and Value

The octal system is also a weighted system. Each digit has a weight based on its position in the number. Weight in octal is eight raised to the power represented by a position, as shown in Table B.3. Once again, the value represented by each weighting is given in decimal terms next to the weight itself. The value of a specific digit is equal to its face value times the weight of its position. For example, a 4 in the third position has the equivalent decimal value 4×64, or 256.

Table B.3   *Octal weights*

Position	Fifth	Fourth	Third	Second	First
Weight	8^4 (4096)	8^3 (512)	8^2 (64)	8^1 (8)	8^0 (1)

To calculate the value of an octal number, multiply the value of each digit by the weight of its position, then add together the results. Figure B.7 shows the weightings for the octal number 3471. As you can see, 3471 is the octal equivalent of decimal 1849.

Figure B.7 *Example of an octal number*

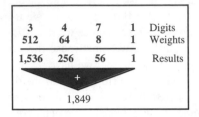

Hexadecimal Numbers

The term *hexadecimal* is derived from the Greek stem *hexadeca,* meaning 16 (*hex* means 6, and *deca* means 10). So the hexadecimal number system is base16. Sixteen is also a power of 2 (2^4). Like octal, therefore, the hexadecimal system is used by programmers to represent binary numbers in a compact form. Hexadecimal uses 16 symbols to represent data: 0, 1, 2, 3, 4, 5, 6, 7, 8, 9, A, B, C, D, E, and F.

> Hexadecimal numbers use 16 symbols: 0, 1, 2, 3, 4, 5, 6, 7, 8, 9, A, B, C, D, E, and F.

Counting in Base 16

The method for counting in the hexadecimal system is the same as that for the decimal, binary, and octal systems except that it is grouped by 16s (see Figure B.8). This time we use symbols 0 through F to count from no objects to 15 objects. Once we reach F, we have used all the available symbols. To continue counting, we must reuse the same symbols, starting again with 0. As with the other systems that we have examined, we now place a 1 in the second column to indicate that we have already used the entire set of symbols once, giving us the compound symbol 10 (0, 1, 2, 3, 4, 5, 6, 7, 8, 9, A, B, C, D, E, F, 10, 11, etc.). In base 16, the 1 in the second position stands for one iteration of 16. The hexadecimal symbol 10, therefore, is the equivalent of decimal 16. Hexadecimal 11 is the equivalent of decimal 17 ($1 \times 16 + 1$), and so on.

We continue counting in this fashion until we reach 1F. At this point, we have used the symbol set twice and so must advance the digit in the second position to 2. Counting continues in this way until we have used the entire symbol set in both positions (FF). At this point, we insert a 1 in the third position, and so on.

Weight and Value

Like the others, the hexadecimal system is a weighted system. Each digit has a weight based on its position in the number. The weight is used to calculate the value represented by the digit. Weight in hexadecimal is 16 raised to the power represented by a

Figure B.8 *Counting in hexadecimal numbers*

0	1	2	3	4	5	6	7	8	9	A	B	C	D	E	F
10	11	12	13	14	15	16	17	18	19	1A	1B	1C	1D	1E	1F ... FF

position, as shown in Table B.4. Once again, the value represented by each weighting is given in decimal terms next to the weight itself. The value of a specific digit is equal to its face value times the weight of its position. For example, a 4 in the third position has the equivalent decimal value 4 ¥ 256, or 1024. To calculate the value of a hexadecimal number, multiply the value of each digit by the weight of its position, then add together the results. Figure B.9 shows the weighting for the hexadecimal number 3471. As you can see, 3471 is the hexadecimal equivalent of decimal 13,425.

Table B.4 *Hexadecimal weights*

Position	Fifth	Fourth	Third	Second	First
Weight	16^4 (65,536)	16^3 (4,096)	16^2 (256)	16^1 (16)	16^0 (1)

Figure B.9 *Example of a hexadecimal number*

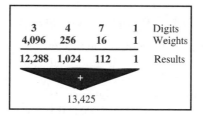

B.2 TRANSFORMATION

The different numbering systems provide different ways of thinking about a common subject: quantities of single units. A number from any given system can be transformed into its equivalent in any other system. For example, a binary number can be converted to a decimal number, and vice versa, without altering its value. Table B.5 shows how each system represents the decimal numbers 0 through 15. As you can see, decimal 13 is equivalent to binary 1101, which is equivalent to octal 15, which is equivalent to hexadecimal D.

Table B.5   *Comparison of four systems*

Decimal	Binary	Octal	Hexadecimal
0	0	0	0
1	1	1	1
2	10	2	2
3	11	3	3
4	100	4	4
5	101	5	5
6	110	6	6
7	111	7	7
8	1000	10	8
9	1001	11	9
10	1010	12	A
11	1011	13	B
12	1100	14	C
13	1101	15	D
14	1110	16	E
15	1111	17	F

From Other Systems to Decimal

As we saw in the discussions above, binary, octal, and hexadecimal numbers can be transformed easily to their decimal equivalents by using the weights of the digits. Figure B.10 shows the decimal value 78 represented in each of the other three systems. In each illustration, the weight of each digit (given as a decimal value rather than a power of the base number) is indicated below the digit itself. Multiplying each digit by its corresponding weight yields a weighted result. The weighted results are then added together to obtain the decimal number that corresponds to the original number.

From Decimal to Other Systems

A simple division trick gives us a convenient way to convert a decimal number to its binary, octal, or hexadecimal equivalent (see Figure B.11).

To convert a number from decimal to binary, divide the number by 2 and write down the resulting remainder (1 or 0). That remainder is the least significant binary digit. Now, divide the result of that division by 2 and write down the new remainder in the second position. Repeat this process until the quotient becomes zero.

In Figure B.12, we convert the decimal number 78 to its binary equivalent. In the first step, we divide 78 by 2, yielding a result of 39 and a remainder of 0. The 0 becomes the least significant digit in our binary number. Next we divide the 39 by 2. This time, the result is 19 with a remainder of 1. The 1 becomes the second digit. And so on. When the resulting quotient reaches 0, the collected remainders are 1001110, the

Figure B.10   *Transformation from other systems to decimal*

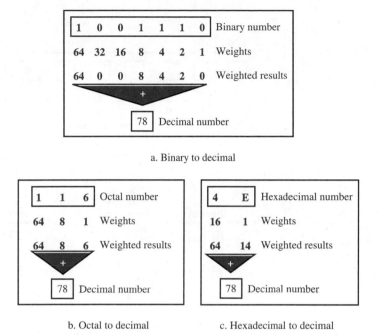

a. Binary to decimal

b. Octal to decimal   c. Hexadecimal to decimal

binary equivalent of 78. To check the validity of this method, we convert 1001110 to decimal using the weights of each position. From left to right:

$$2^6 + 2^3 + 2^2 + 2^1 \quad \Rightarrow \quad 64 + 8 + 4 + 2 \quad \Rightarrow \quad 78.$$

To convert a number from decimal to octal, the procedure is the same but the divisor is 8 instead of 2. To convert from decimal to hexadecimal, the divisor is 16.

From Binary to Octal or Hexadecimal

To change a number from binary to octal, we first group the binary digits from right to left by threes. Then we convert each tribit to its octal equivalent and write the result under the tribit. These equivalents, taken in order (not added), are the octal equivalent of the original number. In Figure B.12, we convert binary 1001110. As you can see, working from the right, $110 = 4 + 2 + 0 = 6$; $001 = 0 + 0 + 1 = 1$; and $1 = 1$. The resulting octal number 116 is the equivalent of binary 1001110.

To change a number from binary to hexadecimal, we follow the same procedure but group the digits from right to left by fours. This time we convert each quadbit to its hexadecimal equivalent (use Table B.5). In Figure B.12, we convert binary 1001110 to hexadecimal. Working from the right, $1110 = $ decimal $14 = $ hex E; $100 = $ hex 4. The hexadecimal equivalent of 1001110, therefore, is 4E.

Figure B.11   *Transformation from decimal to other systems*

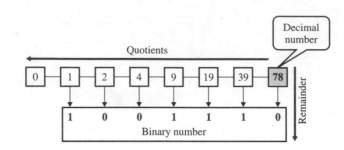

a. Decimal to binary

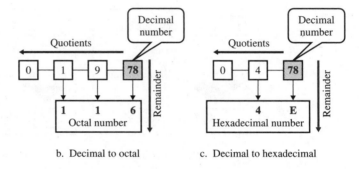

b. Decimal to octal   c. Decimal to hexadecimal

Figure B.12   *Transformation from binary to octal or hexadecimal*

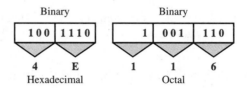

From Octal or Hexadecimal to Binary

To convert from octal to binary, we reverse the procedure above. Starting with the least significant digit, we convert each octal digit into its equivalent three binary digits. In Figure B.13, we convert octal 116 to binary. First, the 6 becomes 110. Next, the 1 in the second position becomes 001. Finally, the 1 in the most significant position becomes 001. Dropping the unnecessary leading 0s gives us 1001110.

To convert a number from hexadecimal to binary, we convert each hexadecimal digit to its equivalent four binary digits, again starting with the least significant digit. In Figure B.13, we convert hexadecimal 4E to binary. First, the E (equivalent to decimal 14) becomes 1110. Then the 4 becomes 0100. Putting the two results together gives us 01001110, or 1001110 once we drop the leading 0.

Figure B.13   *Transformation from octal or hexadecimal to binary*

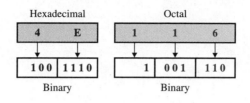

APPENDIX C

REPRESENTATION OF BINARY NUMBERS

Digital processing uses the binary number system as the basis for all operations. Binary arithmetic, with its two symbols 0 and 1, corresponds naturally to the two-state devices, such as switches, used in digital hardware.

Each digit in a binary number is called a bit (**binary digit**). A group of eight bits is called a byte or an octet.

The representation of numbers is limited by the size of the buffer (storage area) used to hold them. In computing, a common buffer size is 16 bits. With 16 available cells, we can represent any binary number of 16 or fewer digits (15 or fewer if we include sign information).

In digital processing, binary numbers can be used and stored in either of two formats: unsigned or signed. *Unsigned* means without a + or - sign, and refers to positive values only. *Signed* numbers can be either positive or negative. Unsigned numbers are represented in only one format. However, computers use three different formats for representing signed numbers: sign-and-magnitude, one's complement, and two's complement (see Figure C.1).

Figure C.1 *Binary representation*

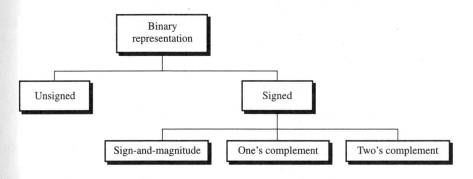

C.1   UNSIGNED NUMBERS

The buffer size limits the amount of space we have in which to store and represent information about a number. All essential information about a given value must be contained within these 16 bits, including whether a value is positive or negative. If a number is unsigned, however, it is assumed to be positive. With no need to indicate the sign, all 16 bits become available to represent digits. In 16 bits, we can represent any whole number between 0 (0000000000000000) and 65,535 (1111111111111111); see Figure C.2.

Figure C.2   *Unsigned*

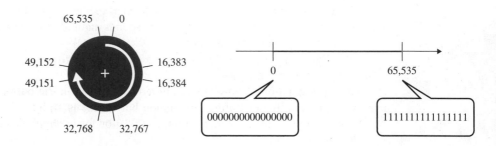

Another way to visualize the limitations of a 16-bit range is with a circle (see Figure C.2). As you can see, with 16 available bits, we can count from 0 to 65,535. When we add 1 to our maximum value of 65,535, we find ourselves back at 0. The process is called modular arithmetic. The most common example of modular arithmetic in everyday life is the 12-hour clock: when you add 1 to 12 you get 1, not 13.

From Decimal to Unsigned

To change a decimal value to its unsigned binary form, follow these steps:
  a. Change the number to its binary form.
  b. Fill in all empty cells on the left with 0s. (If you are using a 16-bit register, you need to fill all 16 cells; with an 8-bit register, you need to fill 8 cells; etc.)

Example C.1

Change 76 to its unsigned representation.

Solution:
  a. 76 in binary is 1001100.
  b. Adding 0s to make the number 16 bits long gives us 0000000001001100.

C.2   SIGNED NUMBERS

Representation of signed binary numbers presents more challenges than does representation of unsigned numbers. Given the same bit limitations, how do we include the sign

(+ or -) in the number? Three methods are commonly used: sign-and-magnitude, one's complement, and two's complement.

Sign-and-Magnitude

In sign-and-magnitude representation, the most significant bit is reserved to indicate the sign. If the bit is 0, the number is positive. If it is 1, the number is negative. Notice that application of this method gives us two 0 values: +0 (0000000000000000) and -0 (1000000000000000). Reserving one bit to show sign also limits the range of values that can be represented in a given number of bits. Given a 16-bit buffer, one cell is now consumed by the sign, leaving only 15 to represent the absolute value of a number. This changes the possible range of numbers that can be represented, as shown in Figure C.3. As you can see, with only 15 possible digits, the range of representable numbers becomes -32,767 to +32,767.

Once again, the circle provides a useful way to visualize a number range. Starting from +0 (0000000000000000), we add 1s, increasing the value until we reach +32,767 (0111111111111111). The next added 1 changes the value to -0 (0111111111111111 + 1 = 1000000000000000). Continuing to advance by 1s, we move around the circle to -32,767 (1111111111111111). The next added 1 changes the available bits to 0000000000000000 (+0), and the cycle begins again (see Figure C.3).

Figure C.3 *Sign-and-magnitude representation*

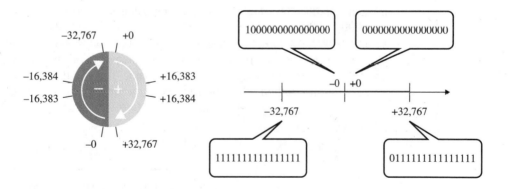

From Decimal to Sign-and-Magnitude

To change a decimal value to its sign-and-magnitude binary form, follow these steps:

a. Ignore the sign.

b. Change the absolute value of the number to its binary form.

c. Fill in all empty cells, except the last one, on the left with 0s (if you are using a 16-bit register, you need to fill 15 cells; with an 8-bit register, you need to fill 7 cells; etc.).

d. Now check the sign: if the number is positive, fill the last cell with 0. If the number is negative, fill the cell with 1.

Example C.2

Change +76 to its sign-and-magnitude representation.

Solution:

a. The absolute value is 76.

b. 76 in binary is 1001100.

c. Adding 0s to make the number 15 bits long gives us 000000001001100.

d. The sign was positive, so the sign-and-magnitude is **0**000000001001100.

Example C.3

Change -77 to its sign-and-magnitude representation.

Solution:

a. The absolute value is 77.

b. 77 in binary is 1001101.

c. Adding 0s to make the number 15 bits long gives us 000000001001101.

d. The sign was negative, so we add a 1 as the last bit: **1**000000001001101.

One's Complement

In the one's complement method, all the bits, not just the most significant, take part in the representation of sign. One's complement is a symmetrical system: numbers are paired with their complements. Complementary numbers are the + and - values of a single absolute value. Adding a number to its complement equals 0. To find the complement of a number, invert all of its digits. For example, inverting the digits of the number 0000000000000001 (+1), gives us 1111111111111110 (-1). This symmetry extends to zero: 0000000000000000 = +0, and 1111111111111111 = -0 (see Figure C.4).

As you can see from Figure C.4, positive numbers in this method use the same digits as those in sign-and-magnitude (and the same digits as the unsigned numbers 0 to 32,767). In this method, also, the sign of a number is immediately apparent from its

Figure C.4 *One's complement*

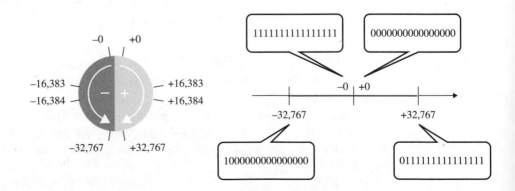

most significant digit. (Positive numbers always start with 0, and negative numbers always start with 1.) However, the numerical representation of negative numbers is very different in one's complement from that in sign-and-magnitude.

One's complement is used in data communications to check the accuracy of a received transmission.

From Decimal to One's Complement

To change a decimal value to its one's complement binary form follow these steps:

a. Ignore the sign.

b. Change the absolute value of the number to its binary form.

c. Fill in all empty cells on the left with 0s. (If you are using a 16-bit register, you need to fill all 16 cells; with an 8-bit register, you need to fill 8 cells; etc.)

d. Now check the sign: if the number is positive, stop here. If the number is negative, complement the digits (invert each 0 to 1 and each 1 to 0).

Example C.4

Change +76 to its one's complement representation.

Solution:

a. The absolute value is 76.

b. 76 in binary is 1001100.

c. Adding 0s to make the number 16 bits long gives us 0000000001001100.

d. The sign was positive, so the one's complement form is 0000000001001100.

Example C.5

Change -77 to its one's complement form.

Solution:

a. The absolute value is 77.

b. 77 in binary is 1001101.

c. Adding 0s to make the number 16 bits long gives us 0000000001001101.

d. The sign was negative, so we complement the number obtained in step c by inverting its digits, giving us 1111111110110010.

Two's Complement

In this method, as in one's complement, all the bits change when the sign of the number changes. The entire number, not just the most significant bit, takes part in the negation process. This time, however, we add a step, resulting in an asymmetrical system with only one representation of 0.

As Figure C.5 shows, having only a single representation of 0 results in the availability of an extra negative number: -32,768. In this way, a 16-bit integer variable can store numbers from -32,768 through +32,767. Note that the absolute value of the maximum integer (+32,767) is one less than the absolute value of the minimum integer (−32,768). Note also that, although this system is numerically asymmetrical, there

Figure C.5   *Two's complement*

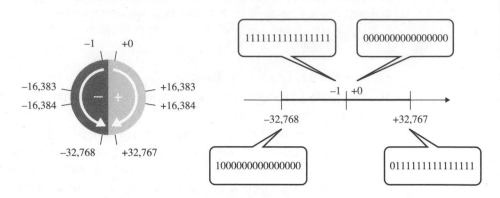

is still an equal number of positive and negative values represented (-1 through -32,768 and 0 through +32,767, or 32,768 possibilities in each range).

An examination of Figure C.5 reveals another interesting fact: in two's complement 0 and -1 are bitwise inverses of each other. They are not complements of each other—adding them together does not yield 0. In fact, 0000000000000000 (0) + 1111111111111111 (-1) = 1111111111111111 (-1). In the same way, +32,767 and −32,768 are inverses of each other. These patterns allow two's complement to replicate decimal arithmetic on the machine level, as we shall see below.

From Decimal to Two's Complement

To change a decimal number to its two's complement form, follow these steps:

a. Ignore the sign.

b. Change the absolute value of the number to its binary form.

c. Fill in all empty cells on the left with 0s. (If you are using a 16-bit register, you need to fill all 16 cells; with an 8-bit register, you need to fill 8 cells; etc.)

d. Now check the sign: if the number is positive, stop here. If the number is negative, complement the digits (invert each 0 to 1 and each 1 to 0) and then add 1 to the resulting number. If adding 1 results in a carry from the most significant digit, that carry is dropped.

Example C.6

Change +76 to its two's complement form.

Solution:

a. The absolute value is 76.

b. 76 in binary is 1001100.

c. Adding 0s to make the number 16 bits long gives us 0000000001001100.

d. The sign was positive, so the two's complement form is 0000000001001100. Note that positive values for all binary forms are the same.

Example C.7

Change -77 to its two's complement form:

Solution:

 a. The absolute value is 77.

 b. 77 in binary is 1001101.

 c. Adding 0s to make the number 16 bits long gives us 0000000001001101.

 d. The sign was negative, so we complement the number, giving us 1111111110110010. Now we add 1 to 1111111110110010, giving us the two's complement: 1111111110110011.

APPENDIX D

ONE'S COMPLEMENT ARITHMETIC FOR CHECKSUM CALCULATION

One's complement arithmetic is defined extensively in discrete mathematics. To understand its application to checksum error detection, however, we need to understand only a few basic concepts.

D.1 FINDING THE COMPLEMENT

As noted in Appendix C, the one's complement of any number is another number such that the sum of the two is equal to 0. The one's complement of A is −A. To complement a binary number, invert every 1 to 0 and 0 to 1 (see Figure D.1).

Figure D.1 *One's complement*

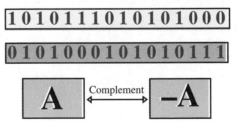

A and −A are one's complement of each other.

```
1 0 1 0 1 1 1 0 1 0 1 0 1 0 0 0
```
```
0 1 0 1 0 0 0 1 0 1 0 1 0 1 1 1
```

A ←Complement→ −A

A surprising corollary to this method of finding the complement by inverting the bits is that we end up with two different representations for the value 0: 0000000000000000, a +0, and its complement, 1111111111111111, −0.

Surprisingly, we have two 0s in one's complement arithmetic.

$+0 \Rightarrow$ 0000000000000000 $-0 \Rightarrow$ 1111111111111111

615

D.2   ADDING TWO NUMBERS

To add two digits in one's complement arithmetic, we proceed as we would if we were interested in the numeric values. In other words, we use the same steps as in base 10 addition, but in base 2. We add the two values in one column together. If the result is less than 2 (0 or 1), the entire sum goes in the corresponding column of the answer. If the result is exactly 2 (10), the 0 goes in that column and the 1 is carried to the next column to the left (the next greater power of 2). If the result is greater than 2 (11), we put the right-hand 1 in the column corresponding to the bits being added, and carry the left-hand 1 to the next column to the left. The box below expresses this process as a series of four simple rules.

> Four simple rules of adding one column:
>
> 1. If there is no 1s, the result is 0.
> 2. If there is only one 1, the result is 1.
> 3. If there are two 1s, the result is 0 and 1 is carried to the next column.
> 4. If there are three 1s, the result is 1 and 1 is carried to the next column.

To add two multibit numbers, we extend this process by two simple steps: First, we add the bits in each column as above, including carries from the lower magnitude columns. Second, if adding the numbers in the last (left-most) column results in a carried 1, that 1 is added to the right-hand column (the one's column). In other words, if the sum of two 5-digit numbers contains six digits, the left-most digit is dropped and 00001 is added to the result.

> Two simple rules for adding two numbers made of two columns or more:
>
> 1. Add the bits in each column.
> 2. If the last column generates a carry, add 1 to the result.

Figure D.2 shows an example of adding two numbers in one's complement where no carry is produced from the last column.

Figure D.2   *Adding in one's complement*

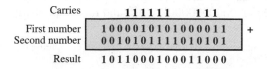

Figure D.3 shows an example of adding two numbers in one's complement where the last column generates a carry. The carry is added to the result.

Figure D.3 *Adding in one's complement with carry from the last column*

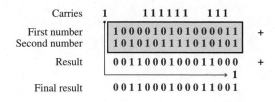

```
Carries          1        111111    111
First number        1000010101000011    +
Second number       1010101111010101
Result              0011000100011000    +
                                    → 1
Final result        0011000100011001
```

Following the above logic, if we add a number to its complement A, the result will be all 1s which, as we have seen, is equal to -0 (see Figure D.4).

> If we add a number with its complement, we get -0, which means all 1s.

Figure D.4 *Adding a number with its complement*

```
+A    1010111010101000    +
−A    0101000101010111
−0    1111111111111111
```

APPENDIX E

FOURIER ANALYSIS

Fourier analysis refers to two techniques used to decompose a signal into its sine wave components (see Figure E.1). The first technique, used to decompose periodic signals, is called a Fourier Series because it reduces a complex periodic signal to a series of simple sine waves. The second technique, used to decompose aperiodic signals, is called a Fourier Transform because it transforms a time-domain signal to a frequency-domain signal that is the envelope of the frequency-domain components.

Figure E.1 *Fourier analysis techniques*

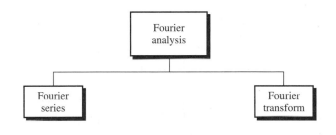

E.1 FOURIER SERIES

The Fourier series allows us to decompose a composite periodic signal into a possibly infinite series of sine waves, each having a different frequency and phase. A periodic signal $x(t)$ can be decomposed as follows:

$$x(t) = c_0 + c_1 \sin(2\pi f_1 t + \phi_1) + c_2 \sin(2\pi f_2 t + \phi_2) + \ldots + c_n \sin(2\pi f_n t + \phi_n) + \ldots$$

The coefficients $c_0, c_1, c_2, c_3, \ldots, c_n$ are the amplitudes of the simple signals. Coefficient c_0 is the amplitude of the signal with frequency 0 (the dc component). Coefficient c_1 is the amplitude of the signal with the same frequency as the original signal. Coefficient c_2 is the amplitude of the signal with a frequency two times that of the original signal, and so on. ϕ_0 is the phase of the signal with frequency 0 (the dc component). ϕ_1 is the phase of the signal with the same frequency as the original signal. ϕ_2 is the phase of the signal with a frequency two times that of the original signal, and so on.

Amplitude and phase are calculated using the Fourier series formulas. We will not give the proof of the Fourier series here; we will mention only how to calculate them. Interested readers can check the proof in any book on advanced mathematics.

To make the calculations simpler, we use the geometric fact that

$$c_n \sin (2\pi f_n t + \phi_n) = a_n \sin (2\pi f_n t) + b_n \cos (2\pi f_n t)$$

which means that any signal can be decomposed into sine and cosine components. Now, calculating a_n and b_n becomes simpler:

$$a_0 = 1/T \int x(t)\, dt$$

$$a_n = 1/T \int x(t)\, dt \cos (2\pi ft)\, dt$$

$$b_n = 1/T \int x(t)\, dt \sin (2\pi ft)\, dt$$

where T is the period of the signal and $f = 1/T$.

Example E.1
Find the coefficients of the Fourier series for the signal in Figure E.2.

Figure E.2 *Example 1*

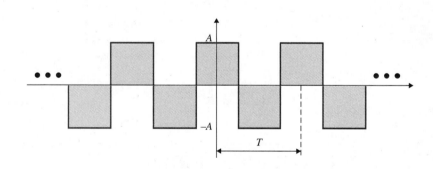

Solution:
Using the formulas shown above, we get:

$$a_0 = 0$$

$$a_1 = 4A/\pi \qquad a_2 = 0 \qquad a_3 = -4A/3\pi \qquad a_4 = 0 \qquad \dots$$

$$b_n = 0$$

Example E.2
Find the coefficients of the Fourier series for the signal in Figure E.3.

Solution:
Using the formulas shown above, we get:

Figure E.3   *Example 2*

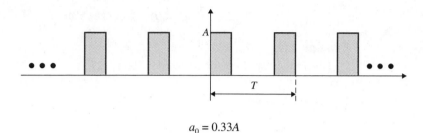

$$a_0 = 0.33A$$

$a_1 = 0.28A$	$a_2 = -0.14A$	$a_3 = 0$	$a_4 = 0.07A$	...
$b_1 = 3A/2\pi$	$b_2 = 3A/4\pi$	$b_3 = 0$	$b_4 = 3A/8\pi$	...

Example E.3

Find the coefficients of the Fourier series for the signal in Figure E.4.

Figure E.4   *Example 3*

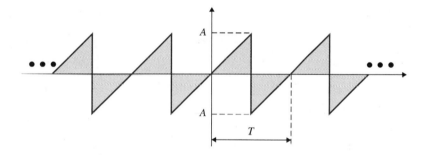

Solution:

Using the formulas shown above, we get:

$$a_0 = 0 \quad a_n = 0$$

$$b_1 = 2A/\pi \quad b_2 = -A/\pi \quad b_3 = 2A/3\pi \quad b_4 = -A/2\pi \quad ...$$

E.2   FOURIER TRANSFORM

The Fourier transform allows us to decompose a composite aperiodic signal into an infinite series of simple sine waves, each having a different frequency and phase. In this case, however, the frequencies are not discrete but rather a continuous spectrum. Transformation changes the time domain to frequency domain and vice versa. Because the spectrum is continuous, the result is an envelope of the frequency-domain components rather than a plot of the components themselves.

To calculate the envelope, the following integrals are used:

$$X(f) = \int X(t)\, e^{-j2\pi ft}\, dt$$

$$X(t) = \int X(f)\, e^{j2\pi ft}\, dt$$

Example E.4

Find the Fourier transform for the signal in Figure E.5.

Figure E.5. *Example 4*

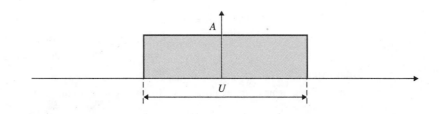

Solution:

Using the integral shown above, we get:

$$V(f) = 2A/2\pi f_0 \sin(2\pi fU/2)$$

APPENDIX F

HARDWARE EQUIPMENT FOR ERROR DETECTION

In this appendix, we discuss the equipment used for error detection. First, three electronic devices are introduced. Then we show how these devices are used to make VRC, LRC, and CRC generators and checkers.

F.1 ELECTRONIC DEVICES

Three electronic devices are used for the generation and analysis of redundancy checks: XOR gates, NOT gates, and shift registers.

XOR Gate

An exclusive or (XOR) gate is an electronic device with two inputs and one output. XOR gates compare two bits of data. If the input bits are equal (both 1s or both 0s), the output of the XOR gate is a 0. If the bits are unequal (one 0 and the other 1), the output of the XOR gate is a 1. Figure F.1 shows the results of passing each of the four possible two-bit combinations through an XOR.

NOT Gate

The NOT gate is an electronic device with one input and one output. The name *NOT* is not an acronym—it means what it says. Any bit input will be output as what it is not. NOT gates invert input by changing 0 to 1 and 1 to 0. They are used in odd-parity generators where a result is generated and then inverted. Figure F.2 shows the output of a NOT gate.

Shift Register

A register is a group of binary storage cells, each of which holds one bit. A register that can move its contents one place to the right or to the left is called a shift register (see Figure F.3).

Figure F.1   *XOR gate*

a. XOR

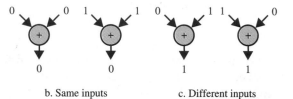

b. Same inputs   c. Different inputs

Figure F.2   *NOT gate*

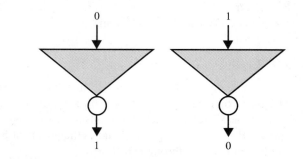

Figure F.3   *Shift registers*

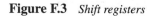

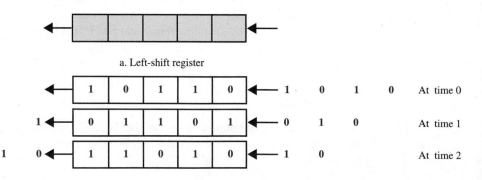

b. Effect of two shifts to the left in a left-shift register

A shift register is connected to a timing pulse. With each pulse, the contents of the register shift one cell to the left (or to the right if it is a right-shift register). Each unit (binary 1 or 0) advances one position. The contents of the last cell get pushed out of the register, and a new unit moves from the waiting stream (if there is one) into the first cell of the register. Figure F.3 shows a left-shift register. A right-shift register behaves the same way but in the opposite direction.

F.2   VRC

As we learned in Chapter 9, the vertical redundancy check (VRC) is used for odd and even parity checking. In this section, we show how we can use electronic devices to make a VRC generator or checker.

VRC Generator

A vertical redundancy check (VRC) generator is a series of XOR gates. The number of gates in the generator is one less than the number of bits in the data unit. The final result is the even-parity bit. Figure F.4 shows how this process works. To generate an odd-parity bit, the output of the last XOR gate is passed through a NOT gate.

Figure F.4   *VRC generator*

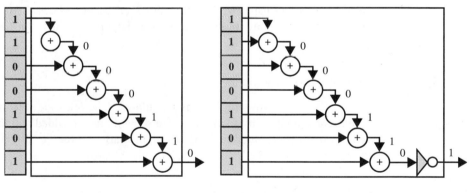

a. Even parity   b. Odd parity

VRC Checker

The VRC checker at the receiving end has one extra XOR gate to accommodate the parity bit. The process is also the same: the output of each XOR gate is passed to the next XOR gate, where it is added to the next bit in the data unit. As with parity generation, an odd-parity checker is identical to an even-parity checker except for the addition of a NOT gate after the last XOR gate.

If the final output is 0, the transmission is assumed to be intact, the parity bit is dropped, and the data are accepted. If the output is 1, the data are rejected. Figure F.5 shows both an even- and an odd-parity VRC checker.

Figure F.5   *VRC checker*

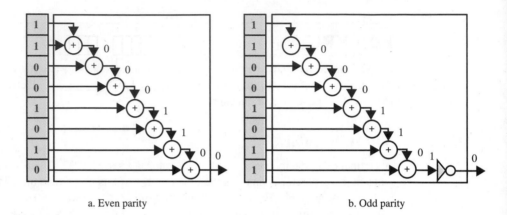

a. Even parity   b. Odd parity

F.3   LRC

As we learned in Chapter 9, the longitudinal redundancy check (LRC) is used for more efficient error checking. In this section, we show how to make an LRC generator and checker.

LRC Generator

Figure F.6 shows how the LRC is calculated. The least significant bits are added together and their parity found; then the second bits are added and their parity found, and so on. The final bit of the LRC is both the parity bit for the LRC data unit itself and the parity bit for all the VRC parity bits in the block.

Figure F.6   *LRC generator*

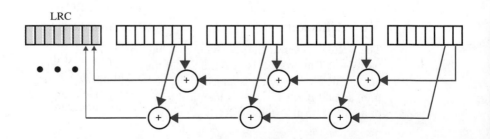

LRC Checker

An LRC checker works like an LRC generator, but we need extra XOR gates. Figure F.7 shows an LRC checker.

Figure F.7   *LRC checker*

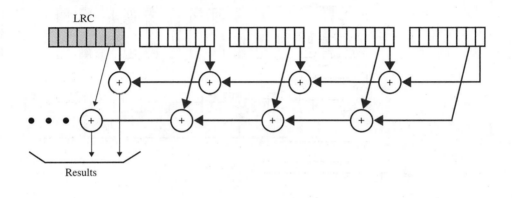

F.4   CRC

As we learned in Chapter 9, the cyclic redundancy check (CRC) is more efficient than VRC or LRC. In this section, we show how to make a CRC generator and checker.

The CRC Generator

Designing a CRC generator from a given polynomial is easily done following these steps:

■ Change the polynomial to a divisor of size $N + 1$. (N is the order of the polynomial.)

■ Make a shift register of size N.

■ Align the shift register cells with the divisor so that the cells are located between the bits.

■ Put an XOR where there is a 1 in the divisor except for the leftmost bit.

■ Make a feedback connection from the leftmost bit to the XORs.

■ Add a switch to direct the data and the generated CRC output.

   Figure F.8 shows the CRC generator derived from the ITU-T polynomial.

   One set of bits moves through the CRC generator to the switch; the other is sent directly to the switch. The switch uses a counter to send the data first and then the remainder (CRC). Figure F.9 shows the generation of the CRC remainder. In each line, the XOR gates add two bits together. After this operation, all bits are then shifted one position to the left. The last line shows the CRC remainder in the shift register.

Figure F.8   *From polynomial to CRC generator*

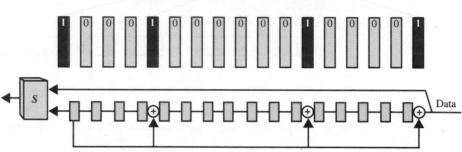

Figure F.9   *An example of a CRC generator*

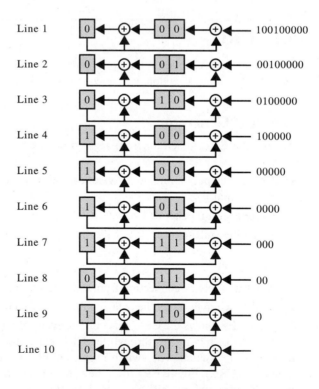

The CRC Checker

The CRC hardware at the receiving end of the transmission works in precisely the same way except that it tests the whole package, including the data and the CRC, to determine the accuracy of the received data (see Figure F.10).

Figure F.10   *CRC checker*

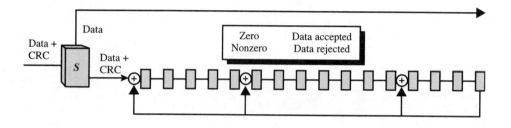

APPENDIX G

HUFFMAN CODING

ASCII and EBCDIC are fixed-length codes. Each ASCII character consists of seven bits. Each EBCDIC character consists of eight bits. Character length does not vary. Although the character E occurs more frequently than the character Z, both are assigned the same number of bits in a given code. This consistency means that every character uses the maximum number of bits, resulting in lengthy encoded messages.

Huffman coding, however, makes coding more efficient. In this mechanism, we assign shorter codes to characters that occur more frequently and longer codes to those that occur less frequently. For example, E and T, the two characters that occur most frequently in the English language, are assigned one bit each. A, I, M, and N, which also occur frequently but less frequently than E and T, are assigned two bits each. C, G, K, R, S, U, and W are the next most frequent and are assigned three bits each, and so on. In a given piece of text, only some of the characters will require the maximum bit length. The overall length of the transmission, therefore, is shorter than that resulting from fixed-length encoding.

Difficulty arises, however, if the bit patterns associated with each character are assigned randomly. Consider the example in Figure G.1. Note that we have purposefully limited the number of characters in the example to only a few from the complete alphanumeric and special character set in order to make the demonstration easier to follow.

Figure G.1 *Bit assignments based on frequency of the character*

E:0	T:1						
A:00	I:01	M:10	N:11				
C:000	D:001	G:010	K:011	O:100	R:101	S:110	U:111

As you can see, each character is represented by a unique bit pattern and is easily distinguishable when presented separately. But what happens when these characters are formed into a data stream? Figure G.2 shows the possible results. Without a predictable character bit length, the receiver may misinterpret the code.

Figure G.2   *Multiple interpretations of transmitted data*

00101010011110
Code sent

0	01	010	100	1	111	0
E	I	G	O	T	U	E

First interpretation

00	10	101	0	01	1	110
A	M	R	E	I	T	S

Second interpretation

001	010	100	111	10
D	G	O	U	M

Third interpretation

Huffman coding is designed to counter this ambiguity while retaining the bit count advantages of a compression code. Not only does it vary the length of the code based on the frequency of the character represented, but each character code is chosen in such a way that no code is the prefix of another code. For example, no three-bit code has the same pattern as the first three bits of a four- or five-bit code (prefix property code).

G.1   CHARACTER TREE

Using the character set from the example above, let's examine how a Huffman code is built.

Before we can assign bit patterns to each character, we assign each character a weight based on its frequency of use. In our example, we assume that the frequency of the character E in a text is 15 percent, the frequency of the character T is 12 percent, and so on (see Figure G.3).

Figure G.3   *Character weights*

E = 15	T = 12	A = 10	I = 08	M = 07	N = 06	C = 05
D = 05	G = 04	K = 04	O = 03	R = 03	S = 02	U = 02

Once we have established the weight of each character, we build a tree based on those values. The process for building this tree is shown in Figure G.4. It follows two basic steps:

1. First we organize the entire character set into a row, ordered according to frequency from highest to lowest (or vice versa). Each character is now a node at the leaf-level of a tree.

2. Next, we find the two nodes with the smallest combined frequency weightings and join them to form a third node, resulting in a simple two-level tree. The weight of the new node is the combined weights of the original two nodes. This node, one level up from the leaves, is eligible to be combined with other nodes. Remember,

Figure G.4   *Huffman tree, part 1*

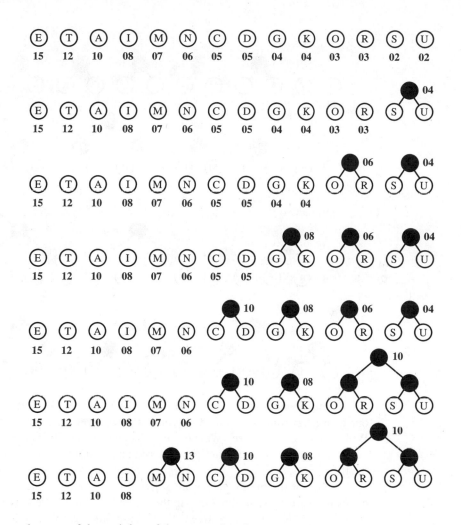

the sum of the weights of the two nodes chosen must be smaller than the combination of any other possible choices.

3. We repeat step 2 until all of the nodes, on every level, are combined into a single tree.

Figure G.4 shows part of this process. The first row of the figure shows step 1, with the leaf-level nodes representing the original characters arranged in descending order of value. In the second row, we locate the two nodes with the smallest values and combine them. As you can see, this process results in the creation of a new node (represented by a solid circle). The frequency value (weight) of this new node is the sum of the weights of the two nodes. In the third row, we combine two more nodes, and so on.

In the sixth row, the nodes with the lowest values are found one level up from the characters rather than among the characters themselves. We combine them into a node two levels up from the leaves. In the seventh row, the lowest value node has a value of 8

Figure G.5   *Huffman tree, part 2*

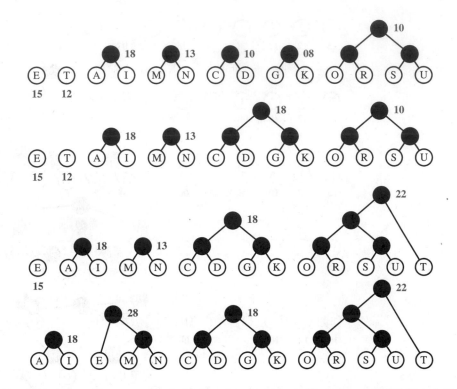

(I) and the second lowest value is 10. But there are three 10s—one at the leaf level (A), one a level up from the leaves (C-D), and one two levels up from the leaves (O-R-S-U). Which should we choose? We choose whichever of the 10s is adjacent to the 8. This decision keeps the branch lines from crossing and allows us to preserve the legibility of the tree.

If none of the higher values are adjacent to the lower value, we can rearrange the nodes for clarity (see Figure G.5). In the figure (third row), we have moved the character T from the left side of the tree to the right in order to combine it with a node on that side. We move the character E for the same reason.

Figure G.6 shows the rest of the process. As you can see, the completed tree results in a single node at the root level (with a value of 86).

G.2   ASSIGNING THE CODES

Once the tree is complete, we use it to assign codes to each character. First, we assign a bit value to each branch (see Figure G.7). Starting from the root (top node), we assign 0 to the left branch and 1 to the right branch and repeat this pattern at each node. Which branch becomes 0 and which becomes 1 is left to the designer—as long as the assignments are consistent throughout the tree.

Figure G.6   *Huffman tree, part 3*

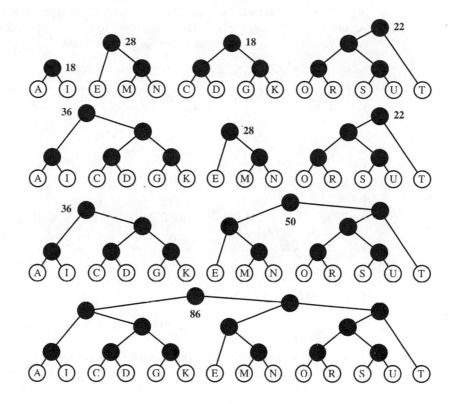

Figure G.7   *Code assignment*

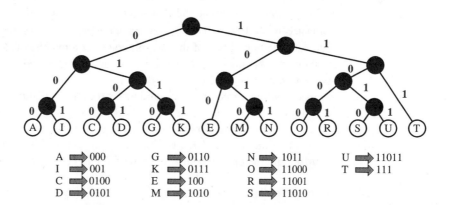

A ➡ 000	G ➡ 0110	N ➡ 1011	U ➡ 11011	
I ➡ 001	K ➡ 0111	O ➡ 11000	T ➡ 111	
C ➡ 0100	E ➡ 100	R ➡ 11001		
D ➡ 0101	M ➡ 1010	S ➡ 11010		

A character's code is found by starting at the root and following the branches that lead to that character. The code itself is the bit value of each branch on the path taken in sequence. In our example, for instance, A = 000, G = 0110, and so on. The code for each character and the frequency of the character is shown in Table G.1. As you can see, no code is the prefix of any other code because each has been obtained by following a different path from the root. The three-bit codes representing the characters E, T, A, and I do not match the first three bits of any four- or five-bit code, and the four-bit codes do not match the first three bits of any five-bit code.

Table G.1 *Code assignment table*

Character	Frequency	Code	Character	Frequency	Code
E	15	100	D	5	0101
T	12	111	G	4	0110
A	10	000	K	4	0111
I	8	001	O	3	11000
M	7	1010	R	3	11001
N	6	1011	S	2	11010
C	5	0100	U	2	11011

G.3   DECODING

A message encoded in this fashion can be interpreted without ambiguity, using the following process:

1. The receiver stores the first three bits received in memory and attempts to match them with one of the three-bit codes. If a match is found, that character is selected and the three bits are discarded. The receiver then repeats this step with the next three bits.

2. If a match is not found, the receiver reads the next bit from the stream and adds it to the first three. It then attempts to find a match among the four-bit codes. If a match is found, the corresponding character is selected and the bits are discarded.

3. If a match is not found, the receiver reads the next bit from the stream and tries to match all five bits to one of the five-bit codes. If a match is found, the character is assigned and the bits are discarded. If not, an error is issued.

Figure G.8 shows a series of bits and their interpretation by the receiver. The receiver reads the first three bits (110) and looks for a match among the three-bit codes. Not finding a match, it adds the next bit (1). It now tries to match the sequence 1101 with a four-bit code. Again finding no match, it adds the next bit (0) and compares 11010 to the five-bit codes. 11010 is found to represent S. S is selected, those five bits are discarded, and the process starts again with the next three bits (101).

Figure G.8   *Unambiguous transmission*

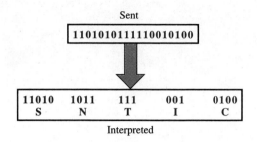

Interpreted

APPENDIX H

IP VERSION 6

With the proliferation of networks and hosts connected to the Internet, the pool of available IP addresses as defined by version 4 is dwindling fast. IPv6 has been designed to handle this problem as well as some other issues. IPv6 will be operational in the near future.

H.1   ADDRESSES

An IPv6 address consists of 16 bytes (octets). It is 128 bits long.

Hexadecimal Colon Notation

To make it easier for users or programs, IP protocol specifies hexadecimal colon notation. In this notation, 128 bits are divided into eight sections, each two bytes in length. Two bytes in hexadecimal require four hexadecimal digits. Therefore, the address consists of 32 hexadecimal digits, with every 4 digits separated by a colon. Figure H.1 shows the concept.

Figure H.1   *Hexadecimal colon notation*

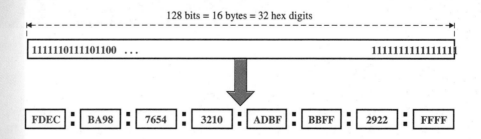

H.2 DATAGRAM

The format of the IPv6 datagram is shown in Figure H.2. Each datagram is composed of a mandatory base header followed by the payload. The payload consists of two parts: optional extension headers and data from an upper layer. The datagram is usually displayed in four-byte rows as shown in Figure H.3. The base header occupies 40 bytes, while the extension headers and data from the upper layer usually contain up to 65,536 bytes of information.

Figure H.2 *IP datagram*

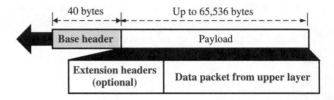

Figure H.3 *IP datagram format*

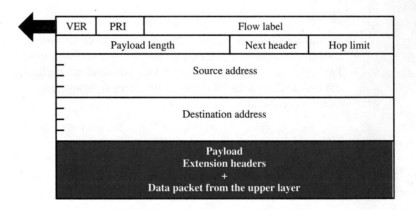

Base Header

The base header consists of eight different fields: version, priority, flow label, payload length, next header, hop limit, source address, and destination address.

- **Version.** The first field defines the version number of the IP. This version is 6 (IPv6), with a binary value of 0110.
- **Priority.** The second field in the IP header defines the priority or the class of the traffic. This is also a four-bit field. Data are divided into two broad classes: non-time-sensitive and time-sensitive. Non-time-sensitive data adapt themselves to the

Figure H.4 *Next header fields*

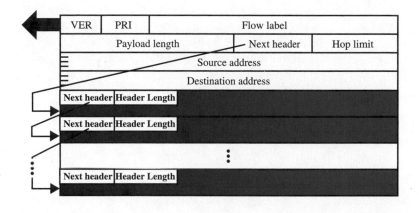

traffic in the network. If the network is congested, the flow of data slows down. An example of this mechanism is file transfer. Conversely, time-sensitive data cannot adapt themselves to the condition of the network. In other words, the transmission speed must remain constant even if traffic is congested. Examples of this type of data are real time audio and video.

- **Flow label.** The three-byte flow label field is designed to provide special handling for a particular flow of data. The flow label is a randomly generated number. The combination of the flow label and the sender IP address creates a unique path identifier that can be used to route the datagrams more efficiently.

- **Payload length.** The payload length field defines the total length of the IP datagram, not including the base header. It is a two-byte field (16 bits) and can define up to 65,536 bytes of payload.

- **Next header.** The next header field defines the header that follows the base header in the datagram. The next header is either one of the optional extension headers used by IP or the header for an upper-layer protocol such as UDP or TCP. Each extension header also contains this field (see Figure H.4).

- **Hop limit.** The hop limit field is the same as the time-to-live field in IPv4.

- **Source address.** The source address field is a 16-byte (128-bit) address. It identifies the original source of the datagram.

- **Destination address.** The destination address field is a 16-byte (128-bit) address. It usually identifies the final destination of the datagram.

Extension Headers

The length of the base header is fixed at 40 bytes. However, to give more functionality to the IP datagram, the base header can be followed by up to six extension headers. The extension headers can add more functionality through services and features such as source routing, fragmentation, authentication, and security.

ANSWERS TO SELECTED PROBLEMS

This section contains solutions to all of the multiple choice questions and to selected exercises from the end of each chapter.

Chapter 1: Introduction

Multiple Choice

1. c   2. b   3. b   4. d   5. c   6. b   7. d   8. b   9. c   10. a

11. a   12. d

Exercises

1. Telecommunication is data communication between two entities that are far apart; telecommunication is therefore a subset of data communication.
5. Networks can make a building secure through the use of an alarm system that is connected to a remote central office and/or through the use of the telephone system to report intruders.

Chapter 2: Basic Concepts

Multiple Choice

1. b   2. c   3. a   4. a   5. b   6. a   7. a   8. a   9. b   10. c

11. c   12. a

Exercises

1. A multipoint connection provides greater efficiency since more than two devices could share the link.

2. For six devices arranged in a fully connected mesh topology:

$$\text{Number of cables needed} = 6 \times (6 - 1) / 2 = 15$$

$$\text{Number of ports needed for each device} = 6 - 1 = 5$$

4. a. Star, ring
   b. Star
   c. Mesh, star
   d. Star, ring

6. a. Full-duplex
   b. Simplex
   c. Half-duplex
   d. Simplex
   e. Half-duplex
   f. Simplex
   g. Half-duplex

Chapter 3: The OSI Model

Multiple Choice

1. b   2. c   3. b   4. b   5. a   6. b   7. c   8. c   9. b   10. d
11. b   12. b   13. a   14. c   15. a   16. c   17. c   18. a   19. b

Exercises

1. The ISO is a standards organization that produced the OSI model.

3. a. Transport
   b. Data link
   c. Application
   d. Physical

5. a. Presentation
   b. Session
   c. Network
   d. Session
   e. Presentation

Chapter 4: Signals

Multiple Choice

1. b   2. b   3. c   4. a   5. a   6. a   7. b   8. a   9. d   10. d

11. c   12. d   13. b   14. a   15. b

Exercises

1. The three characteristics of a sine wave are its amplitude (the maximum value of the strength of the wave as measured in volts, amperes, or watts); its frequency (the number of cycles completed in one second); and its phase (the number of degrees or radians shifted from the origin).

4. Information is what is to be communicated. Signals are the vehicles or tools for carrying information.

6. The points of an analog signal form a smooth and continuous curve with an infinite number of values while the points of a digital signal jump from value to value with a finite number of values.

12. Period = 1 / Frequency
    a. $T = 1/f = 1/24 = 41.7$ ms
    b. $T = 1/f = 1/(8 \times 10^6) = 125$ ns
    c. $T = 1/f = 1/(140 \times 10^3) = 7.14$ µs
    d. $T = 1/f = 1/(12 \times 10^{12}) = 0.0833$ ps

13. Frequency = 1 / Period
    a. $f = 1/T = 1/5$ s $= 0.2$ Hz
    b. $f = 1/T = 1/(12 \times 10^{-6}) = 83.3$ KHz
    c. $f = 1/T = 1/(220 \times 10^{-9}) = 4.55$ MHz
    d. $f = 1/T = 1/(81 \times 10^{-12}) = 12.3$ GHz

Chapter 5: Encoding

Multiple Choice

1. b   2. a   3. d   4. c   5. a   6. b   7. d   8. c   9. d   10. d

11. c   12. d   13. c   14. a   15. b   16. d   17. a   18. c   19. a   20. a

21. d   22. b   23. b   24. b   25. a   26. b   27. c   28. c   29. b   30. d

31. d

Exercises

3. a. ASK or QAM
   b. PSK or QAM
   c. ASK
   d. QAM
   e. FSK
   f. ASK
   g. PSK
   h. QAM

4. QAM is not as susceptible to noise as ASK. QAM is more efficient than PSK because more bits can be sent per symbol. This results in a high transmission rate.

6. The major disadvantage in using NRZ encoding is the potential loss of synchronization due to long strings of 0s (for both NRZ encoding types) or 1s (for NRZ-L encoding). In both RZ and biphase encoding a transition occurs at the middle of each bit. This prevents long time periods at one voltage level and allows for receiver synchronization.

8. a. 2
   b. 2
   c. 2
   d. 3
   e. 2
   f. 2

10. AM is analog-to-analog encoding. ASK is digital-to-analog encoding.

13. Samples / Second = $2 \times$ Highest frequency = 2×4000 = 8000 samples/s

16. a. 1000
    b. 2000
    c. 1500
    d. 6000

20. a. Not enough information
    b. Sampling rate = $2 \times$ Highest frequency = 2×6000 = 12,000 samples/sec
    c. Sampling rate = $2 \times$ Highest frequency = 2×0 = 0 samples/sec, but we need at least one sample.
    d. Sampling rate = $2 \times$ Highest frequency = $2 \times$ Infinity = Infinity; cannot be sampled.

22. a. $BW_t = 10 \times BM_m = 10 \times 12$ KHz = 120 KHz
    b. $BW_t = 10 \times BM_m = 10 \times 8$ KHz = 80 KHz
    c. $BW_t = 10 \times BM_m = 10 \times 1$ KHz = 10 KHz

25. In 8-bit quantization the values range from -127 to $+127$.
    a. $0.91 \times 127 = 116$ ⇨ 01110100
    b. $-0.25 \times 127 = -32$ ⇨ 10100000

c. $0.56 \times 127 = 71$ ⇨ 01000111
d. $0.71 \times 127 = 90$ ⇨ 01011010

Chapter 6: Transmission of Digital Data: Interfaces and Modems

Multiple Choice

1. c   2. d   3. a   4. b   5. d   6. a   7. b   8. d   9. b   10. d

11. c   12. a   13. a   14. a   15. d   16. d   17. d   18. d   19. d   20. b

21. c   22. c   23. b   24. c   25. c   26. a   27. a   28. b   29. a   30. c

31. c   32. b   33. b   34. b   35. d   36. b   37. a   38. d   39. b   40. d

41. d   42. c   43. a   44. a   45. b

Exercises

1. $1000 \times (1 \text{ start bit} + 1 \text{ stop bit}) = 1000 \times 2 = 2000 \text{ extra bits}$

    $1000 \times (8 \text{ bits}) = 8000 \text{ bits}$

    $8000 / (2000 + 8000) = 8000/10{,}000 = 80 \text{ percent efficiency}$

3. The mechanical specification of EIA-232 describes the DTE-DCE interface.
4. The functional specification of EIA-232 defines the functions assigned to each of the 25 pins in DB-25.
9. An unbalanced circuit has one line for signal propagation, while a balanced circuit has two. In the latter, the signals are complements of each other.
16. Telephone communications are traditionally analog. Modems transform digital signals to analog on one end and analog to digital on the other end.
19. In a four-wire system, each pair can be used for each direction. The capacity is therefore two times that of the two-wire system.

Chapter 7: Transmission Media

Multiple Choice

1. b   2. b   3. a   4. b   5. a   6. b   7. b   8. d   9. c   10. c

11. b   12. a   13. a   14. d   15. c   16. b   17. a   18. b   19. a   20. b

21. a   22. d   23. a   24. a   25. c   26. b   27. a   28. d   29. a   30. b

31. c   32. c   33. a   34. b   35. d   36. c

Exercises

1. Crosstalk is the undesired effect of one circuit (channel) on another circuit (channel). Crosstalk can be reduced by shielding each pair of twisted-pair cable.

3. In a fiber-optic cable the light ray needs to travel along a long narrow channel, the core; it does this by successive reflections against the cladding. On the other hand, a refractive ray goes into the cladding and leaves the core area; the information thus does not get propagated; it is lost.

7. Terrestrial microwave transmission is limited by the curvature of the earth and the height of the antennae. Both of these factors are needed to calculate the distance a signal can travel.

8. 22,287.83 miles / 186,000 miles per second = 0.120 seconds = 120 ms

Chapter 8: Multiplexing

Multiple Choice

1. d   2. a   3. d   4. a   5. a   6. b   7. a   8. a   9. b   10. d

11. a   12. a   13. b   14. c   15. b   16. d   17. b   18. d   19. d   20. a

21. c   22. b   23. a

Exercises

1. $BWt = 5 \times 4000 + (5 - 1) \times 200 = 20,000 + 800 = 20,800$ Hz = 20.8 KHz

2.

Bandwidth with guard bands = $7900 - (3 - 1) \times 200 = 7500$ Hz

Bandwidth for each station = 7500 / 3 = 2500 Hz = 2.5 KHz

4. Each device sends 100 characters per second, or 800 bps. One frame consists of one byte from each of the five devices plus one bit for synchronization; each frame is therefore 41 bits.

Frame rate = 100 frames/second

Bit rate = 100 frames/second $\times$ 41 bits/frame = 4100 bps

8. Synchronous TDM is a simple multiplexing technique that assigns a minimum of one slot for each signal source. Asynchronous TDM is more sophisticated and tries to be more efficient. It assumes that not all sources are sending at all times. Therefore, there are usually fewer slots than devices.

12. A modem takes a digital signal and converts it to an analog signal and vice versa. A DSU takes a digital signal and changes its data rate and format to match the available digital line.

16. The sampling rate must be twice the highest frequency component. The highest frequency component is 4000 Hz; therefore, the sampling rate is 8000 samples/second.

18.   2 Gbps / 1.544 Mbps = 1300 T-1 lines

$1,300 \times 24$ voice channels/line = 31,200 channels

Chapter 9: Error Detection and Correction

Multiple Choice

1. d   2. b   3. d   4. a   5. c   6. b   7. c   8. a   9. d   10. c

11. b   12. a   13. b   14. a   15. d   16. b   17. c

Exercises

3. a. 1500 bps $\times$ 0.002 s = 3 bits
   b. 12,000 bps $\times$ 0.002 s = 24 bits
   c. 96,000 bps $\times$ 0.002 s = 192 bits

   The higher the transmission speed, the higher the number of errors for a burst of noise of n seconds.

5. a. 1
   b. 1
   c. 0
   d. 1

11. $2^r \geq m + r + 1$
   a. 5
   b. 5
   c. 5
   d. 7

12. The Hamming code is 100111101111.

   $r_8 = 0$ $r_4 = 1$ $r_2 = 1$ $r_1 = 1$

Chapter 10: Data Link Control

Multiple Choice

1. c   2. a   3. b   4. b   5. c   6. a   7. c   8. b   9. d   10. c

11. c   12. c   13. b   14. d   15. d   16. c   17. b

Exercises

1. Flow control is needed so that the receiver does not become overwhelmed with data. The receiver needs to communicate to the sender how well it is handling the incoming data. Window size, buffer size, and data rate are some of the parameters affecting flow control.

4. The go-back-n ARQ is more popular because selective-reject ARQ requires sorting, sequencing, and storage abilities not needed by go-back-n.

9. a. There is no number on the NAK frame.

   b. The number refers to the damaged frame that must be resent. All frames sent since the last frame acknowledged are retransmitted.

   c. The number refers to the damaged frame that must be resent. No other frames need to be retransmitted.

10. a. The number refers to the receipt of an acceptable frame.

    b. The number refers to the next expected frame.

    c. The number refers to the next expected frame.

11. a. Frames 7 and 0 received successfully.

    b. Frames 7, 0, 1, 2, and 3 received successfully.

    c. Frames 7, 0, 1, and 2 received successfully.

    d. Frames 7 and 0 received successfully; frame 1 arrived damaged.

    e. Frames 7, 0, 1, and 2 received successfully; frame 3 arrived damaged.

    f. Frame 7 arrived damaged.

Chapter 11: Data Link Protocols

Multiple Choice

1. b   2. b   3. a   4. b   5. b   6. b   7. c   8. c   9. d   10. b

11. b   12. b   13. a   14. a   15. a   16. d   17. b   18. b   19. a

Exercises

1. Data transparency means allowing any bit pattern to be used as data without the pattern being mistaken for a control character.

3. The original data are underlined and boldfaced.

   SYN SYN SOH header DLE STX DLE **DLE ETX SYN** DLE **DLE** DLE **DLE ETX** DLE ETX BCC

6. a. RR, F = 1, N(R) = an odd frame number

   b. RR, F = 1, N(R) = an even frame number

   c. REJ, F = 1, N(R) = an odd or even frame number

   d. RNR, F = 1, N(R) = an odd or even frame number

Chapter 12: Local Area Networks (LANs)

Multiple Choice

1. b   2. b   3. a   4. c   5. c   6. c   7. d   8. c   9. b   10. b

11. d   12. b   13. d   14. c   15. d   16. c   17. d   18. a   19. a   20. b

21. a   22. b   23. d   24. a   25. d   26. d   27. d   28. d   29. c   30. a

31. b

Exercises

1. IEEE Project 802.2 takes the data link layer and divides it into two sublayers, the medium access control (MAC) sublayer and the logical link control (LLC) sublayer. The MAC sublayer deals with the movement of a frame through a network and is LAN specific. The LLC, the upper sublayer, handles the end-user functions of the frame and is a protocol common to all LANs.

3. The SSAP and the DSAP are the protocol stack numbers. The MAC frame source address is the physical address of the previous node and the MAC frame destination address is the physical address of the next node.

5. The MAC layer of the IEEE Project 802 defines the type of cable, connections, and signals to be used.

6. The differences between the IEEE Project 802.3 frame and the HDLC I-frame include the following:

   a. The 802.3 frame has a preamble and SFD fields; the HDLC I-frame has a flag field.

   b. The 802.3 frame carries the physical address of both the source and destination; the HDLC I-frame address is the address of the secondary station.

   c. The 802.3 frame has no control field because this field is included in the PDU.

   d. The 802.3 frame has a length PDU field; the HDLC I-frame does not.

   e. There is no ending flag in the 802.3 frame.

8. A baseband signal (a digital signal) is not modulated; a broadband signal (an analog signal) is modulated.

12. The advantages of FDDI over a token ring include the following:

   a. A higher data rate.

   b. The sending of multiple frames when a token is captured.

15. Each of the 16 four-bit data sequences is encoded to five bits. The five-bit sequences are selected such that there can be at most one leading 0 and two trailing 0s. So at most you have a run of three 0s.

Chapter 13: Metropolitan Area Networks (MANs)

Multiple Choice

1. d   2. a   3. d   4. a   5. c   6. d   7. c   8. c   9. a   10. b
11. c

Exercises

2. Six stations are upstream to station 7 on bus A. Seven stations are downstream to station 3 on bus A.
4. The DQDB header address field on a MAN contains a 20-bit VCI. On a LAN this field is all 1s and an additional header is added to carry the MAC physical address.

Chapter 14: Switching

Multiple Choice

1. a   2. b   3. c   4. d   5. b   6. c   7. b   8. d   9. c   10. d
11. b

Exercises

3. a. A TST switch is superior to a single crossbar because fewer crosspoints are needed.
   b. A TST switch is superior to a single TSI because of the reduction in the delay time.
5. $2^{16} = 65,536$ $2^{24} = 16,777,216$

Chapter 15: Integrated Services Digital Network (ISDN)

Multiple Choice

1. c   2. b   3. c   4. d   5. c   6. b   7. d   8. c   9. b   10. a
11. b   12. a   13. b   14. d   15. d   16. a   17. c   18. b   19. a   20. c
21. b   22. a   23. a   24. c   25. a   26. b   27. c   28. b

Exercises

1. The R interface lies between a TE2 and a TA; this interface is not directly part of ISDN and therefore can use any of the EIA standards or V or X standards.

4.

	ASK	2B1Q
Signal	Analog	Digital
Voltage levels	2	4
Bits/voltage level	1	2

Chapter 16: X.25

Multiple Choice

1. d   2. d   3. b   4. c   5. b   6. c   7. c   8. b   9. c   10. a

11. d

Exercises

1. The two types of headers differentiate the size of the packets being transmitted. For the short packet, the sequence number can be a maximum of 7; for the long packet, the sequence number can be a maximum of 127.
3. X.25 provides error control in both data link and network layers.

Chapter 17: Frame Relay

Multiple Choice

1. b   2. c   3. b   4. b   5. a   6. a   7. b   8. d   9. a   10. d

Exercises

1. Flow control in frame relay is actually congestion control. The FECN bit notifies the receiver of incoming congested traffic; the BECN informs the receiver of outgoing congested traffic. Data flow is also influenced by the DE bit, which defines the priority for packet discarding.
3. Advantages of frame relay over X.25 include the following:
   a. More efficient use of bandwidth.
   b. Less buffer space required.
   c. Elimination of network layer functions and some data link layer functions.

Chapter 18: Asynchronous Transfer Mode (ATM)

Multiple Choice

1. d   2. d   3. d   4. b   5. a   6. c   7. c   8. b   9. b   10. a

11. c   12. d   13. b   14. a   15. b   16. d   17. a   18. c

Exercises

1. The whole idea of a cell network is to minimize delay. If a cell network uses the switched virtual circuit approach, the time spent in connection establishment adds to the total delay of the system.

3. Real-time audio and video transmission require minimum and constant delay. Therefore, the data unit size must be the same and as small as possible to prevent variable delay length.

6. If we add 13 bytes of pad to the 47,787 bytes of received data, we can create exactly 996 data units, each consisting of 48 bytes.

$$47{,}787 + 13 \text{ (pad)} + 8 \text{ (trailer)} = 47{,}808 = 996 \times 48$$

Chapter 19: SONET/SDH

Multiple Choice

1. d   2. a   3. b   4. c   5. a   6. a   7. b   8. d   9. c   10. b

11. a   12. d   13. a   14. c   15. b   16. a   17. d   18. d   19. b   20. c

21. b

Exercises

1. An STS multiplexer takes electronic signals, converts them to optical signals, and adds them together. It is used as an interface between an electrical system and an optical system. An add/drop multiplexer only multiplexes or demultiplexes optical signals. It is used only inside an optical system.

4. DS is a hierarchy of digital electrical services. STS is a hierarchy of optical services. DS data rates range from 1.544 Mbps to 274.176 Mbps. STS data rates range from 51.840 Mbps to 9953.280 Mbps.

Chapter 20: Internetworking and Networking Devices

Multiple Choice

1. a   2. d   3. c   4. d   5. b   6. d   7. a   8. d   9. b   10. a

11. a   12. a   13. d   14. c   15. a   16. d   17. b   18. a   19. a   20. b

21. b   22. b   23. c

Exercises

1. An amplifier amplifies the whole signal including any noise. A repeater regenerates the signal by first removing the noise and then amplifying the pure signal.
3. The best reason would be to reduce traffic.
5. The LSP database is a table. The LSP database is compiled from the LSPs received by a node.
8. The only impact router F's table makes on router A's table is the addition of network 92 to the table. For all other entries router A has the lower hop values in its table.

Chapter 21: Transport Layer

Multiple Choice

1. c   2. c   3. c   4. b   5. b   6. c   7. d   8. b   9. c   10. c

11. a   12. b   13. b   14. a   15. d   16. b   17. a

Exercises

1. The data link layer performs its duties on a single network, while the transport layer is responsible for similar duties across multiple networks.
3. a. The left and middle walls are at the same location when acknowledgments for all bytes sent have been received and new data have not yet been sent. The number of bytes that can be sent is equal to the window size.
   b. The middle and right walls are at the same location when no more bytes can be sent until acknowledgments are received.
5. A connection-oriented transport service goes through the following phases:
   a. Establishment of connection.
   b. Transfer of data.
   c. Termination of connection.

Chapter 22: Upper OSI Layers

Multiple Choice

1. c   2. a   3. d   4. b   5. d   6. d   7. d   8. c   9. a   10. d

11. b   12. b   13. d   14. a   15. b   16. b

Exercises

1. A T-disconnect service can abruptly terminate a transport connection at any time during a data transfer. Any data in transit are lost. A session layer graceful close, however, cannot disconnect until the data exchange is complete.

Chapter 23: TCP/IP

Multiple Choice

1. d   2. c   3. d   4. a   5. a   6. d   7. b   8. c   9. d   10. d

11. d   12. a   13. d   14. c   15. b   16. a   17. d   18. c   19. a   20. a

21. d   22. a   23. b   24. a   25. d   26. c   27. c   28. b   29. b   30. a

31. b   32. a   33. b   34. b   35. c   36. d   37. c   38. d   39. d   40. a

41. b   42. c   43. b   44. a   45. b   46. d   47. c   48. d   49. b

Exercises

1. The physical address is associated with the data link layer. The logical address is associated with the network layer. A port address is associated with the application layer.

4. The term *reliable* means that the system can perform sequence control, error control, and loss control.

9. UDP is faster than TCP because no connection establishment or termination is required. Also, less overhead is involved (the header is shorter).

11. One connection in FTP handles control information such as commands, replies, and process updates; the other connection is for the actual transfer of data.

13. In a network address the hostid is all 0s. For a class A network there can be 2^7 networks; for class B, 2^{14}; and for class C, 2^{21}.

14. In class A, a network can have up to $2^{24} = 16,777,216$ hosts. In class B, a network can have up to $2^{16} = 65,536$ hosts. In class C, a network can have up to $2^8 = 256$ hosts.

15. The following shows the answers. Dots are added just to show the boundary of bytes.
    a. 01111100.00100010.00000110.00001001
    b. 00010111.01000011.00000110.00000011
    c. 00000000.00010111.00111000.00000000
    d. 00001100.00100010.01000011.01111101

17. a. 121.0.0.0
    b. 193.23.56.0
    c. not applicable
    d. 142.23.0.0

ACRONYMS

AAL	Application adaptation layer.
ABM	Asynchronous balanced mode.
AM	Amplitude modulation.
AMI	Alternate mark inversion.
ANSI	American National Standards Institute.
ARP	Address resolution protocol.
ARPA	Advanced Research Project Agency.
ARPANET	Advanced Research Project Agency Network.
ARQ	Automatic repeat request.
ASCII	American Standard Code for Information Interchange.
ASK	Amplitude shift keying.
ASN.1	Abstract syntax notation 1.
ATM	Asynchronous transfer mode.
B8ZS	Bipolar 8-zero substitution.
BCC	Block check count.
B-ISDN	Broadband ISDN.
BLAST	Blocked asynchronous transmission
BSC	Binary synchronous communication.
CATV	Community antenna television.
CCITT	Consultative Committee for International Telegraphy and Telephony.
CGI	Common gateway interface.
CLNS	Connectionless network service.
CLTS	Connectionless transport service.
CMIP	Common management information protocol.
CMIS	Common management information services.
CMISE	Common management information service elements.
CONS	Connection-oriented network service
COTS	Connection-oriented transport service
CRC	Cyclic redundancy check.
CS	Convergence sublayer.
CSMA	Carrier sense multiple access.
CSMA/CD	Carrier sense multiple access with collision detection.
CSU	Channel service unit.
DAC	Dual attachment concentrator.
DAS	Dual attachment station.

DCE	Data circuit-terminating equipment.
DDS	Digital data service.
DES	Data encryption standard.
DIB	Directory information base.
DNS	Domain name system.
DPSK	Differential phase shift keying.
DQDB	Distributed queue dual bus.
DSA	Directory system agent.
DSU	Data service unit.
DSU/CSU	Data service unit/channel service unit.
DTE	Data terminal equipment.
DUA	Directory user agent.
EBCDIC	Extended binary coded decimal interchange code.
EDI	Electronic data interchange.
EHF	Extremely high frequency.
EIA	Electronics Industries Association.
EMI	Electromagnetic interference.
EOT	End of transmission.
FCC	Federal Communications Commission.
FCS	Frame check sequence.
FDDI	Fiber distributed data interface.
FDM	Frequency division multiplexing.
FM	Frequency modulation.
FSK	Frequency shift keying.
FTAM	File transfer, access, and management.
FTP	File transfer protocol.
HDB3	High-density bipolar 3.
HDLC	High-level data link control.
Hz	Hertz.
HF	High frequency.
HTML	Hypertext markup language.
HTTP	Hypertext transfer protocol.
ICMP	Internet control message protocol.
IDN	Integrated digital network.
IEEE	Institute of Electrical and Electronics Engineers.
IP	Internetworking Protocol.
IPX	Internetwork packet exchange.
ISDN	Integrated Services Digital Network.
ISO	International Standards Organization.
ITU–T	International Telecommunications Union–Telecommunication Standardizaton Sector.
LAN	Local area network.
LAP	Link access procedure.
LAPB	Link access procedure, balanced.
LAPD	Link access procedure for D channel.
LED	Light-emitting diode.
LF	Low frequency.
LLC	Logical link control.
LRC	Longitudinal redundancy check.
LSP	Link state packet.
MA	Multiple access.
MAC	Medium access control .
MAN	Metropolitan area network.

MAU	Medium attachment unit or multistation access unit.
MF	Middle frequency.
MHS	Message handling system.
MIB	Management information base.
MIC	Media interface connector.
MTA	Message transfer agent.
MTS	Message transfer system.
MTSO	Mobile telephone switching office.
MTU	Maximum transfer unit.
NAK	Negative acknowledgment.
NFS	Network file system.
NIC	Network interface card.
NNI	Network-to-network interface.
NRM	Normal response mode.
NRZ	Non-return to zero.
NRZ-I	Non-return to zero, invert.
NRZ-L	Non-return to zero, level.
NT1	Network termination 1.
NT2	Network termination 2.
NVT	Network virtual terminal.
OC	Optical carrier.
OSI	Open systems interconnection.
PAM	Pulse amplitude modulation.
PBX	Private branch exchange.
PCM	Pulse code modulation.
PDU	Protocol data unit.
PLP	Packet layer protocol.
PM	Phase modulation.
PRI	Primary rate interface.
PSK	Phase shift keying.
QAM	Quadrature amplitude modulation.
RARP	Reverse address resolution protocol.
RIP	Routing information protocol.
RPC	Remote procedure call.
RZ	Return to zero.
SAR	Segmentation and reassembly.
SAS	Single attachment station.
SDH	Synchronous Digital Hierarchy.
SDLC	Synchronous data link control.
SEAL	Simple and efficient adaptation layer.
SFD	Start frame delimiter.
SHF	Superhigh frequency.
SMDS	Switched multimegabit data service.
SMTP	Simple mail transfer protocol.
SNA	Systems Network Architecture.
SNMP	Simple network management protocol.
SONET	Synchronous Optical Network.
SPDU	Session protocol data unit.
STP	Shielded twisted-pair.
STS	Synchronous transport signal.
TA	Terminal adapter.
TCP	Transmission control protocol.

TCP/IP	Transmission control protocol/internetworking protocol.
TDM	Time-division multiplexing.
TE1	Terminal equipment 1.
TE2	Terminal equipment 2.
TFTP	Trivial file transfer protocol.
TPDU	Transport protocol data unit.
TSI	Time-slot interchange.
UA	User agent.
UDP	User datagram protocol.
UHF	Ultrahigh frequency.
UNI	User network interface.
URL	Universal resource locator.
VHF	Very high frequency.
VLF	Very low frequency.
VRC	Vertical redundancy check.
VT	Virtual tributary or virtual terminal.
WAIS	Wide Area Information Service.
WAN	Wide area network.
WWW	World Wide Web.

GLOSSARY

1Base5   The IEEE 802.3 standard for low-data-rate Ethernet. The standard specifies a star topology using twisted-pair cable with a maximum segment length of 500 meters. The data rate is defined to be 1 Mbps. It is also known as starLAN.

10Base-T   The IEEE 802.3 standard for twisted-pair Ethernet. The standard specifies a star topology using twisted-pair cable. The data rate is defined to be 10 Mbps.

10Base2   The IEEE 802.3 standard for Thin Ethernet. The standard specifies a bus topology using thin coaxial cable with a maximum segment length of 185 meters. The data rate is defined to be 10 Mbps. (Also called cheapernet or cheapnet.)

10Base5   The IEEE 802.3 standard for Thick Ethernet. The standard specifies a bus topology using thick coaxial cable with a maximum segment length of 500 meters. The data rate is defined to be 10 Mbps.

100Base-T   A version of the IEEE 802.3 standard for Fast Ethernet. The standard specifies a star topology using twisted-pair cable. The data rate is defined to be 100 Mbps.

A

AAL 1   An AAL layer in the ATM protocol that processes constant-bit-rate data.

AAL 2   An AAL layer in the ATM protocol that processes variable-bit-rate data.

AAL 3/4   An AAL layer in the ATM protocol that processes connectionless or connection-oriented packet data.

AAL 5   An AAL layer in the ATM protocol that processes data with extensive header information from upper layer protocols; also called the simple and efficient adaptation layer (SEAL).

AAL   See *application adaptation layer.*

ABM   See *asynchronous balanced mode.*

abort   To terminate a process abruptly.

abstract syntax notation 1 (ASN.1)   A formal language using abstract syntax for defining the structure of a protocol data unit (PDU).

access control field   A field in a token ring frame containing priority, token, monitor, and reservation bits.

acknowledgment   A response sent by the receiver to indicate the successful receipt and acceptance of data.

active document   In the World Wide Web, a document created at the local site using Java.

active hub   A hub that repeats or regenerates a signal. It functions as a repeater.

address field   A field containing the address of a sender or receiver.

address resolution protocol (ARP)   In TCP/IP, a protocol for obtaining the physical address of a node when the Internet address is known.

Advanced Research Project Agency (ARPA)   The government agency that funded ARPANET.

Advanced Research Project Agency Network (ARPANET)   The packet switching network that was funded by ARPA.

alternate mark inversion (AMI)   A digital-to-digital bipolar encoding method in which the amplitude representing 1 alternates between positive and negative voltages.

AM   See *amplitude modulation.*

American National Standards Institute (ANSI)   A national standards organization that defines standards in the United States.

American Standard Code for Information Interchange (ASCII)   A character code developed by ANSI and used extensively for data communication.

AMI   See *alternate mark inversion.*

amplitude modulation (AM)   An analog-to-analog encoding method in which the amplitude of the carrier wave is a function of the amplitude of the modulating wave.

amplitude shift keying (ASK)   A digital-to-analog encoding method in which the amplitude of the carrier signal represents the digital information.

amplitude   The magnitude of signal strength measured in volts or amperes.

analog data   Data that vary continuously.

analog hierarchy   An AT&T signal classification system.

analog leased service   A public telephone service that provides a dedicated connection between two customers; no dialing is necessary.

analog service   A public telephone service in which the signal is analog.

analog signal   A continuously varying signal.

analog switched service   A common public telephone service that connects two customers temporarily through the use of switching stations and switches; dialing is necessary.

analog transmission   The transfer of information using analog signals.

analog-to-analog encoding   Changing analog information to an analog signal.

angle modulation   See *phase modulation.*

angle of incidence   In optics, the angle formed by a light ray approaching the interface between two media and the line perpendicular to the interface.

angle of reflection   In optics, the angle formed by a reflected light ray at the interface between two media and the line perpendicular to the interface.

angle of refraction   In optics, the angle formed by a refracted light ray at the interface between two media and the line perpendicular to the interface.

ANSI   See *American National Standards Institute.*

aperiodic signal   A signal that has no repeating pattern.

applet   A computer program for creating an active Web document. It is usually written in Java.

AppleTalk   A protocol suite developed by Apple Computer, Inc.

application adaptation layer (AAL)   A layer in ATM protocol that breaks user data into 48-byte payloads.

application layer   The seventh layer in the OSI model; provides access to network resources.

Archie   An automated title-search service on the Internet that finds all files when a name is given. It is short for archive.

ARCnet   A simple local area network using the token access method developed by Datapoint Corporation. It is short for attached resource computing network.

ARP   See *address resolution protocol.*

ARPA   See *Advanced Research Project Agency.*

ARPANET   See *Advanced Research Project Agency Network.*

ARQ   See *automatic repeat request.*

ASCII   See *American Standard Code for Information Interchange.*

ASK   See *amplitude shift keying.*

ASN.1   See *abstract syntax notation 1.*

asynchronous balanced mode (ABM)   In HDLC, a communication mode in which all stations are equal.

asynchronous protocol   A set of rules for asynchronous transmission.

asynchronous TDM   See *asynchronous time-division multiplexing.*

asynchronous time division multiplexing   Time division multiplexing in which link time is allocated dynamically according to whether a terminal is active or not.

asynchronous transfer mode (ATM)   A wide area protocol featuring high data rates, and equal-sized packets (cells); ATM is suitable for transferring textual, audio, and video data.

asynchronous transmission   Transfer of data with start and stop bit(s) and a variable time interval between data units.

ATM   See *asynchronous transmission mode.*

ATM consortium   A group of ATM software and hardware vendors.

ATM forum   A group of ATM parties interested in the promotion and rapid development of ATM.

ATM switch   An ATM device providing both switching and multiplexing functions.

attenuation   Loss of signal strength as the signal travels along a medium.

authentication   Verification of the sender of a message.

automatic repeat request (ARQ)   An error-control method in which correction is made by re-transmission of data.

B

B-channel   An ISDN channel type with a 64 Kbps data rate; the basic user channel; also known as the bearer channel.

B-ISDN   See *broadband ISDN.*

B8ZS   See *bipolar 8-zero substitution.*

backbone   The major transmission path in a network.

balanced circuit   An electrical circuit carrying signals of equal but opposite value.

balanced transmission   Transmission of a signal on a balanced circuit.

bandwidth on demand   A leasing agreement that allows a user the use of a variable number of channels, depending on need.

bandwidth   The difference between the highest and the lowest frequencies of a composite signal. It also measures the information-carrying capacity of a line or a network.

base 2   A number system based on 2 symbols; also called the binary system.

base 8   A number system based on 8 symbols; also called the octal system.

base 10   A number system based on 10 symbols; also called the decimal system.

base 16   A number system based on 16 symbols; also called the hexadecimal system.

baseband   A signal transmitted directly onto a channel without modulating a carrier.

basic rate interface (BRI)   In ISDN, an electrical interface providing two B channels (64 Kbps) and one D channel (16 Kbps). The total data rate is 192 Kbps, which includes some overhead.

baud rate   The number of signal elements transmitted per second. A signal element consists of one or more bits.

BCC   See *block check count.*

bearer services   In ISDN, a service that does not manipulate the content of the transmission.

Bell modems   Modems manufactured by the Bell Telephone Company.

Bellcore   Bell Communication Research; provides research and development resources for the advancement of communications technology.

Bellman-Ford algorithm   An algorithm used to calculate routing tables in the distance vector routing method.

binary number system   A method of representing information using only two symbols (0 and 1).

binary synchronous communication (BSC)   A character-oriented data link protocol developed by IBM; also known as bisync.

bipolar 8-zero substitution (B8ZS)   A digital-to-digital encoding method used in North America that provides synchronization for long strings of 0s.

bipolar encoding   A digital-to-digital encoding method in which 1s are represented by alternating positive and negative voltages.

bit   A binary digit; the smallest unit of information; 1 or 0.

bit rate   The number of bits transmitted per second.

bit stuffing   In bit-oriented protocol, addition of an extra bit (0) to achieve data transparency. In synchronous TDM, the addition of extra bits to equalize different data rates.

bit-oriented protocol   A protocol in which a frame is seen as a bit stream.

bits per second (bps)   A measurement of data speed; bits transmitted per second.

BLAST   See *blocked asynchronous transmission.*

block check count (BCC)   A BSC data frame field for error detection; either a one-character LRC or a two-character CRC.

blocked asynchronous transmission (BLAST)   A protocol similar to XMODEM, but more powerful.

blocking   An event that occurs when a switching network is working at its full capacity and cannot accept more input.

bps   See *bits per second.*

bridge   A network device operating at the first two layers of the OSI model with filtering and forwarding capabilities.

broadband ISDN (B-ISDN)   ISDN with a high data rate based upon cell-relay delivery.

broadband transmission   Transmission of a signal using a modulated carrier wave.

broadcasting   Transmission of a message to all nodes in a network.

brouter (bridge/router)   A device that functions as both a bridge and a router.

browser   An application program that displays a WWW document. A browser usually uses other Internet services to access the document.

BSC   See *binary synchronous communication.*

buffer   Memory set aside for temporary storage.

bulletin board   A repository of information created and used by many on an internetwork.

burst error   Error in a data unit in which two or more consecutive bits have been altered.

bus topology   A network topology in which all computers are attached to a shared medium (often a single cable).

byte   A group of eight bits.

byte rate   The number of bytes transmitted per second.

byte stuffing   In character-oriented protocols, the addition of control character(s) to achieve data transparency.

byte-oriented protocol   See *character-oriented protocol.*

C

carrier   An analog signal whose amplitude, frequency, or phase can be altered to represent data.

carrier sense multiple access (CSMA)   A contention access method in which each station listens to the line before transmitting data.

carrier sense multiple access with collision detection (CSMA/CD)   An access method in which stations transmit whenever the transmission medium is available and retransmit when collision occurs.

CATV   See *community antenna television.*

CCITT   See *Consultative Committee for International Telegraphy and Telephony.*

cell   A small, fixed-size data unit; also, in cellular telephony, a geographical area served by a cell office.

cell network   A network using the cell as its basic data unit.

cell relay   A communication technology using a fixed-size data unit as the packet; used by ATM.

cellular   A wireless communication technique in which an area is divided into cells. A cell is served by a transmitter.

CGI   See *Common Gateway Interface.*

channel   A communications pathway.

channel service unit (CSU)   A device that functions as a digital "modem." It transmits and receives digital signals, performing functions such as filtering and signal shaping.

character-oriented protocol   A protocol in which the basic unit of information is usually an eight-bit character.

cheapernet   See *10Base2.*

cheapnet   See *cheapernet.*

checksum   A field used for error detection. It is formed by adding bit streams using one's complement arithmetic and then complementing the result.

ciphertext   The encrypted data.

circuit switching   A switching technology that establishes an electrical connection between stations using a dedicated path.

cladding   Glass or plastic surrounding the core of an optical fiber; the optical density of the cladding must be less than that of the core.

client   A program that initiates communication with another program called the server.

client server model   The model of interaction between two application programs in which a program at one end (client) requests a service from a program at the other end (server).

CLNS   See *connectionless network service.*

CLTS   See *connectionless transport service.*

CMIP   See *common management information protocol.*

CMIS   See *common management information services.*

CMISE   See *common management information service elements.*

coaxial cable   A transmission medium consisting of a conducting core, insulating material, and a second conducting sheath.

code   An arrangement of symbols to stand for a word or an action.

codec (coder-decoder)   A device that transforms analog data into a digital signal (coder) or a digital signal into analog data (decoder).

collision   The event that occurs when two transmitters send at the same time on a channel designed for only one transmission at a time; data will be destroyed.

combined station   In HDLC protocol, a station that can function as a primary or secondary station at the same time.

common carrier   A transmission facility available to the public and subject to public utility regulation.

common gateway interface (CGI)   A standard for communication between HTTP servers and executable programs. CGI is used in creating dynamic documents.

common management information protocol (CMIP)   The network management protocol defined by the ISO.

common management information service elements (CMISE)   Service elements provided by CMIS for management of a system based on the OSI model.

common management information services (CMIS)   A service that manages a system based on the OSI model.

communication network   A collection of connected devices for the exchange of information.

communication   The exchange of information between two entities.

community antenna television (CATV)   Television using coaxial cable loops; today called cable television.

complex signal   A signal that can be decomposed into more than one sine wave.

compression   The reduction of a message without significant loss of information.

conditioning   Improving the quality of a line through lessening of attenuation and distortion.

congestion   Excessive network or internetwork traffic causing a general degradation of service.

congestion control   A method to manage network and internetwork traffic to improve throughput.

connection establishment   The preliminary setup necessary for a logical connection prior to actual data transfer.

connection request   A message sent to establish a connection.

connection termination   A message sent to end a connection.

connection-oriented network service (CONS)   A network-level data protocol with formal establishment and termination.

connection-oriented service   A service for data transfer involving formal establishment and termination.

connection-oriented transmission   Data transfer involving formal establishment and termination.

connection-oriented transport service (COTS)   A transport level protocol with formal establishment and termination.

connectionless network service (CLNS) A network-level protocol without formal establishment or termination.

connectionless service A service for data transfer without establishment or termination.

connectionless transmission Data transfer without establishment or termination.

connectionless transport service (CLTS) A transport level data transfer protocol without formal establishment or termination

CONS See *connection-oriented network service.*

constellation A plot of the amplitude and phase of signal elements in a composite signal.

Consultative Committee for International Telegraphy and Telephony (CCITT) An international standards group now known as the ITU-T.

contention An access method in which two or more devices try to transmit at the same time on the same channel.

conventional encryption A method of encryption in which the encryption and decryption algorithms use the same key which is kept secret.

convergence sublayer (CS) In ATM protocol, the upper AAL sublayer that adds a header or a trailer to the user data.

COTS See *connection-oriented transport service.*

country domain A subdomain in the domain name system (DNS) that uses two characters as the last suffix.

CRC See *cyclic redundancy check.*

critical angle In refraction, the value of the angle of incidence that produces a 90-degree angle of refraction.

crossbar switch A switch consisting of a lattice of horizontal and vertical paths. At the intersection of each horizontal and vertical path, there is a crosspoint that can connect the input to the output.

crosspoint The junction of an input and an output on a crossbar switch.

crosstalk The noise on a line caused by signals traveling along another line.

CS See *convergence sublayer.*

CSMA See *carrier sense multiple access.*

CSMA/CD See *carrier sense multiple access with collision detection.*

CSU See *channel service unit.*

cycle The repetitive unit of a periodic signal.

cyclic redundancy check (CRC) A highly accurate error-detection method based on interpreting a pattern of bits as a polynomial.

D

D channel (data channel) An ISDN channel used primarily to carry control signals. It can also be used for low-rate data transfer.

DAC See *dual attachment concentrator.*

DAS See *dual attachment station.*

data circuit-terminating equipment (DCE) A device used as an interface between a DTE and a network.

data communication The interchange of information between two or more entities.

data compression The reduction of the amount of data to be transmitted without significant loss of information.

data encryption standard (DES)   The U.S. government standard encryption method for non-military and nonclassified use.

data link layer   The second layer in the OSI model. It is responsible for node-to-node delivery.

data service unit (DSU)   A device used in conjunction with a CSU to ensure proper signal shaping and encoding.

data service unit/channel service unit (DSU/CSU)   A device that functions as a combination of a CSU and a DSU.

data terminal equipment (DTE)   A device that is an information source or an information sink. It is connected to a network through a DCE.

data transfer   The movement of data from one location to another.

datagram   In packet-switching, an independent data unit.

dc component   A zero-frequency component of a signal.

DCE   See *data circuit-terminating equipment.*

DDS   See *digital data service.*

de facto protocol   A protocol that has not been approved by an organized body but adopted as a standard through widespread use.

de jure protocol   A protocol that has been legislated by an officially recognized body.

decimal dotted notation   A notation devised to make the IP address easier to read; each byte is converted to its decimal equivalent and then set off from its neighbor by a period.

decimal number system   A method of representing information using 10 symbols (0, 1... and 9).

decoding   Process of restoring an encoded message to its pre-encoded form.

decryption   Recovery of the original message from the encrypted data.

demodulation   The process of separating the carrier signal from the information-bearing signal.

demodulator   A device that performs demodulation.

demultiplexer   A device that separates a multiplexed signal into its original components.

DES   See *data encryption standard.*

destination address   The address of the receiver of the data unit.

dialog   The exchange between two communicating devices.

DIB   See *directory information base.*

dibit   A unit consisting of two bits.

differential Manchester   A digital-to-digital polar encoding method that features a transition at the middle of the bit interval as well as an inversion at the beginning of each 1 bit.

differential phase shift keying (DPSK)   A variation of PSK in which the change in the phase of the carrier signal represents the digital information.

digital data   Data represented by discrete values or conditions.

digital data service (DDS)   A service featuring a digital leased line using a data rate of up to 56 Kbps.

digital pipe   A high-speed path composed of time-multiplexed channels.

digital signal   A discrete signal with a limited number of values.

digital signature   A method to authenticate the sender of a message.

digital transmission   Data transfer using digital signals.

digital-to-analog encoding   Changing digital information into analog signals.

digital-to-digital encoding   Changing digital information into digital signals.

Dijkstra's algorithm   In link state routing, an algorithm that finds the shortest path to other routers.

directory information base (DIB)   A distributed database containing information in an X.500 directory.

directory service (DS)   A service that can provide the email address of an individual.

directory system agent (DSA)   A part of X.500 that controls DIB.

directory user agent (DUA)   A part of X.500 that provides the interface between an application and DIB.

disconnect   To end a connection.

distance vector routing   A routing method in which each router sends its neighbors a list of networks it can reach and the distance to that network.

distortion   Any change in a signal due to noise, attenuation, or other influences.

distributed processing   A strategy in which services provided for the network reside at multiple sites.

distributed queue dual bus (DQDB)   A protocol defined by IEEE 802.6 to be used as a LAN or MAN.

DNS   See *domain name system.*

domain name system (DNS)   A TCP/IP application service that converts user-friendly names to IP addresses.

downlink   Transmission from a satellite to an earth station.

DPSK   See *differential phase shift keying.*

DQDB   See *distributed queue dual bus.*

DSA   See *directory system agent.*

DSU   See *data service unit.*

DSU/CSU   See *data service unit/channel service unit.*

DTE   See *data terminal equipment.*

DUA   See *directory user agent.*

dual attachment concentrator (DAC)   In FDDI, a device that connects a combination of SASs or DASs to the dual ring. It makes the combination look like a single SAS unit.

dual attachment station (DAS)   In FDDI, a station that can be connected to two rings.

dual bus   Two buses.

duplex mode   See *full duplex mode.*

dynamic document   A Web document created by running an applet at the client.

E

E-lines   The European equivalent of T-lines.

EBCDIC   See *extended binary coded decimal interchange code.*

EDI   See *electronic data interchange.*

EHF   See *extremely high frequency.*

EIA   See *Electronics Industries Association.*

EIA-232   A common 25-pin interface standard developed by the EIA.

EIA-449   An interface standard specifying a 37-pin connector and a 9-pin connector developed by the EIA.

EIA-530   An interface standard based on EIA-449 that uses DB-25 pins.

electromagnetic interference (EMI)   A noise on the data transmission line that can corrupt the data. It can be created by motors, generators, and so on.

electronic data interchange (EDI)   An application that allows the paperless transfer of business information.

electronic mail   A method of sending messages electronically based on mailbox addresses rather than a direct host-to-host exchange.

Electronics Industries Association (EIA)   An organization that promotes electronics manufacturing concerns. It has developed interface standards such as EIA-232, EIA-449, and EIA-530.

email   See *electronic mail.*

EMI   See *electromagnetic interference.*

encapsulation   The technique in which a data unit from one protocol in placed within the data field portion of the data unit of another protocol.

encoding   Transforming information into signals.

encryption   Converting a message into an unintelligible form that is unreadable unless decrypted.

end of transmission (EOT)   In BSC, a frame sent to indicate that no more data are to be sent.

end-to-end message delivery   Delivery of all parts of a message from the sender to the receiver.

ENQ/ACK   A line discipline method used in point-to-point connections. An ENQ frame is transmitted by a station wishing to send data; an ACK is returned if the station is ready to receive the data.

EOT   See *end of transmission.*

error   A mistake in data transmission.

error control   The detection and handling of errors in data transmission.

error correction   The process of correcting bits that have been changed during transmission.

error detection   The process of determining whether or not some bits have been changed during transmission.

error handling   The methods used to detect or correct errors.

error recovery   The ability of a system to resume normal activity after errors are detected.

ether   An imaginary substance believed by the ancients to fill all of outer space.

Ethernet   A local area network using CSMA/CD access method. See *IEEE 802.3.*

even parity   An error detection method in which an extra bit is added to the data unit such that the total number of 1s becomes even.

extended binary coded decimal interchange code (EBCDIC)   An eight-bit character code developed and used by IBM.

extension header   Extra headers in the IPv6 datagram that provide additional functionality.

extremely high frequency (EHF)   Radio waves in the 30 GHz to 300 GHz range using space propagation.

F

facsimile (fax)   The electronic reproduction of a document at a remote site.

fast Ethernet   See *100Base-T.*

fax   See *facsimile.*

FCC   See *Federal Communications Commission.*

FCS   See *frame check sequence.*

FDDI See *fiber distributed data interface.*

FDM See *frequency division multiplexing.*

Federal Communications Commission (FCC) A government agency that regulates radio, television, and wire/cable communications.

fiber distributed data interface (FDDI) A high-speed (100 Mbps) LAN, defined by ANSI, using fiber optics, dual ring topology, and the token passing access method. Today an FDDI network is also used as a MAN.

fiber-optic cable A high-bandwidth transmission medium which carries data signals in the form of pulses of light. It consists of a thin cylinder of glass or plastic, called the core, surrounded by a concentric layer of glass or plastic called the cladding.

file server A computer in a local area network that provides shared access to files.

file transfer, access, and management (FTAM) In the OSI model, an application layer service for remote file handling.

file transfer protocol (FTP) In TCP/IP, an application layer protocol that transfers files between two sites.

filter A device that passes only signals containing certain frequencies.

final bit (F bit) An HDLC control bit sent by the secondary station to indicate whether or not more frames are coming. See *P/F bit.*

flag In HDLC, a field that alerts the receiver of the beginning or ending a frame.

flooding Saturation of a network with a message.

flow control A technique to control the rate of flow of frames (packets or messages).

FM See *frequency modulation.*

forum An organization that tests, evaluates, and standardizes a specific new technology.

Fourier analysis The mathematical technique used to obtain the frequency spectrum of a signal if the time domain representation is given.

Fourier series Fourier analysis for obtaining the spectrum of a periodic signal.

Fourier transform Fourier analysis for obtaining the spectrum of an aperiodic signal.

fragmentation The division of a packet into smaller units to accommodate a protocol's MTU.

frame A group of bits representing a block of data.

frame check sequence (FCS) The HDLC error detection field containing either a two- or four-byte CRC.

frame relay A packet-switching specification defined for the first two layers of the OSI model. There is no network layer. Error checking is done on end-to-end basis instead of on each link.

frequency Number of cycles per second of a periodic signal.

frequency division multiplexing (FDM) A multiplexing method in which the bandwidth of a link is shared by several devices. This is done by dividing the bandwidth of the link into separate bandwidths called channels.

frequency domain plot A diagram showing the changes in the amplitude of a signal with respect to frequency.

frequency modulation (FM) An analog-to-analog encoding method in which the frequency of the carrier wave is a function of the amplitude of the modulating wave.

frequency shift keying (FSK) A digital-to-analog encoding method in which the frequency of the carrier signal represents the digital information.

FSK See *frequency shift keying.*

FTAM See *file transfer, access, and management.*

FTP   See *file transfer protocol.*

full-duplex mode   A transmission mode in which communication can be two way simultaneously.

G

gateway   A device used to connect two separate networks that use different communication protocols.

generic domain   A subdomain in the domain name system (DNS) that uses generic suffixes.

geosynchronous orbit   A fixed orbit at the equatorial plane 22,287.83 miles above the earth.

go-back-*n* ARQ   An error control method in which the frame in error and all following frames must be retransmitted.

gopher   A menu-driven browsing service that searches for documents on the Internet.

group   A level in the AT&T analog hierarchy with a 48 KHz bandwidth.

guard band   In FDM, unused bandwidth between two channels.

guided media   Transmission media with a physical boundary.

H

H-channel   In ISDN, a hybrid channel available in a variety of data rates; suitable for high-data-rate applications.

half-duplex mode   A transmission mode in which communication can be two way but not at the same time.

Hamming code   An error correction code in which redundant bits are inserted in predefined positions.

handshaking   A process to establish or terminate a connection.

Hayes-compatible modem   A class of intelligent modems capable of performing some functions such as automatic answering and dialing.

HDB3   See *high density bipolar 3.*

HDLC   See *high level data link control.*

header   Control information added to the beginning of a data packet.

hertz (Hz)   Unit of measurement for frequency.

hexadecimal colon notation   In IPv6, an address notation consisting of 32 hexadecimal digits, with every 4 digits separated by a colon.

hexadecimal number system   A method of representing information using 16 symbols (0, 1, … 9, A, B, C, D, E, and F).

HF   See *high frequency.*

high density bipolar 3 (HDB3)   A digital-to-digital bipolar encoding method used in Europe and Japan that attempts to control loss of synchronization due to runs of 0s.

high frequency (HF)   Radio waves in the 3 MHz to 30 MHz range using line-of-sight propagation.

high level data link control (HDLC)   A bit-oriented data link protocol defined by the ISO. It is used in X.25 protocol. A subset of it, called link access procedure (LAP), is used in other protocols. It is also a base for many data link protocols used in LANs.

hop count   The number of nodes along a route. It is a measurement of distance in routing algorithms.

horn antenna   An antenna resembling a giant scoop that is used for terrestrial microwave communications.

host   A station or node on a network.

hostid   The part of an IP address that identifies a host.

HTML   See *hypertext markup language.*

HTTP   See *hypertext transfer protocol.*

hub   A central device in a star topology that provides a common connection among the nodes.

Huffman coding   A data compression technique that uses a variable-length code based on the frequency of occurrence of characters.

hybrid topology   A topology composed of more than one basic topology.

hypertext markup language (HTML)   The computer language for specifying the contents and format of a Web document. It allows additional text to include codes that define fonts, layouts, embedded graphics, and hypertext links.

hypertext transfer protocol (HTTP)   An application service for retrieving a Web document.

Hz   See *hertz.*

I

I-frame   In HDLC, an information frame that carries user data and control information.

I.430   An ITU-T standard for BRI physical layer specifications.

I.431   An ITU-T standard for PRI physical layer specifications.

ICMP   See *internet control message protocol.*

IDN   See *integrated digital network.*

IEEE 802.1   The standard developed by IEEE project 802 for local area networks. It covers the internetworking aspect of LANs.

IEEE 802.2   The standard developed by IEEE project 802 for local area networks. It covers the LLC sublayer.

IEEE 802.3   The standard developed by IEEE project 802 for local area networks. It covers the MAC sublayer for networks using the CSMA/CD access method. A formal definition for Ethernet.

IEEE 802.4   The standard developed by IEEE project 802 for local area networks. It covers the MAC sublayer for networks using a ring topology and the token passing access method. A formal definition for token ring.

IEEE 802.5   The standard developed by IEEE project 802 for local area networks. It covers the MAC sublayer for networks using a bus topology and token-passing access method. A formal definition for token bus.

IEEE 802.6   The standard developed by IEEE project 802 for local and metropolitan area networks. It covers the MAC sublayer for networks using the DQDB access method.

IEEE Project 802   A project by IEEE to define LAN standards for the physical and data link layers of OSI model. It divides the data link layer into two sublayers called logical link control (LLC) and medium access control (MAC).

IEEE   See *Institute of Electrical and Electronics Engineers.*

IETF   See *Internet Engineering Task Force.*

inband signaling   A method of signaling in which both control and user data use the same channel.

information services   Network information repositories such as bulletin boards and data banks.

infrared light   Electromagnetic waves with frequencies just below the visible spectrum.

Institute of Electrical and Electronics Engineers (IEEE)   A group consisting of professional engineers that has specialized societies whose committees prepare standards in their area of specialty.

integrated digital network (IDN)   The integration of communication functions using digital technology in a telecommunication network.

integrated services digital network (ISDN)   An ITU-T standard for an end-to-end global digital communication system providing fully integrated digital services.

intelligent hub   A hub that regenerates signals and performs address checking on the data unit. It can function as a bridge.

intelligent modem   A modem that has extra functions such as automatic answering and dialing.

interface   The boundary between two pieces of equipment. It also refers to mechanical, electrical, and functional characteristics of the connection.

International Standards Organization (ISO)   A worldwide organization that defines and develops standards on a variety of topics.

International Telecommunications Union–Telecommunication Standardization Sector (ITU–T)   A standards organization formerly known as the CCITT.

Internet   A global internet that uses the TCP/IP protocol suite.

internet   A collection of networks connected by internetworking devices such as routers or gateways.

Internet Engineering Task Force (IETF)   A group working on the design and development of the TCP/IP protocol suite and the Internet.

Internet Society   The nonprofit organization established to publicize the Internet.

internet control message protocol (ICMP)   A protocol in the TCP/IP protocol suite that handles error and control messages.

internetwork packet exchange (IPX)   Novell's network-level connectionless protocol.

Internetworking Protocol (IP)   The network-layer protocol in the TCP/IP protocol suite governing connectionless transmission across packet-switching networks.

internetworking   Connecting several networks together using internetworking devices such as routers and gateways.

internetworking devices   Electronic devices such as routers and gateways that connect networks together to form an internet.

inverse multiplexing   Diverting one high-speed data stream into multiple lower-speed channels.

ionosphere   The layer of atmosphere above the troposphere containing ions.

IP   See *Internetworking Protocol*.

IP address class   In IPv4, one of the five groups of addresses; classes A, B, and C consist of a netid, hostid, and class ID; class D holds multicast addresses; class E is reserved for future use.

IP address   In IPv4, a 32-bit address that defines a host's connection to its network. In IPv6, a 128-bit address that does the same.

IPng (IP next generation)   See *IPv6*.

IPv4   The Internetworking Protocol version 4. It is the current version.

IPv6   The Internetworking Protocol version 6. A proposed internetworking protocol that features major IP addressing changes.

IPX   See *internetwork packet exchange*.

ISDN   See *Integrated Services Digital Network*.

ISO See *International Standards Organization.*

ITU–T See *International Telecommunications Union–Telecommunication Standardizaton Sector.*

J

Java A programming language used to create active Web documents.

jumbo group The highest level in the AT&T analog hierarchy, with a 16.984 MHz bandwidth.

K

Kermit An asynchronous data link protocol for file transfer.

L

LAN See *local area network.*

LAP See *link access procedure.*

LAPB See *link access procedure, balanced.*

LAPD See *link access procedure for D channel.*

laser Acronym for light amplification by stimulated emissions of radiation. A pure and narrow light beam that can be used as the light source in fiber-optic transmission.

layer One of the seven levels involved in data transmission in the OSI model; each level is a functional grouping of related activities.

LED See *light-emitting diode.*

Lempel-Ziv encoding A data compression method in which pointers are used to refer to repeated strings.

LF See *low frequency.*

light-emitting diode (LED) An electric diode that emits a light signal. Commonly used to drive a multimode fiber.

line configuration The relationship between communication devices and their pathway.

line discipline A data link layer procedure that defines which device has the right to send data; also referred to as access control.

line layer A SONET layer responsible for the movement of a signal across a physical line.

link access procedure (LAP) A bit-oriented data link protocol derived from HDLC.

link access procedure for D channel (LAPD) A LAP protocol defined for the D channel in the ISDN.

link access procedure, balanced (LAPB) A LAP protocol in which stations can function only in the balanced mode.

link state database In link state routing, a database common to all routers and made from LSP information.

link state packet (LSP) In link state routing, a small packet containing routing information sent by a router to all other routers.

link state routing A routing method in which each router shares its knowledge of changes in its neighborhood with all other routers.

LLC See *logical link control.*

local area network (LAN) A network connecting devices inside a single building or inside buildings close to each other.

local loop The link that connects a subscriber to the telephone central office.

logical address   An address defined in the network layer.

logical link control (LLC)   The upper sublayer of the data link layer as defined by IEEE Project 802.2.

longitudinal redundancy check (LRC)   An error detection method dividing a data unit into rows and columns and performing parity checks on corresponding bits of each column.

lossless data compression   A data compression method in which the integrity of the original data is preserved.

lossy data compression   A data compression method in which some insignificant part of the original data can be lost.

low frequency (LF)   Radio waves in the 30 KHz to 300 KHz range.

LRC   See *longitudinal redundancy check.*

LSP   See *link state packet.*

M

MA   See *multiple access.*

MAC   See *medium access control.*

major synchronization point   A synchronization point that must be confirmed before continuation of the session.

MAN   See *metropolitan area network.*

management information base (MIB)   The database used by SNMP that holds the information necessary for management of a network.

Manchester encoding   A digital-to-digital polar encoding method in which a transition occurs at the middle of each bit interval for the purpose of synchronization.

master group   A level in the AT&T analog hierarchy with a 2.52 MHz bandwidth.

MAU   See *medium attachment unit* or *multistation access unit.*

maximum transfer unit (MTU)   The largest size data unit a specific network can handle.

media interface connector (MIC)   A type of interface card used in FDDI.

medium access control (MAC)   The lower sublayer in the data link layer defined by the IEEE 802 project. It defines the access method and access control in different local area network protocols.

medium attachment unit (MAU)   See *transceiver.*

medium bandwidth   The difference between the highest and lowest frequencies a medium can support.

mesh topology   A topology in which each node is directly connected to every other node.

message   Data sent from source to destination.

message handling system (MHS)   The OSI model's application layer service for electronic mail. See *X.400.*

message switching   A switching method in which the whole message is stored in a switch and forwarded when a route is available.

message transfer agent (MTA)   An MHS component that accepts a message, examines it, and routes it.

message transfer system (MTS)   A group of message transfer agents (MTAs).

metropolitan area network (MAN)   A network that can span a geographical area the size of a city.

MF   See *middle frequency.*

MHS   See *message handling system.*

MIB   See *management information base.*

MIC   See *media interface connector.*

microwave   Electromagnetic waves ranging from 2 GHz to 40 GHz.

microwave transmission   Communication using microwaves.

middle frequency (MF)   Radio waves in the 300 KHz to 3 MHz range.

minor synchronization point   A synchronization point that may or may not be confirmed before continuation of the session.

mobile telephone switching office (MTSO)   In cellular telephony, the office responsible for coordinating calls between cell sites and the central office.

modem   A device consisting of a modulator and a demodulator. It converts a digital signal into an analog signal (modulation) and vice versa (demodulation).

modulation   Modification of one or more characteristics of a carrier wave by an information-bearing signal.

monitor station   In the token ring protocol, a station that is responsible for generating and controlling the token.

Morse code   An encoding method in which symbols are represented by the combination of dots and dashes.

MTA   See *message transfer agent.*

MTS   See *message transfer system.*

MTSO   See *mobile telephone switching office.*

MTU   See *maximum transfer unit.*

multicast address   An address used for multicasting.

multicasting   A transmission method that allows copies of a single packet to be sent to a selected group of receivers.

multidrop   See *multipoint.*

multimode graded index fiber   An optical fiber with a core having a graded index of refraction.

multimode step index fiber   An optical fiber with a core having a uniform index of refraction. The index of refraction will change suddenly at the core/cladding boundary.

multiple access (MA)   A line access method in which every station can access the line freely.

multiple bit error   Error in a data unit in which two or more nonconsecutive bits have been altered.

multiplexer   A device used for multiplexing.

multiplexing   The process of combining signals from multiple sources for transmission across a single data link.

multipoint   A line configuration in which three or more devices share a common transmission line.

multistation access unit (MAU)   In token ring, a device that houses individual automatic switches.

N

NAK   See *negative acknowledgment.*

negative acknowledgment (NAK)   A message sent to indicate the rejection of received data.

netid   The part of an IP address that identifies the network.

NetWare   A popular protocol suite and operating system developed by Novell Corporation.

network   A system consisting of connected nodes made to share data, hardware, and software.

network file system (NFS)   A TCP/IP application protocol that allows a user to access and manipulate remote file systems as if they were local. It uses the services of remote procedure call (RPC) protocol.

network interface card (NIC)   An electronic device, internal or external to a station, that contains circuitry that enables the station to be connected to the network.

network layer   The third layer in the OSI model, responsible for the delivery of a packet to the final destination.

network termination 1 (NT1)   In ISDN, devices between a user site and the central office that perform functions related to the first layer of the OSI model.

network termination 2 (NT2)   In ISDN, devices that perform functions related to the first three layers of the OSI model.

network virtual terminal (NVT)   A TCP/IP application protocol that allows remote login.

network-to-network interface (NNI)   In ATM, the interface between two networks.

NFS   See *network file system.*

NIC   See *network interface card.*

NNI   See *network-to-network interface.*

node   An addressable communication device (e.g., a computer or router) on a network.

node-to-node delivery   Transfer of a data unit from one node to the next.

noise   Random electrical signals that can be picked by the transmission medium and result in degradation or distortion of the data.

non-return to zero (NRZ)   A digital to-digital encoding method in which 0s and 1s are represented by specific voltage levels. Contrast with return to zero (RZ).

non-return to zero, invert (NRZ-I)   A type of non-return to zero (NRZ) encoding in which the 1s are represented by a transition at the beginning of the bit interval.

non-return to zero, level (NRZ-L)   A type of non-return to zero (NRZ) encoding in which the level of the voltage determines the bit.

normal response mode (NRM)   In HDLC, a communication mode in which the secondary station must have permission from the primary station before transmission can proceed.

NOT gate   An electronic device that inverts a bit.

NRM   See *normal response mode.*

NRZ   See *non-return to zero.*

NRZ-I   See *non-return to zero, invert.*

NRZ-L   See *non-return to zero, level.*

NT1   See *network termination 1.*

NT2   See *network termination 2.*

null modem   An interface defined to connect two close DTEs without the use of DCEs.

NVT   See *network virtual terminal.*

Nyquist theorem   A theorem that states that to recover the original analog signal from a sampled signal, the sampling rate must be at least twice the highest frequency component of the original signal.

O

OC   See *optical carrier*

octal number system   A method of representing information using eight symbols (0, 1, …, 6, and 7).

octet   Eight bits.

odd parity   An error detection method in which an extra bit is added to the data unit such that the sum of all 1-bits becomes odd.

one's complement   A representation of binary numbers in which the complement of a number is found by complementing all bits.

open system   A set of protocols that allows dissimilar systems to communicate.

open system interconnection (OSI)   A seven layer model for data communication defined by ISO.

optical carrier (OC)   The hierarchy of fiber-optic carriers defined in SONET. The hierarchy defines up to 10 different carriers (OC-1, OC-3, OC-12, …, OC-192), each with a different data rate.

optical fiber   See *fiber-optic cable.*

OSI   See *open system interconnection.*

out-of-band signaling   A method of signaling in which control data and user data travel on different channels.

overhead   Extra bits added to the data unit for control purposes.

P

P/F bit   See *poll/final bit.*

packet header   Control and address information added to the data unit.

packet layer protocol (PLP)   The network layer in X.25 protocol.

packet lifetime   The number of stations a packet can visit before being discarded.

packet   Synonym for data unit; mostly used in the network layer.

packet-switched network   A network in which data are transmitted in independent units called packets.

packet-switching   Data transmission using a packet-switched network.

PAM   See *pulse amplitude modulation.*

parabolic dish antenna   An antenna shaped like a parabola and used for terrestrial microwave communications.

parallel transmission   Transmission in which bits in a group are sent simultaneously, each using a separate link.

parity bit   A redundant bit added to a data unit (usually a character) for error checking.

parity check   An error-detection method using a parity bit.

passive hub   A hub used only for connection; it does not regenerate the signal.

path layer   A SONET layer responsible for the movement of a signal from its optical source to its optical destination.

path   The channel through which a signal travels.

PBX   See *private branch exchange.*

PCM   See *pulse code modulation.*

PDU   See *protocol data unit.*

peer-to-peer protocol   A protocol defining the rule of communication between two equal layers in the OSI model.

period   The time required for a signal to complete one cycle.

periodic signal   A signal that has a repeating pattern.

phase modulation (PM)   An analog-to-analog encoding method in which the phase of the carrier wave is a function of the amplitude of the information-bearing wave.

phase shift keying (PSK)   A digital-to-analog encoding method in which the phase of the carrier signal represents the digital information.

phase shift   The phase change of a signal.

phase   The relative position of a signal in time.

photonic layer   The SONET layer that corresponds to the OSI model's physical layer.

physical layer   The first layer of the OSI model, responsible for the mechanical and electrical specifications of the medium.

piggybacking   The inclusion of acknowledgment on a data frame.

pixel   Picture element; the smallest unit of an image.

plaintext   In encryption/decryption, the original message.

PLP   See *packet layer protocol.*

PM   See *phase modulation.*

point-to-point connection   A dedicated transmission link between two devices.

polar encoding   A digital-to-digital encoding method in which the value of a bit (0 or 1) is represented by two different voltage levels.

poll bit   See *poll/final bit.*

poll   In the primary/secondary access method, a procedure in which the primary station asks a secondary station if it has any data to transmit.

poll/final (P/F) bit   A bit in the control field of HDLC; if the primary is sending, it can be a poll bit; if the secondary is sending, it can be a final bit.

port address   In TCP/IP protocol the address of the executing program (process).

preamble   The seven-byte field of an IEEE 802.3 frame consisting of alternating 1s and 0s that alert and synchronize the receiver.

presentation layer   The sixth layer of the OSI model responsible for translation, encryption, authentication, and data compression.

PRI   See *primary rate interface.*

primary rate interface (PRI)   An ISDN electrical interface providing 23 B channels (64 kbps) and one D channel (64 kbps). The total data rate is 1.544 Mbps, which includes some overhead.

primary station   In primary/secondary access method, a station that issues commands to the secondary stations.

print server   A device that manages printers, print requests, and print queues.

private branch exchange (PBX)   A private telephone system.

private key   In conventional encryption, a key shared by only one pair of devices, a sender and a receiver. In public key encryption, the private key is known only to the receiver.

Project 802   The project undertaken by the IEEE in an attempt to solve LAN incompatibility.

propagation delay   The difference between the time a signal is sent and the time it is received.

protocol converter   A device such as a gateway that changes one protocol to another.

protocol data unit (PDU)   A data unit defined in each layer of the OSI model. In particular, a data unit specified by IEEE 802.2 in the LLC sublayer.

protocol   Rules for communication.

protocol suite   A stack or family of protocols defined for a complex communication system.

pseudoternary encoding   A digital-to-digital encoding method similar to bipolar encoding, but in which the 0-bit (instead of 1-bit) alternates between positive and negative voltages.

PSK See *phase shift keying.*

public key In public key encryption, a key known to everyone.

public key encryption A method of encryption based on a nonreversible encryption algorithm. The method uses two types of keys. The public key is known to the public. The private key (secret key) is known only to the receiver.

pulse amplitude modulation (PAM) The first step in the analog-to-digital encoding process, in which analog information is sampled to create pulses.

pulse code modulation (PCM) An analog-to-digital encoding method in which analog information is sampled, quantized, and converted to a digital signal.

Q

Q.931 The ITU-T standard that defines network layer functions of the ISDN related to the D channel.

QAM See *quadrature amplitude modulation.*

quadbit A unit of data consisting of four bits.

quadrature amplitude modulation (QAM) A digital-to-analog encoding method in which one can change both the amplitude and the phase of a carrier signal to represent digital information.

queue A waiting list.

R

R reference point In ISDN, the interface between a TE2 and a TA.

radio wave Electromagnetic energy in the 3 KHz to 300 GHz range.

RARP See *reverse address resolution protocol.*

receiver The target point of a transmission.

redundancy The addition of bits to a message for error control.

reflection The phenomenon related to the bouncing back of light at the boundary of two media.

refraction The phenomenon related to the bending of light when it passes from one medium to another.

regulatory agency A government agency that protects the public interest.

reliable delivery Receipt of a message without duplication, loss, or out-of-sequence packets.

remote login The process of logging on to a remote computer from a terminal connected to a local computer.

remote procedure call (RPC) A TCP/IP protocol used by NFS.

repeater A device that extends the distance a signal can travel by regenerating the signal.

return to zero (RZ) A digital-to-digital encoding technique in which the voltage of the signal is zero for the second half of the bit interval.

reverse address resolution protocol (RARP) A TCP/IP protocol that allows a host to find its Internet address given its physical address.

reverse domain A subdomain in the domain name system (DNS) that finds the domain name given the IP address.

ring topology A topology in which the devices are connected in a ring. Each device on the ring receives the data unit from the previous device, regenerates it, and forwards it to the next device.

RIP See *routing information protocol.*

route discovery The task of finding the optimum route a data unit must take.

router   An internetworking device operating at the first three OSI layers. A router is attached to two or more networks. It forwards packets from one network to another.

routing algorithm   The algorithm used by a router to determine the optimum path for a packet.

routing information protocol (RIP)   A routing protocol based on the distance vector routing algorithm.

routing table   A table containing information a router needs to route packets. The information may include the network address, the cost, the address of the next hop, and so on.

routing   The process performed by a router.

RPC   See *remote procedure call.*

RS-422 standard   A balanced circuit specification to be used with EIA-449.

RS-423 standard   An unbalanced circuit specification to be used with EIA-449.

RSA encryption   A popular public-key encryption method developed by Rivest, Shamir, and Adleman.

run-length encoding   A compression method in which a run of symbols is replaced by the symbol and the number of symbols.

RZ   See *return to zero.*

S

S reference point   In ISDN, the interface between a TE1 or a TA and an NT.

S-frame   An HDLC frame used for supervisory functions such as acknowledgment, flow control, and error control; it contains no user data.

sampling rate   The number of samples obtained per second in the sampling process.

sampling   The process of obtaining amplitudes of a signal at regular intervals.

SAR   See *segmentation and reassembly.*

SAS   See *single attachment station.*

SDH   See *synchronous digital hierarchy.*

SDLC   See *synchronous data link control.*

secondary station   In poll/select access method, a station that sends a response in answer to a command from a primary station.

section layer   A SONET layer responsible for the movement of a signal across a physical section.

security   The protection of a network from unauthorized access, viruses, and catastrophe.

segmentation and reassembly (SAR)   The lower AAL sublayer in ATM protocol in which a header and/or trailer may be added to produce a 48-byte element.

segmentation   The splitting of a message into multiple packets; usually performed at the transport layer.

select   In poll/select access method, a procedure in which the primary station asks a secondary station if it is ready to receive data.

selective-reject ARQ   An error-control method in which only the frame in error is resent.

self-synchronizing code   A coding scheme that allows for synchronization, often through transition during the bit interval.

sender   The originator of a message.

sequence number   The number that denotes the location of a frame or packet in a message.

serial transmission   Transmission of data one bit at a time using only one single link.

server   A program that can provide services to other programs, called clients.

service access point (SAP)   A type of address that identifies the user of a protocol.

session layer   The fifth layer of the OSI model, responsible for the establishment, management, and termination of logical connections between two end users.

session management   The control and handling of sessions between two end users.

session protocol data unit (SPDU)   The data unit defined in the session layer of the OSI model.

SFD   See *start frame delimiter.*

SHF   See *superhigh frequency.*

shielded twisted-pair (STP)   Twisted-pair cable enclosed in a foil or mesh shield that protects against electromagnetic interference.

shift register   An electronic device made of cells for storing binary digits (bits) in which the bits can be shifted to the right or left.

signal   Electromagnetic waves propagated along a transmission medium.

signed number   A representation of binary numbers including the sign (plus or minus). Signed numbers can be represented using three different formats: sign-and-magnitude, one's complement, and two's complement.

simple mail transfer protocol (SMTP)   The TCP/IP protocol defining electronic mail service on the Internet.

simple network management protocol (SNMP)   The TCP/IP protocol that specifies the process of management in the Internet.

simplex mode   A transmission mode in which communication is one way.

sine wave   The mathematical representation of a pure tone.

single attachment station (SAS)   In FDDI, a station that can be connected only to one ring.

single-bit error   Error in a data unit in which only one single bit has been altered.

single-mode fiber   An optical fiber with an extremely small diameter that limits beams to a few angles, resulting in an almost horizontal beam.

sliding window   A protocol that allows several data units to be in transition before receiving an acknowledgment.

sliding window ARQ   An error control protocol using sliding window concept.

slot   A space for data.

SMDS   See *switched multimegabit data service.*

SMTP   See *simple mail transfer protocol.*

SNA   See *Systems Network Architecture.*

SNMP   See *simple network management protocol.*

SONET   See *Synchronous Optical Network.*

source address   The address of the sender of the message.

source-to-destination delivery   The transmission of a message from the original sender to the intended recipient.

space-division switching   A type of circuit switching in which each connection uses a separate physical path.

SPDU   See *session protocol data unit.*

spectrum   The range of frequencies of a signal.

standard   A basis or model that everyone has agreed to.

standard creation committees   A group that produces a basis or model that everyone has agreed to.

star topology   A topology in which all stations are attached to a central device (hub).

starLAN   A LAN using star topology with a 1 Mbps data rate in which the stations can be daisy-chained.

start bit   In asynchronous transmission, a bit to indicate the beginning of transmission.

start frame delimiter (SFD)   A one-byte field in the IEEE 802.3 frame that signals the beginning of the readable (nonpreamble) bit stream.

static document   On the World Wide Web, a fixed-content document that is created and stored in a server.

static routing   A type of routing in which the routing table remains unchanged.

statistical time division multiplexing   See *asynchronous time-division multiplexing*.

stop bit   In asynchronous transmission, one or more bits to indicate the end of transmission.

stop-and-wait   A flow control method in which each data unit must be acknowledged before the next one can be sent.

stop-and-wait ARQ   An error control protocol using stop-and-wait flow control.

store and forward   Another name for message switching.

STP   See *shielded twisted-pair*.

STS   See *synchronous transport signal*.

subnetwork   Any network on an internet.

supergroup   A level in the AT&T analog hierarchy with a 240 KHz bandwidth.

superhigh frequency (SHF)   Radio waves in the 3 GHz to 30 GHz range using line-of-sight and space propagation.

switch   A device connecting multiple communication lines together.

switched multimegabit data service (SMDS)   A packet-switched service that handles high-speed communications in a MAN.

switched/56   A switched digital service allowing a 56 Kbps data rate.

synchronization points   Reference points introduced into the data by the session layer for the purpose of flow and error control.

synchronous data link control (SDLC)   A precursor of HDLC pioneered by IBM.

synchronous digital hierarchy (SDH)   The ITU-T equivalent of SONET.

synchronous optical network (SONET)   A standard developed by ANSI for fiber-optic technology that can transmit high-speed data. It can be used to deliver text, audio, and video.

synchronous TDM   See *synchronous time-division multiplexing*.

synchronous time-division multiplexing   A method of time-division multiplexing in which multiplexing is done on a fixed, predetermined basis.

synchronous transmission   A transmission method that requires a constant timing relationship between the sender and the receiver.

synchronous transport signal (STS)   A hierarchy of signals for use on a SONET network.

Systems Network Architecture (SNA)   A protocol suite designed by IBM.

T

T reference point   In ISDN, the interface between an NT1 and an NT2.

T-1 line   A 1.544 Mbps digital transmission line.

T-2 line   A 6.312 Mbps digital transmission line.

T-3 line   A 44.736 Mbps digital transmission line.

T-4 line   A 274.176 Mbps digital transmission line.

T-lines   A hierarchy of digital lines designed to carry speech and other signals in digital forms. The hierarchy defines T-1, T-2, T-3, and T-4 lines.

TA   See *terminal adapter.*

TCP   See *transmission control protocol.*

TCP/IP   See *transmission control protocol /internetworking protocol.*

TDM   See *time-division multiplexing.*

TE1   See *terminal equipment 1.*

TE2   See *terminal equipment 2.*

telecommunication   Exchange of information over distance using electronic equipment.

teleconferencing   Audio and visual communication between remote users.

telephony   Voice communication.

teleservice   In ISDN, a service in which the network may change or process the contents of the data.

teletext   A method of broadcasting text using a portion of a TV channel bandwidth.

telex   A method of point-to-point communication using a variety of devices.

TELNET   A TCP/IP protocol for remote login.

terminal adapter (TA)   A device that allows the use of non-ISDN terminals to be connected to ISDN network.

terminal equipment 1 (TE1)   An ISDN standard terminal.

terminal equipment 2 (TE2)   A non-ISDN terminal.

terminator   An electronic device that prevents signal reflections at the end of a cable.

TFTP   See *trivial file transfer protocol.*

thick Ethernet   See *10Base5.*

Thick-net   See *thick Ethernet.*

thin Ethernet   See *10Base2*

Thin-net   See *thin Ethernet*

three-way handshake   A sequence of events for connection establishment or termination consisting of the request, then the acknowledgment of the request, and then confirmation of the acknowledgment.

time to live   See *packet lifetime.*

time-division multiplexing (TDM)   The technique of combining signals coming from low-speed channels to share time on a high-speed path.

time-division switching   A circuit-switching technique in which time-division multiplexing is used to achieve switching.

time-domain plot   A diagram showing the changes in the amplitude of a signal with respect to time.

time-slot interchange (TSI)   The component of a time-division switch that changes the order of frames by a store-and-forward process.

token   A small packet used in token-passing access method.

token bus   A LAN using a bus topology and token-passing access method.

token passing   An access method in which a token is circulated in the network. The station that captures the token can send data.

token ring   A LAN using a ring topology and token-passing access method.

topology   The structure of a network including physical arrangement of devices.

TPDU   See *transport protocol data unit.*

transceiver   A device that both transmits and receives.

transceiver cable   In Ethernet, the cable that connects the station to the transceiver. Also called the attachment unit interface (AUI).

translation   Changing from one code or protocol to another.

transmission control protocol (TCP)   The transport protocol in the TCP/IP protocol suite.

transmission control protocol /internetworking protocol (TCP/IP)   A five-layer protocol suite that defines the exchange of transmissions across the Internet.

transmission medium   The physical path linking two communication devices.

transparency   The ability to send any bit pattern as data without it being mistaken for control bits.

transparent bridge   Another name for a learning bridge.

transparent data   Data that can contain control bit patterns without being interpreted as control.

transport layer   The fourth layer in the OSI model; responsible for reliable end-to-end delivery and error recovery.

transport protocol data unit (TPDU)   The data unit defined in the transport layer of the OSI model.

tree topology   A topology in which stations are attached to a hierarchy of hubs. Tree topology is an extension of star topology with more than one level.

trellis coding   A modulation technique that includes error correction.

tribit   A unit of data consisting of three bits.

trivial file transfer protocol (TFTP)   An unreliable TCP/IP protocol for file transfer that does not require complex interaction between client and server.

troposphere   The layer of atmosphere surrounding the earth.

TSI   See *time-slot interchange.*

twisted pair   A transmission medium consisting of two insulated conductors in a twisted configuration.

two's complement   A representation of binary numbers in which the complement of a number is found by complementing all bits and adding a 1 after that.

U

U reference point   In ISDN, the interface between an NT1 and the rest of the network.

U-frame   An HDLC unnumbered frame carrying link management information.

UA   See *user agent.*

UDP   See *user datagram protocol.*

UHF   See *ultrahigh frequency.*

ultrahigh frequency (UHF)   Radio waves in the 300 MHz to 3 GHz range using line-of-sight propagation.

unbalanced configuration   An HDLC configuration in which one device is primary and the others secondary.

unguided medium   A transmission medium with no physical boundaries.

UNI   See *user network interface.*

uniform resource locator (URL)   A string of characters (address) that identifies a page on the World Wide Web.

unipolar encoding   A digital-to-digital encoding method in which a 0-bit is represented by a zero voltage and a 1-bit is represented by a nonzero voltage or vice versa.

UNIX   The operating system used in the Internet.

unshielded twisted-pair (UTP)   A cable with wires that are twisted together to reduce noise and crosstalk. See also *twisted-pair* and *shielded twisted-pair.*

unsigned number   A representation of binary numbers without sign (plus or minus).

uplink   Transmission from an earth station to a satellite.

urgent data   In TCP/IP, data that must be delivered to the application program as quickly as possible.

URL   See *uniform resource locator.*

user agent (UA)   A component in X.400 protocol that interacts with the user.

user datagram protocol (UDP)   A connectionless TCP/IP transport layer protocol.

user datagram   The name of the packet in the UDP protocol.

user network interface (UNI)   The interface between a user and the ATM network.

V

V series   ITU-T standards which define data transmission over telephone lines.

V.21   The ITU-T standard for 300 bps modems, similar to the Bell modem 103/113.

V.22 bis   The ITU-T standard for 2400 bps modems.

V.22   The ITU-T standard for 1200 bps modems, similar to the Bell modem 212A.

V.32bis   The ITU-T standard for 14,400 bps modems.

V.32   The ITU-T standard for 4800 and 9600 bps modems.

V.34   The ITU-T standard for 28,800 bps modems.

vampire tap   An Ethernet transceiver used in Thick Ethernet (10Base5). The transceiver is housed in a clamp-like device with a sharp metal prong that "bites" Thicknet cable.

Veronica   An automated title-search Internet service that uses gopher.

vertical redundancy check (VRC)   An error-detection method based on per-character parity check.

very high frequency (VHF)   Radio waves in the 30 MHz to 300 MHz range using line-of-sight propagation.

very low frequency (VLF)   Radio waves in the 3 KHz to 30 KHz range using surface propagation.

VHF   See *very high frequency.*

videoconferencing   A service that allows a group of users to exchange information over a network.

videotex   The process of accessing remote databases interactively.

virtual channel identifier (VCI)   A field in an ATM cell header that defines a channel.

virtual circuit   A logical circuit made between the sending and receiving computer. The connection is made after both computers do handshaking. After the connection, all packets follow the same route and arrive in sequence.

virtual path identifier (VPI)   A field in an ATM cell header that identifies a path.

virtual terminal (VT)   The OSI remote login protocol.

virtual tributary (VT)   A partial payload that can be inserted into a SONET frame and combined with other partial payloads to fill out the frame.

virus   Unauthorized software introduced for destructive purposes onto a computer.

VLF   See *very low frequency.*

voice grade channel   A channel used for transmission of speech.

volts   A measure of voltage in an electric circuit.

VRC   See *vertical redundancy check.*

VT   See *virtual tributary or virtual terminal.*

W

WAIS   See *wide area information service.*

WAN   See *wide area network.*

Web   Synonym for World Wide Web (WWW).

Wide Area Information Service (WAIS)   An Internet automated search service that lets users locate documents through key words or phrases.

wide area network (WAN)   A network that uses a technology that can span a large geographical distance.

wireless communication   Data transmission using unguided media.

World Wide Web (WWW)   A multimedia Internet service that allows users to traverse the Internet by moving from one document to another via links that connect them together.

WWW   See *World Wide Web.*

X

X.21   An ITU-T standard defining the interface between a DTE and a DCE.

X.25   An ITU-T standard that defines the interface between a data terminal device and a packet-switching network.

X.400   An ITU-T standard for electronic mail and message handling.

X.500   An ITU-T standard for directory service.

XMODEM   A modem multiple file transfer protocol that ensures the reliable transfer of files between personal computers.

XOR gate   An electronic device that performs the bitwise exclusive-or operation. The output is 0 if the two inputs are equal. Otherwise, it is 1.

Y

YMODEM   A modem multiple file transfer protocol.

Z

ZMODEM   A modem multiple file transfer protocol using a 32-bit CRC for error checking.

REFERENCES

Bates, Bud, and Donald Gregory. *Voice and Data Communications Handbook*. McGraw-Hill, 1996.

Beyda, William J. *Data Communications*, 2nd ed. Prentice Hall, 1996.

Black, Uyless. *Data Link Protocols*. Prentice Hall, 1993.

Black, Uyless. *Emerging Communications Technologies*. Prentice Hall, 1994.

Comer Douglas E. *Internetworking with TCP/IP,* vol. 1. Prentice Hall, 1995.

Comer Douglas E. *The Internet Book*. Prentice Hall, 1995.

Dickie, Mark. *Routing in Today's Internetworks*. Van Nostrand Reinhold, 1994.

Halsall, Fred. *Data Communications*, *Computer Networks and Open Systems,* 4th ed. Addison-Wesley, 1995.

Hardy, James K. *Inside Networks*. Prentice Hall, 1995.

Herrick, Clyde N., and C. Lee McKim. *Telecommunication Wiring*. Prentice-Hall, 1992.

Hioki, Warren. *Telecommunications*, 2nd ed. Prentice Hall, 1995.

Huitema, Christian. *Routing in the Internet*. Prentice Hall, 1995.

Johnson, Howard W. *Fast Ethernet*. Prentice Hall, 1996.

McClimans, Fred J. *Communications Wiring and Interconnections*. McGraw-Hill, 1992.

Morley, John, and Stan Gelber. *The Emerging Digital Future*. Boyd & Fraser, 1996.

Naugle, Matthew G. *Network Protocol Handbook*. McGraw-Hill, 1994.

Partridge, Craig. *Gigabit Networking*. Addison-Wesley, 1994.

Pearson, John E. *Basic Communication Theory*. Prentice Hall, 1992.

Perlman, Radia. *Interconnections: Bridges and Routers*. Addison-Wesley, 1992.

Shay, William A. *Understanding Data Communications and Networks*. PWS, 1994.

Smith, Philip. *Frame Relay*. Addison-Wesley, 1993.

Stallings, William. *Data and Computer Communications,* 5th ed. Prentice Hall, 1997.

Stevens, W. Richard. *TCP/IP Illustrated,* vol. 1. Addison-Wesley, 1994.

Tanenbaum, Andrew S. *Computer Networks,* 3rd ed. Prentice Hall, 1996.

Thomas, Stephen A. *IPng and the TCP/IP Protocols*. Wiley, 1996.

Washburn, Kevin, and Jim Evans. *TCP/IP: Running a Successful Network,* 2nd ed. Addison-Wesley, 1996.

Wright, Gary R., and W. Richard Stevens. *TCP/IP Illustrated,* vol. 2. Addison-Wesley, 1995.

Index